# MYSORE

# MYSORE

## A GAZETTEER COMPILED FOR GOVERNMENT

REVISED EDITION

**B. LEWIS RICE, C.I.E., M.R.A.S**

***Fellow of the University of Madras Director of Archaological Researches***

***late Director of Public Instruction in Mysore and Coorg***

**Vol. II**

MYSORE IN GENERAL

GYAN

*Published by*

GYAN

Gyan Publishing House
5, Ansari Road
Daryaganj, New Delhi-110002
Phone: 011-47034999, 9811692060
E-mail: books@gyanbooks.com

*Distribution Network*
gyanbooks.com
India, USA, Canada, UK, Australia, France



ISBN : 978-81-212-3426-9 (Set)
ISBN : 978-81-212-4858-7 (HB)
First Published, 1887

2nd Impression 2020

*Printed at:* Gyan Press, Delhi.



**Mysore**
Author: B. Lewis Rice

# MYSORE

## A GAZETTEER COMPILED FOR GOVERNMENT

REVISED EDITION

BY

B · LEWIS RICE, C · I · E., M · R · A · S

*Fellow of the University of Madras · Director of Archæological Researches*
*late Director of Public Instruction in Mysore and Coorg*

VOL · II

MYSORE, BY DISTRICTS

Westminster
ARCHIBALD CONSTABLE AND COMPANY
2 WHITEHALL GARDENS S · W
MDCCCXCVII

# CONTENTS OF VOL. II.

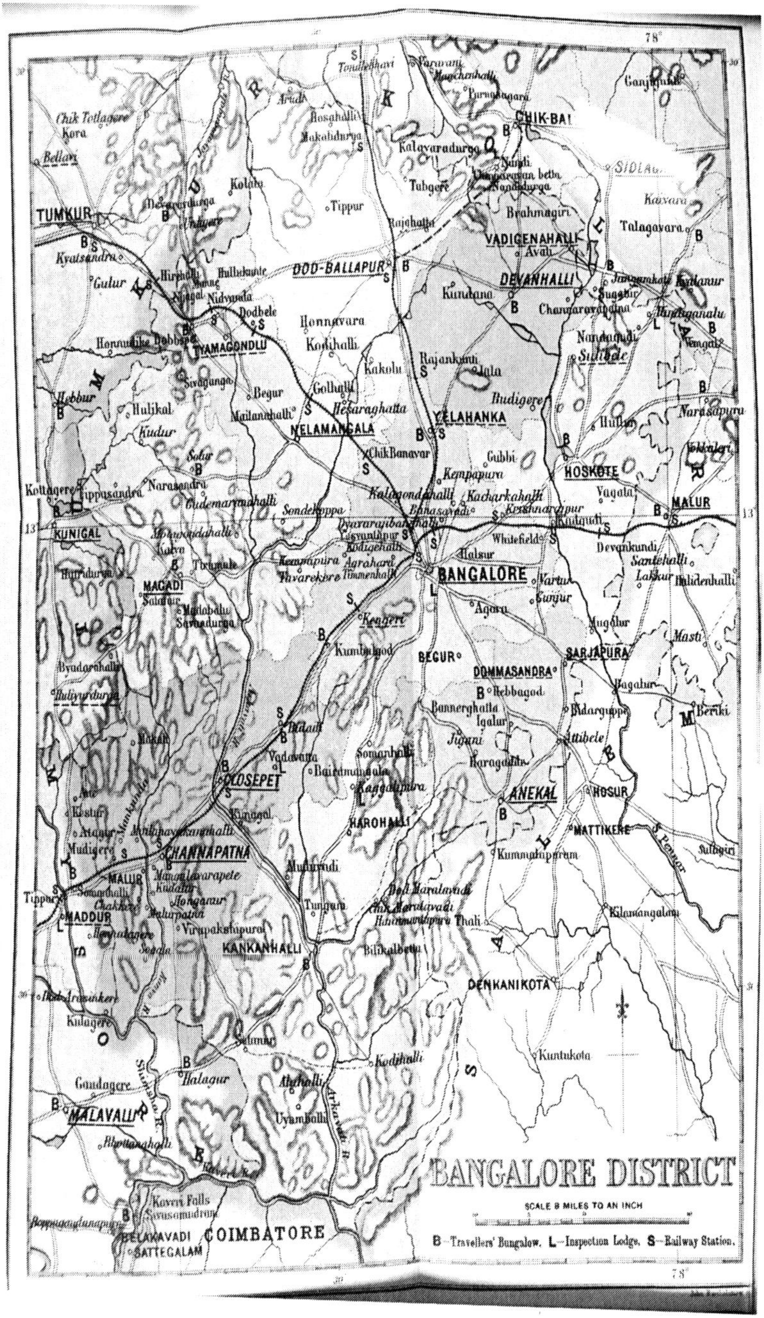
BANGALORE DISTRICT
SCALE 8 MILES TO AN INCH
B—Travellers' Bungalow. L—Inspection Lodge. S—Railway Station.
78°
13°
TUMKUR
DOD-BALLAPUR
CHIK-BAL
VADIGENAHALLI
DEVANHALLI
TYAMAGONDLU
NELAMANGALA
YELAHANKA
HOSKOTE
MALUR
KUNIGAL
MAGADI
BANGALORE
BEGUR
DOMMASANDRA
SARJAPURA
CLOSEPET
HAROHALLI
ANEKAL
HOSUR
MATTIKERE
CHANNAPATNA
MADDUR
KANKANHALLI
DENKANIKOTA
MALAVALLI
BELAKAVADI
COIMBATORE
SATTEGALAM
Kengeri
Whitefield
Nandi
Sivaganga
Savandurga
Halagur
Kavери Falls

# BANGALORE DISTRICT

## GENERAL DESCRIPTION

*Situation.*—A District in the south-east; situated between 12° 14′ and 13° 31′ north latitude, 77° 7′ and 78° 4′ east longitude. Its greatest length is from north to south, the distance between the extreme points being 85 miles. From east to west it measures 60 miles.

*Area.*—The area is 3,061 square miles; of which some 1,398 square miles are under cultivation, and 961 square miles are unculturable and waste, or otherwise not available for cultivation.

*Boundaries.*—It is bounded north-east by the Kolar District, north-west by the Túmkúr District, and south-west by the Mysore District; on the south-east it is bounded by the Salem District of the Madras Presidency, and for 10 miles on the south the river Kaveri separates it from the Coimbatore District of that Presidency, narrowing at one point to what is called the *méke-dáṭu* or Goat's leap.

*Taluqs.*—It is subdivided into the following taluqs: Closepet is a sub-taluq included in Channapatna :—

| No. | Taluq. | Area, sq. Miles. | No. of Hoblis. | No. of Villages or Towns. | Population in 1891. | Per sq. Mile. |
|---|---|---|---|---|---|---|
| 1 | Anekal ......... | 190 | 7 | 223 | 54,834 | 288·60 |
| 2 | Bangalore ...... | 344 | 10 | 370 | 269,683 | 754·88[1] |
| 3 | Channapatna ... | 453 | 10 | 263 | 99,294 | 219·19 |
| 4 | Devanhalli ...... | 232 | 7 | 285 | 53,582 | 230·95 |
| 5 | Dod-Ballapur ... | 341 | 9 | 336 | 65,613 | 192·41 |
| 6 | Hoskote ......... | 271 | 8 | 368 | 60,667 | 223·86 |
| 7 | Kankanhalli ... | 588 | 9 | 272 | 71,868 | 122·22 |
| 8 | Magadi ......... | 367 | 10 | 338 | 64,334 | 175·29 |
| 9 | Nelamangala ... | 275 | 6 | 344 | 63,119 | 229·52 |
| | Total ... | 3,061 | 76 | 2,799 | 802,994 | 262·33 |

[1] Omitting the Town and Cantonment of Bangalore, the rate is 269.

**Physical Features.**—The main portion of the District consists of the valley of the Arkavati, with the Káveri flowing at its southern base. The eastern portion includes the upper basin of the Southern Pinákini (or Pennar), the western a small part of that of the Shimsha.

A line drawn north and south from Nandidroog to the west of Bangalore and thence to Anekal would run along the highest part of the ridge of land which separates the Arkavati valley from that of the S. Pinákini. The elevation of this rising ground at Bangalore, one of the highest parts of the Mysore table-land, is 3,050 feet above the level of the sea, measured at the base of the Resident's flagstaff. At the *mantapam* or watch-tower on the Oyáli-dinne, two miles to the north of Bangalore, which is the highest point, the elevation is 3,118 feet at the base of the observatory.

Parallel with this watershed, which forms the eastern boundary of the Kaveri river system in Mysore, is a broken chain of rocky hills, extending from the west of the Nelamangala taluq, through the taluqs of Magadi, Channapatna, and Kankanhalli, and occasionally rising into lofty mountain peaks, such as Sivaganga and Sávandurga. Beyond this western belt the surface waters, commencing from the west of Magadi, run southwards into the Shimsha.

The central, northern, and eastern portions of the District are open and undulating. The low-lying grounds are occupied with series of tanks for cultivation, formed by embanking the streams of the valleys, and varying in size from small ponds to considerable lakes. The upland tracts are often bare or covered with low scrub jungle. Westward the country is broken and rugged, being composed of a succession of hills and valleys, intersected by rocky and sandy streams, having a great fall. To the south, where the general level of the land declines towards the Kaveri, the hills are closer together and surrounded with thick jungle.

The following heights above the level of the sea will serve to show the general elevation of the upper plain surface. In the centre, Bangalore, High Ground, 3,067 feet; Sompur in the west, 3,088 feet; Betta Halsur in the north, 2,994 feet; Kadgodi in the east, 2,856 feet; Kankanhalli in the south, 2,064 feet.

**Rocks.**[1]—The prevailing rock is gneiss, disrupted by trap seams, dikes and large out-crops, and also by porphyritic and fine-grained granitic rocks, rock crystal, amethystic, smoky and milky quartz. Adularia, pink felspar, chert, corundum, chalcedony, mica and hornblende are found in considerable quantities. Quartzose pebbles, that

[1] The following paragraphs are chiefly from a note by Colonel Puckle.

bear a high polish, are also found in the river beds. Hæmatitic iron ore is abundant, and a nodular limestone of considerable value is found in the valleys, while near Kankanhalli there is a formation of indusial lime, some of which bears a tolerable polish. It is very pure and makes good polished chunam.

*Building Stone.*—The gneissose rock is everywhere abundant and is extensively quarried for building purposes. Large slabs, of from 3 inches to 2 feet in thickness, are readily obtained by the simple application of heat to the surface. Then, by pooling small holes in the required direction and wedging, the stone can be separated with great precision into pieces of almost any dimensions. Pillars thus prepared and 25 feet in length have been extensively employed as telegraph posts, while in the Central College at Bangalore single stones 35 feet high and not more than 15 inches square have been used to support the roof. They are formed into light columns by a coating of chunam, and are a great improvement on the old massive style of brick-in-chunam pillars that took up so much space. Stone is also employed for architraves, for culvert girders up to 8 or 9 feet span (they are not safe above this on account of the preliminary burning process used in quarrying them) and for a variety of other useful purposes. It is easily quarried into a flat-bedded building material, and arches of coursed hammer-dressed stone have been constructed with great economy and success, the face of the work presenting almost the appearance of dressed stone, though in no instance has the chisel been used. Good examples may be seen at Dod-Ballapur, where the first bridge of the kind was built in 1857; at the fifth mile on the Mysore road, where one of 50 feet span is built; at the eighteenth mile on the Túmkúr road, where the newly-constructed bridge stood the rush of water from five tanks, breached at the same time, over its parapets, without a crack being anywhere visible. For partly hammer-dressed and partly chisel-dressed work, the Bangalore Railway Stations offer excellent examples, or the Maharaja's Palace. Thin slabs of stone have also been used for partition walls of houses where economy of space was desirable.

*Road Metal.*—It is used, broken up, for road metal, but from the difference of the decay of the materials composing the rock it does not seem suitable. The tough trap rock, of which there is so large a quantity, might perhaps be substituted for it with advantage, or broken quartz.

**Clays.**—Potters' clay is found in not large quantities, but it is well worked up by the native potters, though their insufficient method of burning the biscuit renders the ware more brittle than it might be.

There are many kaolinitic clays of a highly refractory character, and if these were duly admixed with the potters' clay and hard-fired in proper furnaces, much improvement in the manufactured material would be the result. The white clay is the best and stands great heat. Specimens of it were sent to Mr. Minton, and very favourably reported on, but the coloured kinds were mixed with so much oxide and other foreign matter as, to be pronounced of not much economic value. Excellent fire and cornice bricks, and mouldings of all shapes, can be made of this material, and in a trial made in 1862 an artificial stone was produced that took a fair polish. Materials for glazing pottery are also procurable about Bangalore. In 1883 as many as twenty-four different specimens of clays were sent to the Calcutta Exhibition, and received favourable reports. The clay at Whitefield has attracted special attention at times.

**Soils.**—The prevailing soil is the red or *kempu*. It is a red loam of great fertility, and is found in every variety of colour from light to dark red, and deep chocolate. It generally overlies the metamorphic granite in varying depths from a few inches to several feet. The darker, rich red and chocolate soils are supposed to be the result of the weathering down to mould of the trap rocks, which are everywhere visible in seams and out-crops, having disrupted and overlaid the normal gneissose rock, disintegrating it and tilting the strata in every conceivable way at the points of disruption and contact. Granitic rocks of a porphyritic character are also weathering down in a red soil of much fertility, in which dry crops grow well, and which the natives consider a first-class soil. But the spontaneous growth of fine *hariáli* and of some true grasses, and the rich and healthy appearance of the trees growing in the trap soil, show that any culture will with ordinary attention succeed, and that its capabilities are not sufficiently appreciated. Some cultivators, however, who know its value, state that with proper attention it will yield an eighty-fold return. The decomposition of the normal gneissose rock gives the *saulu* earth, the grey, sandy and sterile soils, and the kaolinitic clays. There are a few isolated tracts of black soil, but not sufficient to induce the special cultivation usual in such ground.

**Climate.**—The climate of Bangalore is noted for its salubrity. It seems well suited to the constitution both of Europeans and natives, epidemics being of rare occurrence and other diseases of a mild character. Those portions of the District lying north and east of Bangalore partake of the same generally healthy character. The taluqs traversed by the western range of hills are, on the other hand, subject to malarious fevers.

From January to March the wind is variable. A pleasant breeze often blows from the south and west in the early morning, but as the sun's heat increases the wind sets strongly from the north-east and gradually drops as sunset approaches. The sky during this season is bright and cloudless. In April the wind chops about suddenly from easterly to westerly, and there are occasional thunder showers. The weather is sometimes sultry and oppressive, at other times storms of wind and dust are prevalent: clouds often bank up heavily in the east and travel round to west, ending not in rain but in a thick dust storm. May is generally sultry, with variable breezes and occasional high winds and thunder storms. Towards the end of the month the wind settles in the S.S.W., in which quarter there is much sheet lightning. In June and July the weather is cloudy, with a high S.W. wind which ought to bring abundance of rain. With some intermission similar weather continues till October, when the wind changes round to the east and north-east, whence the heaviest rains are expected. These continue into November, and are succeeded by bright sunny days and cold foggy mornings. From December to May there is usually little or no rain.

*Temperature.*—The mean temperature deduced from observations at Bangalore is 76·2. The mean diurnal range is 15·6, but the extreme range marked in any one day varies from 18 in October and November to 30 and 32 in February and March. The extreme annual range recently recorded has been 45 degrees, between a minimum of 52 in January 1894 and a maximum of 97 in April of the same year. The following is a summary of mean meteorological results from the registers of the Bangalore observatory for 1893 and 1894, in the former of which the rainfall was about the average, and in the latter, below it.

| 1893. | Barometer. | | | Thermometers. | | | | | | Aqueous Vapour. | | Wind. | | Rain. | | Cloud. | | |
|---|---|---|---|---|---|---|---|---|---|---|---|---|---|---|---|---|---|---|
| | | | | Dry Bulb. | | | | Wet Bulb. | | | | | | | | | Number of Days. | |
| | Red. to 32° F. | Red. to Sea Level. | Daily Range. | Mean. | Max. | Min. | Range. | Mean. | Min. | Pressure in Inches. | Humidity. Per cent. | Daily Velocity Miles. | Mean Direction. | Fall in Inches. | Number of Days. | Mean. Per cent. | Cloudless 10h. to 16 h. | Overcast. |
| | 26+ | 29+ | | | | | | | | | | | | | | | | |
| January | ·946 | ·845 | ·124 | 70·6 | 82·2 | 57·9 | 24·3 | 58·9 | 56·3 | ·428 | 58 | 171 | E.S.E. | 0·03 | 1 | 17 | 13 | 0 |
| February | ·970 | ·846 | ·131 | 74·3 | 86·2 | 61·0 | 25·1 | 61·3 | 58·4 | ·458 | 54 | 129 | S.E. by S. | 0·36 | 3 | 14 | 11 | 0 |
| March | ·932 | ·793 | ·138 | 77·3 | 88·4 | 65·0 | 23·4 | 63·6 | 61·0 | ·499 | 54 | 146 | S.E. by S. | 1·57 | 3 | 15 | 12 | 0 |
| April | ·874 | ·699 | ·129 | 81·5 | 93·6 | 67·4 | 26·2 | 64·2 | 61·1 | ·481 | 45 | 146 | S. | 2·09 | 5 | 22 | 5 | 0 |
| May | ·829 | ·675 | ·123 | 79·0 | 89·4 | 67·8 | 21·6 | 67·4 | 65·3 | ·614 | 62 | 154 | W. | 1·19 | 10 | 47 | 0 | 1 |
| June | ·803 | ·680 | ·089 | 74·5 | 82·3 | 66·4 | 15·9 | 67·1 | 65·2 | ·642 | 75 | 198 | S.W. by W. | 5·96 | 14 | 64 | 0 | 3 |
| July | ·812 | ·700 | ·092 | 72·8 | 79·7 | 66·0 | 13·7 | 66·8 | 65·2 | ·646 | 81 | 173 | W. by S. | 5·84 | 21 | 89 | 0 | 5 |
| August | ·841 | ·727 | ·098 | 73·4 | 80·2 | 65·6 | 14·8 | 66·3 | 64·6 | ·618 | 75 | 194 | W. by S. | 1·91 | 15 | 76 | 0 | 3 |
| Sept. | ·866 | ·750 | ·112 | 73·6 | 81·7 | 64·8 | 16·9 | 65·5 | 63·3 | ·600 | 70 | 178 | W. by S. | 5·31 | 11 | 75 | 1 | 2 |
| October | ·880 | ·779 | ·112 | 70·5 | 79·9 | 64·7 | 15·2 | 66·1 | 64·0 | ·629 | 76 | 105 | — | 9·83 | 18 | 65 | 0 | 1 |
| Nov. | ·936 | ·849 | ·102 | 70·8 | 77·8 | 63·3 | 14·5 | 64·8 | 62·5 | ·633 | 80 | 172 | E. | 2·82 | 10 | 64 | 0 | 6 |
| Dec. | ·989 | ·907 | ·115 | 68·3 | 78·5 | 56 4 | 22·0 | 58·5 | 54·0 | ·460 | 65 | 181 | E. by N. | 0·02 | 1 | 15 | 12 | 0 |
| | 26+ | 29+ | | | | | | | | | | | | | | | | |
| Year | ·889 | ·771 | ·114 | 73·9 | 83·5 | 63·8 | 19·7 | 64·2 | 61·7 | ·559 | 66 | 162 | — | 36·93 | 112 | 47 | 54 | 21 |
| | | | | | | | | | | | | | | Total. | | | Total. | |

| 1894. | Barometer. | | | Thermometers. | | | | | | Aqueous Vapour. | | Wind. | | Rain. | | Cloud. | | |
|---|---|---|---|---|---|---|---|---|---|---|---|---|---|---|---|---|---|---|
| | | | | Dry Bulb. | | | | Wet Bulb. | | | | | | | | | Number of Days. | |
| | Red. to 32° F. | Red. to Sea Level. | Daily Range. | Mean. | Max. | Min. | Range. | Mean. | Min. | Pressure in Inches. | Humidity. Per cent. | Daily Vel. Miles. | Mean Direction. | Fall in Inches. | Number of Days. | Mean. Per cent. | Cloudless 10 h. to 16 h. | Overcast. |
| | 26+ | 29+ | | | | | | | | | | | | | | | | |
| January | ·967 | ·864 | ·120 | 70·6 | 82·3 | 57·3 | 25·0 | 58·4 | 55·5 | ·416 | 55 | 179 | E. by N. | — | — | 19 | 13 | — |
| February | ·978 | ·852 | ·127 | 74·0 | 86·6 | 59·4 | 27·2 | 59·8 | 56·6 | ·423 | 50 | 174 | E.S.E. | 0·22 | 2 | 12 | 17 | — |
| March | ·913 | ·749 | ·138 | 80·4 | 93·0 | 66·2 | 26·8 | 64·5 | 61·3 | ·503 | 49 | 117 | S. | 0·45 | 2 | 20 | 6 | 1 |
| April | ·861 | ·699 | ·130 | 80·9 | 92·0 | 68·1 | 23·9 | 66·9 | 64·2 | ·577 | 56 | 110 | S.W. | 2·91 | 6 | 31 | 1 | — |
| May | ·839 | ·680 | ·123 | 79·3 | 89·7 | 67·8 | 21·9 | 67·7 | 65·1 | 624 | 62 | 136 | W. by N. | 6·49 | 13 | 31 | 3 | — |
| June | ·796 | ·656 | ·089 | 75·8 | 84·2 | 66·2 | 18·0 | 67·1 | 65·0 | ·626 | 69 | 219 | W. by S. | 3·40 | 7 | 70 | — | 2 |
| July | ·818 | ·693 | ·084 | 74·3 | 82·5 | 65·6 | 16·9 | 66·2 | 64·5 | ·582 | 71 | 219 | W.S.W. | 3·47 | 13 | 74 | — | 5 |
| August | ·794 | ·676 | ·103 | 73·7 | 81·2 | 66·0 | 15·2 | 66·9 | 65·1 | ·639 | 78 | 186 | W. | 6·32 | 20 | 84 | — | 2 |
| Sept. | ·830 | ·709 | ·119 | 74·1 | 82·5 | 65·1 | 17·3 | 66·3 | 64·2 | ·626 | 74 | 203 | W. | 1·59 | 12 | 71 | 1 | 3 |
| October | ·871 | ·756 | ·115 | 74·2 | 82·6 | 65·0 | 17·6 | 66·3 | 64·0 | ·627 | 74 | 145 | S.W. by W. | 4·54 | 15 | 61 | — | 1 |
| Nov. | ·967 | ·883 | ·101 | 70·3 | 78·4 | 61·4 | 17·0 | 62·8 | 60·3 | ·556 | 73 | 187 | E. by S. | 2·82 | 6 | 51 | 1 | — |
| Dec. | ·984 | ·894 | ·113 | 69·9 | 79·8 | 58·7 | 21·2 | 59·3 | 57·7 | ·453 | 61 | 197 | E. by N. | — | — | 28 | 10 | — |
| | 26+ | 29+ | | | | | | | | | | | | | | | | |
| Year | ·885 | ·759 | ·114 | 74·8 | 84·6 | 63·9 | 20·7 | 64·4 | 62·0 | ·554 | 64 | 173 | — | 32·21 | 96 | 46 | 52 | 14 |
| | | | | | | | | | | | | | | Total. | | | Total. | |

*Rainfall.*—The mean average rainfall is 35 inches in the year, distributed over from 80 to 90 days. The heaviest fall occurs generally during the prevalence of the N.E. monsoon, about October. As a general rule the showers fall in the afternoon and evening, rainy mornings being of rare occurrence. The accompanying figures, giving the annual fall of rain at Bangalore from the year 1837, will show the extent of variation.

| | In. c. | | In. c. | | In. c. | | In. c. |
|---|---|---|---|---|---|---|---|
| 1837 | 44·3 | 1852 | 55·1 | 1867 | 28·44 | 1881 | 27·44 |
| 1838 | 16 | 1853 | 34·7 | 1868 | 38·89 | 1882 | 36·16 |
| 1839 | 32·4 | 1854 | 29·9 | 1869 | 40·42 | 1883 | 34·80 |
| 1840 | 30·2 | 1855 | 27·1 | 1870 | 31·9 | 1884 | 23·11 |
| 1841 | 38 | 1856 | 48·3 | 1871 | 29·12 | 1885 | 39·75 |
| 1842 | 31·2 | 1857 | 30·4 | 1872 | 40·45 | 1886 | 44·79 |
| 1843 | 37·2 | 1858 | 37·8 | 1873 | 29·16 | 1887 | 33·99 |
| 1844 | 34·4 | 1859 | 26 6 | 1874 | 56·65 | 1888 | 29·45 |
| 1845 | 32·7 | 1860 | 33·2 | 1875 | 22·20 | 1889 | 36·73 |
| 1846 | 40 | 1861 | 30·1 | 1876 | 17·16 | 1890 | 44·08 |
| 1847 | 37·5 | 1862 | 37·3 | 1877 | 39·28 | 1891 | 24·44 |
| 1848 | 40·3 | 1863 | 35·8 | 1878 | 40·81 | 1892 | 26·95 |
| 1849 | 27·8 | 1864 | 37·62 | 1879 | 40·67 | 1893 | 37·04 |
| 1850 | 49·4 | 1865 | 36 | 1880 | 51·70 | 1894 | 31·94 |
| 1851 | 35·3 | 1866 | 33·8 | | | | |

The quantity registered for 1838, only 16 inches, stands by itself, and is exceptionally low, but 1876, with 17·16 inches, was not much better. Omitting these years of singular drought, the range has been from 23·11 inches in 1884 to 56·65 in 1874. The other occasions on which the fall exceeded 50 inches was in 1852, when 55·1 inches were registered, and 1880, with 51·70 inches. Grouping them in the following manner:—

| | | | |
|---|---|---|---|
| below 20 inches | 2 | 35 to 40 inches | 15 |
| 20 to 25 ,, | 3 | 40 to 45 ,, | 9 |
| 25 to 30 ,, | 10 | 45 to 50 ,, | 2 |
| 30 to 35 ,, | 14 | above 50 ,, | 3 |

we find that, in the 58 years, 29, or one-half, had a rainfall below 35, and 29 a rainfall above that. In 24 years the fall was within 10 inches of defect, and in 24 it was within 10 inches of excess. The chances, therefore, are against a fall of less than 25 or more than 45 inches in any one year in general.

**Vegetation.**—*Forest.*—The earliest accounts describe the District as covered with forest, forming a part of the great Dandakáranya. The distinctive names have been preserved of some of the wooded tracts, such as the Chandanáranya (sandal forest) on the Arkavati near Nelamangala; the Ganjáranya (forest of the *abrus precatorius*) around Sivaganga; the Kundáranya (jasmin forest) at Devanhalli, &c.

The following trees and plants enumerated as growing in these woods may be taken to represent the indigenous vegetation:—

| *Sanskrit.* | *Botanical Name.* | *English.* | *Kannada.* |
|---|---|---|---|
| Amalaka ... | Phyllanthus emblica ... | Emblic myrobolan ... | Nelli. |
| Amara, chuta... | Mangifera indica ... | Mango ... ... ... | Mávina mara. |
| Ankotha ... | Alangium hexapetalum... | ... ... ... ... | Udagina gida. |
| Asoka ... ... | Uvaria longifolia ... | Asoka ... ... ... | Asoka. |
| Asvatha, pippala | Ficus religiosa ... ... | Sacred fig ... ... | Arali mara. |
| Badari ... ... | Zizyphus jujuba ... ... | Jujube-tree ... ... | Yagachi. |
| Bilva ... ... | Œgle marmelos ... ... | Bael-tree ... ... | Bilpatre mara. |
| Champaka ... | Michelia champaca ... | Champac ... ... | Sampige. |
| Chandana ... | Santalum album ... | Sandal ... ... ... | Gandada mara. |
| Rakta chandana | Pterocarpus santalinus ... | Red sandal ... ... | Agaru. |
| Hemaksha ... | | | |
| Jaji, malati ... | Jasminum grandiflorum... | Large-flowered jasmin... | Mallige. |
| Jambira ... | Citrus bergamia ... ... | Lime ... ... ... | Nimbe mara. |
| Jambu ... ... | Eugenia jambolana ... | ... ... ... ... | Nerale mara. |
| Kadali ... ... | Musa paradisiaca ... | Plantain ... ... | Bále gida. |
| Kapitta ... | Feronia elephantum ... | Wood apple ... ... | Byálada mara. |
| Kapota ... | | | |
| Karanja, tamala | Pongamia glabra ... | Indian beech ... ... | Honge. |
| Karaviraka ... | Nerium odorum ... ... | Oleander ... ... | Kanigilu. |
| Ketaki ... ... | Pandanus odoratissimus... | Fragrant screw-pine ... | Ketaki. |
| Khadira ... | Acacia catechu ... ... | ... ... ... ... | Táte. |
| Kharjura ... | Phœnix sylvestris ... | Wild date ... ... | Ichalu. |
| Kovidara ... | Bauhinia variegata ... | Mountain ebony ... | |
| Krishnagara ... | | | |
| Kunda ... ... | Jasminum hirsutum ... | Bearded jasmin .. | Mallige. |
| Kuranta ... | Amarantus ... ... | Yellow amaranth ... | Goranti. |
| Kutaja ... ... | Datura ... ... ... | Thorn-apple ... ... | Datturi gida. |
| Langali ... | Gloriosa superba ... | Wild aconite | |
| Lodhra ... | Simplocos racemosa ... | | |
| Madhavi ... | Gœrtnera racemosa ... | ... ... ... ... | Gulagunji. |
| Madhuka ... | Bassia latifolia ... ... | Mahwah ... ... | Ippe. |
| Mallika ... | Jasminum sambac ... | Jasmin ... ... .. | Mallige. |
| Mandara ... | | | |
| Manjula ... | | | |
| Naga ... ... | Cyperus pertenuis ... | | |
| Punnaga ... | Rottleria tinctoria ... | ... ... ... ... | Rangamále. |
| Naga kesara, gajaphuba ... | Mesua ferrea ... ... | ... ... ... ... | Kesara. |
| Narikela ... | Cocos nucifera ... ... | Cocoanut palm ... | Tengina mara. |
| Nichula ... | Baringtonia acutangula ... | | |
| Nimba ... ... | Melia azadiracta... ... | Margosa ... ... | Bevina mara. |
| Nipa ... ... | Nauclea cadamba ... | ... ... ... ... | Kadamba. |
| Palasha, kimsuka ... ... | Butea frondosa ... .. | Bastard teak ... ... | Muttuga. |
| Panasa ... | Artocarpus integrifolia ... | Jack ... ... ... | Halasina mara. |
| Parijata ... | Erythrina fulgens ... | Coral-tree ... ... | Parijata. |
| Patala ... ... | Bignonia suaveolens ... | | |
| Plaksha ... | Ficus infectoria ... ... | Waved-leaf fig ... ... | Basari mara. |
| Rasala ... ... | Saccharum ... ... | Sugar-cane ... ... | Kabbu. |
| Sala ... ... | Shorea robusta ... ... | Sal | |
| Salmala, Kuta salmala } | Bombax pentandrum ... | Silk-cotton tree ... | Búraga. |
| Sami ... ... | Mimosa suma ... ... | Mimosa ... ... ... | Banni mara. |
| Sapta parna ... | Echites sepholaris ... | | |
| Takkola ... | Clerodendron inerme ... | | |
| Tala ... ... | Borassus flabelliformis ... | Palmyra... ... ... | Tále mara. |
| Hintala ... | Phœnix paludosa ... | | |
| Tinduka ... | Diospyros. ... ... | Kind of ebony | |
| Tintrini ... | Tamarindus indica ... | Tamarind ... ... | Hunase. |
| Vakula ... ... | Mimusops elengi ... | ... ... ... ... | Ranja. |
| Vata ... ... | Ficus indica ... ... | Banyan ... ... ... | Alada mara. |

As late as the sixteenth century, when Devanhalli, Dod-Ballapur, Hoskote and other chief places were founded, the original settlers are related to have commenced operations by clearing the surrounding forest.

At the present day the hilly taluqs of Magadi and Kankanhalli contain the greatest proportion of jungle. Trees and bushes grow abundantly, especially in the ravines between the heights. In Kankanhalli there is much fuel jungle and good forest of karachi (*Hardwickia binata*). The best forests in the taluq lie to the east of the Arkavati. Besides acacias, the dindiga (*conocarpus latifolia*) yielding a valuable gum, and the jalári or lac tree (*vatica laccifera*) are abundant. The Channapatna taluq is also hilly, but the tree vegetation is smaller. The remaining taluqs north and east are fairly wooded with trees in the long and hollow valleys of the downs. The most common is the honge (*pongamia glabra*), a valuable tree which fringes many tank bunds and often grows to a large size. Oil is extracted from the seeds, and the leaves are used as manure for sugar-cane. Acacias grow freely, and chennuge (*lagerstrœmia parviflora*) and huluve are frequent. There is much scrub jungle around Ujani-betta and along the western border of the Dod-Ballapur and Nelamangala taluqs.

The different kinds of ficus, the mango, tamarind, mohwah or ippe, jack, and jámun or nerale, all grow well, together with many varieties of acacia, the wood-apple, bael-tree and some bamboo. The sandal grows in Bangalore, Kankanhalli, Magadi and Channapatna taluqs.

Among shrubs and useful bushes are the kakke (*cassia fistula*), tangadi (*cassia auriculata*) and kusambe (*carthamus tinctorius*); also the wild date (*phœnix sylvestris*), which yields toddy.

**Reserved Forests.**—The *State forests* cover an area of 312 square miles. The following are their names and areas :—

| | | | | | |
|---|---|---|---|---|---|
| Bilikal ... ... | 42 | Makali ... ... | 39 | Kabbaldurg ... ... | 12 |
| Savandurg ... ... | 17 | Ragihalli ... ... | 9 | Hultar ... ... | 8 |
| Handigundi ... ... | 30 | Dod Ballapur ... | 13 | Tenginakal ... ... | 16 |
| Chilandadi ... ... | 37 | Mugur ... ... | 34 | Banantimari ... ... | 6 |
| Basavanbetta ... ... | 37 | Kumbalgod ... ... | 2 | Mannugudda ... | 10 |

**Arboriculture.**—*Plantations.*—The great demand for fuel created by the railway and the increasing consumption at Bangalore have led to the formation of fuel plantations both by Government and by private individuals. The common *cassia florida* and the *casuarina muricata* have been largely planted in the reserves. The former grows freely if treated as a pollard, otherwise it is apt to die out suddenly. The latter is the tree principally cultivated of late years. *Avenues* have been planted along all the public roads, 542 miles in length, the best growing indigenous trees being generally employed for the purpose. These consist of the mango, figs, honge, and nerale, which are raised in nurseries and then transplanted.

*Groves* of trees called topes are numerous. They are planted by natives near wells or tanks, as works of merit, for the shelter of travellers. The mango and the ippe appear to be preferred for the purpose in this District. The former is an umbrageous and handsome tree of symmetrical form, and grows well. *Village topes* have also been formed by order of Government, which should prove of great use as camping grounds, besides improving the appearance of the country. The number of topes in 1894 was 2,118, containing 106,103 trees.

*Ornamental trees* have been introduced into the station of Bangalore in great variety. The *poinciana regia* or "flame of the forest," with its splendid scarlet blossoms, has become quite common. The *spathodea*, with a still more gorgeous flower of deep orange tint, is also met with on all sides. Numerous coniferous trees have been cultivated with success, including *araucaria* and other varieties of pine. The Java fig, a graceful and fast-growing tree, with glossy and delicate foliage, has been much planted in gardens, as well as the Moreton Bay chestnut and the *grevillea robusta*. Many of these trees also find their way into the taluq stations and into compounds of the dawk bungalows.

*Hedges* consisting of the thorny *sige háyi* or soap-nut exist round many villages, forming an impenetrable thicket, originally designed as a defence. Such an enclosure formerly surrounded the native town of Bangalore. But hedgerows between the fields are very unusual. The aloe and the kalli or milk hedge (*euphorbia tirucalli*) are most commonly used as fences by native farmers, with the lakkili (*vitex negundo*) and the kádu haraḷu (*jatropha curacus*). The *lantana*, however, bids fair to supersede every other hedge-plant on account of its easy propagation. Unless frequently trimmed it has a tendency to become rank, and spreads itself with wonderful rapidity, choking other vegetation.

**Crops.**—The principal cultivation consists of dry crops, among which the most prominent is rági (*eleusine corocana*), the staple food of the people. Avare or cow-gram (*dolichos lablab*) is sown in lines with the rági, and is the pulse most frequently eaten with it. Jola or millet (*sorghum vulgare*), also sown with the rági, is in this District only used as fodder for cattle. Horse-gram (*dolichos biflorus*) is largely grown in the poorer soils, and as a substitute when rági fails. It is the general food for cattle, and is also used as a pulse for human food. Various oil-seeds are also raised to a considerable extent, such as woḷḷeḷḷu and hucheḷḷu (two kinds of sesamum), and haraḷu (castor-oil). Mulberry cultivation for the support of silk-worms, which forms an important branch of industry among the Muhammadans, at one time much declined owing to the losses arising from continued mortality among the insects, but it has now revived. Opium was produced in Devanhalli and Dod-Ballapur taluqs, until its cultivation was prohibited, and tobacco is grown in several parts.

Paddy cultivation in the Bangalore District (Mr. Ricketts has remarked) is for the most part uncared for by the ryots, whereas much attention is paid to dry crops, which yield in abundance, and also provide for the greater part of the year the necessary fodder for cattle. Excepting at wells and under very large tanks, he is inclined to think that in Bangalore,—where there are no canals,—the wet crops are more uncertain than the dry. A species of blight often attacks paddy crops. The *batáyi* system, too, may have originally led to the ryot's not caring to labour for the benefit of the Government, and thus to expending all his manure and most of his labour on his dry crops. One exception (he adds) must be made as regards wet cultivation, and that is concerning sugar-cane. This product is highly manured and cared for, and yields considerable profits. But sugar-cane is seldom planted in places where a failure of tank-water cannot be supplemented by irrigation from wells.

The success which attended an experimental plantation of coffee near Bangalore has led to land being taken up of late years for the same purpose in maidán parts of the District, but the enterprise has not yet passed out of the experimental stage.

The following is a list of the chief cultivated products of the District :—

| Kannada Name. | Botanical Name. | English Name. |
|---|---|---|
| CEREALS— | | |
| Baragu ... ... | Panicum miliaceum ... | Common millet. |
| Bhatta or Nellu ... | Oryza sativa ... ... | Rice. |
| Godhi ... ... | Triticum sativum ... ... | Wheat. |
| Háraka ... ... | Panicum semiverticillatum.. | |
| Jola ... ... | Sorghum vulgare ... ... | Great millet. |
| Navane ... ... | Panicum italicum ... ... | Italian millet. |
| Rági ... ... | Eleusine corocana ... ... | Rági. |
| Sajje ... ... | Pennisetum typhoideum ... | Spiked millet. |
| Sáme ... ... | Panicum frumentaceum ... | Little millet. |
| PULSES— | | |
| Alasandi ... ... | Vigna catiang ... ... | |
| Avare ... ... | Dolichos lablab ... ... | Cow gram. |
| Hesaru ... ... | Phaseolus mungo ... ... | Green gram. |
| Hurali ... ... | Dolichos biflorus ... ... | Horse gram, kulti. |
| Togari ... ... | Cajanus indicus ... ... | Pigeon pea, doll. |
| Uddu ... ... | Phaseolus radiatus ... | Black gram. |

| Kannada Name. | Botanical Name. | English Name. |
|---|---|---|
| OIL SEEDS— | | |
| Haraḷu ... ... | Ricinus communis ... | Castor-oil. |
| Honge ... ... | Pongamia glabra ... ... | Honge. |
| Huchcheḷḷu or Ramtil | Guizotea abyssinica ... | Foolish oil. |
| Woḷḷellu ... ... | Sesamum indicum ... ... | Gingelli. |
| VEGETABLES (NATIVE)— | | |
| Badane káyi ... | Solanum melongena ... | Brinjal. |
| Bende káyi ... ... | Hibiscus esculentus ... | |
| Bellulli ... ... | Allium sativum ... ... | Garlic. |
| Genasu ... ... | Dioscorea atuleata ... ... | Sweet potato. |
| Jirige ... ... | Cuminum cyminum ... | Cummin seed. |
| Kalle káyi ... ... | Arachis hypogœa ... ... | Ground-nut. |
| Kumbala káyi ... | Cucurbita pepo ... ... | Pumpkin. |
| Mensina káyi ... | Capsicum annuum ... ... | Chilli. |
| Mentya ... ... | Trigonella fœnum græcum... | Fenugreek. |
| Nirulli ... ... | Allium cepa ... ... | Onion. |
| Padavala káyi ... | Trichosanthes anguina ... | Snake gourd. |
| Sasive ... ... | Brassica nigra ... ... | Mustard. |
| Saute káyi ... ... | Cucumis sativus ... ... | Cucumber. |
| Sunti ... ... | Zingiber officinale ... ... | Ginger. |
| MISCELLANEOUS— | | |
| Adike ... ... | Areca catechu ... ... | Areca nut. |
| Bále ... ... | Musa sapientum ... ... | Plantain. |
| Hoge soppu ... | Nicotiana tabacum ... | Tobacco. |
| Hunase ... ... | Tamarindus indica ... | Tamarind. |
| Kabbu ... ... | Saccharum officinale ... | Sugar-cane. |
| Pundi ... ... | Hibiscus cannabinus ... | Dekhan hemp. |
| Sige káyi ... ... | Mimosa abstergens ... | Soap-nut. |
| Tengina káyi ... | Cocos nucifera ... ... | Cocoanut. |
| Viled-ele ... ... | Piper betle ... ... | Betel vine. |

*Garden Produce.*—Besides the productions of the country entered in the foregoing list, vegetables and fruits are raised in large quantities and great variety for the European markets at Bangalore and Madras. Among the former are included potatoes, cauliflowers, peas, asparagus, artichokes, French beans, knolkohl, cabbage, and lettuce; among the latter, apples, peaches, grapes, mangoes, strawberries, figs, guavas, loquats, raspberries, and plantains. The foreign kinds are grown principally in the Bangalore and Devanhalli taluqs.

*Area under Principal Crops.*—The following figures, for 1893, are intended to show approximately the number of acres under cultivation of the chief crops:—Rice, 49,419; rági, 357,448; wheat, 16; other food grains, 91,320; vegetables, 9,250; oil seeds, 15,139; sugar-cane, 3,159; cocoanut and areca nut, 8,943; tobacco, 1,148; mulberry, 3,587; fibres, 741.

**Horticulture.**—Horticulture received much impetus after the establishment of the Agri-Horticultural Society at Bangalore in 1839, but more especially, when that had ceased to exist, by the formation of the Lal Bagh as horticultural and botanical gardens in 1856. A profitable means of livelihood was thus opened to native gardeners, some of whom have set up as florists and seedsmen, replenishing their stocks direct from England. Owing to the profusion of beautiful plants that may with care be successfully cultivated here, much taste has been exhibited in the laying out and adornment of gardens, both public and private. Of roses alone, upwards of 258 varieties have been established; of ferns, more than 160 kinds; of crotons, 122; of ornamental flowering shrubs, brilliant foliage plants, gay annuals and gorgeous-blossomed creepers and orchids, an endless number.[1] There is reason to believe that hybridising and cross-breeding, which have produced such wonderful results in Europe, might be carried out with great success here.

The remarkable adaptation of the climate to the out-door cultivation of plants from different parts of the world will be seen from the following list of some growing in the Lal Bagh without any protection whatever:—

| | |
|---|---|
| From S. America | Achras sapota, eucharis grandiflora, allamanda grandiflora. |
| „ N. America | Magnolia grandiflora, quercus rubra, phlox paniculata. |
| „ Cape of Good Hope | Agapanthus umbillatus, melianthus major, gazania splendens. |
| „ South Sea Islands | Acalypha tricolor, crotons. |
| „ Australia | Castanospermum australe, alsophila latebrosa, coccoloba plotyclada. |
| „ China | Cupressus funebris, farfugium grande, alternanthera sessilis. |
| „ G. Britain | Anagalis carrulea, viola odorata, myosotis arvensis. |
| „ Mexico | Fuchsia fulgens, ageratum mexicanum, agave americana. |

These plants, which in their natural habitats are found at various elevations, are all growing luxuriantly here in the same soil and under the same exposure as the tropical plants of India.[2]

**Wild Animals.**—Early legends tenant the ancient forests which covered the District with the following wild animals:—*simha*, the lion;

[1] The names of the principal genera, taken from the catalogue of the Lal Bagh, Bangalore, have been given in Vol. I., at pp. 85 ff.

[2] From Mr. Cameron's report on the Lal Bagh. An account of the plants of economic value experimentally introduced here has been included in Vol. I., pp. 169 ff.

*sárdúla*, the tiger; *hariṇa*, the deer; *kapi*, the monkey; *bhallúka*, the bear; *kunjara*, the elephant; *srigála*, the jackal; *mahisha*, the buffalo; *biḍála*, the cat; *chamára*, the yak, or perhaps the bison. The lion, it is needless to say, no longer ranges the forest, nor are the elephant, bison, and wild buffalo now to be met with, though the first is said to appear occasionally in the south of the Kankanhalli taluq. But to the remainder on the list may be added the cheetah or panther, the wild hog, and the porcupine. The larger game, which is not plentiful, is mostly confined to the Magadi, Kankanhalli and Closepet taluqs. Of the smaller animals, field-rats are very numerous. The bandicoot, or large pig-rat, infests stables and the neighbourhood of manure pits.

*Birds.*—Jungle fowl, pea-fowl and spur fowl are met with in the woods; bustard, floriken, partridge, quail, rock-pigeon in the open country; snipe, teal and wild duck in the tanks and paddy fields. Birds of bright plumage wing their way in every direction, but none that are not common to the country generally.

*Fish.*—The *bestars* or fishermen are acquainted with the following species of fresh-water fish, caught by them in their nets:—Bále-minu (*sparus spilotus*), ávu minu, korama, kuchchu minu, áne minu, marali minu, gende minu, giralu minu, goddale minu, pakke minu, shígadi minu, handi gorava, súle sasile, yemmechelu minu, malagu minu, hú minu, murave, domme, vonike tatte minu, náyi chelu, kallu korava. Those brought to market at Bangalore are principally obtained in the Dharmámbudhi and Kempámbudhi tanks at Bangalore, the Jigani, Hoskote, Bellandur, Vartur, Tallikere, Anekal, Nelamangala, and Hullur tanks.

**Domestic Animals.**—These consist principally of horses, cows, bullocks, buffaloes, sheep, goats, asses and pigs, dogs and cats. The following figures, for 1893, show approximately the extent of the agricultural live stock of the District:—Cows and bullocks, 375,015: horses, 288; ponies, 3,139; donkeys, 8,827; sheep and goats, 317,063; pigs, 2,210. Elephants and camels were formerly kept by the Commissariat Department. The last-named are said not to thrive here, and only mules are now kept for transport.

*Horses.*—Some horses are bred by the Silahdars from country mares and English, Arab or Australian stallions, imported for the purpose by Government. Excellent horses are sometimes reared, but the want of good pasture prevents horse-breeding on an extensive scale. The market, however, is well supplied annually, by dealers, with horses and ponies from Arabia, Persia, Afghanistan, and Dharwar. Most of the Persian and Afghan horses used to be purchased by the Remount Depôt of the Madras Government at Oosoor. The more powerful Australian horses imported to Madras of late years have, among

Europeans, nearly superseded all others for carriage use, and to a great extent for riding. The average prices of the various descriptions of horses are:—For Arabs and Australians, Rs. 1,000 and upwards; Persians and Gulf Arabs, from Rs. 500; Afghan, from Rs. 400; Dharwar and Mahratta ponies, from Rs. 200; but the demands of polo have sent up the prices of good ponies to high figures. Besides green grass, horses are generally fed on kulti or horse-gram (*dolichos biflorus*), which is given boiled morning and evening, mixed with a certain proportion of bran.

*Bullocks.*—These useful animals, of excellent breed, are plentiful. With the exception of a few buffaloes, they are the only animals used for agricultural labour. An average pair of bullocks will plough two acres of unirrigated land a day. They are fed chiefly on rági straw, ballar or avare (cow-gram), and the residue of the threshings of dry crops. The price of an ordinary pair of plough-bullocks varies from Rs. 30 to 50 and more; but draught bullocks of a superior kind, fit for carriage or dawk purposes, cost from Rs. 70 to 200 and more. With a light carriage they are capable of trotting the usual stage of six miles in an hour. Bullocks employed for this purpose generally have a feed of boiled horse-gram in the evening. The ryots about Bangalore are very fond of rearing bulls. These are bought as calves from dealers, and, being well fed and cared for, are subsequently resold, at considerable profit, to the ryots of other parts who have not the same favourable opportunities as regards climate and grazing for bringing up good cattle. The principal cattle fairs in the District are held in connection with the Gháti Subrahmanya festival in Dod-Ballapur taluq in December, the Madduramma *parishe* at Huskur (Anekal taluq) in March, and the Gangadevi *parishe* at Nallur (Hoskote taluq) in October.

*Cows.*—The common village cows are very inferior animals, owing to the want of proper care and attention. They subsist entirely on the waste lands about the villages and on the stubble-grazing after harvest. Very good cows are reared in Bangalore, where they sell for from Rs. 40 to 80 apiece. They are fed on green fodder, rági straw, and the husks of avare, and should yield from three to five quarts a day when in full milk. Dairy farming on any scale is carried on only in Bangalore, and perhaps to a small extent at Whitefield.

Cattle-shows were held for some years by Government, at which liberal prizes were given, with the view of promoting an improvement in the breed of domestic cattle. Breeding bulls from the Amrit Mahal have also been stationed at favourable places.

*Sheep and Goats.*—These are numerous and thrive well. The wool of the former, however, is of a coarse description, and used only for the manufacture of native blankets and horse-rugs. An account will be found elsewhere of the experimental sheep farm formerly maintained by Government, and the steps since taken to improve the breed. The quality of the mutton sold in Bangalore has been greatly improved by means of prizes offered by the Municipality at the new market.

*Poultry.*—There is as much room for improvement in regard to the rearing of poultry as there is in regard to dairy produce generally. The dunghill and the streets are the principal run of the fowls. The great demand which exists for eggs and poultry has resulted in establishing prices which would probably well remunerate any one engaging in this business. Amateur poultry yards are often kept in Bangalore, in which the best laying and fattening foreign breeds, such as Dorkings, Brahmas, Spanish, &c., are successfully reared, in addition to Guinea-fowl, turkeys, geese, and ducks. Some of the settlers in Whitefield have also taken up poultry-farming. Game cocks are kept by natives of many classes for fighting purposes, and for the same object fighting quails are kept by Muhammadans.

## HISTORY

The earliest historical legends connected with the Bangalore District relate to Nandagudi in the Hoskote taluq, and to Mankunda near Channapatna in the taluq of that name, at both of which places there are signs of ancient remains. The first is said to have been the capital of *Uttunga Bhuja*, whose nephews, the Nanda princes, being imprisoned by him, obtained their release and seized the kingdom through the machinations of a sage named Chanikya. Near where Malur now stands, a king named *Vijayapálá*, of the *soma vamsa* or lunar line, is related to have established a city named *Makunda* or *Muganda* in the *krita yuga* or first age.

Although the name Nandagudi has evidently given rise to confusion between the origin of that place and the incidents of Chandra Gupta's usurpation of Nanda's empire as dramatised in the Mudra Rakshasa, yet the legends exhibit a close connection with the account of the rise of the Andhra or Telugu kings known as the *Kakati* family. "The Kakateya family," says Wilson,[1] "is deduced from the Pandavas, and in general the line proceeds direct from Janamejaya through Satanika to Kshemaka and his two sons, Vijayarka and Somendra. Their sons, named severally Vishnuvardhana and *Uttunga Bhuja*, disagreeing, the

[1] *McK. Coll.* I. cxxvi.

latter quitted Upper India and settled to the south of the Godavari. His son Nanda, who founded the fort of Nandagiri, married the daughter of the Chola king, by whom he had *Vijayapála.*" Another account by Taylor[1] is as follows:—"The lunar line is specified down to Kshemaka. From that line are deduced Vijiyaditya and Somendra. The son of the first was Vishnuvardhana; of the other the son was *Uttunga Bhuja.* These two latter divided the country between them. Vishnuvardhana settled at Dharmapuri[2] on the western bank of the Godavari river. Four hundred villages or towns became subject to him. His son was Nanda, who built a town called Nandagiri, in which the four castes of Hindus were located. His minister was named Dandasasi Nayaka. Nanda formed a marriage alliance with the daughter of a Chola king at Kanjevaram, and, on returning, equitably governed his kingdom. His son was *Vijayapála*, who was munificent." The history from which the above is an extract assigns to *Vijayapála* the date of about 400 A.D., and he may with some probability be taken as identical with the founder of Makunda, whatever the truth may be as regards the origin of Nandagudi.

**Gangas.**—That Makunda was a place of considerable importance as early as the seventh century is beyond doubt, from the fact that at that period Bhúvikrama and Sivamára, two sovereigns of the Ganga line, made it the royal residence. The whole of the District must have been included in the dominions of that dynasty for some centuries before, for it formed part of the Gangavádi Ninety-six Thousand. A subdivision called Chikka Gangavádi, or the Lesser Gangavádi, occupied the valley of the Shimsha, with Honganur (Channapatna taluq) as its chief town. In the eighth century S'rípurusha made Mányapura (Manne in Nelamangala taluq) the royal residence during some part of his reign, and from the Chola references to the place it must have been important long after.

**Pallavas.**—Pallava and Nolamba inscriptions are met with to the east, in Hoskote and Devanhalli taluqs.

**Rashtrakutas.**—An inscription of the time of Akálavarsha occurs in Devanhalli taluq, and one or two in Hoskote taluq may belong to this line.

**Cholas.**—The traces of the Chola conquest in the eleventh century are numerous in the western taluqs. Their inscriptions are found especially in the vicinity of the Ganga city of Makunda, namely, at Malur, Kudalur, and Malúrpatna, the latter indeed receiving the name

[1] *Cat. Rais. Or. MSS.* iii. 481.

[2] There is a village near Nandagudi named Dharmesvara, which professes to be of great antiquity.

of Nikarilichólapura. Mágadi is said to have been founded by a Chola king, and names and inscriptions testify to their influence from there to Nelamangala. In this latter taluq they make a boast of their conquest of Mannai-kaṭakam, the Manne above-mentioned. This part of the country seems to have been named by them the Vikramachóla-maṇḍala. Chola-Ganga, described as the great king of Orissa, is said in an inscription of the twelfth century to have been born in the Hejjáji Twelve of the Kádanur Seventy (Dod Ballapur taluq). To the east we have Chola inscriptions in Hoskote taluq, which it would appear was included in the Kolar country designated the Nikarilichóla-mandala.

**Hoysalas.**—Inscriptions of the Hoysala kings in all parts attest their dominion over the District, and to Víra Ballála, probably the one who reigned from 1172 to 1219, is attributed the adventure which gave Bangalore its name, as related in connection with that place. Vishnu-varddhana's first queen, S'ántala-devi, died at S'ivaganga, which seems to have been a possession of her father's. In the thirteenth century, when the Hoysala territories were divided between Nárasimha III. and his brother, or half-brother, Rámanátha, the latter had the northern parts of the District included in his possessions, and held his court at Kundána in Devanhalli taluq. A number of inscriptions occur, especially in the Yelahanka country, of the last days of the Hoysalas, in the time of Ballála III., when he had his residence at Unnámale (Tiruvannámalai, Trinomalai, South Arcot). In one he is described as living at Virúpákshipura, perhaps the one in Channapatna taluq.

**Yadavas.**—To the time of these kings, who were rivals of the Hoysalas, perhaps belongs the tradition of a city north of the village of Binnamangala in the Nelamangala taluq. The *sthala-purana* of Stambhodadhi (Kammasandra) contains at length an account of how, in the *dvapara yuga* or second age, a prince named *Sumati*, the son of Hemachandra, king of Karnata-desa, came by his father's command from the capital city of Yadu-patna, and, after a march of thirteen days, arrived at Devarayadurga (Tumkur District), where he besieged a robber chief named Andhaka, *alias* Lingaka, for one year, and finally seized and put him to death with all his family and relations; and how he then established a city named *Bhumandana*, on the site above described, and took up his residence there for the security of that part of his father's dominions. This story may possibly relate to Rama-chandra, here corrupted into Hemachandra.

**Vijayanagar.**—Under the *Vijayanagara* sovereigns, who subsequently became paramount in the south, arose the local rulers of greatest note in the modern annals of the District.

**Morasu Wokkalu.**—It is related that about the end of the fourteenth century a party of travellers, consisting of seven farmers with their families, halted at the foot of a hill named Ramaswami-betta, to the east of Nandidurga. From their having arrived in carts they were called the *baṇḍi kápalu* or cart ryots, which may either indicate that carts were an unusual sight or have been equivalent to "carriage people," denoting the possession of greater wealth than those among whom they came to settle. They were of Telugu origin and subsequently became known as the *Morasu Wọkkalu,* a name still borne by a large section of ryots in this District. They were worshippers of Baire Deva, and had the strange custom of amputating the ring and little fingers of the right hand of their daughterss before marriage. The leader of the band was *Rana Baire Gauḍa,* who had been forced to fly from the village of Alur, near Conjeveram, in order to preserve his daughter Doddamma from *mesalliance* with a powerful suitor of lower caste. The fugitives, escaping along the banks of the Palar, were at one point in imminent danger of falling into the hands of their pursuers, when the girl who was the innocent cause of the flight invoking the aid of Ganga and casting her earring into the water as an offering, the river miraculously divided, allowing her whole party to cross, and then interposed its swollen current to baffle the pursuers.

On the night of their encampment on the spot before mentioned Rana Baire Gauda was directed in a dream to settle in that neighbourhood. They accordingly built some huts and formed the village of Ahuti, now Avati, north of Devanhalli. But before long they resolved to separate. *Rana Baire Gauda* remained at Avati and his son was the founder of Devanhalli, Dod-Ballapura and Chik-Ballapura; *Sanna Baire Gauda* betook himself to Holuvanhalli or Korampur, and founded Kortagere (Tuṃkur District); *Timme Gauda* went to Sugatur near Jangamkote, and became the ruler of Kolar and Punganur and the founder of Hoskote, while a descendant of his founded Anekal. The destination of three others is not known, but the seventh established himself at Yelahanka.

**Jaya Gauda.**—This was *Jaya Gauda,* who acquired the title of Yelahanka Nadu Prabhu or lord of the Yelahanka-nad, as a feudatory of the Vijayanagar sovereigns. He ruled for 15 years (1418–1433) and was succeeded by his son *Giḍḍe Gauda.* Being without children, the latter is related to have made a vow to Kempamma, the consort of Baire Deva, that if by her favour he should be blessed with male issue, his descendants ever afterwards should bear her name. The goddess was propitious and he had a son, whom in accordance with his vow he named Kempa Nanja Gauda. After a rule of 10 years (1433–1443)

Gidde Gauda was succeeded by *Kempa Nanja Gauda*. This chief governed his territory with benevolence and justice for the long space of 70 years (1443–1513).

**Kempe Gauda.**—Kempe Gauda, his son, the most distinguished of the line, succeeded, and acquired the favour of Krishna Raya and Achyuta Raya, the kings of Vijayanagar. Once, while making a tour through the Yelahanka-nad, he came to a village named Sivanasamudram, 10 miles south of Yelahanka, and 3 miles south of Bengalúru.[1] The site appearing to him favourable for the erection of a fort, he obtained permission of Achyuta Raya to establish his capital there, and in 1537 built a mud fort and transferred to his new town the name of Bengalúru (Bangalore). As a reward for his zeal and activity, the following places were granted to him by Achyuta Raya, namely, Old Bengaluru, Vartur, Yelahanka, Bevur, Halasur, Tengeri, Talagattapur, Jigani, Kumbalgod, Kanalli, Banavar, and Hesarghatta. The revenue derived from the twelve hoblis amounted to 30,000 pagodas. This accession of wealth was partly devoted to the erection of temples, of which the principal are those of Venkatramana-swami in the fort of Bangalore, of Gavi Gangadharesvara at Gavipura, a mile to the south of the fort, and those of Basavesvara and others in the same neighbourhood. A large tank was formed near these edifices and named the Kempámbudhi after the family goddess.

Not content with feudal honours, the chief now usurped the prerogatives of royalty and established a mint (*ṭankasále*), whence issued the Baire Deva coins. At this period Achyuta Raya, his patron, died, and was succeeded on the Vijayanagar throne by Sadasiva Raya, under the guardianship of Rama Raja. Rumour of Kempe Gauda's proceedings having reached the court, he was summoned to account and cast into prison, his territory being sequestered and added to that of *Jagadeva Ráyal*. After remaining in confinement at Anegundi for five years, he obtained release by the payment of a heavy fine, and his possessions were restored to him. His residence at the metropolis apparently wrought some change in his views, for on his return he is said to have suppressed the custom of amputating the fingers of the marriageable females in his family, considering it incompatible with his dignity as Lord of the country.[2] He appears also to have secretly adopted the worship of Siva in place of that of Baire Deva, the family

[1] This was Hale (or old) Bengalúru, as it was afterwards called, the site of which is pointed out near Koḍigehaḷḷi, north-west of Hebbal tank. The Bangalore District was for a long time called the Sivanasamudram country.

[2] The observance of this barbarous custom continued in some branches of the sect until 1874, when it was prohibited by Government.

god. His rule continued till 1569, being 43 years before and five years after his imprisonment.

His son, *Immaḍi* (or the second) *Kempe Gauda* succeeded to the government. By him were erected the Somesvara pagoda at Halasur, and a number of tanks in various parts. He extended his territory westwards and obtained possession of Savandurga and Magadi, where he built a mud fort and the large temple, now in ruins, of Somesvara, two miles to the west.

**Jagadeva Rayal.**—After the overthrow of the Vijayanagar empire by a Muhammadan confederacy on the field of Talikota in 1564, the dominions of that mighty Hindu sovereignty fell a prey to numerous invaders. The Bijapur and Ahmednagar princes having agreed on different lines of conquest to avoid mutual interference, the forces of the former made many acquisitions to the south. Emboldened by success, an attempt was made on Penugonda, which had for a time been the capital of the ousted kings of Vijayanagar, but whence Timma Raja had transferred the seat of government some years before to Chandragiri. The attack on Penugonda was gallantly repelled by *Jagadeva Ráyal*,[1] a relation of the Raja's, and his services were rewarded by bestowal of a large district which extended his possessions from Baramahal to the Western Ghats. He fixed his capital at Channapatna, which his descendants held till 1630, when it was captured after a long siege by Chama Raja of Mysore, together with Kankanhalli.

In 1638 Ran-dulha Khan, the general of the Adil Shahi prince of Bijapur, captured Bangalore from Kempe Gauda and made it his chief residence, the Gauda retiring to his stronghold on Savandurga.

**Shahji.**—On Ran-dulha Khan's return to court, *Shahji*, father of the celebrated Sivaji, being second in command, was appointed to govern the districts subdued by the Bijapur forces in Karnataka and Dravida, named *Carnatic Bijapur*. With the view of attaching him to the fortunes of the government, he was afterwards granted as a jágir Bangalore, Kolar, Hoskota, Dod-Ballapur and Sira. He fixed his residence at first at Bangalore, but afterwards, when not engaged in military expeditions, lived sometimes at Dod-Ballapur and sometimes at Kolar.

The story of his eventful life is not without romance and demands more than a passing notice. His father, Malloji Bhosla, was an officer, serving with a few men mounted on his own horses, in the Nizam Shahi army, in the time of Malik Amber, the celebrated Abyssinian minister of Ahmednagar. He was, it is said, for many years childless when, in

[1] The *Jug Deo Rayeel* of Wilks.

1594, by virtue of the prayers of Shah Sherif, a Muhammadan saint at Ahmednagar, his wife bore a son, whom in gratitude he named Shah-ji after the holy man. When five years old the boy accompanied his father to an entertainment at the house of his commanding officer, Lukji Jadu Rao, a Mahratta chief of high birth, who was at the head of 10,000 men. Jadu Rao, attracted by the appearance of Shahji, seated him beside his daughter Jeejee, a pretty child of three or four years old, and when they began to play together remarked jestingly that they were a fine pair. But the merriment which this occasioned was checked by Malloji's rising and calling upon his friends to witness that Jadu Rao had formed with him a marriage contract. The chief seemed astonished and was mute. Affecting to treat what had passed as a mere joke, he next day asked Malloji the father to a dinner. But the latter declined the invitation unless Jadu Rao would formally recognize Shahji as his son-in-law, which was indignantly refused.

The crafty father, however, never relinquished the design, and having acquired wealth and a high command, was eventually successful. The marriage of Shahji to Jeejee Bai was accordingly celebrated with great pomp in 1604, and honoured by the presence of the Sultan. The offspring of this union were Sambhaji and the illustrious Sivaji.

In 1620 Shahji, who had succeeded to his father's jágir, distinguished himself in a battle against the Mughals. In 1629 he appears as a supporter of the cause of Khan Jehan Lodi, who had been driven into rebellion by the jealousy of the emperor Shah Jehan. Finding he had adopted a failing cause, and fearing the loss of his jágir, Shahji made a tender of his services to the Mughal emperor, promising, on condition of receiving a safe-conduct and a letter of pardon, to repair to the imperial presence. The indulgence being granted, he came to court accompanied by his immediate dependents and a body of two thousand horse. Having paid his respects to Shah Jehan, he was promoted to the command of 5,000 horse, and not only confirmed in his patrimonial jágir but received a grant for some other districts.

In 1632, dissatisfied with the proceedings of the imperial court, he made overtures to the Bijapur government with such inducements as led to their acceptance. In order to detach him from this alliance his wife and family, who in consequence of his second marriage had separated from him, were seized by the imperialists, but immediately released through the influence of Jeejee Bai's relations, who were adherents of the emperor. Shahji became thenceforward a leading partisan of the Bijapur state, and subdued the Ahmednagar territories, of which he made himself regent. But in 1636 Muhammad Adil Shah was compelled to sue for peace from the emperor. Pardon to

Shahji, on condition of giving up his forts, was one of the articles of the treaty concluded, and from this time his attention was confined to the Carnatic provinces.

In 1649, being suspected of secretly inciting the rebellion of his son Sivaji, he was treacherously seized at an entertainment. On being brought to court he denied all connection with his son's proceedings, but nothing could convince Muhammad Adil Shah of his innocence. Enraged at his supposed contumacy, the king ordered him to be confined in a stone dungeon, the door of which was built up, except a small opening, which he was told would be for ever closed if within a certain period his son did not submit. Through the influence of the Mughal emperor Shah Jehan and others he was saved from a cruel death and released from his dungeon on giving security, but was kept a prisoner at large in Bijapur for four years.

In 1653 Shahji was permitted to return to his government. Soon after his restoration his eldest son Sambhaji, who during his absence had been at the head of affairs, was killed in an expedition. In 1662, with the approval of his sovereign, Shahji, accompanied by his other son Venkoji (or Ekoji),[1] paid a visit to Sivaji and was successful in effecting a reconciliation between him and the Bijapur state.

In 1664 the active career of Shahji was brought to an end, at the age of 70, by a fall from his horse while hunting at Basavapatna, on the banks of the Tungabhadra, in the Shimoga District, where he had joined the Bijapur army to assist in reducing some refractory zamindars. At his death he possessed, besides the estates conferred upon him by Bijapur before mentioned, the fort of Arnee, Porto Novo, and the territory of Tanjore, acquisitions made by conquest.

His son Venkoji, or Ekoji, continued to govern the jágir with the aid of Raghunath Narayan, who had been his father's principal adviser. The latter is described as a person of superior abilities. His relations with the son of his patron were never altogether amicable, though mutual interests prevented an open rupture. But in 1675 Raghunath Narayan left the Carnatic and in course of time entered the service of Sivaji, who received him with distinction. The intention of laying claim to a half share in his father's possessions as an hereditary right had been formed by Sivaji, and with the aid of this new counsellor he matured his plans for an expedition into the Carnatic and the enforcement of his claim. The expediton which set out in 1677, and the negotiations between

[1] *Venkajee* in Duff, *Vencaji* in Elphinstone, *Angojee* or *Ekojee* in Scott, *Eccojee* in Wilks. The latter is no doubt a corruption of the former, in the same way as *Venkata* is often at the present day transformed into *Enkta*. I have attempted to reconcile the spelling of the two forms.

Sivaji and Venkoji are matters of history. By 1678 all the disputed districts had been overrun, and Sivaji's horsemen levied *chouth* and *sardeshmukhi* in every direction, but an amicable arrangement having been come to, Venkoji regained possession the same year. Sivaji died in 1680.

**Mysore Wodeyars.**—Meanwhile the Wodeyars of Mysore, who had gained possession of Seringapatam, were rising to power. In 1654 Kempe Gauda of Magadi had been defeated at Yelahanka by Kanthirava Narasa Raja with great loss and forced to pay a contribution. In 1687 Bangalore also passed into the hands of the Mysore kings in the following manner:—Sivaji was dead, and Venkoji, established on the throne of Tanjore, found his distant dominion of Bangalore to be an expensive and precarious possession, insulated in a great degree by the contending armies which constantly ranged over the intermediate country. He therefore determined to sell it to the highest bidder, and Chikka Deva Raja, who, taking advantage of the general anarchy, had been gradually extending his possessions, finally agreed to purchase it for three lakhs of rupees (£30,000). He accordingly sent a detachment to occupy the new purchase and to pay the money. But the negotiation having been long protracted had become a matter of notoriety, and attracted the attention of Harji Raja, the Mahratta commander-in-chief at S'enji, and of Aurangzeb, who had just raised the siege of Golkonda. These powers, entertaining a high opinion of the importance of Bangalore, sent each a detachment from their distant and opposite stations to anticipate the Raja of Mysore. Khasim Khan, the general of Aurangzeb, by forced marches along the west of the Ghats, arrived first, and the place being in a dismantled state preparatory to its sale, fell into his hands almost without opposition. The detachment of Harji Raja, finding themselves forestalled, marched back as they came. The imperial colours, however, were hoisted for only four days on the ramparts of Bangalore. For Khasim Khan, who had more important objects in view, resolved to accept the terms still offered by the Mysore Raja, as he would thereby obtain a large sum of money and eseape the necessity of leaving a detachment to occupy the place. At the same time its use as a point of communication would still be preserved. Thus, in July 1687, this important town became a part of the Mysore kingdom.

At Dod-Ballapura is an interesting inscription of the thirty-second year of Aurangzeb (1689), recording its capture by Khasim Khan and its bestowal upon a descendant of one of the courtiers at Delhi.

In 1728 Deva Raja, Dalavayi of Dodda Krishna Raja, made an attack upon Magadi with a view of replenishing the treasury, which had been heavily drained by the contributions levied by the Muhammadans and the Mahrattas. Kempe Gauda imprudently allowed himself to be surrounded in the weak fort of Magadi and was forced to surrender at discretion. He was carried to Seringapatam as a state prisoner, and there ended his days, the last of his line. The impregnable fortress of Savandurga, with the accumulated plunder of nearly two hundred years, thus fell into the hands of the Mysore army.

In 1749 the siege of Devanhalli was undertaken, in which Haidar Ali first distinguished himself as a volunteer horseman, and here his son and successor Tipu was afterwards born. In 1758 the fort and district of Bangalore were conferred on Haidar as a jágir in recognition of his distinguished services. In 1759 the Mahrattas under Gopal Hari invested Bangalore and surprised Channapatna, but both places were relieved by his address. In 1761 he obtained from Basalat Jang the cession of Hoskote and of Dod-Ballapur, the jágir of Abbas Kuli Khan. From this year dates his usurpation of the Mysore throne, from which period therefore the District was under the Muhammadan rule of himself and of his son and successor, Tipu Sultan.

In 1791 Bangalore was captured from Tipu by the British under Lord Cornwallis, to whom also Devanhalli and other places submitted. Savandurga, Ramgiri, Sivangiri and other hill forts were taken. On the death of Tipu in 1799 the District was included by the treaty of Seringapatam in the territory of the Mysore Raja. Under the native government which followed, the Bangalore and Kolar Districts constituted the Bangalore Faujdari, which was afterwards called the Bangalore Division, until the formation of the Nundydroog Division in 1863, when the name Bangalore was confined to the District. The most important topical changes that occurred in the District during this period were the foundation of Closepet in 1800, and the establishment of the British Cantonment at Bangalore in 1809, the latter of which events has added so greatly to the wealth and prosperity of the surrounding country.

On the Rendition in 1881, the site of the Bangalore Cantonment was made over as an Assigned Tract to the British Government, who at the same time surrendered to Mysore the island of Seringapatam. In 1882 were established the Eurasian and Anglo-Indian colonies of Whitefield and Sausmond, in the east of the Bangalore taluq. The Closepet Sub-Division, comprising the taluqs of Channapatna, Magadi and Kankanhalli, was formed in 1884.

In 1888 the fort of Bangalore was given up to the Mysore civil authorities, being no longer required for military purposes, the Residency and grounds being added to the Assigned Tract in exchange.

## POPULATION

*Number.*—The entire population of the District is 802,994, according to the census of 1891, the number of males being 399,486, and of females 403,508.

*Density.*—This gives 262·33 persons to a square mile, a higher rate than in any other District of the Province. But the result is largely affected by the presence of the Town and Cantonment of Bangalore, the united population of which is 180,366. Excluding these from the calculation, the density of population in the District is 204·17 persons per square mile. Individual taluqs show a much higher rate. The most thickly peopled at the time of the census was Anekal, where there were 288·6 persons to a square mile. In Bangalore (taluq only) the rate was 269, in Dod-Ballapur 231, in Nelamangala 229·5, in Hoskote 223·9, in Channapatna 219·2.

*By Religion.*—The numbers professing each of the principal forms of faith are as follows :—

| Religions. | Above 15. | | Under 15. | | Total. | Percentage. |
|---|---|---|---|---|---|---|
| | Male. | Female. | Male. | Female. | | |
| Hindus ... ... ... | 224,716 | 229,913 | 126,251 | 127,257 | 708,137 | 88·2 |
| Muhammadans ... ... | 21,654 | 20,557 | 13,737 | 13,279 | 69,227 | 8·5 |
| Jains ... ... ... | 576 | 477 | 272 | 253 | 1,578 | 2 |
| Christians ... ... | 7,660 | 7,222 | 4,596 | 4,531 | 24,009 | 3·0 |
| Others .. ... ... | 18 | 11 | 6 | 8 | 43 | — |
| Total ... | 254,624 | 258,180 | 144,862 | 145,328 | 802,994 | |

**Increase.**—The following table compares the statistics according to the *khâneshumâri* accounts of 1853-4 with those obtained in the censuses of 1871, 1881 and 1891 :—

| Taluq. | 1853-4. | 1871. | 1881. | 1891. |
|---|---|---|---|---|
| Anekal ... ... ... ... ... ... | 23,596 | 55,828 | 44,423 | 54,834 |
| Bangalore ... ... ... ... ... | 267,717 | 231,666 | 233,571 | 269,683 |
| Channapatna ... ... ... ... ... | 66,535 | 109,304 | 87,484 | 99,294 |
| Devanhalli ... ... ... ... ... | 45,117 | 57,815 | 44,079 | 53,582 |
| Dod-Ballapur ... ... ... ... . | 46,732 | 77,375 | 52,021 | 65,613 |
| Hoskote ... ... ... ... ... | 38,194 | 65,694 | 51,903 | 60,667 |
| Kankanhalli ... ... ... ... ... | 47,136 | 84,551 | 65,323 | 71,868 |
| Magadi ... ... ... ... ... ... | 51,011 | 86,156 | 50,295 | 64,334 |
| Nelamangala ... ... ... ... ... | 32,468 | 73,844 | 50,565 | 63,119 |
| Total ... ... ... | 618,506 | 842,233 | 679,664 | 802,994 |

Some of the variations are due to redistribution of taluqs, and to changes in the limits of the District. There was an apparent increase on the whole up to 1871 equivalent to 33·9 per cent. in 18 years. But 25 per cent., as we have seen (Vol. I.), was due to defective enumeration in the early record. The loss inflicted by the famine of 1877–8 sent down the total 19·3 per cent. by 1881, but it had risen again 18·14 per cent. by 1891. The net result may be stated at an increase of 3·6 per cent. in 38 years.

**Classes.**—Classified according to sources of livelihood and nationality, the population is composed as follows :—

| | No. | Per cent. |
|---|---|---|
| A—Agricultural... ... ... ... ... | 293,790 | 36·58 |
| B—Professional... ... ... ... ... | 40,988 | 5·10 |
| C—Commercial... ... ... ... ... | 60,191 | 7·24 |
| D—Artisan and Village Menial ... ... | 273,885 | 34·10 |
| E—Vagrant Minor Artisans and Performers... | 40,216 | 5·00 |
| Races and Nationalities ... ... ... | 93,252 | 11·61 |
| Others, not stated ... ... ... ... | 672 | ·08 |

The castes or classes which number over 10,000 are the following, in order of strength. These account for 716,289, or 89·35 per cent., of the population :—

| | | | | | |
|---|---|---|---|---|---|
| Wokkaliga ... | 225,511 | Bráhmana ... | 29,882 | Native Christians... ... | 15,656 |
| Holeya ... ... | 81,369 | Tigala ... ... | 29,192 | Beda ... ... | 15,339 |
| Musalmans ... | 69,227 | Banajiga ... | 28,437 | Panchála ... | 14,046 |
| Mádiga ... ... | 46,128 | Neyigára ... | 23,862 | Agasa ... ... | 11,447 |
| Kuruba ... ... | 41,407 | Wodda ... | 20,846 | Maráta ... | 10,616 |
| Lingáyita[1] ... | 32,894 | Golla ... .. | 20,430 | | |

The most numerous classes of Wokkaliga are the Gangaḍikára (105,284), Morasu (53,360), Reḍḍi (24,466), Kunchaṭiga (11,840), and Vellála (6,048). Of Musalmans, the Shekhs number 38,923, Pathans 12,057, and Saiyids 11,407. The largest sects of Brahmans are Baḍaganáḍ (5,311), Mulikináḍ (3,816), Deshasta (3,410), and S'rívaishnava (3,354). Of Banajigas the most numerous are Telugu Banajigas (12,896), Bale Banajigas (4,183), Seṭṭi Banajigas (3,673), and Linga Banajigas (3,187, included under Lingáyita). The Bale and Seṭṭi are mostly in the Civil and Military Station of Bangalore. Of the Neyigára, the Devánga number 10,791, and Togaṭa 5,556. Mannu Woḍḍa number 8,390, and Kallu Woḍḍa 5,640. Of the Panchála, 13,230 are classed as goldsmiths, 647 as blacksmiths, and 216 as brass and coppersmiths.

Besides the above the following are important trading classes :—Nagarta (5,289), Komaṭi (4,766), and Mudali (1,625); also 161 Baniya, the latter being all in the Civil and Military Station of Bangalore.

[1] Of this sect 1,045 besides are included in Wokkaliga.

**Agricultural Stock.**—The returns for 1893 show that there were then in the District (exclusive of the Civil and Military Station of Bangalore), 375,015 cows and bullocks, 288 horses, 3,139 ponies, 8,827 donkeys, 317,063 sheep and goats, 2,210 pigs, 34,532 buffaloes, 81,019 ploughs, 2 boats, and 16,347 carts.

**Tanks and Wells.**—There were, in the same limits, at the same period, 1,988 Government tanks (of which 1,324 were reported to be in good order), 400 Inam tanks, 16,725 wells, and 354 canals.

**Dwellings.**—The number of occupied houses throughout the District was 141,232, of which 43,975 were in towns, and 97,257 in villages.

**Towns.**—The District contains 16 towns, with a total population of 251,721, made up of 183,821 Hindus, 416 Jains, 46,860 Musalmans, 20,586 Christians, and 38 others. The latter are, all but 2, in the Civil and Military Station of Bangalore, and include 23 Brahmos and 6 Parsis.

The following are the names of the towns, with the population of each. All have municipalities :—

| Town | Population | Town | Population |
|---|---|---|---|
| Bangalore, C. & M. Station | 100,081 | Magadi ... ... ... | 4,852 |
| ,, City ... ... | 80,285 | Nelamangala ... ... | 4,171 |
| | | Vadigenhalli ... ... | 3,970 |
| Total | 180,366 | Tyamagondlu ... ... | 3,748 |
| Channapatna ... ... | 9,160 | Kankanhalli ... ... | 3,484 |
| Anekal ... ... ... | 7,419 | Sarjapur ... ... ... | 3,017 |
| Dod-Ballapur ... ... | 7,141 | Yelahanka ... ... ... | 2,668 |
| Devanhalli ... ... | 6,693 | Dommasandra ... ... | 2,284 |
| Closepet ... ... ... | 6,236 | Kengeri ... ... ... | 1,622 |
| Hoskote ... ... ... | 4,890 | | |

**Villages.**—The total number of *asali* or primary villages in 1891 was 2,799, to which were attached 1,646 *dákhali* or secondary villages or hamlets. Of the first, 2,171 were Government villages, 46 sarvamánya, 345 jódi, and 237 káyamgutta. The following are the details by taluqs, given in two different ways :—

| Taluq. | Populated. | | De-populated. | Classified. | | | | Total. |
|---|---|---|---|---|---|---|---|---|
| | Vil-lages. | Ham-lets. | | Govern-ment. | Sarva-mánya. | Jódi. | Káyam-gutta. | |
| Anekal ... | 192 | 34 | 31 | 186 | 3 | 11 | 23 | 223 |
| Bangalore ... | 328 | 237 | 42 | 264 | 4 | 26 | 76 | 370 |
| Channapatna .. | 249 | 315 | 14 | 235 | 13 | 7 | 8 | 540 |
| Devanhalli .. | 242 | 25 | 43 | 195 | 1 | 66 | 23 | 285 |
| Dod-Ballapur... | 296 | 120 | 40 | 266 | 6 | 48 | 16 | 336 |
| Hoskote ... | 307 | 28 | 61 | 259 | 3 | 88 | 18 | 368 |
| Kankanhalli ... | 237 | 370 | 35 | 255 | 4 | 2 | 11 | 272 |
| Magadi ... | 297 | 354 | 41 | 252 | 2 | 56 | 28 | 338 |
| Nelamangala ... | 302 | 163 | 42 | 259 | 10 | 41 | 34 | 344 |

**Great Festivals.**—The principal concourse of people occurs at the following religious festivals:—

At *Lagumainhalli*, Dod-Ballapur taluq, on the occasion of the *Ghati Subrahmanya rathotsava*, held for twelve days from from *Pushya suddhu 3rd*, during which 20,000 people assemble.

At *Tirumale* in Magadi taluq, where 10,000 people come together for the *Ranganathaswami parishe*, lasting ten days from full moon in Chaitra.

In *Bangalore*, the *Rangaswami rathotsava* in Ballapur-pet, and the *Dharma Rayan parishe* in Halsur-pet, are both held in April about the same time. The former lasts seven days from the 9th and attracts 3,000 people, the latter for twelve days from the 7th and attracts 5,000 people, principally Tiglar, who celebrate the festival at night.

At *Hoskote*, on full moon day in Vaishakha, 5,000 people keep the *Dharma Rayan karaga*.

There are also gatherings of 5,000 people at Huskur (Anekal taluq) for three days from *Phálguna bahula 3rd*; at Hunasanhalli (Channapatna taluq) for five days in *Chaitra*; and at Sivaganga (Nelamangala taluq) for seven days from *Chaitra* full moon. At the latter place 4,000 people assemble for five days in *Phálguna*; and also at Bannerghatta (Anekal taluq) for three days from *Phálguna bahula 6th*; at Sugganhalli (Magadi taluq) for five days in *Phálguna*; and at Malur (Channapatna taluq) for one day from *Vais'ákla suddha 11th*.

**Fairs.**—The largest weekly fairs are the following:—

| Place. | Taluq. | Day. | No. of Visitors. |
|---|---|---|---|
| Vagata ... ... | Hoskote ... ... | Sunday ... ... | 2,000 |
| Hindiginalu ... | ,, ... ... | Monday ... ... | 3,000 |
| Muduvadi ... ... | Kankanhalli ... | ,, ... ... | 1,500 |
| Closepet ... ... | Closepet ... ... | Tuesday ... ... | 4,000 |
| Krishnarajpur ... | Bangalore ... | ,, ... ... | 2,000 |
| Harohalli ... ... | Kankanhalli ... | Wednesday ... | 1,500 |
| Kankanhalli ... | ,, ... ... | Thursday ... | 2,000 |
| Dod-Ballapura ... | Dod-Ballapura ... | ,, ... ... | 3,000 |
| Nelamangala ... | Nelamangala ... | Friday ... ... | 2,500 |
| Tubgere ... ... | Dod-Ballapura ... | Saturday ... ... | 1,500 |

**Vital Statistics.**—The birth-rate of the District in 1893–4 was 19·8 per mille of the population, while the death-rate was 12·8 per mille. The births registered numbered 14,314, being 7,419 males, and 6,895 females. The total number of deaths registered was 8,848. Excluding the Civil and Military Station, 3,802 were deaths of males and 3,511 of females; of which 6,389 occurred among Hindus, 554 among Muhammadans, and 370 among other classes. The causes of death registered (inclusive of Civil and Military Station) were : from diseases—cholera 112, small-pox 131, fevers 4,345, bowel complaints, 399 ; from injuries—suicide 23, wounds or accidents, 123, snake-bite or wild beasts, 15 ; all other causes 3,640.

**Diseases.**[1]—*Endemics.*—The chief endemic disease is malarious fever, which prevails extensively in some of the taluqs, *viz.*, Closepet, Magadi, and Kankanhalli, and is very frequently attended with enlargement of the spleen. It likewise prevails in all the other taluqs, but not so severely. It is not generally fatal when properly treated. I am not aware that any improvement is taking place in this disease. In some years it occurs severely in certain taluqs, and during others there is a comparative freedom from it. It is difficult to assign any special cause for the origin of the malaria which gives rise to this fever, but, generally speaking, it may be stated that when the rains and seasons are favourable fever is less prevalent. It is most frequent at the commencement and close of the monsoons. Even Bangalore is not exempt from malarious fever, but the type is less marked, and cases met with easily treated. With the exception of malarious fever I am not aware that any other class of disease is endemic in this District.

In Bangalore, of late years, many cases of typhoid fever have occurred among Europeans, but I have never seen a well-marked case in a native. Measles and whooping-cough are also frequently met with, and occasionally diphtheria. Pneumonia in natives, and congestion of the liver in Europeans, are exceedingly common. Syphilis may perhaps be said to be almost endemic both in Bangalore and in the District generally. It prevails extensively, and when neglected, as it often is, assumes a very virulent form.

*Epidemics.*—Cholera becomes epidemic occasionally. When it occurs it generally commences in February or March, and prevails more or less until the commencement of the cold season. In the epidemics that have hitherto occurred, the first cases are generally supposed to have been imported from infected districts in the Madras Presidency.

Small pox is always more or less prevalent in the District during the hot season and commencement of the rains. I do not think the disease is worse or more fatal in this District than in other countries. During some years the disease is comparatively dormant. Vaccination is carried on in every taluq by a staff of vaccinators, but the system is capable of improvement."

The annual deaths from cholera and small-pox since 1881 were as follows :—

[1] Contributed by Dr. Oswald when Surgeon to the Mysore Commission.

| | Cholera. | | Small-pox. | | Cholera. | | Small-pox. |
|---|---|---|---|---|---|---|---|
| 1881 ...... | 2 | ... | 897 | 1888 ...... | 67 | ... | 858 |
| 1882 ...... | 6 | ... | 620 | 1889 ...... | 456 | ... | 777 |
| 1883 ...... | 5 | ... | 995 | 1890 ...... | 31 | ... | 391 |
| 1884 ...... | 20 | ... | 820 | 1891 ...... | 94 | ... | 493 |
| 1885 ...... | 91 | ... | 522 | 1892 ...... | 172 | ... | 1,142 |
| 1886 ...... | 0 | ... | 595 | 1893 ...... | 112 | ... | 140 |
| 1887 ...... | 205 | ... | 284 | | | | |

As cholera is constantly imported by pilgrims returning from Tirupati and other places, quarantine camps and chattrams have been provided at important railway stations for the purpose of affording travellers and pilgrims accommodation close by and passing them on to their destinations with as little delay as possible, thereby preventing their wandering into towns in search of food and shelter. But Surgeon-Colonel McGann, the head of the Medical Department, impresses upon Government "the importance of improving village sanitation. Every advance in that direction, in the way of improving and conserving the water-supply, and promoting general cleanliness, by preventing the storage of manure in the streets and back-yards of houses, and preventing, as far as possible, the defilement of the ground in and immediately around towns and villages would be a distinct gain, would improve the general health of the people, diminish their liability to fevers, bowel complaints and cholera, and tend to check the spread of the last-named disease on its occurrence amongst them." In order to reduce the mortality from small-pox, he strongly urges the introduction of a Compulsory Vaccination Act as the only effectual course.

A severe epidemic of dengue occurred in Bangalore in the latter part of 1872. It was confined chiefly to the native population, and seems to have been imported, as it was prevailing in many parts of India. Influenza was epidemic in 1890.

*Medical Relief.*—Dispensaries, with trained Hospital Assistants in charge, have been established at all taluq stations; and qualified native midwives are supplied to every taluq.

## TRADE

**Manufactures.**—An account has already been given (in Vol. I) of the steam cotton, woollen and silk-mills established at Bangalore, also of the steam oil-mills, soap and candle factories, iron foundry, etc. The most general manufactures, carried on all over the District, are those of cotton cloths and coarse woollen blankets or *kamblis*. The following is a list of cloths made, with prices; the higher prices include silk borders, with more or less admixture of silk.

**Cotton Fabrics.**—*Women's cloths.*—Eight yards long, 1¼ yard wide—chár kane shíre, Rs. 15 to 100; gasgase or sásave kandangi, Rs. 10 to 30; mungi, Rs. 25 to 35; sálári, Rs. 8 to 20; kádigannu, Rs. 6 to 35; kempu chandrakáli, Rs. 5 to 50; bilipatla, Rs. 4 to 40; gulál chukki, Rs. 6 to 30; kalás mungi, Rs. 20 to 30; bánagere or jóda sálári, Rs. 10 to 25; kari chandrakáli, Rs. 5 to 50; kadle-banna or kadle-putáni, Rs. 25 to 40; nimbávali, Rs. 10 to 30.

*Men's cloths.*—Págu, Rs. 5 to 20; rummál, Rs. 3 to 100; panche, Rs. 2½ to Rs. 30; dhótra, Rs. 4 to 40; sálya, Rs. 8 to 15; vastra, As. 4 to Rs. 5; dupati, Rs. 2½ to 5; tale-batte, As. 6.

*Tape* (navár) for bedding is made at Sarjapur, and *satranji* or cotton carpets. *Tent cloth* of strong texture is made by the convicts at Bangalore; *dosuti* for the outside and *dangari* for the inside.

**Woollen Fabrics.**—*Woollen kamblis.*—Kari kambli, the ordinary black or dark grey kind; jhádi kambli, quilted; gangadikár kambli one corner stitched up with a tassel so as to form a hood.

*Carpets* made in Bangalore are noted for their excellent and durable qualities.[1] The common drugget carpet with reversible pattern is called *jamkhána* and costs from 8 As. to 1¼ Rupee a square yard; the rugs and pile carpets, *ratna kambli*, cost from Rs. 4 a square yard. The art has been carried to great perfection in the Central Jail, the carpets made in which, of Persian and Turkish designs, are in great demand even for England, at from Rs. 12 a square yard.

**Silk Fabrics.**—Silks of stout durable texture and costly patterns are largely made by *patvegars* in Bangalore and sold by weight at from Rs. 4 and 5 a tola.

*Raw silk.*—The production of raw silk, an industry confined to the Muhammadans, declined for many years owing to continued mortality of the worms. The attempt to establish a Silk Filature Company at Kengeri in 1866 was on that account a failure. The industry has now revived, as either through importation or climatic changes, a healthy breed of insects has been established.

**Metal Manufacture.**—In Magadi taluq much iron is made and some steel. *Steel wire* of a superior quality for strings of musical instruments is made at Channapatna.

*Gold* and *Silver lace* is also made at Bangalore. *Lacquered ware* and *toys* are well-known manufactures of Channapatna.

**Oils.**—The extraction of oils forms an important branch of industry. These consist of castor-oil of two kinds, the inferior description

[1] *See* also Vol. I, p. 537.

obtained from the large seed being called lamp oil; ground-nut oil, caron oil, and gingelli oil, of good and inferior kinds. They are more fully described, with their uses, under Oil-pressing.

The manufacture may also be mentioned of *coir* ropes and matting; of *goni* bags or sacks; and of *bamboo* matting and baskets.

**Arts.**—The arts of printing, bookbinding, lithography and photography are pursued in Bangalore, with electro-plating, boot and shoe-making, smiths' work of all kinds, and carpentering in all its branches, including coach-building and furniture-making. The variety of handicrafts is too numerous to specify, and is probably on the increase owing to the demand of a growing population.

**Marts.**—The chief marts of trade, in addition to that of Bangalore, are at Channapatna, Dod-Ballapur, Sarjapur, Vadagenhalli, Tyamagondal, and Hindiginal.

## REVENUE

The revenue of the District for five years is exhibited in detail in the following table :—

| Items. | 1890-1. | 1891-2. | 1892-3. | 1893-4. | 1894-5. |
|---|---|---|---|---|---|
| Land revenue ... | 10,55,594 | 10,88,501 | 11,35,915 | 12,00,221 | 11,94,261 |
| Forests ... ... | 1,28,689 | 1,33,399 | 1,22,432 | 1,45,729 | 1,36,266 |
| Mohatarfa ... | 41,420 | 41,183 | 42,055 | 41,461 | 27,697 |
| Abkari ... ... | 1,43,556 | 3,25,352 | 7,47,755 | 7,36,131 | 7,87,220 |
| Sayar ... ... | 5,499 | 6,546 | 4 883 | 98 | 159 |
| Salt ... ... | 18 | 12 | 12 | 12 | 15 |
| Public Works ... | 1,635 | 1,491 | 2,529 | 1,166 | — |
| Stamps ... ... | 1,44,331 | 1,83,510 | 1,56,525 | 1,67,269 | 1,61,247 |
| Law and Justice ... | 22,976 | 34,819 | 9,282 | 6,777 | 10,239 |
| Registration ... | — | — | — | 21,502 | 21,529 |
| Jails ... ... | — | — | — | 1,481 | 1,524 |
| Education ... | — | — | — | 13,475 | 15,592 |
| Police ... . | 62 | 37 | 49 | 22 | 121 |
| Other items ... | 33,395 | 38,502 | 60,825 | 13,050 | 11,172 |
| Total Rs. ... | 15,77,175 | 18,53,352 | 22,82,262 | 23,48,394 | 23,67,042 |

The items which are blank in the first three years are included in some of the other heads.

## COMMUNICATIONS

**Railways.**—The railways radiating from the Bangalore City station are—the Branch Railway to Madras, broad gauge, running east to Jalarpet, of which about twenty-three miles are in this District, with stations at Bangalore Cantonment, Krishnarajpuram, Whitefield and Devankundi; the Mysore State Railway, metre gauge, running south-west to Mysore and Nanjangud, of which about forty-two miles are in this District, with stations at Kengeri, Bidadi, Closepet, Channapatna and Mudgere; the Southern Mahratta Railway, metre gauge, running north to Guntakal, and from Yesvantpur junction north-west to Harihar and Poona. Of each of these about 35 miles are in this District, with stations on the former at Yesvantpur, Yelahanka, Rajankunti, Dod-Ballapur, and Maklidroog; on the latter, at Yesvantpur, Chik Banavar, Golhalli, Dodbele, and Nidvanda.

**Roads.**—The length of *Provincial roads* is 227 miles, maintained at an annual cost of Rs. 40,690. *District roads* amount to 429 miles, costing for upkeep Rs. 26,695 a year. The particulars regarding each class of roads are given below :—

| Provincial Roads. | Miles. | Cost. |
|---|---|---|
| Suburban and municipal roads in Bangalore ... ... | 21 | Rs.8,400 |
| Madras—Cannanore road ... ... ... ... ... | 66 | 9,900 |
| Bangalore—Kadapa road ... ... ... ... ... | 14 | 1,680 |
| Salem—Bellary road ... ... ... ... ... | 50 | 10,000 |
| Bangalore—Bellary road ... ... ... ... ... | 27 | 4,050 |
| Bangalore—Hindupur road ... ... ... ... ... | 26 | 3,900 |
| Bangalore—Mangalore road ... ... ... ... | 23 | 2,760 |
| Total ... | 227 | Rs.40,690 |

| District Roads. | Miles. | Cost. |
|---|---|---|
| Bangalore—Kankanhalli road ... ... ... ... | 44 | 3,960 |
| Kankanhalli—Kodihalli road ... ... ... ... | 9 | 360 |
| Closepet—Magadi road ... ... ... ... ... | 20 | 1,200 |
| Closepet—Kankanhalli road ... ... ... ... | 16 | 800 |
| Channapatna—Satanur road ... ... ... ... | 20 | 1,000 |
| Hoskote, Kadgodi, Anekal railway feeder ... ... | 30 | 1,500 |
| Channapatna—Halgur road ... ... ... ... | 8 | 320 |
| Attibele—Mattikere road ... ... ... ... ... | 3 | 150 |
| Hoskote—Sulibele road ... ... ... ... ... | 6 | 150 |
| Hoskote—Malur railway feeder ... ... ... ... | 7 | 350 |
| Kolar—Sompur road .. ... ... ... ... | 39 | 1,950 |
| Hoskote—Sidlaghatta road ... ... ... ... | 12 | 600 |
| Bangalore—Vartúr road ... ... ... ... ... | 8 | 400 |
| Bangalore—Anekal road ... ... ... ... ... | 27 | 2,025 |

D 2

| District Roads. | Miles. | Cost. |
|---|---|---|
| Bangalore—Dommasandra road ... ... ... ... | 10 | 600 |
| Iggalur—Anekal—Gumlapur road ... ... ... | 11 | 550 |
| Bangalore—Magadi—Hulyurdroog road ... ... ... | 38 | 3,800 |
| Nelamangala—Golhalli—Dod-Ballapur railway feeder... | 21 | 1,260 |
| Dobbspet—Sivaganga road ... ... ... ... | 4 | 200 |
| Bégur—Tyamagendal—Manne road ... ... ... | 10 | 500 |
| Dobbspet—Koratigere road ... ... ... ... | 6 | 360 |
| Devanhalli—Dod-Ballapur road ... ... ... ... | 10 | 600 |
| Devanhalli—Vadagenhalli road ... ... ... ... | 6 | 300 |
| Venkatapura—Devanhalli road ... ... ... ... | 3 | 90 |
| Bangalore—Nandidroog road ... ... ... ... | 6 | 300 |
| Dod-Ballapur cross roads ... ... ... ... ... | 6 | 300 |
| Gudimaranhalli—Magadi road ... ... ... ... | 10 | 600 |
| Magadi—Kunigal road ... ... ... ... ... | 10 | 600 |
| Bannerghatta cross road ... ... ... ... ... | 1 | 100 |
| Kodihalli—Satanur road ... ... .. ... ... | 16 | 1,200 |
| Gunjur—Sausmond road ... ... ... ... ... | 3 | 150 |
| Bangalore suburban roads ... ... ... ... ... | 7 | 420 |
| Total ... | 429 | Rs. 26,695 |

**Accommodation for Travellers.**—*Dak Bungalows* or rest houses, originally intended for European officials and travellers, have been built at the stations named in the accompanying list, where the class is shown to which each belongs. Brahman kitchens have been built in the compounds for vegetarian Hindu officials.

*First Class*: Closepet. *Second Class*: Bidadi, Channapatna, Devanhalli, Dod-Ballapur, Hebbagod, Sompur, Solur, Yelahanka. *Third Class*: Anekal, Kankanhalli, Kumbalgod, Magadi.

*Musáfirkhánas* for the accommodation of native travellers are maintained by Government at Anekal, Dod-Ballapur, Golhalli, Harohalli, Hindiginal, Kadgodi, Kankanhalli, Nelamangala.

## GAZETTEER

**Agara.**—A village in Bangalore taluq, about five miles south-east of Bangalore, head-quarters of the hóbli of the same name. Population 746. Contains large tanks, which inscriptions show were in existence in the 8th century. The Artillery practice ground is on the Agram plain.

**Alsur** (Ulsoor),—*see* Halasúr.

**Anekal.**—A taluq in the south-east. Area 190 square miles. Head-quarters at Anekal. Contains the following hóblis, villages and population :—

| No. | Hoblis. | Vil-lages. | Ham-lets. | Villages Classified. | | | | Population. |
|---|---|---|---|---|---|---|---|---|
| | | | | Govern-ment. | Sarva-mánya. | Jodi. | Kayam-gutta. | |
| 1 | Anekal ... ... | 27 | 3 | 25 | — | 2 | — | 11,523 |
| 2 | Attibele ... ... | 23 | 4 | 21 | — | 2 | — | 6,293 |
| 3 | Bidarguppe ... | 40 | 2 | 33 | — | — | 7 | 8,704 |
| 4 | Hárgadde ... | 32 | 5 | 25 | — | 4 | 3 | 4,701 |
| 5 | Iggalur ... ... | 33 | 2 | 25 | 2 | 3 | 3 | 6,072 |
| 6 | Jigani ... ... | 36 | 16 | 28 | 1 | — | 7 | 6,769 |
| 7 | Sarjapur ... ... | 32 | 2 | 29 | — | — | 3 | 10,772 |
| | Total ... | 223 | 34 | 186 | 3 | 11 | 23 | 54,834 |

*Principal places, with Population.*—Anekal, 7,719; Sarjapur, 3,017; Dommasandra, 2,284; Attibele, 1,613; Jigani, 1,418.

The taluq was increased by the addition of the Sarjapur and Bidarguppe hóblis, on the breaking up of the Sarjapur taluq, in 1873.

The *S. Pinákini* runs along the eastern side and receives nearly the whole drainage. The western side is jungly and marked by a continuous range of hills, through which several rivulets, uniting under the name of the *Suvarnamukhi*, descend to the Arkavati at the lower level of Kankanhalli. The taluq consists of two principal valleys, which collect all the smaller streams running eastward: the southernmost extends from Anekal to Attibele; through the northern flows the *Sanatkumára*, which joins the S. Pinákini near Hosur, in the Salem District, five miles beyond the Mysore boundary.

Except in the western parts the soil is fertile and well cultivated, but a somewhat better rainfall in those parts, owing to the proximity of hills, allows of the growth of rice without artificial irrigation. The principal dry crops are the ordinary ragi, gram, &c. The wet crops consist chiefly of paddy and sugar-cane. In favourable seasons two crops of rice are grown under large tanks. The sugar-cane is of a superior kind. There are many gardens of the betel vine, with some areca and cocoanut plantations. Minor garden produce is raised by Tigalas in the south-east. Mulberry cultivation is also met with here and there. The Sanatkumára supplies several small channels and tanks. Its waters are further utilised by means of pikota wells.

Iron ore is collected and smelted in the western parts of the taluq. Common cotton cloths are made at Anekal, Dommasandra and other places. Raw silk is produced at Anekal and Sarjapur. At this latter place muslins of various patterns, turbans, and small cotton carpets are made.

The revenue settlement was introduced in 1891. The area of the taluq was thus distributed :—

| | | |
|---|---|---|
| Culturable (dry, 49,934 ; wet, 7,699 ; garden, 2,212) | ... | 59,845 |
| Unculturable (including village sites, &c.) ... ... | ... | 42,506 |
| Inam (with Commissariat kavul 450)... ... ... | ... | 19,400 |
| Total area, acres | ... | 121,751 |

Of the culturable area 7,434 acres were waste.

The total revenue under all heads for 1891–2 (15 months) was Rs. 1,46,612 ; and for 1892–3 it was Rs. 1,44,823. The land revenue from Government lands in those years was thus apportioned :—

| Cultivation. | 1891-92. | | 1892-93. | |
|---|---|---|---|---|
| | Area. | Assessment. | Area. | Assessment. |
| Dry ... ... | 40,897 | 65,764 | 41,596 | 66,936 |
| Wet ... ... | 5,885 | 31,321 | 5,972 | 31,822 |
| Garden ... | 2,028 | 9,855 | 2,043 | 9,950 |
| Total ... | Ac. 48,810 | Rs. 1,06,940 | Ac. 49,611 | Rs. 1,08,708 |

The average rainfall at Anekal for twenty-five years (1870–94), and at the other places for two years (1893–94), was as follows :—

| | Jan. | Feb. | Mar. | April | May | June | July | Aug. | Sept. | Oct. | Nov. | Dec. | | Year. |
|---|---|---|---|---|---|---|---|---|---|---|---|---|---|---|
| Anekal ... | 0·12 | 0·17 | 0·48 | 1·00 | 4·45 | 2·36 | 3·70 | 5·61 | 5·53 | 6·18 | 2·65 | 0·78 | ... | 33·03 |
| Attibele... | — | 0·80 | 0·13 | 1·59 | 4·02 | 5·10 | 2·68 | 3·21 | 3·33 | 7·61 | 1·95 | — | ... | 30·42 |
| Hebgod... | — | 0·89 | 0·30 | 1·81 | 5·53 | 6·58 | 3·92 | 4·04 | 3·16 | 6·29 | 1·93 | — | ... | 34·95 |

The trunk road from Bangalore to Salem runs through the taluq, from north-west to south-east, with a branch road to Anekal from near Hebbagod. From Attibele in the same main road there are branches south to Mattikere, south-west to Anekal and north to Sarjapur. From this place there is a road to Whitefield Railway station, with a branch to Bangalore through Agara. There is also a road from Bangalore to Anekal by way of Bannerghatta. Local roads run from Anekal to Mattikere, and from Anekal towards Denkanikota. One from Anekal to Kankanhalli has also been traced.

**Anekal.**—A town situated in 12° 42′ N. lat., 77° 43′ E. long., 22 miles south-east of Bangalore. Head-quarters of the Anekal taluq, and a municipality. The direct road from Bangalore is by Bannerghatta, but there is also a cross road from the Hosur road beyond Hebbagod.

| Population in 1891. | Males. | Females. | Total. |
|---|---|---|---|
| Hindus ... ... ... ... | 3,219 | 3,475 | 6,694 |
| Muhammadans ... ... ... | 317 | 326 | 643 |
| Christians .. ... ... ... | 44 | 38 | 82 |
| Total ... ... | 3,580 | 3,839 | 7,419 |

The suburbs are Bendarhalli, population 100, and Bahadurpur, 200. A fair is held every Friday, attended by 400 persons.

The origin of the name—*áne-kal*, hailstone—is not known. The town was founded about 1603 by Chikka Timme Gauda, a descendant of the original Sugatur chief. The general of the Bijapur State, after seizing Timme Gauda's hereditary possession of Hoskote, granted him Anekal, which formed a hóbli of that pargana. He thereupon erected the fort and temple, constructed the large tank to the west, and set on foot such improvements as tended to the opulence and prosperity of the town. After a reign of thirty years he died, and was succeeded by his son Timme Gauda. The latter reigned twenty years, and left the territory to his son Dodda Timme Gauda, in whose time Anekal was conquered by the Mysore Rája. The chief, however, remained in possession, paying an annual tribute of 2,000 rupees, and died shortly after, having completed a long reign of 60 years. His son Vira Nanjana Timme Gauda then ruled for 24 years, and was in turn succeeded by his son Jama Gauda. This chief, in common with many others, was expelled by Haidar and his possessions were annexed to Mysore.

| Municipal Funds. | 1892–93. | 1893–94. | 1894–95. | 1895–96. |
|---|---|---|---|---|
| Income (opening balance Rs. 2,478) ... ... | Rs. 2,336 | Rs. 2,001 | Rs. 4,065 | Rs. 4,300 |
| Expenditure ... ... | 4,687 | 3,659 | 3,770 | 4,420 |

**Arades'ahalli.**—A Jódi village in Devanhalli taluq, four miles south-west of Kundána. Population 390. Contains some old stone inscriptions, one of Akálavarsha, and two relating to the Punnáḍ kings (*see* Vol. I, p. 312).

**Arkavati.**—A tributary of the Kávéri, flowing through the District from north to south and receiving the drainage of all the country between the central watershed and the western chain of hills. Its reputed source is a well on Nandidroog, on the south-west. Thence entering the Dod-Ballapur taluq it forms several large tanks, as at Dod-Ballapur, Kakolu and Hesarghatta; and passing through the east of the Nelamangala taluq, receives in the south the *Kumadvati* from the west. It then flows through the Magadi taluq, passing east of Savandurga. Penetrating between Ramgiri and Sivangiri near Closepet, it runs through the Channapatna taluq in a south-easterly direction past Closepet and Kúnagal, which are on the left bank, into Kankanhalli taluq. Near Muduvadi-durga it is joined on the north by the *Vrishabhávati* and then runs due south, leaving Kankanhalli on the right bank, and discharges into the Kávéri on the southern frontier. The length of the main stream is about 120 miles.

The greater part of its course from Magadi onwards is through a wild country amid rocky hills, precipices and thick jungle. Its waters are therefore little utilized in those parts for purposes of cultivation. Though never entirely dry, it presents in the hot season the usual aspect of a sandy bed with a little current of water flowing at one side. Holes scooped in the sand furnish a ready means of water supply to the dwellers on the banks. In the rains, when the freshes come down, it is a formidable stream, swollen by mountain torrents and bearing along in its irresistible force logs of timber and uprooted trees torn from the forests on its banks. It is bridged in three places for roads from Bangalore, namely, 5 miles east of Nelamangala, 10 miles east of Magadi, and at Closepet. The calculations for the second of these gave a maximum flood discharge of 50,000 cubic feet per second, with an ordinary monsoon discharge of 3,500.

**Avati.**—Properly *Ahuti*, a village in the Devanhalli taluq, 4 miles north of the kasba, on the road to Chik-Ballapur. Head-quarters of the Avati hobli. Population 975.

It is historically interesting as being the original settlement of the seven enterprising farmers from Kanchi, whose story holds so prominent a place in the annals of the Bangalore, Kolar and Tumkur Districts. The three sons of Baire Gauda, the leader, it will there be seen, established themselves as chiefs of Devanhalli, Dod-Ballapur and Chik-Ballapur respectively. Timme Gauda became lord of Sugatur Nad, obtained the title of Chikka Ráyal, restored Kolar and founded Hoskote; while his descendants became the chiefs of Punganur and Anekal. Sanna Baire Gauda settled at Holavanhalli and founded Koratigere. Jaya Gauda became lord of Yelahanka Nad and founder of Bangalore, his descendants being the chiefs of Magadi.

**Bairan-durga.**--A hill in the north-west of the Magadi taluq near Kudúr. It was fortified by the Mahrattas about 1609 and, with Hulikal, formed into a separate pargana. It was purchased twenty years afterwards by the Mysore Rája, who appointed Timma Nayak as governor. He improved and strengthened the fortifications, which consisted of three lines of defence and some outworks on the north and east faces, built the temple of Bairava at the summit, and changed the name of the hill from Abdul Bandar to Bairan-durga. The works were demolished and the town removed to Kudúr by order of Tipu Sultan in 1792, on account of its unhealthiness and a deficiency of water.

**Bangalore.**—A taluq near the centre. Area 344 square miles. Head-quarters at Bangalore. Contains the following hóblis, villages and population :—

| No. | Hoblis. | Vil-lages. | Ham-lets. | Villages Classified. | | | | Population. |
|---|---|---|---|---|---|---|---|---|
| | | | | Govern-ment. | Sarva-mánya. | Jodi. | Kayam-gutta. | |
| 1 | Agara ... ... | 45 | 13 | 39 | — | 1 | 5 | 12,777 |
| 2 | Bangalore ... | 1 | 19 | 1 | — | — | — | 180,366 |
| 3 | Bégur ... ... | 38 | 13 | 27 | — | 3 | 8 | 9,709 |
| 4 | Halasúr[1] ... ... | 14 | 14 | 10 | — | 1 | 3 | 5,274 |
| 5 | Kengeri ... ... | 86 | 90 | 65 | 1 | 6 | 14 | 16,943 |
| 6 | Krishnarajpur ... | 33 | 9 | 20 | — | 3 | 10 | 6,744 |
| 7 | Vartúr ... ... | 34 | 5 | 30 | — | 3 | 1 | 8,828 |
| 8 | Yelahanka ... | 77 | 6 | 46 | 2 | 7 | 22 | 12,380 |
| 9 | Yesavantapur ... | 42 | 49 | 26 | 1 | 2 | 13 | 16,662 |
| | Total ... | 370 | 237 | 264 | 4 | 26 | 76 | 269,683 |

*Principal Places, with Population.*—Bangalore, 180,366 (Civil and Military Station, 100,081, City, 80,285); Yelahanka, 2,668; Bégur, 2,074; Kengeri, 1,746; Banasavádi, 1,556; Timmenhalli, 1,464; Kálagondahalli, 1,244; Gunjur, 1,215; Valagerepálya, 1,208; Vartúr, 1,143; Devarajibanhalli, 1,075; Krishnarájpura, 1,056; Kodigehalli, 1,003.

The taluq was increased in 1870 by the addition of the Krishnarajpur and Yelahanka hóblis from the old Yelahanka taluq, and in 1873 by the Begur and Vartur hóblis from the Sarjapur taluq, and Kengeri hóbli from the Kengeri taluq. By these accessions its limits were restored to nearly what they were in 1799.

The greater part of the taluq drains to the east, the waters being collected into two streams, which, forming continuous chains of tanks, fall into the S. Pinákini. The northern of these commences beyond Yelahanka and, uniting near Hebbal with a stream from the north, flows into the S. Pinákini at Kadgodi. The southern runs from Vasantapur, past Vartur, into the same near the Patandur hill. In the western part of the taluq a stream from Oyali Dinne feeds the Vrishabhavati, which, rising near Gavipura, flows past Kengeri and Bidadi to the Arkavati in Kankanhalli.

[1] The name has now been changed to Kasba Bangalore hobli.

The south-west is rocky and hilly; the remainder being composed of open, well-cultivated country, undulating much towards the north-west. Some of the principal elevations are those at Dod-Bettahalli (3,158 feet), in the north; at Banavar (3,108 feet), in the north-west; at Kotnur (3,118 feet) in the south; at Banasvadi (3,029 feet) in the east. From the Oyali Dinne (3,118 feet), north of Bangalore, was measured the base line of the Great Trigonometrical Survey, for 7 miles north-east, to near Gubbi. There are numerous quarries around Bangalore of gneissose stone, which is not only largely employed for every variety of building in the town, but transported to distant places.

The prevailing soil is the red, on which are cultivated ragi and the commonly associated dry crops. Paddy and sugar-cane are grown on the lands under tanks. In the immediate neighbourhood of Bangalore, especially on the south, numerous kinds of fruits and vegetables are raised for the European market, such as apples, peaches, grapes, mangoes, strawberries, &c.; cauliflowers, peas, knol-kohl, cabbage, lettuce, &c. Coffee cultivation to the south-east of Bangalore has proved of late years very successful, and plantations are being opened in other parts.

The weaving of cotton cloths is the most extensive native manufacture. These are of the ordinary as well of superior kinds. Coarse woollen blankets and goni for bags are also made. But the most important local arts are those of silk-weaving and carpet-making in the City of Bangalore, regarding which and other arts pursued in Bangalore more particular mention will be found elsewhere.

The taluq is intersected in all directions by roads radiating from Bangalore, and, except on the south-east, by railways.

The revenue settlement was introduced into the Bangalore, Agara, Halsur and Yesvantpur hoblis in 1872; Yelahanka, Krishnarajpur and Kengeri, in 1875; Begur and Vartur in 1877.

The total revenue under all heads for 1891–2 (15 months) was Rs. 2,13,287, and for 1892–3 it was Rs. 2,13,116. The land revenue from Government lands in those years was thus apportioned:—

| Cultivation. | 1891–2. | | 1892–3. | |
|---|---|---|---|---|
| | Area. | Assessment. | Area. | Assessment. |
| Dry .. ... ... | 71,114 | 84,853 | 71,854 | 85,594 |
| Wet ... ... ... | 7,078 | 31,346 | 7,269 | 32,420 |
| Garden ... ... ... | 3,840 | 25,979 | 3,772 | 25,640 |
| Total ... ... | Ac. 82,032 | Rs. 1,42,178 | Ac. 82,895 | Rs. 1,43,654 |

The following was the average rainfall for 25 years (1870–94) at Bangalore, and for 2 years (1893–4) at the other stations :—

| | Jan. | Feb. | Mar. | April | May | June | July | Aug. | Sept. | Oct. | Nov. | Dec. | Year. |
|---|---|---|---|---|---|---|---|---|---|---|---|---|---|
| Bangalore ... | 0·07 | 0·27 | 0·83 | 1·14 | 4·67 | 3·39 | 4·51 | 6·49 | 6·00 | 7·40 | 2·71 | 0·42 | ... 37·90 |
| Hebbál (Butts) | — | 0·30 | 1·00 | 1·55 | 5·73 | 4·43 | 4·13 | 4·58 | 5·20 | 5·71 | 2·75 | — | ... 35·38 |
| Krishnarájpur | — | 1·36 | 0·39 | 1·99 | 3·36 | 2·89 | 2·03 | 3·80 | 5·34 | 5·41 | 1·96 | — | ... 28·53 |
| Vartur ... | — | 1·40 | — | 1·62 | 4·20 | 3·79 | 3·41 | 4·16 | 4·90 | 7·54 | 4·15 | — | ... 35·17 |
| Yelahanka ... | — | 0·09 | 2·42 | 1·34 | 3·61 | 5·04 | 4·24 | 3·67 | 3·06 | 3·28 | 1·22 | — | ... 27 97 |

**Bangalore.**—Chief town, situated 12° 57′ N. lat. and 77° 35′ E. long. The seat of government for the Province of Mysore, and head-quarters of the former Mysore Division and present Bangalore District of the Madras Army. Population 180,366. It covers an area of 20¼ square miles, and consists of two separate parts, namely, the City (the Péṭe or old native Town of Bangalore Proper), and the Civil and Military Station (formerly called the Cantonment).

Its name *Bengaḷúru*, of which Bangalore is a corruption, is said to be derived from *bengaḷu*, a kind of beans, to account for which the following story is related:—One day, when king Vira Ballála was hunting, he became separated from his attendants, and losing his way, wandered about till nightfall. At last, faint and weary, he came upon a solitary hut, in which was an old woman, to whom he applied for something to eat. She had nothing better to offer him than some *bengaḷu*, green beans boiled in a little water, which however he was glad enough to get, and sharing them with his horse passed the night under shelter of the lowly hut. The incident speedily became known, and the village (*úru*) which sprung up thence took the name of Bengalúru. This was situated to the north of Kodigehalli, and after Kempe Gauda had given the name to his new capital was called old or Hale Bengalúru. At each of the cardinal points is an old watch-tower,[1] which marks, it is said, the limits to which it was predicted the town would extend. The prophecy has now been more than fulfilled.

**City.**—Bangalore City includes the Fort on the south, and extends to the Maharaja's Palace on the north. Two large extensions have been added to it in recent years—the northern, from the Race-course northwards, and the western, from the Fort westwards. It includes 19 suburbs, and occupies an area of 8¼ square miles.

[1] The one to the north is on the Oyálidinne, overlooking the Rifle Butts; the one to the east is on the rock of the Halsur waterworks; the one to the south is above the quarry on the east of the Lal Bagh; and the one on the west is near Gavipur, at the northern end of the Kempámbudhi tank bund. This one has lost its dome.

| Population in 1891. | Males. | Females. | Total. |
|---|---|---|---|
| Hindus (with 226 Jains and 2 Sikhs)... | 34,167 | 33,221 | 67,388 |
| Muhammadans ... ... ... ... | 5,519 | 4,953 | 10,472 |
| Christians ... ... ... ... | 1,187 | 1,238 | 2,425 |
| Total ... ... | 40,873 | 39,412 | 80,285 |

In 1894 there were 10,800 houses, of which 537 were terraced, 437 tiled, 8,992 mud-roofed, and 834 thatched. The estimated annual rental value was Rs. 4·59 lakhs.

The town itself was originally surrounded by a deep ditch and a thickset thorny hedge, which had served as a defence against the Mahratta cavalry. It was stormed by the British in 1791, and a cenotaph is erected near the Halsur gate to Colonel Moorhouse and other officers who lost their lives in the attack. The hedge was cleared away about 30 years ago, and the ditch has been filled up and built upon. The orthodox number of gates (*bágilu*) was eight, to correspond with the eight cardinal points, but after improvements have added several new ones. The principal are the Yelahanka gate on the north, the Halasur gate on the east, the Fort and Mysore gates on the south, the Agrahara and Sondekoppa gates on the west, and the Bale gate on the north-west.

The town is divided into numerous péṭe or quarters. But the Doḍḍa-péṭe (High-street) running from the Yelahanka gate in the north to the Fort gate in the south, separates the two comprehensive divisions of Déshada péṭe on the west from Nagarta péṭe on the east. This line is crossed at right angles by a street running from the Halasur gate on the east to the Sondekoppa gate on the west. The intersection of these two main roads is styled the *chauk*, or square, near to which is situated the Taluq Cutcherry.

Between the Fort and Mysore gates is an excellent public market. Siddi Kaṭṭe, the quarter in which many Brahman officials live, occupies, it is said, the site of an old tank, built at the expense of Siddi, a lady of the Kempe Gauda family. The City Railway-station is on the west of the Dharmámbudhi tank, and its advent has caused a great transformation on that side of the town. The houses forming the quarters of the railway staff are chiefly to the west of the station, where there are also a church and a chapel.

Owing to the circumstances of its origin, the rapid growth of the town, and the various hands through which it has passed, the streets in the old parts are often narrow and mostly irregular in appearance. The atter defect has been to some extent remedied by the construction of stone drains along both sides of the principal streets, which has also promoted the cleanliness of the town. Many streets, too, have been widened as far as possible. Substantially built and imposing edifices may be seen in Chikka-péṭe and other parts, belonging to wealthy natives, but their effect is a good deal lost from their scattered positions. Bangalore, however, presents a lively specimen of a Hindu town, the main streets being generally crowded with pedestrians, among whom vehicles of all kinds, from the carriage or brougham of the high official to the rude jatka of the merchant trader and the slow and heavily-laden bullock-cart, thread their difficult way by dint of continual vociferous shouts.

The open stalls or bazaars on either side of the Doḍḍa-péṭe and other thoroughfares display their wares arranged on tiers of shelves, all within reach of the owner, who sits comfortably ensconced among them. Customers stand in the street to make their bargains, or squat on a small ledge in front of the shop for a preliminary chat with the proprietor. Those of a trade generally flock together, so that many shops containing the same description of goods will be found side by side. In the Grain market (Taragu-péṭe) a perfect block of carts stops the way, their contents being discharged in heaps into the street, where they are measured before being stored. In the Cotton market (Arale-péṭe) the verandahs of the warehouses are piled with bulging bales. Arrangements have been made to remove these markets to the western extension, a railway siding being constructed for their convenience.

In the quieter and more private parts of the town the floor and ground at the entrance to the houses will be seen carefully washed with purifying cowdung, and pleasingly decorated with numerous geometrical figures, which are drawn afresh by the women with lines of white chalk every morning, while the lintel of the door is decked with mango leaves strung on a thread as a sign of welcome. On all sides may be seen women, with water jars and shining brass vessels, grouped round the public wells and fountains, or on their way to a tank with baskets of clothes. The peculiar odours of eastern bazaars pervade the streets; mendicants go from house to house sounding their conchs or gongs; and the universal babel gives evidence of the out-door life of the people.

The water supply of the native town was hitherto derived principally from the Dharmámbudhi tank on the north-west. From this reservoir water was laid on to the streets and drawn out by the people as required from the square troughs or basins constructed at convenient points. The residents of the north-east quarter resorted to the Sampangi tank, the bed of which is now a polo ground. The well-water in the town is mostly brackish. But at a cost of 19½ lakhs a pure and abundant water supply has now been provided, drawn from the Hesarghatta tank, 13 miles to the north-west. The water is pumped up to the top of a hill at Banavar, and from there runs by gravitation through cast-iron pipes to the settling and filter-beds above Sankey's reservoir to the west, and thence to a subterranean reservoir at the Race-course, whence it is distributed in iron mains to all parts of the City, and drawn off at stand-pipes or hydrants at suitable points in the streets.

The drainage of the Péṭe is collected into one main channel, which runs out from the southern side and is continued as far as the Sunnakal tank, a distance of two or three miles, where the sewerage is applied to agricultural purposes.

The *Fort* is no longer used for any military purpose, and is now a part of the City. The original Fort was of mud, and is said to have been erected in 1537 by Kempe Gauda, Prabhu of Yelahanka and ancestor of the Magadi chiefs. Under its Hindu masters, namely, the Magadi gaudas, the Mahratta governors subordinate to the Adil Shahi princes of Bijapur, and lastly the Mysore Wodeyars, the Fort retained its old character, with no doubt some additions to its strength. But under the Muhammadans the fortress was enlarged and rebuilt of stone. This work is attributed to a Khiledar named Ibrahim Sahib, and was carried out in 1761, the first year of Haidar Ali's reign. The form of the Fort is oval, with round towers at proper intervals. It had, when captured by the British in 1791, five powerful cavaliers, a fausse-bray, a good ditch and covered way without palisades, but the glacis was imperfect in some parts. The two gateways, one in the north and the other in the south, were called the Delhi and Myṣore gates respectively. The former, which opened towards the Péṭe, was a handsome structure in the best style of Muhammadan military architecture, and consisted of several gates surmounted by traverses.[1] But there being no ditches between the gates, an enemy taking possession of the works over the first gateway had a ready communication with all the others, which the British troops who stormed the Fort at this point took advantage of.

Within the Fort the principal building was the *Mahal* or palace (on the plan of one at Sira), which, though the walls were of mud, was not without some degree of magnificence. The building was of two storeys. A large open court in front was surrounded by a corridor, in the centre of which, opposite the palace, was the *naubat khâna* or raised band-stand.

[1] The old tortuous entrance through seven gates was given up some thirty years ago and a straight entrance pierced through the wall at the side of the Delhi gate. Openings in the walls have also now been made for a wide road running east and west through the Fort, on which some new buildings have been erected.

The upper storey of the palace contained the public and private apartments of the Sultan and his ladies, with two balconies of state from which he gave audience. Paint and false gilding decorated the walls.

Buchanan thus describes the arrangements of the building as he saw it in 1800 :—" On the upper story it contains four halls, each comprising two balconies of state for the prince, and each balcony faces a different *cutcherry* or court for giving audience. No persons, except a few trusty guards, were admitted into the hall with the Sultan ; but at each end of the court was erected a balcony for the officers of the highest rank. The inferior officers occupied a hall under the balcony of the prince, open in front, and supported by columns as high as the roof of the upper story. The populace were admitted into the open court, in which there were fountains for cooling the air. At each end of the hall are private apartments, small, mean, and inconvenient. The bath consists of a small room, in which a person may sit, and have water poured over him. . . . There were two apartments for the ladies. One, for the principal wife, contains a *cutcherry*, where, like the Sultan, she gave audience to the concubines, and to the ladies of the Musalman chiefs. The other apartment belonged to the concubines. It is a square court, having at the two sides a corridor, under which the women sat at their meals and amusements." [1]

When the Fort was restored to Tipu at the peace of 1792, he dismantled it, but after 1799 Purnaiya had it completely restored on the former foundation. On the removal of the British garrison from Seringapatam in 1809, some of the troops had their quarters in the Fort, where the General Commanding and many of the European residents also lived. The arsenal was not transferred to it till about 1823. From 1831 the principal departments of the Administration were accommodated in the palace above described, until in 1868 the new Public Offices in Cubbon Park were completed, the removal to which carried away the few remaining European residents. The palace having partly fallen in the greater part was demolished, but the Government Press remained there till the present building was erected for it. The arsenal had been given up, when the military guards were withdrawn and the Fort was handed over to the Civil authorities on the 2nd October 1888. What remains of the palace is used for the Forest, Police and Excise offices.[2] The Municipal office is also in the Fort.

[1] An inscription found in it says it was begun in 1778 and completed in 1789. The dates are expressed in phrases, meaning " Abode of happiness " and " Envy of heaven."

[2] Besides the fort itself, and the remains of the palace, objects of interest pointed out are :—a dungeon near the Delhi gate in which Colonel (afterwards Sir David) Baird was confined in 1794, preparatory to exchange of prisoners with the British, and in front of the palace, a well at which he was made to draw water in order that the Sultan's ladies might see him.

Outside, on the east, are the Lascar Lines, a quarter inhabited by large numbers of the lower orders of natives. On the west side, south of the Mysore road, is the new western extension, Chámarájendrapéṭe, with a large Government Hospital under construction; north of that road are the barracks of the Barr or Mysore infantry.

The most prominent buildings and places in the City limits are, the Maharaja's Palace, to the north-east, near the Cantonment Railway station; the Public Offices in Cubbon Park, with the Band Promenade around Sir Mark Cubbon's statue, and the Tennis Courts and Museum lower down. In the road from the Public Offices to the Yelahanka gate are the Government Press, the Central College and Meteorological Observatory, the District Cutcherry, with St. Martha's Hospital and the Maternity Hospital beyond to the east, and the Central Jail to the west. North of the Jail is the Race-course with the Silahdar lines to the west. Between the Race-course and the Golf Links is a new quarter composed of houses mostly in the European style, occupied by the leading Durbar officials. The cotton-mills are on the north-west, close to the Southern Mahratta Railway line, and the fine building of the woollen-mills to the south-west, also close to the line.

No account of Bangalore would be complete without a notice of the Lal Bagh. This beautiful pleasure garden, situated about a mile to the east of the Fort, appears to have been first laid out in the time of Haidar Ali (perhaps after one at Sira) and enlarged in the time of Tipu Sultan.

Dr. Buchanan, writing in 1800, says :—"The gardens are extensive, and divided into square plots separated by walks, the sides of which are ornamented with fine cypress-trees. The plots are filled with fruit-trees and pot-herbs. The Musalman fashion is to have a separate piece of ground allotted for each kind of plant. Thus one plot is entirely filled with rose-trees, another with pomegranates, and so forth. The walks are not gravelled, and the cultivation of the whole is rather slovenly, but the people say that formerly the gardens were well kept. Want of water is the principal defect of these gardens; for in this arid country everything during the dry season must be artificially watered. The garden of Tippoo is supplied from three wells, the water of which is raised by the *capily*, or leather-bag, fastened to a cord passing over a pulley, and wrought by a pair of bullocks, which descend an inclined plane. This the workmen say is a much more effectual machine than the *yatam*. Hyder's garden is watered from a reservoir, without the assistance of machinery. The taste of Hyder accorded more with the English than that of his son. His walks are wider, his cypress-trees are not so much crowded; and in the means for watering the plots there is not so much masonry or bricklayers' work employed. There is, indeed, so much of these in the parts of Tippoo's garden, which he probably considered the finest, as almost to cover the ground, and to leave nothing but holes, as it were, through which the trees grow."

During the latter part of Tipu's rule, and for long after, the Lal Bagh was supervised by two Darogas, father and son. The former, named Muhammad Ali, seems to have been invested with considerable powers and was able to do a good deal for his charge; but under Abdul Khader, the son, whose authority was probably more limited, the garden became an ill-kept jungle of fruit-trees. In 1836, Sir Mark Cubbon made over the Lal Bagh to the Agri-Horticultural Society, then newly formed in Bangalore, and assisted them with convict labour. But the Society came to an end in 1842 and restored the garden to Government. In 1856, on the recommendation of Dr. Hugh Cleghorn, it was formed into a Horticultural Garden, and a professional Superintendent was obtained from Kew for its management. This system has continued to the present time and the gardens have a wide-spread reputation. Flower and fruit shows have all along been held twice a year, in July or August and in January or February, when numerous prizes are awarded, and there is a keen competition among exhibitors, of whom the greater number are native gardeners.

The Lal Bagh contains a rare and valuable collection of tropical and sub-tropical plants, together with indigenous and foreign fruit-trees. The stock is constantly replenished by exchanges and donations or importations. Being situated under a tank, the cultivation is easily supported by irrigation. A menagerie adds to its attractions. Since the Rendition it has been extended to the east and now contains nearly 100 acres. A handsome and spacious glass house, the foundation-stone of which was laid by the late Prince Albert Victor of Wales, has been erected as an Exhibition Hall. A complete collection is being made of coloured botanical drawings of indigenous plants, for which a native artist is employed.

*City Municipality.*—The administration of the City Municipality is conducted under the Municipal Regulations as amended by Mysore Regulations III of 1888 and I of 1890. The privilege of election was granted in 1892. The Municipal Board is now composed of a President and five *ex-officio* members appointed by Government, and of fourteen elected members,[1] two for each Division or Ward as per margin.[2] The number of qualified electors in 1894 was 4,543, of whom 1,926 actually voted.

Names of Divisions.
I. Palace.
II. Balepete.
III. Manavartipete.
IV. Halsurpete.
V. Nagartapete.
VI. Lal Bagh.
VII. Fort.

[1] It has lately been ordered that half the twenty members, including the President, shall be nominated by Government, and half elected.

[2] There were eight Divisions at first, but in 1893 the Palace and High Ground Divisions were amalgamated into the Palace Division.

To the end of 1895 the Deputy Commissioner was the *ex-officio* President and was assisted by a paid Vice-President. A separate paid President has since been appointed and the office of Vice-President abolished. In connection with the new western and northern extensions, a special City Improvements Committee was for a time appointed by Government, to carry out the apportionment and sale of sites, and to promote the suitable laying out and early occupation of the new quarters. Their operations thus relieved and assisted the work of the Board.

The following are statements of the Municipal income and expenditure for four years to 1894–5:—

| Receipts. | 1891–92. | 1892–93. | 1893–94. | 1894–95. |
|---|---|---|---|---|
| Octroi ... ... ... ... | Rs. 20,230 | Rs. 21,129 | Rs. 25,444 | Rs. 28,345 |
| Taxes on houses and buildings ... | 26,272 | 18,712 | 16,931 | 19,599 |
| Licenses ... ... ... ... | 15,200 | 14,584 | 24,290 | 24,553 |
| Mohatarfa... ... ... ... | 19,946 | 15,798 | 12,710 | 18,749 |
| Rents ... ... .. ... | 6,918 | 6,946 | 7,867 | 8,249 |
| Fines ... ... ... ... | 69 | 5 | 11 | 6 |
| Miscellaneous ... ... ... | 16,333 | 21,936 | 31,481 | 26,093 |
| Deposits ... ... ... ... | — | 3,523 | 5,430 | 2,387 |
| Opening balance ... ... | — | 7,338 | 8,415 | 12,508 |
| Total Municipal Receipts ... | Rs. 1,04,968 | Rs. 1,09,971 | Rs. 1,32,579 | Rs. 1,40,489 |
| Contributions ... ... ... | 7,260 | 7,160 | 20,624 | 9,879 |
| Jubilee Fund ... ... ... | 2,899 | — | — | — |
| Special Improvement Funds ... | 25,160 | 27,820 | — | — |
| Special Irrigation Fund ... ... | — | 12,256 | — | — |
| Grand total ... ... | Rs. 1,40,287 | Rs. 1,57,207 | Rs. 1,53,203 | Rs. 1,50,368 |

| Expenditure. | 1891–92. | 1892–93. | 1893–94. | 1894–95. |
|---|---|---|---|---|
| Head Office charges ... ... | Rs. 7,795 | Rs. 5,286 | Rs. 8,860 | Rs. 9,969 |
| Collections ... ... .. | 8,553 | 8,761 | 8,209 | 7,748 |
| Conservancy ... ... ... | 16,845 | 17,937 | 18,039 | 18,667 |
| Registration of Births and Deaths | 694 | 786 | 786 | 786 |
| Lighting charges ... ... ... | 5,617 | 7,983 | 8,101 | 9,675 |
| Public works ... ... ... | 38,037 | 33,832 | 50,029 | 41,128 |
| Charitable grants... ... ... | 19,105 | 15,713 | 16,650 | 16,593 |
| Education ... ... ... ... | 7,888 | 8,408 | 7,992 | 7,510 |
| Miscellaneous ... ... ... | 1,971 | 2,849 | 12,369 | 17,170 |
| Total Municipal Funds ... | Rs. 1,05,505 | Rs. 1,01,555 | Rs. 1,31,035 | Rs. 1,29,246 |
| Jubilee Fund ... ... ... | 2,899 | — | — | — |
| Special Improvement Funds ... | 14,414 | 38,257 | — | — |
| Contributions ... ... ... | 7,100 | 7,160 | 9,660 | 7,400 |
| Closing balance ... ... ... | — | 10,235 | 12,508 | 13,722 |
| Grand total ... ... | Rs. 1,29,918 | Rs. 1,57,207 | Rs. 1,53,203 | Rs. 1,50,368 |

**Civil and Military Station.**—Till the Rendition in 1881 this was known as the Cantonment (called *Daṇḍu*[1] by Hindus, and

[1] Pronounced Dhundoo and Lushker.

*Lashkar*[1] by Musalmans). It was then made over to the British Government as an Assigned Tract, and is under the administration of the Resident. It is situated to the north-east of Bangalore Proper, and was established in 1809, on the removal of the British garrison from Seringapatam, which had proved too unhealthy for the troops. It includes 18 suburbs and covers an area of 12½ square miles.

The parade ground extends two miles east and west and is surrounded by a ride or mall, the Rotten Row of the station. At its western end, on a commanding site, stand the Residency, with the fine range of Mysore Public Offices rising out from the wooded grounds of Cubbon Park, and the Post Office. The north side of the parade ground is occupied by the guard houses of the Native Infantry regiments, with lines for the men some distance at the back. Further east stands St. Andrew's Kirk, and beyond that come the main-guard, the bakery for the troops and the barracks of the British Infantry. At the east end, and southerly from Trinity Church, are situated the extensive Artillery and Cavalry barracks[1] and lines, with the native town of Halasur on the north. On the south side of the parade ground are St. Mark's Church, the Bowring Institute, the United Service Library, the Mayo Hall and the Gymkhana, besides some fine shops. From this direction thoroughfares lead south to the quarters known as Shoolay and Richmond Town, where numerous European pensioners and Eurasians live. Beyond this again are the Native Cavalry and Arab lines, and All Saints' Church.

The Cantonment bazaar, a native town in itself, lies in a valley to the north of the Infantry lines. It contains a commodious and well-kept Market, the Bowring Civil Hospital, numerous imposing stores for the sale of European goods, and large native buildings. To the north of this again is the populous district of St. John's Hill, inhabited by great numbers of European pensioned soldiers, whose neat little cottages, with the spire of the parish church rising up in their midst, give the place somewhat the appearance of an English village. To the east of St. John's Hill are the lines of the Sappers and Miners, on the north, Cleveland Town, and on the west, the Pioneer lines and the Cantonment Railway-station.

Among the buildings deserving a more particular notice are the Residency, the Convent Schools, the Roman Catholic Cathedral and St. Mary's Church, the Mayo Hall, the Kirk, the Cavalry barracks, etc. Near the New Market will be seen more than one ornamental mosque, and the *gopura* or tower of the Halsur pagoda is a good specimen of the Hindu pyramidal architecture.

[1] The Cavalry barracks occupy the site of what was the old Race-course.

The population of the Civil and Military Station is classified as follows :—

| Population in 1891. | Males. | Females. | Total. |
|---|---|---|---|
| Hindus (with 176 Jains) ... ... | 28,844 | 29,407 | 58,251 |
| Muhammadans ... ... ... | 12,210 | 11,682 | 23,892 |
| Christians— | | | |
| Europeans ... ... ... ... | 3,262 | 1,723 | 4,985 |
| Eurasians ... ... ... ... | 1,127 | 1,522 | 2,649 |
| Natives ... ... ... ... | 4,726 | 5,542 | 10,268 |
| Others (23 Brahmos, 6 Parsis, &c.) ... | 20 | 16 | 36 |
| Total ... ... | 50,189 | 49,892 | 100,081 |

An analysis of the population according to occupations, gives the following results as to means of livelihood :—

| | Males. | Females. | Totals. | | Per cent. |
|---|---|---|---|---|---|
| Government— | | | | | |
| Administration ... ... ... | 1,825 | 1,777 | 3,602 | | |
| Defence ... ... ... ... | 6,843 | 4,424 | 11,267 | | |
| | | | | 14,869 | 14·85 |
| Pasture and agriculture ... ... ... | 3,187 | 2,793 | | 5,980 | 5·27 |
| Personal and household service ... | 8,625 | 8,182 | | 16,807 | 16·79 |
| Preparation and supply of material substances ... ... ... ... | 14,538 | 15,886 | | 30,424 | 30·39 |
| Commerce, transport and storage ... | 4,810 | 4,568 | | 9,378 | 9·37 |
| Professions, learned and artistic ... | 2,662 | 2,977 | | 5,639 | 5·63 |
| Indefinite— | | | | | |
| Unskilled labour ... ... ... | 3,966 | 5,076 | 9,042 | | |
| Undefined ... ... ... ... | 299 | 432 | 731 | | |
| | | | | 9,773 | 9·76 |
| Independent of work— | | | | | |
| Property or alms ... ... ... | 690 | 882 | 1,572 | | |
| Pensions ... ... ... ... | 2,744 | 2,895 | 5,639 | | |
| | | | | 7,211 | 7·20 |

Good water is obtained from wells in some parts of the Cantonment, but in several quarters, among others the Cavalry barracks, there is no water. These barracks are supplied from the large Halsur tank and wells adjacent to it, from which the water is pumped up by an engine to the top of a rock and thence distributed in pipes. The Cantonment bazaar and Sepoy lines get water from a chain of reservoirs known by the name of Miller's tanks. There is also a tank for Shoolay.

The water supply being inadequate for the growing demands of the town, Sankey's Reservoir was designed, by the Chief Engineer after whom it is named, in order to remedy the want. It provided for collecting and storing the rain-flow over an area of 2½ square miles on the high ground to the north-west, about 3 miles distant, such land as was under the plough being thrown out of cultivation. The run-off from the surface was conducted by means of contour channels to the reservoir, which again was connected with Miller's tanks, and afterwards with the Dharmámbudhi also. Work was begun in 1875, but was interrupted and virtually stopped by the famine. The reservoir was eventually made serviceable by 1882, the total cost having amounted tc $5\frac{3}{4}$ lakhs.[1]

But even this scheme, though affording material help, it became evident would not suffice to provide for the water supply of the Civil and Military Station, much less for that of the whole of Bangalore. A prize for the best essay on the subject was offered to public competition, and schemes and opinions of extraordinary diversity have been brought forward since by a succession of Engineer officers, several of them specially appointed by the Government of India to report upon the whole question. Indeed, there is scarcely a site or a tank for miles round Bangalore that has not formed a part of one or another project. The latest proposal was the formation of a reservoir in the Maligal valley, about 7 miles distant on the Magadi road. Meanwhile the Mysore Government have completed the Hesarghatta scheme for the supply of the City, and it seems probable that the Civil and Military Station will also be provided for from the same source. The matter is of urgency in relation to the public health.

The drainage of the bazaar and Cantonment is carried by a large sewer, passing through a tunnel in the Halsur tank, to some distance beyond Halsur, where it is applied to cultivation.

*Administration.*—An *imperium in imperio*, under the control of the Resident, the Assigned Tract is provided with the various departments of administration, separate from those of the Mysore Government.

*Land.*—The area for cultivation is a little over five square miles, of which only about two-fifths are Government land (375 acres of it unculturable); the rest belongs to káyamgutta, jodi, and sarvamánya villages. The revenue work continued under the Deputy Commissioner of the Bangalore District till the 1st of April 1884, when it was made over to the Station District Magistrate as Collector, and he is aided by an Amildar. In *Legislation*, all Acts, Rules, and Regulations in force before the Rendition continued in force; but in 1883–4 a revised list of such as applied to the Civil and Military Station was issued by the Government of India, declaring to what extent and with what modifications they were to be the law. Other enactments have since

[1] In 1892–93, owing to the drought, Hebbal tank was temporarily connected with Sankey's reservoir, and additional water pumped up for the use of Bangalore, both City and C and M Station.

been extended to the Civil and Military Station from time to time. The *Police* force is composed of a District Superintendent, with (in 1894) 48 subordinate officers and 278 constables, costing Rs. 62,653. The Courts of *Criminal Justice* are the Bench of Honorary Magistrates (established in September 1888), with third-class powers in regard to offences under sections 352 and 405 of the Indian Penal Code, and 34 of Act V of 1861, or against Municipal Regulations and bye-laws the penalty for which does not exceed Rs. 50; the Court of the Second Magistrate, with powers of the first class; that of the District Magistrate (who took the place of the previous Town and Cantonment Magistrate); and the Sessions Court. The powers of a High Court were vested in the Chief Judge of Mysore till May 1884, when they were transferred to the Resident, and the other courts above-named established. The duties of Civil and Sessions Judge were united in one officer till August 1891, when the Assistant Resident was made Sessions Judge, and a post of District Judge was created. The receipts in Criminal Courts for 1894–5 amounted to Rs. 8,377, and the charges to Rs. 25,357. The number of cases brought to trial was 2,726, involving 4,212 persons. The great majority were disposed of by the Bench of Magistrates. There is no separate jail, the Bangalore Central Jail being close at hand. For *Civil Justice* there are the Munsiff's Court, established in January 1887, under the Second Magistrate, with jurisdiction up to Rs. 500; the District Court, with unlimited jurisdiction, and the Small Cause Court with jurisdiction up to Rs. 500, both these being under the Civil Judge, who also hears appeals from the Munsiff. The Resident exercises the powers of a High Court. The receipts in 1894–5 were Rs. 35,679, and the charges Rs. 19,861. The number of suits for disposal was 2,911. For *Registration* the Assistant-Resident has been Inspector-General since July 1886, relieving the Mysore officer; the District Judge is the District Registrar; and the work of Sub-Registrar, previously held by the Second Magistrate, was, in October 1888, given to the Amildar. There were 1,681 documents registered in 1894–5. The receipts were Rs. 6,434, and the charges Rs. 699.

The Resident's Treasury, besides dealing with the accounts of the Assigned Tract, is the medium through which the subsidy from the Mysore State is paid, and it disburses a variety of charges connected with the Military, Ecclesiastical, Post Office, Telegraph, and other services, as well as pensions, leave allowances, and other items. The total receipts in 1894–5 were over 98 lakhs, and the disbursements nearly 95. The District Magistrate was made also Treasury officer in October 1888, the separate post being abolished. The accounts are in the first instance audited at Madras, after which the transactions which pertain to the Residency and to the Assigned Tract are transferred to the books of the Government of India. The revenue surplus, previously credited to Mysore, is since 1884-5 retained by the Government of India. It will suffice in this place to give the *Revenue* and *Expenditure* of the Assigned Tract for the past five years :—

| Receipts. | 1890-91. | 1891-92. | 1892-93. | 1893-94. | 1894-95. |
|---|---|---|---|---|---|
| Land Revenue ... ... ... | 4,599 | 3,692 | 3,125 | 5,417 | 4,445 |
| Stamps ... ... ... ... | 65,026 | 61,833 | 71,666 | 62,763 | 68,562 |
| Excise ... ... ... ... | 3,88,045 | 3,41,594 | 4,26,328 | 4,35,297 | 4,62,136 |
| Forest ... ... ... ... | — | — | — | — | 2,038 |
| Registration... ... ... ... | 6,023 | 5,792 | 5,923 | 6,421 | 6,175 |
| Law and Justice—Courts of Law... | 2,375 | 3,319 | 2,719 | 3,593 | 3,452 |
| Police ... ... ... ... | 1,384 | 1,380 | 1,550 | 1,762 | 1,683 |
| Scientific and other minor departments ... ... ... ... | — | — | 1,051 | 1,223 | 1,483 |
| Other items ... ... ... ... | 36 | 56 | 22 | 64 | 630 |
| Total ... ... Rs. | 4,67,488 | 4,17,666 | 5,12,384 | 5,16,540 | 5,50,604 |

| Disbursements. | 1890-91. | 1891-92. | 1892-93. | 1893-94. | 1894-95. |
|---|---|---|---|---|---|
| Refunds and drawbacks ... ... | 4,377 | 5,214 | 4,889 | 3,648 | 5,539 |
| Land Revenue ... ... ... | 1,731 | 1,741 | 1,745 | 1,735 | 1,741 |
| Stamps ... ... ... ... | 653 | 651 | 690 | 696 | 729 |
| Excise ... ... ... ... | — | 7,584 | 26,570 | 13,732 | 12,248 |
| Registration... ... ... ... | 685 | 622 | 694 | 579 | 699 |
| Law and Justice—Courts of Law... | 48,924 | 45,878 | 41,939 | 47,237 | 44,633 |
| ,, ,, Jails ... ... | 3,550 | 4,238 | 3,474 | 4,477 | 4,524 |
| Police ... ... ... ... | 61,121 | 62,319 | 63,709 | 62,220 | 62,838 |
| Education ... ... ... ... | 28,945 | 27,815 | 29,495 | 34,667 | 35,852 |
| Medical ... ... ... ... | 4,437 | 4,410 | 4,329 | 8,855 | 4,767 |
| Scientific and other minor departments ... ... ... ... | — | — | 885 | 1,011 | 1,134 |
| Superannuation ... ... ... | 1,654 | 1,677 | 1,742 | 1,552 | 1,477 |
| Stationery and printing ... ... | 1,497 | 1,316 | 1,385 | 1,589 | 1,524 |
| Miscellaneous ... ... ... | 7,489 | 7,408 | 7,728 | 6,770 | 6,568 |
| Civil works ... ... ... ... | 5,025 | 5,025 | 5,025 | 5,025 | 5,025 |
| Total ... ... Rs. | 1,70,088 | 1,75,898 | 1,94,299 | 1,93,793 | 1,89,298 |

The principal item of Revenue is under Excise, and is derived from the lease of farms, grant of licenses, and the levy of duties. Arrack is supplied from the Durbar distillery, which has the exclusive privilege of manufacture and wholesale vend, the Station paying a proportionate share of the expenses for maintenance and testing. Separate contracts are made for toddy, ganja, beer and opium. The entry under Forest relates to the sale of sandalwood growing in the Station. The heading Scientific and Minor Departments accounts for fees of the Primary and Secondary School examinations, as also do the entries per contra. In the Disbursements, the entry against Jails represents the cost of feeding prisoners from the C and M Station committed to the Bangalore Central Jail.

The *Medical* institutions are the Bowring Civil Hospital and the Halsur Dispensary. The latter was established in March 1884, when also the Bowring Hospital was placed in charge of the Residency Surgeon. The numbers treated in 1894–5 at the Hospital were 1,985 in-door, and 22,809 out-door patients; at the Dispensary 8,559, all out-door. Of the in-door, 459 were Europeans or Eurasians, and of the out-door 2,392. The remainder were 227 in and 8,770 out, Musalmans; 763 and 14,611, Hindus; 536 and 5,556, other classes. *Education* continued to be supervised till December 1888, gratuitously, by the Director of Public Instruction in Mysore, who was assisted by his Deputy Inspector. It was then added to the charge of the Inspector of Schools, Madras Western Circle, an old officer of the Mysore Educational Department, and on his transfer in 1894 to the Central Circle, he still retained the charge. There are no Government schools in the Civil and Military Station, all being Aided schools. Inspection is therefore the main duty that devolves on Government. The Inspector visits Bangalore in June, July and August for that purpose, and a Sub-Deputy Inspector is stationed here permanently. Probably no place in India of the size of Bangalore is better provided with the means of education for all classes, and nowhere is a more earnest attention devoted to the subject than on the part of the various private agencies at work. The following are the statistics for three periods:—

| Aided. | 1881–82. | | | | 1887–88. | | | | 1894–95. | | | |
|---|---|---|---|---|---|---|---|---|---|---|---|---|
| | For Boys. | | For Girls. | | For Boys. | | For Girls. | | For Boys. | | For Girls. | |
| | No. | Pupils | No. | Pupils | No. | Pupils | No. | Pupils | No. | Pupils | No. | Pupils |
| Arts Colleges ... ... | 1 | 10 | — | — | 2 | 41 | — | — | 1 | 14 | — | — |
| Secondary Schools ... | 14 | 291 | 7 | 91 | 16 | 746 | 9 | 226 | 11 | 1,953 | 10 | 1,054 |
| Primary Schools ... | 23 | 1,884 | 15 | 877 | 26 | 2,082 | 20 | 1,391 | 13 | 790 | 13 | 908 |
| Special ... ... .. | 1 | 91 | — | — | 1 | 157 | 1 | 10 | — | — | — | — |
| Total ... ... | 39 | 2,276 | 22 | 968 | 45 | 3,026 | 30 | 1,627 | 25 | 2,757 | 23 | 1,962 |
| Unaided Schools ... | 52 | 1,537 | 14 | 592 | 49 | 1,965 | 9 | 334 | 55 | 1,805 | 10 | 846 |
| Total ... ... | 91 | 2,813 | 36 | 1,560 | 94 | 4,991 | 39 | 1,961 | 80 | 4,562 | 33 | 2,808 |
| General total ... ... | 127 schools<br>4,373 pupils | | | | 133 schools<br>6,952 pupils | | | | 113 schools<br>7,370 pupils | | | |

According to caste or creed, the last total includes 1,934 Europeans or Eurasians, 1,081 Native Christians, 3,054 Hindus, 1,372 Muhammadans, and 29 others. The expenditure on English education was Rs. 89,724, and on Vernacular education Rs. 13,889. It was distributed among the schools of the various religious denominations as follows :—

| Denomination. | Government. | | Private. | | Total. | Per cent. |
|---|---|---|---|---|---|---|
| | Imperial. | Municipal. | Fees. | Other Sources. | | |
| Church of England ... | 10,140 | 1,320 | 6,949 | 7,404 | 25,813 | 24·92 |
| Church of Scotland ... | 3,600 | 360 | 9,857 | 1,138 | 14,955 | 14·43 |
| Roman Catholic ... | 6,563 | 600 | 8,767 | 14,376 | 30,306 | 29·25 |
| Wesleyan Mission ... | 1,740 | 1,937 | 2,832 | 4,469 | 10,978 | 10·59 |
| Lutheran Mission ... | — | 250 | 12 | 529 | 791 | ·76 |
| Hindu ... ... ... | 4,800 | 900 | 4,200 | 4,154 | 14,054 | 13·56 |
| Muhammadan ... ... | 1,200 | 1,868 | 223 | 3,425 | 6,716 | 6·49 |
| Total ... Rs | 28,043 | 7,235 | 32,840 | 35,495 | 1,03,613 | 100·00 |

The only College is St. Joseph's, which is of the second grade, educating to the standard of the First in Arts examination, and attended by both Europeans and Natives. The principal High schools are Bishop Cotton's, St. Andrew's, Baldwin, and Convent schools, for Europeans; with Narrainswami Mudaliar's for natives.

*Station Municipality.*—The municipal administration was conducted under the Bangalore Municipal Regulations of 1871 as amended by Government notification of the 28th April 1881, until superseded by the Regulations of 1883. The District Magistrate is the President, and the Board is composed of six *ex-officio* and eighteen non-official members, the latter being elected. There are six Divisions or Wards, as per margin, and the elected Commissioners are so apportioned as to represent the several classes in each. There are thus six Europeans and Eurasians, four Muhammadans, and eight Hindus and others.[1] Elections at first took place as vacancies occurred, but in 1888 the rule was amended so as to secure a general election every two years. The Fort formed Division VII, and was represented by an extra Commissioner till given up in 1888. A tax on arts, professions, trades and callings was introduced on the 1st January 1884. The contribution for one-third cost of Police was also exchanged for the charges of the Bowring Hospital. The maintenance of the military roads was undertaken in 1884–5, a contribution

Divisions.
I. Halsur (Ulsoor).
II. Southern.
III. East General Bazaar.
IV. West General Bazaar.
V. Cleveland Town.
VI. High Ground.

[1] The following was the distribution laid down by the election rules passed in 1890 :—

Divisions. I. III. II. V. IV. VI.
Eur. (I. III.) 1, (II.) 3, (V.) 1, (IV. VI.) 1 = 6;

Divisions. I. II. III. V. VI. IV.
Muh. (I. II. III. V. VI.) 2, (IV.) 2 = 4;

Divisions. I. II. III. IV. V. VI.
Hin. (I.) 1, (II.) 1, (III.) 3, (IV.) 2, (V. VI.) 1 = 8.

being received for the purpose.[1] Hackney carriage rules were introduced on the 1st April 1885. Octroi duties were abolished from the 1st April 1887, but Town Duties on tobacco, &c., were again imposed in 1892. The following is a statement of receipts and expenditure for three years:—

| Receipts. | 1892-93. | 1893-94. | 1894-95. |
|---|---|---|---|
| Collections— | | | |
| Town duties on tobacco, &c. ... ... ... | 43,066 | 46,762 | 47,130 |
| Tax on houses, buildings, and lands ... ... | 40,207 | 38,437 | 48,916 |
| Tax on oil-mills and carts ... ... ... ... | 1,212 | 1,144 | 1,126 |
| Lighting tax ... ... ... ... .. ... | 12,135 | 9,875 | 11,896 |
| Tax on Arts, &c.— | | | |
| Tax on arts, professions, and trades ... ... | 11,611 | 12,066 | 15,835 |
| Slaughter-house fees ... ... ... ... ... | 24,933 | 24,750 | 27,600 |
| Other license fees ... ... ... ... ... | 13,998 | 19,695 | 22,215 |
| Rents, &c.— | | | |
| Rents on buildings and lands ... ... ... | 672 | 744 | 1,241 |
| Market rents ... ... ... ... ... ... | 11,868 | 11,871 | 12,012 |
| Cattle pounds ... ... ... ... ... | 1,573 | 1,669 | 1,777 |
| Miscellaneous collections ... ... ... ... | 34,753 | 38,688 | 46,385 |
| Extraordinary— | | | |
| Refunds and interest ... ... ... ... | 448 | 1,217 | 1,273 |
| Fines from Magistrates' Courts ... ... ... | 1,589 | 1,797 | 2,142 |
| Transfers and contributions ... ... ... | 46,602 | 46,776 | 47,711 |
| Total ... ... Rs. | 2,44,667 | 2,55,491 | 2,87,259 |

| Expenditure. | 1892-93. | 1893-94. | 1894-95. |
|---|---|---|---|
| Collections— | | | |
| For town duties on tobacco, &c. ... ... ... | 9,178 | 9,561 | 10,401 |
| For tax on houses, buildings, and lands ... ... | 3,284 | 3,144 | 3,200 |
| For tax on professions and trades ... ... ... | 811 | 816 | 1,177 |
| Markets, &c. ... ... ... ... ... | 3,253 | 3,228 | 3,334 |
| Head Office charges ... ... ... ... | 4,105 | 4,583 | 4,875 |
| Supervision and Management— | | | |
| Salary of officers ... ... ... ... ... | 11,510 | 11,510 | 12,037 |
| Public Works— | | | |
| Supervision ... ... ... ... ... ... | 4,095 | 4,245 | 4,763 |
| Original works ... ... ... ... ... | 34,484 | 60,002 | 17,721 |
| Repairs ... ... ... ... ... ... | 37,355 | 47,093 | 41,219 |
| Compensation for purchase of houses ... ... | 166 | 1,652 | 3,000 |
| Education ... ... ... ... ... ... | 6,496 | 7,077 | 7,444 |
| Charitable Grants— | | | |
| Hospital and Dispensary ... ... ... | 25,842 | 26,312 | 27,509 |
| Vaccination ... ... ... ... ... ... | 2,212 | 2,333 | 2,289 |
| Grants in aid to charitable institutions ... ... | 3,315 | 3,925 | 3,985 |
| Conservancy ... ... ... ... ... ... | 36,944 | 38,361 | 39,975 |
| Lighting ... ... ... ... ... ... ... | 15,151 | 15,832 | 15,220 |
| Fairs and exhibitions ... .... ... ... ... | 373 | 366 | 420 |
| Miscellaneous— | | | |
| Cattle pounds ... ... ... ... ... | 1,466 | 1,439 | 1,490 |
| Registration of vital statistics ... ... ... | 1,017 | 1,007 | 1,019 |
| Other items, and charges from Reserve ... ... | 19,306 | 20,552 | 22,920 |
| Advances to be recovered ... ... ... ... | — | 1,375 | 11,360 |
| Total ... ... Rs. | 2,20,363 | 2,64,413 | 2,35,357 |

[1] The length of municipal roads is 65 miles; of military roads, 21; and suburban roads, 7½.

**Bannerghatta.**—A sacred hill in the Anekal taluq, 10 miles south of Bangalore. Its height is 3,271 feet above the level of the sea. On the occasion of the *rathotsava* in honour of Sampangi Ramaswami, held for three days from Phalguna bahula 6th, there is an assemblage of 4,000 people.

**Begur.**—A village in Bangalore taluq, about 8 miles south of Bangalore. Head-quarters of the hóbli of the same name. Population 2,074. An elaborately sculptured stone from here, now in the Bangalore Museum, is a memorial to the local chief, named Nágattara, who, in about 920, fell in the war between the Ganga king Ereyappa and the Nolamba king Bíra Mahendra, while attacking the elephants in the army of the Nolamba prince Ayyapa Deva.

**Channapatna.**—A taluq in the south-west. Area 427 square miles. Head-quarters at Channapatna. Contains the following hóblis, villages and population :—

| No. | Hóblis. | Vil-lages. | Ham-lets. | Villages classified. | | | | Popula-tion. |
|---|---|---|---|---|---|---|---|---|
| | | | | Govern-ment. | Sarva-manya. | Jodi. | Kayam-gutta. | |
| 1 | Bairamangala ... ... | 27 | 42 | 23 | 1 | 1 | 2 | 6,633 |
| 2 | Biḍadi ... ... ... | 21 | 21 | 16 | 1 | — | 4 | 5,275 |
| 3 | Channapatna ... ... | 14 | 16 | 13 | — | 1 | — | 14,938 |
| 4 | Closepet ... ... | 17 | 48 | 17 | — | — | — | 9,916 |
| 5 | Honganúr ... ... | 24 | 31 | 23 | — | — | 1 | 8,218 |
| 6 | Kúnagal ... ... | 31 | 42 | 29 | — | 1 | 1 | 6,179 |
| 7 | Mákali ... ... ... | 34 | 44 | 28 | 5 | 1 | — | 10,769 |
| 8 | Malúr ... ... ... | 18 | 12 | 16 | 2 | — | — | 11,190 |
| 9 | Múdigere ... ... | 29 | 10 | 28 | — | 1 | — | 8,127 |
| 10 | Virúpákshipur ... ... | 48 | 49 | 42 | 4 | 2 | — | 18,049 |
| | Total ... ... | 263 | 315 | 235 | 13 | 7 | 8 | 99,294 |

*Principal places, with Population.*—Channapatna, 9,160; Closepet, 6,236; Malúr, 2,161; Mangalavárpete, 1,973; Honganúr, 1,705; Kúdalúr, 1,508; Biḍadi, 1,391; Sogála, 1,350; Chekkere, 1,255; Malúrpatna, 1,078.

In 1873 Channapatna was formed into a sub-taluq of the Closepet taluq, with the Channapatna, Malúr and Múdigere hóblis; but in August 1892 its former status was restored, and Closepet made its sub-taluq, each with 5 hóblis (*see* Closepet).

The taluq may be divided into two parts with regard to its physical features. The northern and north-western part is traversed by several ranges of hills, contains large tracts of waste land, more or less covered with scrub-jungle, and is generally devoid of tanks and other artificial irrigation works. The southern and south-western parts are plain, contain more populous villages, and are studded with tanks, some of which are of considerable importance.

The *Arkavati* flows past Closepet and Kúnagal through the west, and the *Kanva* past Malur through the east, both running from north to south. The course of the former is surrounded with lofty hills, precipices and jungle, which are characteristic of much of the taluq. Its waters are therefore little used for purposes of cultivation, except that it is fringed with a multitude of mulberry gardens, irrigated by lifts from the stream. Its tributary, the *Vrishabhávati*, joins it in the extreme west. The Kanva, on emerging from the hills a short distance north of Malur, enters on a broad and fertile valley of wet and garden land, which continues to the limits of the taluq. This river is dammed near Abbur, and is made to feed several good tanks. The principal hills picturesquely grouped around the town of Closepet are Ramgiri (which formerly gave its name to the taluq), Sivangiri, Sidlukal, and Achalbetta.

Owing to the broken nature of the country the soil is very varied. The produce of wet cultivation, consisting of paddy, cocoanuts, betel-leaf, plantains, and sugar-cane, is considerable. Numbers of cocoanut gardens are formed along the lower course of the Kanva river, the soil being well adapted for the purpose, and water tapped a few feet from the surface. The trees are watered only when young: on arriving at maturity they are left to depend upon rainfall and subsoil moisture. Much raw silk is produced at Closepet and Channapatna and exported, though disease among silkworms for many years destroyed the industry. The annual production is estimated at 1,850 maunds, valued at nearly 3 lakhs. Channapatna is one of the principal manufacturing and trading towns in the country. Coarse cotton cloths are woven in many parts of the taluq.

The whole of this region formed part of the Ganga dominions, Mankunda having been the royal residence in the seventh century. The western part of the taluq was included in the district of Chikka Gangavádi, whose chief town was Honganur. Under the Chola kings Malúrpatna and Kúḍalúr were important places. Subsequently, after having formed part of the Hoysala kingdom, the entire stretch of territory east and west between the Ghats was conferred by the fallen Vijayanagar sovereign upon Jagadeva Ráyal, for his services in defending Penugonda. He made Channapatna his capital. In 1630 it was taken by the Rája of Mysore and the territory absorbed into the Mysore kingdom.

The revenue settlement was introduced in 1893, except in Bidadi hóbli, which was settled in 1879, when a part of the Magadi taluq.

The area of the taluq was thus distributed :—

| | | |
|---|---|---|
| Culturable (dry, 91,136; wet, 5,855; garden, 8,442) | ... | 105,433 |
| Unculturable (including village sites, &c.) ... | ... ... | 99,183 |
| Inam villages ... | ... ... ... ... ... ... | 28,230 |
| State forests, plantations, and kavals | ... ... ... | 40,202 |
| Total area | ... | Acres 273,048 |

Of the culturable area 6,324 acres were waste.

The total revenue under all heads for 1891–2 (15 months) was Rs. 155,950, and for 1892–3 it was Rs. 156,494. The land revenue from Government lands in those years was thus apportioned :—

| Cultivation. | 1891–92. | | 1892–93. | |
|---|---|---|---|---|
| | Area. | Assessment. | Area. | Assessment. |
| Dry ... ... ... | 60,218 | 53,630 | 61,098 | 54,387 |
| Wet ... ... ... | 4,229 | 24,617 | 4,267 | 25,695 |
| Garden ... ... ... | 6,540 | 29,849 | 6,544 | 29,864 |
| Total... ... | Ac. 70,987 | Rs. 1,08,096 | Ac. 71,909 | Rs. 1,09,945 |

The following was the average rainfall for 25 years (1870–1894) :—

| | Jan. | Feb. | Mar. | April | May | June | July | Aug. | Sept. | Oct. | Nov. | Dec. | | Year. |
|---|---|---|---|---|---|---|---|---|---|---|---|---|---|---|
| Channapatna... | 0·03 | 0·05 | 0·22 | 1·37 | 4·05 | 3·00 | 3·37 | 6·06 | 6·15 | 8·92 | 2·91 | 0·83 | ... | 36·96 |
| Closepet ... | 0·03 | 0·03 | 0·45 | 1·18 | 3·75 | 2·30 | 2·71 | 4·42 | 4·48 | 6·21 | 2·36 | 0·24 | ... | 28·16 |

The railway from Bangalore to Mysore runs through the middle of the taluq from north-east to south-west, with stations at Bidadi, Closepet, Channapatna and Múdgere. Alongside of the railway is the old trunk road to Mysore. From Closepet a road runs south-east to Kankanhalli, and one north to Magadi. From Channapatna there is a road south-east to Sátanur, with a branch to Halagur.

**Channapatna,** or **Chennapatna.**—A town situated in 12° 38′ N. lat. 77° 13′ E. long., 37 miles south-west of Bangalore, on the Bangalore-Seringapatam road. Head-quarters of the Channapatna taluq, and a municipality. The industrial portion of *Channapatna*, the handsome city, is called *Sukravár-péṭe*, Friday bazaar, and contains 6,381 of the population. The suburbs are Kottanhalli (857) and Godamodu (544.)

| Population in 1891. | Males. | Females. | Total. |
|---|---|---|---|
| Hindus (with 1 Jain) ... ... | 2,532 | 2,658 | 5,190 |
| Muhammadans ... ... ... | 1,761 | 2,187 | 3,948 |
| Christians ... ... ... ... | 13 | 9 | 22 |
| Total ... ... | 4,306 | 4,854 | 9,160 |

The fort appears to have been built about 1580 by *Jagadeva Râyal*,[1] who made Channapatna the capital of the territory, yielding it is said a revenue of nine lakhs of pagodas, bestowed upon him for his gallant defence of Penugonda, by the fallen Vijayanagar prince, to whom his daughter was married. Possessions which included such widely distant places as Mulbagal and Periyapatna, Kankanhalli and Budihal, thus suddenly acquired, must have formed a government more extensive than consolidated. The original possessions of the family were in Baramahal. Buchanan states that they were of the Telugu Banajiga caste and rose to power about the fourteenth century. The following names are given of the Ráyals of this line who ruled at Channapatna :—Ranoji Raya, Immaḍi Jagadeva, 15 years; Mummaḍi Jagadeva, 8 years; Kumára Jagadeva, 7 years; and Ankusha Raya, 16 years. The fort stood a long siege in 1630, when it was captured by Chama Raja Wodeyar of Mysore. In 1759 it was surprised by the Mahratta army under Gopal Hari, but was speedily released by Haidar Ali. It was repaired by the Dewan Purniah and contains portions of a palace erected for a relative of the then Maharaja, but has become much depopulated by reason of extreme unhealthiness from fever.

The Péṭe lies to the north-east of the fort. It is celebrated for the manufacture of lacquered ware and toys, of fine steel wires for strings of musical instruments, and of glass bracelets, of all of which an account will be found elsewhere. It is the residence of a large number of Muhammadans belonging to the Labbe and Daira sects, who trade with the western coast.

North of the péṭe are two large Muhammadan tombs, one erected in memory of Akil Shah Kadiri, the religious preceptor of Tipu, and the other in honour of Sayyid Ibrahim, a commandant of Bangalore, distinguished for his humanity to the English prisoners taken by Tipu.

| Municipal Funds. | 1892-93. | 1893-94. | 1894-95. | 1895-96. |
|---|---|---|---|---|
| Income (opening balance Rs. 1,460) | 5,027 | 3,518 | 3,895 | 4,065 |
| Expenditure ... ... ... | 5,606 | 3,893 | 3,486 | 4,288 |

**Closepet.**—A Sub-Division of the Bangalore District, composed of Channapatna, Magadi and Kankanhalli taluqs. Also a sub-taluq of the Channapatna taluq. The hóblis of the sub-taluq are Bairamangala, Bidadi, Closepet, Kúnagal and Mákali (for details *see* Channapatna taluq).

[1] By Wilks called *Jug Deo Rayeel*; by Buchanan, *Jacadeva Raya*; by Mackenzie, *Jagadeorian*.

**Closepet.**—A town on the left bank of the Arkávati, situated in 12° 40′ N. lat. 77° 12′ E. long., 30 miles south-west of Bangalore, on the Bangalore-Seringapatam road. Head-quarters of the Closepet Sub-Division and of the Closepet sub-taluq, and a municipality.

| Population in 1891. | Males. | Females | Total. |
|---|---|---|---|
| Hindus ... ... ... ... ... ... | 1,983 | 2,103 | 4,086 |
| Muhammadans ... ... ... ... ... | 1,061 | 993 | 2,054 |
| Christians ... ... ... ... ... ... | 43 | 53 | 96 |
| Total ... ... | 3,087 | 3,149 | 6,236 |

A fair is held every Tuesday, attended by about 4,000 persons.

Closepet, by natives pronounced *Kulis-pêṭe*, is so named after Sir Barry Close, Resident at the court of Mysore. There is an inscription on a pillar in the town to this effect in Persian and Kannada. It is generally called in Kannada *Hosapêṭe*, in Hindustani *Navipêṭ*, both meaning the new town. It is also called *Rámgiri*, from a neighbouring hill, at foot of which the original town stood. Closepet was founded in 1800 by the Dewan Purnaiya, for greater security of the high road, which there passed through a wild and jungly tract. It was at the same time made the head-quarters of the Bargeer, or irregular horse. The horse-breeding establishment of the Silahdars, since removed to Kunigal (Tumkur District), was formerly at Closepet.

The town has an agrahara at the side of the river, with a temple of Arkes'vara, and a chatram established by Purnaiya. The Muhammadans here are largely engaged in the rearing of silkworms. This industry was brought nearly to a stand by the disease which for some years destroyed the insects: those engaged in it emigrating in large numbers to the coffee districts. But the industry has now revived.

| Municipal Funds. | 1892-3. | 1893-4. | 1894-5. | 1895-6. |
|---|---|---|---|---|
| Income (opening balance, Rs. 1,938) | 2,717 | 2,940 | 2,975 | 2,810 |
| Expenditure ... ... ... ... | 3,018 | 2,953 | 3,634 | 4,503 |

**Devanhalli.**—A taluq in the north-east. Area 232 square miles. Head-quarters at Devanhalli. Contains the following hoblis, villages and population :—

| No. | Hoblis. | Villages. | Hamlets. | Villages classified. | | | | Population. |
|---|---|---|---|---|---|---|---|---|
| | | | | Govern-ment. | Sarva-mánya. | Jódi. | Kayam-gutta. | |
| 1 | A'vati ... ... | 34 | 2 | 26 | 1 | 3 | 4 | 6,239 |
| 2 | Búdigere ... | 26 | 10 | 18 | — | 7 | 1 | 7,062 |
| 3 | Channaráypatna | 37 | 2 | 33 | — | 4 | — | 6,058 |
| 4 | Devanhalli ... | 56 | 1 | 42 | — | 9 | 5 | 12,212 |
| 5 | Jála ... ... | 48 | 3 | 25 | — | 17 | 6 | 8,317 |
| 6 | Kundána .. | 60 | 7 | 32 | — | 22 | 6 | 7,698 |
| 7 | Vadigenhaḷḷi ... | 24 | — | 19 | — | 4 | 1 | 5,996 |
| | Total ... | 285 | 25 | 195 | 1 | 66 | 23 | 53,582 |

*Principal places, with Population.*—Devanhalli, 6,693; Vadigenhaḷḷi, 3,970; Búdigere, 1,591.

The taluq was abolished in 1882, but re-established in 1886. The Ṣ. Pinákini forms a part of its eastern boundary, and receives all the smaller streams. The country undulates in gentle curvatures, the valleys being fertile and well cultivated. The elevated parts are covered with low jungle. There are a few small hills and rocks to the north and west, but generally speaking it is an open country, healthy and well supplied with good water.

In addition to the usual dry and wet crops, there was, until prohibited, some cultivation of the poppy for opium. Potatoes of good quality are raised in considerable quantities. Pamelos attain a large size. Coffee cultivation has been recently commenced on an extended scale in the west. Sugar of superior quality was formerly manufactured, under the instruction of some Chinese brought over for that purpose by Tipu Sultan. A few coarse cotton cloths and cumblis are made.

An early place of importance in the taluq appears to have been Nellurpatna in the east, a town which has lain for centuries in ruins. In the thirteenth century Kundána seems to have been the royal residence of the Hoysala king Rámanátha, who had possession of the south and east of the Hoysala dominions. Devanhalli was subsequently founded by one of the family of refugees who, settling at Avati, became the founders of the Magadi, Chik-Ballapur, and other lines of chiefs. Vadigenhaḷḷi, which is largely populated by merchants, is one of the chief trading-places in the Bangalore District.

The revenue settlement was introduced in 1885, at the time when the taluq had been broken up and portions annexed to other taluqs. Thus Kundana hobli was assigned to Dod-Ballapur taluq, Jála hobli to Bangalore taluq, and Devanhalli hobli to Chik-Ballapur taluq. The wet rates were found to be generally so high as to be prohibitive, in consequence of which all available manure was applied exclusively to the dry fields, and much rice land was waste. The batayi system which prevailed was also unfavourable to cultivation in many ways. The new Survey rates have rectified these matters. In the north of the taluq *talpargis*, or surface springs, are numerous, and the supply of water from them almost unfailing. Channels led off from these talpargis irrigate rice and sugar-cane extensively. When the water ceases to flow of itself, a *yáta* is erected, and the water thus lifted at the fountain head. Wells are very numerous, and water is found with certainty almost anywhere in the low-lying lands, not far from the surface.

The total revenue under all heads for 1891–2 (15 months) was Rs. 1,24,394, and for 1892–3 it was Rs. 1,35,105. The land revenue from Government lands in those years was thus apportioned :—

| Cultivation. | 1891–2. | | 1892–3. | |
|---|---|---|---|---|
| | Area. | Assessment. | Area. | Assessment. |
| Dry ... ... ... | 27,750 | 49,533 | 28,356 | 50,568 |
| Wet ... ... ... | 3,132 | 19,063 | 4,564 | 28,003 |
| Garden ... ... ... | 2,398 | 13,476 | 2,465 | 13,886 |
| Total ... ... | Ac. 33,280 | Rs. 82,072 | Ac. 35,385 | Rs. 92,457 |

The following was the average rainfall for 25 years (1870–94) at Devanhalli, and for two years (1893–4) at the other places :—

| | Jan. | Feb. | Mar. | Apl. | May | June | July | Aug. | Sept. | Oct. | Nov. | Dec. | Year. |
|---|---|---|---|---|---|---|---|---|---|---|---|---|---|
| Devanhalli | — | 0·05 | 0·26 | 0·65 | 3·94 | 3·08 | 2·59 | 3·75 | 4·22 | 3·95 | 2·06 | 0·26 ... | 24·82 |
| Chikka Jála | — | 0·30 | 1·20 | 2·52 | 5·74 | 4·68 | 3·92 | 4·02 | 3·47 | 6·76 | 1·94 | — ... | 34·55 |
| Vadigenhaḷḷi | — | 0·03 | 0·20 | 2·39 | 3·13 | 4·76 | 3·08 | 4·40 | 4·78 | 8·90 | 2·72 | 0·23 ... | 34·62 |

The railway from Bangalore to Guntakal runs through the south-west, and has a station at Rájankunti. The taluq is crossed from south to north by the old Bangalore-Bellary road, and from east to west by the Kolar Dod-Ballapur road. There is also a short road from Devanhalli to Nandidroog.

**Devanhalli.**—A town situated in 13° 15′ N. lat. 77° 44′ E. long., 23 miles north of Bangalore, on the old Bangalore-Bellary road. Head-quarters of the Devanhalli taluq, and a municipality.

| Population in 1891. | Males. | Females. | Total. |
|---|---|---|---|
| Hindus ... ... ... ... ... ... | 3,066 | 3,231 | 6,297 |
| Muhammadans ... ... ... ... ... | 191 | 201 | 392 |
| Christians ... ... ... ... ... ... | 3 | 1 | 4 |
| Total ... ... | 3,260 | 3,433 | 6,693 |

A fair is held every Wednesday, attended by 500 persons.

Devanhalli appears to have been originally a small village, named Devandoḍḍi from Deva its headman. About the year 1501 Malla Baire Gauda, a son of one of the refugees from Kanchi who settled at Avati, being led by auspicious omens, formed the resolution of building a fort on the spot. The consent of Deva Gauda was obtained with difficulty, and only after the bestowal of liberal compensation and the promise that the new town should bear his name. A fort, the remains of which were formerly visible inside the present one, was accordingly erected by Malla Baire Gauda and named Devanhalli, or Devanḍhalli. He conferred the government upon his brother Sanna Baire Gauda, who succeeded in bringing a large tract of the surrounding country under cultivation. He reigned 40 years and was succeeded by his son Baire Gauda, who reigned 25 years. The following chiefs succeeded to the government, each being the son of the preceding. Dayál Baiche Gauda ruled 37 years, Mudda Baire Gauda 20 years, Immadi Sanna Baire Ganda 37 years, Gopal Gauda 35 years, Dodda Baire Gauda 54 years, and Rangappa Gauda only 10 months. The latter dying without issue, was succeeded by his relative Chikkappa Gauda of Chik-Ballapur, three months after whose accession Devanhalli was invested by the Mysore army under Nanja Raj. It fell in 1749 after a gallant defence of 8 months and was thenceforward annexed to Mysore.

In this siege Haidar Ali, the future ruler of the country, first gained distinction as a volunteer horseman, and at Devanhalli his son and successor Tipu was born. These circumstances were sufficient to invest the place with peculiar interest in the eyes of the family.[1] Haidar therefore commenced rebuilding the fort. It was built of stone, in the form of an oval, flanked with circular bastions and two cavaliers on the eastern face, and was not quite completed when invested in 1791 by the army under Lord Cornwallis, to whom it easily submitted. When the fort was erected, the old péṭe surrounding it to the south and east was levelled to the ground, to prevent its sheltering the besiegers in case of an attack, and a new one on rising ground half a mile to the westward was afterwards erected, called the Sultan Péṭe. This was soon deserted for the old quarter after the capture.

| Municipal Funds. | 1892-3. | 1893-4. | 1894-5 | 1895-6. |
|---|---|---|---|---|
| Income (opening balance, Rs. 1,531) ... | 1,284 | 1,308 | 2,406 | 2,870 |
| Expenditure ... ... ... ... | 2,418 | 1,494 | 2,174 | 3,537 |

[1] The site of Haidar's house is still pointed out, to the west of the fort.

**Dod-Ballapur.**—A taluq in the north-west. Area 341 square miles. Head-quarters at Dod-Ballapur. Contains the following hoblis, villages and population :—

| No. | Hoblis. | Villages. | Hamlets. | Villages classified. | | | | Population. |
|---|---|---|---|---|---|---|---|---|
| | | | | Govern-ment. | Sarva-mánya. | Jodi. | Kayam-gutta. | |
| 1 | Dod-Ballapur ... | 46 | 7 | 37 | — | 9 | — | 12,944 |
| 2 | Honnavára ... | 28 | 4 | 25 | — | 3 | — | 4,913 |
| 3 | Hosahalli ... | 35 | 19 | 28 | — | 5 | 2 | 5,178 |
| 4 | Hullukunṭe ... | 63 | 28 | 48 | — | 11 | 4 | 9,099 |
| 5 | Kákólu ... ... | 31 | 11 | 20 | 2 | 5 | 4 | 7,439 |
| 6 | Kódihalli ... | 25 | 14 | 24 | — | — | 1 | 6,851 |
| 7 | Rájaghaṭṭa ... | 25 | 10 | 21 | — | 3 | 1 | 5,492 |
| 8 | Tippúr ... ... | 39 | 5 | 32 | 1 | 3 | 3 | 6,405 |
| 9 | Túbagere ... | 44 | 22 | 31 | 3 | 9 | 1 | 7,292 |
| | Total ... | 336 | 120 | 266 | 6 | 48 | 16 | 65,613 |

The only place in the taluq with population exceeding 1,000 is Dod-Ballapur.

This taluq is bounded on the north by a hilly range through which a pass descends to the low country of Goribidnur. The N. Pinákini rises on the north-eastern frontier and immediately leaves the taluq. Near the same spot rises the Arkavati, which, flowing S.S.W., receives the drainage of the entire taluq and supplies several large tanks, particularly at Dod-Ballapur, Kakolu, and Hesarghatta. The country is open and in general free from very sensible irregularities of surface. All the west, some parts of the south, and the neighbourhood of the hills on the frontier are covered with jungle, the pasturage in which forms a source of revenue.

The soil generally is good. Besides the usual crops, some tobacco is cultivated and a small quantity of potatoes. Coffee cultivation is being introduced in the east. Weavers are numerous in Dod-Ballapur and cloths of the commoner descriptions are manufactured throughout the taluq to a considerable extent. Sericulture, which for many years was at a standstill, is again making progress. The famine of 1877-8 affected this taluq more severely than any other in the Bangalore District.

Passing over the times of the Gangas,[1] the Cholas and the Hoysalas, the country at a later period formed part of the dominions of Malla Baire Gauda, the founder of Devanhalli, who, resigning that possession

[1] Chola-Ganga, called the great king of Orissa, is said in inscriptions to have been born in the Hejjáji Twelve of the Kádanúr Seventy, which are both in this taluq (*see* Vol. I., p. 317).

to his brother, and led by auspicious omens, founded the present Dod-Ballapur. With the countenance of the Vijayanagar king, who maintained a shadow of the former state at Penugonda, he speedily subdued all the neighbouring tract of country, forming the Goribidnur and Gudibanda taluqs, and possessed himself of a territory yielding a revenue of a lakh of pagodas. His descendants continued to rule this dominion until it was subdued by the Bijapur army under Randulha Khan. The Mahrattas subsequently held it for a short time, when it was taken in 1689 by the Mughals under Khasim Khan and dismembered. After annexing the north to Chik-Ballapur, and other parts to Sira, the remainder was formed into a jágir yielding a revenue of 54,000 pagodas, and bestowed on a general named Ali Khuli Khan On his death it passed to his son, and afterwards formed a part of the province of Sira, until subdued by Haidar and incorporated with the State of Mysore.

The revenue settlement was introduced in 1881. Alternate forcing of the revenue, under the batayi system, and checking it under an erroneous system of wet rates, it was found, had exhausted as well as misdirected the resources of the taluq. But the new settlement remedied these defects. The soils are best in the south, and worst in the north and north-east. They range from light red to dark brown, the latter being generally found in the low-lying lands. The red soils have a large admixture of sand. Talpargis or surface springs are numerous.

The total land revenue for 1891-2 (15 months) was Rs. 1,57,620, and for 1892-3 it was Rs. 1,77,943. The amount realized from Government lands was thus apportioned :—

| Cultivation. | 1891-92. | | 1892-93. | |
|---|---|---|---|---|
| | Area. | Assessment. | Area. | Assessment. |
| Dry ... ... ... | 60,035 | 79,937 | 61,044 | 81,160 |
| Wet ... ... ... | 5,240 | 27,445 | 7,466 | 41,019 |
| Garden ... .. ... | 1,296 | 9,547 | 1,344 | 9,912 |
| Total ... | Ac. 66,571 | Rs. 1,16,929 | Ac. 69,854 | Rs. 1,32,091 |

The following was the average rainfall at Dod-Ballapur for 25 years (1870-1894).

| Jan. | Feb. | Mar. | April | May | June | July | Aug. | Sept. | Oct. | Nov. | Dec. | | Year. |
|---|---|---|---|---|---|---|---|---|---|---|---|---|---|
| 0·01 | 0.11 | 0·46 | 0·77 | 2·61 | 2·37 | 2·82 | 4·37 | 5·04 | 5·77 | 2·55 | 0·77 | ... | 27·65 |

The Bangalore-Guntakal Railway crosses the east of the taluq, with stations at Dod-Ballapur and Maklidrug. The Nandi-Sompur road runs through the taluq from east to west. From Dod-Ballapur roads issue north to Goribidnur, east to Devanhalli, south-east to Yelahanka, and south-west to Nelamangala.

**Dod-Ballapur.**—A town on the right bank of the Arkavati, situated in 13° 18′ N. lat. 77° 26′ E. long., 27 miles north-west of Bangalore, with which it is connected by rail and road. Head-quarters of the Dod-Ballapur taluq, and a municipality.

| Population in 1891. | Males. | Females. | Total. |
|---|---|---|---|
| Hindus (with 2 Jains) ... ... ... | 3,039 | 3,105 | 6,144 |
| Muhammadans... ... ... ... | 510 | 476 | 986 |
| Christians ... ... ... ... | 5 | 6 | 11 |
| Total ... ... ... | 3,554 | 3,587 | 7,141 |

A fair held on Thursday is attended by 3,000 people.

*Doḍḍa Baḷḷápura*, Great Ballapur, is so named to distinguish it from *Chikka-Baḷḷápura*, Little Ballapur. Similarly, in Hindustani it is called *Bara-Baḷḷapur* and in Telugu *Pedda-Ballápuram*. It is said to derive its name from the circumstance that a cow used to drop a *baḷḷa* of her milk daily over a certain ant-hill, an omen which led to the foundation of the town.

It was an important place of trade in the twelfth century under the Hoysala kings. But Malla Baire Gauda of Avati, the founder of Devanhalli, was also the founder of the present Doḍ-Baḷḷápur. He was revolving in his mind the import of the omens he had witnessed in hunting, when the god Adi Narayana was revealed in a dream as the dweller in the ant-hill above mentioned. A temple and fort were shortly erected, the jungle cleared and cultivation encouraged. Obtaining authority from the king at Penugonda to punish the neighbouring refractory pallegars, Malla Baire Gauda speedily possessed himself of territory yielding a revenue of a lakh of pagodas. In the government of this he established his brother Havali Baire Gauda, who died after a prosperous reign of 20 years and was succeeded by his son Dodda Havali Baire Gauda. He ruled 25 years and was followed by his son Havali Baire Gauda, who ruled for 40 years. On his death Chikkappa Gauda, the heir, being a minor, the government was for a time conferred on Tammanna Gauda, the nephew and Dalavayi of the late chief. He discharged the trust reposed in him with zeal and fidelity for ten years, when he died, and Chikkappa Gauda, now come to years of maturity, succeeded. Three years after his accession Doḍ-Ballapur was besieged and taken by the Bijapur army under Randulha Khan. After 40 years of possession by that power it was surrendered to the Mahrattas, by whom the fort was enlarged and various temples erected. In ten years it was invested by the Mughals under Khasim Khan, and yielded in 1689 after an obstinate defence of two months.[1] Dod-Ballapur and a part of the surrounding country were then formed into a jágir yielding a revenue of 54,059 pagodas, and bestowed on a favourite general named Ali Khuli Khan. He enjoyed it only for a short time and died. It was next bestowed on his son Durga Khuli Khan, then Subadar of Sira, which however he shortly after relinquished and retired to Dod-Ballapur, but only enjoyed it for one year. It remained attached to the government of Sira for 49 years, when it was seized by the Nizam, and bestowed as a jágir on Abbas Khuli Khan. In 1761 it was captured by Haidar Ali and has ever since been subject to Mysore.

The fort, of which only the name remains, is said to have been erected with stones from the ruins of Rajaghatta. There are remains of several fine buildings and tanks in the fort, the principal, now almost destroyed, being the Ashur Khana erected by Abbas Khuli Khan, and a fine well with three flights of stairs leading down to it and a very stout stone grating over the water. At the west of the town is the *darga* or tomb of a saint named Mohiuddin Chishti, said to have died nearly 200 years ago. It is built of materials taken from Hindu temples. The town extends lengthwise north and south for above two miles. Cotton cloths in great variety are made here.

| Municipal Funds. | 1892–3. | 1893–4. | 1894–5. | 1895–6. |
|---|---|---|---|---|
| Income (opening balance Rs. 3,302) | 1,722 | 1,993 | 4,052 | 4,265 |
| Expenditure ... ... ... | 3,095 | 2,950 | 4,056 | 5,605 |

**Domlur.**—A suburb of Bangalore, on the east, included in the Civil and Military Station. Population 792. On an old temple are some Grantha and Tamil inscriptions of the time of the Hoysala king Víra-Rámanátha, the thirteenth century. The name of the village was Dombalur or Tombalur, perhaps Tumbalur, which may be a clue to the title of one of the earliest Kannada authors (*see* Vol. I., p. 496). It also had the Brahman name of Des'imánikka-paṭṭana.

[1] This capture is recorded on a stone in the fort, which bears a Hoysala inscription of 1267 A.D. The idolatrous symbols at the top have been removed and the Persian inscription has been engraved in their place.

**Dommasandra.**—A village in the north-east of Anekal taluq, 3 miles west of Sarjapur, and a municipality.

| Population in 1891. | Males. | Females. | Total. |
|---|---|---|---|
| Hindus ... ... ... ... | 916 | 918 | 1,834 |
| Muhammadans ... ... ... | 232 | 213 | 445 |
| Christians ... ... ... | 2 | 3 | 5 |
| Total ... ... ... | 1,150 | 1,134 | 2,284 |

There is a considerable weaver population, and the Dommasandra cloths are in good repute.

| Municipal Funds. | 1892-3. | 1893-4. | 1894-5. | 1895-6. |
|---|---|---|---|---|
| Income (opening balance Rs. 865)... | 451 | 329 | 686 | 745 |
| Expenditure ... ... ... | 685 | 682 | 1,275 | 1,267 |

**Duckworth.**—One of the Eurasian and Anglo-Indian settlements (*see* Whitefield) in the east of the Bangalore taluq. It is 10 miles east of Bangalore, and 2 miles south of Sausmond. It was the outcome of proposals by Dr. Duckworth, after whom it is named, for assisting military pensioners and people of small means to settle on the land and acquire homes for themselves. His scheme provided for an allotment of 150 acres to a batch of ten families (preference being given to Government pensioners) at the rate per family of 10 acres of arable land for cultivation, and 5 acres for pasturage and fuel planting. Grain seed, implements and cattle, to be supplied gratis at starting, and for a period of 12 months a supplementary allowance of Rs. 10 a month to be made to each family, to be spent in improving the land. Some of the first settlers seem to have turned out badly, but in 1886 there were 7 resident, and 4 non-resident settlers. Their holdings were from 10 to 12 acres of land each, with a cottage built by the Association at the cost of about Rs. 120.

**Gangavara.**—A village in Devanhalli taluq, on the right bank of the S. Pinákini, near the head of the Hoskote tank. Population 405. The inscriptions and remains show that it was a place of some importance in the eighth century under the Gangas, and subsequently under the Cholas. The Somes'vara temple has some picturesque fluted pillars with a seated lion for the pedestal.

**Gavipur.**—A suburb of Bangalore City, about a mile south-west of the Fort. Population 733.

Its chief feature is the cave temple of Gavi Gangádharesvara, the Sivite emblems attached to which, carved on a gigantic scale out of solid stone, are curious specimens of the mason's art. They consist of the *trisúla* or trident, the *chhatri* or umbrella, and the *ḍamaruga* or double drum, each being 15 feet or more in height and proportionately wide. They were executed in the time of Kempe Gauda.

**Halasur.**[1]—One of the suburbs of the Civil and Military Station of Bangalore, situated north-east of the Cantonment, close to the large tank of the same name. It appears to have been founded by Kempe Gauda, under the following circumstances. The surrounding country was then covered with forest, into which he had wandered from Yelahanka in pursuit of game, and being much fatigued, laid himself down under the shade of a tree. In his sleep the god Somes'vara, formerly worshipped on that spot by Mandava rishi, and which lay buried in the sand, appeared in a dream, and revealing to him the existence of a hidden treasure, bid him therewith erect a temple, promising at the same time the divine favour. He accordingly secured the treasure and built the Somes'vara pagoda, employing, it is said, a sculptor from Belur, a descendant of the famous Jakanáchári, to ornament the walls with scenes from the marriage of Siva and Parvati. The *gopura* is an imposing structure in the Dravidian style. The village of Halasur was also built, containing residences for the attendant Brahmans, and made the kasba of 33 villages, from each of which one *koḷaga* for each *kanḍaga* of grain was appointed to be given as an endowment for the maintenance of the religious services. There is another temple on a large scale, dedicated to Subba Raya, but unfinished. The village is a prosperous one and contains several wealthy residents of Tamil origin.

**Hindiginal.**—A trading village in the north-east angle of the Hoskote taluq, near where the Kolar-Vadigenhalli road crosses the Bangalore-Kadapa road. Population 1,020.

**Honganur.**—A village about 5 miles south of Channapatna, head-quarters of the hobli of the same name. Population 1,705. In the time of the Ganga kings it was the chief town of Chikka Gangaváḍi, a district which occupied most of the valley of the Shimsha.

**Hoskote.**—A taluq in the east. Area 271 square miles. Head-quarters at Hoskote. Contains the following hoblis, villages and population :—

[1] The form Alsur (Ulsoor) is due to the Tamil pronunciation, there being no aspirate in that language.

| No. | Hoblis. | Villages. | Hamlets. | Villages classified. | | | | Population. |
|---|---|---|---|---|---|---|---|---|
| | | | | Government. | Sarvamánya. | Jodi. | Kayamgutta. | |
| 1 | Gubbi ... ... | 46 | 2 | 29 | — | 16 | 1 | 6,091 |
| 2 | Hoskóṭe ... ... | 29 | 6 | 23 | 1 | 4 | 1 | 9,694 |
| 3 | Hullúr ... ... | 52 | 1 | 39 | — | 12 | 1 | 6,636 |
| 4 | Káḍgoḍi ... .. | 29 | 2 | 19 | — | 10 | — | 5,850 |
| 5 | Mugalúr ... ... | 44 | 2 | 27 | 1 | 14 | 2 | 8,351 |
| 6 | Nandaguḍi ... | 54 | 11 | 35 | — | 11 | 8 | 8,908 |
| 7 | Súlibele ... ... | 64 | 2 | 49 | — | 11 | 4 | 7,971 |
| 8 | Vágaṭa ... ... | 50 | 2 | 38 | 1 | 10 | 1 | 7,166 |
| | Total ... | 368 | 28 | 269 | 3 | 68 | 19 | 60,667 |

*Principal places, with Population.*—Hoskote, 4,917; Sulibele, 1,927; Hindiginál, 1,020.

At the time of the British conquest Hoskote included Jangamkote, Malur, Masti, and Sarjapur. The hobli of Mugalur was added to it in 1873 from Sarjapur taluq.

Towards the north the S. Pinákini forms the western boundary. After entering the taluq it supplies the large tank at Hoskote, and thence flows southwards past Kadgodi, where it receives a stream from the Bangalore taluq on the west. With the exception of some low hills on the north, the country is open and easily crossed in all parts. The tracts best cultivated are those bordering on the S. Pinákini and the neighbourhood of Nandagudi eastwards. From Nandagudi southwards and along the Bangalore road the soil is stony and unfertile. Some cultivation is carried on of potatoes, and formerly the poppy was also grown, in addition to the usual wet and dry crops. Considerable attention is given to the cultivation of hay for the Bangalore market, especially in the neighbourhood of Hoskote.

At Nandagudi are traces of former buildings, of which it is related that they mark the site of Patalipur, the capital of Uttunga Bhuja Raya, whose nine nephews, the Nava Nanda, being imprisoned by him, were released by the schemes of Chanikya. The story is taken from the Mudra Rakshasa, a play on the successful usurpation of Chandra Gupta and the establishment of the Nanda kings. In a similar manner Dharmesvara, in the same neighbourhood, is connected with Dharma Raya and the Pandus. They are stated to have been rendered insensible by the poisonous exhalation of a well made by Duryodhana for their destruction. This incident is said to be sculptured on a pillar at the temple over the spot. Two masons, engaged in the repairs of this temple 60 years ago, are related to have fallen down senseless from the exhalation on shifting the stones covering the well.

The country at times belonged to the Gangas, and to the Pallavas or Nolambas. The Cholas followed, but subsequently it formed part of the Hoysala dominions, and on their partition, went with the Tamil territory to Rámanátha. Eventually, under Vijayanagar, it became a possession of the Sugatur family, one of whom erected Hoskote, or the new fort, as distinguished from Kolar, and settled traders in the place. Afterwards it became a part of the territory administered by Shahji, the representative of the Bijapur princes, and changing hands several times, was finally ceded to Haidar in 1761, and united to the kingdom of Mysore.

The revenue settlement was introduced in 1886. The total land revenue in 1891–2 (15 months), was Rs. 1,58,592, and for 1892–3 it was Rs. 1,67,983. The amount realized from Government lands was thus apportioned :—

| Cultivation. | 1891–2. | | 1892–3. | |
|---|---|---|---|---|
| | Area. | Assessment. | Area. | Assessment. |
| Dry ... ... ... | 38,062 | 68,303 | 38,496 | 69,140 |
| Wet ... ... ... | 3,921 | 24,930 | 5,301 | 33,884 |
| Garden ... ... .. | 2,421 | 13,573 | 2,558 | 13,827 |
| Total ... ... | Ac. 44,404 | Rs. 1,06,806 | Ac. 46,355 | Rs. 1,16,851 |

The average rainfall at Hoskote for 25 years (1870–1894) and at Kádgodi for 2 years (1893–4) was as follows :—

| | Jan. | Feb. | Mar. | Apl. | May | June | July | Aug. | Sept. | Oct. | Nov. | Dec. | | Year. |
|---|---|---|---|---|---|---|---|---|---|---|---|---|---|---|
| Hoskote | — | 0·21 | 0·39 | 0·59 | 3·44 | 1·88 | 2·66 | 3·61 | 4·05 | 4·81 | 2·60 | 0·53 | ... | 24·77 |
| Kádgodi | — | 0·90 | 2·12 | 1·62 | 3·66 | 2·71 | 4·14 | 3·46 | 4·28 | 7·26 | 2·26 | — | ... | 32·41 |

The Bangalore branch of the Madras Railway crosses the south of the taluq, with stations at Whitefield and Devankundi. The Bangalore-Kolar road runs through the taluq from west to east, and gives off at Hoskote roads to Kadapa, to Jangamkote and to Sulibele northwards, to Malur eastwards, and to Kádgodi southwards.

**Hoskote.**—A town on the left bank of the S. Pinákini, situated in 13° 4′ N. lat., 77° 48′ E. long, 16 miles E.N.E. of Bangalore, on the Bangalore-Kolar road, and 6 miles north-east of the Whitefield Railway station. Head-quarters of the Hoskote taluq, and a municipality.

| Population in 1891. | Males. | Females. | Total. |
|---|---|---|---|
| Hindus .. ... ... ... ... ... | 2,060 | 2,108 | 4,168 |
| Muhammadans ... ... ... ... ... | 363 | 341 | 704 |
| Christians ... ... ... ... ... ... | 11 | 7 | 18 |
| Total ... ... | 2,434 | 2,456 | 4,890 |

At the Amritesvara *rathotsava*, held for ten days from Vaishakha suddha 11, there is an assemblage of 4,000 people. On full moon day in the same month, Dharma Rayan *karaga* is attended by 5,000 people.

*Hosa-kôṭe*, new fort, so called to distinguish it from Kolar, was built about 1595 by Timme Gauda, the chief of Sugatur, who had recently settled at Kolar and obtained from the Penugonda sovereign the title of Chikka Ráyal. The superiority of the soil to that of Kolar induced him to fix on the new site, as well as the facility with which the waters of the S. Pinákini might there be dammed for purposes of irrigation. The large Hoskote tank, with an embankment two miles long, which forms when full a sheet of water not less than ten miles round, bears testimony to the sagacity of his choice. Raising an armed force, he subdued Anekal, Mulbagal and Punganur, and added them to his possessions. He ruled till 1632. Shortly after, the territory was conquered by the Bijapur army, and subsequently conferred as a jágir on Shahji, the governor of Karnatak Bijapur, who resided at Bangalore. On the capture of these districts by the Mughal troops under Khasim Khan in 1663, they became part of the province of Sira. In 1756 Hoskote was taken by the Mysore army, but was subdued the following year by the Mahrattas. It changed hands several times, until finally ceded to Haidar Ali and annexed to Mysore in 1761.

| Municipal Funds. | 1892–3. | 1893–4. | 1894–5. | 1895–6. |
|---|---|---|---|---|
| Income (opening balance, Rs. 782) ... | 1,166 | 1,231 | 2,227 | 2,228 |
| Expenditure ... ... ... ... | 1,865 | 1,258 | 2,117 | 2,713 |

**Hulikal.**—A village in the north of Magadi taluq, head-quarters of the hobli of the same name. Population 673.

It is said to have been founded in 1310 by the Hoysala king, under the following circumstances :—A sannyasi named Guriachinta, who had gained his favour, lived at the foot of the adjacent hill called Ramalinga

Betta. On a certain day one of the holy man's bullocks, attacked by a tiger, not only threw off its assailant but killed it. This being reported to the king, he considered it a happy omen and ordered the hill to be fortified, naming it, in memory of the incident, *huli-kallu*, tiger-rock, or, according to the tradition of the place, *huli-kollu*, tiger-kill. It subsequently came into the possession of Baiche Gauda of Koratigere, whose descendants held it as tributaries of the Mysore kings. The chief was expelled by Tipu Sultan and the place annexed to Mysore.

**Huskur.**—A village in Bidarguppe hobli, Anekal taluq. Population 778.

A fair takes place on Friday, attended by 300 people. A festival (*parishe*) is held for five days from Phalguna bahula 3rd, in honour of Madhuramma, at which 3,000 persons assemble and as many as 10,000 bullocks are brought for sale.

Colonel Boddam gave the following account of a visit to the cattle fair in 1871 :—"There are peculiarities about this fair; it is essentially one for low castes, both human and bovine. There is a superstition that cholera and cattle plague are averted by worship at the Huskur temple (a very insignificant one) at this time; consequently all the idol cars of the surrounding villages are dragged to the temple, each with about forty bullocks and their owners and a rabble; usually there are not less than 25 of these cars, run up like high Chinese pagodas on a framework of bamboo and covered with gaudy paintings of Hindu deities. The religious ceremonies last five days, and then the cattle fair is held, after which the cars are taken back; on an average about 10,000 bullocks are collected, but the greater portion of them are inferior cattle. Looking over the lot, I found all the good caste animals were born outside the Province, principally at Mahadeseo. I only came upon one good animal bred in this District; the mother was said to be of fine breed. As a rule the people do not keep fine cows; they are content with the small cows of the country for giving milk, and do not attend to breeding. This year, owing to many people being still engaged in threshing their grain, which had been delayed by the recent unusual rains, there were less idol cars brought (15 only), and fewer bullocks—not 8,000 in all."

**Kankanhalli.**—A taluq in the south. Area 588 square miles. Head-quarters at Kankanhalli. Contains the following hoblis, villages, and population :—

| No. | Hoblis. | Villages. | Hamlets. | Villages classified. | | | | Population. |
|---|---|---|---|---|---|---|---|---|
| | | | | Govern-ment. | Sarva-mánya. | Jodi. | Kayam-gutta. | |
| 1 | Hárohalli ... ... | 25 | 44 | 25 | — | — | — | 7,589 |
| 2 | Kánkánhalli ... | 35 | 54 | 30 | 1 | — | 4 | 12,169 |
| 3 | Kodihalli ... ... | 49 | 46 | 46 | 1 | 1 | 1 | 9,950 |
| 4 | Maralavádi ... | 30 | 30 | 30 | — | — | — | 5,877 |
| 5 | Mudvádi ... ... | 19 | 38 | 18 | — | — | 1 | 6,166 |
| 6 | Sátanúr ... ... | 37 | 35 | 37 | — | — | — | 8,309 |
| 7 | Somanhalli ... | 20 | 30 | 15 | 1 | — | 4 | 6,203 |
| 8 | Tungani ... ... | 29 | 37 | 27 | — | 1 | 1 | 7,631 |
| 9 | Uyamballi ... | 28 | 56 | 27 | 1 | — | — | 7,974 |
| | Total ... | 272 | 370 | 255 | 4 | 2 | 11 | 71,868 |

*Principal places, with Population.*—Kánkánhalli, 4,986; Hárohalli, 2,632; Kaggalipura, 1,175; A'lahalli, 1,113; Kodihalli, 1,098; Dodda Maralavádi, 1,089; Hanumantapura, 1,028.

The taluq is bounded on the south by the Kaveri, and traversed from north to south by its tributary the Arkavati. The southern half of the taluq is a succession of hills and forests, affording extensive grazing grounds, in proximity to the river Kaveri. The principal heights near Kankanhalli are: on the west, Banati Mari Betta, 3,422 feet above the level of the sea, Narsimha Deva Betta, and Mudvadi Betta; on the east, Bilikal Betta and Koppa Betta, the latter 2,822 feet in elevation.

The Arkavati is joined on the west near Mudvadi by the Vrishabhavati from Bangalore, which itself receives a little higher up the Suvarnamukhi from Anekal taluq. Another considerable stream from the same quarter unites with the Arkavati at Kankanhalli, as well as two further south, one on the west and one on the east. Ragi, avare, and the castor-oil plant form the principal cultivation of the open parts. Tamarinds and cocoanuts are also important products, as well as mulberry. But the soils are for the most part inferior, and generally very shallow and rocky.

The taluq was included in the territory granted to Jagadeva Rayal, and by him the fort of Kankanhalli seems to have been erected. It was captured along with Channapatna by the Mysore Raja in 1630.

The revenue settlement was sanctioned in 1896. The area of the taluq is thus distributed:—

| | |
|---|---|
| Culturable (dry, 94,316; wet, 1,671; garden, 2,651) . . . . | 98,638 |
| Unculturable (including village sites, &c.) . . . . . . | 175,264 |
| Inam villages . . . . . . . . . . . . | 13,825 |
| Forests (84,391) and kavals (6,003) . . . . . . . | 90,394 |
| Total area acres . | 378,121 |

Of the culturable area 4,263 acres are waste.

The total revenue for 1891-2 (15 months) was Rs. 1,04,879, and for 1892-3 it was Rs. 1,00,183. The revenue realized from Government lands was thus apportioned :—

| Cultivation. | 1891-2. | | 1892-3. | |
|---|---|---|---|---|
| | Area. | Assessment. | Area. | Assessment. |
| Dry ... ... ... | 56,900 | 55,990 | 58,079 | 57,014 |
| Wet ... ... ... | 988 | 6,270 | 1,025 | 6,460 |
| Garden ... ... ... | 2,637 | 8,032 | 2,656 | 7,978 |
| Total ... | Ac. 60,525 | Rs. 70,292 | Ac. 61,760 | Rs. 71,452 |

The following was the average rainfall at Kankanhalli for 25 years (1870-94):—

| Jan. | Feb. | Mar. | April | May | June | July | Aug. | Sept. | Oct. | Nov. | Dec. | | Year. |
|---|---|---|---|---|---|---|---|---|---|---|---|---|---|
| 0·04 | 0·16 | 0·32 | 1·25 | 3·81 | 2·49 | 2·42 | 4·25 | 4·57 | 5·58 | 1·78 | 0·39 | ... | 27·06 |

There is a road from Kankanhalli to the railway at Closepet. Also a road from Bangalore to Kankanhalli, continuing west to Mysore. There is a cross road from Satanur to Channapatna, and one from Kankanhalli to Kodihalli.

**Kankanhalli.**—A town on the right bank of the Arkavati, situated in 12° 33′ N. lat. 77° 29′ E. long., 36 miles south of Bangalore, on the Bangalore-Malvalli road, and 17 miles from the railway at Closepet. Head-quarters of the Kankanhalli taluq, and a municipality.

| Population in 1891. | Males. | Females. | Total. |
|---|---|---|---|
| Hindus ... ... ... ... ... | 1,558 | 1,557 | 3,115 |
| Muhammadans... ... ... ... | 190 | 179 | 369 |
| Total... ... ... | 1,748 | 1,736 | 3,484 |

A fair held on Thursday is attended by 2,000 people.

The existing fort of Kankanhalli appears to have been erected by Jagadeva Rayal, the chief of Channapatna, who in order to do so is said to have displaced a smaller structure owned by one Kánakána, whence the name (but see below). It was captured by Chama Raja of Mysore in 1630.

The principal feature in the fort is the ancient temple of Ranganatha, much out of repair. The town was twice burned or laid waste by Tipu Sultan to prevent its being of use to the British army on their march to Seringapatam. The beasts of prey increased so much in consequence that during the last two years of his reign eighty persons were carried away by tigers from within the walls of the fort. Except on the north it is surrounded at a short distance by lofty mountains and thick jungle. On the banks of the Arkavati are many cocoanut gardens.

The alliteration of the name excites attention and arouses curiosity as to its derivation. Buchanan has the following remarks on the subject:—"I went three cosses to Kankaranhalli, commonly called Kankanhalli. The former name is universally said by the natives to be the proper one; but the derivation which they give of it seems very forced. *Kanikarna*, they say, is the genitive case of *kanikar*, which in the Tamil language signifies a proprietor of land: and *halli*, in the language of Karnata, is a village." In a note he adds: "The name of this village is properly *Kanya-karna*, composed of two Sanskrit words, *kanya*, virgin, or the goddess Bhavani, and *karna*, ear." This cannot be said to throw much light on the question.

An inscription of the 13th century gives the name as Káṇikáṛahaḷḷi, which accords with the first explanation.

| Municipal Funds. | 1892-3. | 1893-4. | 1894-5. | 1895-6. |
|---|---|---|---|---|
| Income (opening balance Rs. 595)... | 1,233 | 1,128 | 1,888 | 1,882 |
| Expenditure... ... ... ... | 1,868 | 1,077 | 1,660 | 2,264 |

**Kengeri.**—A town in the Bangalore taluq, 9 miles south-west of Bangalore, on the Bangalore-Mysore railway. It is a municipality, and till 1873 was the head-quarters of a taluq of the same name.

| Population in 1891. | Males. | Females. | Total. |
|---|---|---|---|
| Hindus ... ... ... ... ... | 733 | 702 | 1,435 |
| Muhammadans ... ... ... | 91 | 94 | 185 |
| Christians ... ... ... ... | 2 | — | 2 |
| Total ... ... ... | 826 | 796 | 1,622 |

Kengeri or *Ten-géri*, southern street or road, appears formerly to have been of greater extent than it is now, but was destroyed by Tipu to prevent its giving shelter to the army of Lord Cornwallis. The town was for a short time the seat of the raw silk trade. In 1866 Signor de Vecchj, an Italian gentleman, noticing the then depressed condition of the industry, made exertions, with the assistance of the Government, for its revival. He attributed the mortality of the silk-worms to degeneracy owing to continued propagation from the same stock, to feeding on inferior species of leaf, and to want of care in rearing. The raw silk produced was also deteriorated in value from negligent methods of reeling. In order to remedy these defects, cartoons of silk-worm eggs were imported from Japan and freely distributed, superior kinds of mulberry-trees (*Moris sinensis*, *M. perotetra*, *M. alba*, and *M. nigra*) were grown from cuttings and seed, and finally a steam factory for Silk Filature was established at Kengeri, with eighty basins. The hands employed in this delicate process were female orphans from the Bangalore Convent, under the charge of native nuns. These measures produced their natural effect, and a great impetus was given for a time to sericulture. Not only were cocoons bought to any extent for filature, but the refuse silk (*chussum*), not taken into consideration before, became an important article in the market. But the severe drought of 1866 proved disastrous to the imported worms. Fresh were obtained in two successive seasons. After all, however, the eradication of disease among the worms was not effected, and the business was at length given up.

| Municipal Funds. | 1892-3. | 1893-4. | 1894-5. | 1895-6. |
|---|---|---|---|---|
| Income (opening balance Rs. 1,449) | 441 | 444 | 895 | 985 |
| Expenditure ... ... ... ... | 1,035 | 932 | 1,521 | 1,123 |

**Kudalur.**—A village on the left bank of the Kanva, about 4 miles south-east of Channapatna. Population 1,508. In the time of the Cholas it was an agrahara called Rajaraja-chaturvedimangala. Haidar Ali gave it as an inám to a fakir.

**Kundana.**—A village about 7 miles west of Devanhalli. Population 386. Seems to have been the Kundaṇi which was the royal residence of the Hoysala king Rámanátha in the 13th century.

**Magadi.**—A taluq in the west. Area 367 square miles. Head-quarters at Magadi. Contains the following hoblis, villages, and population; Bidadi and Tavarekere having been added in 1873:—

| No. | Hoblis. | Villages. | Hamlets. | Villages classified. | | | | Population. |
|---|---|---|---|---|---|---|---|---|
| | | | | Govern-ment. | Sarva-mánya. | Jodi. | Kayam-gutta. | |
| 1 | Gudemáranhaḷḷi ... | 30 | 24 | 16 | — | 14 | — | 5,572 |
| 2 | Hulikal ... ... | 20 | 25 | 20 | — | — | — | 3,902 |
| 3 | Kudúr ... ... | 20 | 36 | 18 | 1 | — | 1 | 6,199 |
| 4 | Mádabálu ... ... | 40 | 29 | 31 | — | 5 | 4 | 4,740 |
| 5 | Mágadi ... ... | 42 | 60 | 30 | — | 8 | 4 | 10,320 |
| 6 | Nárasandra ... | 19 | 24 | 18 | — | — | 1 | 3,539 |
| 7 | Sátanúr ... ... | 38 | 37 | 25 | — | 9 | 4 | 7,513 |
| 8 | Sólúr ... ... | 43 | 27 | 34 | 1 | 8 | 2 | 6,997 |
| 9 | Távarekere ... | 49 | 51 | 33 | — | 4 | 12 | 8,353 |
| 10 | Tippasandra ... | 37 | 41 | 29 | — | 8 | — | 7,199 |
| | Total ... | 338 | 354 | 252 | 2 | 56 | 28 | 64,334 |

*Principal places, with population.*—Magadi, 4,915; Gudemaranhalli, 1,419; Tavarekere, 1,323; Kudur, 1,263; Motagondahalli, 1,137; Solur, 1,120.

A hilly and jungly taluq, through the south-east portion of which the Arkavati runs, forming in some parts the boundary. Its bed being deep and generally surrounded by hills, the country adjoining derives little benefit from it as to cultivation. The streams of the north-east flow into the Arkavati; those of the centre and west flow south, forming the Kanva; those of the north-west flow south-west into Kunigal. The loftiest mountain is Sávandroog, 4,024 feet above the sea. It is surrounded by deep defiles, covered with rocks and jungle, among which is situated the Sávandroog state forest, 17 square miles in extent. Bairandurga is a conspicuous hill, formerly fortified. Much bamboo and various kinds of timber are met with in the southern parts of the taluq. There are several productive tanks, the one at Tippasanḍra being very extensive.

The soil generally is a shallow red mould mixed with stones, not very fertile unless when the rains set in plentifully and at the right seasons. The crops consist chiefly of those raised without irrigation, ragi, gram, avare, togari, &c. Tobacco is grown to some extent.

The Cholas appear to have held the district in the 12th century, followed by the Hoysalas. From them it is said to have been wrested by Pratapa Rudra of Orangal, and soon after to have been conquered by Harihara, king of Vijayanagar. The deputy of the Vijayanagar sovereigns, Sámanta Ráya by name, taking advantage of the feebleness of the government, declared his independence, and the country was held by his descendants to the third generation, when Kempe Gauḍa, the chief of Bangalore, obtained possession. In his family it remained till 1728, when it was captured by the Raja of Mysore.

The revenue settlement was introduced in 1879. The total revenue for 1891-2 (15 months) was Rs. 1,50,164, and for 1892-3 it was Rs. 1,52,650. The revenue realized from Government lands was thus apportioned:—

| Cultivation. | 1891-2. | | 1892-3. | |
|---|---|---|---|---|
| | Area. | Assessment. | Area. | Assessment. |
| Dry ... ... ... | 65,528 | 71,256 | 68,392 | 73,909 |
| Wet ... ... ... | 5,419 | 21,479 | 5,766 | 22,886 |
| Garden ... ... ... | 2,321 | 10,675 | 2,342 | 10,776 |
| Total ... | Ac. 73,268 | Rs. 1,03,410 | Ac. 76,500 | Rs. 1,07,571 |

The following was the average rainfall at Magadi for 25 years (1870–94) and at the other stations for two years (1893–4):—

| | Jan. | Feb. | Mar. | April | May | June | July | Aug. | Sept. | Oct. | Nov. | Dec. | Year |
|---|---|---|---|---|---|---|---|---|---|---|---|---|---|
| Magadi ... | 0·04 | 0·03 | 0·52 | 1·18 | 4·34 | 2·84 | 3·04 | 4·44 | 4·64 | 6·36 | 2·03 | 0·38 | ... 29·84 |
| Solur ... ... | — | 0·60 | 0·80 | 0·80 | 5·50 | 2·60 | 3·25 | 2·70 | 2·86 | 4·50 | 1·25 | — | ... 24·86 |
| Tavarekere | 0·01 | 0·49 | 0·88 | 2·58 | 3·68 | 3·93 | 3·73 | 4·35 | 3·85 | 10·12 | 0·08 | — | ... 33·70 |

The road from Bangalore to Kunigal runs through Magadi, whence there are roads to Huliyurdurga, to Closepet, and to Solur. The high road from Nelamangala to Kunigal passes through the north of the taluq.

**Magadi.**—A town situated in 12°57′ N. lat., 77°17′ E. long., 29 miles west of Bangalore, with which it is connected by road. Head-quarters of the Magadi taluq, and a municipality.

| Population in 1891. | Males. | Females. | Total. |
|---|---|---|---|
| Hindus (with 11 Jains) ... ... ... ... | 2,123 | 2,232 | 4,355 |
| Muhammadans ... ... ... ... ... | 262 | 235 | 497 |
| Total ... ... | 2,385 | 2,467 | 4,852 |

There is a tradition that Magadi was founded in 1139 by a Chola king, who, in the course of an expedition to that part, heard that in early times it had been the residence of some holy rishis. It soon passed into the hands of the Hoysala kings, and after them into those of the Vijayanagar line. In the time of Achyuta Ráya of that house, Sámanta Ráya was appointed Adhikári, or manager of the district. He enlarged the town and fortified the height of Sávandurga, in return for which that part of the country was granted him as an *amara* or jágir. He enjoyed it for 28 years, from 1543 to 1571, and was succeeded by his son Sampaja Ráya. He governed for 17 years and repaired the temple of Rangaswami at Tirumale. His son Chikka Ráya or Múlaka Ráya, after ruling 16 years, threw himself in a fit of madness into the pool on the droog and was drowned. He left no children, and Gangappa Náyak, the *talári* or watchman of Balakara, taking advantage of the confusion, seized the government and strove to enrich himself by plunder. But Immaḍi Kempe Gauḍa of Bangalore marched against him, took the place and put him to death. Kempe Gauḍa being shortly after ousted from Bangalore, retired to Magadi, which is thenceforward identified with that family, whose history is given elsewhere. Magadi was captured by the Mysore army in 1728 and the chief carried prisoner to Seringapatam, where he died, the last of his line.

The fort is now deserted. The Péṭe is built on a slope to the north. Beyond the eastern end is the village of Tirumale, and some distance from the western end a large temple of Somesvara in ruins.

| Municipal Funds. | 1892-3. | 1893-4. | 1894-5. | 1895-6. |
|---|---|---|---|---|
| Income (opening balance, Rs. 675) ... | 1,637 | 1,677 | 2,949 | 3,071 |
| Expenditure ... ... ... ... | 3,095 | 2,131 | 3,918 | 3,723 |

**Malur.**[1]—A village on the banks of the Kanva. Head-quarters of the Malur hobli, Channapatna taluq. Population 2,161.

Most of the residents are Brahmans of the Srivaishnava sect: they give the village the name of Rájendrasimha-nagara. There are several ruined temples in the place, and a number of Chola inscriptions; but the large temple of Aprameyaswami is maintained in good order. The sage named Vijnánes'vara yogi here composed his celebrated *bhdshya* or commentary on the code called the Yajnavalkya Smriti.

**Malurpatna.**[1]—A village on the right bank of the Kanva, about 3 miles south of Malur in Channapatna taluq. Population 1,078.

It contains a number of ruined temples and inscriptions of the Ganga and Chola periods. It was originally called Manalúr, but the Cholas gave it the name of Nikarili Cholapura. In 1764 Haidar Ali granted Malurpatna as an inam to a fakir.

**Mankunda.**—A village in the west of Channapatna taluq, about 2 miles north of Mudigere. Population 658.

In the 7th century the Ganga kings Bhúvikrama and S'ivamára appear to have made this the royal residence, removing from Talakád. The place was probably destroyed in the Chola invasion.

**Manne.**—A village in the north of Nelamangala taluq, about 5 miles north of Tyamagondlu. Population 702.

Under the name of Mányapura it was a royal residence of the Ganga kings in the 8th century, in the time of S'ripurusha. It was captured and destroyed by the Cholas at the beginning of the 11th century, and as Mannai-kattakam, is referred to in their inscriptions as one of their principal conquests. Several ruined temples attest its magnificence, and its extent is shown by the tradition that the city included Chik Hejjaji and Belavangala, 8 miles or more to the east.

**Nelamangala.**—A taluq in the west. Area 275 square miles. Head-quarters at Nelamangala. Contains the following hoblis, villages and population :—

[1] The *a*, it should be observed, is short, which causes the name to sound like *Molur*.

| No. | Hoblis. | Villages. | Hamlets. | Villages classified. | | | | Population. |
|---|---|---|---|---|---|---|---|---|
| | | | | Govern-ment. | Sarva-mányа. | Jodi. | Kayam-gutta. | |
| 1 | Begur ... ... | 46 | 13 | 36 | 1 | 8 | 1 | 6,685 |
| 2 | Doddabele ... | 57 | 18 | 51 | — | 3 | 3 | 11,634 |
| 3 | Mailanahalli ... | 47 | 15 | 32 | — | 7 | 8 | 9,365 |
| 4 | Nelamangala ... | 72 | 30 | 44 | 4 | 11 | 13 | 13,294 |
| 5 | Nijagallu ... | 75 | 56 | 63 | 5 | 5 | 2 | 13,194 |
| 6 | Sondekoppa ... | 47 | 31 | 33 | — | 7 | 7 | 8,947 |
| | Total ... | 344 | 163 | 259 | 10 | 41 | 34 | 63,119 |

*Principal places, with population.*—Nelamangala, 4,171; Tyamagondal, 3,748; Sondekoppa, 1,624; Hesarghaṭṭa, 1,051.

This taluq was formed out of the old parganas of Nelamangala, Doḍḍabele and Nijagallu. It is drained on the east and south by the Arkavati, and on the west by the Kumadvati, an affluent of the former, both flowing southwards in deep and rocky channels. The Garudáchala rises in the north-west and takes a northerly course into the Tumkur District. A chain of mountains runs through, and in some places bounds the taluq on the west, the chief heights being Sivaganga (4,559 feet above the sea) and Nijagal. The country on this side is hilly, broken and jungly. The other parts are open and contain some large valleys in which excellent tanks have been formed, one at Tyamagondal, fed by the Kumadvati, being the largest.

The soil is generally a red mould, shallow and gravelly, dependent for its cultivation on abundant and seasonable rains. The dry crops are chiefly ragi, ballar, savé and gram: the wet crops paddy, sugar-cane and some wheat. Iron ore is obtained in some parts.

In the 8th century Manne was a place of great importance, under the Gangas, and in the 11th century Mannai-náttu was still the chief district, under the Cholas. The Hoysalas soon after succeeded, and in the temporary partition of their territories in the 13th century this part of the country fell to the share of Ramanatha, who had the Tamil districts. After sharing in the fortunes of Dod-Ballapur and Bangalore, Nelamangala was apparently acquired by the Mysore Rajas at the same time as the latter place.

The revenue settlement was introduced in 1878. The total revenue realized in 1891–2 (15 months) was Rs. 1,61,666, and in 1892–3 it was Rs. 1,66,280. The revenue realized from Government lands was thus apportioned :—

| Cultivation. | 1891–2. | | 1892–3. | |
|---|---|---|---|---|
| | Area. | Assessment. | Area. | Assessment. |
| Dry ... ... ... | 66,903 | 71,195 | 68,897 | 72,894 |
| Wet ... ... ... | 6,141 | 27,190 | 6,671 | 29,822 |
| Garden ... ... ... | 2,001 | 10,293 | 2,024 | 10,433 |
| Total ... ... | Ac. 75,045 | Rs. 1,08,678 | Ac. 77,592 | Rs. 1,13,149 |

The following was the average rainfall at Nelamangala for 25 years (1870–1894):—

| Jan. | Feb. | Mar. | April | May | June | July | Aug. | Sept. | Oct. | Nov. | Dec. | | Year. |
|---|---|---|---|---|---|---|---|---|---|---|---|---|---|
| — | 0·19 | 0·33 | 0·67 | 3·29 | 2·64 | 2·10 | 4·28 | 3·75 | 5·02 | 1·44 | 0·49 | ... | 24·10 |

The Bangalore-Harihar railway runs through the northern half of the taluq, with stations at Golhalli, Dodbele and Nidvanda. The Bangalore-Tumkur road goes through Nelamangala and Sompur or Dobbspet, where it meets the road from Kolar *viâ* Dod-Ballapur. A short cross road connects Tyamagondal with both. The Hassan road branches off at Nelamangala to the south-west. There is also a road from Nelamangala to Dod-Ballapur, and a short one from Dobbspet to Sivaganga.

**Nelamangala.**—A town situated in 13° 6′ N. lat., 77° 27′ E. long., 16 miles north-west of Bangalore on the Bangalore-Tumkur road. Head-quarters of the Nelamangala taluq, and a municipality.

| Population in 1891. | Males. | Females. | Total. |
|---|---|---|---|
| Hindus ... ... ... .. ... ... | 1,783 | 1,729 | 3,512 |
| Muhammadans ... ... ... ... ... | 334 | 317 | 651 |
| Christians ... ... ... ... ... ... | 4 | 4 | 8 |
| Total ... ... | 2,121 | 2,050 | 4,171 |

A fair is held on Friday, attended by 2,500 people.

On or near the site of Nelamangala formerly stood a large city, so it is said, to which tradition gives the name of Bhumandana. It is said to have been founded by Sumati, son of Hemachandra, king of Karnataka, whose capital was Yadupatna. Having succeeded in an expedition against a robber chief at Devaraydurga, he took up his residence at Bhumandana for the security of that part of his father's dominions. The actual history has been given above under the taluq. Nelamangala appears to have been transferred to the Mysore Rajas along with Tyamagondal at the time when Bangalore was purchased from the Mughal general Khasim Khan. This was in 1687.

| Municipal Funds. | 1892-3. | 1893-4. | 1894-5. | 1895-6. |
|---|---|---|---|---|
| Income (opening balance Rs. 2,754) ... | 1,132 | 2,201 | 2,470 | 2,259 |
| Expenditure ... ... ... ... | 1,443 | 2,953 | 2,315 | 3,727 |

**Nellurpatna.**—A ruined city 5 miles south-east of Devanhalli. It is stated to have been of great extent and ruled by a rich and powerful line of kings. In the time of the last of these, named Chauda Raya, the city was captured, after maintaining an obstinate defence for three years, during which the enēmy was twice forced to raise the siege. Its fall was due to an act of treachery on the part of the king's daughter, who, being married to the chief of Gubbi in the Hoskote taluq, had accompanied her husband to the war, and made known the existence of the subterranean passage by which the city was supplied with water from a distance. Chauda Raya is said to have blown up his palace, containing his family and treasures, while the enemy were scaling the walls.

**Nijagal.**—A hill, also called S'úragiri, in the north-west of the Nelamangala taluq, accessible only on the north and east. The fort which formerly occupied the summit owed its strength more to nature than to art, and was the scene of many desperate encounters. The péṭe has been for many years almost deserted, the inhabitants having removed to Tyamagondal. The present population is 158.

**Pennar.**—*See* Pinákini.

**Pinakini.**—The Southern or Dakshina Pinákini, a river flowing through the eastern parts of the District. It is better known to European geographers as the Southern Pennár. The continuous curve formed by the course of the N. and S. Pinákini, which both rise near the hill of Nandi, sacred to Siva, may probably account for their receiving the name of Pinákini, from *pináka*, the bow of Siva. This is the only designation by which the streams are known to the Kannaḍa people[1]; but it seems also to be called the Ponnaiyár in the Tamil country.

The S. Pinákini rises in the Chenna Kesava hill, east of Nandidroog. Its course, after entering the Bangalore District, is southwards through the Devanhalli and Hoskote taluqs, where it forms the Jangamkote and Hoskote tanks, the latter one of the largest sheets of water in the

[1] It is also the ancient name in Tamil works, as appears from a stanza of the poetess Avvaiyar, in which the *Pináka* is given as the southern boundary of Tondamandalam. Quoted by Ellis in *Mirási Rights.*

country. Continuing south, it leaves the Mysore a little to the east of the town of Sarjapur and enters the Bagalur estate. Thence, turning eastwards, it makes its way through the Eastern Ghats near the town of Krishnagiri and, after traversing the Salem and South Arcot Districts of Madras, falls into the Bay of Bengal near Fort St. David, a few miles north of Cuddalore. The length of its entire course is 245 miles, of which about 50 miles from the source are in the Mysore. It is estimated that 85·60 per cent. of the water of this portion is stored for agricultural purposes.

**Ramgiri.**—A picturesque hill, at one time fortified, on the left bank of the Arkavati, three miles north of Closepet. It formerly gave its name to the taluq, the town of Ramgiri being at its base. The place was captured by the British in 1791. On the foundation of Closepet the residents removed to the new settlement.

**Sarjapur.**—A town in the Anekal taluq, 12 miles north-east of the kasba, and a municipality. Till 1873 it was the head-quarters of a taluq of the same name.

| Population in 1891. | Males. | Females. | Total. |
|---|---|---|---|
| Hindus ... ... ... ... ... | 1,232 | 1,279 | 2,511 |
| Muhammadans ... ... ... ... | 265 | 241 | 506 |
| Total ... ... ... | 1,497 | 1.520 | 3,017 |

A small fair is held on Sunday, visited by 100 people.

Cotton cloths, carpets and tape are made here in considerable quantities. Formerly it appears that muslins of fine quality were woven.

Sarjapur, with 18 other villages, was formerly a jágir, held from the Mughals on condition of maintaining a military force for the service of the emperor. The jágir was confirmed by successive rulers, as appears from some interesting *sanads* exhibited to me several years ago. (1) Grant in Persian, by Dilávar Khan, Subahdar of Sira, in the name of Alamgír, Pádsháh i Ghází. (2) Grant in Mahratti, by Mádhava Ráo, minister of the Peshwa. The seal bore the inscription, *Rájá Rám narapati, harsha nidhán, Mádhav Ráv Ballál pradhán.* At the joinings of the paper and at the end were small seals, with the words *lékhan símá.* (3) Grant by Haidar Ali, in Mahratti, signed with Haidar's autograph, and sealed with the words *Fatte Haidar.* (4) Grant by Lord Cornwallis, written in Persian, on white paper sprinkled with gold dust. Signed *Cornwallis*, and sealed with the Persian words *Sálár e . . . Inglistán.* Initialled at the back G. F. C. (5) Grant in Persian, by Captain Cherry. Seal in Persian, with the words *George Frederick Cherry, khâyim jang, fidvi e Kampani Angrezi Bahádúr.* (6) Grant in Persian, by Captain Read, dated 1791. Seal in Persian, *Alexander Read Bahádúr.*

The grants were cancelled by Purnaiya, who, finding the Jágírdár wanted to sell his villages, bought him out. There is now no jágir.

| Municipal Funds. | 1892-3. | 1893-4. | 1894-5. | 1895-6. |
|---|---|---|---|---|
| Income (opening balance Rs. 1,941) | 653 | 607 | 1,193 | 1,280 |
| Expenditure ... ... ... ... | 1,217 | 1,329 | 2,771 | 1,679 |

**Sausmond.**—One of the Eurasian and Anglo-Indian settlements in the east of the Bangalore taluq (*see* Whitefield). It is 12 miles from Bangalore, and 3 miles south of Whitefield. Named after Dr. Sausman, now President of the Association. It originally contained 926 acres, but only 812 were occupied and the rest relinquished. In 1889 there were 45 families belonging to the settlement, of whom 25 were non-resident. The Report for 1895 says:—"The land is for the most part in the hands of the wealthier members of the community, and there are only six families that come within the term poor. The former are mostly absentees, but have agents to supervise the working of their farms and give employment to some of the poorer settlers. They have greatly improved their holdings by growing coffee, fruit-trees, casuarinas, &c. A dairy has been successfully started by one of them."

**Savandurga.**—A mountain in the Magadi taluq, 7 miles south-east of the kasba, and familiarly called the Magadi hill. It is an enormous mass of granite, rising to 4,024 feet above the level of the sea, and standing on a base eight miles in circumference. The summit consists of two peaks, separated by a chasm, each being independent of the other, and abundantly supplied with water. One is called the Kari or black peak, the other the Bili or white peak.

The hill appears to have been first fortified in 1543 by Sámanta Ráya, the officer appointed to the charge of the Magadi district by Achyuta Ráya, the king of Vijayanagar. Taking advantage of the feebleness of the government, and relying no doubt on the natural strength of his position, he made himself independent, and took up his residence on the droog, with a force of 8,000 men, officered by 8 gurikars. He died in 1571 and was succeeded by his son Sampaja Ráya. He ruled for 17 years, and was followed by his son Chikka Ráya, who, after a rule of 16 years, threw himself in a fit of madness into the chasm and was drowned, leaving no issue. Ganga, the *tálári*, or watchman of Gudamarnhalli, seized the place and began plundering in order to enrich himself. But Immaḍi Kempe Gauḍa of Bangalore put him to death, secured the stronghold for his own family, and changed its name from *Sámanta-durga* to *Sávana-durga.* He soon had need of the retreat, being driven out of Bangalore by the Bijapur army. His descendants held Sávandurga till 1728, when Deva Rája, Dalavayi of Mysore, obtained possession and carried Mummaḍi Kempe Gauḍa, the chief, prisoner to Seringapatam, where he ended his days, the last of his line. The name of Krishnarája-giri then given to the droog has not survived. The memorable capture of Sávandurga in 1791 by the British under Lord Cornwallis is thus described by Wilks:—

"Colonel Stuart encamped within three miles of the place on the 10th of December, and immediately commenced the arduous labour of cutting a gun-road through the rugged forest to the foot of the rock, a work which, added to the difficulties of dragging iron twenty-four pounders over precipices nearly perpendicular, called for a degree of incessant exertion and fatigue which could scarcely have been exceeded.

The batteries opened on the 17th, and the breach in what was named the lower wall of the rock, although at least fifteen hundred feet higher than its base, was deemed practicable on the 20th. Immediately overlooking it, at a precipitous height, and perfectly well situated for destroying, by the usual artillery of rocks and stones, everything that should attempt to ascend beyond the breach, was a range of ancient wall. Lord Cornwallis had come from the camp, distant seven miles, to witness the assault; the grenadiers were ordered to their stations, and the garrison was seen to be collecting behind this wall. This observation fortunately prevented the assault on that day; the experiment was made of pointing with sufficient elevation by receiving the trail of the gun carriage into an excavation behind the platform. The execution was not only perfect, but the wall was found to be so frail that a few discharges must dislodge its defenders. The arrangements for the ensuing day were founded on the fact thus opportunely ascertained. The batteries were prepared for the purpose, and in the morning the requisite number of guns were directed against this wall with the most perfect success; every person behind it was dislodged, and the storming party, having been placed without observation within twenty yards of the breach, the assault commenced by signal at eleven o'clock in the forenoon.

The defenders had been so unexpectedly dislodged from their appointed positions that no new disposition had been made. The assailants accordingly ascended the rock without the slightest opposition, clambering up a precipice which, after the service was over, they were afraid to descend. The eastern citadel was completely carried; and the assailants, on reaching the summit of the rock, had the satisfaction to descry a heavy column of infantry, destined to reinforce the garrison, in full march to enter the place, which would have been effected if the assault had been postponed even for half an hour. A division of the assailants, after descending considerably above the breach, had been directed to turn to the right along a path which had been observed to be practised by the garrison, leading along the side of the rock to the western citadel. The killedar of that citadel, observing the defenders of the eastern rock to be driven from their post above the breach, and the assailants to have begun climbing up, sallied with the view of taking them in flank, but was unexpectedly met among the rocks by the division described ; and, at the same instant, a few well-directed shot from the batteries fell with great execution among his troops. He retreated in surprise and dismay, followed with great energy by the English troops. At this instant the assailants, who had gained the highest eminence of the eastern rock, obtained a distinct view of the pursuit ; they observed the killedar to fall just as he approached the gate of his citadel, and the pursuers to enter with the fugitives. Everything was carried within one hour from the commencement of the assault ; and an enterprise which had been contemplated by Lord Cornwallis as the most doubtful operation of the war, was thus effected in twelve days from the first arrival of the troops, and five of open batteries, including the day of assault, with a moderate amount of casualties in the previous operations, and in the assault itself his Lordship had not to regret the loss of a single life."

**Sivaganga.**—A sacred hill in the north-west of the Nelamangala taluq, whose acute conical peak rises to a height of 4,559 feet above the level of the sea. On the east its outline is supposed to resemble a bull, on the west Ganesha, on the north a serpent, and on the south a linga. The number of steps leading to the top is said to equal the number of yojanas hence to Benares. The place is therefore called Dakshina Kási, and an ascent to the top is vicariously as meritorious as a pilgrimage to the holy city. The puránas give it the name of Kakudgiri. Coming down to historical times, it is mentioned by its present name in the twelfth century as the place where Santala Devi died, the first queen of Vishnuvardhana of the Hoysala line, and also as one of the distant points to which the Lingáyit faith, recently established by Basava, the minister of Bijjala, king of Kalyána, had extended.

The northern face is occupied with numerous sacred buildings, many of which were erected at the expense of Kempe Gauḍa, the chief of Magadi. The two principal temples, dedicated to Gangádharesvara and Honna Devamma, are formed out of large natural caverns, the ascent to which is by an imposing flight of stone steps. There are eight springs or tirthas on the hill, one of which, contained in a deep and extremely narrow cleft of the rock, is named the Pátála Ganga or Ganges of the lower regions. The level of the water in this is said to rise several feet during the hot season and to sink during the rains, an effect due to natural causes, but regarded as miraculous. On the eastern face is a Lingáyit establishment called the Ráchoṭi maṭh. The remaining sides are covered with low jungle, in which and in the caves around bears and other wild animals may be met with. At the extreme summit are two pillars, from beneath one of which about a quart of water oozes on the day of the winter solstice or *makara-sankrânti.* The attendant priests receive the tiny stream in a vessel, and devoting half to the god, convey the other half to the palace at Mysore.

The village of Sivaganga is at the northern base of the hill. Population 535. The houses are entirely of stone and form a single street through which the car is drawn at religious festivals. At the entrance to the village is a lofty towered gateway. The math having become involved in great pecuniary difficulties, the revenues of the religious endowments are, on the wish of the gúru, being managed by the Muzrai department.

**Sivan-giri.**—A fortified hill near Closepet, on the right bank of the Arkavati, opposite to Ramgiri. It surrendered to the British in 1791 without much resistance.

**Sulibele.**—A village in the north of Hoskote taluq, head-quarters of the hóbli of the same name, and a municipality. Population 1,927.

This part of the country in the 10th century was in the hands of the Nolambas, and subsequently of the Cholas. In modern times, under Vijayanagar, it was part of the province belonging to the Sugatur family.

| Municipal Funds. | 1892-3. | 1893-4. | 1894-5. | 1895-6. |
|---|---|---|---|---|
| Income (opening balance Rs. 459)... | 897 | 908 | 971 | 994 |
| Expenditure ... ... ... ... | 496 | 875 | 928 | 1,437 |

**Tirumale.**—A village 2 miles east of Magadi, and included in it. Population 630.

A large festival (*párishe*) is held for eight days in April, in honour of Ranganathaswami, whose temple is the principal feature of the place. On this occasion 10,000 people assemble from the surrounding taluqs.

**Tyamagondal.**—A mercantile town and municipality, 11 miles north-west of Nelamangala, with which it is connected by a branch road from Begur. It is about midway between the Nidvanda and Dodbele railway stations, not more than 3 miles from either.

| Population in 1891. | Males. | Females. | Total. |
|---|---|---|---|
| Hindus ... ... ... ... ... | 1,477 | 1,503 | 2,980 |
| Muhammadans ... ... ... ... | 403 | 362 | 765 |
| Christians ... ... ... ... | 2 | 1 | 3 |
| Total ... ... ... | 1,882 | 1,866 | 3,748 |

The town increased to its present dimensions on the desertion of Nijagal, and contains a considerable number of merchants and traders in grain. Some large tanks have been formed in the vicinity by intercepting the waters of the Kumadvati.

| Municipal Funds. | 1892-3. | 1893-4. | 1894-5. | 1895-6. |
|---|---|---|---|---|
| Income (opening balance Rs. 2,574) | 1,019 | 2,990 | 4 235 | 2,225 |
| Expenditure ... ... ... .. | 2,286 | 3,314 | 4 449 | 4,350 |

**Vadigenhalli.**—A mercantile town and municipality, 7 miles north-east of Devanhalli, on the Kolar-Nandi road.

| Population in 1891. | Males. | Females. | Total. |
|---|---|---|---|
| Hindus ... ... .. ... ... | 1,854 | 1,933 | 3,787 |
| Muhammadans ... ... ... ... | 83 | 100 | 183 |
| Total .. ... ... | 1,937 | 2,033 | 3,970 |

A fair held on Friday is attended by 300 people.

The principal trade of Vadigenhalli is in the hands of Nagarta merchants, and consists of the import and export of cotton. The two temples of Nagaresvara and Kesava were erected about fifty years ago, and the designs are said to be taken from temples at Kanchi.

| Municipal Funds. | 1892-3. | 1893-4. | 1894-5. | 1895-6. |
|---|---|---|---|---|
| Income (opening balance Rs. 2,793) | 658 | 623 | 1,745 | 1,790 |
| Expenditure ... ... ... ... | 1,478 | 1,945 | 2,884 | 1,999 |

**Vasantapur.**—A village 5 miles south of Bangalore. Population 112. It is in no way remarkable but for an old temple of Vallabharáya-swami, which is a favourite resort for native wedding parties from Bangalore.

**Whitefield.**—The principal of the Eurasian and Anglo-Indian settlements in the east of the Bangalore taluq; named after Mr. D. S. White, the founder of the original Association in Madras. It is 2 miles south of the railway station of the same name (formerly called Kadgodi station) and 12 miles east of Bangalore.

The Eurasian and Anglo-Indian Association in Mysore (numbering 213 members in 1895) was formed in November 1879, for the purpose of co-operation among the members in improving the condition of families belonging to those communities. This object was to be attained by promoting industrial and agricultural pursuits among them.

A boot and shoe factory was started, and as long as it was open proved successful; arrangements were also made for apprenticeship to other trades; and an Art and Industrial Institute was in view, where poor women and girls could be employed in needlework and fancy work, and in making Indian condiments and jams. But the main reliance was on the land scheme, which aimed at the formation of agricultural settlements or colonies. The Mysore Government readily lent its aid by a grant in July 1881 of nearly 4,000 acres of land, selected by the Association, to be held free of assessment for the first five years. With the help of Sir James Gordon, special sanction was obtained for holding a lottery in order to raise funds for starting the scheme. One lakh was thus obtained, but half of it was allotted for prizes. The original intention was to establish four colonies, as follows :—

| | | |
|---|---|---|
| Glen Gordon[1] ... ... | 527 acres | In the Srigandha Kaval, 8 miles west of Bangalore, on the Magadi road. |
| Haldwell Green ... ... | 757 ,, | |
| Whitefield ... ... | 542 ,, | 12 miles east of Bangalore, as above described. |
| Sausmond ... ... | 926 ,, | |

But this was found to be more than the Association could accomplish. They therefore, in July 1883, relinquished the lands of the Kaval and also the outlying lands of Sausmond, the Mysore Government having sanctioned their giving up any of the lands either absolutely or in favour of any specified individual or individuals. The terms on which the lands retained were held were further modified in November 1884 in the following manner :—No assessment was to be levied on village sites, and on land set apart for common pasturage. On the rest, the assessment was remitted for 3 years more; half rates to be levied in the 4th year, and full rates thereafter.

Whitefield in 1889 contained 25 families, of whom 6 were non-resident. In 1894, in accordance with the wishes of the settlers, the Association transferred its right of occupancy to them, so that they became the registered tenants and paid their assessment direct to Government, but as members of the Association they are bound by its rules as to the disposal of the land.[2] The report for 1895 gives the number of permanent residents at that time as 115. From it is also gathered the following information :—Whitefield now embraces two plots of land, the larger being the grant made by the Mysore Government to the Association, and the smaller consisting of the lands of Pattandur, leased by the late Mr. White from the Jodidar.

[1] The first was named after Sir James Gordon, and the second after a prominent member of the Association.

[2] Claims to control on the part of the Madras Association have led to serious dissensions, but these it is believed are now at an end.

The number of landowners in Whitefield proper is 26, but all the available holdings have been taken up and there is no room left for expansion in this direction, but land can be had in Pattandur from Mrs. White. The number of houses built on the farms is 14, and cottages on the village site 12. There are 8 houses in Pattandur, also a Roman Catholic chapel and parsonage. In Whitefield there is a Protestant church, where Church of England and Dissenting services are regularly held alternately, and a parsonage is under erection. There is a good school, with 31 pupils, aided and inspected by Government. Room is also provided for the residence of the Head-Master and his wife, who assists him in teaching. The Association has also established a Family Benefit Fund, and offers various prizes and scholarships for promoting education and athletic sports.

**Yelahanka.**—A town 10 miles north of Bangalore, on the railway to Guntakal and on the Bangalore-Chikballapur road; a municipality. Till 1871 it was the head-quarters of a taluq of the same name.

| Population in 1891. | Males. | Females. | Total. |
|---|---|---|---|
| Hindus ... ... ... ... ... | 1,208 | 1,284 | 2,492 |
| Muhammadans ... ... ... ... | 90 | 78 | 168 |
| Christians ... ... ... ... | 4 | 4 | 8 |
| Total ... ... ... | 1,302 | 1,366 | 2,668 |

Yelahanka is historically interesting as being one of the oldest places in the District. As Ilaipákka under the Cholas, and Elahakka under the Hoysalas, it gave its name to all the surrounding country.[1] It was the first possession of Jaya Gauḍa, the progenitor of the Kempe Gauḍa line of chiefs, who founded Bangalore and subsequently became identified with Magadi and Savandurga. Jaya Gauḍa obtained the title of Yelakanka Nad Prabhu in about 1420, and the place remained in possession of his family for 230 years, when it was captured by the Mysore Raja.

A car festival held for 10 days from Chaitra suddha 8th in honour of Venugopala is attended by 2,000 people.

| Municipal Funds. | 1892-3. | 1893-4. | 1894-5. | 1895-6. |
|---|---|---|---|---|
| Income (opening balance Rs. 413)... | 502 | 527 | 1,049 | 1,249 |
| Expenditure ... ... ... ... | 1,443 | 452 | 1,082 | 2,010 |

[1] The form Yelahanka probably arose from the old Prakrit custom of indicating a duplicated consonant by a round dot, like that used to express a nasal, for which latter purpose it is now exclusively employed.

KOLAR DISTRICT
SCALE 8 MILES TO AN INCH
B—Travellers' Bungalow. L—Inspection Lodge. S—Railway Station.
ANANTAPUR
TUMKUR
BANGALORE
SALEM
MUHAMMADABAD
TAMBALLAPALLI
MUDIVEDU
TARICONDA
MADANAPALLI
RAMASAMUDRAM
PUNGANUR
CHIK-BALLAPUR
SIDLACHATTA
CHINTAMANI
SRINIVASPUR
GORIBIDNUR
GUDIBANDA
BAGEPALLI
CHILIMUTTUR
HINDUPUR
PARIGI
HOSUR
DOD-BALLAPUR
VADIGENAHALLI
DEVANHALLI
YELAHANKA
NELAMANGALA
HOSKOTE
MALUR
KOLAR
MULBAGAL
BOWRINGPET
GOLDMINES
KUPPAM
KANGUNDI
BEGUR
SARJAPURA
SOMPALLI
RANGASAMUDRAM
PEDDATIPPASAMUDRAM
GHATTU
KOTTAKOTA KURABALAKOTA

# KOLAR DISTRICT

## GENERAL DESCRIPTION

*Situation.*—A District in the east of Mysore, situated between 12° 48′ and 13° 57′ north latitude and 77° 26′ and 78° 39′ east longitude. Its greatest length is from north to south, about 85 miles, but from east to west an equal distance may be measured between the furthest points.

*Area.*—The area is 3,168 square miles.

*Boundaries.*—The Bangalore and Tumkúr Districts bound it on the west. On all other sides it is surrounded by Districts of the Madras Presidency, having Anantapur on the north, Kadapa and North Arcot on the east, and Salem on the south.

*Divisions.*—The Chik Ballapur Sub-Division was formed in November 1891, comprising the Chik Ballapur, Goribidnur and Bagepalli taluqs. The District contains the following taluqs, Gudibanda being a sub-taluq of Bagepalli.

| No. | Taluq. | Area in square miles. | No. of Hoblis. | No. of Villages or Towns. | Population. |
|---|---|---|---|---|---|
| 1 | Bagepalli ... ... | 447 | 8 | 374 | 58,086 |
| 2 | Bowringpet .. ... | 335 | 7 | 444 | 71,042 |
| 3 | Chik Ballapur ... ... | 250 | 5 | 272 | 51,592 |
| 4 | Chintamani ... ... | 503 | 6 | 326 | 49,888 |
| 5 | Goribidnur ... ... | 341 | 7 | 272 | 71,990 |
| 6 | Kolar ... ... ... | 299 | 6 | 332 | 72,543 |
| 7 | Malur ... .. ... | 269 | 6 | 424 | 54,180 |
| 8 | Mulbagal ... ... | 361 | 6 | 355 | 56,269 |
| 9 | Sidlaghatta ... ... | 363[1] | 6 | 350 | 58,077 |
| 10 | Srinivaspur ... ... | ... | 7 | 329 | 46,463 |
| | Total ... | 3,168 | 64 | 3,478 | 591,030 |

**Physical Features.**—The District occupies that portion of the Mysore table-land immediately bordering on the Eastern Ghats. But the frontier touches the Ghats only in the north-east and south: between those points it recedes from the range to a mean distance of 15 miles.

The chief watershed lies in the north-west, in and around Nandidroog, the height of which is 4,851 feet above the sea. The streams which spring from this elevated region, said to be the birthplace of seven

[1] Included in Chintamani.

rivers, radiate in all directions, receiving the drainage of the intermediate tracts of country. The Arkavati and Northern Pinákini (or Pennár), rising to the west of Nandidroog, flow one to the south and the other to the north ; the Chitravati and Pápaghni rise in the north and have a north-easterly course : the Pálár and Southern Pinákini (or Pennár) springing from the eastern side, run eastward and southward respectively. Of these several streams the Arkavati and most of the S. Pinákini belong to the Bangalore District. The main part of the Kolar District comprises the head of the Pálár river system on the south and that of the N. Pinákini on the north, separated by an imaginary line from Chik-Ballapur to S'rinivaspur.

The principal chain of mountains runs north from Nandidroog, the highest point, through Gudibanda, as far as Penugonda and Dharmavaram in the Anantapur District. More or less parallel with the Nandidroog range, and from 30 to 40 miles to the east of it, is a line of hills entering the District due north of Gumnayakanpalya, and separating the valleys of the Chitravati and Pápaghni. At the frontier the range is known as the Dongala or Dokkala-konda. After a considerable interval it reappears in the isolated peaks of Murugamale, Ambájidurga (4,399 feet) and Rahmandurga (4,227 feet). Thence, forming the chain of hills to the west of the town of Kolar (highest point 4,026 feet), it is continued in the Vokkaleri and Tyakal hills to the south.

A third line of low hills, represented in places merely by mounds or rising ground, commences near S'rinivaspur, and, preserving the same general direction as the former, passes to the east of Kolar, and extends through the southernmost parts of the Bowringpet taluq to Kangundi, Kuppam and the Ghats.

The hills still more to the east incline in some places to a circular arrangement, enclosing elevated valleys which are occupied by villages. This configuration appears at Mudimadagu and Sunṇakal.

The central and eastern parts of the District, forming the valley of the Pálár, are undulating and well cultivated, the general level varying between 2,786 feet at Kolar, 2,970 feet at Malur, and 2,989 feet at the foot of Ambajidurga. A considerable depression occurs in the valley of the N. Pinákini towards Goribidnur, the height of Hindupur just beyond the boundary being only 2,068 feet, and of Penugonda 1,677 feet. The outlying districts along the northern frontier mark with alternate rise and fall the descent to the level of the Anantapur country. On the east, the Mugli and Naikaneri passes to the plains of the so-called Carnatic are some distance beyond the boundary.

**Tanks.**—In no District has the tank system been more fully developed, as none offered equal facilities for the purpose. The entire water of the Pálár is intercepted for purposes of irrigation, while of the N. Pinákini and its affluents upwards of 85 per cent. of the drainage is similarly utilized. The series of tanks form a marked feature in the landscape when surveyed from a height, as from Nandidroog, whence 400 can be readily counted. The total number for the District is 5,497, covering an area of upwards of 120,000 acres.

The Pálár chain of tanks consists of the Somámbudhi, Jannagatta, Mudvadi, Chillapalli, Manigatta, Holali, Betamangala, and Rámságar tanks, which are at a mean distance of four or five miles from each other, extending through the Kolar and Bowringpêt taluqs. The Kolar, Nangali and Kurbur tanks are also connected with the same system. The largest of the above and in the whole District is the Rámságar. The particulars given below show the capacity and dimensions of some principal tanks of the Pálár system. To these may be added the tanks of the S'rinivaspur sub-taluq, namely, the Bagavadu, irrigating 663 acres, the Ronur 280 acres, the Kolatur 150 acres, and the Lakshmansagar 226 acres.

| Name of tank. | Embankment. | | | | No. of Sluices. | No. of acres irrigated. |
|---|---|---|---|---|---|---|
| | Length. | Height. | Depth. | | | |
| | | | At base. | At top. | | |
| Rámságar ... ... ... | ft. 1,500 | 45 | 150 | 18 | 4 | 1,500 |
| Betamangala ... ... | 4,152 | 24 | 89 | 12 | 2 | 700 |
| Somambudhi ... ... | 5,475 | 18 | 74 | 10 | 3 | 1,500 |
| Kolar ... ... ... | 6,000 | 18 | 90 | 10 | | 800 |
| Nangali ... ... ... | 4,272 | 21 | 50 | 8 | | 1,112 |
| Kurubur ... ... ... | 3,732 | 20 | 70 | 9 | | 450 |

The head waters of the S. Pinákini form the Kandavara and Gopalkrishna tanks at Chik-Ballapur, irrigating 625 and 715 acres, and Katamachanhalli tank, lower down in the same taluq, irrigating 540 acres. The surplus waters of the Gopalkrishna tank feed the Ammankere and Bellútikere, two large tanks at Sidlaghatta, irrigating 350 acres each. The Bhadrana tank irrigates 1,600 acres.

The N. Pinákini and its affluents the Chitravati and Pápaghni supply many important tanks. Of these the Bairasagar at Gudibanda is one of the largest in the District. Others are the Vatadahoshalli, a very deep tank north-west of Gudibanda, formed by embanking a gorge between two chains of hills; two tanks at Hudugur, irrigating 434 and 408 acres, one at Nagaragere, irrigating 391 acres, and one at Namagondlu, irrigating 376 acres, all in the same taluq. South-west of

Goribidnur is the Purnasagara tank, irrigating 250 acres. The tank at Periasandra, formed by the Chitravati, irrigates 256 acres.

| Name of tank. | Embankment. | | | | No. of Sluices. | No. of acres irrigated. |
|---|---|---|---|---|---|---|
| | Length. | Height. | Depth. | | | |
| | | | At base. | At top. | | |
| Bairsagar ... ... ... | ft. 4,032 | 27 | 94 | 18 | 5 | 1,100 |
| Vatadahoshalli ... ... | 1,923 | 51 | 185 | 6 | 2 | 1,500 |
| Srinivasa-sagara ... ... | 2,100 | 40 | 117 | 20 | 3 | 1,200 |
| Venkata-sagara ... ... | 1,293 | 42 | 110 | 20 | 2 | 990 |

*Channels.*—In addition to the numerous tanks of the District, a few small channels are drawn from the N. Pinákini in Goribidnur taluq, and from the Chitravati near Bagepalli in Bagepalli taluq. Some anicuts built across streams and large water-courses in the Chik-Ballapur, Gudibanda, Bagepalli, and Sidlaghatta taluqs, also supply water for a good deal of cultivation.

**Rocks.**—The rocks of the District are for the most part similar to those of the adjoining District of Bangalore, being composed of gneiss, but with a smaller admixture of mica, and a paler felspar. The low hills previously referred to, which cross the course of the Pálár and run south through the Bowringpet taluq, are composed of a soft ferruginous clay slate. They are flat at their tops and mostly barren, with a soil about them of fine argillaceous red earth. Gold has long been found close to the surface near these hills in considerable quantities, either mixed with the soil or interspersed in quartzy stones. It almost invariably occurs either in thin veins or disseminated in grains in the veins and beds of quartz, associated with iron ore, and sometimes with platinum. Mining operations were also carried on from a remote period by the natives of Mysore, but had long been abandoned by them. Deep mining by Europeans has now established here the most valuable gold mines in India.

**Soils.**—The soil on the high grounds is red and gravelly, with very often rocks of gneiss or granite, of little cohesion, appearing on its surface. The lower parts of these high grounds are intersected by nullahs or deep ravines, torn up by the torrents of water precipitated from the heights in the rainy season. The tops of the ridges are usually very barren, producing nothing but a small jungle. The soil in the valleys is a good and loamy mixture, formed of the finer particles of the decomposed rocks, washed down and deposited during the rains.

On the first ascent from the valley the soil is of a middling quality, suited for dry grains, and is a mixture of loam, sand and oxide of iron, with a portion of vegetable and animal matter. Higher up, towards the top of the ridge, a siliceous sand prevails in the soil, which is on that account adapted only for horse-gram. Below the superficial soil there is commonly a bed of gravel, which immediately covers a gneissic or granitic rock, very often in a state of disintegration considerably advanced.

**Climate.**—The climate does not differ materially from that of the Bangalore District. So far as reliance can be placed on the register of observations, the mean temperature at Kolar is about 80·5° of Fahrenheit. The average rainfall, on the other hand, is considerably less, being only from 29 to 30 inches. This is doubtless due to the influence of the mountain ranges running through the west of this and the Bangalore District, which intercept much of the rain brought by the monsoon from the south-west quarter. So that this District is mainly dependent on the north-east monsoon. The description given in the preceding paragraphs will show, however, the abundance of the water supply with which the District is, notwithstanding, enriched.

It is generally a healthy country, remarkably so in the neighbourhoods of Chik-Ballapur and Kolar, which are probably not surpassed in that respect by any other parts of the Province. Kolar and the towns east and south of it were formerly much visited with cholera and other epidemics, originating among the crowds of travellers continually passing through the Ghats to and from Madras and the large towns of the Carnatic, more especially among bands of pilgrims to the shrine of Tirupati. The diversion of this passenger traffic to the railway, and the successful carrying out of sanatory operations by the municipal boards, have almost freed that portion of the District from the scourge of diseases for the prevalence of which it was at one time notorious. But the recent influx of labourers from so many different parts to the gold mines has led to outbreaks of cholera among them from time to time.

*Temperature.*—From the accompanying table, compiled as well as the data allowed from observations taken at Kolar in 1873 and 1874,[1] it appears that a maximum heat of 94° and 95° was experienced in April and May respectively. The minimum temperature was 57°, registered in February; during January and March it reached 59°.

| | Max. | Min. | | Max. | Min. |
|---|---|---|---|---|---|
| January ... | 75 | 59 | July ... | 86 | 73 |
| February ... | 81 | 57 | August .. | 86 | 73 |
| March ... | 83 | 59 | September | 83 | 70 |
| April ... | 94 | 65 | October ... | 79 | 69 |
| May ... | 95 | 70 | November | 78 | 75 |
| June ... | 83 | 69 | December . | 74 | 67 |

[1] No more recent registers are procurable.

The extreme annual range of the thermometer was 38°. The means of maximum and minimum temperature were 83·08 and 67·16, giving a general average of 75·12.

*Rainfall.*—The rainfall at Kolar shows an annual average of 29·24 inches, based upon the observations for 25 years (1870–94). The register by months is given under each taluq. The average annual rate for the 25 years at other taluq stations was as in the margin.

| | | | |
|---|---|---|---|
| Bagepalli | ... 18·44 | Gudibanda | ... 28·50 |
| Bowringpet | ... 28·81 | Málur... | ... 27·98 |
| Chik-Ballapur | . 31·50 | Mulbagal | .. 30·44 |
| Chintamani | ... 27·14 | Sidlaghatta | ... 27·74 |
| Goribidnur | ... 23·56 | Srinivaspur | ... 27·51 |

The actual annual fall at Kolar has been registered as follows :—

| | | | | | |
|---|---|---|---|---|---|
| 1868 | ... ... 47·65 | 1877 | ... ... 32·63 | 1886 | ... ... 29·70 |
| 1869 | ... ... 30·00 | 1878 | ... ... 42·80 | 1887 | ... ... 40·15 |
| 1870 | ... ... 18·64 | 1879 | ... ... 26·49 | 1888 | ... ... 33·52 |
| 1871 | ... ... 22·45 | 1880 | ... ... 30·40 | 1889 | ... ... 34·54 |
| 1872 | ... ... 26·48 | 1881 | ... ... 36·00 | 1890 | ... ... 27·37 |
| 1873 | ... ... 25·12 | 1882 | ... ... 33·09 | 1891 | ... ... 16·61 |
| 1874 | ... ... 37·66 | 1883 | ... ... 41·56 | 1892 | ... ... 30·72 |
| 1875 | ... ... 16·52 | 1884 | ... .. 23·73 | 1893 | ... ... 29·20 |
| 1876 | ... ... 12·19 | 1885 | ... ... 25·60 | 1894 | ... ... 26·74 |

Out of the 27 years the average has been exceeded in 15. In only 4 years has the fall been less than 20 inches, and in 4 it has been above 40.

**Vegetation.**—The only forest containing trees of large growth is in the neighbourhood of Nandidroog. On several of the hills in the District the soil is a shallow blackish vegetable mould lying on rock, and though trees and bushes grow abundantly they never attain any size. In the northern taluqs near Gumnayakanpalya and Gudibanda the hills are very barren, and produce only stunted bushes of bandrike, tangadi, dodonæa, barleria, small devadari (*sethia indica*), beppale (*wrightia tinctoria*), and a few bushes of *butea frondosa* and *cassia fistula*. In portions of these taluqs wild tamarinds are abundant, and in the plains are topes of mango, mohwah or ippe, and tamarinds. The reserved forest of 142½ square miles in the Narasimhadeva hill consists principally of bamboos and stunted *dindiga* trees.

The hills in the south-east corner of the Bowringpet taluq are covered with a profuse but small growth of various common fuel trees, among which tamarinds are not uncommon. In the Chik-Ballapur taluq the bábúl and tópál (*acacia leucophlœa*) grow freely, and near Nandidroog there is much jálári (lac tree), chiefly in the west and south-west of the hill. The vegetation up to the fort walls is frequently dense, but of no size. Within the enclosure are several fine champakas, and the growth of all trees is better. Acacias are also common in groves in Kolar, Mulbagal, Sidlaghatta, and Srinivaspur. In this last-named sub-taluq is a jungle, covering in all perhaps some 11 square miles, besides the Ráyalpád forest of over 34 square miles. At the bases and on the lower slopes of the Ráyalpád hills the scrub is of a superior description, several bushes of *cassia auriculata* running up to six and seven feet in height. The trees hereabouts average 20 feet; they consist chiefly of pachári, cheninge, navaládi, small dévadári, huluvé, yenne maddi, ralé, wild tamarind, jálári, a few shisham, and a few káráchi, while high up on the Mudimadagu hill is some bad teak. Near the top of this hill, and all round and about the large Sunnakal hill, bamboos are abundant, also jálári or lac trees.

In the Málur taluq there are fewer trees, and the uncultivated plains are covered with the ordinary scrub, mixed with euphorbias, which are also common in the Kolar taluq. Many villages in parts of this District are surrounded with stout and high hedges, in which banyans and bhair (*zizyphus jujuba*) trees are common and well grown. Cocoa-nut trees are principally cultivated in the Mulbagal and Goribidnur taluqs, and areca in the latter. Near Mudavádi in Kolar taluq, there are good fuel tracts, which, as well as the Kolar hills, supply the town of Kolar with firewood. The sandal is scarce, but attempts have been made to propagate it in the Nandi forest.

Besides the *State forests* reserved at Nandi, Narasimhadeva-betta, and Ráyalpád, already mentioned, there are the Agara jungles of 15 square miles in Mulbagal taluq, the Kamsandra jungles of 26 square miles in Bowringpet taluq, and the Valsebetta forest of 4¼ square miles in Goribidnur taluq.

There are also 32 plantations under the Forest department, covering an area of 16¼ square miles, and 10 plantations under the Revenue department, occupying a little more than 3 square miles. The following list shows their distribution :—

| Taluq. | Forest. | | Revenue. | |
|---|---|---|---|---|
| | No. | Acres. | No. | Acres. |
| Bowringpet ... ... ... | 4 | 354 | — | — |
| Chik-Ballapur ... ... ... | 4 | 1,483 | 1 | 45 |
| Gudibanda ... ... ... ... | — | — | 1 | 88 |
| Kolar ... ... ... ... | 2 | 2,127 | 2 | 119 |
| Málur ... ... ... ... | 12 | 3,912 | 1 | 56 |
| Mulbagal ... ... ... ... | 2 | 355 | — | — |
| Sidlaghatta ... ... ... ... | 3 | 2,047 | 4 | 1,620 |
| Srinivaspur ... ... ... ... | 5 | 134 | 1 | 78 |
| Total ... ... | 32 | 10,412 | 10 | 2,006 |

Several private casuarina plantations have sprung up in the vicinity of the railway in Málur and Bowringpet taluqs. None of the forests in the District yield good timber trees of any size. Babul and toppal grow freely, and the former is here considered durable timber, being used for buildings and carts. The District is rich in honge trees (*pongamia glabra*), which grow more luxuriantly here than in other parts of the State. They are most useful to the ryots; the leaves and flowers being excellent manure for rice fields, the seeds yielding oil for lamps, and the wood being used for fuel.

The planting of avenues along the public roads and of village topes has been successfully carried out. Up to the 30th of June 1893 there were 490 miles planted with avenues, and 8,087 acres occupied with groves containing 382,699 trees, all planted by the ryots.

**Agricultural Produce.**—The cultivated products are similar to those of the Bangalore District, but owing to the large number of tanks there is a greater proportion of wet and garden cultivation. Potatoes are extensively cultivated in the rich valleys of Chik-Ballapur and Sidlaghatta taluqs. Poppy cultivation, now prohibited, was formerly a source of great profit to the ryots. A little coffee is grown at Nandidroog, and mulberry in the Chik-Ballapur, Sidlaghatta, and Kolar taluqs.

The number of acres cultivated with rice in 1893 was 40,476, wheat 69, other food grains 322,906, oil seeds 11,508, sugar-cane 7,492, fibres 60, tobacco 826, vegetables 27,032, mulberry 1,751.

The kinds of rice grown in the district are *doḍḍa baira, giḍḍa baira, doḍḍa kembatti, saṇṇa kembatti, arsina kembatti, gutti saṇṇa, bili saṇṇa, sukadds, punagarâj, yálakki bhatta, puṭṭa bhatta, tóka nellu, kari tóka nellu, and gandhasale.*

The following list shows the quantity and value of each article of produce raised in the District, and the quantity and value exported:—

| Name. | | | Produced. | | Exported. | |
|---|---|---|---|---|---|---|
| Kannada. | Botanical. | English. | Quantity. | Value. | Quantity. | Value. |
| | CEREALS. | | Tons. | Rs. | Tons. | Rs. |
| Baragu ... | Panicum miliaceum | — | 46 | 725 | — | — |
| Bhatta ... | Oryza sativa ... ... | Rice ... ... | 3,200 | 22,400 | 360 | 25,200 |
| Godhi ... | Triticum aristatum | Wheat ... ... | 3 | 896 | — | — |
| Háraka ... | Panicum semiverticillatum ... .. | — | 429 | 9,000 | 71 | 1,500 |
| Jola ... | Holcus sorghum ... | Maize ... ... | 15 | 1,050 | — | — |
| Navane ... | Panicum italicum ... | Italian millet | 29 | 800 | — | — |
| Ragi ... | Cynosurus corocanus | Ragi ... .. | 18,940 | 1,325,400 | 9,066 | 634,620 |
| Sajje ... | Holcus spicatus ... | Spiked millet | 86 | 2,400 | — | — |
| Sáme ... | Panicum frumentaceum ... ... ... | Little millet | 286 | 8,000 | — | — |

| Name. | | | Produced. | | Exported. | |
|---|---|---|---|---|---|---|
| Kannada. | Botanical. | English. | Quantity. | Value. | Quantity. | Value. |
| | PULSES. | | Tons. | Rs. | Tons. | Rs. |
| Avare ... | Dolichos lablab ... | Cow gram ... | 714 | 60,000 | — | — |
| Hesaru ... | Phaseolus mungo ... | Green gram... | 35 | 3,920 | — | — |
| Hurali ... | Dolichos uniflorus | Horse gram... | 1,100 | 77,000 | — | — |
| Kadale ... | Cicer arietinum ... | Bengal gram | 1,200 | 182,400 | — | — |
| Togari ... | Cajanus indicus ... | Dholl ... ... | 60 | 8,400 | — | — |
| Uddu ... | Phaseolus minimus | Black gram... | 40 | 4,600 | — | — |
| | OIL SEEDS. | | | | | |
| Haralu ... | Ricinus communis | Castor oil ... | 500 | 35,000 | 36 | 6,000 |
| Kád Haralu | — | Wild ,, ... | 36 | 725 | — | — |
| Honge ... | Pongamia glabra ... | Honge ,, ... | 1,714 | 96,000 | 214 | 13,500 |
| Wollellu... | Sesamum orientale | Gingelli oil... | 71 | 10,000 | — | — |
| | VEGETABLES. | | | | | |
| Arisina ... | Curcuma longa ... | Turmeric ... | 25 | 4,600 | — | — |
| Bellulli ... | Allium sativum ... | Garlic ... ... | 56 | 7,800 | 24 | 3,300 |
| Kottambari bija .. | Coriandrum sativum | Coriander seed | 37 | 6,000 | 7 | 750 |
| Mensina káyi ... | Capsicum annuum | Chilly ... ... | 84 | 16,250 | 16 | 4,875 |
| Mentya ... | Trigonella fœnum grœcum ... .. | Fenugreek .. | 51 | 5,400 | 23 | 2,400 |
| Nirulli ... | Allium cepa .. ... | Onion ... ... | 171 | 12,000 | 64 | 4,500 |
| Sásive ... | Sinapis dichotoma | Mustard ... | 28 | 2,400 | — | — |
| Sunti ... | Ammomum zinziber | Dry ginger ... | 25 | 11,500 | — | — |
| | MISCELLANEOUS. | | | | | |
| Adike ... | Areca catechu ... | Areca nut ... | 1 | 240 | — | — |
| Alala káyi | Terminalia chebula | Gall nut ... | 6 | 640 | — | — |
| Bále ... | Musa sapientum ... | Plantain ... | 48 | 9,040 | 32 | 6,000 |
| Géru bija | Semicarpus anacardium ... ... ... | Marking nut | ¼ | 160 | — | — |
| Hoge soppu | Nicotiana tabaccum | Tobacco ... | 6 | 8,600 | — | — |
| Hunase ... | Tamarindus indica | Tamarind ... | 857 | 80,000 | 214 | 20,000 |
| Kalle káyi | Arachis hypogœa | Ground nut... | 643 | 18,000 | 271 | 8,000 |
| Sige káyi | Mimosa abstergens | Soap nut ... | 54 | 15,000 | 18 | 3,400 |
| Tenginu káyi ... | Cocos nucifera ... | Cocoanut ... | No. 94,800 | 2,962 | 40,000 | 1,250 |
| Viledeie ... | Piper betel ... | Betel leaf ... | Bundles. 254,000 | 15,000 | — | — |

**Wild Animals.**—Owing to the absence of large forests there is not much cover for wild beasts. A few bears are met with in the Mekalnaikanpalya and Budikota jungles; cheetahs and wild boar in the Nandidroog, Mudimadagu, Sunnakal and Dokkal-konda hill ranges. Unfrequented parts of the District, where there is shelter, are the resorts of hyenas, jackals, antelopes, porcupines, and hares. The mungoose and other small animals find protection in the thick hedges around villages.

*Birds.*—The wild birds are similar to those of the Bangalore

District. A large kind of vulture takes shelter and breeds on the almost inaccessible top of Worlakonda, a large hill between Peresandra and Gudibanda.

*Fish* are stated to be not so plentiful as the number of streams and tanks would lead one to expect, but large fish are found in the Betamangala and Ramasagara tanks.

**Domestic Animals.**—The indigenous bulls of the district are of a diminutive breed. Large-sized ones are imported by ryots from the woodlands and jungles on the Madras frontier, and reared either for local use or for sale at places below the Ghats. Buffaloes are generally met with throughout the District as well as sheep and goats. Gumnayakanpalya is noted for a superior breed of sheep, sold at moderate prices.

Large *cattle fairs* are held at Nandi, Vanarasi, Vokkaleri, and Avani, as well as at the Gháṭi Subrahmanya festival on the Goribidnur-Dodballapur border, mentioned in connection with the Bangalore District. The fair at Nandi is held for 15 days from Sivarátri, on the occasion of the Nandisvara car-festival. It is attended by 20,000 people, and 10,000 bullocks are brought for sale. The Vánarási fair is held for 15 days in April, in honour of Iralappa, and is visited by 5,000 people. No less than 10,000 bullocks are brought to the market. The fair at Avani is in honour of Rámalinga. It lasts for 10 days from Sivarátri, and attracts a concourse of 10,000 people with 20,000 bullocks.

*Cattle shows* instituted by Government were at one time held at Nandi, in connection with the festival above mentioned, at which bulls and bullocks from all the surrounding country are brought together, and thousands of animals change owners. Colonel Pearse, describing the show of 1872, says: 'I rode over the whole of the ground where the cattle were picketed, and the lowest computation was that quite 10,000 head were assembled, many of them remarkable for power, symmetry, and good hard condition, with the fine bold spirited look of the old Amrit Mahal breed specially apparent; and as on this occasion no false and mischievous rumours were spread tending to alarm the ryots and lead to a misunderstanding regarding the intentions of Government, the very cream of these cattle was produced at the show ground on the evening of the 12th of March. The bulls were very fine, and some of the bullocks were truly magnificent animals. Selection was not only a work of time but a really difficult task. Quite 500 pairs were brought into the enclosure, and the value placed on some by the owners was very high, the asking price for one pair being Rs. 800. The spirit of competition was most gratifying, and no owners in any part of the world could have been more eager to attract attention than the ryots at the Nandi Cattle Show. This show was exclusively composed of cattle from the Bangalore and Kolar Districts.'

*Poultry.*—The town of Kolar and the villages adjacent to it are noted for turkeys, which are reared in large numbers for export to Bangalore, Bellary, and other places.

## HISTORY

On tracing back the history of the District the usual legends are encountered. These are associated principally with Avani in the Mulbagal taluq, which is identified with Avántika-kshetra, one of the ten chief sacred places in India. Here Valmiki, the author of the Ramayana, it is said, lived, and here Rama remained for some time on his way back to Ayodhya after the conquest of Lanka. Hither, too, Sita retired on being rejected by her husband, and, under the protection of the sage Valmiki, gave birth to her twin sons Kusa and Lava, to whom he became the preceptor.

The hills to the west of Kolar, called the Satasringa parvata or hundred peaked mountains, are also made the scene of the story of Renuka and Parasu Rama, and there the latter is said to have revenged upon Kártaviryárjuna the murder of his father Jamadagni, committed in order to obtain possession of Surabhi, the cow of plenty. The *koláhala* or "shouting" consequent on this feat is represented to have given the town its name, since shortened into Kolar.

At both places the Pandavas are stated to have lived in the course of their wanderings: Kaivára is said to be Ekachakrapura, and Sádali is said to have been founded by Sahadeva, the youngest of the brothers. At Kúdumale the gods are said to have mustered their forces previous to assaulting the mythical city of Tripura.

**Mahavalis.**—From inscriptions it may be gathered that the Mahávali or Bána kings were in possession of the country east of the Pálár river early in the Christian era. Traces of them are found throughout the Mulbagal and Chintamani taluqs, as well as in Bowringpet taluq.

**Gangas.**—In about the second century the Gangas either founded or became masters of Kolar, from which, as long as their dynasty was in power, or for nearly a thousand years, they took the title *Kuvalálapuravares'vara.* The narrative of their migration to this place is given in Vol. I., p. 311. But, as there stated (p. 316), among the Kalinga Ganga inscriptions, one of 1118, from Vizagapatam, contains a very full and circumstantial account connected with Kolar. According to it,

Gángeya, the progenitor of the line, was succeeded by the following eighteen kings :—

| | | |
|---|---|---|
| Virochana | Saur ánga | Jayasena (II) |
| Samvedya | Chitrámbara | Jitavirya |
| Samvedin | Sáradhvaja | Vrishadhvaja |
| Dattasena | Dharma (Dhammeba) | Pragalbha (Pragarbba) |
| Soma | Parikshit | Koláhala |
| Ams'udatta | Jayasena | Virochana (II) |

Koláhala, the last but one of these, it says, "built the city named Koláhala, in the great Gangavádi vishaya." After eighty kings (not named), in succession to Virochana (II), had enjoyed the city of Koláhala, there arose Virasimha, who had five sons,—Kámárnava, Dánárnava, Gunárnava, Márasimha and Vajrahasta. The first of these, giving over his own territory to his paternal uncle (not named), set out with his brothers to Kalinga, where he founded a new Ganga dynasty. As grants have lately been discovered in the names of some of these kings, it may be well to give the list, with the number of years each is said to have ruled (see *Ep. Ind.*, iv., 186).

| | | | | | |
|---|---|---|---|---|---|
| Kámárnava I ... | 36 | Jitánkus'a[1]... ... | 15 | Gundama II ... | 3 |
| Dánárnava... ... | 40 | Kaligalánkus'a ... | 12 | Madhu Kámárnava VI ... ... | 19 |
| Kámárnava II ... | 50 | Gundama I ... | 7 | Vajrahasta V ... (crowned in 1038). | 30 |
| Ranárnava... ... | 5 | Kámárnava IV ... | 3 | Rájarája ... ... | 8 |
| Vajrahasta II ... | 15 | Vinayáditya ... | 3 | Chola Ganga (crowned in 1078). | |
| Kámárnava III ... | 19 | Vajrahasta IV ... | 35 | | |
| Gunárnava ... | 27 | Kámárnava V ... | ½ | | |

Whatever truth there may be in this account, it is undoubted that the Gangas of Mysore came into conflict with the Bánas from the first, and occupied nearly all the District down to the eleventh century.

**Pallavas.**—Their principal rivals in the east, however, were the Pallavas of Kanchi, who in general ruled over the tracts east of a line from about Goribidnur, through Nandi, to Avani and Hunkunda. The Gangaru Thousand was an important province in this region.

**Vaidumbas.**—Of these kings occasional inscriptions are found in Chintamani and Bagepalli taluqs.

**Cholas.**—There is a traditional account of the foundation of Kolar to the following effect. A herdsman named Kola discovered a hidden treasure, which the king Uttama Chola hearing of, sent for him to Kanchi the capital, and being warned in a vision by Renuka in the form of Koláhalamma, erected a temple in her honour, founded the city of Koláhala, and invested Kola with the government. The name

[1] Instead of this and the following name, two grants have Vajrahasta III, 40 (or 44), while Gundama is said to have ruled 3 years, and Kámárnava IV, 35. Vajrahasta V is also given 33 years.

is with equal probability derived from *Kola hala*, Kola's plough, the implement which turned up the treasure. Be this as it may, the hoblis of Yerkalve, Mulbagal, Murgamale, and Betamangala were annexed to the new settlement, in the enjoyment of which Kola and his descendants continued under the Chola dynasty. Of that line Vira Chola, Vikrama Chola, and Raja Narendra Chola are stated to have erected shásanas at Siti betta, Avani, Mulbagal, and other places in the vicinity.

This tradition is evidently based on some confused reminiscence of certain names and historical events. From the records of the period we know that the Cholas subverted the power of the Gangas by the capture of Talakád in about 1004, and speedily possessed themselves of all the south and east of Mysore. The important city of Koláhala, or Kolar, thus became subject to them, together with the whole of the present Kolar District. In accordance with their usual system, they gave the name of Nikarilichola-mandala to the District, and formed it into sub-divisions, of which Jayamkondachola-valanád was towards the south.

At a later period we find a family of Chola-Gangas ruling over the parts around Kolar, of whom, in the thirteenth century, we have the names of Uttama Chola-Ganga, Vikrama Chola-Ganga and others.

**Hoysalas.**—But before this, or in about 1117, the Hoysalas under Vishnuvardhana captured Talakád, and drove out the Cholas from Mysore. KoláIa is specially mentioned among the conquests of this king, and the lower ghat of Nangali is specified as the eastern boundary of his kingdom. On the death of Somesvara, in 1254, a partition of the Hoysala dominions took place between his two sons, and the Kolar District was included in the Tamil provinces, which fell to the share of Rámanátha. In the next reign the kingdom was again united under Ballála III., but the ancestral capital of Dorasamudra or Halebíḍu having been destroyed by the Musalman invaders in 1326, we find him residing, among other places, at Hosavíḍu (the new capital), now Hosur in Goribidnur taluq.

**Vijayanagar.**—The empire of Vijayanagar was founded in the fourteenth century, and Bukka Ráya I. made the same place, called Hosapaṭṭana, his residence for a time, and it may have been then the eastern boundary of the kingdom. Under Deva Ráya it appears that Mulbagal was the principal place in the District, and in the fifteenth century we find two brothers, Lakhana Danáyak and Mádanna Danáyak, as the Heggade Devas or chiefs who were governing there as representatives of the supreme power. But we may now revert to the annals of the principal modern local rulers.

*Timme Gauḍa.*—The history of the Bangalore District has already introduced us to the story of Baire Gauda and the band of refugees of the Morasu Wokkal tribe, who, escaping from Kanchi, settled at Avati in the Devanhalli taluq. On their agreeing to separate, *Timme Gauḍa*, one of the seven, took up his abode at Sugaṭur, near Jangamkote. This was about the year 1418. Another Sugaṭur near Kolar lays claim to be the place, but apparently without foundation.

Soon afterwards Timme Gauḍa repaired to the Vijayanagar court, and having ingratiated himself with the authorities, returned with the title of Náḍ Prabhu, or Lord of the Sugaṭur Náḍ. In course of time he discovered a hidden treasure, which, as it was in a tract claimed by Yerra Ganga and Challava Ganga, two men of the Yerralu tribe[1], he did not disturb, but resorted again to court, where he received the command of a small body of men. While thus employed he had an opportunity of rendering signal service by rescuing some members of the royal family who had fallen into the hands of the Mughals.[2] For this gallant act he was rewarded with the title of *Chikka Ráyal*, and soon after returned with royal permission to appropriate the treasure he had discovered and with extended authority. He accordingly repaired the fort of Kolar, built Hoskote (the new fort), and possessed himself of Mulbagal, Punganur and the adjacent parts, turning out the descendants of Lakhana and Madanna. To Kolar he added the hoblis of Vemgal, Bail Sugaṭur, Kaivara, Buradagunte, and Budikote. At this period some Lingáyit traders, headed by Chikkanna S'etti and Kalasanna S'etti, leaving the Bijapur country on account of troubles there, placed themselves under the protection of *Chikka Ráyal Timme Gauḍa*, who with wise policy appointed the former as Patna S'etti of Kolar and the latter of Hoskote, thus attracting merchants and settlers to these two towns. He further favoured the same sect by erecting Jangamkote for their *jangama* or priest.

*Immaḍi* (or the second) *Chikka Ráyal Timme Gauḍa* succeeded. On his death he divided the territory between his two sons. To *Mummaḍi* (or the third) *Chikka Ráyal Timme Gauḍa* he granted Hoskote, and Kolar to Timme Gauḍa. The latter ruled for five years under the name of *Sugaṭur Timme Gauḍa*, and was succeeded by his son *Timme Gauḍa*, who in turn was followed by his son *Chikka Ráyal Timme Gauḍa*.

**Shahji.**—In the middle of the sixteenth century the District appears

[1] A wandering tribe identical with, or closely related to, the Korachar. They are known in Coorg as Yeravas. For a full account, quoted from Mr. Stokes, see *Nellore Manual* under Yerukalas, p. 154. But this story may be only a reminiscence of Ganga or Chola Ganga rule.

[2] Another account says of the Palegar of Chingleput.

to have been in a disturbed state owing to the incursions of some robber chiefs, until it was subdued by the Bijapur army, and placed under the governorship of *Shahji* in 1639. The latter bestowed the Punganur district upon Chikka Ráyal Timme Gauḍa in place of Kolar, the charge of which he committed to his own son Sambhaji. On the death of whom, his son Soorut Singh managed Kolar, and subsequently it formed part of the territories of Venkoji or Eccoji.

During his government the Mughal army under Khasim Khan conquered this part of the District, which was thenceforward attached to the province of Sira for 70 years, during part of which time Fatte Muhammad, father of Haidār Ali, was Faujdar, with Budikote as his jágir. It next passed into the hands of the Mahrattas, of the Nawab of Kadapa, and then of Basalat Jang, chief of Adoni and brother of the Nizam. Kolar and Hoskote were ceded by the last named in 1761 to Haidār Ali, who regarded Kolar with peculiar interest as being the country of his birthplace and connected with his family. Mulbagal and Kolar were taken for a time by the British in 1768. In 1770 the Mahrattas under Madhu Rao again seized the District, but it was recovered by Haidār. In 1791 it was a second time taken by the British under Lord Cornwallis, but restored at the peace of 1792, since when it has been incorporated with the State of Mysore.

*Malla Baire Gauḍa.*—The history of the north-western part of the District carries us back again to the band of exiles at Avati. Their leader Baire Gauḍa had three sons, the youngest of whom, Malla Baire Gauḍa, we have seen, in connection with the Bangalore District, providing for his eldest brother Sanna Baire Gauḍa by founding Devanhalli, and for the second brother Havali Baire Gauḍa by founding Dod-Ballapur.

Having accomplished these undertakings, *Malla Baire Gauḍa*, about the year 1478, when on a visit to the ancient temple of Varada rajaswami at Kandavara, went out hunting northwards along the tank bank with his son Mare Gauḍa. As they approached Kodi Manchanhalli, the site of the present Chik-Ballapur, they were surprised to see a hare turn upon the hounds. As this indicated heroic virtue in the soil, it was resolved to erect there a fort and petta, for which the consent of the Vijayanagar sovereign was obtained. Chik-Ballapur was accordingly founded, and long remained in the possession of *Mare Gauḍa* and his descendants, who extended the territory by the purchase of Sidlaghatta and strengthened themselves by fortifying Nandidroog, Kalavaradroog, Gudibanda and Itikaldroog. The annals of this house are given elsewhere.

Chik-Ballapur, which was assisted by Murári Rao, the chief of Gutti, was exposed to the rival contests of the Mahrattas and the Mysoreans until taken in 1762 by Haidar Ali, who carried the chief as a captive to Bangalore, and subsequently removed him to Coimbatore. The family were kept prisoners there until released by the British army and reinstated by Lord Cornwallis in 1791, but on peace being made with Tipu Sultan, they were again forced into exile, and the district was included in the territory of Mysore.

## POPULATION

*Number.*—According to the *khâneshumâri* returns for 1853–4, the population at that time was 461,979. The total population as ascertained at the regular census periods since has been as follows :—

| — | Males. | Females. | Total. |
|---|---|---|---|
| 1871 ... | 309,635 | 309,269 | 618,954 |
| 1881 ... | 228,193 | 232,956 | 461,129 |
| 1891 ... | 297,655 | 293,375 | 591,030 |

The diminution after 1871 is of course due to the great famine; and the disproportion of the sexes in 1881 may probably be traced to the same cause. The disparity of the sexes in 1891 no doubt arises from the preponderance of male labour in the gold mines.

*Density.*—There are thus 186·6 persons to a square mile. The taluqs most thickly peopled are Kolar, with 253·6 to the square mile; Bowringpet with 212·1; and Goribidnur with 211·1. Next follow Chik-Ballapur with 206·3, and Malur with 201·4. The lowest is Bagepalli, with only 129·9 to the square mile.

*By Religion.*—Classified according to religious belief the following are the numbers and percentage under each head :—

| Religion. | Above 15. | | Under 15. | | Total. | Per-cent-age. |
|---|---|---|---|---|---|---|
| | Males. | Females. | Males. | Females. | | |
| Hindus .. ... ... | 184,809 | 180,233 | 93,342 | 96,348 | 554,732 | 93·85 |
| Muhammadans ... ... | 10,689 | 8,984 | 6,623 | 6,109 | 32,405 | 5·48 |
| Jains ... ... ... | 326 | 277 | 153 | 140 | 896 | ·15 |
| Christians ... ... ... | 1,201 | 779 | 511 | 505 | 2,996 | ·51 |
| Parsi ... ... ... | 1 | — | — | — | 1 | — |
| Total ... ... | 197,026 | 190,273 | 100,629 | 103,102 | 591,030 | |

*Increase.*—The following table compares the statistics by taluqs according to the *khdneshumdri* accounts of 1853-4 with those obtained in the censuses of 1871, 1881 and 1891:—

| Taluq. | 1853-4. | 1871. | 1881. | 1891. |
|---|---|---|---|---|
| Bagepalli ... ... ... | 61,526 | 66,382 | 50,821 | 58,086 |
| Bowringpet ... ... | 45,460 | 62,662 | 51,288 | 71,042 |
| Chik-Ballapur ... ... | 60,942 | 59,273 | 41,450 | 51,592 |
| Chintamani ... ... | 89,330 | 96,886 | 66,131 | 79,151 |
| Goribidnur ... ... | 26,087 | 76,400 | 58,676 | 71,990 |
| Kolar ... ... ... | 47,264 | 73,721 | 59,048 | 75,834 |
| Malur ... ... ... | 38,845 | 58,971 | 44,545 | 54,180 |
| Mulbagal ... ... ... | 44,686 | 70,606 | 53,389 | 61,327 |
| Sidlaghatta ... ... | 47,839 | 81,872 | 55,786 | 67,828 |
| Total ... ... | 461,979 | 646,773 | 481,134 | 591,030 |

Some of the variations are due to redistribution of taluqs, and to changes in the limits of the District. There was an apparent increase in the whole up to 1871 equivalent to 40 per cent. in eighteen years. But 25 per cent. must be allowed for defective enumeration in the early account. The famine of 1877-8 sent down the total 25·6 per cent. by 1881, but it had risen again 18·5 per cent. by 1891. The net result may be stated at an increase of 2·34 per cent. in thirty-eight years.

*Classes.*—Classified according to sources of livelihood and nationality, the population is composed as follows:—

| | | No. | Per cent. |
|---|---|---|---|
| A. | Agricultural ... ... ... ... | 186,108 ... | 31·48 |
| B. | Professional ... ... ... ... | 31,939 ... | 5·40 |
| C. | Commercial ... ... ... ... | 55,079 ... | 9·32 |
| D. | Artisan and Village Menial ... ... | 208,998 ... | 35·36 |
| E. | Vagrant minor Artisans and Performers | 73,173 ... | 12·38 |
| | Races and Nationalities... ... ... | 35,402 ... | 5·98 |
| | Others, not stated ... ... ... | 331 ... | ·05 |

The castes or classes which number over 10,000 are the following, in order of strength. These account for 487,713, or 82·51 per cent. of the population:—

| | | | | | |
|---|---|---|---|---|---|
| Wokkaliga | ... 163,160 | Banajiga | ... 36,296 | Bráhmana | ... 23,325 |
| Holeya | ... 57,665 | Kuruba | ... 35,304 | Wodda ... | ... 23,090 |
| Beda ... | ... 47,329 | Musalmans | ... 31,759 | Tigala ... | ... 10,156 |
| Mádiga | ... 39,607 | | | | |

The most numerous classes of Wokkaligas are the Morasu (84,263), and Reddi (40,267). Of the Banajigas the Telugu Banajigas (26,222) predominate. Of Musalmans, the Shekhs number 8,831, Saiyids 6,541, and Pathans 4,937. The chief Brahman seats are Mulikináḍ (2,986), Baḍaganáḍ (2,771), Des'astha (2,503), and Ulchakamme (2,030).

**Stock.**—The *agricultural stock* in 1893 included 29,733 carts and 81,673 ploughs; the *manufacturing stock* consisted of 4,890 looms—namely, 2,653 for cloths, 1,732 for cumblies, 13 for girdles, and 21 for goni, besides 471 proprietary looms. The number of oil-mills was 456, of which 365 are of stone and 91 wooden.

A number of iron sugar-cane mills have also been introduced, some of them manufactured at the iron works in Chik-Ballapur.

**Dwellings.**—Houses of the better sort number 682, occupied by 6,233 tenants, and those of the inferior sort 123,964, with 584,797 inhabitants. Houses of the first class are most numerous in the Chik-Ballapur, Sidlaghatta and Bowringpet taluqs, and after these in the Kolar and Chintamani taluqs.

**Towns and Villages.**—The towns and villages, according to population, may be classified as follows :—

| | No. | Pop. | | No. | Pop. |
|---|---|---|---|---|---|
| Over 10,000 ... | 2 | 22,771 | 1,000 and under 2,000 | 29 | 39,969 |
| 5,000 and under 10,000 ... | 3 | 18,871 | 500 ,, 1,000 | 126 | 86,672 |
| 3,000 ,, 5,000 ... | 2 | 7,024 | 200 ,, 500 | 722 | 212,312 |
| 2,000 ,, 3,000 ... | 3 | 7,928 | Under 200 | 1,958 | 195,483 |

Those with a population exceeding 5,000 are :

| | | | |
|---|---|---|---|
| Kolar ... ... ... | 12,551 | Sidlaghatta ... ... | 6,572 |
| Chik-Ballapur ... ... | 10,623 | Mulbagal... ... ... | 5,026 |

The Kolar gold-fields, reckoned as the fifth, do not form a regularly constituted town.

The number of municipal towns is 11, all taluq or sub-taluq head-quarters. There are altogether 2,865 villages and 785 hamlets populated, with 608 villages depopulated.

**Great Festivals.**—The following religious festivals are the most numerously attended in the District :—

At *Nandi*, Chik-Ballapur taluq, on the occasion of the *Nandis'vara rathotsava*, held for fifteen days from Magha bahula 14th, which attracts 20,000 people.

At *Avani*, Mulbagal taluq, where 10,000 people attend the festival of *Ramalinga*, lasting for fifteen days from the same date.

At *Vánarási*, Kolar taluq, 5,000 people assemble at the festival of *Iralappa*, held for fifteen days in April.

At *Srinivasa-samudra*, or Melahalli, Bowringpet taluq, 2,coo people keep the festival of *Gangamma* for fifteen days from full moon in Vaishakha.

Near the hill of *Ullerhalli*, Malur taluq, 5,000 people collect at the *Bhúpatamma parishe*, held for eight days from new moon in Phalguna.

The *Yeldur játre*, Mulbagal taluq, lasts eight days from full moon in Chaitra, and attracts 5,000 people.

At *Ronakunte*, Chintamani taluq, 20,000 people come to the *Venkatramana-swami rathotsava*, held for fifteen days from full moon in Ashádha.

At *Tirupati*, Malur taluq, 5,000 people assemble at the Venkataramana car-festival, which lasts for five days in April, when 6,000 cattle are brought for sale.

At *Melur*, in Sidlaghatta taluq, the Gangádevi parishe is held for ten days from Chaitra bahula 5th, when 6,000 people collect and 10,000 bullocks are brought for sale.

At *Bowringpet*, 5,000 people attend the Kodanda-Ramasvami car-festival, held for ten days in Vaisakha, when 5,000 cattle are brought for sale.

At *Vokkaleri*, the Markandes'vara car-festival, held for eight days from new moon in Magha, attracts 2,000 people, who bring 1,600 bullocks for sale.

**Fairs.**—The following is a list of the largest weekly fairs :—

| Place. | Taluka. | Day. | No. of Visitors. |
|---|---|---|---|
| Chintamani ... ... | Chintamani ... ... | Sunday ... | 3,000 |
| Uriga ... ... ... | Bowringpet ... ... | " | 1,000 |
| Sidlaghatta ... ... | Sidlaghatta ... ... | Monday ... | 2,000 |
| Peresandra ... ... | Chik-Ballapur... ... | " | 2,000 |
| Mulbagal ... ... | Mulbagal ... ... | Tuesday ... | 5,000 |
| Tayalur ... ... ... | " ... ... | Wednesday | 1,000 |
| Kolar ... ... ... | Kolar ... ... ... | Thursday... | 2,000 |
| Malur ... ... ... | Malur ... ... .. | " | 1,000 |
| Bowringpet ... ... | Bowringpet ... ... | Friday ... | 2,000 |
| Manchenhall ... ... | Goribidnur ... ... | " | 1,000 |
| Yeldur ... ... ... | Mulbagal ... ... | " | 1,000 |
| Chik-Ballapur ... ... | Chik-Ballapur ... | Saturday ... | 2,000 |
| Tirupati ... ... ... | Malur ... ... ... | " | 1,500 |

**Vital Statistics.**—The following are particulars of the number of births and deaths registered in the District :—

| — | Births. | | | Deaths. | | |
|---|---|---|---|---|---|---|
| | M. | F. | Total. | M. | F. | Total. |
| 1891 ... | 5,817 | 5,449 | 11,266 | 4,475 | 4,146 | 8,621 |
| 1892-3 ... | 5,006 | 5,037 | 10,043 | 4,187 | 4,243 | 8,430 |
| 1893-4 ... | 5,577 | 5,426 | 11,003 | 3,621 | 3,372 | 6,993 |

The most prevalent causes of mortality are indicated in the following statement :—

| — | 1891. | 1892-3. | 1893-4. |
|---|---|---|---|
| Cholera ... ... ... | 564 | 137 | 136 |
| Smallpox ... ... | 402 | 527 | 267 |
| Fevers ... ... ... | 4,968 | 5,417 | 4,216 |
| Bowel Complaints ... | 277 | 182 | 197 |

## REVENUE

The revenue of the District for ten years is exhibited in the following table :—

| Items. | 1883-4. | 1884-5. | 1885-6. | 1886-7. | 1887-8. |
|---|---|---|---|---|---|
| Land Revenue ... ... | 9,70,020 | 9,62,044 | 1,01,534 | 10,25,591 | 10,43,127 |
| Forests ... ... ... | 3,344 | 3,805 | 3,704 | 5,547 | 7,746 |
| Abkari ... ... ... | 32,833 | 49,105 | 49,231 | 50,715 | 57,833 |
| Mohatarfa ... ... | 30,670 | 32,420 | 34,926 | 37,442 | 40,033 |
| Sayar ... ... ... | 1,234 | 1,204 | 919 | 473 | 410 |
| Salt pans ... ... ... | 984 | 2,041 | 941 | 1,733 | 2,667 |
| Stamps ... ... ... | 37,159 | 39,878 | 45,780 | 42,463 | 44,886 |
| Post Office ... ... | 4,850 | 5,077 | 5,433 | 5,039 | 5,738 |
| Law and Justice ... ... | 6,256 | 5,798 | 7,185 | 6,595 | 7,276 |
| Police ... ... ... | 63 | 27 | 46 | 206 | 266 |
| Public Works ... ... | 2,047 | 2,817 | 3,966 | 4,085 | 6,679 |
| Miscellaneous ... ... | 5,784 | 8,266 | 19,033 | 22,513 | 18,475 |
| Total Rs. ... | 10,95,244 | 11,12,482 | 11,72,698 | 12,02,402 | 12,35,136 |

| Items. | 1888-9. | 1889-90. | 1890-1. | 1891-2. | 1892-3. |
|---|---|---|---|---|---|
| Land Revenue ... ... | 10,22,672 | 10,80,601 | 11,01,782 | 10,82,747 | 11,90,394 |
| Forests ... ... ... | 12,206 | 21,366 | 29,980 | 27,057 | 25,158 |
| Abkari ... ... ... | 58,003 | 58,449 | 80,327 | 1,87,366 | 4,65,598 |
| Mohatarfa ... ... | 45,989 | 47,979 | 45,806 | 45,699 | 45,384 |
| Sayar ... ... ... | 274 | 129 | 36 | 703 | 2,140 |
| Salt pans ... ... ... | 4,557 | 5,737 | 4,858 | 764 | 5,813 |
| Stamps ... ... ... | 45,156 | 57,443 | 51,762 | 62,554 | 56,826 |
| Post Office ... .. | 6,364 | 63 | 9 | 74 | — |
| Law and Justice ... ... | 8,471 | 11,929 | 13,286 | 16,866 | 13,398 |
| Police ... ... ... | 823 | 533 | 175 | 408 | 344 |
| Public Works ... ... | 2,398 | 4,023 | 4,903 | 2,788 | 925 |
| Miscellaneous ... ... | 13,333 | 16,640 | 13,052 | 14,495 | 14,787 |
| Total Rs. ... | 12,20,246 | 12,95,892 | 13,45,976 | 14,41,521 | 18,20,767 |

## TRADE

**Manufactures.**—The principal manufacture of the District arises out of the extensive cultivation of sugar-cane, and consists of jaggory, molasses, and sugar.

Cotton cloths, and coarse woollen blankets are made in various parts, as well as the ordinary pottery of the country.

The rearing of silkworms and production of raw silk, an industry extensively pursued by the Muhammadans, is successfully carried on in the Kolar, Sidlaghatta and Chik-Ballapur taluqs.

**Exports.**—The following list of exports will serve to illustrate the articles produced in the District :—

| Articles. | | Quantity. | Average Value. |
|---|---|---|---|
| Cotton cloths ... ... ... | No. | 13,460 | Rs. 26,960 |
| Blankets ... ... ... | ,, | 9,000 | 13,500 |
| Honge seed ... ... ... | Tons | 214 | 13,500 |
| Sugar ... ... ... ... | ,, | 964 | 3,15,000 |
| Sugar-candy ... ... ... | ,, | 2 | 1,050 |
| Jaggory ... ... ... ... | ,, | 535 | 81,250 |
| Molasses ... ... ... | ,, | 850 | 38,950 |
| Bangles ... ... ... ... | ,, | 32 | 6,000 |
| Butter and ghee ... ... | ,, | 2 | 1,800 |
| Sealing wax ... ... ... | ,, | 1 | 500 |

**Imports.**—The imports are thus returned :—

| Articles. | | Quantity. | Average Value. |
|---|---|---|---|
| Cotton cloths ... ... ... | No. | 12,800 | Rs. 46,510 |
| ,, thread ... .. ... | Tons | 42 | 40,000 |
| Silk cloths ... ... ... | No. | 1,000 | 26,500 |
| Blankets ... ... ... | ,, | 7,000 | 21,000 |
| Carpets ... ... ... ... | ,, | 4,500 | 9,000 |
| Castor-oil ... ... ... | Tons | 9 | 45,000 |
| Gingelli oil ... ... ... | ,, | 7 | 4,200 |
| Jaggory ... ... ... ... | ,, | 117 | 17,625 |
| Cooking utensils ... ... | No. | 4,500 | 45,000 |
| Bangles ... ... ... ... | Tons | 200 | 46,000 |
| Baskets ... ... ... ... | No. | 60,100 | 10,012 |
| Brass ... ... ... ... | Tons | 42 | 44,000 |
| Butter and ghee ... ... | ,, | 9 | 9,900 |
| Coir rope ... ... ... | No. | 65,000 | 8,250 |
| Goni ... ... ... ... | ,, | 5,000 | 1,100 |
| Fuller's earth ... ... ... | Tons | 5 | 450 |
| Indigo ... ... ... ... | ,, | 2 | 6,600 |
| Mats ... ... ... ... | No. | 42,000 | 5,800 |
| Paper ... ... ... | Reams | 109,000 | 32,700 |
| Sea-salt .. ... ... ... | Tons | 2,000 | 313,600 |
| Stone pots ... ... ... | No. | 18,000 | 1,600 |

## COMMUNICATIONS

**Railways.**—The Bangalore Branch Railway runs through the south of the District. Ascending the Ghats near Kuppam in a north-west direction, it enters the Bowringpet taluq, and keeps that course to the Junction at Bowringpet, eleven miles from Kolar. Thence it continues due west through Málur taluq. The Gold Fields Railway runs for ten miles east and south from the Bowringpet Junction to the Mysore mine. The Bangalore-Guntakal Railway passes through the Goribidnur taluq from south to north.

**Roads.**—The length of *Provincial roads* is 187 miles, maintained at an annual cost of Rs. 25,860. Of *District roads* there are 345 miles, costing for upkeep Rs. 20,465 a year. The particulars regarding each class are given below :—

*Provincial Roads.*

| | Miles. | Cost. |
|---|---|---|
| Madras-Cannanore road ... ... ... | 43 | 5,160 |
| Bangalore-Kadapa road ... ... ... ... | 40 | 4,000 |
| Kadapa road railway feeder ... ... ... | 33 | 4,950 |
| Bangalore-Bellary road ... ... ... ... | 34 | 3,400 |
| Bangalore-Hindupur road ... ... ... | 20 | 2,400 |
| Kolar Gold Mines railway feeder ... ... | 17 | 5,950 |
| | Ms. 187 | Rs. 25,860 |

*District Roads.*

| | Miles. | Cost. |
|---|---|---|
| Kolar-Málur-Hosur railway feeder ... ... | 26 | 3,900 |
| Mulbagal-Goribidnur road ... ... ... | 75 | 3,750 |
| Kolar-Sompur road ... ... ... ... | 36 | 1,800 |
| Chintamani-Bagepalli road ... ... ... | 35 | 1,750 |
| Mulbagal railway feeder ... ... ... | 19 | 1,520 |
| Kolar-Venkatagirikote road ... ... ... | 25 | 1,250 |
| Peresandra-Dibburhalli road ... ... ... | 25 | 1,250 |
| Yellampalli-Chelur road ... ... ... | 20 | 1,000 |
| Málur-Masti railway feeder ... ... ... | 12 | 600 |
| Hoskote-Sidlaghatta road ... ... ... | 11 | 550 |
| Málur-Narsapur railway feeder ... ... ... | 10 | 500 |
| Bangalore-Nandidroog road ... ... ... | 9 | 450 |
| Budikote railway feeder ... ... ... ... | 8 | 400 |
| Nandi-Heggadihalli road ... ... ... | 7 | 350 |
| Gudibanda-Chenrayanhalli loop line ... ... | 5 | 300 |
| Dod Ballapur-Maddagiri road ... ... ... | 10 | 300 |
| Chik Ballapur-Nandidroog road ... ... | 4 | 200 |
| Chinnasandra-Chintamani road ... ... | 3 | 150 |
| Hoskote-Málur railway feeder ... ... ... | 4 | 120 |
| Venkatapur-Devanhalli road ... ... ... | ½ | 25 |
| | Ms. 344½ | Rs. 20,465 |

**Accommodation for Travellers.**—*Dak Bungalows* or rest-houses for officials and travellers are situated at the stations named in the accompanying list, where the class is shown to which each belongs. Brahman kitchens are attached to most of them.

*First Class.*—Bowringpet, Urigam.

*Second Class.*—Kolar, Chik-Ballapur, Málur, Nandi.

*Third Class.*—Bagepalli, Chintamani, Dibburhalli, Goribidnur, Jangamkote, Motumakalpalli, Mulbagal, Narsapur, Peresandra, Ráyalpád, Srinivaspur, Talagavara, Vémgal.

*Chatrams* for the accommodation of native travellers are kept up by Government at Kolar, Bowringpet, Mulbagal, and Málur.

# GAZETTEER

**Ambajidurga.**—A detached hill in the Chintamani taluq, three miles west-south-west of Chintamani. The summit, which is 4,399 feet above the level of the sea, was fortified by Tipu Sultan, but taken by the British in 1791. Until 1873 the surrounding hoblis formed a taluq called after this hill, with head-quarters at Chintamani.

**Avani.**—A village and hill in the Mulbagal taluq, eight miles south-west of the kasba; head-quarters of the hobli of the same name. Population, 723.

The region is said to be the *Avántika-kshetra*, one of the ten places of greatest sanctity in India. The hill is related to have been the residence of the poet Valmiki, author of the Ramayana, and thence to have been called *Válmiki-parvata*. Rama is said to have encamped here for some time on his return from the expedition against Lanka or Ceylon, and hither Sita, when subsequently banished by her husband, is stated to have come and given birth to her twin sons, finding in Valmiki a protector for herself and a preceptor for her children. It is mentioned in a Bána inscription, the professed date of which is 339, and in a later inscription is called the Gayá of the south.

There is a considerable group of temples dedicated to Rama, Lakshmana, Bharata, and Satrughna, as well as to Vali and Sugriva. But earlier than these was a temple erected in the ninth century, to the memory of her husband, by the Kadamba princess who was married to the Nolamba king Bira Mahendra (*see* Vol. I., p. 307). A memorial to a certain Tribhuvana-karttar Deva, who died in 961, states that he governed A'vani for forty years, during which he built fifty temples, and constructed several tanks. Inscriptions of the Pallavas, the Cholas, the Hoysalas and the Vijayanagar kings found there show the importance attached to the place for several centuries.

The temples were repaired in the fourteenth century by Ilavanji Raya and Vasudeva Raya, who came, together with a merchant named Navakoti[1] Narayan Shetti, from Kumbhakona. A guru of the Smarta sect resides here. To the great annual festival, held for ten days from Magha bahula 14th, in honour of Ramalinges'vara (the linga set up by Rama), 10,000 people resort and 20,000 bullocks are brought for sale.

**Bagepalli.**—A taluq in the north, formerly till 1882 called Gumnáyakanpálya. Area 447 square miles. Head-quarters at Bágepalli.

[1] The title *Nava-koti*, or nine crores, indicates a millionaire possessed of wealth to that amount, reckoned in pagodas.

Includes the Guḍibanḍa sub-taluq, and contains the following hoblis, villages and population :—

| No. | Hoblis. | Villages. | Hamlets. | Villages Classified. | | | | Population. |
|---|---|---|---|---|---|---|---|---|
| | | | | Government. | Sarvamánya. | Jodi. | Kayamgutta. | |
| 1 | Bágepaḷḷi ... ... | 45 | 29 | 38 | — | 5 | 2 | 8,371 |
| 2 | Billúr ... ... | 41 | 42 | 39 | — | 2 | — | 7,422 |
| 3 | Chéḷúr ... .. | 36 | 25 | 34 | — | 1 | 1 | 6,610 |
| 4 | Guḍibanḍa ... | 71 | 7 | 66 | — | 3 | 2 | 7,097 |
| 5 | Gúḷúr ... ... | 30 | 18 | 27 | — | 2 | 1 | 6,548 |
| 6 | Miṭṭemari ... ... | 38 | 33 | 33 | — | 5 | — | 6,553 |
| 7 | Pálya ... ... | 38 | 45 | 33 | — | 4 | 1 | 8,423 |
| 8 | Sóménhaḷḷi ... | 75 | 19 | 72 | — | 1 | 2 | 7,062 |
| | Total ... | 374 | 218 | 342 | — | 23 | 9 | 58,086 |

*Principal places, with population*:—Guḍibanḍa, 1,957; Bágepalli, 1,389; Chákavél, 1,296; Miṭṭemari, 1,019; Gúlúr, 971.

A rugged and hilly taluq, the centre of which is crossed from north to south by the Dongala-konda hills. The south-eastern portion is watered by the Pápaghni, which receives a considerable stream named the Vandaman, rising near Pátpálya. On the frontier, near Chelur, the Pápaghni forms a very large tank, called the Vyása-samudra, after Vyásaráya-svámi, a guru of the Mádhva Brahmans, by whom it is said to have been constructed. Through the western side of the taluq flows the Chitravati, which near Bágepalli is dammed by anicuts, and supplies some small channels for irrigation. In the open country east and west of the hills there are many good tanks, the number in the taluq altogether being 481. The most productive part is probably the north-eastern. But much of the surface of the country is broken and irregular and unfit for cultivation. The neighbourhood of the hills, except where there are fruitful valleys, is covered with low jungle. Iron ore is found and manufactured in great quantities. The taluq produces a good breed of sheep.

The revenue settlement was introduced in 1885, except in the Guḍibanḍa and Sómenhalli hoblis, which had been settled in 1876. The unculturable area in the former was 133,335 acres, or 208⅓ square miles.

The total revenue demand for 1891–2 (fifteen months) was Rs. 1,34,127, and for 1892–3 it was Rs. 1,64,494. The amounts under Land revenue were Rs. 1,02,765 and Rs. 1,14,121 respectively.

The average annual rainfall at Bágepalli for twenty-five years (1870–94), has been as follows:—

| Jan. | Feb. | Mar. | Apr. | May | June | July | Aug. | Sept. | Oct. | Nov. | Dec. | ... | Year. |
|---|---|---|---|---|---|---|---|---|---|---|---|---|---|
| — | — | 0·20 | 0·38 | 1·60 | 1·88 | 1·84 | 2·83 | 2·93 | 4·20 | 2·24 | 0·34 | ... | 18·44 |

The old road from Bangalore to Bellary runs through the west of the taluq from south to north. From Bágepalli there are roads east to Chelur and south-east to Chintamani. From the high road there is also a branch west to Guḍibanḍa and to the railway at Goribidnur.

**Bagepalli or Bagenhalli.**—A small frontier town on the right bank of the Chitravati, about sixty miles north-west of Kolar, on the old Bangalore-Bellary road. Head-quarters of the Bágepalli taluq and a municipality.

| Population in 1891. | Males. | Females. | Total. |
|---|---|---|---|
| Hindus ... ... ... ... ... ... ... | 508 | 543 | 1,051 |
| Muhammadans ... ... ... ... ... | 98 | 88 | 186 |
| Total ... ... | 606 | 631 | 1,237 |

There were formerly, it is said, three towns near this spot, namely, Gaḍadampatna, at Devargudipalli, two miles to the east; Kárkúr, at the village of that name, two miles to the south-east; and Kunṭlúr, on the banks of the Chitravati, to the west. Inscriptions show that the first of these was in existence in the fourteenth century.

The place now derives all its importance from being the taluq head-quarters. An attempt was made some years ago to remove it to the left bank of the river for the sake of communication with the high road, but without success, as the people could not be induced to move and rebuild their houses on the new site.

| Municipal Funds. | 1892–3. | 1893–4. | 1894–5. | 1895–6. |
|---|---|---|---|---|
| Income ... ... ... ... ... | 321 | 305 | 398 | 697 |
| Expenditure... ... ... ... ... | 442 | 451 | 529 | 973 |

**Betamangala.**—An old town on the right bank of the Palar, which till 1864 gave its name to and was the head-quarters of what is now the Bowringpet taluq. It is eighteen miles south-east of Kolar, with which it is connected by road. A road from Bowringpet to Mulbagal also passes through it. Population 1,160.

A fair held on Friday is attended by 1,000 people.

The name is a contraction of Vijayáditya-mangala, derived from the

Bána king Vijayáditya, probably its founder. Two old inscribed stones worshipped in a temple under the name of Gangamma, are of the dates 904 and 944, the Nolamba period. The large tank was repaired in the time of the Nolamba king Iriva Nolamba, about 950. It again breached and was restored in 1095 by Chokkimaya, general of the Hoysala prince Vishnuvardhana, while encamped at Nangali, after a victorious expedition to the countries in the east below the Ghats.

The town lost its importance on the opening in 1864 of the railway, which diverted the former large passenger traffic, and the removal, owing to increasing unhealthiness, of the taluq head-quarters to the newly-formed town of Bowringpet.

**Bowringpet.**—A taluq in the south-east, formerly called Betamangala. Area 335 square miles. Head-quarters at Bowringpet. Contains the following hoblis, villages and population :—

| No. | Hoblis. | Villages. | Hamlets. | Villages Classified. | | | | Population. |
|---|---|---|---|---|---|---|---|---|
| | | | | Government. | Sarvamánya. | Jodi. | Kayamgutta. | |
| 1 | Bétamangala ... | 77 | 2 | 64 | — | 12 | 1 | 8,666 |
| 2 | Bowringpet ... | 86 | 5 | 70 | 2 | 12 | 2 | 15,463 |
| 3 | Búdikóte ... ... | 71 | 18 | 53 | 1 | 16 | 1 | 8,531 |
| 4 | Dásarahosahalli ... | 62 | 10 | 51 | 1 | 9 | 1 | 12,633 |
| 5 | Kámasandra ... | 50 | 11 | 41 | — | 9 | — | 6,584 |
| 6 | Kyásamballi ... | 57 | 21 | 41 | 3 | 11 | 2 | 7,383 |
| 7 | Rámaságara ... | 41 | 5 | 33 | 2 | 5 | 1 | 4,658 |
| | (Gold Mines) ... | — | — | — | — | — | — | 7,124 |
| | Total ... | 444 | 72 | 353 | 9 | 74 | 8 | 71,042 |

*Principal places, with population* :—Gold Mines, 7,124; Bowringpet, 2,613; Uriga, 1,540; Búdikóṭe, 1,339; Bétamangala, 1,160.

The river Palar runs through the taluq from north-west to south-east, and forms the large Bétamangala and Ramasagar tanks. The west of the taluq is crossed from north to south by the auriferous tract, generally uncultivated and marked by low flat hills, in which have now been formed the Kolar Gold mines. The southern borders of the taluq abut upon the Eastern Ghats, and are rugged and jungly.

The revenue settlement was introduced in 1890.

The total revenue demand for 1891-2 (fifteen months) was Rs. 2,03,390, and for 1892-3 it was Rs. 3,68,709. The amounts under Land revenue were Rs. 1,16,840 and Rs. 1,20,231 respectively.

The average annual rainfall for twenty-five years (1870-94) at

Bowringpet, and for two years (1893–4) at the other stations was as follows:—

| | Jan. | Feb. | Mar. | Apr. | May | June | July | Aug. | Sept. | Oct. | Nov. | Dec. | Year. |
|---|---|---|---|---|---|---|---|---|---|---|---|---|---|
| Bowringpet ... | 0·02 | 0·01 | 0·55 | 1·19 | 2·61 | 2·41 | 2·06 | 4·22 | 4·02 | 6·97 | 3·88 | 0·87 | ... 28·81 |
| Betamangala ... | — | 0·25 | — | 0·83 | 2·38 | 3·06 | 5·33 | 2·25 | 4·31 | 6·10 | 2·45 | — | ... 26·96 |
| Gold Mines ... | — | — | — | 0·40 | 4·12 | 1·97 | 3·81 | 1·80 | 1·50 | 3·09 | 1·70 | — | ... 18·39 |

The Madras Branch Railway from Bangalore to Jalarpet enters the taluq in the west and turns south at Bowringpet, which is the junction for the Gold Fields Railway. There are stations at Bowringpet and Kamasandra in the former, and at four places—Balaghat, Urigam, Champion Reef, and Mysore Mine—on the latter. From Bowringpet there are roads north to Kolar, east to Bétamangala, south-west to Búdikóṭe, and a loop road east south and west through the gold mines to Kamasandra. There is also a road fom Bétamangala to Kolar.

**Bowringpet.**—A new town, situated at the former Kolar Road, now Bowringpet station of the Bangalore Branch Railway, to which it owes its origin. It includes the previously existing villages of Maramatlu and Hosingere, and was established in 1864 on the opening of the railway, being named after Mr. Bowring, then Chief Commissioner. It lies eleven miles south of Kolar, with which it is connected by a road. Head-quarters of the Bowringpet taluq, and a municipality.

| Population in 1891. | Males. | Females. | Total. |
|---|---|---|---|
| Hindus ... ... ... ... ... ... ... | 978 | 911 | 1,889 |
| Muhammadans... ... ... ... ... ... | 404 | 295 | 699 |
| Christians ... ... ... ... ... ... | 14 | 11 | 25 |
| Total ... ... | 1,396 | 1,217 | 2,613 |

A fair held on Friday is attended by 2,000 people and 700 bullocks. Owing to its proximity to the gold-fields, and its being the junction for the Gold Fields Railway, it has become one of the most important places in the District.

| Municipal Funds. | 1892–3. | 1893–4. | 1894–5. | 1895–6. |
|---|---|---|---|---|
| Income ... ... ... ... ... | 2,136 | 1,888 | 1,503 | 2,486 |
| Expenditure ... ... ... .. | 2,508 | 2,932 | 2,282 | 3,925 |

**Brahma-giri** or **Yarg-konda.**—A hill of the Nandidroog range, rising to 4,657 feet above sea-level. It stands to the south-west of Nandidroog, being connected with it by a saddle. The trees on the hill form part of the reserved plantations of the Forest Department.

**Budikote.**—A large village in the Bowringpet taluq, eight miles south-west of the kasba, situated between the two branches of the Markanda river near their point of junction. Head-quarters of the Búdikóṭe hobli. Population 1,339.

A small fair held on Monday is visited by 600 people. *Búdi-kóṭe*, fort of ashes, is said to derive its name from the immense holocausts performed there at some remote period. It was the birth-place of Haidar Ali, and formed the jágir of his father Fatte Muhammad on his receiving the appointment of Faujdar of Kolar under the Subadar of Sira.

**Chennakesava-betta or Channarayan-betta.** — One of the Nandidroog hills and the reputed source of both Northern and Southern Pinákini or Pennar. Height above the sea 4,762 feet. It is five miles south-west of Chik-Ballapur and contiguous to Nandidroog on the north-west. The forest on it is one of those reserved by the State. At one part on the top is a large cave connected with a temple. The hill was also at one time called Baynes' hill, after an officer who built a small bungalow there, and died in 1807.[1]

**Chik-Ballapur.**—A Sub-Division, formed in November 1891, comprising the taluqs of Chik-Ballapur, Bágepalli and Goribidnur. Head-quarters at Chik-Ballapur.

**Chik-Ballapur.**—A taluq in the west. Area 250 square miles. Head-quarters at Chik-Ballapur.

Contains the following hoblis, villages and population :—

| No. | Hoblis. | Villages. | Hamlets. | Villages Classified. | | | | Population. |
|---|---|---|---|---|---|---|---|---|
| | | | | Government. | Sarvamánya. | Jodi. | Kayamgutta. | |
| 1 | Chik-Ballápur ... | 72 | 11 | 49 | 2 | 17 | 4 | 23,925 |
| 2 | Mandikal ... ... | 57 | 15 | 47 | 1 | 6 | 3 | 3,960 |
| 3 | Nandi ... ... | 57 | 16 | 40 | — | 15 | 2 | 10,526 |
| 4 | Perésandra ... ... | 20 | 35 | 18 | — | 1 | 1 | 4,323 |
| 5 | Púrnaságara ... ... | 66 | 27 | 53 | — | 11 | 2 | 8,858 |
| | Total ... | 272 | 104 | 207 | 3 | 50 | 12 | 51,592 |

*Principal places, with population*:—Chik-Ballapur, 10,623; Nandi, 997.

The taluq, composed as it is of a lofty range of mountains, with rivers rising on either side, besides detached clusters of hills, presents a

[1] Welsh says of him that he was conversant with all the country languages, and of a most indefatigable nature. No man knew better how to rule the Brinjaris, or itinerant grain dealers, which enabled him to make most surprising marches, and thus ensure regular supplies to the army of General Wellesley, who made him Town Major of Seringapatam.

great variety of soil and aspect. The Nandidroog range runs north and south through the western side, the hills of Dibbagiri, Brahmagiri or Vargkonda, Channakesava-betta, Hariharesvara-betta, and Kalavara-durga being included in the taluq, besides the lofty peak of Nandidroog itself. The valley between this mountain and Brahmagiri encloses the principal forest in the District, in a part of which coffee is cultivated. Of the passes through the chain, the Manchenhalli ghat, through which a road connects Chik-Ballapur and Goribidnur, is the chief. A road to Dod-Ballapur runs through a pass called the Basavan kanive to the north of Nandidroog, but a level road from Nandi has been carried round the base of the hills to meet the other beyond.

Around this spot and within a few miles of Chik-Ballapur the S. Pinákini rises on the east of the range, flows through the tanks of the town, and bends southwards to Jangamkote. The Chitravati rises in the north-east and continues that direction past Perésandra. The N. Pinákini rises on the west and flows north-west into Goribidnur. The Arkavati, rising near the same spot, takes a south-west course to Dod-Ballapur.

The soil on the table-land about Chik-Ballapur and Nandi, and to the west of the range, is of great fertility and extremely favourable for the cultivation of the sugar-cane. Much of the Perésandra hobli, on the other hand, is unfavourable to husbandry, abounding with deep ravines and broken ground, through which the streams from the mountains and high lands westward fall into the low country about Sadali.

Besides the fortifications of Nandidroog there are several buildings in the taluq deserving of mention, among others the temple of Umá-mahesvara at Nandi, decorated with some delicate stone carving, and of Rangaswami at the *ranga sthala* 2 miles west of Chik-Ballapur.

The revenue settlement was introduced in 1884. The unculturable area is 82,062 acres, or 128¼ square miles, and the area of the Nandi State forest is 2,749 acres, or nearly 4¼ square miles. The total revenue demand for 1891–2 (15 months) was Rs. 1,43,567, and for 1892–3 it was Rs. 1,78,257. The amounts under Land revenue were Rs. 79,316 and Rs. 83,622 respectively.

The average rainfall for 25 years (1870–94) has been as follows at Chik-Ballapur:—

| Jan. | Feb. | Mar. | Apl. | May | June | July | Aug. | Sept. | Oct. | Nov. | Dec. | Year. |
|---|---|---|---|---|---|---|---|---|---|---|---|---|
| 0·04 | 0·08 | 0·53 | 0·87 | 3·29 | 2·97 | 3·69 | 4·96 | 5·77 | 6·05 | 2·74 | 0·51— | 31·50 |

The old Bangalore-Bellary road crosses the taluq from south to north through Chik-Ballapur, whence there are roads east to Sidlaghatta, west to Goribidnur, and south-west to Nandi and Dod-Ballapur. A road from Kolar to Dod-Ballapur passes through Nandi. A short branch connects the south-eastern foot of Nandidroog with the high road near Devanhalli. A line of rail is proposed connecting Chik-Ballapur with the railway at Dod-Ballapur.

**Chik-Ballapur.**—A large town 36 miles north-west of Kolar, on the old Bangalore-Bellary road. Head-quarters of the Sub-Division and of the taluq bearing the same name, and a municipality.

| Population in 1891. | Males. | Females. | Total. |
|---|---|---|---|
| Hindus ... ... ... ... ... | 4,580 | 4,865 | 9,445 |
| Muhammadans ... ... ... ... | 548 | 504 | 1,052 |
| Christians ... ... ... ... ... | 61 | 64 | 125 |
| Parsi ... ... ... ... ... ... | 1 | — | 1 |
| Total ... ... | 5,190 | 5,433 | 10,623 |

Chikka Ballápura, or Little Ballápur, is so called to distinguish it from Doḍḍa-Ballápura. In Hindustani it is called Chóṭa Ballápúr, and in Telugu, Chinna Ballápuram. It was founded about 1479 by *Malla Baire Gauḍa*, youngest son of Baire Gauda, the leader of the refugees who settled at Avati. The village which originally occupied the site was called Kodi Manchanahalli, in the vicinity of which Malla Baire Gauda, while hunting, observed a hare turn upon the hounds, and was led by this indication of *ganḍu bhúmi*, or male soil, to make proposals for the erection of a fort and petta there to Baiche Gauda and Baire Gauda, the joint patels. But permission of the Vijayanagar sovereign being necessary, Mari Gauda, the chief's son, was despatched thither and returned with a favourable reply. The moment determined on by the Brahmans as the most lucky for laying the foundation of the fort was to be proclaimed when Malla Baire Gauda and the workmen were on the spot, by the sound of a conch such as is carried by beggars. But unluckily one of that fraternity passing at the time sounded his shell, which being taken for the signal agreed on, the work was commenced half an hour too soon, in consequence of which it was foretold that the government should continue in that family only 300 years.

On its completion, *Mari Gauḍa* was appointed governor of the new state and ruled for 24 years. His son *Doḍḍa Baire Gauḍa* succeeded. He reigned only 3 years and was followed by his son *Rangappa Gauḍa*, who held the government for 42 years. Dying without issue, he was succeeded by his brother *Jogi Baire Gauḍa*, who ruled for 30 years, and was followed by his son *Doḍḍa Baire Gauḍa* for 46 years. The latter left no issue, but his wife *Venkaṭamma* carried on the government with the aid of confidential officers for 15 years longer, and at her death appointed *Mari Gauḍa*, a grandson of Jogi Baire Gauḍa's whom she had brought up from an infant, to succeed her.[1] After a reign of 45 years, through some defect or imbecility in his management, he was deposed, and succeeded by his eldest brother *Anni Gauḍa*, he being only the fifth son. The new ruler, during a reign of 18 years, purchased Sidlaghatta for 100,000 pagodas, annexed it to his territory, and died after amassing a fortune of 20 lakhs of pagodas. The brother who had been deposed appears to have been put in possession of Sadali and Itikaldurga as a jágir. Anni Gauda's son *Havali Baire Gauḍa* succeeded, but after 4 months was deposed, on account of his tyranny and oppression, being succeeded by his nephew *Baiche Gauḍa*, who ruled 16 years.

During his time the Mysore army under Kanthirava, the Dalavayi, attempted to reduce the fort. But the Mahrattas, to whom Baiche Gauda applied, forced him to raise the siege, and in a severe battle near Kotikonda, defeated and slew him, cutting off his head. Baiche Gauda soon after purchased and annexed Burdagunta. At his death he was succeeded by his son *Doḍḍa Baire Gauḍa*, who during a reign of 2 years re-conquered those parts of the dominion which had submitted to Kanthirava during the siege of the capital. He was succeeded by his brother *Venkaṭa Narayan Gauḍa*, who ruled 35 years, and was followed by his son *Baiche Gauḍa*. The latter after 9 months was deposed, and his uncle *Chikkappa Gauḍa* took the government.

Three years after his accession, Haidar Ali appeared before the town, and after a siege of three months, during which many attempts were made to carry the fort by storm and mining, which from the pallegar's knowledge of counter-mining was unsuccessful, a treaty was concluded by which the Mysore army was to withdraw on condition of the chief's paying 500,000 pagodas and a golden head in the room of Kanthirava's, particularly insisted on by Haidar. Part of the sum was paid on the spot, and a confidential officer left to receive the balance. But no sooner had Haidar removed to Devanhalli than Chikkappa Gauḍa communicated with Murári Rao, the chief of Gutti, who at once sent a reinforcement. Putting these troops in possession of the fort, the Gauḍa with his family took refuge at Nandidroog. Haidar, immediately on hearing of it, retook the fort, severely punishing the defenders by mutilation, and shortly after sent a force to reduce Nandidroog, Kalavaradroog, Gudibanda, Itikaldroog and Kotikonda. The pallegar and his family were kept close prisoners in Bangalore, where Chikkappa Gauda died, without issue. A report being circulated that a rescue would be attempted, the other prisoners were removed to Coimbatore.

When Haidar visited Coimbatore some time after and desired them to be brought before him, they all attended except Baiche Gauda, the

[1] Another account says he was a son of the Devanhalli chief and adopted by her.

one that had been deposed, whose pride was averse to saluting the conqueror. Unwilling to hurt the old man's sensibility, Haidar ordered that he should be admitted through a low door, intending to accept the bending down with his head forward in passing through it as a salute and return the compliment. But the obstinate Gauda, to prevent Haidar having even that gratification, presented one of his feet first, on which he was put into irons and close confinement.

A younger member of the family, named Narayan Gauda, was afterwards re-instated by Lord Cornwallis and put in possession of Chik-Ballapur, which Tipu's troops had evacuated in order to defend Nandi-droog. He declined assistance, preferring to rely on his own resources, which Tipu hearing of, made a sudden attack upon the fort, took and demolished it after a feeble resistance. On the capture of Nandidroog by the British in 1791, the chief was again in possession for a short time, but on the conclusion of peace with Tipu could no longer retain his power.

The town has been improved of late years by several large buildings for Sub-Division offices, Munsif's Court, &c. The London Mission have also made a principal out-station here. There is an iron foundry under native management, and the silk industry is largely pursued.

| Municipal Funds. | 1892–3. | 1893–4. | 1894–5. | 1895–6. |
|---|---|---|---|---|
| Income (opening balance Rs. 5,465) ... | 4,758 | 5,080 | 4,673 | 6,277 |
| Expenditure ... ... ... ... | 8,888 | 8,738 | 5,883 | 11,588 |

**Chintamani.**—A taluq in the east, till 1873 called Ambájidurga, and then till 1882 called Sriniváspur. Area 503 square miles. Head-quarters at Chintámani. Contains the following hoblis, villages and population :—

| No. | Hoblis. | Villages | Ham-lets. | Villages Classified. | | | | Population. |
|---|---|---|---|---|---|---|---|---|
| | | | | Govern-ment. | Sarva-mánya. | Jodi. | Kayam-gutta. | |
| 1 | Ambájidurga ... | 66 | 5 | 58 | — | 5 | 3 | 8,197 |
| 2 | Chintámani... ... | 69 | 6 | 61 | 2 | 4 | 2 | 13,667 |
| 3 | Iragampalli... ... | 45 | 8 | 42 | — | 2 | 1 | 6,037 |
| 4 | Kaivára ... ... | 55 | 2 | 51 | 1 | 1 | 2 | 8,851 |
| 5 | Mungánhalli ... | 31 | 11 | 28 | — | 2 | 1 | 6,121 |
| 6 | Murugamale ... | 60 | 7 | 53 | — | 6 | 1 | 7,015 |
| | Total ... | 326 | 39 | 293 | 3 | 20 | 10 | 49,888 |

*Principal places, with population*:—Chintámani, 3,839; Muragamale, 978.

The taluq naturally divides itself into two distinct tracts. That which lies to the north of the roads from Chintámani to Bagepalli and to Kadapa respectively, is a *kal s'ime* or stony tract, draining to the north; all to the south of it is a *kempu bail s'ime* or open rolling country composed of red soil, draining to the south. Though the latter is the more favourable for general cultivation, the former has greater facilities for storing the drainage, both tanks and wells in that part being very good. Sugar-cane is largely grown and thrives well. Cocoa-nut and areca nut, on the other hand, are raised in very small quantities and are poor. Of the crops produced on dry fields, the ragi is of a superior description and highly esteemed. Fine topes of mango, tamarind and other trees are common. The honge is abundant everywhere.

Blankets and coarse cloth are manufactured in some parts, as well as a finer cloth for kamarbands. Gunny for sacking is woven at Dimbala and Ronur.

Inscriptions show that the Bánas, the Vaidumbas, the Pallavas, the Cholas, the Hoysalas, and the Vijayanagar kings have at various times occupied this part of the country, until the Mahrattas in modern times gained an ascendancy for short periods.

The revenue settlement was introduced in 1887. The unculturable area is 202,201 acres, or nearly 316 square miles: the area of inam villages is 17,075 acres, or about 26⅔ square miles. The total revenue demand for 1891–2 (15 months) was Rs. 2,05,640, and for 1892–3 it was Rs. 2,52,058. The amounts under Land revenue were Rs. 1,56,467 and Rs. 1,74,369 respectively.

The average rainfall at Chintámani for 25 years (1870–94) was as follows:—

| Jan. | Feb. | Mar. | Apl. | May | June | July | Aug. | Sept. | Oct. | Nov. | Dec. | Year. |
|---|---|---|---|---|---|---|---|---|---|---|---|---|
| — | 0·07 | 0·22 | 0·92 | 2·63 | 2·26 | 2·37 | 3·18 | 4·02 | 6·46 | 3·56 | 1·45 | ... 27·14 |

The old Bangalore-Kadapa high road runs through the taluq from south-west to north-east, being met at Muragamale by one from Kolar through Srinivâspur. From Chintámani there are roads west to Sidlaghatta, north-west to Bagepalli, north to Chelur, and east to Srinivâspur and Mulbagal, with a short one south to the Kadapa high road.

**Chintamani** (more properly *Chintámaṇipêṭ*).—An important commercial town, 27 miles north-north-west of Kolar; head-quarters of the Chintámani taluq, and a municipality.

| Population in 1891. | Males. | Females. | Total. |
|---|---|---|---|
| Hindus (with 3 Jains) ... ... ... | 1,525 | 1,582 | 3,107 |
| Muhammadans ... ... ... ... | 372 | 359 | 731 |
| Christians ... ... ... ... ... | 1 | — | 1 |
| Total ... ... | 1,898 | 1,941 | 3,839 |

The town is named after its founder Chintámani Rao, a Mahratta chief, and is the seat of the Komatis or banking class. Considerable trade is carried on in gold, silver, and precious stones, besides other merchandise. Pomegranates grow here to a large size. A low hill commanding the town on the north-west was formerly fortified.

| Municipal Funds. | 1892–3. | 1893–4. | 1894–5. | 1895–6. |
|---|---|---|---|---|
| Income ... ... ... ... ... | 2,200 | 2,082 | ,223 | 4,144 |
| Expenditure ... ... ... ... | 6,083 | 2,565 | 2,732 | 3,052 |

**Chitravati.**—An affluent of the N. Pinákini. It rises in the Hari haresvara hill, north of Nandidroog, and flowing north-east between the Worlakonda hill and Bagepalli, leaves Mysore a few miles north of the latter. Thence, entering the Anantapur District, it runs north past Kodikonda, after which, turning north-east again, it supplies the Bukkapatna and Dharmávaram tanks, and ends its course near Gaudalur of the Kadapa District, where it unites with the N. Pinákini or Pennar. The stream is dammed near Bagepalli in several places, from which channels are led off which irrigate a considerable extent of paddy land in the Bagepalli taluq.

**Dibbagiri.**—The terminal hill southwards of the Nandidroog range, properly Divigiri.

**Dokkala-konda**, or *Dongala konda.*—The Robber hills (Telugu), so named from their affording a shelter to the banditti who used to plunder the neighbouring country. The hills are on the Mysore frontier in the north of the Bagepalli taluq.

**Goribidnur.**—A taluq in the north-west. Area 341 square miles. Head-quarters at Goribidnur. Contains the following hoblis, villages and population :—

| No. | Hoblis. | Villages | Hamlets. | Villages Classified. | | | | Population. |
|---|---|---|---|---|---|---|---|---|
| | | | | Government. | Sarvamánya. | Jodi. | Kayamgutta. | |
| 1 | Bommasandra ... | 16 | 9 | 16 | — | — | — | 5,700 |
| 2 | Dádináyakanpálya... | 69 | 22 | 63 | — | 2 | 4 | 11,833 |
| 3 | Goribidnur ... ... | 36 | 12 | 27 | 2 | 2 | 5 | 14,617 |
| 4 | Hosúr ... ... | 42 | 11 | 38 | 1 | 2 | 1 | 14,192 |
| 5 | Manchenhalli ... | 54 | 19 | 36 | 2 | 14 | 2 | 13,943 |
| 6 | Nágaragere... ... | 26 | 13 | 21 | 1 | 2 | 2 | 5,033 |
| 7 | Toṇḍebhávi ... | 29 | 19 | 28 | — | 1 | — | 6,672 |
| | Total ... ... | 272 | 105 | 229 | 6 | 23 | 14 | 71,990 |

*Principal places, with population.*—Hosur, 2,574; Manchenhalli, 1,989; Goribidnur, 1,765; Idagur, 1,514; Toṇḍebhávi, 1,444; Dádináyakanpálya, 1,428; Hudagur, 1,409; Námagondlu, 1,379; Minakingurike, 1,172; Narsinganhalli, 1,140; Varavani, 1,038; Mudagere, 1,030.

The taluq was extended in 1886 by the addition of some neighbouring hoblis. It is composed of the basin of the N. Pinákini, which river runs through it from south-east to north, being confined between the Nandidroog range of mountains on the east and a chain of hills from Mákalidurga on the west. The Kumadvati or Kundar, a tributary of the N. Pinákini, rising on the west of Mákalidurga in Bangalore District, flows through the taluq from south to north and then enters the Maddagiri taluq of the Tumkur District. A small stream from the east of Mákalidurgá waters the Toṇḍebhávi hobli and joins the N. Pinákini a little to the east of Bommasandra.

The level of the taluq is considerably lower than that of the neighbouring parts of the District, the descent being marked on the south by the Nagralpille kanave on the Dod-Ballapur frontier, and by the Manchenhalli ghat on the east. The soil is loose and fertile, especially in the neighbourhood of the chief town, where water is easily procurable almost at the surface, not only from channels from the river but from shallow wells of never failing water, the sides of which are protected with wicker baskets to prevent their falling in. Sugar-cane, paddy, turmeric, and ground-nut are extensively cultivated; cocoanut and areca-nut especially near Varavani. The wild custard-apple grows abundantly on the hills, where also iron ore is plentiful.

The revenue settlement was introduced in 1880. The total revenue demand for 1891–2 (fifteen months) was Rs. 1,82,778, and for 1892–3 it was Rs. 2,42,214. The amounts under Land revenue were Rs. 1,33,570, and Rs. 1,43,730 respectively.

The average rainfall at Goribidnur for twenty-five years (1870–94) was as follows :—

| Jan. | Feb. | Mar. | Apl. | May | June | July | Aug. | Sept. | Oct. | Nov. | Dec. | Year. |
|---|---|---|---|---|---|---|---|---|---|---|---|---|
| — | 0·12 | 0·15 | 0·52 | 2·61 | 2·05 | 2·09 | 3·80 | 4·68 | 5·41 | 1·88 | 0·25 | 23·56 |

The Bangalore-Guntakal railway runs through the middle of the taluq from south to north, with stations at Tondebhavi, Goribidnur and Dod-Kurugod. The old road to Hindupur is close alongside the railway, and from Goribidnur there are roads east to Gudibanda and south-east to Chik-Ballapur. There is also a road westwards from Tondebhavi to Maddagiri.

**Goribidnur.**—A town on the left bank of the N. Pinákini, fifty-six miles north-west of Kolar, on the Bangalore-Guntakal railway, and the Dod-Ballapur-Hindupur road. Head-quarters of the Goribidnur taluq, and a municipality.

| Population in 1891. | Males. | Females. | Total. |
|---|---|---|---|
| Hindus (with 16 Jains) ... ... ... | 748 | 743 | 1,491 |
| Muhammadans ... ... ... ... | 137 | 132 | 269 |
| Christians ... ... ... ... ... | 5 | — | 5 |
| Total ... ... | 890 | 875 | 1,765 |

It is stated to have been in ancient times the residence of Vidura, an uncle of the Pandavas, and thence called *Vidurúr.* A peepul tree of great age, said to have been planted by him, is still an object of worship, under the name of the Vidur-asvattha, near Dod-Kurugod, four miles to the north. In modern times the town became a possession of the chief of Dáḍináyakanpálya, eight miles to the east, who gave it as a dowry to his daughter, and after her name it was called *Gauri Vidurúr.* The Muhammadans corrupted it into *Gori Bidnúr*, a form to which some *goris* or tombs erected by them near the town seem to give countenance. The fine tomb at Hire Bidnur, the other side of the river, is that of Husen Shah Mirza, one of the Bijapur nobles. The one at Goribidnur is of the same period, in memory of a saint named Bakhári Vali.

The place lies low, 2,252 feet above the sea, and differs from all other parts of the District, bearing a resemblance, it is said, in some of its features to Conjeveram. The climate is hot, the soil loose and fertile, water abundant and easily procurable almost at the surface. The town is rising much in importance owing to the advent of the railway, and the establishment of a sugar factory by Messrs. Arbuthnot & Co. of Madras.

| Municipal Funds. | 1892-3. | 1893-4. | 1894-5. | 1895-6. |
|---|---|---|---|---|
| Income ... ... ... ... ... | 761 | 1,452 | 1,422 | 1,398 |
| Expenditure ... ... ... ... | 1.039 | 1.975 | 1,945 | 3,681 |

**Gudibanda.**—A sub-taluq included in Bagepalli taluq, to the west; composed of the Gudibanda and Somenhalli hoblis. Head-quarters at Gudibanda. Till 1882 it was a separate taluq.

**Gudibanda.**—A town in the Nandidroog range of hills, fifty-eight miles north-west of Kolar. Head-quarters of the Gudibanda sub-taluq, and a municipality.

| Population in 1891. | Males. | Females. | Total. |
|---|---|---|---|
| Hindus (with 27 Jains) ... ... ... | 685 | 727 | 1,412 |
| Muhammadans ... ... ... ... | 235 | 216 | 451 |
| Total ... ... | 920 | 943 | 1,863 |

It is situated at the southern foot of a *banḍa* or rock, of domelike shape, surmounted by a *guḍi* or temple, whence the name. Guḍibanḍa, with the jungly tract in its vicinity, was given to *Havali Baire Gauda*, on the capture of Dod-Ballapur by Khasim Khan. It was then the haunt of freebooters, and little or no improvements were made in cultivation till some time after, when he had address enough to conciliate them, and they became useful husbandmen. He first built the fortifications on the rock called Old Gudibanda, and some time after fortified the present rock, and dying without issue was succeeded by his wife's brother *Ráma Gauḍa*. This gave umbrage to Baiche Gauḍa of Chik-Ballapur, the line of succession of his family being thereby interrupted, which he endeavoured to recover by proposing a marriage between his son and Rama Gauḍa's daughter, and requested Ráma Gauḍa to pay him a visit at Chik-Ballapur to settle the terms. But this he declined, agreeing, however, to meet him half-way between their respective capitals. They accordingly had an interview near Mandikal, attended by their forces. After several apparently friendly conversations, one of Ráma Gauḍa's servants, whom Baiche Gauḍa had gained over, on a signal given, stabbed his master in the back. Gudibanda was thereby annexed to Chik-Ballapur, perhaps about the year 1689.

| Municipal Funds. | 1892-3. | 1893-4. | 1894-5. | 1895-6. |
|---|---|---|---|---|
| Income ... ... ... ... ... | 502 | 487 | 461 | 921 |
| Expenditure ... ... ... ... | 629 | 682 | 565 | 1,098 |

**Gumnayakanpalya.**—A village in the Bágepalli taluq, to which, till 1882, it gave a name, and was formerly the head-quarters. It is 10 miles east of Bágepalli. Population 229.

*Gumma-náyakana-pálya* is a small fortified circular rock in the midst of jungle, rising about 150 feet above the surrounding hilly tract, and to the eastward of the range. It appears to have been originally dependent on Pátpálya, the residence of a Bédar named Pápa Náyak. A settlement was subsequently made there by *Gumma Náyak* and *Lakka Náyak*, two brothers from Devarajhalli, who discovered a hidden treasure, and induced some neighbours to join them. Asylum was also given to a band of freebooters from Kadapa, on condition of receiving half the plunder they might obtain. For their protection Lakka Náyak, about the year 1364, built a line of defence round the rock, naming the place after his brother, now dead. On a visit he paid to a neighbouring fair he was impressed with the state and retinue maintained by other pallegars and became desirous of increasing his consequence. He accordingly encouraged immigrants from the neighbouring districts to join his standard on condition of enjoying three-fourths of the produce of their lands and added to his forces. On his death, in 1372, he was succeeded by his son *Masal Náyak*, who, taking advantage of Pápa Náyak's death, subdued Patpalya and other places. He was succeeded in 1412 by his son *Kadrappa Náyak*, to whose honour it is related that he introduced many wise regulations and appointed village accountants to superintend and encourage cultivation. The withdrawal of the robbers protected by the former rulers was the consequence of these politic measures. The estimable Kadrappa Náyak died in 1472. Of his six sons, *Narsimha Náyak*, the eldest, ruled 3 years, *Kadrappa Náyak*, the second son, 7 years. *Masal Náyak*, the next son, then succeeded. During his tenure of power he gained possession, by force or stratagem, of some neighbouring pályams, and died in 1500 of a mortification in his back. His brother *Vira Náyak* succeeded, and pursuing the same policy died in 1532, "little esteemed or regretted." His son, *Vasanta Náyak*, after a quiet rule of 5 years, was followed by *Lakka Náyak*, son of the latter. He was shortly summoned to pay tribute to the Penugonda sovereign, to which he consented. At the same time he strengthened the fortifications of Gumnayakanpálya, constructed a large tank to the west and improved the town.

Nothing of interest is related of the succeeding rulers, during whose time various conquests were made, until the accession of *Narsimha Náyak*. He is described as a weak prince, on which account a daḷaváyi was appointed, named Sani Narsimaya. He was a man of ambitious views, and by his successful conquests, including that of Itikaldurga, gained such an ascendency in the state that Rámakka, the Náyak's wife, regarded with apprehension his growing power. When, therefore, the Mahratta army under Murári Rao appeared before the capital, she opened negotiations with the view of getting rid of the minister. He, however, coming to know this, offered them battle, and broke up their camp. Rámakka's situation now became daily more critical, as she had gone too far to withdraw, and was entirely in the daḷaváyi's power. She therefore secretly offered to all the neighbouring chiefs from whom conquests had been made an unconditional surrender of the places they had lost, provided they would combine against the minister. The latter opposed the confederate forces with his usual bravery. But they gaining intelligence that his resources were nearly at an end, cut the bank of the tank and forced him to capitulate. He requested permission to retire with his family and private property. This the allies refused, but through the advice of Rámakka the terms were ultimately agreed to, and Sani Narsimaya retired to Chik-Ballapur, where he died of a broken heart. The pályam was soon after reduced by the army of Haidar Ali, and Narsimha Náyak with his wife Rámakka were taken prisoners, first to Guramkonda and then to Seringapatam. The chief died on his way, his reign having lasted 64 years.

**Hariharesvara-betta.**—A two-peaked hill rising to 4,122 feet above sea-level, north of Nandidroog, and one of the same range. It is the reputed source of the Chitravati.

**Hosur.**—A large village in the Goribidnur taluq, 6 miles south-west of the kasba. Population 2,574.

A fair held on Saturday is attended by 500 people. Under the name of Hosaviḍu, the new camp or residence, it was for a time occupied by the Hoysala king Ballála III., who may have been its founder, and may have named it with reference to Halebiḍu, his old residence or capital of Dorasamudra, which had been destroyed by the Musalmans. As Hosapaṭṭana it apparently formed in 1355 one of the boundary towns of the early Vijayanagar kingdom under Bukka Raya I. (*see* Vol. I., p. 346), and was a royal residence. It probably lost its importance when the Bijapur power was overcome by the Mughals in 1687, and is now greatly reduced in population and extent from what it was even a few years ago, the population in 1871 being 5,751, and in 1891 only 2,574.

**Hunkunda.**—A village in the Dásarahosahalli hóbli of the Bowringpet taluq, about 8 miles north by east of the kasba, near the Kolar-Betamangala road. Population 329.

It seems, from the numerous inscriptions there, to have been a frontier station down to the 10th and 11th centuries, where much fighting took place. It was successively in the possession of Mahávali Bánarasa, the Nolamba kings Ayyapa and Dilípayya, the Ganga king Márasimha, and Uttama Chola Ganga.

**Kaivara.**—A village in Chintámani taluq, 7 miles east by south of the kasba, near the Bangalore-Kadapa road. Head-quarters of the Kaivara hobli. Population 1,287.

There are several old temples in the place, which is said to have been formerly called Ekachakrapura, celebrated in the history of the Pándavas. One of the temples is said to have been founded by them. The inscriptions are of the time of Ganga Perumál in the 13th century, and of the Vijayanagar kings afterwards.

**Kalavara-durga** or **Skandagiri.**—The most prominent height to the north of Nandidroog, from which it is 5 miles distant, forming part of the same range. The summit, 4,749 feet above the sea, was formerly fortified and directly commanded the town of Chik-Ballapur. The Pápaghni is said to have its source in this hill. The fort was taken by the British in 1791 and has been dismantled.

**Kaundinya.**—An affluent of the Pálár. It rises in the Kurudumale hill near Mulbagal. Taking an easterly course, after feeding some smaller tanks, it falls into the large one at Nangali. Thence crossing the frontier near the village of Potenagavara, it turns south-east near Palamner, and flows into the Pálár near Gudiyatam.

**Kumadvati** or **Kundar.**—A tributary of the N. Pinákini. It rises in the Bangalore District, west of Mákalidurga, and in its course northwards flows through the Goribidnur taluq, whence it enters the Tumkur District in Maddagiri taluq.

**Kolar.**—A taluq in the centre towards the south. Area 299 square miles. Head-quarters at Kolar. Contains the following hoblis, villages and population :—

| No. | Hoblis. | Villages. | Hamlets. | Villages Classified. | | | | Population. |
|---|---|---|---|---|---|---|---|---|
| | | | | Government. | Sarvamánya. | Jodi. | Kayamgutta. | |
| 1 | Hólúr ... ... | 54 | 1 | 43 | — | 9 | 2 | 8,762 |
| 2 | Huttúr ... ... | 50 | 5 | 34 | — | 14 | 2 | 8,932 |
| 3 | Kólár ... ... | 61 | -- | 52 | 2 | 5 | 2 | 20,417 |
| 4 | Sugatúr ... ... | 44 | 5 | 36 | — | 6 | 2 | 6,872 |
| 5 | Vémagal ... ... | 57 | 4 | 43 | 1 | 3 | 10 | 14,928 |
| 6 | Vokkaléri ... .. | 68 | 5 | 54 | 1 | 10 | 3 | 12,632 |
| | Total ... | 334 | 20 | 262 | 4 | 47 | 21 | 72,543 |

*Principal places, with population.*—Kolar, 12,148; Vokkaléri, 1,674; Kyálnur, 1,599.

The Palar runs through the northern and eastern parts of the taluq: the western side is occupied with the ranges of the Kolar and Vokkaléri hills. It is generally well cultivated, including even the table-land on the Kolar hills. There are 300 tanks, of which at least ten may be called large. There are also numerous fine wells, especially in the south, with water close to the surface. The dry crop soils are generally red, mixed with sand. The best soil is found in Holur and the old Dalsanur hoblis, where also stretches of black soil are met with. Silk-worms are reared in many of the villages, the silk being exported.

The revenue settlement was introduced in 1889. The unculturable area is 83,587 acres, or 130½ square miles; the area of inám villages is 29,937 acres, or nearly 46 square miles, and that of plantations 302 acres. The total revenue demand for 1891–2 (15 months) was Rs. 1,88,895, and for 1892–3 it was Rs. 2,40,685. The amounts under Land revenue were Rs. 1,41,882 and Rs. 1,56,678 respectively.

The average rainfall for 25 years (1870–94) at Kolar, and for two years (1893–4) at the other stations was as follows:—

| | Jan. | Feb. | Mar. | Apl. | May | June | July | Aug. | Sept. | Oct. | Nov. | Dec. | Year. |
|---|---|---|---|---|---|---|---|---|---|---|---|---|---|
| Kolar ... | 0·09 | 0·04 | 0·45 | 1·22 | 2·96 | 3·27 | 2·80 | 3·96 | 4·78 | 5·51 | 3·31 | 0·84 | ... 29·24 |
| Mudavadi ... | 0·11 | 0·15 | 0·42 | 1·52 | 3·09 | 1·88 | 2·82 | 3·30 | 1·19 | 7·18 | 2·18 | — | ... 23·84 |
| Vemgal ... | — | — | 0·60 | 0·50 | 3·20 | 3·65 | 2·53 | 5·05 | 2·90 | 3·44 | 2·93 | — | ... 24·80 |

The old Bangalore-Madras road passes through Kolar, running west to east, from Hoskote to Mulbagal. From Kolar there are also roads south to the railway at Bowringpet, north to Srinivaspur, north west to Nandi, south-west to Malur, and south-east to Betamangala. There is also a short road from Vemgal leading to Malur.

**Kolar.**—The chief town of the District, situated in 13° 6′ N. lat., and 78° 7′ E. long., 43 miles east-north-east of Bangalore by road, but connected with it by rail from the station at Bowringpet, 11 miles to the south.

| Population in 1891. | Males. | Females. | Total. |
|---|---|---|---|
| Hindus (with 18 Jains) ... ... ... ... | 4,681 | 4,544 | 9,225 |
| Muhammadans ... ... ... ... ... ... | 1,043 | 1,491 | 2,534 |
| Christians ... ... ... ... ... ... | 186 | 203 | 389 |
| Total ... ... ... | 5,910 | 6,238 | 12,148 |

Kolar is a place of great antiquity, but has passed through so many vicissitudes, and been so devastated by warfare in modern times, that but little now remains in it that is ancient. It was founded by the Gangas early in the Christian era, if not in existence before. Though Taḷakád was their capital, the title "Lord of the city of Kuvalála" (or Kolála,—the old names of Kolar), is assumed by all the Ganga kings down to the 11th century, and also by the Chálukya princes whose mother was of the Ganga family. When the Ganga power was overthrown by the Cholas in about 1004, Kolar passed into the hands of the latter, and from inscriptions it would appear that the existing temple of Koláramma may have been erected in the time of Rájendra Chola. Early in the next century the Hoysalas drove out the Cholas from Mysore, and Kolála is specially mentioned among the conquests of Vishnuvardhana. When, in the latter half of the 13th century, a partition of the Hoysala dominions took place between the two sons of Somésvara, Kolar was included in the Tamil districts, and fell to the share of Rámanátha. But even up to this time a family of Chola-Gangas continued in power there, who still bore the title "Lord of the city of Kuvalála."

Passing over the early Vijayanagar period, we come to the 15th century, in which Timme Gauḍa, with the title of Chikka Ráyal, received authority to repair the fort of Kolar. Bijapur next subdued the place, and in 1639 Shahji, father of the celebrated Sivaji, became the Governor of this, with other Districts), and often resided there. The Mughals took it 50 years later, and in about 1720 Fatte Muhammad, father of Haidar Ali, became Faujdar of Kolar, under the Subadar of Sira, who had a residence on the Kolar hills. After various fortunes, Kolar was ceded to Haidar Ali in 1761. It was subsequently at times again lost to Mysore. In 1768 it was taken by the English under Colonel Donald

Campbell. In 1770 it was taken by the Mahrattas under Madhu Rao. In 1791 it was again taken by the English under Lord Cornwallis, but at the peace of 1792 was restored to Tipu Sultan, and since then has been included in the Mysore territory.

The Makbára or tomb of Haidar Ali's father is one of the principal old buildings, and is still maintained with an endowment. The fort walls were levelled about 20 years ago and the ditch filled up. Many new streets were at the same time laid out. The Kolar tank on the east is a fine sheet of water. The town contains the usual District offices for Deputy and Assistant Commissioners, School, Dispensary, Barracks, &c. There is also an orphanage, now under the Methodist Episcopal Mission.

The old roads by the Mugli and Naikaneri passes from Madras and the districts east of the Ghats to Bangalore united at Kolar and, before superseded by the railway, brought a continual influx of travellers and pilgrims to the town from both sides. The result was frequent outbreaks of cholera, as a hot-bed for which fell disease Kolar was long notorious. The diversion of this heterogeneous stream of humanity, no less than superior sanatory arrangements, have entirely freed it of that scourge for many years. Scorpions abound, whose sting is unusually venomous and often fatal. A pit under the entrance to the Kolaramma temple is full of scorpions, which make a hissing noise on being disturbed, and among the offerings presented at the temple it is customary to include the figure of a scorpion in silver. The mulberry is cultivated for the rearing of silkworms. Turkeys are reared in large numbers for export to Bangalore, Bellary and other places. Cumblies or coarse blankets are also manufactured. A large fair takes place on Thursday, attended by 2,000 people, and 700 cattle.

| Municipal Funds. | 1892-3. | 1893-4. | 1894-5. | 1895-6. |
|---|---|---|---|---|
| Income ... ... ... ... ... | 7,243 | 7,564 | 7,102 | 7,412 |
| Expenditure ... ... ... ... ... | 7,735 | 8,243 | 6,145 | 8,854 |

**Kolar-betta** or hills, also bear the name of Satasringa parvata, the hundred peaked hills. The range extends along the north west of the town of Kolar, the highest point being 4,026 feet above the sea. The hills present a barren and rocky appearance on all sides, but on the top is an extensive plateau occupied by villages and irrigated fields. A perennial spring on the east side, named the Antara Ganga or subterranean Ganges, is esteemed sacred.

The legends connected with these hills have been referred to in the historical summary. Two centuries ago they were fortified, and here the Mughal general Khasim Khan, the first Subadar of Sira, for some time resided. The fort was destroyed by the Mahrattas.

**Kolar Gold Fields.**—These are in the south of the Bowringpet taluq, to the east of a low ridge of hills of which Betaráyan hill, 3,199 feet above sea level, is the most conspicuous point. They are connected by the Gold Fields railway with the Bangalore-Madras line at Bowringpet, and a road runs through them from Bowringpet to Kamasandra, where there is also a railway station. Information regarding the geology and the recent history and development of these gold fields has already been given in Vol. I. Upwards of 35½ square miles have been leased for gold-mining in the District,-and the following thirteen companies are now at work (arranged alphabetically).

| Company. | Capital. | Company. | Capital. |
|---|---|---|---|
| Balaghat ... ... ... | £200,000 | Mysore West .. ... | £150,000 |
| Champion Reef ... ... | 220,000 | Mysore Wynaad ... ... | 150,000 |
| Gold Fields of Mysore ... | 275,000 | Nine Reefs ... ... ... | 62,500 |
| Indian Consolidated ... | — | Nundydroog ... ... | 220,000 |
| Kolar Central (East) ... | 200,000 | South East Mysore ... | — |
| Mysore ... ... ... | 250,000 | Urigam (Ooregum)... ... | 265,000 |
| Mysore Reef ... ... | 200,000 | | |

The original Kolar Concessionaires' Company has gone into liquidation, and the blocks held by it are either owned by the Companies above mentioned or sub-leased to the Gold Fields of Mysore Company. Mysore, Urigam, Nundydroog and Champion Reef are the only mines where operations have so far been attended with satisfactory results.

**Kuruda-male.**—Or more correctly Kúḍu-male, is the hill 4 miles north-west of Mulbagal, at the foot of which are the ruins of several large temples, with sculpture attributed to Jakanachari, but apparently restored by Ilavanji Raya and his companions from the south, mentioned in the account of Avani. The principal are those of Somesvara and Ganesha. The elevation of the hill is 3,312 feet above the level of the sea. The gods, it is said, on going to make war on Tripura, mustered their forces at this place, whence the name *Kúḍu-male* or hill of assembly. The Kaundinya, a tributary of the Palar, has its source here, which is said to have been the site of the hermitage of Kaundinya rishi.

**Kushavati.**—There are two streams in the District of this name, one a tributary of the Pápaghni, and the other of the Chitravati. The former rises from the Vali Isvara hill near the boundary of the Punganúr zamindari, and after forming the Yerakálave tank in this District crosses the frontier north-westwards near Mursanpalli. It then goes

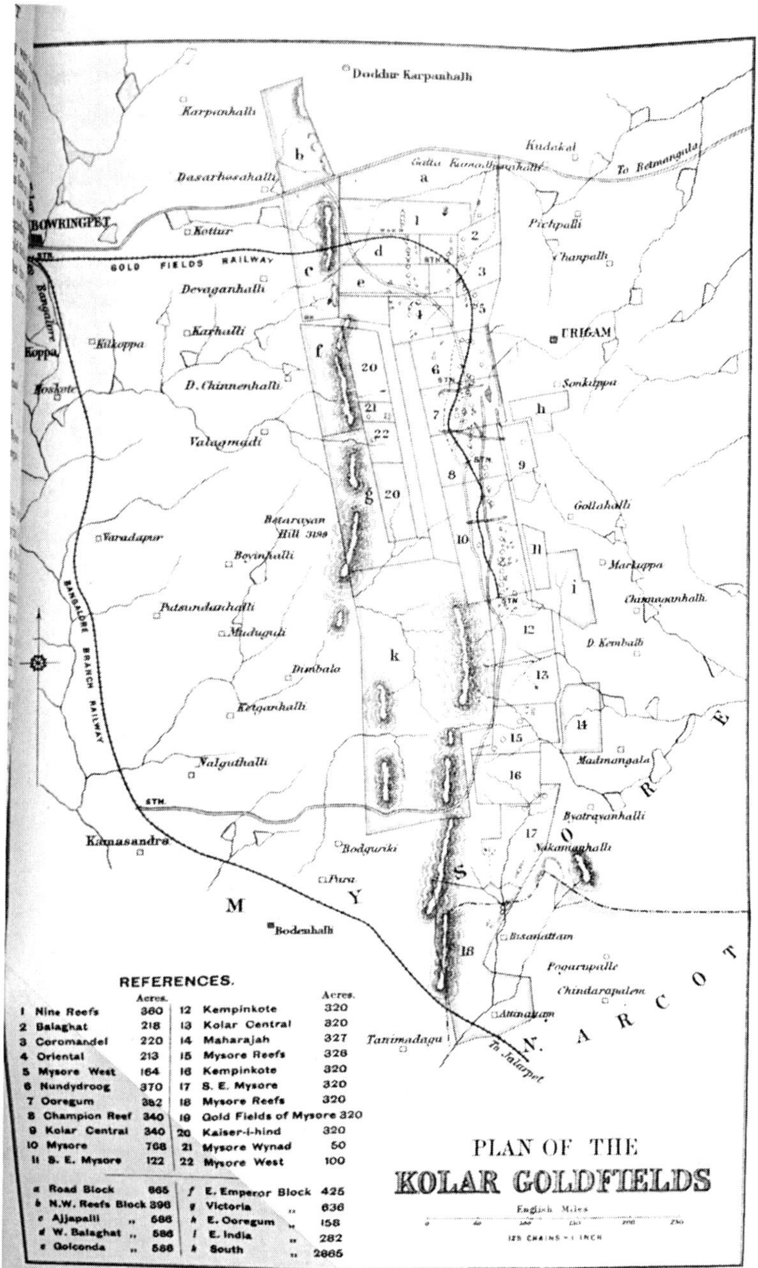

Doddur Karpanhalli
Karpanhalli
Kudakal
To Betmangala
Dasarhosahalli
BOWRINGPET
Kottur
Pichpalli
Chanpalli
GOLD FIELDS RAILWAY
Devaganhalli
Karhalli
Kilkoppa
Koppa
URIGAM
Sonkuppa
D. Chinnenhalli
Valagmadi
Gollahalli
Betarayan Hill 3189
Varadapur
Bovinhalli
Markuppa
Chinnaganhalli
Putsandanhalli
Mudugudi
D. Kembali
BANGALORE BRANCH RAILWAY
Dimbala
Ketganhalli
Nalguthalli
Madmangala
Byotrayanhalli
Kamasandre
Bodguriki
Nakamanhalli
Pura
M Y S O R E
Bodenhalli
Bisanattam
Pogarupalle
Chindarapalem
Attanattam
Tanimadagu
To Jalarpet
N. A R C O T
REFERENCES.
Acres.
1 Nine Reefs 360
2 Balaghat 218
3 Coromandel 220
4 Oriental 213
5 Mysore West 164
6 Nundydroog 370
7 Ooregum 382
8 Champion Reef 340
9 Kolar Central 340
10 Mysore 768
11 S. E. Mysore 122
12 Kempinkote 320
13 Kolar Central 320
14 Maharajah 327
15 Mysore Reefs 328
16 Kempinkote 320
17 S. E. Mysore 320
18 Mysore Reefs 320
19 Gold Fields of Mysore 320
20 Kaiser-i-hind 320
21 Mysore Wynad 50
22 Mysore West 100
a Road Block 865
b N.W. Reefs Block 396
c Ajjapalli „ 586
d W. Balaghat „ 586
e Golconda „ 588
f E. Emperor Block 425
g Victoria „ 636
h E. Ooregum „ 158
i E. India „ 282
k South „ 2665
PLAN OF THE
KOLAR GOLDFIELDS
English Miles
125 CHAINS = 1 INCH

to Tippasandra tank of Madanpalli, in the Kadapa District, and ultimately falls into the Pápaghni.

The other Kushávati rises from Avalu-konda, or cow-hill, to the north of Nandidroog; and, after forming the Bairsagara tank before the town of Gudibanda, runs in a northerly direction, almost parallel to the Bangalore-Bellary high road, and falls into the Chitravati some miles beyond the frontier.

**Madivala.**—There are several places so called in this District, and in the east of the Bangalore District, each of which has a large Siva temple with many inscriptions in Grantha and Tamil characters. The name is a euphemism for a washerman, but seems here to indicate a holy place. The following are those in Kolar District:—

| Taluq. | Hobli. | Taluq. | Hobli. |
|---|---|---|---|
| Bowringpet... ... | Bowringpet. | Kolar ... ... | Vemgal. |
| ,, ... ... | Kyasamballi. | ,, ... ... | Vokkaleri. |
| Chintamani ... | Sómayájulapalli. | Málur ... ... | Málur. |
| ,, ... ... | 'Irugampalli. | Mulbagal ... | Mallanayákanhalli. |

The oldest appears to be the one near Málur, which has inscriptions dating in 988; also one of Hoysala Ramanatha, the 13th century. Most of the others have grants either by Chola, Hoysala, or Vijayanagar kings.

**Malur.**—A taluq in the south-west. Area 269 square miles. Head-quarters at Málur. Contains the following hoblis, villages and population:—

| No. | Hoblis. | Villages | Hamlets. | Villages Classified. | | | | Population. |
|---|---|---|---|---|---|---|---|---|
| | | | | Government. | Servamánya. | Jodi. | Kayamgutta. | |
| 1 | Huladénhalli ... | 90 | 7 | 80 | — | 9 | 1 | 6,157 |
| 2 | Lakkúr ... ... | 40 | 5 | 27 | — | 12 | 1 | 8,588 |
| 3 | Málúr ... ... | 102 | 1 | 63 | 6 | 28 | 5 | 15,177 |
| 4 | Másti ... ... | 63 | 3 | 51 | — | 11 | 1 | 8,027 |
| 5 | Narasápura ... ... | 47 | 3 | 31 | — | 10 | 6 | 7,337 |
| 6 | Tyákal ... ... | 82 | 6 | 72 | — | 9 | 1 | 8,894 |
| | Total ... ... | 424 | 25 | 324 | 6 | 79 | 15 | 54,180 |

*Principal places, with population.*—Málur, 3,185; Másti, 1,859; Lakkúr, 1,617; Narsápur, 1,246; Santehalli, 1,013.

The taluq was abolished in 1881 but restored in 1886. It lies along the watershed separating the valleys of the Pálár and S. Pinákini. The elevated tracts are bare or covered with low jungle. The most fertile part extends along the eastern side from Narsápura down to Másti, through which flow streams which are tributary to the S. Pinákini. One of these, rising south-west of the Vokkaleri hills, is named the Márkanda. There are as many as 385 irrigation tanks, of which 55 are of good size. Excellent potatoes are grown in the taluq. The predominant soil is red, of considerable depth, but much mixed with sand. It is best in Málur and Lakkúr hoblis, but towards the hills of Narsápur and Tyákal becomes inferior, changing to grey and falling off in depth. This is the case also in the south, where rocks, moreover, crop up at intervals.

The taluq is crossed from east to west by the Bangalore Branch of the Madras Railway, which has stations at Málur and Tyákal. From Málur there are roads to Hoskote, to Narasápur, to Kolar, to Másti, and to Hosur in the Salem District.

The revenue settlement was introduced in 1890. The unculturable area is 67,102 acres, or nearly 105 square miles. The area of inám villages is 34,353 acres, or 53⅗ square miles: that of plantations is 1,834 acres. The total revenue demand for 1891-2 (15 months) was Rs. 1,26,476, and for 1892-3 it was Rs. 1,47,391. The amounts under Land revenue were Rs. 1,00,590, and Rs. 1,05,520 respectively.

The average rainfall at Málur for 25 years (1870-94), and at the other station for two years (1893-4) was as follows :—

| | Jan. | Feb. | Mar. | Apl. | May | June | July | Aug. | Sept. | Oct. | Nov. | Dec. | Year. |
|---|---|---|---|---|---|---|---|---|---|---|---|---|---|
| Málúr ... | 0·02 | 0·19 | 0·35 | 0·86 | 3·89 | 2·05 | 2·60 | 4·18 | 6·02 | 5·18 | 2·24 | 0·40... | 27·98 |
| Narsapur. | — | — | 0·48 | 2·20 | 5·20 | 3·95 | 3·68 | 4·71 | 4·09 | 5·15 | 2·13 | 0·10... | 31·69 |

**Malur.**—A town 18 miles south-west of Kolar, on the Bangalore Branch Railway. Head-quarters of the Málur taluq, and a municipality.

| Population in 1891. | Males. | Females. | Total. |
|---|---|---|---|
| Hindus (with 5 Jains) ... ... ... | 1,424 | 1,492 | 2,916 |
| Muhammadans ... ... ... ... | 128 | 131 | 259 |
| Christians ... ... ... ... ... | 5 | 5 | 10 |
| Total ... ... | 1,557 | 1,628 | 3,185 |

A fair held on Thursday is attended by 1,000 people, and an equal number of bullocks are brought for sale.

It is said to have originally borne the name of *Mallikà-pura* or jasmin town, from being surrounded with the gardens which supplied garlands to the Márkandésvara temple on the Vokkaleri hill, the village forming part of the endowments of the temple. In the 16th century it was one of the possessions of Timme Gauda, the chief of Hoskote. From him it was captured by the Bijapur army and held as a jágir by several mansubdars. Subsequently it was farmed from the

Mahrattas by Hrida Rám Singh, a Rajput zamindar, who enlarged it and gave it the name of *Málur.* His descendants continued in possession until the subjection of the country by Haidar Ali.

By road it is connected with Hoskote on the north-west, with Kolar on the north-east, and with Hosur in the Salem District on the south. Also with Narsápur and Másti.

| Municipal Funds. | 1892-3. | 1893-4. | 1894-5. | 1895-6. |
|---|---|---|---|---|
| Income ... ... ... ... ... | 1,022 | 945 | 990 | 1,550 |
| Expenditure ... ... ... ... | 1,257 | 1,389 | 1,370 | 2,288 |

**Manchenhalli.**—A village in the Goribidnur taluq, on the right bank of the N. Pinákini, 9 miles east of the kasba, on the Chik-Ballapur-Goribidnur Road. Head-quarters of the hobli of the same name. Population 1,989.

The car festival of Rama-deva is held for 6 days from full moon in Chaitra, and is attended by 800 people.

**Markanda.**—A tributary of the S. Pinákini, is formed by two branches, one rising from the south-west of the Vokkaleri hills, and the other from the Tyakal hills. Both unite on the south-east of the town of Budikote in the Bowringpet taluq. The stream then strikes towards the south, and soon after leaves the District, descending the Ghats towards the east of Ankusgiri, where it joins the Vrishabhávati.

**Masti.**—A village in the Malur taluq, 9 miles south of the kasba, with which it is connected by road. Head-quarters of the Másti hobli. Population 1,859.

A fair held on Wednesday is attended by 500 people.

*Másti* appears to have been founded in the 16th century by *Chokka Babati*, a petty chief from the neighbourhood of Conjeveram, who fled to save his daughter from disgrace by the ruler of that country. He was summoned to Vijayanagar, where, having rendered some important military service, he was confirmed by Achyuta Raya in the possession of a territory yielding a revenue of 20,000 pagodas, and made Másti his capital. His successors subsequently acquired Ankusgiri, with which the family became identified. On the capture of Kolar by the Mahrattas, Másti was united to Hoskote and shared in the after fortunes of the District, until annexed to Mysore by the conquests of Haidar Ali.

**Melur.**—A village in the Sidlaghatta hobli, of the Sidlaghatta taluq, about 6 miles south of the kasba. Population 839.

A cattle fair takes place in connection with the Gangadevi *parishe*, held for 10 days from full moon in Chaitra. It is attended by 10,000 people, and bullocks to the same number are brought for sale.

**Mulbagal.**—A taluq in the east. Area 361 square miles. Headquarters at Mulbagal. Contains the following hoblis, villages, and population :—

| No. | Hoblis. | Villages | Hamlets. | Villages Classified. | | | | Population. |
|---|---|---|---|---|---|---|---|---|
| | | | | Government. | Sarvamánya. | Jodi. | Kayamgutta. | |
| 1 | 'Avani ... ... | 75 | 16 | 62 | 1 | 10 | 2 | 11,788 |
| 2 | Bairakúr ... ... | 61 | 17 | 55 | 1 | 3 | 2 | 10,946 |
| 3 | Duggasandra ... | 35 | 14 | 34 | 1 | — | — | 6,675 |
| 4 | Mallináyakanhalli ... | 93 | 12 | 82 | 5 | 4 | 2 | 10,109 |
| 5 | Mulbágal ... ... | 58 | 14 | 50 | 6 | 1 | 1 | 12,099 |
| 6 | Uttanúr ... ... | 30 | 11 | 21 | — | 5 | 4 | 4,652 |
| | Total ... ... | 352 | 84 | 304 | 14 | 23 | 11 | 56,269 |

*Principal places, with population.*—Mulbagal, 3,763; Táyilúr, 1,363; Nangali, 1,124; Agara, 1,040.

The taluq is drained on the west by the Pálár, the streams on the east also running into that stream below the Ghats in the North Arcot District after an easterly and southerly course. Excepting the range of hills extending north from Mulbagal, the taluq is well cultivated, especially eastwards towards Nangali. The chief feature of the taluq is the quantity of rock cropping up everywhere in the shape of rocky hills and hillocks, composed of loose boulders of gneiss. Large boulders are promiscuously scattered about everywhere, and masses of sheet rock all over the country. There are some rocky hills of considerable altitude near Mulbagal and Avani. The watershed runs nearly north and south through the centre of the taluq, the fall of the land to the west being gentle and to the east abrupt and steep. To the west there are rolling downs, broad valleys, and generally shallow tanks: to the east there are narrow valleys, deep tanks, much broken ground and rocky ridges. The number of tanks, large and small, is no less than 460. Irrigation from tanks is greatly supplemented by water from wells, which are usually open pits, only built up with stone where the *yáta* is placed, and with the water close to the surface, often flush with it.

The dry crop soil is generally poor, grey and sandy. In the wet lands there is much sand and clay, and efflorescence of potash is not uncommon.

The revenue settlement was introduced in 1887. The unculturable area is 108,125 acres, or nearly 169 square miles. The area of inám villages is 22,970 acres, or nearly 35 square miles. The total revenue demand for 1891–2 (15 months) was Rs. 1,66,265, and for 1892–3 it was Rs. 2,00,987. The amounts under land revenue were Rs. 1,29,519 and Rs. 1,47,931 respectively.

The average rainfall at Mulbagal for 25 years (1870–94) was as follows:—

| Jan. | Feb. | Mar. | Apl. | May | June | July | Aug. | Sept. | Oct. | Nov. | Dec. | | Year. |
|---|---|---|---|---|---|---|---|---|---|---|---|---|---|
| 0·15 | 0·16 | 0·44 | 0·83 | 3·20 | 2·78 | 2·72 | 4·35 | 4·14 | 5·61 | 4·90 | 1·16 | ... | 30·44 |

**Mulbagal**—or more properly *Múdla-bágalu*, eastern gate, so called from being situated at the eastern pass from the table-land of Mysore to the temple of Tirupati. The name also appears as Muluváyi in old inscriptions, which conveys the same meaning. It is an important town, 18 miles east-north-east of Kolar, on the old Bangalore-Madras road by the Mugli pass. Head-quarters of the Mulbagal taluq, and a municipality.

| Population in 1891. | Males. | Females. | Total. |
|---|---|---|---|
| Hindus ... ... ... ... ... ... ... | 1,592 | 1,812 | 3,404 |
| Muhammadans... ... ... ... ... ... | 829 | 782 | 1,611 |
| Christians ... ... ... ... ... ... | 11 | — | 11 |
| Total ... ... ... | 2,432 | 2,594 | 5,026 |

Some ancient temples exist near the town, and the tomb of a saint named Haidar Wali attracts great numbers of Muhammadans to the place on the celebration of his anniversary. Pilgrims to Tirupati who pass through Mulbagal from all the western countries go through the preliminary ceremony of purification by shaving their heads and bathing in a pond named Narsimha tirtha. Sugar cane and fine paddy are cultivated in the neighbourhood, Mulbagal sugar and Mulbagal rice being esteemed the best in the District. The former is prepared by Musalmans employed by Brahmans.

The taluq formed part of the Mahávali or Bána territory from early in the Christian era. Towards the close of the 10th century the Pallavas became the overlords, and the Vaidumbas held some of the north. It was the seat of government for the Kolar country when first brought under the sway of the Vijayanagar kings, who were represented by two officers named Lakkana Danáyak and Mádana Danáyak. It subsequently came under the control of Timme Gauda of Hoskote, and shared in the fortunes of the District as elsewhere related. It was besieged by the British in June 1768, under Colonel Campbell, and betrayed by the killedar. The British field deputies afterwards took it upon them to put Muhammad Ali's troops in charge, who, in their turn, again betrayed it to Haidar. But it was recovered in October by Colonel Wood, who, after very severe fighting amidst the congeries of granite rocks and boulders scattered over the whole surface of the plain, defeated all the efforts of Haidar and his vastly superior force to prevent its recapture.

| Municipal Funds. | 1892-3. | 1893-4. | 1894-5. | 1895-6. |
|---|---|---|---|---|
| Income ... ... ... ... ... | 1,846 | 1,883 | 2,029 | 3,532 |
| Expenditure ... ... ... ... | 2,600 | 1,944 | 2,466 | 4,205 |

**Nandi.**—A village in the Chik-Ballapur taluq, at the north-eastern base of Nandidroog. Head-quarters of the Nandi hobli. Population 997.

It contains a large temple dedicated to Bhoga Nandisvara, which is surrounded with Chola inscriptions in the Grantha character. The foundation of the village is attributed to Baire Gauda of Avati, but the temple is much older. A Pallava and several Chola inscriptions are in the court yard. The village was for some years a British military station, till the troops were removed in 1808. Writing in 1809, Colonel Welsh says:—"The Pettah (that is, the present Sultanpet) is extensive, and was formerly connected with the foot of the hill by a line of works and deep ditch, now out of repair and useless; it had very good bazars in it, and the place altogether is famous for the best potatoes and soft sugar in the Peninsula; while the gardens abound in almost every fruit and vegetable of Europe and Asia combined." A large annual fair takes place at the Sivarátri festival, attended by 20,000 people. The best bullocks reared in the country are brought for sale then, and as much as Rs. 1,000 is said to have been offered for a pair of draught bullocks. A cattle show was held by Government at this season for several years, and prizes were distributed, but in 1874 the show was transferred to Bangalore.

**Nandidroog** (*Nundydroog*).—A famous fortified hill in the Chik-Ballapur taluq, 31 miles north of Bangalore, at the termination of a range of mountains, of which it is the highest point, running north to Penugonda and the Bellary District. There is an extensive plateau at the top, sloping to the west, in the centre of which is a large hollow, containing a wood and a well-constructed tank, called the *Amrita-sarovara* or lake of nectar, fed by perennial springs. The four sides are built round with stone steps, which diminish as they descend, until they meet in a point at the bottom, where there is a small shrine.

From the earliest period, and throughout their time, the Gangas had the title "Lord of Nandagiri," and the hill was then a Jain place Owing to subsequent changes, and the extensive quarrying of stone in recent times for the fortifications and buildings, all traces of this have disappeared, except perhaps the name Sravana-tirtha, given to a deserted and now inaccessible well at the edge of the precipice on the south. But in the Gopinatha hill, on the north-east, is an ancient Jain inscription, whose opening words are like those of the Ganga grants, and which claims that the *chaitya* there was founded by Ráma, the son of Das'aratha, and subsequently repaired by Kunti, the mother of the Pándus! The name Nandagiri (hill of pleasure) was changed to Nandigiri (hill of Nandi, the bull of S'iva) in the 11th century, under the Cholas. As the Jain inscription above-mentioned begins by invoking the first Tirthankara, Vrishabhà, whose name means bull, this may have helped towards suggesting the appellation. That the Sivites at once appropriated the hill is evident from the old inscription in the cave near the Bull temple (Nellikáyi Basava) on a ledge on the east, which records that a Saiva ascetic from Sriparvata took up his abode there. The situation of the well before spoken of, as well as that of the original entrance to the temple, may indicate that the tremendous fracture and landslip which produced the perpendicular precipice on this side as it is now, strewing the saddle below with immense boulders and laying bare in the middle of its face the great cavern known as the Asura cave and the Tiger cave, may have occurred after this period. There is evidence that the present Bhoga Nandis'vara temple, at the village of Nandi, near the north-eastern base, has been in existence from Pallava, Chola and Hoysala times; and the Yoga Nandis'vara temple at the summit must be at least as old. On the latter is an inscription of the end of the 11th century, which states that a robber chief then ascended the hill, with a force, in order to seize the hidden treasure supposed to be there, but did not succeed. On the Vira-bhadra temple under the cliff, near one of the gateways on the north, below the Sheristadar's house, is an inscription showing that it was in existence at the end of the 14th century.

The hill was probably first fortified by the Chik-Ballapur chiefs, but the extensive fortifications whose ruins now surround the summit were erected by Haidar Ali and Tipu Sultan, after its seizure by the Mahrattas under Madhu Rao in 1770. A precipitous cliff at the south-west angle is pointed out as Tipu's Drop, being the place over which prisoners are said to have been hurled by the orders of that ruler. Haidar's Drop is on a small hill to the north, near the village of Nandi. Beneath the cliff over which prisoners were thrown is a cave in which many Europeans were confined. This is the place described in Meadows Taylor's *Tippoo Sultaun*.

This formidable stronghold, Nandidroog, was captured by the British army under Lord Cornwallis in 1791. The siege and assault, which were under the command of Major Gowdie, are thus described by Wilks.

Every fortified place the English had hitherto seen in Mysore exhibited evidence of the extraordinary attention paid by Tipu Sultan to the repair and improvement of this important branch of national defence, but the works of Nandidroog, a granite rock of tremendous height, seemed to have engrossed in a peculiar degree his design of rendering it impregnable; and its defence was committed to Latf Ali Beg, an officer who had always merited the highest distinction both from Haidar and Tipu. There was no choice with regard to the face to be attacked, because except on the west the precipice was inaccessible. That point had been strengthened by a double line of ramparts; and the foundation was laid for a third, which ultimately aided the assailants in forming their last lodgment. The defence was highly respectable, the ammunition of the cannon was well reserved, and the jinjals, or wall-pieces, were served with peculiar steadiness and skill; the labour was excessive of working regularly up the face of a steep and craggy mountain to breaching distance, and dragging cannon to the batteries; but in twenty-one days two breaches were effected; one in the exterior rampart, and the other in an outwork, and it was resolved to give the assault and form a lodgment for the farther operations against the interior works. The assailants received, however, a particular direction for endeavouring to enter with the fugitives, while the division allotted to forming the lodgment should be employed in providing cover; and in order that every possible impression might be made on the minds of the garrison Lord Cornwallis moved the army to the immediate vicinity: some additional flank companies were ordered in to lead the assault, and General Medows, with the usual spirit which animated him on such occasions, desired to take the immediate direction of the service.[1]

The assault was given by clear moonlight on the morning of the 19th of October; the arrangements of defence were excellent, and particularly the masses of granite reserved till this period to be rolled down the rock with tremendous effect, but the lodgment was within one hundred yards of the breach, and although the garrison was perfectly alert, the ardour and rapidity of the assailants surmounted every obstacle, and they pressed the fugitives so closely as to prevent their effectually barricading the gate of the inner rampart. It was forced after a sharp conflict, and the place

[1] Shortly before the assault, while all were waiting the signal in silence, one of the soldiers inadvertently whispered something about a mine. "To be sure there is," said General Medows, "and it is a mine of gold;" a smothered laugh ran along the ranks and produced the proper impression.

was carried with the loss in the assault of only thirty killed and wounded, chiefly by the stones tumbled down the rock, and in the whole siege one hundred and twenty.

A regiment was stationed at the foot, between Nandi and Sultanpet, from 1799 to 1808. It was during this period that the fruit-garden near the large tank was planted by Colonel Cuppage. The present dwelling houses on the droog were erected in about 1848[1], the remains of an old tower or fort on the highest point being removed for the site of the principal one. The salubrity of the spot led to its becoming a resort in the hot season for European officials from Bangalore, and the large house at the summit was long the favourite retreat of Sir Mark Cubbon. The temperature, especially at nights, is on the average ten degrees cooler than that of the plain 1,800 feet below. Except on the west, where it is united to a certain height with the adjoining range, Nandidroog presents an almost perpendicular rocky face. The present name is composed of *Nandi*, the sacred bull of Siva, and *durga*, hill fort. The principal old pilgrim ascent was by regularly formed steps beginning on the north side, and continuing on the west, connecting the temple in the village below with the temple at the top. The steps have now been taken entirely up the north side. A bridle path has since been carried from the bottom of the saddle on the south up the western face, the ascent by which is 4 miles long. At one point another bridle path meets it from the Basavan Kanive, or Bull pass, on the north-west, where there is a large stone bull. A rude flight of steps on the south side, known as the coolie path, forms a short cut for pedestrians. There is also a very steep foot path from the north-east angle.

The summit, 4,851 feet above the level of the sea, commands an extensive view over the Kolar and Bangalore Districts, the hundreds of shining tanks scattered over the country, of which it is said 400 can be counted, forming a marked feature in the scene. Kalavara-durga or Skandagiri (4,749 feet) is a conspicuous height on the north, formerly fortified. Brahma-giri or Varg-konda (4,657 feet) on the south-west, and Chenna-Kesava or Chenna-Rayan betta (4,762 feet) on the north-west, are partially connected with Nandidroog. The following rivers radiating in all directions have their sources in either this hill or those in the immediate neighbourhood. The Northern Pennár or Uttara Pinákini rises on the north-west in Chenna Kesava-betta, and can be traced for a long distance through the Manchenhalli

[1] By Colonel Hill (Glentilt), Sir Mark Cubbon, and his Secretary, Captain Cunningham (Oaklands); also one lower down, by his Sheristadar, between the inner and outer fortifications, looking over the pass.

valley to Goribidnur. The Southern Pennár or Dakshina Pinákini rises in the same hill, and flows south through the large Jangamkote and Hoskote tanks. The Arkavati rises in a well on the south-west of Nandidroog, between the two lines of fortification, and flows south-west to Dod-Ballapur. The Pálár is said to rise in the well near the eastern summit. On the north-east the Pápaghni and Chitravati may be discerned, the former of which rises in Kalavara-durga, and the latter in the Harihares'vara hill.

On the first heavy fall of rain following upon a long period of dry weather, myriads of lights are seen at night along the valley of the Northern Pennár, and towards the north, resembling the lamps in the streets of a great city—a phenomenon which has not been satisfactorily explained.[1] In the large cave on the south, almost inaccessible, black tourmaline is found in considerable quantities. The forest surrounding the mountain, as well as that on the neighbouring hills, is reserved by the State. It contains an occasional cheeta or panther, and numbers of wild pig; also pea-fowl and jungle-fowl.

**Nangali.**—A village in Mulbagal taluq, close to the eastern frontier, on the Kolar-Chittur road. Population 1,124.

It was an important frontier station from the time of the Hoysalas in the twelfth century, and is constantly enumerated among the conquests of Vishnuvardhana. Some large tanks exist in the neighbourhood.

**Palar.**—A river said to rise in a well near the summit of Nandidroog on the east, where the water of the little spring reputed as the immediate source used formerly to flow, as in the natural way, through a small stone bull, since mutilated. If however this be accepted as the source, it follows that the stream must at some point cross the S. Pinákini—a difficulty which the natives easily set aside by the hypothesis, for which there is no evidence, that it runs underground at that place. The river more probably springs from the neighbourhood of Kaivara, to the west of Ambajidurga and Rahmanghur. It first becomes visible, it is said, at Gautama guḍḍa, a small hill southward of Kaivara. From Jangamkote it flows eastward, until ten miles

[1] By some they are called *corpse candles*. Others consider them to be (and this seems the right explanation) the lights of the villagers used in the capture of the winged white ants, which issue from the ground at such times in countless profusion and are cooked and eaten by the lower orders as a great delicacy. Large coops of open wicker work are placed around the holes, surmounted by torches formed of the stem of an inferior kind of sugar cane. The insects, attracted by the light, fall in thousands into the hollows scooped below, where, as their wings drop off, they remain heaped together till gathered up.

Mr. Walhouse has suggested that the effect may be due to the mole cricket (*gryllotalpa vulgaris*), which emits a light that is often confounded with the *ignis fatuus*. *Ind. Ant.* IV, 47.

beyond Kolar, at the village of Yenandahalli, it receives an important tributary and directs its course south-south-east. Flowing through the Bowringpet taluq, where it forms the large Betamangala and Ramasagara tanks, it leaves the Mysore and enters North Arcot, near the village of Gundlapalli in the Kangundi zamindari. Running southwards to the west of Kangundi, it bends to the north-east past Vaniambadi and flows through the North Arcot and Chingalpat Districts, passing Vellore, Arcot and Kánchivaram (or Conjeveram), and falls into the Bay of Bengal south of Sadras.

The name *Pál-ár*, which means milk river, is rendered in Sanskrit into Kshira-nadi, the designation of the stream in the puranas. Its length in the District is about 47 miles, the entire drainage of its catchment basin, or 1,036 square miles, being utilized for cultivation.

**Papaghni.**—An affluent of the N. Pinakini. It rises in Kalavara-durga or Skandagiri, north of Nandidroog, and taking a north-easterly course, flows through the Bagepalli taluq into the Kadapa District, where, after forming the Vyasa-samudram and other large tanks, it unites with the N. Pinakini near Kamalapur. The name *Pápa-ghni*, signifying sin-destroyer in Sanskrit, denotes the purifying efficacy of its waters. A dam is carried across the stream near Burudukunte, whereby irrigation is provided for 180 acres of land. The famous large tank of Vyasa-samudram is a few miles below this point, on the Kadapa frontier, and is said to have been constructed by Vyasa Rayaswami, the guru of the Madhva Brahmans. The discharge of the stream in maximum flood has been gauged as 5,244 cubic feet per second.

**Pinakini.**[1]—The Northern or Uttara Pinákini, the Northern Pennár of European geographers, rises in the Chenna Kesava hill, north-west of Nandidroog, and flowing north-west past the town of Goribidnur, enters the Penugonda taluq of the Anantapur District. Thence, crossing a projecting angle of Pavugada taluq, it re-enters the Anantapur District and, turning eastward, passes through the Kadapa and Nellore Districts, finally discharging its waters into the Bay of Bengal near the town of Nellore.

Its principal tributaries from this District are the Pápaghni and the Chitravati. The total length of the main river and its chief affluents within the Province has been estimated at 167 miles, with a catchment basin of 2,280 square miles, of the drainage of which 85·35 per cent. has been intercepted for purposes of cultivation.

From an inscription at Kallodi we learn that the water supply of Penugonda was drawn from this part of the river. Bukka Raya, the son of Harihara Raya, ordered his chief engineer, Singaya Bhatta, in

[1] For S. Pinákini *see* Bangalore District.

1389 to "bring the Henne river (the Pennár or Hennár) to Penugonda." And he accordingly led a channel, remains of which may still be seen, to the Siruvara tank, naming it the Pratápa Bukka Ráya channel.

**Rahman Ghur.**—A conspicuous hill-fort in Chintamani taluq, rising to 4,227 feet above the level of the sea, which surrendered to the British in 1791. A large boulder on the western side near Kaivara, is crossed by belts of a brown colour, and from a crevice in the side a liquid resembling blood is said to issue at the time of Sivarátri, which kites and crows eagerly eat. The story is that Bhima, one of the Pandu brothers, imprisoned a giant under the mountain, who yearly turns upon his side and causes his wounds to bleed afresh. Tipu Sultan, mortified at the capture by the British of Nandidroog, which he had deemed impregnable, proposed to abandon it and strengthen Rahmanghur instead, but the design was not carried out.

**Sadali.**—A village in the north-west of the Sidlaghatta taluq, 18 miles north of the kasba, on the road to Bagepalli. Population 1,145.

A great antiquity is attributed to this village. It is said to have been founded by Sahadeva, the youngest of the Pandu brothers, and thence called Sahadeva-patna, since abbreviated into Sádahalli or Sádali. The spot was selected by Saka rishi, whom he had come to visit, and with whom he had an interview where Gumnayakanpalya now stands. The village changed hands several times until annexed to the Sira suba and bestowed as a jágir on two Muhammadan chiefs, who, to prevent its falling a conquest to the Kadapa navab, privately disposed of it, about 1459, to Dodda Baiche Gauda of Chik-Ballapur.

**Sidlaghatta.**—A taluq in the centre towards the north. Area 363 square miles. Head-quarters at Sidlaghatta. Contains the following hoblis, villages, and population :—

| No. | Hoblis. | Villages. | Hamlets. | Villages Classified. | | | | Population. |
|---|---|---|---|---|---|---|---|---|
| | | | | Government. | Sarvamanya. | Jodi. | Kayamgutta. | |
| 1 | Basettihalli ... | 61 | 13 | 54 | — | 1 | 6 | 6,810 |
| 2 | Chilakalnerpu ... | 45 | 14 | 36 | — | 7 | 2 | 6,756 |
| 3 | Ganjigunte ... | 52 | 7 | 42 | — | 9 | 1 | 5,645 |
| 4 | Jangamkote ... | 56 | 2 | 36 | 4 | 5 | 11 | 9,026 |
| 5 | Sádali ... ... | 38 | 14 | 32 | 1 | 5 | — | 7,271 |
| 6 | Sidlaghatta ... | 98 | 3 | 77 | — | 10 | 11 | 23,469 |
| | Total ... | 350 | 53 | 277 | 5 | 37 | 31 | 58,977 |

*Principal places, with population.*—Sidlaghatta, 6,572 ; Jangamkote 1,504 ; Sádali, 1,145.

The taluq forms the valley of the Pápaghni, which river crosses it in a north-easterly direction. The S. Pinákini drains the south-west angle and forms two large tanks at the kasba. The northern parts of the taluq, marking the continuation of the Dongala-konda hills, are stony and rugged. The remaining parts are fertile and well cultivated. In the former the dry crop soils are, as a rule, poor and stony or sandy. In the vicinity of the rivers, however, black soil is not uncommon. To the south of Sidlaghatta the dry crop soil is usually reddish, of fair quality. The irrigated lands are generally superior, rich brown loam being very common. Wet cultivation receives special attention in the north, and the abundance of *honge* trees there (*pongamia glabra*) provide, in their leaves and branches, the manure required for the rice-fields. In the south, on the contrary, ragi is the staple crop, but potatoes also occupy a considerable area, as well as sugar-cane. The manufactures consist principally of ordinary women's cloths, cumblies, glass bangles, sack cloth, and thread.

The revenue settlement was introduced in 1885. The unculturable area is 130,290 acres, or 203½ square miles. The area of inam villages is 31,011 acres, or nearly 48½ square miles; that of forests is 1,157 acres. The total revenue demand for 1891–2 (15 months) was Rs. 1,58,370, and for 1892–3 it was Rs. 2,00,238. The amounts under land revenue were Rs. 1,21,798 and Rs. 1,44,190 respectively.

The average rainfall for twenty-five years (1870–94) at Sidlaghatta, and for two years (1893–4) at Jangamkote was as follows :—

| | Jan. | Feb. | Mar. | Apl. | May | June | July | Aug. | Sept. | Oct. | Nov. | Dec. | Year. |
|---|---|---|---|---|---|---|---|---|---|---|---|---|---|
| Sidlaghatta... | 0·01 | 0·06 | 0·58 | 0·67 | 2·99 | 2·84 | 2·85 | 3·87 | 4·71 | 5·57 | 2·90 | 0·69 | 27·74 |
| Jangamkote . | — | — | — | 0·97 | 2·98 | 3·09 | 2·60 | 3·19 | 1·97 | 5·74 | 1·98 | — | 22·56 |

From Sidlaghatta there are roads west to Chik-Ballapur, east to Chintamani, and south to Jangamkote and Hoskote. The Bangalore-Kadapa high road passes through the south-east angle and the Chintamani-Bagepalli road crosses through the taluq a little above the middle. The Kolar-Nandi road runs along the southern limit through Jangamkote.

**Sidlaghatta.**—A large town, 30 miles north-west of Kolar, on the Srinivaspur-Chik-Ballapur road. Head-quarters of the Sidlaghatta taluq and a municipality.

| Population in 1891. | Males. | Females. | Total. |
|---|---|---|---|
| Hindus ... ... ... ... ... | 2,686 | 2,831 | 5,517 |
| Muhammadans ... ... ... ... | 534 | 505 | 1,039 |
| Christians ... ... ... ... ... | 12 | 4 | 16 |
| Total ... ... | 3,232 | 3,340 | 6,572 |

Sidlaghatta is said to have been founded about 1524 by Shivangi Gauda. His father, named Kempe Gauda, appears to have been an outlaw from Ujanipatna, who, with a band of freebooters, settled at Abalod, north of Sidlaghatta. The gang were captured during some depredations near Vellore and put to death. Shivangi Gauda extended his power on all sides from Sidlaghatta by conquest, and his family held possession for 87 years. The Mahrattas then subdued and held it for 45 years, when it was taken by the Mughals. It afterwards again became subject to the Mahrattas, who sold it to Anni Gauda, the chief of Chik-Ballapur.

For about five miles round Sidlaghatta there occurs a kind of laterite, called *chaṭṭu*, which differs from ordinary laterite in allowing of the growth of large trees, as on a hill south of the town. Reduced to clay it forms a very durable plastering for walls, and applied to roofs makes them permanently watertight.

| Municipal Funds. | 1892-3. | 1893-4. | 1894-5. | 1895-6. |
|---|---|---|---|---|
| Income ... ... ... ... ... | 2,811 | 2,807 | 2,823 | 4,351 |
| Expenditure ... ... ... ... | 5,765 | 4,567 | 3,594 | 5,911 |

**Siti-betta.**—A hill in the Vemgal hobli, Kolar taluq. It has a temple of Kála Bhairava, and is an important sacred place of the Morasu Wokkalu tribe, who preponderate in this District. Inscriptions at the place show that the name is contracted from Siripati, through Sihati. They are of the time of the Chola kings, of Ganga Perumál, the Hoysala king Ballála III., and of the Vijayanagar period.

**Srinivaspur.**—A taluq to the east. Head-quarters at Srinivaspur. Contains the following hoblis, villages and population :—

| No. | Hoblis. | Villages. | Hamlets. | Villages classified. | | | | Population. |
|---|---|---|---|---|---|---|---|---|
| | | | | Govern-ment. | Sarva-mánya. | Jodi. | Kayam-gutta. | |
| 1 | Aḍḍagal ... ... | 52 | 17 | 50 | 1 | 1 | — | 6,011 |
| 2 | Dalsanúr ... ... | 25 | — | 25 | — | — | — | 3,291 |
| 3 | Nelavanki ... | 55 | 14 | 47 | — | 6 | 2 | 6,852 |
| 4 | Ráyalpáḍ ... | 40 | 18 | 38 | — | 2 | — | 4,367 |
| 5 | Sómayájalpaḷḷi ... | 66 | 13 | 57 | — | 8 | 1 | 9,896 |
| 6 | Srinivászpur ... | 63 | 3 | 57 | — | 4 | 2 | 10,988 |
| 7 | Yeldúr ... ... | 28 | 11 | 27 | — | — | 1 | 5,058 |
| | Total ... | 329 | 76 | 301 | 1 | 21 | 6 | 46,463 |

*Principal places, with population.*—Srinivászpur, 2,741 ; Yeldúr, 1,049.

The taluq was reduced in 1882 to a sub-taluq under Chintamani, but restored as a taluq in 1897, with the addition of Yeldúr hobli from Mulbagal and Dalsanúr from Kolar. The taluq is bounded on the north and north-east by ranges of hills connected with the Eastern Ghats, among which are situated the two clusters of hills enclosing the elevated picturesque valleys of Mudimadagu and Sunnakal. The former is a circular basin, inaccessible on all sides except at the north and south, where there are passes leading to the country around. The village of Mudimadagu is situated in the centre of the valley, and some twenty villages in other parts of it. The group to the south also forms a circle, in the middle of which stands the village of Sunnakal. The only outlet now used is towards the west. There are four villages in the valley, and the scenery here is described as more picturesque than at Mudimadagu. Both these groups of hills are covered with thick jungle, and have been the strongholds of petty chiefs who held sway over the surrounding country. From the neighbourhood of Yeldur commence the low flat hills which indicate the auriferous tract extending to the southernmost limits of the District. Further description is included in that of Chintamani taluq

The average rainfall at Srinivaspur for twenty-five years (1870–94) was as follows:—

| Jan. | Feb. | Mar. | Apr. | May | June | July | Aug. | Sept. | Oct. | Nov. | Dec. | | Year. |
|---|---|---|---|---|---|---|---|---|---|---|---|---|---|
| 0·03 | 0·46 | 0·43 | 0·71 | 2·76 | 2·38 | 2·61 | 4·03 | 5·85 | 5·21 | 2·98 | 0·36 | ... | 27·51 |

The Bangalore-Kadapa road runs through the taluq in a north-east direction, and is joined at Tadgol by a road from Kolar through Srinivaspur. The Mulbagal-Chintamani road also passes through Srinivaspur. The Madanapalli and Chinna-Tippasamudram stations of the South Indian Railway from Vellore to Dharmávaram are close to the north-east angle of the taluq.

**Srinivaspur.**—A town 15 miles north-north-east of Kolar, with which it is connected by road. Head-quarters of the Srinivaspur taluq, and a municipality.

| Population in 1891. | Males. | Females. | Total. |
|---|---|---|---|
| Hindus ... ... ... ... ... | 952 | 1,044 | 1,996 |
| Muhammadans ... ... ... ... | 358 | 376 | 734 |
| Christians ... ... ... ... ... | 8 | 3 | 11 |
| Total ... ... | 1,318 | 1,423 | 2,741 |

It is better known to the natives of the District by its old name of Pápanpalli. The Divan Púrnaiya, when he visited the place on his return from a pilgrimage to Tirupati, gave it the present name, calling it after his son Srinivasa Múrti. Rough bits for horses and other articles of iron are manufactured here.

At Gúlgánpode, about two miles to the east, is pointed out the site of an ancient city, said to have been called Haralukóte. Two Mahávali inscriptions, of the time of Bánarasa and Vikramáditya, were excavated by me there some years ago,[1] and a Pallava inscription dating in 768 was also found.

| Municipal Funds. | 1892-3. | 1893-4. | 1894-5. | 1895-6. |
|---|---|---|---|---|
| Income ... ... ... ... ... | 874 | 825 | 920 | 1,566 |
| Expenditure... ... ... ... ... | 1,355 | 1,103 | 967 | 1,628 |

**Vanarasi.**—A village in the Holur hobli of Kolar taluq, seven miles north of Kolar. Population 357.

It is the seat of a large annual festival held for fifteen days in April, in honour of Iralappa, when 5,000 people assemble and a cattle fair takes place, to which 10,000 bullocks are brought for sale.

**Vrishabhavati.**—A tributary of the S. Pinákini. It rises from the east of the Vokkaleri hills, passes by Sulikunte, and crosses the railway at the Bowringpet station. It then feeds the tank of Kuppam, and passing by Kendoti, leaves the District three miles beyond it. The stream descends into the plains by the Singarlapalli pass, receives the waters of the Markanda near Ankusgiri, and falls into the S. Pinákini near Krishnagiri.

[1] See *Ind. Ant.* X., 36. This was, I believe, the first discovery of the Mahávali or Bána dynasty.

TUMKUR DISTRICT
SCALE 8 MILES TO AN INCH
B—Travellers' Bungalow. L—Inspection Lodge. S—Railway Station.
CHITALDROOG
SIDDAVVANAHALLI
HIRIYUR
HOSDURGA
KADUR
HULIYAR
CHIKNAYAKANHALLI
HONNAVALLI
TIPTUR
TURUVEKERE
CHANNARAYAPATNA
NAGAMANGALA
MYSORE
GUBBI
TUMKUR
KUNIGAL
SIRA
MADDAGIRI
KORATIGERE
MADAKASIRA
PAVUGADA
AMARAPURAM
KUNDARPIDURGA
MULAKALEDU
CHANGAVARA
ANANTAPUR
HINDUPUR
HUSENAPURA
RODDAM
DOD-BALLAPUR
NELAMANGALA
TYAMAGONDLU
KOLAR
HOSKOTE

# TUMKUR DISTRICT

## GENERAL DESCRIPTION

*Situation.*—A District in the centre and north-east, situated between 12° 15′ and 14° 15′ north latitude, and between 76° 30′ and 77° 25′ east longitude. Its extreme length is from north to south 96 miles, and its greatest breadth from east to west 69 miles.

*Area.*—The area is 4,154 square miles; of which 1,667 square miles are under cultivation, and 1,604 square miles unculturable.

*Boundaries.*—It is bounded on the north by the Anantapur District of the Madras Presidency, on the east by the Kolar and Bangalore Districts, on the south by the Mysore District, and on the west by the Chitaldroog, Kadur and Hassan Districts.

*Divisions.*—It is subdivided into the following taluqs. The sub-taluqs are: Huliyár, included in Chiknáyakanhaḷḷi; Koraṭigere, in Maddagiri; and Turuvekere, in Tiptúr.

| No. | Taluq. | Area in sq. miles. | No. of Hoblis. | No. of Villages or Towns. | Population in 1891. |
|---|---|---|---|---|---|
| 1 | Chiknáyakanhaḷḷi ... ... | 532 | 7 | 279 | 51,620 |
| 2 | Gubbi ... ... ... ... | 552 | 8 | 421 | 73,570 |
| 3 | Kunigal ... ... ... ... | 381 | 7 | 291 | 66,502 |
| 4 | Maddagiri ... ... ... | 596 | 11 | 483 | 97,973 |
| 5 | Pávugaḍa ... ... ... | 532 | 7 | 145 | 53,377 |
| 6 | Síra ... ... ... ... | 599 | 8 | 253 | 68,327 |
| 7 | Tiptúr ... ... ... ... | 510 | 9 | 391 | 78,867 |
| 8 | Tumkúr ... ... ... ... | 452 | 9 | 473 | 90,782 |
| | Total ... ... | 4,154 | 66 | 2,736 | 581,018 |

Gubbi is the former Kadaba taluq; and Tiptúr, the former Honnavalli taluq. Pávugaḍa taluq, which is separated from the rest by the intervening Madaksira taluq of the Madras Presidency, was transferred to this District from Chitaldroog in 1882. It was in the same year that the sub-taluqs were formed.

**Physical Features.**—A considerable range of hills, forming the eastern boundary of the Krishna river system in Mysore, runs north and south through the eastern parts of the District. Entering its limits from the north, with Kámandurga (3,537 feet) and Nidugal (3,485 feet) in Pávugada taluq, it is continued by Midagesi-durga (3,414 feet), and includes the prominent peaks of Maddagiri-durga (3,935 feet), Channaráyan-durga (3,744 feet), Koratigiri (2,906 feet), Devaráyadurga (3,940 feet), Nijagal (3,569 feet), Hutari-durga (3,713 feet), and Huliyur-durga (3,086 feet). It is a part of the range running through the west of the Bangalore District, represented by Sivaganga and Sávandurga.

The streams issuing from these hills are of small size, the principal being the Jayamangali, which rises in Devaráyadurga and flows north-east into the N. Pinákini; and the Shimsha, which rises to the south of the same hill and flows southwards towards the Káveri. The N. Pinákini has a course of only a few miles across the extreme north-east corner of the District, in the Pávugada taluq.

West of the chain of hills above mentioned, a low range, commencing near Kibbanhalli, runs north-west past Chiknáyakanhalli and connects with the central belt of the Chitaldroog District. The watershed separating the river system of the Krishna northwards from that of the Káveri southwards may be defined by a line drawn east and west from Koratigere to Tiptúr; while the main chain of mountains forms the western limit of the upper N. Pinákini basin.

The open parts of the District maintain a generally even level above the sea, the height at Tumkúr being 2,678 feet. At Kunigal it has been determined as 2,520 feet; at Kibbanhalli it is 2,734, at Maddagiri 2,462, east of Holuvanhalli 2,479. But the situation of Síra is much lower, being only 2,160 feet above the sea. This depression is evident to the eye from the neighbourhood of the Shibi temple.

The southern taluqs, except around Huliyurdurga, where the country is wooded and hilly, consist of undulating plains, interspersed with clumps of tall and well-grown trees, where stone is scarce, except on occasional ridges or hillocks. Cocoanut and other palms are confined to the vicinity of tanks. Farther north, large plantations of cocoanuts occupy even the dry lands, especially in Gubbi, Tiptúr and Chiknáyakanhalli taluqs. After crossing Tumkúr eastwards, the park-like appearance of that taluq changes, north of Devaráyadurga, to the scenery of a hill country intersected by cultivated valleys: the hills and their skirts being for the most part covered with shrubs, interspersed with trees which remain verdant through the greater part of the year.

To the north-east extends a very fertile tract, irrigated from perennial springs, reached at a depth of only a few feet below the surface. These springs, called *talpargis*, form a marked and peculiar feature of the Maddagiri taluq, as well as of the adjoining taluqs of the Madras Presidency. The water obtained from the spring-heads is either conducted directly by narrow channels to the fields, or a *kapile* well is constructed, from which the water is raised by two or four bullocks. Where the soil is not sandy, springs may be tapped at short distances from each other.

**Rocks.**—The majority of the rocks are similar in formation to those of the Bangalore District. But near Síra westwards the stratified hills make their appearance, running in straight lines in various directions. They are quite bare of trees, but in the wet season have a green appearance from the long hill grass (*anthistiria barbata*), which is almost the only vegetation that grows on them. These hills are mostly covered at top with a kind of magnetic iron-stone, that withstands the decomposing powers of the air and water much longer than the lower parts of the hills, which seem to be composed of ferruginous slate clay.

In the south-west, near Turuvekere, is a celebrated quarry, situated in Karekal-guḍḍa, a ridge about half a mile long, a hundred yards wide, and from twenty to fifty feet in perpendicular height. This ridge runs nearly north and south in the common direction of the strata of the country, and is surrounded on all sides by the common gray granite, which, as usual, is intersected in all directions by veins of quartz and felspar ; but neither of these enter the quarry. The stone is called *kare-kallu* or black stone by the natives, who give the same appellation to the quartz impregnated with iron, and to the brown hæmatites ; and in fact they all run very much into one another, and differ chiefly in the various proportions of the same component parts, but have a certain general similitude easily defined, and are found in similar masses and strata. The black stone of this place is an amorphous hornblend, containing minute but distinct rhomboidal lamellar concretions of basaltine. It is probably the same stone as that which by the ancients was called Basaltes. The surface of the ridge is covered with irregular masses, which, where they have been long exposed to the air, in the natural process of decay lose their angles first. When these masses have thus become rounded, they decay in concentric lamellæ ; but where the rock itself is exposed to the air, it separates into plates of various thicknesses nearly vertical and running north and south. In the sound stone there is not the smallest appearance of a slaty texture, and it splits in the wedges in all directions. The north end of the ridge is the lowest, and has on its surface the largest masses, but the natives have always contented themselves with splitting detached blocks and have never ventured on quarrying the solid rock itself, where much finer pieces might be procured than have ever yet been obtained. The great *basava*, or bull, at Turuvekere is the finest piece of the wrought rock to be seen, and is exquisitely polished. The pillars of Haidar Ali's mausoleum at Seringapatam are said to have been obtained from here. Very handsome vases might be made of the stone polished. In the same neighbourhood is a quarry of pot stone, which is formed into small vessels and pencils.

In the hills east of Chiknáyakanhaḷḷi is found a hard whetstone or novaculite, used by natives for polishing diamonds and to compound medicines upon. The auriferous characteristics of the schistose rocks in the Chiknáyakanhaḷḷi band have been described in Vol. I, p. 49.

**Metals and Minerals.**—Iron ore is largely obtained from the hill sides in Chiknáyakanhaḷḷi, either upon or at a very small distance below the surface. The metal is also smelted from the black sand brought down by streams from the rocks in Maddagiri and Koratigere. The Chiknáyakanhaḷḷi iron is esteemed the best, and is principally manufactured from the quarries of Dore guḍḍa. The hæmatite or limonite obtained in the same neighbourhood is much used by braziers for polishing the utensils made by them. As yellow ochre it furnishes a dye, and is also applied as a colour-wash to walls of houses. Corundum or emery stone is found in small quantities in Turuvekere, and limestone or chunam in most of the taluqs.

**Soils.**—Except the taluqs of Maddagiri, Chiknáyakanhaḷḷi, and the eastern and northern parts of Síra and Koratigere respectively, the soil is described as generally hard and poor, requiring much labour and manure to render it productive. Acres on acres may be seen in some parts on which there is nothing but scattered stunted shrub, without even a blade of grass. This has no reference to the superior land irrigated by tanks, nálas and spring channels, as these soils of the taluqs above referred to are exceptionally remarkable for their fertility. Pasture land is abundant, but poor, except in the Amrit Mahal kávals throughout the District.

The southern and western taluqs may be described as most abundant in the red soil and contain large tanks. The eastern taluqs abound in sandy soil, the northern contain some black.

**Climate.**—The District generally enjoys the reputation of having an even, pleasant and healthy climate, agreeing alike with natives and Europeans. In the south and south-west the climate greatly resembles that of Bangalore; the high elevation, the red soil, and the greenness of the surface among the hills contributing to moderate the temperature. From Síra northwards the lower level of the country and the prevalence of black soil raise the temperature more to that of the adjoining Bellary District. The eastern side of every range of hills is said to be perceptibly warmer than the western.

*Temperature.*—The following averages are given from observations at Tumkúr of the dry bulb thermometer at 9.30 A.M. and 3.30 P.M. during each month of 1873 and 1874. No observations appear to have been made in more recent years. The temperature is thus seen to be tolerably equable. For nine months in the year it is never very unpleasantly hot; the nights in the hottest months are comparatively cool. The hot season is from the middle of February to the middle of May. The average range of the thermometer throughout the year in the observatory at Tumkúr was from 74° to 83° at noon.

| Months. | 1873. | | 1874. | |
|---|---|---|---|---|
| | 9.30 A.M. | 3.30 P.M. | 9.30 A.M. | 3.30 P.M. |
| January ... ... ... ... | 68 | 71 | 73 | 75 |
| February ... ... ... ... | 75 | 79 | 80 | 82 |
| March ... ... .. ... | 79 | 84 | 84 | 86 |
| April ... ... ... ... | 79 | 84 | 87 | 88 |
| May ... ... ... ... | 81 | 84 | 78 | 81 |
| June ... ... ... ... | 76 | 80 | 75½ | 76½ |
| July ... ... ... ... | 73½ | 77 | 73 | 74½ |
| August ... ... ... ... | 72 | 77½ | 73 | 74½ |
| September... ... ... ... | 72½ | 78 | 71½ | 73 |
| October ... ... ... ... | 73 | 75 | 72½ | 74½ |
| November... ... ... ... | 74 | 78 | 72 | 74 |
| December... ... ... ... | 72 | 74 | 69 | 71 |

*Rainfall.*—The average annual rainfall, calculated on the amount registered in each year at Tumkúr from 1837 to 1874, was 32·7 inches, falling on from 40 to 50 days. The average, calculated on 25 years' rainfall from 1870 to 1894, is 37·36. The following are the actual figures :—

| | In. c. | | In. c. | | In. c. | | In. c. | | In. c. |
|---|---|---|---|---|---|---|---|---|---|
| 1837 | 26 | 1849 | 31·6 | 1861 | 37·8 | 1873 | 21·78 | 1884 | 21·26 |
| 1838 | 13·8 | 1850 | 36·3 | 1862 | 33·8 | 1874 | 36·24 | 1885 | 24·86 |
| 1839 | 31·2 | 1851 | 31·3 | 1863 | 28·8 | 1875 | 16·52 | 1886 | 52·29 |
| 1840 | 22·7 | 1852 | 57·4 | 1864 | 41·8 | 1876 | 16·99 | 1887 | 31·20 |
| 1841 | 29·2 | 1853 | 21·1 | 1865 | 25·3 | 1877 | 34·98 | 1888 | 38·36 |
| 1842 | 27·5 | 1854 | 30 | 1866 | 34·7 | 1878 | 44·56 | 1889 | 57·75 |
| 1843 | 42 | 1855 | 22·5 | 1867 | 34·23 | 1879 | 34·82 | 1890 | 34·69 |
| 1844 | 24·7 | 1856 | 39·6 | 1868 | 32·69 | 1880 | 37·93 | 1891 | 21·61 |
| 1845 | 26·5 | 1857 | 22·1 | 1869 | 26·11 | 1881 | 27·38 | 1892 | 41·34 |
| 1846 | 56·9 | 1858 | 55·6 | 1870 | 41·11 | 1882 | 39·32 | 1893 | 48·13 |
| 1847 | 31·5 | 1859 | 26·4 | 1871 | 34·55 | 1883 | 40·45 | 1894 | 40·73 |
| 1848 | 17·2 | 1860 | 30 | 1872 | 31·5 | | | | |

The annual average at other taluq and sub-taluq stations, based on the register for 25 years (1870–1894), has been :—

| | | | |
|---|---|---|---|
| Chiknáyakanhalli ... ... | 22·86 | Maddagiri ... ... ... | 19·36 |
| Gubbi ... ... ... ... | 31·55 | Pávugada ... ... ... | 18·58 |
| Huliyár ... ... ... | 24·93 | Síra ... ... ... ... | 15·15 |
| Koratigere ... ... ... | 21·55 | Tiptúr ... ... ... ... | 27·77 |
| Kunigal ... ... ... | 30·38 | Turuvekere ... ... ... | 25·08 |

**Vegetation.**—The principal forest in the District is on the slopes of the Devaráyadurga hills. Farther north the hills around Koratigere are clothed with good fuel jungle. Near Maddagiri the vegetation improves in appearance and variety. On the western range of hills running north from Kibbanhalli, there is a forest of karachi (*hardwickia binata*), extending from Bukkapatna northwards to Gangarapente.

The following are the reserved or State forests in the District :—

| | Sq. m. | | Sq. m. |
|---|---|---|---|
| Devaráyadurga ... ... ... | 30 | Huliyurdurga ... ... ... | 30 |
| Maddagiri... ... ... ... | 32 | Kudare-kanave ... ... ... | 21 |
| Bukkapatna ... ... ... | 50 | Kemplapura... ... ... ... | 1¼ |

There are also nine Forest plantations, covering 963 acres, and three Revenue plantations. Of these, three are for sandal, and the others for casuarina and cassia.

The best wooded taluqs are those which include the great eastern range of hills—namely, Tumkúr, Koratigere, Maddagiri, and the old Huliyurdurga taluq. In these, too, sandal grows. The south-western taluqs are well occupied with trees in topes, and such as have planted themselves in valleys and hedges. Cocoanut gardens are numerous, and in some parts the *butea frondosa* grows abundantly in waste lands. The north and centre of the Síra taluq is badly supplied with wood, but the wild custard-apple grows in profusion in the plains.

With the exceptions above noted the tree vegetation resembles that of the adjoining Districts on the east.

**Cultivation.**—A list will be given below of the principal crops raised in the District by dry cultivation, as well as of the garden produce of irrigated grounds. Lands are generally manured to the extent of the annual collections of manure and refuse in the house or cattle yard of each landholder. Near large towns, or where municipalities are established, town refuse is freely bought and sells well.

Manure is conveyed to the fields on platform carts surmounted with large wicker baskets, or in gunny bags on buffaloes or on men's heads; and is chiefly composed, in addition to the village and town refuse, of ashes and silt, which are carefully collected in pits and used for the dry lands; while vegetable manure, especially leaves of the shrub karanj, and sheep's dung are used for wet lands.

*Tanks and Wells.*—The number of Government tanks in the District is 2,254, of which 605 are classed as large, yielding a revenue of more than Rs. 300. The large one at Kunigal, when full, is 14 miles in circumference. The Maidalada, Kallamballa, Kadaba, Mallaghatta, and Dipambudhi tanks are all large reservoirs, the last-named being about 30 feet deep at the lowest point. Another large tank, recently constructed, is the Borankanave, in Chiknáyakanhaḷḷi taluq. The number of wells is 13,495. There are also 145 tanks in Inam villages.

*Crops.*—The cereals, pulses and oil-seeds cultivated are the same as those of the Bangalore District. Cotton and indigo are grown to a small extent in Maddagiri and Pávugaḍa taluqs.

The following is a list of miscellaneous products :—

| Kannada. | Botanical. | English. |
|---|---|---|
| Adike ... ... | Areca catechu ... ... | Areca-nut. |
| Hoge soppu ... | Nicotiana tabaccum ... | Tobacco. |
| Kabbu ... ... | Saccharum officinale ... | Sugar-cane. |
| Kalle kayi ... ... | Arachis hypogœa ... ... | Ground-nut. |
| Mensina kayi ... | Capsicum annuum ... ... | Chilly. |
| Tengina kayi ... | Cocos nucifera ... ... | Cocoanut. |
| Uppu Nérle ... | Morus ... ... ... | Mulberry. |
| Viled-ele ... ... | Piper betle ... ... ... | Betel vine. |

*Garden Produce.*—The names of vegetables and fruit raised in the District exhibit the variety of garden produce. Under the former may be mentioned brinjals, cucumbers, pumpkins, onions, garlic, potatoes, cabbages, beans, peas, ginger: the latter includes mangoes, oranges, figs, grapes, apples, peaches, strawberries, gooseberries, loquats, pomegranates, plantains, limes, citron, guavas, &c.

*Acreage under principal Crops.*—The number of acres under rice cultivation in 1893 was 61,208, wheat 84, ragi 428,864, other food grains 272,622; oil-seeds 38,408, sugar-cane 899, cotton and fibres 3,866, tobacco 2,775, vegetables 26,885, cocoanut and areca-nut 44,756, mulberry 818.

**Wild Animals.**—The larger game is very scarce, and pretty nearly confined to the preserved forest tracts around Devaráyadurga, where tiger, panther, bear, and wild hog may be met with. In the jungly parts of Síra taluq, deer may sometimes be found and occasional cheetahs. There are also deer about the plantations in Gubbi taluq.

*Birds* of prey are stated to be very numerous.

**Domestic Animals.**—Among bullocks, those of Maddagiri, Turuvekere, and parts of Kadaba are highly esteemed on account of their breed, but the cattle generally resemble those of the other Districts on the east. Buffaloes are commonly used both for agricultural and dairy purposes. Swine are numerous in certain localities. Cows are plentiful, but poor in size, breed, and yield of milk. Sheep are not of the highest quality, but a good breed is met with in Chiknáyakanhaḷḷi and the taluqs to the south and west. Those of Maddagiri, Midagesi and that side are considered less valuable.

## HISTORY

Omitting the legends that the Kadaba tank was constructed by the orders of Rama, when encamped in the neighbourhood; that the emperor Nriga was cured of leprosy by bathing in the Nagini, the stream that forms the Kunigal tank; and that Salivahana was born at Hale Tanduga near Turuvekere: the place in this District claiming the highest antiquity is the village of Sampige in Gubbi taluq. It is said to be the site of Champaka-nagara, the capital of Sudhanva, son of a king named Hamsa Dhvaja. There was a Haihaya prince of this name, of whom the following account is given.[1] "Tradition asserts that at the end of the Satyayuga a monarch named Sudhyumna presided over the destinies of the East. Of his descendants, one son, Nila Dhwaja, got the throne of Mahishmati; a second, Hamsa Dhwaja, became monarch of Chandrapur; and the third received the kingdom of Ratanpur." In later times the village of Kaidala near Tumkúr is said to have been a large city named Kríḍápura, and the birth-place of the famous sculptor and architect Jakanachari. The legend regarding Devaráyadurga and its capture from a robber chief, named Andhaka or Lingaka, by Sumati, son of Hemachandra, king of Karnataka, and the subsequent foundation of a city by Sumati near Nelamangala have already been related in connection with the Bangalore District.

**Gangas.**—The Tumkúr country was from an early period in possession of the Gangas, and an inscription of the tenth century spells the name as *Tummegúru*, which may mean the country of the *tumme* or *tumbe*, a common fragrant herb (*leucas indica*). Among other records of the Gangas, a grant by Nava Káma (679–713) was obtained at Hebbur, and inscriptions of S'rípurusha (726–777) occur at Midagesi, and of Satyavákya Nolambakulántaka (963–974) at Kibbanhalli.

**Nolambas.**—The Noḷambas or Noṇambas, who were of Pallava

[1] *Central Provinces Gazetteer*, Int., l.

descent (*see* Vol. I, p. 307), have left many memorials throughout the east of the District. They had a capital city at Penjeṟu or Henjeṟu, in Tamil called Pperuncheṟu, which I have identified with Hemavati, situated on the northern border of Síra taluq, in Madaksira. Its name occurs in a number of professedly very ancient inscriptions,[1] as well as in certain legends, and the existing remains show that it must have been a place of considerable importance. The Noḷambas had their stronghold at Nidugal, which is only a few miles to the east, in Pávugaḍa taluq. In the ninth century they were in matrimonial alliance with the Gangas, Nolambádhirája having married Jáyabbe, younger sister of the Ganga king Nítimárga. He also assigned to each of his other queens certain villages in the Síra country. The Noṇaba ryots, who are more numerous in this District than anywhere else, are representatives of the subjects of the old Noṇamba kingdom, the Nonambaváḍi Thirty-two Thousand, of which a further account will be found under Chitaldroog District (*see* also under Gubbi, and Vol. I, p. 230).

**Hoysalas.**—The Hoysalas, whose inscriptions are numerous, succeeded the Gangas, and there are no regular Chola remains in this District. But the Hoysalas subdued Irungola, a chief whose capital was at Henje.u and his stronghold at Nidugal, and the line of kings to which he belonged had the title "Lords of Oreiyúr," the ancient Chola capital, now called Warriore, at Trichinopoly, and style themselves Chola kings. They profess to be descended from Karikála Chóla, through a king called Mangi or Kali Mangi. His successors were Bebbi or Bíchi, Govinda, Irungola (I), Malli Deva or Bhoga, Brahma or Barma, whose wife was Báchala Devi, and their son Irungola (II), called Irungola-Deva Chóla-mahárája. A representative of the line, named Víra Bomma, who had a minister Baicheya or Chaicheya, seems to have been still in power at Nidugal in the thirteenth century.

From Turuvekere the king Narasimha I appears to have obtained his wife Lokamma or Lokámbika, whose name is perpetuated in that of the neighbouring village of Lokammanhalli, granted by her as an endowment to a temple. It is in his reign that we first meet with the singular name A'nebiddasari or A'nebiddajari, meaning "the steep where the elephant fell," as that of the náḍ or district which included the Devaráyadurga hills and the central and southern parts of the Tumkúr taluq. It must have been in use, however, before that, and continued in use during the Vijayanagar period. The steep itself seems to have been on Devaráyadurga, at a spot called A'negondi.

[1] See my *Ep. Carn.*, Mysore, I, Intro., p. 2, and *Coorg Gaz.*, p. 95.

When, after the death of Somes'vara, a partition was made of the Hoysala dominions between his two sons, the share which, along with the Tamil districts, fell to Rámanátha, did not extend west of the Devaráyadurga hills, and a line from Urudigere to Hebbur, with one from there east to Lakkur in Malur taluq (Kolar District), would pretty well define the western and southern limits of his territory in the Mysore country.

**Chalukyas.**—The later of the Henjeṛu Chola inscriptions and the earliest of the Hoysala inscriptions in the District acknowledge the supremacy of the Chálukyas, and the records of this line are met with throughout the western taluqs, Tipṭúr and Chiknáyakanhaḷḷi. Under them, the Hoysalas Vinayáditya and Vishnuvardhana (at the beginning of his reign) are represented as ruling over the Gangavádi Ninety-six Thousand, and Nárasimha as ruling over both that and the Nonambavádi Thirty-two Thousand.

**Vijayanagar.**—The Vijayanagar empire arose in the fourteenth century and many traces exist of the rule of its kings throughout the District. It was under this sovereignty that several feudatory states arose of local interest.

The *Nidugal* chiefs were descended from Harati Tippa Raja or Tippa Náyaka, whose possessions were in the north-east of the Chitaldroog District, under which an account of him will be found. At his death he divided his territory among his seven sons. But on the invasion of the country by the Bijapur army, the descendants of these were driven out of their estates, and Timmanna Nayak, who had lost Dodderi, retired to the hill of Nidugal, which he fortified. There the family long remained, paying to Síra a tribute of 3,000 pagodas. On the capture of Síra by Haidar Ali in 1761, the Nidugal chief, also called Timmanna Nayak, submitted to the conqueror, who imposed on him a tribute of 7,000 pagodas and the supply of 300 men. Subsequently, while accompanying Tipu Sultan in the expedition against Mangalore, he fell ill, and when at the point of death, was compelled to sign a letter relinquishing his territory and ordering his son Hottana Nayak to deliver it up to the governor of Chitaldroog. Possession was at once taken, and Hottanna Nayak and his brother were sent as prisoners to Chitaldroog and thence to Seringapatam, where they were put to death when the British army ascended the Ghats.

That of *Holavanhalli* or Korampur, in the east, was founded by Baire Gauda or Vira Gauda, one of the band of refugees that settled in the fifteenth century at Avati, Devanhalli taluq, and whose history is so prominent in connection with the Bangalore and Kolar Districts. The newly-acquired territory of Holavanhalli does not seem to have been long enjoyed by this family, when it was conquered by the chief of Magadi, who gave it to his own brother Ankana Gauda. The Baire Gauda then ruling, with his eldest son Dodda Baiche Gauda, repaired to the Musalman court at Síra, where he was not only well received but was invested with an important command. Meanwhile, the younger son, Sanna Baiche Gauda, apparently preferring his own people, sought protection from the chief of Dod-Ballapur, who, after a time, sending a force, reduced Holavanhalli. Sanna Baiche Gauda was placed in the government and Ankana Gauda with his family was imprisoned at Hulikal. But within two years the Síra army attacked Dod-Ballapur and captured it. Baire Gauda fell in the siege, and in recognition of his services the eldest son, Dodda Baiche Gauda, was invested with the government of Holavanhalli, with an increase of territory. Subsequent members of the family fortified Koratigere, subdued the neighbouring hoblis belonging to Devaráyadurga, Makalidurga and Channaráya-durga, and waged war successfully with the chief of Maddagiri. The successes of the Mysore army soon reduced these possessions, which were finally annexed by Haidar Ali.

The *Maddagiri* line of chiefs arose in a similar manner, and extended their possessions over the north of the District, fortifying Maddagiri, Channaráya-durga and other points. In 1678 the joint rulers, Rama Gauda and Timma Gauda, on the capture of their capital by Deva Rája, the dalavayi of Mysore, were taken prisoners and conveyed to Seringapatam. They were afterwards released and granted Midagesi as an estate.

The *Hágalvádi* chiefs appear to have had their origin from a *talári* of Yerrakatta, afterwards known as Sál Náyak, who, on the overthrow of the Vijayanagar government, became the leader of a band of freebooters, and succeeded in capturing Kandikere and Shettikere. He afterwards assisted the Penugonda army with a force on condition of being confirmed in his conquests, and when that army was defeated, escaped to his own country with such plunder as he could secure, including, it is said, twelve elephants. Chiknáyakanhaḷḷi, the seat of government, had been founded and named after his brother, when Honnavalli, Turuvekere, and Nonavinkere were added to their possessions. It was on the completion of these enterprises that he is said to have taken the name of Sál Náyak, from the idea that his conquests extended in a *sálu* or line. The Chiknáyakanhaḷḷi country changed hands several times, being held alternately by the Muhammadans and the Mahrattas, until reduced by the Mysore army in the time of Chikka Deva Raja.

At *Hebbur* a small zamindari was formed under Hale Gauda and

Timma Gauda, which, being seized for a time by Kempe Gauda of Magadi, who owned the southern parts of the District, and then by the Hágalvádi chief, was finally united to Mysore.

**Bijapur.**—The overthrow of the Vijayanagar empire on the field of Talikota in 1564 opened the way for many invaders. The Bijapur army under Ran-dulha Khan overran all the north of the District in 1638, and Síra, with Dod-Ballapur, Bangalore, Hoskote, and Kolar, forming what was called Carnatic Bijapur, were placed under the government of Shahji (*see* Bangalore District).

**Mughals.**—On the capture of Golkonda and Bijapur by Aurangzeb in 1687, and the conquest of their territories by the Mughal army, Síra was made the capital of the new province,—consisting of the seven parganas of Basvapatna, Budihal, Síra, Penugonda, Dod-Ballapur, Hoskote, and Kolar,—placed under Khasim Khan as Subadar or Faujdar of the Carnatic. This officer applied himself with energy and success to the task of regulating and improving the District. In 1698 he was killed at Dodderi, and the distinguished general Zulfikar Khan succeeded. Another governor named Rustam Jang is said to have built the fort and petta, and by his wise administration of affairs to have obtained the title of Bahadur and the name of Kaifiyat Khan. In 1757 Síra was taken by the Mahrattas, and restored two years after, on the conclusion of peace with Mysore. In 1761 it was taken by Haidar, in alliance with Basalat Jang, who had conferred upon him the title of Navab of Síra. In 1766 it fell again into the hands of the Mahrattas by the defection of Haidar's brother, and in 1774 was reconquered by Tipu. The Mahrattas once more occupied it for a short time in 1791 on marching to join the army of Lord Cornwallis.

The following is a professed list of the Subadars of Síra under the Mughal government, as given in the Mackenzie MSS :—

| | | | |
|---|---|---|---|
| Khasim Khan ... ... ... | 1686 | Ghalib Khan ... ... ... | 1713 |
| Atish Khan ... ... ... | 1694 | Darga Khuli Khan ... ... | 1714 |
| Kurad Manur Khan ... ... | 1697 | Abid Khan ... ... ... | 1715 |
| Dhakta Manur Khan ... ... | 1704 | Mulahavar Khan ... ... | 1716 |
| Pudad Ulla Khan ... ... | 1706 | Darga Khuli Khan ... ... | 1720 |
| Davud Khan ... ... ... | 1707 | Abdul Rasul Khan ... ... | 1721 |
| Sadat Ulla Khan ... ... | 1709 | Tayar Muhammad Khan ... | 1722 |
| Amin Khan ... ... ... | 1711 | Dilavar Khan ... ... | 1724–1756 |

**Mysore Rajas.**—The foregoing accounts have, in order to present a continuous narrative of the history of each chiefdom, necessarily anticipated to some extent the steps by which the various parts of the District were brought under the rule of the Mysore Rajas. But it was Chikka Deva Raja who, at the end of the 17th century, effected the conquest of all the territory which was not appropriated by the Bijapur government established at Síra. Thus Ketasamudra, Kandikere, Handalagere, Gulur, Tumkúr and Honnavalli, are enumerated among his conquests. After which he seized Jadakanadurga and changed its name to Chikkadevarayadurga (now Devaráyadurga). Maddagiri, Midagesi, Bijjavara and Channarayadurga were also subdued in his reign. The remainder of the District fell to Mysore on the conquest of Síra by Haidar Ali in 1761.

At the beginning of the present century the District was embraced in the Maddagiri Faujdari. After the British assumption in 1832 the Tumkúr District was formed, and with that of Chitaldroog constituted the Chitaldroog Division. At the reorganization of 1863 this Division was broken up, and Tumkúr became one of the Districts of the new Nundydroog Division. In 1882 it was extended so as to include Chitaldroog as a Sub-Division. In 1886 Chitaldroog was restored as a District, but Pávugaḍa taluq remained as part of Tumkúr District.

## POPULATION

*Number.*—The population of the District is 581,018 according to the census of 1891, 291,237 being males and 289,781 females.

*Density.*—This gives 139·9 persons to the square mile. The most thickly peopled taluqs at the time of the census were Tumkúr, where the number was 200·8 to the square mile, Kunigal, Maddagiri and Tiptúr, where the rate was 174·5, 164·4 and 154·6 respectively. The most sparsely populated were Chiknáyakanhaḷḷi, with only 97, and Pávugaḍa, with 100·3 per square mile.

*By Religion.*—Dividing the population among the different religious classes, and separating adults from children, we get the following results:—

| Religion. | Above 15. | | Under 15. | | Total. | Per cent. |
|---|---|---|---|---|---|---|
| | Male. | Female. | Male. | Female. | | |
| Hindus ... ... | 179,955 | 175,615 | 96,897 | 100,379 | 552,846 | 95·13 |
| Muhammadans ... | 7,590 | 7,342 | 5,247 | 5,062 | 25,241 | 4·34 |
| Jains ... ... | 747 | 633 | 296 | 280 | 1,956 | 0·33 |
| Christians... ... | 253 | 192 | 148 | 150 | 743 | 0·13 |
| Others ... ... | — | — | — | — | 232 | — |
| Total ... | 188,545 | 183,782 | 102,588 | 105,871 | 581,018 | — |

*Increase.*—The following table compares the statistics according to the *khâneshumâri* accounts of 1853-4 with those obtained in the censuses of 1871, 1881 and 1891.

| Taluq. | 1853-4. | 1871. | 1881. | 1891. |
|---|---|---|---|---|
| Chiknáyakanhalli ... ... ... | 30,187 | 62,949 | 38,268 | 51,620 |
| Gubbi ... ... ... ... | 33,367 | 91,423 | 57,588 | 73,570 |
| Kunigal ... ... ... ... | 78,388 | 75,416 | 51,250 | 66,502 |
| Maddagiri ... ... ... ... | 92,045 | 115,665 | 75,294 | 97,973 |
| Pávugada ... ... ... ... | 37,078 | 62,178 | 42,732 | 53,377 |
| Síra ... ... ... ... ... | 42,663 | 75,815 | 51,780 | 68,327 |
| Tiptúr ... ... ... ... | 59,862 | 88,750 | 65,606 | 78,867 |
| Tumkúr ... ... ... ... | 59,908 | 116,830 | 70,113 | 90,782 |
| Total... ... ... | 433,498 | 689,026 | 452,631 | 581,018 |

The redistribution of taluqs, and changes in the limits of the District are responsible for some of the variations. There was an apparent increase in the first 18 years of 37·08 per cent., but the early estimate was shown to be 25 per cent. too low. The famine inflicted a loss which sent down the total of 1871 by 34·3 per cent. in the succeeding census of 1881. There was a recovery of 28·36 per cent. by 1891. The net result appears as an increase of 7·22 per cent. in 38 years.

**Classes.**—With reference to means of livelihood and nationality the population may be classified as follows :—

| | | No. | Per cent. |
|---|---|---|---|
| A. | Agricultural... | 215,091 | 37·01 |
| B. | Professional ... | 31,876 | 5·49 |
| C. | Commercial ... | 40,135 | 6·91 |
| D. | Artisan and Village Menial | 208,800 | 35·95 |
| E. | Vagrant Minor Artisans and Performers... | 58,686 | 10·10 |
| | Races and Nationalities | 25,984 | 4·47 |
| | Others, not stated ... | 214 | 0·03 |

The castes or classes which number over 10,000 are the following. These account for 502,498, or 86·32 per cent. of the population :—

| | | | | | |
|---|---|---|---|---|---|
| Wokkaliga... | 179,206 | Kuruba ... | 38,186 | Tigala ... | 14,718 |
| Madiga ... | 48,283 | Musalman ... | 23,724 | Wodda ... | 13,386 |
| Beda ... | 43,370 | Holeya ... | 23,616 | Banajiga ... | 12,408 |
| Lingáyita ... | 38,789[1] | Brahman ... | 17,007 | Uppara ... | 11,568 |
| Golla ... | 38,237 | | | | |

The most numerous classes of Wokkaliga are Gangadikara (64,478), Kunchatiga (44,231), Nonaba (30,654), and Reddi (11,123). Amongst Brahmans the most numerous sects are Badaganad (3,988), Hoisaniga

[1] The Nonaba, included in Wokkaliga, are also Lingáyits.

(1,466), Sirnad (1,242), Mulikinad (1,157), Desastha (1,082), and Ulchakamme (1,044). Of Banajigas, the Setti (5,340), and Telugu Banajigas (3,932) are the most numerous. There are also 7,019 Linga Banajigas included in Lingáyits. Komatis number 5,304. Of the Panchala, 7,636 are Akkasale. Of the Neyigara, 4,545 are Devanga and 1,694 Togata. Kadu Golla number 16,406; Hálu Kuruba, 20,193; Kallu Wodda, 4,948; Mannu Wodda, 4,661. Among Musalmans, the Shekhs (14,247), Pathans (4,462) and Sayyids (3,009) preponderate.

*Agricultural Stock.*—There were in 1893 the following:—364,319 cows and bullocks, 66,551 buffaloes, 3,119 horses and ponies, 6,779 mules and donkeys, 547,849 sheep and goats, 12,268 carts and 91,652 ploughs.

*Tanks and Wells.*—At the same period there were 2,254 Government tanks, of which 605 are large, yielding a revenue of over Rs. 300 each, and 145 Inam tanks. The wells numbered 13,495.

**Towns.**—The District contains 14 municipal towns, with a population of 45,350, composed of 37,101 Hindus, 288 Jains, 7,465 Musalmans and 496 Christians. The following is the list:—

| | | | |
|---|---|---|---|
| Tumkúr ... ... ... | 11,086 | Tiptúr ... ... ... | 2,260 |
| Chiknáyakanhalli ... ... | 4,863 | Turuvekere ... ... ... | 1,610 |
| Kunigal ... ... ... | 4,406 | Pávugada ... ... ... | 1,558 |
| Gubbi ... ... ... | 4,187 | Bellavi ... ... ... | 1,510 |
| Síra ... ... ... ... | 3,595 | Huliyurdurga ... ... | 1,482 |
| Maddagiri ... ... ... | 3,536 | Kadaba ... ... ... | 1,467 |
| Koratigere ... ... ... | 2,358 | Huliyar ... ... ... | 1,432 |

*Villages.*—The total number of *asali* or primary villages was 2,736 in 1891, to which were attached 1,492 *dákhali* or secondary villages or hamlets. The following are the details:—

| Taluq. | Populated | | Depopulated. | Classified. | | | | Total. |
|---|---|---|---|---|---|---|---|---|
| | Villages. | Hamlets. | | Government. | Sarvamanya. | Jodi. | Kayamgutta. | |
| Chiknáyakanhalli ... | 236 | 130 | 43 | 273 | ... | 6 | ... | 279 |
| Gubbi ... ... | 350 | 214 | 71 | 415 | ... | 6 | ... | 421 |
| Kunigal ... ... | 276 | 261 | 15 | 254 | 8 | 24 | 5 | 291 |
| Maddagiri ... ... | 409 | 182 | 74 | 408 | 10 | 39 | 26 | 483 |
| Pávugada ... ... | 137 | 81 | 8 | 140 | 2 | 2 | 1 | 145 |
| Síra ... ... ... | 211 | 122 | 42 | 246 | 2 | 5 | ... | 253 |
| Tiptúr ... ... | 358 | 253 | 33 | 383 | 3 | 5 | ... | 391 |
| Tumkúr ... ... | 386 | 249 | 87 | 425 | 12 | 32 | 4 | 473 |
| Total ... | 2,363 | 1,492 | 373 | 2,544 | 37 | 119 | 36 | 2,736 |

**Great Festivals.**—The principal concourse of people occurs at the following religious festivals :—

At *Síbi,* in Tumkúr taluq, 10,000 people assemble during the *Narasimhaswámi rathótsava,* held for fifteen days from full moon day of Mágha.

At *Yediyur,* Kunigal taluq, on the occasion of the *Siddesvara játre,* lasting five days, from Chaitra suddha 3rd, 10,000 people come together.

At *Ságasandra,* Chiknáyakanhaḷḷi taluq, 4,000 people collect together on full moon day of Chaitra, for the *Ammana játre.*

At *Devaráyadurga,* Tumkúr taluq, at *Holalgunda,* Kunigal taluq, and at *Peddahalli,* Tiptúr taluq, respectively, the *Narasimhaswámi rathótsava,* the *Umámahésvara rathótsava* and the *Ammana játre* are held from full moon day in Phálguna, the first lasting five days, the second three days, and the third one day. Each attracts 3,000 people.

At *Tumkúr,* 3,000 people celebrate the *Lakshmíkánta* and *Gangádharésvara rathótsavas* held, the former on the 7th, and the latter on the 14th of Mágha suddha, for one day each.

**Fairs.**—The following are the largest weekly fairs :—

| Place. | Taluq. | Day. | No. of Visitors. |
|---|---|---|---|
| Bellavi ... ... | Tumkúr ... | Monday ... ... | 3,000 |
| Gubbi ... ... | Gubbi ... | Thursday .. ... | 1,000 |
| Tiptúr ... ... | Tiptúr ... | Saturday and Sunday... | 10,000 |

**Vital Statistics.**—The birth-rate of the District in 1893–4 was 20·79 per mille of the population, while the death-rate was 13·34 per mille. The number of births registered was 12,074, of which 6,192 were males and 5,882 females. The total of deaths registered was 7,749; of these, 4,055 were males and 3,694 females. Of the deaths 7,160 occurred among Hindus, 323 among Muhammadans, and 266 among other classes. The following were the causes of death registered: from diseases,—cholera 18, small-pox 756, fevers 4,232, bowel complaints 340; from injuries,—suicide 4, wounds or accidents 122, snake-bite or wild beasts 38, all other causes 2,209.

## REVENUE

The revenue of the District for five years is shown in the statement below :—

| Items. | 1891-2. | 1892-3. | 1893-4. | 1894-5. | 1895-6. |
|---|---|---|---|---|---|
| Land Revenue ... | 11,04,193 | 11,84,430 | 12,55,881 | 12,64,433 | 12,85,213 |
| Forests ... ... | 37,495 | 22,874 | 27,937 | 30,680 | 37,167 |
| Mohatarfa ... ... | 48,946 | 51,009 | 49,359 | 40,563 | 40,814 |
| Abkari ... ... | 1,98,432 | 2,72,405 | 2,86,681 | 2,97,027 | 2,99,612 |
| Sayar... ... ... | 51,356 | 48,075 | 44,967 | 41,855 | 40,624 |
| Salt ... ... ... | 2,573 | 4,954 | 4,802 | 3,464 | 5,109 |
| Stamps ... ... | 53,679 | 47,664 | 52,471 | 55,104 | 56,251 |
| Law and Justice ... | 13,985 | 12,548 | 4,299 | 4,788 | 4,544 |
| Registration ... ... | ... | ... | 7,589 | 7,436 | 7,770 |
| Education ... ... | ... | ... | 5,417 | 6,951 | 7,427 |
| Police ... ... | 64 | 48 | 18 | 32 | 33 |
| Public Works ... | 8,202 | 6,310 | ... | ... | ... |
| Other items ... ... | 17,263 | 24,865 | 25,502 | 17,642 | 14,317 |
| Total Rs. ... | 15,36,188 | 16,75,182 | 17,64,923 | 17,69,975 | 17,98,881 |

## TRADE

The trade of the District, though followed by many other castes or classes, is principally in the hands of the Lingáyits. Their chief emporium is at Gubbi, but there are also extensive marts at Bellávi, Turvekere, Tiptúr and Chiknáyakanhaḷḷi, to which the trade of the southern Mahratta country, and of the Bellary, Vellore, and Madras districts is attracted, as well as that of the west and south of the Mysore country. The Lingáyit merchants generally have either extensive connections or branch agencies at Dharwar and Nagar.

The articles of merchandise and course of trade may be gathered from the following statement :—

At Gubbi, areca-nut, pepper and cardamoms are imported from Nagar and transmitted to Vellore and Wallaja; whence nutmegs, mace and European cloths are obtained in exchange and exported to Nagar. Sugar, sugar-candy and silk, the produce of Bangalore, together with cocoanuts raised on the spot, are sent to Dharwar; whence cotton and thread are received in return, part of which goes to Nagar.

At Chiknáyakanhaḷḷi and Honnavalli, the cocoanuts and food-grains cultivated in these taluqs are sent to Bangalore, in exchange for jaggory, sugar and sugar-candy.

From Honnavalli, Turvekere and other marts, cocoanuts, iron, steel, tobacco and silk are exported to Dharwar and the southern Mahratta country; and cotton, thread, kusumba and Persian dates received in exchange; much of which goes to Bangalore by way of Síra and Tumkúr.

At Bargur in Síra and Hampasandra in Maddagiri, a trade is carried on between Bangalore and Bellary; sugar, sugar-candy and European piece-goods from the former being exchanged for cotton from the latter.

The following is given as a statement of the different articles of trade dealt with, and the approximate value of each as exported or imported :—

| Articles. | Exports. | | Imports. | |
|---|---|---|---|---|
| | 1891-2. | 1892-3. | 1891-2. | 1892-3. |
| Food-grains ... ... ... | 38,16,383 | 39,64,583 | 3,54,960 | 3,98,651 |
| Condiments, including chillies, tamarinds, salt and pepper ... | 16,400 | 19,940 | 41,632 | 53,582 |
| Oil-seeds, oil and ghee .. ... | 1,76,400 | 1,94,652 | 35,550 | 43,984 |
| Sugar and jaggory ... ... | 46,580 | 49,836 | 1,02,880 | 1,32,403 |
| Nuts ... ... ... ... | 3,53,310 | 3,42,384 | 7,380 | 9,843 |
| Silk, cotton, and other articles ... | 7,980 | 8,492 | 11,44,760 | 11,49,631 |
| Metals ... ... ... ... | ... | ... | 86,410 | 93,311 |
| Sundries ... ... ... ... | 50,986 | 54,896 | 1,51,280 | 1,53,124 |
| Total Rs. ... ... | 44,68,039 | 46,34,783 | 19,24,852 | 20,34,529 |

**Manufactures.**—There are in the District 116 forges for the manufacture of iron and steel, 101 silk looms, 431 salt-pans, 2,990 cotton and 1,822 woollen looms, and 426 oil-mills.

The principal articles of manufacture are coarse cotton cloths, woollen blankets, both plain and black-and-white check, those prepared at Chiknáyakanhaḷḷi being the best; rope, made from cotton thread or the fibre of the cocoanut or wild aloe, from hemp and munji grass; besides strong tape. Furniture, carts and palanquins; toys, instruments and tools for all trades, agricultural implements, cooking utensils, baskets, millstones, brass, copper and stone idols or images, native musical instruments, iron and steel swords, daggers, and knives, silk, gold and silver ornaments, glass bangles, oils, earth-salt, dyes, sealing-wax, tobacco, spirits and drugs are also largely manufactured or prepared.

The importation of English piece-goods has destroyed the formerly thriving manufactures of chintz in Síra and Midagesi, the imported cloths being superior and cheaper.

Silk is chiefly produced in Kunigal, Kadaba, Koratigere and Síra; sparingly in Tumkúr.

## COMMUNICATIONS

**Railways.**—The Southern Mahratta Railway, from Bangalore to Poona, runs through the District for 58½ miles, from east to west, with stations at Hirehalli, Tumkúr, Gubbi, Nittur, Yelladbagi, Banasandra, Kardi, Tiptúr and Konehalli.

**Roads.**—The length of *Provincial roads* is 189 miles, maintained at an annual cost of Rs. 24,675. *District roads* cover 423 miles, costing for upkeep Rs. 25,940 a year. The particulars regarding each class of roads are given below.

| *Provincial Roads.* | Miles. | Cost. |
|---|---|---|
| Salem-Bellary road | 52 | 6,500 |
| Tumkúr-Bellary road | 66 | 6,600 |
| Bangalore-Honavar road | 54 | 9,450 |
| Bangalore-Mangalore road | 17 | 2,125 |
| Total | 189 | 24,675 |

| *District Roads.* | Miles. | Cost. |
|---|---|---|
| Tumkúr-Maddur road | 44 | 3,520 |
| Nelligere-Síra road | 50 | 3,500 |
| Bisalramanagudi-Huliyar road | 26 | 2,600 |
| Kibbanhalli-Huliyar road | 21 | 2,100 |
| Banavar-Síra road | 41 | 2,050 |
| Vediyur-Tiptúr road | 31 | 1,240 |
| Síra-Maddagiri road | 23 | 1,150 |
| Tumkúr Station road | 8 | 1,150 |
| Maddagiri-Dod-Ballapur road | 18 | 900 |
| Holalkere-Huliyar road | 16 | 800 |
| Kibbanhalli-Turuvekere road | 11 | 770 |
| Sira-Amrapura road | 25 | 750 |
| Tumkúr-Chelur road | 14 | 700 |
| Gubbi-Hebbur | 12 | 600 |
| Hassan-Tiptúr road | 7 | 560 |
| Tumkúr-Urudigere road | 11 | 550 |
| Hiriyur-Huliyar road | 6 | 480 |
| Dobbspet-Koratigere | 15 | 450 |
| Huliyar-Banavar road | 12¼ | 360 |
| Chellakere-Pávugada road | 7 | 350 |
| Bangalore road-Amratur | 7 | 350 |
| Tiptúr-Chanraypatna road | 6 | 300 |
| Bellavi-Timmarajanhalli road | 5 | 250 |
| Konehalli Station road | 2¾ | 240 |
| Nittur " " | 1 | 80 |
| Madaksira-Pávugada road | 2 | 60 |
| Karadi Station road | ⅝ | 50 |
| Tiptúr " " | ¼ | 20 |
| Chelur-Hágalvádi road | ½ | 10 |
| Total ... Miles | 423 | Rs. 25,940 |

**Accommodation for Travellers.**—*Dak Bungalows*, or rest houses, originally intended for European officials and travellers, are kept up at the stations named in the accompanying list, where the class is shown to which each belongs. Brahman kitchens are erected for vegetarian Hindu officials.

*First Class.*—Devaráydurga, Kunigal, Tumkúr. *Second Class.*—Kibbanhalli, Síra, Tiptúr. *Third Class.*—Ankasandra, Badavanhalli, Hebbur, Huliyar, Kallambella, Koratigere, Maddagiri, Mayasandra, Midagesi, Nelhal, Nittur, Turuvekere, Yediyur.

*Musáfirkhánas* for the accommodation of native travellers are maintained at Gubbi, Sibi, Síra, and Tumkúr.

## GAZETTEER

**Bellavi.**—A town in Tumkúr taluq, 9 miles north-west of Tumkúr, and a municipality.

| Population in 1891. | Males. | Females. | Total. |
|---|---|---|---|
| Hindus (with 40 Jains) .. ... ... | 604 | 756 | 1,360 |
| Muhammadans ... ... ... ... | 70 | 80 | 150 |
| Total ... .. ... | 674 | 836 | 1,510 |

The streets are wide, with uniform shops on either side. All the surrounding places depend on the weekly fair held here on Monday, at which trade is carried on to the value of Rs. 20,000. It is a great mart, especially for export products. The well-water is generally brackish, but a well of sweet water exists outside the town, where also there is a good tank.

| Municipal Funds. | 1892-3. | 1893-4. | 1894-5. | 1895-6. |
|---|---|---|---|---|
| Income ... ... ... ... ... | 385 | 508 | 527 | 901 |
| Expenditure ... ... ... .. | 479 | 605 | 595 | 897 |

**Bhasmangi.**—A fortified hill in the Maddagiri taluq, 26 miles north of Tumkúr, close to the frontier. On the summit is the temple of Bhasmangesvara. The original fortifications are said to have been erected by Budhi Basavappa Nayak, of mud and stone. But when Haidar Ali captured the place in 1768, he dismantled the old fort and erected a superior structure of stone and brick, with a mahal or palace. The hill has a perennial supply of water. Some Bedars live half way up, and cultivate the fields below.

**Búdihál.**—A ruinous town in the Chiknáyakanhaḷḷi taluq, 9 miles west-north-west of Huliyar, on the road to Hosdurga. Head-quarters of the Búdihál hobli. Population, 1,209.

Búdihál formerly gave its name to a taluq, of which it was the chief town. It appears to have been founded by an officer from Vijayanagar, of the Golla caste, named Siriman or Sirimaya Nayak, to whom the surrounding district was granted as an estate yielding a revenue of 10,000 pagodas, of which half was paid as tribute. He settled first at Sujikal, but the incident of a hare turning on the hounds pointed out the site of the present Búdihál as a spot suitable for a fort, which was accordingly erected. and named Bhútipura. The next ruler, Kumára Mallappa Nayak, withheld the tribute, on which an army was marched against him and the district placed under Narsinga Rao as governor. There are several inscriptions of the Vijayanagar kings in the fort, dated in the sixteenth century.

After the fail of Vijayanagar, Búdihál was seized by the Tarikere chiefs, but was soon added to the conquests of the Bijapur army, and subsequently formed a district of the province of Síra under the Mughals. The pallegar of Chitaldroog and the Mahrattas had in turn possessed it, when in 1761 it yielded to Haidar Ali. The Mahrattas took it again in 1771, but it was recovered in 1774. In 1790 it was once more in the hands of the Mahrattas, but was restored on the conclusion of peace in 1792. It was one of the last places at which the insurgents under the Tarikere pallegar created disturbances in 1831.

**Channaraya-durga.**—A conspicuous but deserted hill-fort in the Maddagiri taluq, situated midway between Koratigiri and Maddagiri, rising to 3,744 feet above the sea. Formerly the head quarters of a taluq bearing the same name. It appears to have been originally fortified by Chikkappa Gauda of Maddagiri, and named Allimenstikallu. In his family it remained for a long period, when it was taken by the Mahrattas, and Rama Gauda, at that time the chief, took refuge in Maddagiri. In two years, however, he retook it, but only to hold it for eight years longer. It was then captured by Komaraiya, general of the Mysore Raja, and Dodda Arasu placed in charge. Its name was also changed to Prasanna-giri. It was subsequently taken by Haidar, and after six years by the Mahrattas under Mádhava Ráo, and after a like period retaken by Tipu. At the entrance are inscriptions of the Mahratta generals S'ripant pradhán and Mádhava Ráv Ballál pradhán. In the latter, dated in 1766, the hill is called Chandráyadurga.

**Chiknayakanhalli.**—A taluq in the west. Area 532 square miles. Head-quarters at Chiknáyakanhaḷḷi. Contains the following hoblis, villages and population:—

| No. | Hoblis. | Villages. | Hamlets. | Villages Classified. | | | | Population. |
|---|---|---|---|---|---|---|---|---|
| | | | | Government. | Sarvamânya. | Jódi. | Kayamgutta. | |
| 1 | Búdihál ... ... | 37 | 8 | 37 | — | — | — | 6,860 |
| 2 | Chiknáyakanhaḷḷi | 41 | 24 | 38 | — | 3 | — | 9,766 |
| 3 | Handanakere ... | 45 | 35 | 44 | — | 1 | — | 6,769 |
| 4 | Huliyár ... ... | 46 | 7 | 46 | — | — | — | 10,038 |
| 5 | Kandikere ... | 42 | 16 | 41 | — | 1 | — | 5,209 |
| 6 | S'eṭṭikere ... .. | 40 | 29 | 40 | — | — | — | 6,963 |
| 7 | Yelanaḍu ... ... | 28 | 11 | 27 | — | 1 | — | 6,015 |
| | Total ... | 279 | 130 | 273 | — | 6 | — | 51,620 |

*Principal places, with population.*—Chiknáyakanhaḷḷi, 4,863; Huliyár, 1,432; S'eṭṭikere, 1,259; Búdihál, 1,209; Kenkere, 1,147.

The east of the taluq is crossed by a chain of low bare hills running northwards, the streams on both sides of which also flow north and run into a feeder of the Vedavati in Síra taluq. These hills are part of the auriferous tract described as the Chiknáyakanhaḷḷi gold-field (*see* Vol. I, p. 49). The land west and south of the hills is fertile and well cultivated. A stream starting from the south of S'eṭṭikere runs north to Huliyár, and one from Yelanaḍu runs north-west by Búdihál to the Vedavati in Holalkere taluq. From the humidity of the fogs which form on the range of hills the crops are often preserved from failure in dry seasons. The principal export trade is confined to cocoanut and areca-nut.

The revenue settlement was introduced in 1879. The total revenue demand for 1891–2 (15 months) was Rs. 1,46,403, and for 1892–3 it was Rs. 1,68,080.

The average rainfall at Chiknáyakanhaḷḷi and Huliyár for twenty-five years (1870–94) and at the other places for two years (1893–4) was as follows:—

| | Jan. | Feb. | Mar. | April | May | June | July | Aug. | Sept. | Oct. | Nov. | Dec. | Year. |
|---|---|---|---|---|---|---|---|---|---|---|---|---|---|
| Chiknáyakanhaḷḷi | 0·04 | 0·04 | 0·33 | 0·96 | 3·48 | 2·47 | 2·13 | 2·49 | 3·79 | 4·72 | 2·01 | 0·40 | ... 22·86 |
| Huliyár ... | — | 0·11 | 0·18 | 1·56 | 2·45 | 1·78 | 1·98 | 1·27 | 4·98 | 6·50 | 3·25 | 0·87 | ... 24·93 |
| Búdihál ... | — | 0·40 | 0·55 | 2·78 | 6·21 | 2·16 | 0·80 | 0·39 | 2·15 | 5·54 | 1·97 | — | ... 22·95 |
| Mattigatta | — | 0·37 | 0·20 | 2·20 | 3·75 | 3·47 | 4·89 | 1·92 | 0·91 | 3·71 | 1·24 | 0·06 | ... 22·72 |

From Banasandra Railway-station there is a road north to Chiknáyakanhaḷḷi and Huliyár, from which place roads radiate eastwards to Síra, north to Hiriyur, west to Hosdurga northwards and Banavar southwards, and south-west to Honnavalli and the Konehalli Railway-station.

**Chiknayakanhalli.**—A town situated in 13° 25′ N. lat. 76° 41′ E. long., 40 miles west-north-west of Tumkúr, on the Turvekere-Huliyár road, 9 miles north of the Bangalore-Shimoga road, and 12 miles north of the Banasandra Railway-station. Head-quarters of the taluq of the same name, and a municipality.

| Population in 1891. | Males. | Females. | Total. |
|---|---|---|---|
| Hindus (with 2 Jains) ... ... ... | 2,137 | 2,302 | 4,439 |
| Muhammadans ... ... ... ... | 202 | 217 | 419 |
| Christians ... ... ... ... ... | 3 | 2 | 5 |
| Total ... .. ... | 2,342 | 2,521 | 4,863 |

It derives its name from Chikka Náyaka, one of the chiefs of the Hágalvádi house. The town was plundered and the fort destroyed by the Mahrattas under Parasu Ram Bhao, when marching to join the army of Lord Cornwallis before Seringapatam. The residents, it is said, foreseeing the treatment the town would receive, had hidden their most valuable effects and retired to the neighbouring hills. But they were not destined thus to escape. For when the Mahratta army returned to Síra, the wealthy inhabitants were enticed to return by assurances of protection and by a daily distribution of charity to Brahmans. The leading men were then seized and forced by torture to disclose where their treasures were hid. Plunder to the value of Rs. 500,000 thus fell into the hands of the Mahrattas.

It is a prosperous town, surrounded on all sides by plantations of cocoanut and areca palms. Their produce, together with the coarse cotton cloths, white and coloured, manufactured in the place, are largely sold at the weekly fair. Many of the inhabitants act as carriers to the merchants of Nagar and Bangalore. Seven of the temples are endowed with land or money, the principal being one dedicated to Anjaneya. The town is dependent on the tank for fresh water.

| Municipal Funds. | 1892-3. | 1893-4. | 1894-5. | 1895-6. |
|---|---|---|---|---|
| Income ... ... .. ... ... | 1,468 | 1,734 | 1,727 | 3,349 |
| Expenditure ... ... ... ... | 963 | 1,016 | 1,643 | 3,104 |

**Devarayadurga.**—A fortified hill 9 miles east of Tumkúr, situated amidst wild and picturesque scenery and extensive forest. It consists of three distinct terraces or elevations, and is well supplied with springs. Near the summit, which is 3,940 feet above the level of the sea, is a small temple, connected with the principal one on the lower level, dedicated to Durga Narasimha. On the intermediate terrace are three European houses, forming a retreat for the hot weather. The fortifications are carried round the three elevations, and must in former days have been of considerable strength.

Tradition relates that a robber chief named Andhaka or Lingaka had his stronghold here, and that he was subdued by Sumati, a prince whose father, Hemachandra, was king of Karnata and ruled in Yadupatna. On thus accomplishing the enterprise on which he had been sent, Sumati is related to have established the city of Bhumandana near the present Nelamangala (Bangalore District), and taken up his residence there for the protection of that part of his father's kingdom.

Under the Hoysalas there seems to have been on the hill a town called Anebiddasari or Anebiddajari, which long gave its name to the surrounding district, especially the country to the west and south. The name means "the steep where the elephant fell," and the incident out of which it arose appears to have happened at a spot on the hill now known as Anegondi, or the elephant pit, below the peak called Karigiri, or the elephant hill. A rogue elephant, which the local purana describes as a *gandharva* who had assumed that form, suddenly appeared before the town, to the great consternation of the people, and after doing considerable mischief to the tank there, madly tried to walk up the steep rock on the west, when he slipped, fell back, and was killed. Under the Vijayanagar kings the use of the same name continued, and a large tank named Bukkasamudra, after one of the earliest of them, was formed by throwing an embankment across the gorge from which the Jayamangali riyer has its source. Remains of the embankment and of the adjacent town can still be traced.

The hill was in the possession of a chief named Jadaka, and called Jadakanadurga, when it was captured in about 1696 by Chikka Deva Raja of Mysore, by whom the present fortifications were erected and who gave his name to it, since shortened into Devaráya-durga. The temples were built by Kanthirava Raja of Mysore, and are the scene of a great annual festival resorted to by 3,000 people. They contain jewellery and other property of the god to the value of Rs. 10,000 and are endowed with an annual grant of Rs. 848.

**Dore-gudda.**—A hill in the Chiknáyakanhaḷḷi taluq, of which there is a tradition that, owing to extensive excavations for the extraction of iron ore, it fell in, burying the miners of seven villages with all their cattle. It is still one of the principal sources whence the ore is obtained.

**Garudachala.**—A stream which rises on the frontier of the District, south-east of the Devaráydurga group of hills, and flowing north into Koratigere, unites with the Jayamangali near Holavanhalli or Korampur.

**Gubbi.**—A taluq in the middle. Area, 552 square miles. Headquarters at Gubbi. Contains the following hoblis, villages and population :—

| No. | Hoblis. | Villages. | Hamlets. | Villages classified. | | | | Population. |
|---|---|---|---|---|---|---|---|---|
| | | | | Government. | Sarvamánya. | Jódi. | Kayamgutta. | |
| 1 | Chelúr ... ... | 61 | 18 | 61 | — | — | — | 8,755 |
| 2 | Chitnahalli .. | 51 | 45 | 50 | — | 1 | — | 11,199 |
| 3 | Dandinasivara ... | 40 | 21 | 39 | — | 1 | — | 6,448 |
| 4 | Gubbi ... ... | 46 | 27 | 46 | — | — | — | 13,032 |
| 5 | Hágalvádi ... | 59 | 16 | 59 | — | — | — | 6,084 |
| 6 | Kadaba ... ... | 41 | 26 | 40 | — | 1 | — | 7,237 |
| 7 | Kallúr ... ... | 49 | 49 | 46 | — | 3 | — | 9,797 |
| 8 | Nittúr ... ... | 74 | 12 | 74 | — | — | — | 11,018 |
| | Total ... | 421 | 214 | 415 | — | 6 | — | 73,570 |

*Principal places, with population* :—Gubbi, 4,187 ; Kadaba, 1,467 ; Hágalvádi, 1,288 ; Kallúr, 1,282 ; Chelúr, 1,047.

The taluq till 1886 was called Kadaba. It is watered by the Shimsha, which flows through the middle from north to south, past Gubbi and Kadaba, where it forms a very large tank. At Kallúr it is joined by the Nága from the west, and continues south. On the north-west of the taluq are the chains of bare hills separating Hágalvádi from Chiknáyakanhalli, which belong to the auriferous tract. The remainder of the taluq is generally an open country and well watered. The soil is mostly a red mould, shallow and gravelly.

The revenue settlement was introduced in 1882. The total revenue demand for 1891–2 (15 months) was Rs. 1,92,786 and for 1892–3 it was Rs. 2,40,951.

The average rainfall at Gubbi for 25 years (1870–94) and at the other places for two years (1893–4) was as follows :—

| | Jan. | Feb. | Mar. | April | May | June | July | Aug. | Sept. | Oct. | Nov. | Dec. | Year. |
|---|---|---|---|---|---|---|---|---|---|---|---|---|---|
| Gubbi .. | 0·03 | 0·03 | 0·22 | 1·67 | 3·00 | 3·03 | 3·77 | 5·02 | 5·82 | 5·60 | 2·82 | 0·54 | 31·55 |
| Chitnahalli | — | — | 0·65 | 0·75 | 3·15 | 2·31 | 1·99 | 1·05 | 2·05 | 7·95 | — | — | 19·90 |
| Kadaba ... | — | 0·57 | 0·30 | 0·93 | 1·31 | 4·52 | 3·89 | 1·34 | 4·23 | 8·37 | 0·30 | — | 25·76 |

The railway from Bangalore to Poona crosses the taluq from east to west, somewhat south of the middle, with stations at Gubbi, Niṭṭúr, and Yelladbági. The Bangalore-Shimoga trunk road runs nearly alongside the railway, and at Niṭṭúr is crossed by a road running north to Síra, and south by Nelligere to Seringapatam. There is also a road from Gubbi south-east to Hebbur, and one from Hágalváḍi, running east through Chelúr and Bellávi to Tumkúr. There is also a road connecting Hágalváḍi with the road to Huliyár.

**Gubbi.**—An important trading place, situated in 12° 19′ N. lat. 77° E. long., 13 miles west of Tumkúr, on the Bangalore-Poona railway and the Bangalore-Shimoga road. Head-quarters of the Gubbi taluq, and a municipality.

| Population in 1891. | Males. | Females. | Total. |
|---|---|---|---|
| Hindus ... ... ... ... ... | 1,807 | 1,865 | 3,672 |
| Muhammadans ... ... ... ... | 210 | 207 | 417 |
| Jains ... ... ... ... ... ... | 35 | 28 | 63 |
| Christians ... ... ... ... ... | 14 | 21 | 35 |
| Total ... ... .. | 2,066 | 2,121 | 4,187 |

It is the *entrepôt* for the areca-nut trade between the Nagar Malnád and Wallajapet in the North Arcot District, as well as for the wolágra or internal trade of the neighbourhood. It is said to have been founded over 400 years ago by the Gauda of Hosahalli, two miles distant, and called Amaragonda-pura. He claimed to be a descendant of Honnappa Gauda, hereditary chief of the Nonaba Wokligas, who lived 700 years ago, and owned a district yielding a revenue of 3,000 pagodas. The family were first made tributary by the Mysore Rajas, to whom they paid 500 pagodas a year. Haidar increased the tribute to 2,500, leaving them little better than renters, and Tipu dispossessed them altogether. They are now in the position of ordinary cultivators, but their rank is acknowledged in their own tribe.

Gubbi formerly suffered much from the party spirit of the contending sects of Komatis and Banajigas or Lingáyits, and was at one time in imminent danger of abandonment from this cause. During the administration of Purnaiya, the erection of a temple by the Komatis to a virgin who had cast herself into the flames to avoid dishonour, excited the previous animosity of the opposite party to such a degree that the town was ordered to be divided by a wall in order to separate the quarters of the two factions. An Amildar was at length chosen from the party which appeared least in the wrong, and with the help of the Brahmans and peaceably disposed inhabitants order was gradually restored, although the extreme measure of slaughtering an ass in the main street was threatened, which would have compelled all Hindus to abandon the town.

At Gubbi is one of the chief annual fairs in the country, frequented by merchants from great distances. The neighbourhood produces coarse cotton cloths, both white and coloured, blankets, sack-cloth, areca-nut of the kind called wolágra (or neighbouring), cocoanuts, jaggory, tamarind, capsicum, wheat, rice, ragi, and other grains; lac, steel, and iron; all of which here find a ready sale or exchange, as the imports are large, and it is an intermediate mart for all goods passing through the Peninsula in almost every direction. It is computed that at the weekly fair there are sold from 50 to 100 loads of areca-nut produced in the neighbouring districts of Síra, Hágalváḍi, Chiknáyakanhaḷḷi, Búdihál, Honnavalli and Gubbi; as well as from 20 to 40 loads of kopri or dry cocoanut from the same districts. Taking the load at 8 maunds of 40 Sultani seers, there are thus sold annually at this mart alone 335 tons of areca-nut, and 134 tons of cocoanut, the produce of the neighbourhood, representing a money value of Rs. 2,18,400 and Rs. 33,280 respectively.

Of the coarse cloths made in the vicinity by the Dévángas, Togatas and Holeyas 100 pieces on the average are sold at each fair, representing an annual value of about 15,000 rupees. There are, however, many other fairs in the surrounding country where these products are also sold to a considerable extent.

| Municipal Funds. | 1892-3. | 1893-4. | 1894-5. | 1895-6. |
|---|---|---|---|---|
| Income ... ... ... ... ... | 1,384 | 1,599 | 1,777 | 2,932 |
| Expenditure ... ... ... ... | 1,638 | 1,837 | 1,355 | 3,141 |

**Hagalvadi.**—A village in the Gubbi taluq, 25 miles north-east of the kasba. Population, 1,288.

Lingáyits and Kurubas are the prevailing classes in the place. The chief produce of the neighbourhood is areca-nut, and inferior kamblis are manufactured. It was the original possession of the line of chiefs named from it, who built Chiknáyakanhaḷḷi and owned all the west of the District. When subdued by the Mysore Raja they gave up the rest of their territory in order to retain Hágalváḍi free of tribute. Haidar Ali subsequently compelled them to pay for this also, and his son dispossessed them altogether.

**Hebbur.**—A large village in the Tumkúr taluq, 15 miles south of Tumkúr, on the road to Kunigal. Population, 1,646.

The place is said to have been founded by two brothers named

Hale Gauda and Timme Gauda. It was at first called Heb-huli (great or royal tiger), from the circumstance that a bullock attacked by a tiger had driven it off and pursued it, with the other cattle and their owners, until it was killed. The courage of the cattle was attributed to the peculiar virtue of the spot, pointing it out as suitable for the construction of a fort. Accordingly, the carcase of the tiger being burnt, the limits of the fort were marked out with its ashes, and the erection was completed with the countenance of the Vijayanagar king. The name was subsequently changed from Hebhuli to Hebbur, the great town, and Katti Kamanna was appointed as the king's agent; Hale Gauda and Timme Gauda being made patels of Hebbur, Kallesapura and Ramanhalli. The agent, however, instead of supplying his patron's exchequer, spent the public money in erecting temples, forming tanks, &c. For his insolence on being summoned to court to account for his proceedings, he was condemned to have both his eyes put out and to be expelled from the royal territories. A descendant of the Gaudas was next placed in charge, but after Vijayanagar was taken by the Muhammadans, Kempe Gauda of Magadi captured Hebbur, and held it for many years. It was then taken by the Chiknáyakanhaḷḷi chief, and from him by Chikka Deva Raja of Mysore. A quarter of a century later it again changed hands, falling a prey to the Mughal army, but in course of time was regained by the Mysore Raja. For two years before the usurpation of Haidar Ali, again, it was in the hands of the Mahrattas. The place has thus seen many vicissitudes.

**Heggere.**—A village six miles west of Huliyár. Population, 901. It contains some ruined temples and various Chálukya and Hoysala inscriptions which indicate that it was at one time an important place.

**Hemavati.**—A village on the extreme northern frontier of Síra taluq, in Madaksira. It has been identified by me as the site of the ancient Nolamba or Pallava capital called in inscriptions Penjeru or Henjeru (*see* Nidugal). It contains a number of large ruined temples and other remains which attest its former importance. The principal temple now kept up is that of Henjerappa, who, according to some accounts, was a man. The whole site is strewn with lingas of enormous size.

**Holavanhalli.**—A village on the Jayamangali river, in the Maddagiri taluq, 5 miles east of Koratigere. Population, 1,459.

It is said to have been formerly called Korampur, the inhabitants being a few persons of low caste whose chief was Holava Gauda. To them Baire Gauda, one of the Kanchi refugees who settled at Avati (Bangalore District), or a descendant of the same name, proposed to establish a fort and péte at Korampur, to which the people would agree only on condition that the place should be called after their Gauda, whence its present name. Baire Gauda became tributary to the Vijayanagar kings, and obtained from them a grant of 33 villages in Kolahalli and the neighbourhood, together with other lands, yielding altogether 6,000 pagodas a year. During seven years Baire Gauda greatly improved his estate, when it was seized by the chief of Magadi, who placed his brother Ankana Gauda in charge of it. Seven years later it was taken by Havali Baiche Gauda of Dod-Ballapur; but in two years Dod-Ballapur was itself captured by the Navab of Síra. Baire Gauda, who had joined the Síra army, was killed in this enterprise, but Holavanhalli was restored to his eldest son Dodda Baiche Gauda, with additions to the estate, on condition of paying a tribute. The fort and péte of Koratigere were built some time after by a member of this family, and the hoblis of Gundakal, Irkasamudra, Sageri, Kolála and Dásarahalli annexed, yielding altogether a revenue of 26,000 pagodas, subject to a tribute of 3,000 pagodas and the maintenance of a military force. The local chiefs continued in possession as tributary, successively, to the Mysore Rajas, the Mahrattas and the Navab of Síra, and afterwards to Haidar Ali, on whose death, in 1782, Holavanhalli was annexed to Mysore. In 1792 Lord Cornwallis reinstated one of the family, named Dodda Rama Baire Gauda, but on the withdrawal of the confederate forces, Tipu reduced the place and resumed possession.

**Honnavalli.**—A town in the Tiptúr taluq, 8 miles north-west of the kasba. Population 2,102.

The place derives its name from Honnu-amma, the tutelary goddess who in a vision directed Somes'vara, one of the chiefs of Harnhalli (Hassan District), to found the town. It contains many Brahmans, and is situated amid cocoanut plantations, which produce a rare kind, named, from the delicious milk contained in the young nut, the Gangá-páni, or water of the Ganges. The town depends chiefly on one well for drinking purposes.

**Huliyar.**—A town situated in 13° 35′ N. lat., 76° 36′ E. long., 14 miles north by west of Chiknáyakanhaḷḷi. Head-quarters of the Huliyár sub-taluq included in Chiknáyakanhaḷḷi taluq, and a municipality.

| Population in 1891. | Males. | Females. | Total. |
|---|---|---|---|
| Hindus ... ... ... ... ... | 614 | 572 | 1,186 |
| Muhammadans ... ... ... ... | 117 | 129 | 246 |
| Total ... ... ... | 731 | 701 | 1,432 |

The addition of Kenkere, an adjoining suburb, would raise the population to 2,579. Huliyár was formerly the head-quarters of the Búdihál taluq, but in 1886 was made the chief town of the sub-taluq named after itself. Inscriptions of the Chálukyas and other remains indicate that the place may, in early times, have been of some importance. Latterly, in the sixteenth century, it was included in the possessions of the chiefs of Hágalváḍi. It then passed into the hands of the Muhammadans, and formed part of the province of Síra. Haidar Ali subdued it in common with the rest of the District, and thus annexed it to Mysore.

| Municipal Funds. | 1892-3. | 1893-4. | 1894-5. | 1895-6. |
|---|---|---|---|---|
| Income ... ... ... ... ... | 356 | 391 | 401 | 758 |
| Expenditure ... ... ... ... ... | 378 | 362 | 411 | 681 |

**Huliyurdurga.**—A town in the Kunigal taluq, 40 miles south of Tumkúr, at the junction of roads from Kunigal and Magadi. Head-quarters of the hobli of the same name, and a municipality.

| Population in 1891. | Males. | Females. | Total. |
|---|---|---|---|
| Hindus ... ... ... ... ... | 582 | 636 | 1,218 |
| Muhammadans ... ... ... ... | 134 | 130 | 264 |
| Total ... ... ... | 716 | 766 | 1,482 |

Till 1873 it was the head-quarters of a taluq of the same name. The place is surrounded with jungle, and derives its name from *huli*, tiger, which animal used to abound in the neighbourhood. The town and the fortifications of the hill commanding it, rising to 3,096 feet above the level of the sea, were erected by Kempe Gauḍa, the chief of Magadi. Muhammadans and Lingáyits form the principal classes of the population.

| Municipal Funds. | 1892-3. | 1893-4. | 1894-5. | 1895-6 |
|---|---|---|---|---|
| Income ... ... ... ... ... | 195 | 242 | 291 | 670 |
| Expenditure ... ... ... ... | 243 | 163 | 174 | 866 |

**Hutri-durga.**—A fortified hill in the south-west of the Kunigal taluq, rising to 3,713 feet above the sea. The fort was taken by Lord Cornwallis in 1792.

**Jayamangali.**—An affluent of the N. Pinákini. It rises in Devaráyadurga, in a gorge called the Jálada-gondi, and flowing in a northerly direction into the Maddagiri taluq, receives the Garudáchala near Holavanhalli from the east, and farther on, near Rampura, the Suvarnamukhi from the west. Thence, continuing its course through the east of the Maddagiri taluq, it flows into the N. Pinákini near Parigi in the Anantapur District. In the sandy bed are formed a number of *kapile* wells, and *talpargi* or spring-head streams are drawn from the channel.

**Kadaba.**—A town in the Gubbi taluq, on the right bank of the Shimsha, 7 miles south-west of the kasba, on the road from Niṭṭúr to Mayasandra. Head-quarters of the hobli of the same name, and a municipality.

| Population in 1891. | Males. | Females | Total. |
|---|---|---|---|
| Hindus ... ... ... ... ... | 695 | 729 | 1,424 |
| Muhammadans ... ... ... ... | 23 | 20 | 43 |
| Total ... ... ... | 718 | 749 | 1,467 |

Till 1886 it gave its name to the taluq now called Gubbi, and was at one time the head-quarters of the taluq.

It is said to owe its name to Kadamba rishi, who performed penance here on the banks of the Shimshupa, as the Shimsha is called in the local purana. Rama, on his return from Lanka, is said to have encamped here, and at the request of Sita, the river, which was too narrow for the convenience of all the followers, was dammed so as to expand into the present large tank. There is a settlement of Sri Vaishnava Brahmans here, which seems to have been formed in the time of the reformer Rámánujáchárya, who, fleeing from the Chola country, took refuge with the Hoysala king.

**Kaidala.**—A village in Gulur hobli, 3 miles south of Tumkúr, containing the ruins of two fine temples. Population 577.

It appears to have been formerly the capital of a state, and is said to have borne the name of *Kriḍa-pura.* It is also reported to be the native place of Jakanáchári, the famous architect and sculptor to whose wonderful skill is attributed all the finest temple carving in the Province, as at Halebíd, Bélur, &c. Tradition relates that Jakanáchári's career began while Nripa Ráya was ruling in Kriḍápura. He then left his native place and, entering the service of various courts, produced the works by which his fame is to this day upheld. After his departure, a son, Dankanáchári, was born to him, who, when grown up, set out in search of his father, neither having ever seen the other. At Belur the young man found the Chennakésava temple in course of erection, and—so the story goes—remarked that one of the images had a blemish. As this would be fatal to its claim as an object of worship, the architect, who was no other than Jakanáchári himself, hastily vowed to cut off his right hand if any defect could be found in an image he had carved. To test the matter the figure was covered with sandal paste, which dried on every part except around the navel. In this on examination was found a cavity the son had detected, containing a frog and some sand and water. Mortified at the result, Jakanáchári cut off his right hand, and inquiries as to who his critic was, led to the unexpected discovery of their mutual relationship. Subsequently Jakanáchári was directed in a vision to dedicate a temple to the god Kesava in Kriḍápura, his native place. Thither he accordingly returned, and no sooner was the temple completed than his right hand was restored. In commemoration of this incident the place has ever since been called *Kai-daḷa*, the restored hand.

The Gangesvara temple contains inscriptions stating that it and the Narayana temple were erected in 1150, in the reign of the Hoysala king Nárasimha, by a chief named Gúle Báchi. The name is there spelled Kaydáḷa, and there is nothing in support of the above story.

**Karekal-gudda.**—A hill in the south-east of the Tiptúr taluq, containing an old quarry of fine black hornblende, which has been extensively applied to the construction of temples. The quarry is situated about half a mile east from the village of Kádahalli.

**Koratigere.**—A sub-taluq included in Maddagiri taluq. The hoblis belonging to it are Channarayadurga, Holavanhalli, and Koratigere.

**Koratigere.**—A town situated on the left bank of the Suvarnamukhi, in 13° 31′ N. lat., 77° 17′ E. long., 16 miles north of Tumkúr, on the Tumkúr-Maddagiri road. Head-quarters of the Koratigere sub-taluq, and a municipality.

| Population in 1891. | Males. | Females. | Total. |
|---|---|---|---|
| Hindus ... ... ... ... ... | 1,052 | 1,064 | 2,116 |
| Muhammadans ... ... ... ... | 127 | 115 | 242 |
| Total ... ... ... | 1,179 | 1,179 | 2,358 |

The fort and péte were founded by one of the Holavanhalli chiefs, who removed the seat of government hither. The former is in ruins, having been dismantled by Tipu Sultan. Glass bangles are manufactured in the town. The people are dependent for drinking on the river water, which is procurable at all seasons. The well water is brackish.

| Municipal Funds. | 1892-3. | 1893-4. | 1894-5. | 1895-6. |
|---|---|---|---|---|
| Income ... ... ... ... ... | 618 | 698 | 802 | 1,228 |
| Expenditure ... ... ... ... | 572 | 616 | 757 | 1,264 |

**Kundar** or **Kumadvati.**—A stream which rises near Mákalidurga in the Dod-Ballapur taluq, and flowing northwards through the Goribidnur and Maddagiri taluqs, runs into the N. Pinákini just beyond the frontier of the Province, near the town of Hindupur in the Anantapur District. Its extreme length is about 30 miles.

**Kunigal.**—A taluq in the south-east. Area 381 square miles. Head-quarters at Kunigal. Contains the following hoblis, villages and population:—

| No. | Hoblis. | Villages. | Hamlets. | Villages classified. | | | | Population. |
|---|---|---|---|---|---|---|---|---|
| | | | | Government. | Sarvamánya. | Jodi. | Kayamgutta. | |
| 1 | Amritúr ... ... | 56 | 26 | 45 | 1 | 9 | 1 | 11,291 |
| 2 | Bédarahalli .. | 29 | 36 | 28 | — | 1 | — | 6,375 |
| 3 | Huliyúrdurga ... | 49 | 29 | 39 | 7 | 1 | 2 | 7,917 |
| 4 | Hutridurga ... | 34 | 59 | 28 | — | 5 | 1 | 9,233 |
| 5 | Kottagere ... | 33 | 41 | 29 | — | 3 | 1 | 8,196 |
| 6 | Kunigal ... ... | 31 | 29 | 29 | — | 2 | — | 11,491 |
| 7 | Yediyúr ... ... | 59 | 41 | 56 | — | 3 | — | 11,999 |
| | Total ... | 291 | 261 | 254 | 8 | 24 | 5 | 66,502 |

*Principal places, with population.*—Kunigal, 4,406; Amritúru, 1,621; Huliyúrdurga, 1,482.

The Shimsha runs along the western and part of the southern border. From the large tank at Kunigal it receives a stream called the Nágini. The south-east is occupied by the continuation of the great hill range which runs north to the Maddagiri taluq. The country around Huliyúrdurga, and between that place and Kunigal, is very hilly and jungly, the ground being rocky and barren. To the northward and westward the soil is fertile and well cultivated.

Early in the ninth century the Kuningil country, which apparently corresponded with the Kunigal taluq and neighbouring parts, was being governed by Vimaláditya, a Chálukya prince who was the nephew of

Cháki Rája, the Ráshtrakúta viceroy ruling the Ganga territories during the imprisonment of the Ganga king.

The revenue settlement was introduced in 1881. The area of the taluq (including Koppa hobli, since transferred to Mandya taluq) was thus distributed :—

| | | |
|---|---|---|
| Culturable (dry, 135,225 ; wet, 10,825 ; garden, 3,948) | ... | 149,998 |
| Unculturable (including roads, village sites, &c.) | ... ... | 82,220 |
| Inam villages (37,776), Amrit Mahal kavals (5,458) | ... ... | 43,234 |
| Total acres ... | ... ... | 275,452 |

Of the culturable area, 49,834 acres were unoccupied. The total revenue demand for 1891–2 (15 months) was Rs. 1,33,652, and for 1892–3 it was Rs. 1,58,772.

The average rainfall at Kunigal for 25 years (1870–94) was as follows :—

| Jan. | Feb. | Mar. | April | May | June | July | Aug. | Sept. | Oct. | Nov. | Dec. | Year. |
|---|---|---|---|---|---|---|---|---|---|---|---|---|
| 0·02 | 0·14 | 0·34 | 1·19 | 3·64 | 2·77 | 3·59 | 4·49 | 5·68 | 6·33 | 1·98 | 0·21 | 30·38 |

The Bangalore-Hassan road passes through Kunigal, whence also there are cross roads to Tumkúr, and *viâ* Huliyurdurga to Maddur.

**Kunigal.**—A town situated in 13° 2′ N. lat. 77° 5′ E. long., 22 miles south of Tumkúr, on the Bangalore-Hassan road. Head-quarters of the Kunigal taluq, and a municipality.

| Population in 1891. | Males. | Females. | Total. |
|---|---|---|---|
| Hindus ... ... ... ... ... | 1,529 | 1,706 | 3,235 |
| Muhammadans ... ... ... ... | 568 | 542 | 1,110 |
| Christians ... ... ... ... ... | 26 | 35 | 61 |
| Total ... ... ... | 2,123 | 2,283 | 4,406 |

The derivation of the name is said to be *kuni-gal*, dancing stone, Siva having danced here. But from early inscriptions it would appear that the original form of the name was Kuningil or Kunigil.

Three streams rising in Sivaganga, whose names are Naḷini, Nágini and Kamala, are said here to unite their waters. Their virtue is such that a king from the north, named Nriga chakravarti, is said to have been cured of leprosy by bathing in them, and to have constructed the large tank in consequence. A party of seven Lipi jógís, it is said, subsequently came from the Himálayas and obtained a large treasure from the bed of the tank, after killing the seven-headed serpent which guarded it. The tank is estimated to be fourteen miles round when full. The foundation of the fort is attributed to a Víra Kambala Ráya in 1290. It afterwards came into the possession of the Magadi chief, who enlarged the town and fort. Owing to a low type of fever, the place at one time became very unhealthy. The Stud Farm for the breeding of horses for the Mysore Silahdars, formerly at Closepet, has been long established here.

| Municipal Funds. | 1892-3. | 1893-4. | 1894-5. | 1895-6. |
|---|---|---|---|---|
| Income ... ... ... ... ... | 1,281 | 1,358 | 1,313 | 2,334 |
| Expenditure .. ... ... ... | 998 | 1,370 | 1,277 | 3,464 |

**Maddagiri.**—A taluq in the north-east. Area 596 square miles. Head-quarters at Maddagiri. Contains the following hoblis, villages and population :—

| No. | Hoblis. | Villages. | Hamlets. | Villages classified. | | | | Population. |
|---|---|---|---|---|---|---|---|---|
| | | | | Government. | Sarvamánya. | Jodi. | Kayamgutta. | |
| 1 | Channaráyadurga | 60 | 27 | 57 | 1 | 2 | — | 9,049 |
| 2 | Doddéri... ... | 59 | 20 | 52 | 2 | 4 | 1 | 8,361 |
| 3 | Holavanhalli ... | 63 | 43 | 47 | 4 | 8 | 4 | 12,525 |
| 4 | Itagadibbanhalli. | 29 | 9 | 25 | — | 2 | 2 | 7,150 |
| 5 | Kodigenhalli ... | 25 | 9 | 20 | — | 4 | 1 | 9,628 |
| 6 | Koratigere ... | 43 | 16 | 40 | 1 | 2 | — | 7,946 |
| 7 | Maddagiri ... | 64 | 18 | 52 | 2 | 6 | 4 | 10,958 |
| 8 | Midagési ... | 43 | 13 | 39 | — | 3 | 1 | 8,422 |
| 9 | Puravara ... | 49 | 14 | 35 | — | 3 | 11 | 10,785 |
| 10 | Rantavalalu ... | 26 | 8 | 21 | — | 4 | 1 | 4,843 |
| 11 | Teriyúr ... | 22 | 5 | 20 | — | 1 | 1 | 8,306 |
| | Total ... | 483 | 182 | 408 | 10 | 39 | 26 | 97,973 |

*Principal places, with population.*—Maddagiri, 3,536; Koratigere, 2,541; Kodigenhalli, 1,727; Holavanhalli, 1,459; Kadagatturu, 1,405; Itagadibbanhalli, 1,345; Rampura, 1,345; Midagési, 1,039; Nittarhalli, 1,026; Chandragiri, 1,023.

The taluq is crossed from north to south by the lofty chain of mountains including Channaráya-durga, Maddagiri-durga and Midagési-durga. The valleys to the west of the range and south of Maddagiri have a greater elevation than the other parts of the taluq. The open country to the north-east is crossed at one corner by the N. Pinákini, nearly parallel with which, on the west, flow its affluents, first the Kumadvati and then the Jayamangali. This is a very fertile tract of country, with water easily obtainable, at a few feet below the surface, from *talpargis* or spring heads. All the wet and dry crops of the eastern Districts, as well as the fruits grown in Bangalore, are successfully cultivated.

The revenue settlement was introduced in 1877. The total revenue demand for 1891–2 (15 months) was Rs. 2,31,803, and for 1892–3 it was Rs. 2,82,898.

The average rainfall for 25 years (1870–94) at Maddagiri, and for two years (1893–4) at the other places, was as follows:—

| | Jan. | Feb. | Mar. | April | May | June | July | Aug. | Sept. | Oct. | Nov. | Dec. | Year. |
|---|---|---|---|---|---|---|---|---|---|---|---|---|---|
| Maddagiri ...... | 0·04 | 0·02 | 0·25 | 0·55 | 2·20 | 2·15 | 2·19 | 2·75 | 3·02 | 4·22 | 1·60 | 0·37 | 19·36 |
| Badavanhalli ... | — | 0·10 | 0·25 | 0·48 | 1·13 | 3·28 | 2·08 | 1·00 | 3·50 | 3·55 | 0·68 | — | 16·05 |
| Iṭagadibbanhalli | — | 0·03 | 0·50 | 1·65 | 2·60 | 2·38 | 1·88 | 1·31 | 2·44 | 8·49 | 1·37 | — | 22·65 |

The Tumkúr-Pávugaḍa road runs through the taluq from south to north, by way of Koraṭigere, Maddagiri and Miḍagési. At Maddagiri it is crossed by a road going south-east to the Tondebhavi Railway-station, and west to Sira. From Koraṭigere there is a road south to Dobbspet in Nelamangala taluq.

**Maddagiri.**—A town situated in 13° 39′ N. lat. 77° 16′ E. long., 24 miles north of Tumkúr, on the Tumkúr-Pávugaḍa road. Head-quarters of the taluq bearing the same name, and a municipality.

| Population in 1891. | Males. | Femal·s. | Total. |
|---|---|---|---|
| Hindus... ... ... ... ... ... | 1,339 | 1,399 | 2,738 |
| Muhammadans ... ... ... ... | 357 | 405 | 762 |
| Jains ... ... ... ... ... ... | 22 | 14 | 36 |
| Total ... ... ... | 1,718 | 1,818 | 3,536 |

It is surrounded on all sides by hills, the continuation of the north and south range which traverses the east of the District. The town derives its name from Madhu-giri, or honey hill, at the northern base of which it is situated. The two large temples of Venkatramana-swami and Mallesvara, standing side by side, are conspicuous objects. A very graceful ornament is carried round under the eaves of the roof of the latter, representing doves or pigeons, of about life size, in every natural attitude.

The erection of the original fort and town is ascribed to a local chief named Raja Hira Gauḍa. The circumstance of a stray sheep having returned from the hill dripping with wet led to the discovery that it was well supplied with springs of water. This being reported by the shepherds of the neighbouring village of Bijavara, the advantages of the situation were so apparent that the town was established, and mud fortifications constructed on the hill for its protection. About 1678, while Rama Gauḍa and Timma Gauḍa, descendants of the founder, were ruling in Maddagiri, they incurred the hostility of the Raja of Mysore. The dalavayi Devaraj was therefore sent against it, who, after a siege of a year, took the place and led the Gauḍas with their families captive to Seringapatam. They were, however, released and sent back to Midagési, which was left to them out of their lost possessions.

The fortifications of Maddagiri were greatly increased by Haidar Ali, and the place was the seat of a valuable trade, containing a hundred houses of weavers alone. Hither in 1763, on the conquest of Bednur, he sent as prisoners both the Rani and her lover, and also even the pretender Chenna Basavaiya, for whose rights he had ostensibly been fighting, and here they remained until the capture of the place by the Mahrattas in 1767. The Mahratta chief Madhava Rao held possession of Maddagiri for seven years, and when forced by Tipu in 1774 to retire, plundered the town of everything he could carry away. With the usual exaggeration its wealth is said to have been so great that he disdained to remove anything less valuable than gold. Tipu bestowed on it the name of Fattehábád, city of victory, and made it the capital of a surrounding district yielding a revenue of six lakhs of pagodas. But his exactions had nearly ruined the place, when the destruction was completed by the Mahrattas in 1791. Balvant Rao, one of Parasu Ram Bhao's officers, besieged it, though without success, for five months, having under his command a large army, according to native accounts, of 20,000 men. It was principally composed of banditti assembled by the palegars formerly driven from their strongholds, who had ventured back under the protection of Lord Cornwallis. On the conclusion of peace they were speedily dispersed by the Sultan, but not before they had devastated all the neighbouring country. Of 500 Mahratta horse who had joined this rabble, it is said that only 20 men, with their chief, escaped. On the conclusion of the third Mysore war and the death of Tipu, Maddagiri was included in the new territory of Mysore.

Though its prosperity has somewhat revived, the town has never recovered from the ravages of the Mahratta army. It has, however, an extensive trade in brass, copper, and silver vessels of every description. There are also manufactures of iron, steel, coarse cloths and cumblis, and weekly interchange is held with the markets at Tiptúr, Bellary and Hindupur in the Anantapur District, as well as with Bangalore. The chief article of export is rice, especially that called *chinnada saláki*, or golden stick, which is much cultivated and eagerly sought by Bangalore merchants, as it is esteemed to be the best in the Province. The cattle here are finer than those ordinarily seen in other parts of the District. The town, as well as the whole taluq, owes its prosperity to the richness of the soil, and the springs peculiar to this region, which abound everywhere near the surface, so that in the worst of seasons an unfailing supply of water is obtainable for the crops, while the well-water is generally sweet.

| Municipal Funds. | 1892-3. | 1893-4. | 1894-5. | 1895-6. |
|---|---|---|---|---|
| Income ... ... ... ... ... | 1,086 | 1,332 | 990 | 1,880 |
| Expenditure ... ... ... ... | 1,110 | 1,167 | 1,243 | 2,158 |

**Maddagiri-durga.**—A bold fortified hill commanding the town of Maddagiri. The summit is 3,935 feet above the level of the sea. The only access is on the northern face, which slopes upwards at a steep angle, presenting large sheets of bare rock that scarcely allow of foothold except when perfectly dry. In time of war the garrison, it is said, were accustomed to pour oil down these rocky inclines, to prevent the assailing force from mounting the hill. The history of the fortress has already been given in connection with that of the town of Maddagiri. The present formidable lines of defence were erected by Haidar, as stated by a rude inscription in Kannada over one of the upper gateways. There are many springs and ponds of water on the hill, with large granaries and store-houses, formed out of caverns or excavated in the rock. "The view of Madhu giri, on approaching it from the east," says Buchanan, "is much finer than that of any hill-fort I have seen. The works here make a very conspicuous appearance, whereas in general they are scarcely visible, being hidden by the immensity of the rocks on which they are erected."

**Midagesi.**—A town in the Maddagiri taluq, at the eastern base of the Midagési-durga, 12 miles north of the kasba, on the Tumkúr-Pávugaḍa road. Head-quarters of the Midagési hobli. Population, 1,039.

It is said to be named after a princess who was burned here with the corpse of her husband. Ránis of the same family continued to govern it until conquered by Chikkappa Gauḍa, of whose family it remained the chief possession long after they had been deprived of Maddagiri and Channaráya-durga. In 1761 it was reduced by Haidar Ali, and six years later by the Mahrattas, from whom it was recovered by Tipu in 1774. During the invasion of Lord Cornwallis a descendant of Chikkappa Gauḍa returned to the town, but finding on the conclusion of peace that it must revert to Tipu, plundered it of the little that had escaped Mahratta rapacity, and did not leave it until Kamar-ud-Din was approaching with a large force. Under the Muhammadan government, Midagési was the residence of an Asoph, and afterwards the head-quarters of a taluq, which was finally incorporated with Maddagiri.

**Muganayakankote.**—A town in the Gubbi taluq, 15 miles east of the kasba. Population, 977.

It is strongly fortified with mud walls, and before the last incursion of the Mahrattas contained a fine market, consisting of a wide street lined with cocoanut-trees. A somewhat droll account is given of the Mahratta attack on the place, which was repulsed by the inhabitants with the utmost gallantry. Parasu Ram Bhao while at Síra despatched, it is said, a force of 500 horse with 2,000 irregular foot and one gun to capture the fort. Its defence was undertaken by 500 peasants from the neighbourhood, who had two small guns and 100 matchlocks; slings and stones being the only other weapons. The market was destroyed to prevent its giving shelter to the attacking party. The siege was maintained for two months, but though the Mahrattas repeatedly fired their gun, they never once, says the local historian, succeeded in hitting the fort! Disheartened by their ill-success and the loss of two or three of their men, the enemy abandoned the siege and retired, not one of the defendants having been hurt.

**Nidugal.**—A fortified hill in the Pávugaḍa taluq, 14 miles west of the kasba, with a village of the same name on the south and east. Head-quarters of the Nidugal hobli. Population, 310.

The lofty pointed peak of *Niḍu-gal*, literally the long or high stone or rock, rising to 3,722 feet above sea-level, is a conspicuous object throughout the north-east of the country, and it was at all times a formidable stronghold. In the ninth and tenth centuries it was held by the Nolamba kings, who were of the Pallava family, and whose capital was at Henjeru, now called Hemavati. Subsequently it was in possession of a line of kings of Chola descent, prominent among whom was Irungola, acknowledging the supremacy of the Chálukyas, whose name occurs as one of the opponents of the Hoysala king Vishnuvardhana in the twelfth century. The Hoysalas appear to have finally captured the place in the time of Ballala II. Under the Vijayanagar kings, a line of chiefs, whose progenitor was Tippa Raja of Harati, held Nidugal. In 1761 they submitted to Haidar Ali on his conquest of Síra, and were finally ousted by Tipu, who took the last representative as a prisoner to Seringapatam, and put him to death when the British army ascended the Ghats. A fuller account is contained in the history of the District.

The hill was surrounded with six lines of fortifications. That round the summit was called Kálanjana-giri and Kálahasti-kóṭe; the second fort was Bhairavan-kóṭe; the third, Basavan-kóṭe; the fourth, Chennaráyan-kóṭe (the palace of the chiefs was here); the fifth, Allamdevar-kóṭe and Bestar-kóṭe; the sixth, Vírabhadra-kóṭe. Within the fourth and sixth forts are many ruined temples.

**N. Pinakini.**—The Uttara Pinákini or Northern Pennar has a course of only a few miles through the extreme north-east corner of the District, in Pávugaḍa taluq. For a fuller account of the river see Kolar District.

**Pavugada.**—A taluq in the north-east. Area 532 square miles. Head-quarters at Pávugaḍa. Contains the following hoblis, villages and population :—

| No. | Hoblis. | Villages. | Hamlets. | Villages classified. | | | | Popula-tion. |
|---|---|---|---|---|---|---|---|---|
| | | | | Govern-ment. | Sarva-mânya. | Jódi. | Kayam-gutta. | |
| 1 | Gummagaṭṭa ... | 8 | 10 | 7 | 1 | — | — | 4,451 |
| 2 | Hosakóte ... | 23 | 8 | 22 | — | — | 1 | 8,458 |
| 3 | Mugadálbeṭṭa ... | 24 | 23 | 24 | — | — | — | 8,524 |
| 4 | Niḍugal ... ... | 24 | 15 | 23 | 1 | — | — | 5,713 |
| 5 | Pávugaḍa ... | 26 | 15 | 24 | — | 2 | — | 9,795 |
| 6 | Ponnasamudra ... | 22 | 4 | 22 | — | — | — | 6,216 |
| 7 | Rácharlu ... | 18 | 6 | 18 | — | — | — | 10,220 |
| | Total ... | 145 | 81 | 140 | 2 | 2 | 1 | 53,377 |

*Principal places, with population.*—Pávugaḍa, 1,930; Hosakóṭe, 1,608; Gummagaṭṭa, 1,335; Byádanúr, 1,120; Husenpura, 1,052; Kámandurga, 945.

This taluq till 1886 was attached to the Chitaldroog District. It forms a large projection from the north-eastern frontier of Mysore, attached to it by a narrow neck less than five miles in width, and is separated from the remainder of the District by the intervening Madaksira taluq of the Anantapur District. The N. Pinákini runs across the extreme east and in some parts forms the boundary on that side. From Niḍugal northwards the taluq abounds in rocky hills, many of which are crowned with fortifications. Ranges of hills also form the outer boundary of the Rácharlu hobli, a separate tract entirely to the east of the N. Pinákini; and there is a thick cluster on the south, between the frontier and Madaksira.

The soil is sandy and abounds with *talpargis* or springs of water, which may be tapped at short distances from each other. In some parts of the taluq the wells, instead of being dug in the sand, require to be cut through a soft porous rock. Paddy, ragi, navane, and horse-gram are grown in abundance, but all the dry and wet crops of the District are raised more or less, as well as tobacco and cotton. Iron and rice are exported to Bangalore, Bellary, Karnul and other places.

The revenue settlement was introduced in 1872. The total revenue demand for 1891–2 (15 months) was Rs. 96,971, and for 1892–3 it was Rs. 1,15,146.

The average annual rainfall at Pávugaḍa for 25 years (1870–94) was as follows :—

| Jan. | Feb. | Mar. | April | May | June | July | Aug. | Sept. | Oct. | Nov. | Dec. | Year. |
|---|---|---|---|---|---|---|---|---|---|---|---|---|
| — | — | 0·25 | 0·76 | 2·11 | 2·49 | 1·21 | 2·41 | 3·19 | 3·86 | 2·00 | 0·30 | 18·58 |

The chief road is one from Maddagiri through Madaksira to Pávugaḍa and the north. There is also a road from Pávugaḍa east through Rodda to the railway at Penugonda, and one west to Chellakere. A road from Madaksira to Penugonda also crosses the south-east of the taluq. The old Bangalore-Bellary road ran through Rácharlu.

**Pavugada.**—A town situated in 14° 16′ N. lat., 77° 21′ E. long., at the southern base of the hill so named, 60 miles north of Tumkúr, on the road from Maddagiri, and 19 miles west of the railway at Penugonda. Head-quarters of the Pávugaḍa taluq, and a municipality.

| Population in 1891. | Males. | Females. | Total. |
|---|---|---|---|
| Hindus (with 21 Jains) ... ... ... | 711 | 708 | 1,419 |
| Muhammadans ... ... ... ... | 67 | 65 | 132 |
| Christians ... ... ... ... ... | 3 | 4 | 7 |
| Total ... ... ... | 781 | 777 | 1,558 |

*Pávu-gaḍa* or *Pámu-gonḍa*, snake hill, is said to have been so named from a remarkable stone that was discovered there, with the figure of a snake upon it. The place was the haunt of a body of freebooters, who subsisted by plundering the neighbouring country, when it was captured by Bálappa Náyak, the founder of the Pávugaḍa line of palegars. He was one of three brothers of the Yerra Golla caste, who, about 1585, coming from Gutti, entered into the service of Havali Baire Gauda, palegar of Chik-Ballapur (Kolar District). This chief, having no children, adopted Bálappa Náyak, and when summoned to aid the king at Penugonda in an attack upon Gutti, sent him in command of the contingent. Bálappa Náyak, from his local knowledge, was enabled to surprise Gutti, and was rewarded with a grant of Pallavola and other villages. It was after obtaining this estate that he seized Pávugaḍa and fortified the hill. At a later period a conflagration broke out at Penugonda, owing to a powder magazine being struck by lightning. Venkatpati Ráya was absent at the time, but Bálappa Náyak, hastening to the place, extinguished the spreading flames, for which service he was invested with the title of palegar, and received a large accession of territory.

This—with occasional losses from attacks by the palegars of Ratnagiri, Niḍugal and Ráydurga, and the Mahrattas—his descendants continued to govern until the place was taken by the forces of Haidar Ali, when the chief, Timmappa Náyak, and his family, were sent as prisoners to Maddagiri. In 1777, when engaged in operations against Chitaldroog, Haidar visited Pávugaḍa and ordered the erection of the present fortifications. The palegar of Rácharlu was at the same time made prisoner and sent to Penugonda, his territory being annexed to Pávugaḍa. When Maddagiri was taken by the Mahrattas, co-operating with Lord Cornwallis against Seringapatam, Timmappa Náyak obtained release, and took possession again of Pávugaḍa. But on the conclusion of peace could not keep the place against Tipu.

The hill of Pávugaḍa rises to 3,026 feet above the level of the sea.

| Municipal Funds. | 1892-3. | 1893-4. | 1894-5. | 1895-6. |
|---|---|---|---|---|
| Income ... ... ... ... ... | 368 | 418 | 531 | 953 |
| Expenditure ... ... ... ... | 414 | 382 | 695 | 903 |

**Sampige.**—A village in the Gubbi taluq, four miles west of Kadaba. Population, 582.

It is stated to be the site of Champaka nagara, the capital of Sudhanva, of whom an account is given in the Jaimini Bhárata.

**Sibi.**—A village in the Síra taluq, 15 miles north of Tumkúr, on the Tumkúr-Chitaldroog road. Population, 875.

It is remarkable only for the temple of Narasimha, at which there is a great annual festival in the month of Mágha, attended by 10,000 people. The origin of the temple is thus related. In the days when there were no roads and the place was covered with jungle, a certain merchant carrying grain on pack bullocks halted at Sibi. But when his pot of rice was set on to boil on a small projecting rock, its contents turned to the colour of blood and he with his attendants and bullocks fell down in a swoon. While in this unconscious state Narasimha appeared to him in a vision and, revealing that the stone was his abode, commanded the merchant to build a temple over it in atonement for the desecration committed.

The small temple then erected was replaced by the present large building during this century under the following circumstances: Three brothers living at Tumkúr, who had enriched themselves by farming the revenue of the District in the days of Tipu, subsequently sought to atone for their oppressions by works of charity. To Nallappa, the eldest, Narasimha in a vision offered eternal happiness on condition of his building and endowing the temple at Sibi. This was accordingly accomplished in ten years by the three brothers. It is an ordinary structure, surrounded by a high stone wall. The approach is lined on either side with mean stone sheds for the accommodation of visitors to the annual festival. Shops to the number of 400 are then opened by merchants from Dharwar, Bellary, Bangalore, Chitaldroog, Kumbhakonam and other distant places, and trade is carried on to the value, it is said, of several lakhs of rupees.

**Shimsha.**—An affluent of the Kaveri, also called the Shimshupa, the Kadamba and the Kadaba-kola. It rises to the south of Devaraydurga and flowing south-west through the Gubbi taluq, forms the large Kadaba tank. Thence running southwards, it unites near Kallur with the Nága, which feeds the Turuvekere tank, and further on, in the Kunigal taluq, with the Nágini from the Kunigal tank. Afterwards, turning east, it skirts the hills west of Huliyurdurga and pursues a southerly course into the Mandya taluq of the Mysore District.

**Sira.**—A taluq in the north. Area 599 square miles. Headquarters at Síra. Contains the following hoblis, villages, and population :—

| No. | Hoblis. | Villages. | Hamlets. | Villages classified. | | | | Population. |
|---|---|---|---|---|---|---|---|---|
| | | | | Government. | Sarvamánya. | Jódi. | Kayamgutta. | |
| 1 | Agrahára ... | 30 | 19 | 30 | — | — | — | 8,894 |
| 2 | Baragúr ... ... | 27 | 10 | 24 | 1 | 2 | — | 7,084 |
| 3 | Bukkapaṭna ... | 45 | 3 | 45 | — | — | — | 5,867 |
| 4 | Hulikunṭe ... | 24 | 16 | 24 | — | -- | — | 11,147 |
| 5 | Kallambelle ... | 12 | 21 | 12 | — | — | — | 5,610 |
| 6 | Náḍúr ... ... | 36 | 15 | 35 | — | 1 | — | 10,539 |
| 7 | Síra ... ... | 46 | 36 | 43 | 1 | 2 | — | 15,608 |
| 8 | Tarúr ... ... | 33 | 2 | 33 | — | — | — | 3,578 |
| | Total... ... | 253 | 122 | 246 | 2 | 5 | — | 6,8327 |

*Principal places, with population.*—Síra, 3,595; Sibi, 3,379; Chengávara, 2,517; Modalúru, 1,718; Hemmadore, 1,339; Nádúr, 1,181; Halénahalli, 1,131; Bukkapatna, 1,113; Kóṭha, 1,027; Mélukunṭe, 1,023.

The taluq was transferred to this District from Chitaldroog in 1866. It is at a considerably lower level than the rest of the District. It is crossed from east to west by a stream which flows into the Vedávati, and whose course is marked by cocoa-nut gardens. The tracts adjoining Madak-sira are fertile and well watered. The soil in other parts is mostly rocky and hard. Along the west there is a good deal of jungle, from Bukkapaṭna northwards.

The revenue settlement was introduced in 1870. The total revenue demand for 1891–2 (15 months) was Rs. 1,59,492, and for 1892–3 it was Rs. 1,97,613.

The average rainfall at Síra for 25 years (1870–94), and at the other places for 2 years (1893–4) was as follows:—

| | Jan. | Feb. | Mar. | April | May | June | July | Aug. | Sept. | Oct. | Nov. | Dec. | Year. |
|---|---|---|---|---|---|---|---|---|---|---|---|---|---|
| Síra ... ... | 0·06 | 0·03 | 0·14 | 0·67 | 2·02 | 2·17 | 1·44 | 1·88 | 2·96 | 3·20 | 0·35 | 0·23 | 15·15 |
| Bukkapaṭna ... | — | 0·59 | 0·86 | 2·28 | 2·73 | 3·32 | 0·86 | 0·85 | 1·61 | 4·61 | 2·36 | — | 20·07 |
| Kallambelle ... | — | — | 0·58 | 1·19 | 2·05 | 1·83 | 2·20 | 2·85 | 1·60 | 6·64 | 0·79 | — | 19·73 |

The Bangalore-Bellary road passes through Síra, from whence also there is a road through Huliyar to the west, and to Maddagiri on the east, with one north to Amarapuram in Madaksira. The Seringapatam road branches off to the south at Kallambelle.

**Sira.**—A town situated in 13° 44′ N. lat. 76° 58′ E. long., 33 miles north-north-west of Tumkúr, on the Tumkúr-Chitaldroog road. Head-quarters of the Síra taluq, and a municipality.

| Population in 1891. | Males. | Females. | Total. |
|---|---|---|---|
| Hindus (with 13 Jains) ... ... ... | 1,260 | 1,255 | 2,465 |
| Muhammadans ... ... ... .. | 532 | 593 | 1,125 |
| Christians ... ... ... ... ... | 3 | 2 | 5 |
| Total ... ... ... | 1,795 | 1,850 | 3,595 |

The foundation of the town and fort is attributed to Rangappa Nayak, the chief of Ratnagiri, the selection of the site being due, as is commonly related of other forts in the country, to the turning of a hare upon the hounds while in pursuit—an indication of heroic soil. Before the fort was completed, Síra and its dependencies were conquered by Ran-dulha Khan, general of the Bijapur state. Malik Husen, then appointed governor, completed the fort and enclosed the town with mud walls. Malik Rihan was Subadar from 1638 to 1650.

The capture of Bijapur by Aurangzeb in 1687 was speedily followed by the conquest of the Carnatic districts dependent on it. Síra was made the capital of the new province south of the Tungabhadra,—composed of the seven parganas of Basvapatna, Budihal, Síra, Penukonda, Dod-Ballapur, Hoskote, and Kolar,—with Harpanhalli, Kondarpi, Anegundi, Bednur, Chitaldroog, and Mysore as tributary states. Khásim Khán was appointed as the first governor, under the designation apparently of Faujdár Diván, a title, however, which was often altered according to circumstances. He introduced the Muhammadan revenue system, elsewhere described, and governed with ability until 1698, when, being surprised by the Mahrattas and the chief of Chitaldroog at Dodderi while in the conveyance of a large treasure, he either committed suicide to avoid disgrace or was killed by them. Zulifikar Khan succeeded, but a governor named Rastam Jang or Chak appears to have most distinguished himself by his administration, gaining the title of Bahádur and the name of Kaifiyat Khán. The last of the Mughal governors of Síra, which shared in many of the contests between the rivals for the Subadari of the Dekhan, was Dilávar Khán, from whom the place was taken in 1757 by the Mahrattas.

In 1761, Haidar, having entered into alliance at Hoskote with Basálat Jang and received from him the title of Naváb of Síra, at once took the place and thence extended his conquests all over the north. In 1766 the brother-in-law of Haidar was induced by the Mahrattas to yield up Síra, which remained in their hands till retaken by Tipu in 1774, since which time it has been attached to Mysore, except for a short period when it was occupied by the Mahratta army co-operating with the British against Seringapatam.

Síra attained its highest prosperity under Dilávar Khán and is said to have contained 50,000 houses. An elegant palace erected by him, now all ruined, was the model on which those of Bangalore and Seringapatam were built. A fine garden was also made, called the Khán Bágh, which was kept up by Haidar, and may have suggested the Lál Bágh at Bangalore. The ruins of a large quarter, to which tradition assigns the name of Láṭapura, may yet be seen to the north-west of the fort. Tipu forcibly transported 12,000 families from Síra to form a population for his new town of Shahar Ganjam on the island of Seringapatam. These vicissitudes and the inroads of the Mahrattas reduced the town to 3,000 houses. There are now only about 700, much scattered. The Jama Masjid, of hewn stone (date 1696), is deserving of mention, and the tomb of Malik Rihan (date 1650). The fort, well built of stone, is surrounded with a moat and a fine glacis.

A large tank to the north irrigates the subjacent lands. The soil around is favourable to the growth of the cocoa-nut, the dried kernel of which is the staple article of export. The population consists largely of Kurubar, who manufacture cumblis or coarse blankets, of wool imported from Davangere, Kankuppa and Madaksira. These are exported to Walaji, Kaudial or Mangalore, Bangalore, Mysore, Ganjam, Nagar and Coorg. The prices range from 8 annas to 12 rupees according to quality and texture, the entire trade being of the annual value of Rs. 5,000. Some years ago chintzes were largely manufactured, and a glazed kind found a ready sale among the higher classes. But the importation of English piece goods has put a stop to the native manufacture. Common sealing-wax continued to be made, but it was far inferior to the kind now prepared in England specially for India.

| Municipal Funds. | 1892-3. | 1893-4. | 1894-5. | 1895-6. |
|---|---|---|---|---|
| Income ... ... ... ... ... | 1,500 | 1,571 | 1,404 | 2,383 |
| Expenditure ... ... ... ... | 1,158 | 2,085 | 2,018 | 2,843 |

**Sitakal.**—A village in the Kolála hobli of the Tumkúr taluq. Population 976.

Brass utensils are largely manufactured by Bhogars or braziers, and there is an extensive trade in cotton.

**Suvarnamukhi.**—A stream which rises in Channaráya-durga. Flowing at first south-east, on emerging from the hills it turns to the north-east, and passing Koratigere, after a course of about 15 miles runs into the Jayamangali.

**Tiptur.**—A taluq in the south-west. Area 510 square miles. Head-quarters at Tiptur. Contains the following hoblis, villages and population :—

| No. | Hoblis. | Villages. | Hamlets. | Villages classified. | | | | Popula-tion. |
|---|---|---|---|---|---|---|---|---|
| | | | | Govern-ment. | Sarva-mánya. | Jódi. | Kayam-gutta. | |
| 1 | Dabbegatta ... | 34 | 14 | 33 | — | 1 | — | 6,489 |
| 2 | Hálkurike ... | 29 | 26 | 26 | 2 | 1 | — | 4,974 |
| 3 | Honnavalli ... | 45 | 35 | 45 | — | — | — | 8,932 |
| 4 | Ichanúr ... ... | 40 | 13 | 40 | — | — | — | 5,925 |
| 5 | Kibbanhalli ... | 30 | 28 | 29 | — | 1 | — | 5,952 |
| 6 | Máyisandra ... | 65 | 30 | 65 | — | — | — | 13,374 |
| 7 | Nonavinkere ... | 36 | 28 | 36 | — | — | — | 8,354 |
| 8 | Tiptur ... ... | 51 | 36 | 50 | — | 1 | — | 13,190 |
| 9 | Turuvekere ... | 61 | 43 | 59 | 1 | 1 | — | 11,677 |
| | Total ... | 391 | 253 | 383 | 3 | 5 | — | 78,867 |

*Principal places, with population.*—Tiptur, 2,378; Honnavalli, 2,102; Turuvekere, 1,610; Nonavinkere, 1,462; Hálkurike, 919.

The taluq, till 1886, was called Honnavalli; and at the same period Turuvekere, transferred from the old Kadaba taluq, was made a sub-taluq.

The taluq is generally undulating, with here and there slight elevations, which can scarcely be called hills. In the extreme north and west there are rocky hills, spurs of the Hirekal-gudda hills. On the south-east, near Dabbegaṭṭa, are some hills yielding a fine black hornblende, which has been formerly much quarried for pillars of temples and other public buildings. In the northern parts the soils are more or less gravelly; in the centre and south they are reddish, with an admixture of sand in the high-lying, and dark brown in the low-lying lands. In Ichanúr there is an extensive area of stony soil of an inferior description. There are numerous tanks, some of them, especially in the south, being of considerable size. The principal dry crops are ragi, avare, horse-gram, chillies, and tobacco, with patches of castor and other oil plants. Rice is the general wet crop, sugar-cane cultivation being very limited. Some wheat is also produced. The gardens are almost entirely cocoa-nut, both irrigated and unirrigated. Areca-nut is limited to gardens specially well situated and having a good water supply. In these are also grown betel-leaf, plantains, and vegetables, while in the dry cocoa-nut gardens rági and sáme are produced. The cocoa-nuts of Honnavalli are celebrated for their flavour. The taluq suffered very much in the famine of 1877–8.

The revenue settlement was introduced in 1880. The area of the taluq at that time was thus distributed:—

| | |
|---|---|
| Culturable (dry, 127,550; wet, 3,980; garden, 17,472) ... ... | 149,002 |
| Unculturable (roads, village sites, &c.) ... ... ... ... | 54,826 |
| Inam villages (4,977), Amrit Mahal kavals (10,705) ... ... | 15,682 |
| Total acres | 219,510 |

Of the culturable area, 63,746 acres were waste. The total revenue demand for 1891–2 (15 months) was Rs. 2,01,062, and for 1892–3 it was Rs. 2,28,448.

The average rainfall for 25 years (1870–94) at Tiptur and Turuvekere, and for 2 years (1893–4) at the other places (except Honnavalli, which is only for 1894) was as follows:—

| | Jan. | Feb. | Mar. | April | May | June | July | Aug. | Sept. | Oct. | Nov. | Dec. | Year. |
|---|---|---|---|---|---|---|---|---|---|---|---|---|---|
| Tiptur ......... | — | 0·03 | 0·22 | 2·04 | 3·32 | 1·65 | 2·04 | 2·64 | 4·61 | 7·18 | 3·21 | 0·83 | 27·77 |
| Turuvekere ... | 0·18 | 0·02 | 0·14 | 1·47 | 2·92 | 2·98 | 1·87 | 2·75 | 4·22 | 6·25 | 1·72 | 0·56 | 25·08 |
| Honnavalli ... | — | — | — | 1·20 | 1·20 | 2·80 | — | 2·20 | 1·76 | 6·10 | 2·53 | — | 17·79 |
| Kibbanhalli ... | — | — | 0·80 | 1·73 | 3·95 | 3·18 | 3·75 | 1·65 | 2·85 | 6·46 | 0·90 | — | 25·27 |
| Mayisandra ... | — | 0·18 | 0·38 | 1·40 | 5·04 | 1·79 | 3·32 | 2·95 | 5·73 | 11·19 | 2·58 | — | 34·56 |
| Nonavinkere | — | 0·38 | 0·38 | 3·35 | 4·38 | 2·18 | 5·47 | 1·38 | 5·56 | 5·85 | 1·49 | — | 30·42 |

The Bangalore-Poona Railway runs through the taluq from east to west, with stations at Banasandra, Karodi, Tiptur, and Konehalli. The trunk road from Bangalore to Shimoga passes through in the same direction, a little north of the railway line. From Tiptur there are roads south-west to Hassan, south to Chanraypatna, and south-east to

Turuvekere. This latter continues on to Mayisandra, where it meets the Gubbi-Seringapatam road, with a branch to Yediyur. From Turuvekere a road runs north to Banasandra Railway-station, Chiknayakanhalli, and Huliyar. From Konehalli Railway-station, in the west, there is a road north to Honnavalli and Huliyar.

**Tiptur.**—A large trading-place, situated in 13° 15′ N. lat. 76° 32′ E. long., 46 miles west of Tumkúr, on the Bangalore-Poona Railway and the Tumkúr-Shimoga road. Head-quarters of Tiptur taluq, and a municipality.

| Population in 1891. | Males. | Females. | Total. |
|---|---|---|---|
| Hindus (with 5 Jains) ... ... ... | 903 | 954 | 1,857 |
| Muhammadans ... ... ... ... | 196 | 198 | 394 |
| Christians ... ... ... ... ... | 4 | 5 | 9 |
| Total ... ... ... | 1,103 | 1,157 | 2,260 |

It is the seat of a great weekly fair, which lasts from Saturday morning till noon on Sunday. Merchants attend from Dharwar, Bellary, Madras, Salem and other places, the value of the commodities exchanged being Rs. 30,000 a week.

| Municipal Funds. | 1892-3. | 1893-4. | 1894-5. | 1895-6. |
|---|---|---|---|---|
| Income ... ... ... ... ... | 1,910 | 2,083 | 2,015 | 3,315 |
| Expenditure ... ... ... ... | 2,004 | 2,444 | 2,180 | 3,672 |

**Tumkur.**—A taluq in the east. Area 452 square miles. Head-quarters at Tumkúr. Contains the following hoblis, villages and population :—

| No. | Hoblis. | Villages. | Hamlets. | Villages classified. | | | | Population. |
|---|---|---|---|---|---|---|---|---|
| | | | | Government. | Sarvamánya. | Jódi. | Kayamgutta. | |
| 1 | Bellávi ... ... | 31 | 14 | 30 | — | — | 1 | 5,862 |
| 2 | Gúlúr ... ... | 55 | 24 | 46 | 3 | 6 | — | 9,343 |
| 3 | Hebbúr ... ... | 48 | 43 | 44 | — | 4 | — | 10,007 |
| 4 | Honnuḍike ... | 34 | 16 | 30 | — | 4 | — | 6,422 |
| 5 | Koláła ... ... | 51 | 13 | 40 | — | 10 | 1 | 5,756 |
| 6 | Kora ... ... | 68 | 25 | 65 | 3 | — | — | 9,471 |
| 7 | Toṭlagere ... | 32 | 9 | 30 | 1 | 1 | — | 4,190 |
| 8 | Tumkúr... ... | 60 | 32 | 53 | 1 | 5 | 1 | 21,790 |
| 9 | Uruḍigere ... | 94 | 73 | 87 | 4 | 2 | 1 | 17,941 |
| | Total ... ... | 473 | 249 | 425 | 12 | 32 | 4 | 90,782 |

*Principal places, with population.*—Tumkúr, 11,086; Kyátasandra, 1,960; Hebbúr, 1,646; Bellávi, 1,510; Urudigere, 1,068; Chik Toṭlagere, 1,021; Honnuḍike, 979; Sitakal, 976.

The east of the taluq is occupied by the Devaráydurga hills, which are surrounded with forest. The Jayamangali rises in them on the north, but during its short course in this taluq is of little benefit, owing to the rocky and rugged nature of the country surrounding its banks. The tracts south of the hills are well supplied with tanks, fed by streams which ultimately unite to form the Shimsha. The country around Tumkúr is very fertile and highly cultivated; to the westward it is less fruitful. The undulating nature of the country being favourable to the formation of tanks, there are extensive gardens of areca-nut and cocoa-nut, as well as the usual paddy cultivation. The streams, though none of them large enough to supply channels, are yet of great assistance to agriculture, the water after the rains being distributed from them to the adjoining fields by *yáta* and *kapile* wells.

The revenue settlement was introduced in 1871. The area of the taluq at that time was thus distributed:—

| | | |
|---|---|---|
| Culturable (dry, 152,516; wet, 14,652; garden, 4,860) | ... | 172,028 |
| Unculturable (including roads, tanks, village sites, &c.) | ... | 66,768 |
| Total acres | | 238,796 |

Of the culturable area, 29,675 acres were waste. The total revenue demand for 1891–2 (15 months) was Rs. 1,83,178, and for 1892–3 it was Rs. 2,53,148.

The average rainfall at Tumkúr for 25 years (1870–94) and at the other places for two years (1893–4) was as follows:—

| | Jan. | Feb. | Mar. | April | May | June | July | Aug. | Sept. | Oct. | Nov. | Dec. | Year. |
|---|---|---|---|---|---|---|---|---|---|---|---|---|---|
| Tumkúr ... | 0.09 | 0.08 | 0.35 | 1.34 | 4.14 | 4.19 | 4.80 | 5.78 | 6.90 | 7.06 | 2.14 | 0.49 | 37.36 |
| Bellávi ... | — | — | — | 1.30 | 5.01 | 3.78 | 2.71 | 2.40 | 0.56 | 7.44 | 0.35 | — | 23.55 |
| Hebbur ... | — | 0.20 | 1.45 | 2.89 | 5.20 | 3.35 | 3.70 | 2.00 | 2.05 | 7.05 | 1.15 | — | 29.04 |
| Nelhal ... | — | 0.13 | 0.78 | 2.75 | 4.30 | 3.98 | 5.53 | 2.93 | 1.50 | 9.50 | 1.45 | — | 32.85 |
| Urdigere | — | — | 0.45 | 0.88 | 2.35 | 5.20 | 4.82 | 3.79 | 2.09 | 10.93 | 1.45 | — | 31.96 |

The Bangalore-Poona Railway runs through the taluq from east to west, with stations at Hirehalli and Tumkúr. The Bangalore-Shimoga road is close alongside the railway. From Tumkúr there are trunk roads north-west to Chitaldroog and north-east to Maddagiri and Pavugada; with a road south to Kunigal, connecting at Hebbur with one from Gubbi on the west.

**Tumkur.**—The chief town of the District, situated in 13° 20′ N. lat. 77° 9′ E. long., 43 miles north-west of Bangalore, with which it is connected by rail and road.

| Population in 1891. | Males. | Females. | Total. |
|---|---|---|---|
| Hindus ... ... ... ... ... | 4,205 | 4,366 | 8,571 |
| Muhammadans .. ... ... ... | 1,023 | 1,010 | 2,033 |
| Jains ... ... ... ... ... ... | 59 | 49 | 108 |
| Christians ... ... ... ... ... | 211 | 163 | 374 |
| Total ... ... ... | 5,498 | 5,588 | 11,086 |

It is prettily situated at the south-western base of the Devaráy-durga group of hills, on elevated ground, near the waste weir of a large tank. The town is surrounded with gardens of plantains, areca and cocoa-nut palms, and betel vines, besides many groves of well-grown trees. The well water is generally brackish, but three wells close to the town yield sweet drinking water. Some of the streets are wide, forming thoroughfares for the high roads to Bangalore, Bellary, Shimoga and the coffee districts in the west. The native houses are mostly mud-built, of one storey and tiled. Of the European dwellings, which are somewhat scattered, the principal lie to the north beyond the town, but the advent of the railway has, of late years, increased the importance of the southern part.

Tumkúr is said originally to have formed part of a territory whose capital was Kaidala, now an insignificant village three miles to the south of it. Its name is said to be derived from *ṭumuku*, a small drum or tabret, the place having been granted to the herald or tom-tom beater of the Kaidala raja. But the earliest form of the name, as given in an inscription of the tenth century, is Tummegúru (*see* above, p. 161). From the twelfth century it formed a part of the A'nebid-dasari or A'nebiddajari district (*see* p. 177). Kante arasu, one of the Mysore family, is said to have formed the present town, consisting of a fort, the walls of which have now been levelled, and a péte to the east of it.

The Deputy Commissioner's court is a conspicuous circular building of three storeys. The town contains the usual District offices, a High School, and other public buildings. It is the residence of a European Missionary of the Wesleyan Society, who have here a chapel and several schools.

| Municipal Funds. | 1892–3. | 1893–4. | 1894–5. | 1895–6. |
|---|---|---|---|---|
| Income ... ... ... ... ... | 7,618 | 8,353 | 8,658 | 14,786 |
| Expenditure ... ... ... ... | 7,177 | 7,639 | 7,990 | 17,872 |

**Turuvekere.**—A town in the Tiptur taluq, 8 miles south of the

Banasandra Railway-station. Head-quarters of the sub-taluq of the same name, and a municipality.

| Population in 1891. | Males. | Females. | Total. |
|---|---|---|---|
| Hindus ... ... ... ... ... | 702 | 780 | 1,482 |
| Muhammadans ... ... ... ... | 71 | 57 | 128 |
| Total ... ... ... | 773 | 837 | 1,610 |

Its ancient name is said to have been Narasimha-pura. It contains three fine temples, in two of which, dedicated to Chennigaráya-swámi and Virabhadra, are inscriptions making gifts of agraharas in the time of the Hoysala king Narasimha, of whose queen Lokamma or Lokámbika it appears to have been the native place. Facing the temple of Gangádharesvara is a recumbent bull of large size, elaborately carved in black hornblende from Karekal-gudda, and still retaining a brilliant polish. About 30 years after its foundation Turuvekere appears to have been captured by the Hágalvádi chief named Sál Nayak, who committed the government to his brothers Chikka Náyak and Anne Náyak. By them the outer fort was built, the tank enlarged and other improvements made. In 1676 it was taken by Chikka Deva Rája of Mysore and has ever since been a part of the Mysore territory, Lingáyits form a principal part of the population. Till 1873 it was the chief town of a separate taluq, named after it.

The inhabitants depend for water entirely on the tank, which is fed by a stream called the Nága and contains much lotus.

| Municipal Funds. | 1892–3. | 1893–4. | 1894–5. | 1895–6. |
|---|---|---|---|---|
| Income ... ... ... ... ... ... | 661 | 570 | 492 | 634 |
| Expenditure ... ... ... ... | 678 | 560 | 571 | 645 |

**Yediyur.**—A village in the Kunigal taluq, 12 miles south west of the kasba, on the Bangalore Hassan road. Head-quarters of the Yediyur hobli. Population, 477.

A large festival, called Siddesvara játre, is held here for five days from Chaitra suddha 7th, at which 10,000 people assemble.

# MYSORE DISTRICT

## GENERAL DESCRIPTION

*Situation.*—The Mysore District forms the southernmost portion of the Province, and is situated between 11° 36′ and 13° 35′ north latitude, 75° 76′ and 77° 24′ east longitude. The greatest length from east to west is about 97 miles; from north to south the extreme distance is about 102 miles.

*Area.*—The area of the District is 5,517 square miles, of which 1,914 square miles are under cultivation, and 2,356 square miles unculturable and waste.

*Boundaries.*—It is bounded on the north by the Hassan and Tumkúr Districts; east by the Bangalore District and the Coimbatore Collectorate; south by the Nilgiri and Malabar Collectorates; west by Coorg.

*Divisions.*—The District was extended to its present dimensions in 1882 and 1886, and is composed of thirteen taluqs and one jágir. Five taluqs—Krishnarájpet, Malavalli, Mandya, Nágamangala, and Seringapatam—form the French Rocks Sub-Division, which was constituted in 1882. Maddúr is a sub-taluq under Mandya.

| No. | Taluq. | Area. square miles. | No. of Hoblis | No. of Villages or Towns. | Population in 1891. | Per square mile. |
|---|---|---|---|---|---|---|
| 1 | Chámarájnagar ... ... ... | 479 | 10 | 179 | 91,250 | 190·50 |
| 2 | Gundlupet ... ... ... ... | 544 | 6 | 179 | 63,036 | 115·87 |
| 3 | Heggadadevankote ... ... ... | 621 | 5 | 262 | 61,226 | 98·59 |
| 4 | Hunsúr ... ... ... ... | 672 | 10 | 412 | 113,271 | 168·59 |
| 5 | Krishnarájpet ... ... ... ... | 424 | 6 | 362 | 91,453 | 215·69 |
| 6 | Malavalli ... ... ... ... | 391 | 7 | 223 | 85,910 | 219·79 |
| 7 | Mandya ... ... ... ... | 452 | 12 | 301 | 99,783 | 220·76 |
| 8 | Mysore ... ... ... ... ... | 322 | 8 | 150 | 134,684 | 418·27[1] |
| 9 | Nágamangala ... ... ... ... | 401 | 5 | 354 | 69,265 | 172·73 |
| 10 | Nanjangúd ... ... ... ... | 384 | 9 | 199 | 97,374 | 201·49 |
| 11 | Seringapatam ... ... ... ... | 274 | 11 | 210 | 85,242 | 311·10 |
| 12 | Tirumakúdlu Narsipúr ... ... | 217 | 7 | 138 | 83,454 | 384·67 |
| 13 | Yedatore ... ... ... ... | 234 | 7 | 180 | 74,262 | 316·93 |
| 14 | Yelandúr Jágir ... ... | 102 | 4 | 26 | 31,754 | 311·31 |
| | Total ... ... | 5,517 | 107 | 3,175 | 1,181,964 | 214·24 |

[1] Omitting the City of Mysore, the rate is 188·31.

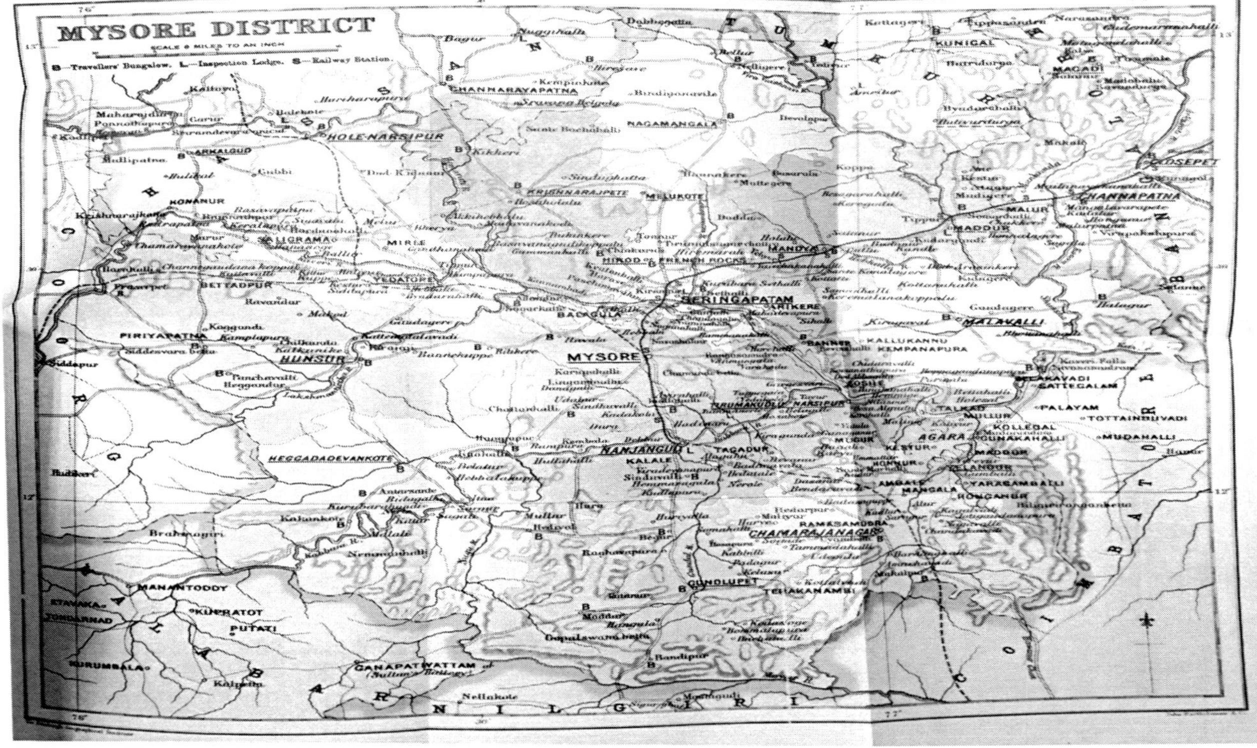
MYSORE DISTRICT
SCALE 8 MILES TO AN INCH
B—Travellers' Bungalow. L—Inspection Lodge. S—Railway Station.
HOLE-NARSIPUR
ARKALGUD
KONANUR
SALIGRAMA
YEDATORE
BETTADPUR
PIRIYAPATNA
HUNSUR
HEGGADADEVANKOTE
CHANNARAYAPATNA
NAGAMANGALA
KRISHNARAJPETE
MELUKOTE
MANDYA
SERINGAPATAM
MYSORE
NANJANGUD
TAGADUR
KALALE
CHAMARAJANAGAR
GUNDLUPET
MALAVALLI
KUNIGAL
MAGADI
CLOSEPET
CHANNAPATNA
MADDUR
MALUR
KOLLEGAL
PALAYAM
TOTTAINDUVADI
MUDAHALLI
SATTEGALAM
KALLUKANNU
KEMPANAPURA
MANANTODDY
PUTATI
KURUMBALA
GANAPATWATTAM
(Sultan's Battery)
Nellakote
Siddapur
N I L G I R I
C O O R G
M A L A B A R
C O I M B A T O R E

The following are the names of taluqs which have been altered:—Hunsúr was formerly Periyapatna; Krishnarájpet was Attikuppa; Seringapatam was Ashtagram; and Tirumakúdlu Narsipúr was Talakád.

**Physical Features.**—The river Káveri, besides forming the boundary for some distance both on the western and eastern sides, traverses the District from north-west to east, receiving the tributaries Hémávati, Lókapávani and Shimsha on the north, and the Lakshmantirtha, Kabbani and Honna Hole or Suvarnávati on the south.

Lofty mountain ranges covered with vast forests, the home of the elephant, shut in the western, southern, and some parts of the eastern frontier. The only break in this mighty barrier is to the south-east, where the Káveri takes its course towards the Ghats and hurls itself down the falls of Gagana Chukki and Bar Chukki at the island of Sivasamudram. The principal range of hills within the District is the Biligirirangan in the Yelandúr Jágír at the south-eastern extremity, rising to a height of 5,091 feet above the level of the sea. Next to these the isolated hills of Gópálswámi in the south near Gundlupet, 4,770 feet above sea-level, and of Bettadpur in the north-west (4,389 feet), are the most prominent heights, with Chámundi hill (3,489 feet) south of Mysore. The French Rocks (2,882 feet), to the north of Seringapatam, are conspicuous points of a line culminating in the sacred peak at Melukote (3,589 feet). Short ranges of low hills appear along the southern parts of the District, especially in the south-west. On the east, in Malavalli taluq, are encountered the hills which separate the valleys of the Shimsha and Arkavati, among which Kabbál-durga (3,507 feet) has gained an unenviable notoriety.

An undulating table-land, fertile and well watered by perennial rivers, whose waters, dammed by noble and ancient anicuts, enrich their banks by means of canals; such has the Mysore District been described. Here and there granite rocks rise from the plain, which is otherwise unintermittent and well wooded. There is a gradual fall in the level of the country from west to east, Yelwal being 2,826 feet above the sea, Mysore 2,525, and Seringapatam 2,337. The extreme south forms a terai of dense and valuable but unhealthy forest, occupying the depression which runs along the foot of the Nilagiri mountains, the lowest part of which is the remarkable long, steep, trench-like ravine,[1] sometimes called the Mysore ditch, which forms the boundary on this side, and in which now flows the Moyár.

*Channels*.—The irrigated fields under the numerous channels drawn from the Káveri and its tributaries cover many parts of the District with rich tracts of verdure. For within this District alone there are

[1] *See* Vol. I., p. 27.

nine anicuts on the Káveri, seven on the Lakshmantirtha, five on the Hemavati, one on the Shimsha, one on the Nugu, two on the Suvarnavati (besides temporary ones erected annually), one on the Kabbani, and one on the Gundal. The total length of channels running is 691 miles, yielding a revenue of more than 4 lakhs a year. The importance of these works, which will be more fully described under each river, may be estimated from the following statement:—

| Name of River. | Name of Anicut. | Name of Channel. | Length in miles. | Area irrigated in acres. | Revenue in Rupees (1890). |
|---|---|---|---|---|---|
| Káveri ... | Krishnaráj katte | Kattepura ... | 36 | 3,865 | 19,864 |
| | Alale katte ... | Saligram series... | 24 | 2,884 | 18,361 |
| | | Mirle series ... | 38 | 3,110 | 20,811 |
| | Chunchan katte | Ramasamudram | 41 | 4,300 | 25,809 |
| | Adagur katte ... | Tippur ... ... | 22 | 590 | 4,089 |
| | Madad katte ... | Chikdevarayságar | 71 | 13,737 | 89,571 |
| | Devaráya ... | Devaraya ... | 18 | 1,657 | 12,787 |
| | Balmuri... ... | Virja-nadi ... | 41 | 7,330 | 45,888 |
| | Bangárdoddi ... | Bangárdoddi ... | 9 | 820 | 5,632 |
| | Rámaswámi ... | Rámaswámi ... | 30 | 3,104 | 16,793 |
| | | Rájaparamesvari | 21 | 1,848 | 9,771 |
| | Mádhava mantri | Mádhava mantri | 18 | 2,939 | 13,677 |
| Suvarnavati ... | Gajanur... ... | Bhandikere ... | 9 | 354 | 1,541 |
| | Hongalvadi ... | Hongalvadi ... | 15 | 1,706 | 7,439 |
| | | Sargur ... ... | 3 | 223 | 1,191 |
| | | Marlahalli ... | 3 | 309 | 1,601 |
| | | Alur, new ... | 4 | 158 | 1,401 |
| | | ,, old .. | — | 136 | 1,374 |
| | | Homma ... | 4 | 371 | 1,890 |
| | | Hosahalli ... | 4 | 189 | 1,156 |
| | | Kudlur ... ... | 6 | 30 | 192 |
| | | Honganur ... | — | 1,686 | 8,197 |
| Lakshmantirtha | Hanagod ... | Hanagod series | 66 | 4,101 | 18,265 |
| | Katte Malalvadi | Katte Malalvadi | 11 | 509 | 2,520 |
| | Hangarhalli ... | Sarayur ... ... | 11 | 463 | 1,753 |
| | | Husainpur ... | 11 | 675 | 3,246 |
| | Manchaballi ... | Manchaballi ... | 10 | 406 | 2,392 |
| | Sagar katte ... | Anandur ... | 20 | 1,317 | 7,278 |
| | | Ayarhalli ... | 4 | 147 | 718 |
| Hemavati ... | Mandigere ... | Mandigere ... | 27 | 2,720 | 20,007 |
| | Hemagiri ... | Hemagiri ... | 17 | 19 | 126 |
| | Akkihebbal ... | Akkihebbal ... | 7 | 378 | 2,724 |
| | Kalhalli ... | Kalhalli ... | 8 | 22 | 149 |
| | Danáyakan katte | Kannambádi ... | 14 | 1,125 | 8,047 |
| Kabbani ... | | Rampur ... | 32 | 1,367 | 8,020 |
| Nugu ... ... | Lakshmanapura | Lakshmanapura | 5 | 297 | 1,401 |
| Shimsha ... | Maddur ane ... | Maddur ane ... | 12 | 1,090 | 6,453 |
| | | Kemman ... | $5\frac{1}{2}$ | 472 | 3,183 |
| | | Vaidyanathpur... | $3\frac{1}{4}$ | 254 | 1,492 |
| | | Bairan ... ... | 2 | 379 | 2,800 |
| | | Chamanhalli ... | $2\frac{3}{4}$ | 805 | 4,961 |
| | | Total ... | $685\frac{1}{2}$ | 68,060 | 4,04,670 |

**Rocks.**—The geological formation is principally of granite, gneiss, quartz, and hornblende. In many places these strata are overlaid with laterite. Stone for masonry, principally common granite, is abundant throughout the District. Black hornblende of inferior quality, and potstone are also found. Quartz is abundant, and is chiefly used for road metalling. Corundum occurs in Hunsúr taluq. In Singanamáranhalli the corundum beds were found by Mr. Holland (of the Geological Survey of India) to be associated "with an intrusion of olivine-bearing rocks, similar to those of the Chalk Hills near Salem, and large masses of a rock composed of a highly ferriferous enstatite with magnetite and the iron-alumina spinel, hercynite. The association here is very strikingly like that of the rocks in which the corundum (emery) occurs in the Cortland series of New York State, where there is a development of pyroxenic granulites and ultra-basic rocks, presenting characters precisely similar to those of the charnockite and norite series in South India. A similar association of corundum with hercynite, magnetite, and rhombic pyroxenes has been described on the eastern edge of the Bohemian Forest—the original home of the mineral hercynite."

**Minerals.**—Gold dust is sometimes found in the jungle streams of Heggadadevankóte taluq. Mining for gold has been experimentally begun near Nanjangud, and exploration for the same purpose near Bannur. Altogether more than 10,000 acres have been taken up for gold-mining. Iron abounds in the rocky hills throughout the District, but is worked only in Heggadadevankóte and Malavalli taluqs. The iron ore of the Malavalli taluq is procured from the Sravana hills near Tippur. The smelting furnaces are at Halgur and Husgur. The iron of Malavalli is considered the best in the Mysore territory. Of the quantity produced, about half was exported in a crude state: the remainder was manufactured in the taluq into nearly every description of implements, and of these the larger proportion were exported in various directions. But the indigenous iron manufacture has much declined and become nearly extinct during recent years, being unable to compete with importations from England and other European countries.

Stones containing magnetic iron are occasionally turned up by the ploughshare near Dévanúr of the Nanjangud taluq. The natives hold this ore in high esteem for medicinal purposes, and a magnetic cup was one of the many devices for prolonging life pressed upon the Raja who died in 1868 by his hakims. They have also a strange belief that milk boiled in a magnetic cup will not boil over. It is smelted in the same manner as common iron.

Talc (abhraka) is found in several taluqs. It is used for putting a gloss on baubles employed in ceremonies. Native doctors hold it in high esteem for flux cases. It occupies the rents and small veins in decomposing quartz, but its laminæ are not large enough to serve for glass. The natives commonly believe that it indicates the presence of diamonds.

Asbestos (kalnár) is found in abundance in Chamrajnagar taluq. It is used by native physicians as an antiphlogistic.

Nodules of flint called chakmukki are found in the east of the District. It was formerly the material for gun flints, and is even now used by the ryots for striking a light with tinder.

**Soils.**—The red soil is abundant and prevails throughout the District, but of the more fertile black soil, one of the most valuable tracts in the country runs through the south-east in the Chamrajnagar taluq and the Yelandur jágír. In the latter there is probably not a single acre of uncultivated land, excepting on the hills.

**Climate.**—The climate is hotter than that of the Bangalore District, and exhibits greater extremes. While the mean annual temperature is a little over 77, the minimum has been recorded of 50 in January, and the maximum of 100 in March and April. But for the intermittent fevers which prevail during the cold months the climate would be healthy.

*Temperature.*—The mean meteorological results of observations made at Mysore during 1894 and 1895 are here given as illustrating the monthly variations of the climate.

| 1894. | Barometer. Red. to 32° F. | Barometer. Red. to Sea Level. | Barometer. Daily Range. | Thermometers. Dry Bulb. Mean. | Thermometers. Dry Bulb. Max. | Thermometers. Dry Bulb. Min. | Thermometers. Dry Bulb. Range. | Thermometers. Wet Bulb. Mean. | Thermometers. Wet Bulb. Min. | Aqueous Vapour. Press. Inches. | Aqueous Vapour. Humidity. Per cent. | Wind. Daily Vel. Miles. | Wind. Mean Direction. | Rain. Fall Inches. | Rain. Number of Days. | Cloud. Mean. Per cent. | Cloud. No. of Days. Cloudless 10 h. and 16 h. | Cloud. No. of Days. Overcast. |
|---|---|---|---|---|---|---|---|---|---|---|---|---|---|---|---|---|---|---|
| | 27+ | 29+ | | | | | | | | | | | | | | | | |
| Jan. . | .451 | .874 | .122 | 72.2 | 83.2 | 59.5 | 23.7 | 60.2 | 57.2 | .456 | 56 | 245 | E. by N. | 0.00 | — | 29 | 9 | — |
| Feb. . | .455 | .859 | .138 | 75.7 | 87.6 | 62.2 | 25.4 | 63.4 | 60.0 | .532 | 58 | 236 | E. by S. | 0.01 | 1 | 13 | 14 | — |
| Mar. . | .400 | .780 | .150 | 80.8 | 92.3 | 68.3 | 24.0 | 68.2 | 66.6 | .585 | 57 | 204 | S. by E. | 1.02 | 4 | 27 | 7 | 1 |
| April . | .357 | .738 | .142 | 80.4 | 91.4 | 68.2 | 23.2 | 69.3 | 67.0 | .660 | 63 | 209 | S.W. by W. | 5.75 | 12 | 36 | — | — |
| May . | .339 | .721 | .130 | 80.2 | 91.0 | 68.5 | 22.5 | 69.1 | 66.9 | .644 | 62 | 261 | W. by S. | 4.07 | 11 | 33 | — | — |
| June . | .308 | .712 | .084 | 76.2 | 84.5 | 67.2 | 17.3 | 67.6 | 65.7 | .635 | 70 | 394 | W. by S. | 1.88 | 12 | 73 | — | 2 |
| July . | .330 | .742 | .082 | 75.4 | 84.1 | 66.4 | 17.7 | 67.0 | 65.4 | .611 | 69 | 399 | W. by S. | 0.70 | 12 | 74 | — | 4 |
| Aug. . | .309 | .717 | .102 | 75.5 | 83.7 | 67.0 | 16.6 | 68.0 | 66.2 | .657 | 74 | 344 | W.S.W. | 3.85 | 16 | 82 | — | 6 |
| Sept. . | .337 | .742 | .120 | 76.0 | 85.4 | 65.9 | 19.5 | 67.0 | 65.0 | .616 | 68 | 319 | W. by S. | 0.68 | 7 | 67 | 1 | 4 |
| Oct. . | .364 | .772 | .130 | 76.0 | 84.8 | 66.2 | 18.6 | 67.5 | 65.5 | .638 | 71 | 208 | S.W. by W. | 10.04 | 15 | 59 | — | 4 |
| Nov. . | .447 | .872 | .117 | 72.9 | 81.1 | 63.8 | 17.3 | 69.8 | 62.7 | .578 | 70 | 246 | E. by S. | 1.32 | 3 | 59 | 1 | 4 |
| Dec. . | .462 | .887 | .129 | 72.4 | 82.7 | 60.2 | 22.5 | 61.3 | 58.3 | .483 | 59 | 251 | E. | 0.00 | — | 17 | 10 | — |
| | 27+ | 29+ | | | | | | | | | | | | | | | | |
| Year . | .380 | .785 | .121 | 76.1 | 86.0 | 65.3 | 20.7 | 66.1 | 63.9 | .591 | 65 | 276 | — | 29.32 | 93 | 47 | 42 | 25 |
| | | | | | | | | | | | | | | Total. | | | Total. | |

| 1895. | Barometer. | | | Thermometers. | | | | | | Aqueous Vapour. | | Wind. | | Rain. | | Cloud. | | |
|---|---|---|---|---|---|---|---|---|---|---|---|---|---|---|---|---|---|---|
| | | | | Dry Bulb. | | | | Wet Bulb. | | | | | | | | | No. of Days. | |
| | Red. to 32° F. | Red. to Sea Level. | Daily Range. | Mean. | Max. | Min. | Range. | Mean. | Min. | Press. Inches. | Humidity. Per cent. | Daily Velocity Miles. | Mean Direction. | Fall Inches. | Number of Days. | Mean. Per cent. | Cloudless 10h. and 16h. | Overcast. |
| | 27+ | 29+ | | | | | | | | | | | | | | | | |
| Jan. . | ·448 | ·865 | ·133 | 73·3 | 84·3 | 60·5 | 23·8 | 62·1 | 57·9 | ·540 | 65 | 208 | E. by N. | — | — | 17 | 12 | — |
| Feb. . | ·453 | ·854 | ·145 | 76·5 | 88·3 | 63·1 | 25·2 | 61·5 | 58·5 | ·457 | 50 | 180 | E.S.E. | — | — | 4 | 18 | — |
| Mar. . | ·385 | ·759 | ·150 | 81·2 | 93·4 | 67·6 | 25·8 | 63·6 | 60·5 | ·455 | 44 | 177 | S.E. | — | — | 20 | 9 | — |
| April . | ·357 | ·738 | ·156 | 81·2 | 92·4 | 69·4 | 23·0 | 67·8 | 65·3 | ·596 | 57 | 178 | S.S.W. | 4·91 | 12 | 50 | 1 | — |
| May . | ·346 | ·722 | ·132 | 81·2 | 92·2 | 69·4 | 22·8 | 68·7 | 66·7 | ·610 | 57 | 254 | W.S.W. | 2·17 | 12 | 44 | 4 | 3 |
| June . | ·308 | ·709 | ·094 | 77·1 | 84·9 | 68·5 | 16·4 | 68·8 | 67·1 | ·652 | 70 | 312 | W.S.W. | 4·77 | 20 | 77 | — | 8 |
| July . | ·348 | ·770 | ·078 | 74·0 | 81·1 | 66·6 | 14·5 | 66·9 | 65·5 | ·619 | 74 | 341 | W. by S. | 2·23 | 19 | 93 | — | 17 |
| Aug. . | ·325 | ·737 | ·100 | 75·3 | 83·3 | 66·7 | 16·6 | 67·2 | 65·8 | ·628 | 71 | 289 | W. | 3·24 | 17 | 84 | — | 7 |
| Sept. . | ·355 | ·758 | ·123 | 76·6 | 85·7 | 66·6 | 19·1 | 67·1 | 65·3 | ·601 | 65 | 261 | W. by S. | 4·32 | 10 | 74 | — | 4 |
| Oct. . | ·373 | ·785 | ·124 | 75·7 | 83·3 | 67·2 | 16·1 | 68·0 | 66·3 | ·643 | 71 | 177 | S.E. by S. | 10·21 | 12 | 76 | — | 6 |
| Nov. . | ·466 | ·886 | ·115 | 74·4 | 82·9 | 64·1 | 18·7 | 64·6 | 62·3 | ·543 | 61 | 177 | E. | 1·21 | 5 | 51 | 3 | 6 |
| Dec. . | ·441 | ·870 | ·124 | 71·3 | 81·1 | 59·3 | 21·9 | 59·8 | 56·7 | ·435 | 54 | 233 | E. by N. | 0·11 | 2 | 46 | 4 | 5 |
| | 27+ | 29+ | | | | | | | | | | | | | | | | |
| Year . | ·384 | ·788 | ·123 | 76·5 | 86·1 | 65·6 | 20·3 | 65·5 | 63·2 | ·565 | 62 | 232 | — | 33·17 | 109 | 53 | 51 | 56 |
| | | | | | | | | | | | | | | Total. | | | Total. | |

*Rainfall.*—The average annual rainfall at Mysore, calculated on the observations for 26 years (1870–95), is 29·78 inches. The register by months is given under each taluq. The average annual rate for the 26 years at other taluq stations was as follows:—

| | | | |
|---|---|---|---|
| Chamrajnagar ... ... ... | 20·68 | Mandya ... ... ... | 29·94 |
| Gundlupet ... ... ... | 23·66 | Nagamangala ... ... ... | 27·41 |
| Heggadadevankóte ... ... | 24·82 | Nanjangud ... ... ... | 26·06 |
| Hunsúr... .. ... ... | 30·57 | Seringapatam ... ... ... | 27·97 |
| Krishnarajpet ... ... ... | 27·79 | T. Narsipur ... ... ... | 29·02 |
| Malavalli ... ... ... | 26·33 | Yedatore ... ... ... | 27·03 |

The parts lying immediately at the base of the Nilagiri and Western Ghat ranges receive, it appears, a smaller proportion of rain than the more open tracts, owing doubtless to the interception of the south-west monsoon by the mountains. There is generally no rain during the first three months of the year.

The actual annual fall at Mysore has been registered as follows:—

| | | | | | | | |
|---|---|---|---|---|---|---|---|
| 1837 ... | 22·7 | 1852 ... | 52·8 | 1867 ... | 28·46 | 1882 ... | 38·99 |
| 1838 ... | 20·2 | 1853 ... | 37·8 | 1868 ... | 29·22 | 1883 ... | 37·69 |
| 1839 ... | 11·7 | 1854 ... | 20·5 | 1869 ... | 31·37 | 1884 ... | 21·50 |
| 1840 ... | 15·8 | 1855 ... | 34·8 | 1870 ... | 35·63 | 1885 ... | 30·54 |
| 1841 ... | 33·1 | 1856 ... | 26·8 | 1871 ... | 27·38 | 1886 ... | 33·82 |
| 1842 ... | 23·8 | 1857 ... | 30·3 | 1872 ... | 26·28 | 1887 ... | 38·77 |
| 1843 ... | 22·6 | 1858 ... | 30·2 | 1873 ... | 23·17 | 1888 ... | 23·80 |
| 1844 ... | 34·6 | 1859 ... | 27·8 | 1874 ... | 28·71 | 1889 ... | 32·09 |
| 1845 ... | 34·1 | 1860 ... | 30·7 | 1875 .. | 20·22 | 1890 ... | 35·66 |
| 1846 ... | 27·2 | 1861 ... | 30·2 | 1876 ... | 22·80 | 1891 ... | 26·84 |
| 1847 ... | 25·4 | 1862 ... | 35·9 | 1877 ... | 31·68 | 1892 ... | 40·02 |
| 1848 ... | 26·9 | 1863 ... | 31·4 | 1878 ... | 31·72 | 1893 ... | 33·48 |
| 1849 ... | 25·4 | 1864 ... | 32·2 | 1879 ... | 26·28 | 1894 ... | 25·45 |
| 1850 ... | 36·7 | 1865 ... | 30·6 | 1880 ... | 46·34 | 1895 ... | 32·10 |
| 1851 ... | 22·6 | 1866 ... | 35·4 | 1881 ... | 23·54 | | |

The greatest fall occurred in 1852, when 52·8 inches were measured. This was a year of unusual rain throughout the south of the country. But in 1874, when a like excess occurred in Bangalore, Mysore had scarcely the normal quantity. In 1880 both were abundantly favoured, but in 1892 Mysore had an excess and Bangalore a deficiency.

**Vegetation.**[1]—In this District lies the great belt of forest which, commencing on the west at the Fraserpet bridge, about 10 miles north-west of Periyapatna, extends continuously for 80 miles to a point a few miles south-east of Bandipura in the Gundlupet taluq. From the Fraserpet bridge to the Viranahosahalli jungle in Periyapatna, the Mysore portion of this belt varies from 1½ to 3 miles in breadth, and contains in abundance honné,[2] matti,[3] arsentega,[4] dindiga,[5] navaĺadi,[6]

[1] From Captain van Someren's Forest Report. [2] Pterocarpus marsupium.
[3] Terminalia tomentosa. [4] Nauclea cordifolia. [5] Conocarpus latifolia. [6] Vitex alata.

udi,[1] huluve, banni, a few blackwood-trees, and here and there patches of ill-grown stunted teak. Here the belt increases suddenly to 5 or 6 miles in breadth, and a portion of it is known as the Viranahosahalli jungles. The jungles of Metikuppa and Hunasekuppa adjoin the Viranahosahalli jungles, and between Bisalvádi on the west and Rámpura on the banks of the Nugu in the east, is that portion of the Heggadadevankóte taluq, which, measuring about 20 miles in length by 7 to 10 in breadth, contains the teak forests of Bisalvádi, Kákankóte, Bégúr and Ainúru Márigudi. Crossing the Nugu and passing through some thriving villages, a walk of about three miles brings one to the jungles of Berambádi and Bandipura in the Gundlupet taluq. From Bandipura up to Yelandur the belt of forest again narrows. Much sandalwood is intermixed with it, very little teak is seen, open glades are common, and the country is very hilly.

The only other wooded portion of this District is the eastern taluq of Malavalli. There kárachi[2] is not uncommon round the Basavanabetta hill, and bamboos are abundant. Honné, matti, and ippe[3] are abundant, but the vegetation generally is poor. The dindiga-tree, which yields a valuable gum, grows abundantly.

The Hunsúr taluq has a comparatively heavy rainfall in the west, where it borders Coorg, and several very fine specimens of mangoes, tamarinds and banyans grow round the villages. In this and the Heggadadevankote taluqs to the south, the fields are frequently divided by quick hedges or bamboo fences, among which bushes of various kinds have sprung up, and which much favour the growth of sandalwood. This marking off of fields by hedges is not common in Mysore. Parts of Periyapatna are covered with thousands of the date-palm (*P. sylvestris*), growing in the waste lands, and further south on the road to Heggadadevankote are two large fuel tracts known as the Paduvakote and Janapanahalli jungles; much of the tree vegetation would, if enclosed, grow up into useful timber. The Heggadadevankote taluq has much forest in it, and the bábúl is very common in fields.

The taluq of Mysore has no forest, but bábúl-trees grow all over it in the fields. There are several planted topes of mangoes and banyans, and the jámun-tree grows well in many parts. Some thriving cocoa- and areca-nut gardens are scattered throughout it. The taluq of Seringapatam is well irrigated by channels, and grows much rice and sugar-cane, as does the taluq of Tirumakudlu Narsipur in the east; but trees, except in planted groves, are scarce. Yedatore, another rice-growing taluq, is also bare of forest or large tracts of jungle; but the

[1] Bignonia falcata. [2] Hardwickia binata. [3] Bassia latifolia.

high waste-lands are covered with the *cassia auriculata*, and frequently the *cassia fistula*, both of which yield fuel for the use of the surrounding home population. The taluq of Mandya is very thinly wooded, and Maddur sub-taluq is not much better. Gundlupet and Chamarajnagar in the south are well off in this respect, the latter especially so, for in addition to the wood growing close by in the Ummattúr hóbli, and the jungles in the vicinity of Punjur, the Biligirirangan hills are near at hand. It is a well-watered land, full of paddy fields and rich gardens, strongly fenced in. The Nanjangud taluq has no lack of wood for home consumption.

**Forests.**—The *State Forests* are Ainúr Márigudi, 39 square miles in extent; Begur, 42 square miles; Kákankóte, 36 square miles; Viranhoshalli, Metikuppa and Hunasekuppa, 47 square miles; all in Heggadadevankote taluq. In Gundlupet taluq are the Bandipur, 25 square miles in extent, and Bérambádi, 50 square miles. There are also Chamrajnagar, 40 square miles; Narayandurg, 15; and Hasuvin Kával Sandal reserve, 1½. *District Forests* have been formed at Paduvakote and Janapanhalli, between Hunasur and Antarsante; on Basavanbetta, and between Halgur and the banks of the Káveri in Malavalli taluq; near the line of State forests running from Bandipúr and Anechaukur; and near Atgulipur and Punjur on the road passing Hardanhalli to the Hásanur ghat. There are also 24 plantations under the Forest Department, occupying 1,439 acres. There were in 1895 topes or groves to the number of 2,416, containing 81,402 trees; and 844 miles of road had been planted with avenues.

Attention has been directed to the great drain on the teak forests of the Mysore District, which has been going on from the time of the taking of Seringapatam, or even before that, and which threatens to exhaust the supply. One cause has been that, while in many other parts of India the forests were comparatively untouched owing to want of roads, there were trunk lines of communication passing through several of the forests in the Mysore District, admitting of easy access and the removal of teak and other timber. Teak seedlings are, no doubt, found more or less frequently in these forests, but the undergrowth and surroundings of an old forest seem not to be favourable to the raising of teak seedlings. The formation of regular teak plantations is therefore being carried out in places where the growth of this valuable timber, the demand for which is ever on the increase, may be free and unimpeded; the climate and soil of Mysore in certain parts being specially favourable for its propagation.

**Cultivation.**—The following is a list of the cultivated products of the District:—

| Kanarese. | Botanical. | English. |
|---|---|---|
| **CEREALS.** | | |
| Baragu ... ... | Panicum miliaceum .. | Common millet. |
| Bhatta ... .. | Oryza sativa... ... ... | Rice. |
| Godhi ... ... | Triticum aristatum ... ... | Wheat. |
| Háraka ... ... | Panicum semiverticillatum... | |
| Jóla ... ... | Holcus sorghum ... ... | Great millet. |
| Kambu ... ... | Holcus spicatus ... ... | Spiked millet. |
| Navane ... ... | Panicum italicum ... ... | Italian millet. |
| Rági ... ... | Eleusine corocana ... ... | Ragi. |
| Sáme ... ... | Panicum frumentaceum ... | Little millet. |
| **PULSES.** | | |
| Avare ... ... | Dolichos lablab ... ... | Cow gram. |
| Chennangi ... | Lens esculenta ... ... | Lentil. |
| Hesaru ... ... | Phaseolus mungo ... ... | Green gram. |
| Hurali ... ... | Dolichos uniflorus ... ... | Horse gram. |
| Kadale ... ... | Cicer arietinum ... ... | Bengal gram. |
| Tadugani ... | Dolichos catiang ... ... | |
| Togari ... ... | Cajanus indicus ... .. | Pigeon pea, doll. |
| Uddu ... ... | Phaseolus minimus ... ... | Black gram. |
| **OIL SEEDS.** | | |
| Achchellu ... | Sesamum orientale ... ... | Gingelli. |
| Huchchellu ... | Guizotea oleifera ... ... | Wild gingelli. |
| Haralu ... ... | Ricinus communis ... ... | Castor-oil. |
| **MISCELLANEOUS.** | | |
| Arale ... ... | Gossypium indicum ... | Cotton. |
| Káphi ... ... | Coffea arabica ... .. | Coffee. |
| Hoge soppu ... | Nicotiana tabaccum ... | Tobacco. |
| Kabbu ... ... | Saccharum officinale ... | Sugar-cane. |
| Sanabu ... ... | Crotolarea juncea ... ... | Country hemp. |
| Uppu nérle ... | Morinda ... ... ... | Mulberry. |

The crops both wet and dry are classed under two heads, according to the season in which they are grown, *hainu* and *káru*. The season for sowing both wet and dry hain crops opens in July, that for sowing kár wet crops in September, and for kár dry crops in April. It was not uncommon in former times for the ryots to obtain annually both hain and kár crops from their wet lands, the hain being the better of the two. It may however be doubted whether their aggregate out-turn in the year was greater than it is at present, as, without plentiful manuring, two crops a year tax wet land very severely. Now, owing to the yearly repair of the channels, and also in part to want of water, it is only under a few rain-fed tanks in the east of the District that both hain and kár crops are obtained from the same wet lands in one year.

On dry lands it is usual to grow two crops in the same year, the latter being a minor grain, if the land is fertile enough to admit of it. Thus horse gram, kadale, hesaru, &c., are often put in immediately after jóla has been reaped. But of grains which form the staple food of the people, such as rági and jóla, the land will only admit of one crop a year as a rule, consequently the ryots are obliged to choose between a hain or kár crop. In the northern taluqs, Yedatore, Mysore, Seringapatam, Mandya and Malavalli, hain crops are preferred, because their growth is then more influenced by the monsoon. But in the southern or Malnad taluqs, the ryots generally find a kár crop more desirable, because while their jungle springs and the rain, which there falls more frequently, afford them a tolerable supply of water all the year round, the south-west monsoon, which falls with greater force on the forest land, would render ploughing operations in June laborious.

The kár crops of paddy are further divided into Tula kár, Kumbha kár, and Mésha kár. When the ryots are well supplied with bullocks and labour, then the Kumbha kár crop is sown at the most favourable season, that is at the end of September. But sometimes, owing to deficiency of the aforementioned requirements, part of the crop is sown before and part after the proper season. The former is known as Tula kár and the latter as Mésha kár. The Tula kár is an inferior crop. Under rain-fed tanks especially, which require some time to fill, the rice harvest is often very late, for many ryots are averse to trusting to future rain, and will not put in their seed until the tank is full.

All crops can be grown as either hain or kár with the exception of certain sorts of paddy, cotton, wheat, gram, (which however is sometimes grown as manure for a wet crop,) háraka, bargu, jírige, kadale, tadagani, huchchellu, coriander, chillies and turmeric, which are grown as hain only.

The extensive system of irrigation channels gives special prominence to paddy and sugar-cane cultivation and other wet crops. Owing to the richness of the soil a liberal crop usually rewards the ryot without that constant manuring which is necessary in most other districts. The following is a list of varieties of rice known in the District: doḍḍa bhatta, or dappa bhatta, kembhatta, késari, puṭráj bhatta, chambe, kavaḍaga, kari bhatta, punuguráj, ból mallige, ganḍa sarige, chinna sarige, kendalu, sukadás, bilé bhatta, kare káru, jírige sanna, haladi sanna, arsina sanna, kár sanna, kaliyúr sanna, saláki sanna, góbi sanna, sakláti sanna, bangár kaḍḍi, munḍuga or murḍuga (bara bhatta). The last named is grown by *bengár* or dry cultivation, and only needs a moist situation and a fair supply of rain. It has been found impossible to define exactly the season at which each is grown, on account of the different observances of each taluq in this respect. The usual period which elapses before the paddy arrives at maturity is six months, but two or three varieties, karé káru, for instance, require only $3\frac{1}{2}$ months, while others, such as doḍḍa bhatta and mundaga require seven months. The *sanna* paddy is of superior quality to the others, and from it table rice is cooked.

As is the case throughout India, there are three methods of rice cultivation, both in hain and kár: the *bara bhatta* or *punaji*, in which the seed is sown dry on the field; the *mole bhatta*, in which the seed is not sown until it has sprouted through being soaked in water and packed in leaves; and the *náṭi*, by which method the seed is first sown very thick in a small plot of ground and transplanted into the field when the shoots are a foot high. The last is the most common, and yields the best crop.

All the varieties of rice can be cultivated according to the *náṭi* or transplantation mode, with the exception of one, that one the coarsest of all, which is known in different taluqs under the several names of mundaga, muradaga, kannel bhatta and bara bhatta, being subject to the rules laid down for the bara bhatta (broad cast) or punaji method.

Rágí (*eleusine corocana*) is the staple food of the District. The poorer classes and those who gain their bread by manual labour are here greatly prejudiced against rice, and fully appreciate the strengthening qualities of rágí. The varieties of rági are kempa or yelchegan, huluparé, kari, boliga, hasargambi, kari banḍuga, bili banḍuga and kari kádi. Of these, the two first are the most esteemed, and the two last held in least repute. The different kinds are not usually separated, three or four being often sown in the same field. Owing to the exhaustive nature of rági, the land on which it is sown will not ordinarily support another crop during the same year. There are, however, exceptions to this rule. Rági straw is reckoned the best fodder for cattle, and they will thrive and work on it alone without requiring gram, which is not the case with respect to paddy-straw. It also supplies a very nourishing but too heating fodder for horses when grass is scarce. This grain thrives best on a rich red soil, and grows either in the hain or kár season.

Tobacco is grown extensively in Hunsúr and Yedatore taluqs and is of a superior quality at Bettadpur. Cotton is grown in the rich black soil which is most abundant in Chamarajnagar, Nanjangud, Tirumakudlu Narsipur and Mandya. Coffee cultivation has been tried but apparently with most success in the region of the Biligirirangan hills. Much attention was paid to promoting mulberry cultivation in the eastern taluqs for the support of silk-worms, but the same fatality for long attended the efforts to rear healthy insects as in other parts. This has now been overcome.

*Area under principal crops.*—The following figures show the number of acres cultivated in 1892 with the chief crops:—Rice 97,475, wheat 5,911, other food grains 922,546, oil seeds 68,528, sugar-cane 2,505, cotton 1,218, tobacco 5,115, vegetables 6,973, cocoanut and areca-nut 30,453, mulberry 6,289.

**Wild Animals.**—The range of elephants extends through nearly the whole belt of jungle which fringes the south and part of the east and west of the District. They are supposed to breed chiefly in the Biligirirangan hills. In former years they were a constant source of ruin to the ryots in most of the southern taluqs, and even now they sometimes cause considerable damage to the crops in Heggadadevankote, Hunsúr, and Chamarajnagar. But their numbers were found to be decreasing so fast, owing to increased cultivation, that extinction appeared imminent, and on the recommendation of Colonel Elliot, C.B., Commissioner of Ashtagram, the indiscriminate killing and snaring of elephants was provided against by an order of the Chief Commissioner, which appeared in the year 1868. It is now illegal to destroy elephants unless they prove destructive to the crops, in which case a special licence must be obtained. An account of the Keddah department formed in 1874 for the capture and taming of elephants, and of the operations under this head since, has been given in Vol. I., p. 179. Notwithstanding all the captures made, the numbers do not seem to diminish so much as might be expected, considerable catches having been made in 1896 and 1897.

Tigers are most numerous in the Heggadadevankote and Hunsúr taluqs, in the former being met with everywhere. But, except in some portions of the north, they are found wherever there is sufficient jungle to give them cover. Their numbers have greatly decreased within the last 100 years, owing to the spread of firearms among the inhabitants and increase of cultivation. During the year 1891 only two people in all were killed by these wild beasts in this District—a remarkable example of the increase of civilization since the last century, when all the inhabitants of a village were frequently driven away by the ravages of tigers. Buchanan gives a curious account of Periyapatna in this respect. In his time, tigers had taken possession of the inner fort, and especially of the temples, to such an extent that it was unsafe to enter it even in the day time, and the inhabitants of the outer fort were compelled to shut themselves up at sunset.

The usual method of destroying tigers is to mark one down in a thick patch of jungle, and surround it with a strong net about 300 yards in circumference. It is then easily despatched. Great skill is shown by the shikaris, who are generally of either Bedar or Uppaliga caste, in following this plan. Another way is to hang up a loose net across where the tiger is expected to go. He is then driven towards it and, as it falls on him as soon as touched, gets entangled in its folds, when he is killed with spears.

Panthers are common all over the District. Bison are abundant throughout the ranges frequented by elephants. Bears are found in the highlands, but not now in very great numbers. Sámbar are not uncommon, and spotted deer are numerous in the south of the District. Antelope are now scarce owing to the great numbers shot and snared, and it is to be feared that unless preserving is resorted to this animal will become extinct in the District.

*Birds.*—Peafowl and jungle fowl are common in most of the jungles; bustard on the plains.

*Fish.*—The following are the Kannada names of the larger fish found in the District: kurab or handi, genḍe, báḷe, beli, kochal, muchal, ravu, avul, hávu (a kind of eel), argin, kal-kove, kal-korma, giral, kun, godle, chani, kotu, kari, kechal, charl, chupped, báchanige. Most of these are good eating; some are found only in particular localities, but many are found not only in the rivers but also in the tanks.

**Domestic Animals.**—The finest cattle in the District, and indeed in Southern India, are the *Amrit Mahal* or Sultan's breed, which is supposed to have been originally obtained by Haidar Ali from a conquered pálégar. The breed was maintained with the greatest care by Tipu Sultan, and fell into British hands after the taking of Seringapatam. It was then placed under the Mysore Government, but subsequently, in 1813, the Commissariat Department of Madras assumed charge of the breed. In 1860 Sir Charles Trevelyan ordered the sale of all the herds, but a few years' experience showed the inexpediency of this measure, and in 1865 the Madras Government sanctioned the re-purchase of 4,000 cows and 100 bulls of the Amrit Mahal breed. Owing to five years' neglect it was with some difficulty that this number was collected, although 13,000 head had been sold in 1860. A large number had found their way to Egypt, being bought for the service of the Khedive. The herds were almost entirely in the hands of the Madras Government until 1882, when the establishment was taken over by the Mysore Government, under an agreement to supply the Madras Government with a certain number every year, as might be required, at a stipulated price. The breed is scattered in herds throughout the Mysore Province, the depôt being at Hunasur in this District. The *kávals* or grazing grounds are all over the province, the largest being at the Súle-kere tank in Shimoga and at Hanagód near Hunasur. The cattle are driven from one to another according to the state of the grazing.

The cattle of this breed are as superior to those of any other as a thorough-bred horse is to an ordinary roadster. Their great speed is equalled by their capacity of endurance. With them Haidar Ali marched 100 miles in two days and a half to the relief of Chidambram, and with them both Haidar and Tipu were generally enabled to draw off their guns in the face of an enemy. That the breed had not deteriorated was shown in the Afghan war, when they proved their superiority to all the other cattle employed, often remaining upwards of 16 hours in the yoke.

In height, bullocks of the Amrit Mahal breed often reach 54 inches, bulls measure from 45 to 50, and cows from 40 to 45, with frames stout in proportion. The horns are long, and generally thin at the root, the forehead prominent, and the head rather large. In colour, the bulls preferred for breeding are iron-grey or slate-coloured: after being gelt, they gradually become white, a colour of which bulls are seldom born. The cows are generally white, or iron-grey: a mottled brown is not uncommon, but black or light red are seldom or never seen. One of the chief characteristics of the breed is found in their feet, which are remarkably sound and strong. The cows do not yield much milk, which is, however, very rich. These cattle are always in the open air, not being housed at night like the other Mysore breeds. During the wet weather they are all driven down to the Hunasur jungles on the borders of Coorg. They are not worked till they are six years old. This breed is not prolific, the average of births being about 50 per cent. on the number of cows.

The *Hallikár* is a local breed chiefly found in the hands of a few well-to-do patels. It closely resembles the Amrit Mahal: in fact, if the cattle of this breed were taken in hand and had the same care bestowed on them, they would probably equal the former, to which they are doubtless akin. The bulls of this breed are commonly iron-grey or slate-coloured: the cows iron-grey. The latter, like those of the Amrit Mahal breed, are bad milkers. The rearing of Hallikár cattle receives special attention in the Nágamangala taluq, particularly in and about Karadihalli.

*Madesvara betta* or *Madhugiri* is the name given to the large cattle found generally on the borders of the Coimbatore District. The bullocks of this breed are equal in point of size to the Amrit Mahal, but have neither the endurance nor the speed of the latter, and soon knock up in a long stage, especially when ill-fed: their feet, too, are seldom so hard and sound. White, mottled-brown, and light red are the colours most commonly met with. These cattle may also be known by their pendulous dewlaps and long loose sheaths, in which points they differ from both Amrit Mahal and Hallikár. The cows are excellent milkers. The finest specimens of this variety are to be met with at Ganjam near Seringapatam, where the merchants are in the habit of picking them up young and feeding them well till they are old enough to work, by which means they attain great size.

The cattle ordinarily seen in a Mysore village are of a poor description. This is partly owing to want of care and to starvation, and partly to the indiscriminate system of breeding in vogue. Government interference and aid is urgently needed here. The breed will continue to deteriorate until good bulls are introduced and a Government breeding farm organized. Where good grazing is plentiful some improvement in the breed is perceptible, especially on the Coorg frontier; but everywhere there is room for improvement.

Buffaloes, sheep, goats, swine and asses are numerous. The Kurumbars, a jungle tribe, easily tame the young of the wild hog, and there appears to be little or no distinction between the domesticated and wild breeds.

The live stock of the District consisted in 1893 of 685,100 cows and bullocks, 4,259 horses and ponies, 9,163 asses, 653,920 sheep and goats, and 4,745 pigs.

## HISTORY

A District traversed by the sacred stream of the Kávéri is assuredly not wanting in puranic legends, associated with every rapid, bend, island and hill in its course. But until a key to these tediously monotonous stories is discovered, if key there be, they must remain unmeaning and unprofitable fables.

Next to the Páṇḍu expedition sent by Yudhishthira, and Sahadeva's attack on Mahishmati, described with such singular details in the Mahá Bhárata (*see* above, Vol. I., p. 280), one of the oldest legends of an historical character, and not connected with the Kávéri, relates to a city named Maṇipura, in Kannada Haraḷukóṭe, the site of which is pointed out three miles south-east of Chamrajnagar. It is stated to be the Manipura mentioned in the Mahá Bhárata, the princess of which, named Chitrangada, was married by Arjuna, one of the Páṇḍu princes.[1] Babhruváhana, the son of this marriage, in course of time became king of Manipura. A fight afterwards took place between father and son, owing to the horse destined by Yudhishthira for the asvamedha, the defence of which devolved on Arjuna, having in the course of its wanderings to the Dakshina or south country come to Manipura.[2] Babhruváhana, according to the local account, ruled the country wisely and all his people were happy. The rains fell at the right seasons and the crops were abundant. Thus was Manipura equal to

[1] Adi Parva, 7826—7883. [2] Asvamedhika Parva, 2303—2431.

Indraprastha. This prosperity invited an attack from two giants named Niváta and Kavacha, who bore a grudge against Arjuna. But Babhruváhana applying to his father for assistance, the latter came to the rescue and destroyed them. He then appointed Anjaneya or Hanumanta as guardian of the place and set up his image at each of the gates. The city is said to have been six miles square, with a gate on every side, the position of each being still indicated by an image of Anjaneya. The inscriptions at the place are of the Hoysala kings, 800 years old.

The earliest mention of Mysore or Mahishúr is referred to the time of Asoka in 245 B.C., when, on the conclusion of the third Buddhist convocation, a *thero* was despatched to Mahisha-maṇḍala, as to Banavasi and other countries, for the purpose of establishing the religion of Buddha. Of other events of those early times, so far as they are connected with this District, we have no certain knowledge until the rise of the Gangas. But an old Jain work of the 10th century says that Bhadrabáhu, when he came to the south in the 3rd century B.C., with Chandra Gupta, and died on the journey at Sravana Belgola (*see* Vol. I., p. 287), was on his way to the Punnáṭa country. This must be the Punnáḍ described below, and corresponds with the Pounnata mentioned by Ptolemy, whence beryl was obtained in the Roman period.

**Gangas.**—The Ganga dynasty appears to have been established in the 2nd century, and the Ganga kings ruled over the greater part of Mysore till about 1004, their principal territory being known as the Gangavádi Ninety-six Thousand. They claim Kuvalála or Kolar as their original city in this country, but tradition credits them with a capital called Skandapura, which is supposed to have been at Gajalhaṭṭi, on the Moyár, near its junction with the Bhaváni, beyond the south of the Chámarájnagar taluq, west of Satyamangalam. However, in the 3rd century the capital was established at Talakád on the Kávéri, in Tirumakúdal Narsipur taluq. At this period the south of the Mysore District was occupied by a kingdom called the Punnáḍ Ten Thousand, whose capital was at Kittipura, identified by me with Kittúr on the Kabbani, in Heggadadevankote taluq. This Ten Thousand country may correspond with the Padi-nád or Ten-nád country of later times, of which the name survives in Hadinád. In the 5th century the Ganga king Avinita married the daughter of the Punnáḍ Rája, Skandavarmá, and his son Durvinita seems to have absorbed Punnáḍ into the Ganga dominions. Though Talakád continued to be the Ganga capital, the royal residence was apparently removed to Makunda (Channapatna taluq) in the 7th century, and in the 8th century to Manne (Nelamangala taluq).

Early in the 9th century the *Ráshṭrakúṭas*, whose capital was Mányakheta (Malkhed in the Nizam's Dominions), seized and imprisoned the Ganga king, and appointed their own viceroy to administer the Ganga territories. An inscription of the Ráshṭrakúṭa prince Kambharasa, or Ranávaloka, probably the first viceroy, occurs in Heggadadevankote taluq.

Eventually the Ganga king was restored to power, and in the 10th century there were matrimonial alliances and the greatest intimacy between the Gangas and the Ráshṭrakúṭas. This was especially the case in the time of Bútuga, who married the Ráshṭrakúṭa king's sister, and whose son married the Ráshṭrakúṭa king's daughter. He had secured the Ganga throne by putting to death the rightful heir, Ráchamalla, his brother, or half-brother. But an inscription in Heggadadevankote taluq shows that the chiefs of Bayal-náḍ and other parts refused to recognize his claims and fought for Ráchamalla. At this period the Cholas were at war with the Ráshṭrakúṭas, and, led by their king Rájáditya, apparently entered the Mysore country in order to attack them, when Bútuga, by some treachery, killed the Chola king at a place called Takkola[1] and brought the war to an end. This was in 950.

**Cholas.**—But in about 1004 a formidable invasion by the Cholas took place, under the command of Rájendra Chola, son of the reigning king Rájarája. They succeeded in capturing Talakád and overthrew the Ganga power, which had ruled over Mysore for nearly a thousand years. Giving to Ṭalakád the name of Rájarájapura, the Cholas speedily possessed themselves of all the country in Mysore south of the Kávéri, together with that east from Seringapatam, along with the Bangalore and Kolar Districts. In accordance with their usual policy they imposed their own names on the conquered provinces, and the south of the Mysore District thus became the Mudikonda Chola-mandala, the part in which Talakád was situated being called the Rájendra Chola-valanáḍ. Towards the west, partly in Mysore and partly in Coorg, they subdued the Changálva kings of Nanjaráyapattana and Piriyapattana, who in consequence received the name Kulóttunga-Chola-Changálva.

**Hoysalas.**—Meanwhile the Hoysalas, whose capital was at Dorasamudra (Halebid in the Belur taluq), had been gradually increasing in power. Vinayáditya, who came to the throne in 1047, subdued the Malapas or hill-chiefs, who may be identical with the Danáyaks of Beṭṭadakóṭe (on the Gópálswámi hill, Gundlupet taluq). From the account given in Vol. I, p. 336, it will be seen that during the confusion that ensued on the break-up of the Ganga power, nine

[1] Possibly the Tati-hole, a stream described by Buchanan (I, 413), at Hanur in Coimbatore District, to the south of Sivanasamudra.

brothers, called the Nava Danáyak, established themselves at Beṭṭadakóte, and after splitting into two hostile parties, the four victorious ones got possession of Nanjangud and overran all the hill region from the south of Coorg to Goa, and from Satyamangala to the Bisale Ghat.

But soon after 1104 the Hoysalas gained a much greater accession of power under Bitti Deva (afterwards called Vishnuvardhana), who retook Talakád and drove the Cholas out of Mysore. The capture of Talakád itself was effected by his general Ganga Rája, who was a representative of the old Ganga kings. Vishnuvardhana recovered all the Ganga dominions and took the title of Vira Ganga. In 1117 he claims to be ruling over a territory extending from Nangali (Mulbagal taluq) in the east to Barkanur (in South Kanara) in the west, and from Kongu (Salem and Coimbatore), Chera (Travancore) and Anamale (the hills of that name) in the south to Sávimale (? in Dharwar) in the north. The career of the Hoysalas is given in detail in the chapter on History. It will suffice here to say that on the final destruction of Dorasamudra by the Muhammadans in 1326, it was to Tondanur (Tonnur in Seringapatam taluq) that the Hoysala king retired.

**Vijayanagar.**—In the 14th century the Hoysala dominion came to an end, and the Vijayanagar sovereigns next became paramount throughout the south. Narasa, the founder of the second dynasty, captured Seringapatam in about 1495. A viceroy known as the Sri Ranga Ráyal, from Srirangapattana (Seringapatam) the seat of his government, levied tribute in their name on the neighbouring chiefs, and had under his direct jurisdiction the districts of Patna Ashtagram and Mysore Ashtagram, with outlying territories to the west. In the 16th century Jagadeva Ráyal of Channapatna (Bangalore District) held sway over the eastern and some of the northern parts of the District. At the same time a line of kings was ruling Padinád, in the south of the District, with a city at Yelandur. There were also chiefs at Ummattúr, Múgúr and other places.

**Mysore Wodeyars.**—Among the feudatory chiefs the Woḍeyars of Mysore, the account of whose origin is given in the first part of this work, rapidly rose to a position of independence. After evading the payment of tribute on various pretexts, Rája Woḍeyar, in 1610, succeeded in gaining possession of Seringapatam. The mode in which this was accomplished is involved in some obscurity. "The prevailing tale states that the viceroy Tirumal Ráj, or Sri Ranga Ráyal, as he is sometimes called, being afflicted with the rájpora, or royal boil, the disorder most fatal to opulent and luxurious Indians, retired to the holy temple of Talakád, with the view of being cured by the interposition of the idol, or breathing his last before the sacred shrine; and that previously to his departure he had selected Ráj Woḍeyar of Mysore for the confidential trust of administering the government in his absence; and in the event of his death, of transferring it to his kinsman and heir the Woḍeyar of Ummatur.

But on adverting to the animosities and jealousies which had prevailed for many years between these two persons, and the recent attempt of the viceroy, only three years before, to remove Ráj Woḍeyar by assassination, we must reject as contrary to all probability the tale of this singular bequest of confidence and friendship.

Forty-six years had now elapsed since the subversion of the empire from which the viceroy had derived his original powers. This sinking and fugitive state, foiled in the attempt to re-establish its government at Penugonda, had now renewed its feeble efforts at Chandragiri. The viceroy himself was worn down with age and disease: his government, long destitute of energy, had fallen into the last stage of disorganization, faction, and imbecility: it is not improbable that, foreseeing its impending destruction, he concluded the best compromise in his power with his destined conqueror; and the manuscript of Nagar Pootia even details the names of the persons, probably of his own court, who had combined (as it is stated, with the permission of Venkatapati Raya, who then reigned at Chandragiri) to compel him to retire. All that can be determined with certainty is, the quiet retirement of Tirumal Ráj to Talakád, where he soon afterwards died; and the peaceable occupation by Ráj Woḍeyar of the fort of Seringapatam, which thenceforth became the seat of the government of his family. It is certain that until this period the Rajas of Mysore openly professed the religion of the Jangam; but many circumstances afford room to conjecture that it was about this time that they adopted the insignia and ceremonies of the sect of Vishnu; and as the whole of the old court had been of that persuasion, it is highly reasonable to suppose that the real or ostensible conversion of the new Raja was one of the fundamental conditions of their conspiring to depose the viceroy."[1]

The extensive possessions of Jagadeva Ráya of Channapatna were absorbed in 1630, and the subsequent conquests of the Mysore Rajas speedily brought within their dominion a territory which, at the death of Chikka Deva Raja in 1704, extended from the Palni hills, south of the Coimbatore country, to Midagesi in the north of the Tumkúr District, and from the borders of Coorg to Vaniambadi and Carnatic Ghur. That sovereign had with judicious policy maintained a friendship with Khasim Khan, the Mughal general from whom he had purchased Bangalore, now governor of Sira, and through him with the

[1] Wilks, *Hist. Sk. I.* 27.

court of Aurangzeb. On the death of Khasim Khan, in 1699, he sent an embassy to the emperor, then at Ahmednagar, with the view of obtaining a recognition of his extended authority, on which occasion it is alleged that the privileges were conferred of sitting on an ivory throne and of using a signet bearing the title of Jagat Deva Raja.

It is unnecessary in this place to follow the fortunes of the royal family throughout their subsequent career up to 1761, the date of Haidar Ali's usurpation of power; or to describe the conquests whereby this ruler enlarged the Mysore territories, including that of the rich capital of Bednur; the various wars in which he and his son Tipu Sultan engaged; the siege of Seringapatam by the British in 1792; its capture in 1799, the fall of Tipu and the restoration of the Hindu raj. These events have found full and able historians and are described elsewhere, in the chapter on History in Vol. I.

After 1799 Mysore became the capital in place of Seringapatam. In 1809, owing to the increasing unhealthiness of the latter, the British troops were removed to Bangalore. A native regiment was quartered at Hiróḍ, or the French Rocks, a healthy spot a few miles to the north, until 1867, when it was removed to a new cantonment at Mysore. But the site chosen for this, about three miles to the north, proved so feverish that the troops reverted to French Rocks, until the regiment was withdrawn altogether, in 1881.

The District formed at first part of the Patnada Ráyaḍa or Subáyana, and afterwards of the Ashtagram Faujdari. The latter, in 1862, merged in the Ashtagram Division, which included the Districts of Mysore and Hassan. Divisions had been abolished before the Rendition in 1881, and the island of Seringapatam was then made over to Mysore. In 1882 the District was extended by the addition of several taluqs from the Hassan District, which was also abolished. There were thus fourteen taluqs and three sub-taluqs, besides Yelandur jágir, included in the Mysore District, of which five taluqs and one sub-taluq were formed into the French Rocks Sub-Division. In 1886 the Hassan District was restored, but the limits of the Mysore District remained as they now are, embracing the French Rocks Sub-Division.

## POPULATION

*Number.*—The total population of the District, according to the census of 1891, is 1,181,814, composed of 580,737 males and 601,077 females.

*Density.*—There are thus 214·24 persons to a square mile. But the population of the City of Mysore, which numbers 74,048, slightly affects the result; excluding this, we obtain 200·82 persons per square mile.

Tirumakudal Narsipur is the most densely populated taluq, containing 384·67 persons to the square mile. The rate in Yedatore, which is next, is 316·93, in Yelandur 311·31, in Seringapatam 311·10. There are four other taluqs which exceed the average for the District.

*By religion.*—The following table shows the numbers under the principal religious heads :—

| Religion. | Above 15. | | Under 15. | | Total. | Percentage. |
|---|---|---|---|---|---|---|
| | Male. | Female. | Male. | Female. | | |
| Hindus ... ... | 339,160 | 363,386 | 214,268 | 211,346 | 1,128,160 | 95·46 |
| Muhammadans ... | 15,542 | 14,999 | 9,165 | 8,795 | 48,501 | 4·10 |
| Jains ... ... ... | 720 | 659 | 388 | 391 | 2,158 | 0·18 |
| Christians ... ... | 906 | 911 | 565 | 565 | 2,947 | 0·25 |
| Others (17 Parsis, 27 Sikhs, 4 Jews) ... | 15 | 19 | 8 | 6 | 48 | — |
| Total ... ... | 356,343 | 379,974 | 224,394 | 221,103 | 1,181,814 | — |

*Increase.*—The following figures compare the estimates of population in the *khâneshumâri* accounts of 1853–4 with the numbers recorded in the censuses of 1871, 1881 and 1891.

| Taluq. | 1853–4. | 1871. | 1881. | 1891. |
|---|---|---|---|---|
| Chamarajnagar ... ... ... | 70,750 | 82,214 | 75,224 | 91,250 |
| Gundlupet .. ... ... ... | 33,657 | 58,620 | 54,404 | 63,036 |
| Heggadadevankote ... ... | 31,995 | 55,703 | 63,794 | 61,226 |
| Hunsúr ... ... ... ... | 74,730 | 116,632 | 113,334 | 113,271 |
| Krishnarajpet ... ... ... | 53,511 | 84,512 | 74,188 | 91,453 |
| Malavalli ... ... ... ... | 49,510 | 75,603 | 71,852 | 85,910 |
| Mandya ... ... ... ... | 70,822 | 99,873 | 79,640 | 99,783 |
| Mysore ... ... ... ... | 89,537 | 119,011 | 120,364 | 134,684 |
| Nagamangala ... ... ... | 52,528 | 74,825 | 54,615 | 69,265 |
| Nanjangud ... ... ... ... | 36,995 | 93,972 | 85,261 | 97,374 |
| Seringapatam .. ... ... | 66,506 | 77,548 | 77,671 | 85,242 |
| Tirumakudlu Narsipur ... ... | 39,560 | 72,466 | 71,286 | 83,454 |
| Yedatore ... ... ... ... | 37,978 | 66,370 | 61,358 | 74,262 |
| Yelandur ... ... ... ... | (25,000) | 27,459 | 28,103 | 31,754 |
| Total ... ... ... | 733,079 | 1,104,808 | 1,031,094 | 1,181,964 |

Some of the differences are due to redistribution of taluqs and changes in the limits of the District. Up to 1891 there was an apparent increase in the total of 65·81 per cent. in 18 years. But 25 per cent. must be allowed for defective estimate in the *khâneshumâri* accounts. The famine caused the total to be reduced by 6·67 per cent. in 1881, but it rose again in 1891 by 14·63 per cent. The net result may be stated at an increase of 29 per cent. in 38 years.

*Classes.*—Classified according to occupation and nationality, the population consists of the following divisions :—

| | | No. | | Per cent. |
|---|---|---|---|---|
| A. | Agricultural ... ... ... ... ... | 400,851 | ... | 33·91 |
| B. | Professional ... ... ... ... ... | 68,252 | ... | 5·77 |
| C. | Commercial ... ... ... ... ... | 115,778 | ... | 9·79 |
| D. | Artisan and Village Menial ... ... ... | 529,884 | ... | 44·83 |
| E. | Vagrant Minor Artisans and Performers ... | 14,439 | ... | 1·22 |
| | Races and Nationalities ... ... ... | 51,469 | ... | 4·35 |
| | Others, not stated ... ... ... ... | 1,141 | ... | 0·09 |

The following are the largest castes or classes, those which number over 10,000, in order of strength. These account for 1,077,364 or 91·16 per cent. of the population :—

| | | | | | |
|---|---|---|---|---|---|
| Wokkaliga ... | 325,557 | Musalmán ... | 45,483 | Agasa ... ... | 19,435 |
| Holeya ... | 173,003 | Bráhmana ... | 42,998 | Banajiga ... | 17,811 |
| Lingáyita[1] ... | 155,184 | Uppára ... ... | 34,717 | Kumbára ... | 16,136 |
| Kuruba ... | 115,805 | Panchála ... | 32,225 | Gániga ... ... | 15,634 |
| Besta ... ... | 59,550 | Mádiga ... ... | 23,816 | | |

By far the most numerous class of Wokkaliga are the Gangadikára (271,935), then the Telugu Wokkaliga (9,216). Of the Kuruba, 91,441 are Hálu Kuruba. Of the Besta, 26,034 are Parivára. Of Musalmans the Shekhs number 28,634, Pathans 7,586 and Sayyids 7,327. The largest sect of Brahmans is the Srivaishnava (6,289), then Hala Kannadiga (5,580), Smárta (3,904), Desastha (3,608), and Badaganád (3,298). Of the Panchála, 18,498 are Akkasále. Of Banajigas, the Telugu (6,438) are the most numerous, then Dása (5,410).

**Stock.**—The *agricultural stock* in 1893 consisted of 22,220 carts and 152,848 ploughs. The *manufacturing stock* included 4,933 looms for cloth, 1,451 for kambli, 239 for girdles, 32 for goni, and 13 for carpets. There are also 1,295 wooden oil-mills.

**Tanks.**—The number of tanks in the District is returned as 2,000.

**Dwellings.**—The dwellings of the people in 1892 consisted of 194,854 houses, of which 166 were terraced, 26,454 tiled, and the rest thatched. The Mysore, Seringapatam, Nanjangud, and Tirumakudlu Narsipur taluqs contain the largest number of first and second class houses.

**Towns and Villages.**—The District contains 19 Municipal towns, with a population of 140,520, composed of 112,937 Hindus, 929 Jains, 24,354 Musalmans, 2,252 Christians, 17 Parsis, 27 Sikhs, and 4 Jews. The last three are all in Mysore. The following are the towns, with the population of each :—

[1] There are also 5,088 included in Wokkaliga.

| | | | |
|---|---|---|---|
| Mysore ... ... ... ... | 74,048 | Nagamangala ... ... ... | 2,667 |
| Seringapatam ... ... ... | 12,551 | French Rocks ... .. ... | 2,470 |
| Nanjangud ... ... ... | 6,421 | Yedatore ... ... ... ... | 2,413 |
| Malavalli ... ... ... | 5,639 | Mandya ... ... ... ... | 2,348 |
| Hunsur ... ... ... ... | 5,141 | Maddur ... .. ... ... | 2,217 |
| Chamarajnagar ... ... ... | 4,675 | Sargur ... ... ... ... | 1,746 |
| Gundlupet ... ... ... | 4,022 | Krishnarajpet ... ... ... | 1,662 |
| Saligrama ... ... ... | 3,788 | Tirumakudlu Narsipur ... ... | 1,650 |
| Sosale ... ... ... ... | 3,033 | Heggadadevankote ... ... | 1,295 |
| Melukote ... ... ... | 2,734 | | |

The total number of *asali* or primary villages in 1891 was 3,175, to which were attached 1,701 *dákhali* or secondary villages or hamlets. Of the former 2,759 were populated and 416 depopulated. Government villages numbered 2,818, and inám villages 357—namely, sarvamánya 245, jódi 73, and káyamgutta 39.

**Great Festivals.**—The principal concourse of people occurs at the following religious festivals :—

At *Seringapatam*, on the occasion of the *Rathasaptami utsava*, held for one day in January, when 20,000 people come together. At the same place 10,000 people assemble during the *Brindávanótsava*, kept up a single night in October or November.

At *Melukote*, during the *Vairanudi utsava*, held for 12 days from Phalguna or Chaitra suddha 5, more than 10,000 people assemble.

At *Ganjam*, where 20,000 people collect for the *Karighatta játre*, held for one day in February or March.

At *Sante Kasalgere*, Mandya taluq, where 12.000 people assemble for the *Chaudésvara játre*, held in March.

At *Bettahalli* or *Mudukdore* in Tirumakudlu Narsipur taluq, where 10,000 people come together on the occasion of *Mallikárjunaswami játre*, lasting 15 days in January or February.

At *Holalu*, Mandya taluq, 6,000 people celebrate the *Patnada Amman játre*, in February.

At *Boppagaudanpura*, Tirumakudlu Narsipur taluq, 4,000 people assemble for the *Manteswami játre*, held for three days in March or April.

At the *Chamundi hill*, on the occasion of the *Chamundéswari Amma rathotsava*, held in October, 4,000 people attend.

At *Marhalli*, Malavalli taluq, where 3,000 people come together for the *Narasimhaswami rathotsava*, which lasts for five days in May.

At *Satanur*, in Mandya taluq, 3,000 people assemble for the *Bire Deva játre*, held once in four or five years.

At *Mugur*, Tirumakudlu Narsipur taluq, the *Tibba Devi játre*, lasting for 10 days in December or January, is attended by 2,000 people.

At *Chunchankatte* in Yedatore taluq, 2,000 people come to the *játre*, which lasts for 20 days in January.

Below the *Chunchanagere* hill in Nagamangala taluq, 10,000 people come to the *Gangádharesvara játre*, held for 15 days from Phalguna suddha 3.

At *Somanhalli*, in the same taluq, *Ammana játre* held for five days from Margasira suddha 14, attracts 4,000 people.

**Fairs.**—The largest weekly fairs are the following :—

| Place. | Taluq. | Day. | No. of Visitors. |
|---|---|---|---|
| Santemarahalli... ... | Chamarajnagar ... | Tuesday ... ... | 3,000 |
| Sátanúr... ... ... | Malavalli ... ... | ,, ... ... | 1,000 |
| Nidugatta ... ... | Mandya ... ... | Wednesday... ... | 2,000 |
| Ganganur ... ... | Tirumakudlu Narsipur | Thursday ... ... | 1,000 |
| Hiród ... ... ... | Seringapatam ... | ,, ... ... | 2,000 |
| Mandya... ... ... | Mandya ... ... | ,, ... ... | 1,000 |
| Terakanambi ... ... | Gundlupet ... ... | ,, ... ... | 3,500 |
| Malavalli . ... ... | Malavalli ... ... | Friday ... ... | 1,000 |

**Vital Statistics.**—*Births.*—The number of births registered in the District during the year 1893–4 was 17,447; of which 9,076 were of males and 8,371 of females. This gives a birth-rate of 14·76 per mille of the population.

*Deaths.*—The number of deaths registered was 7,407 males and 6,495 females, making a total of 13,902. The death-rate was thus 11·76 per mille of the population.

Of the whole number of deaths 7,918 were from fevers, 535 from bowel complaints, 821 from small-pox, 385 from cholera, 219 from injuries—namely, suicide 20, wounding or accidents 155, snake-bite or killed by wild beasts 44: from all other causes 4,024.

*Diseases.*—The most prevalent disease in the District is malarious fever. It is usually of the intermittent type, and in the great majority of cases tractable. In the most feverish taluqs, however, splenic enlargement and visceral congestions are not unfrequent. Attacks are most common and severe in the cold season, and when the wind is easterly. The outbreak of cholera seems generally to commence early in the year, about April. It is very rare to hear of a case in the cold season.

Although, owing to the elevation of the District and the consequent coolness of temperature, Europeans generally enjoy fair health, fever is somewhat prevalent among them during the months of December, January and February; and exposure to the sun is perhaps more deleterious than in a hotter climate. Both Europeans and natives enjoy the best health during the prevalence of the south-west monsoon, at which period the climate is agreeable and invigorating.

*Dispensaries.*—There are 15 taluq dispensaries, the number of patients treated in which during 1892–3 was 89,827.

## REVENUE

The subjoined is a statement showing the revenue of the District for five years:—

| Items. | 1890-1. | 1891-2. | 1892-3. | 1893-4. | 1894-5. |
|---|---|---|---|---|---|
| Land revenue ... ... | 15,64,535 | 15,92,944 | 16,30,338 | 16,99,188 | 17,38,171 |
| Forests... ... ... | 6,20,140 | 6,85,166 | 4,56,140 | 5,01,585 | 4,29,455 |
| Mohatarfa ... ... | 68,069 | 67,888 | 71,530 | 71,063 | 61,529 |
| Abkari ... ... ... | 2,86,062 | 3,82,127 | 3,84,092 | 5,86,599 | 5,83,989 |
| Sáyar ... ... ... | 6,712 | 6,503 | 5,083 | 2,063 | 2,166 |
| Salt ... ... ... | 1,361 | 1,042 | 860 | 1,235 | 1,236 |
| Public Works ... ... | 5,468 | 73,674 | 70,172 | 3,723 | — |
| Stamps ... ... | 1,68,294 | 2,27,383 | 2,00,691 | 1,98,189 | 1,96,991 |
| Law and Justice ... | 35,653 | 46,945 | 41,889 | 14,666 | 15,623 |
| Police ... ... ... | 2,824 | 2,735 | 682 | 50 | 152 |
| Other items ... ... | 21,983 | 21,991 | 29,494 | 63,667 | 65,326 |
| Total Rs.... ... | 27,81,101 | 31,08,398 | 28,90,971 | 31,42,038 | 30,94,638 |

## TRADE

**Manufactures.**—The articles manufactured in the District are cotton cloths, cumblis, brass utensils, earthenware and jaggory, both cane and date. A little silk weaving is also carried on. Coarse country paper used to be made at Ganjam and Yedatore, but the manufacture has long ceased. The cloths of the best quality are made in Mysore and Ganjam, but in nearly every village the ryots manufacture sufficient to supply their own wants.

Government factories connected with the Commissariat were long maintained at Hunasur; consisting of a blanket manufactory, a tannery and leather manufactory, and a wood yard where carts and waggons were built. Although these have been abolished, the District continues to reap the advantage which they conferred in training workmen after the European model. Many of them still remain at Hunasur and are capable of turning out boots, knapsacks, &c., of good quality, some of which have been bought by Government for the use of native regiments and the police. What was formerly the Government Tannery is now in the hands of an enterprising native. For tanning purposes the American sumach (*cæsalpinia coriaria*), introduced by Dr. Wallich in 1842, and called by the natives divi-divi, used to be considered the best. Excellent cumblis also continue to be made at Hunasur, but the large importation of English blankets has tended to throw them out of the market. Nearly all the country carts used in the District are built at the same place. There are also extensive pulping works for coffee, which is sent here from the Coorg estates.

Another important factory, established in 1847 by private enterprise, formerly in operation at Palhalli, under the designation of the Ashtagram Sugar Works, was closed some years ago, on the departure and death of the proprietors. Jaggory produced by the ryots from the sugar-cane and from the date-palm was here bought and refined into sugar on a large scale. The process is elsewhere described. Prizes, medals and other honours were awarded to the produce of the Ashtagram Sugar Works at the Universal Exhibitions of London, Paris, &c. The factory had, while in operation, an important influence on cultivation in the neighbourhood, especially of wet lands.

**Commerce.**—The principal exports of the District are: rice, rági, jola, chenna, horse-gram, betel-leaves, oil-seeds, silk, tobacco, hides, sugar, sandalwood and sheep; and the imports: hardware, piece goods, ghee, cotton, wheat and salt. But this list is liable to variation every year as the seasons are bad or good. There is a great demand for grain from the west coast and Coimbatore, and the Nilgiri market derives a portion of its supplies from the Mysore District. There is also considerable trade with Bangalore and Madras. Commerce is not confined to any one caste and a large number of the traders are Musalmans; there are also a great many Lambánis employed, principally on the Nilgiri road.

The large merchants are chiefly residents in the town of Mysore; and are for the most part of the Kunchigar caste. They employ agents throughout the District to purchase up the grain, in many cases giving half the price in advance before the harvest is reaped. By this means a few men of large capital are able, in a certain minor degree, to regulate the market.

Much of the trade of the country is carried on by means of weekly fairs or santés, which are largely resorted to, and at Chunchankatte in the Yedatore taluq there is a great annual fair, which lasts for a month. It is upon these that the rural population are mainly dependent for their supplies.

The following is an approximate statement of exports and imports in 1892–3:—

| Articles. | | Exports. | | Imports. | |
|---|---|---|---|---|---|
| | | Tons. | Value in Rs. | Tons. | Value in Rs. |
| Areca-nut | ... | 35½ | 19,845 | 189½ | 1,00,931 |
| Castor-oil seed | ... | 1,517 | 1,45,545 | 510½ | 48,512 |
| Copper | ... | — | — | 85½ | 79,645 |
| Cotton and cotton thread | .. | 4 | 2,216 | 161½ | 1,09,280 |
| Country cloths | No. | 5,000 | 5,000 | 80,000 | 80,000 |
| Gall-nut | .. | 370 | 69,084 | 200½ | 40,020 |
| Ghee | ... | — | — | 250 | 2,56,750 |
| Horse-gram | ... | 2,000 | 1,54,000 | 500½ | 38,500 |
| Hides | No. | 60,213 | 60,213 | 3,000 | 3,000 |
| Iron and steel | ... | — | — | 600 | 86,620 |
| Paddy and rice | ... | 21,930 | 12,91,080 | 11,900 | 5,86,900 |
| Paper | Reams | — | — | 10,000 | 15,000 |
| Pearls | No. | — | — | 4,500 | 22,500 |
| Piece goods | No. | 10,000 | 40,000 | 87,500 | 3,50,000 |
| Pottery | No. | 48,000 | 3,000 | 16,000 | 10,000 |
| Rági | ... | 28,000 | 15,68,000 | 5,020 | 2,81,120 |
| Salt | ... | — | — | 4,200 | 4,70,400 |
| Silk, raw | ... | — | — | 1¾ | 16,308 |
| Silk cloths | No. | — | — | 105,000 | 6,30,000 |
| Sugar and jaggory | ... | 726 | 1,08,000 | 370 | 85,740 |
| Tobacco | ... | 120 | 67,200 | 50¼ | 28,150 |
| Wheat | ... | — | — | 300¾ | 60,750 |

## COMMUNICATIONS

**Railways.**—The Mysore State Railway, metre gauge, runs through the District for about 60 miles. Entering to the east of Maddur, it passes on south-west through Mandya, Yeliyur and French Rocks stations, where it turns south and continues through Seringapatam, Paschima-váhini or Pachiván, Mysore and Kadakola to Nanjangud.

**Roads.**—The following table shows the number of roads in the District, their length, and cost in Rupees for annual up-keep:—

PROVINCIAL ROADS.

| | Miles. | Cost. |
|---|---|---|
| Madras-Cannanore road | 82 | 12,300 |
| Bangalore-Nelligere road, minor branches | 61 | 10,370 |
| Mysore-Manantoddy road | 56 | 6,720 |
| Nanjangud-Hassanur Ghat road | 45 | 3,150 |
| Gundlupet-Sultan's Battery road | 22 | 2,339 |
| Mysore-Yelwal road | 12 | 1,800 |
| Mangalore road *viâ* Mercara | 28 | 4,200 |
| Mangalore road *viâ* Manjarabad Ghat | 18 | 2,250 |
| Total | 324 | Rs. 43,129 |

DISTRICT ROADS.

| | Miles. | Cost. |
|---|---|---|
| Mandya-Bannur road ... | 15 | 750 |
| Mysore-Bangalore road *viâ* Kankanhalli ... | 46 | 2,525 |
| Seringapatam-Sosile-Sivasamudram road ... | 42 | 1,680 |
| Sosile-Narsipur road ... | 2 | 120 |
| Yelwal-Hassan road ... | 25 | 2,000 |
| Sagarkatte-Ramnathpur road ... | 24 | 1,200 |
| Yedatore-Tippur road ... | 4 | 160 |
| Hampapur-Ramnathpur road ... | 18 | 540 |
| Bherya-Saligram road ... | 6 | 180 |
| Hunsur Begur road ... | 46 | 2,760 |
| Hunsur-Yedatore road ... | 14 | 700 |
| Hunsur-Hanagod road ... | 9 | 270 |
| Mysore-Mahadevapur road... | 10 | 400 |
| Mysore-Talkad-Sivasamudram road ... | 33 | 1,650 |
| Nanjangud-Hura road ... | 18 | 540 |
| Gundlupet-Chamrajnagar road ... | 20 | 1,000 |
| Nanjangud-Narsipur road ... | 17 | 850 |
| Kaulandi-Kollegal road ... | 15 | 600 |
| Chamrajnagar-Narsipur road ... | 21 | 840 |
| Fraserpet-Bettadpur-Hadya road ... | 19 | 400 |
| Hassan-Periyapatna-Cannanore road ... | 21 | 1,060 |
| Mysore suburban road ... | 13 | 1,600 |
| Channapatna-Halgur road ... | 5 | 200 |
| Tumkur-Maddur road ... | 10 | 800 |
| Mandya-Koppa railway feeder ... | 12 | 480 |
| Maddur-Kaveri Falls road ... | 29 | 290 |
| Mysore Railway Station-Sivapura road ... | 1 | 50 |
| Mandya-Basaral road ... | 16 | 560 |
| Mandya-Melukote road ... | 6 | 240 |
| Lingarajchatra-Kannambadi road ... | 18 | 810 |
| Seringapatam-Chanraypatna road ... | 37 | 5,550 |
| Attikuppa-Nagamangala road ... | 25 | 875 |
| Kikkeri-Ipya road ... | 6 | 240 |
| Palhalli-Kalasavadi road ... | 2 | 80 |
| Yediyur-Tiptur road ... | 3 | 150 |
| Nelligere-Sira road ... | 6 | 360 |
| Nelligere-French Rocks Station road ... | 35 | 2,800 |
| Jakkanhalli-Melukote road ... | 4 | 206 |
| Total ... | 653 | Rs. 35,516 |

**Accommodation for travellers.**—For the accommodation of European travellers, *Dák bungalows* or rest houses of the classes specified below have been built at the following stations, with Brahman kitchens for vegetarian Hindus:—

*First Class.*—Hunsur, Somanhalli.

*Second Class.*—Antarsante, Bandipur, Gundlupet, Hampapura, Krishnarajpet, Maddur (Gundlupet taluq), Malvalli, Mandya, Periyapatna, Settahallii and Yelval.

*Third Class.*—Atagulipura, Bannur, Begur, Bilikere, Chamrajnagar, Chetnahalli,

Chinkurli, French Rocks, Heggadadevakote, Kadakola, Kakankote, Kikkari, Nagamangala, Nelligere, Panchavalli, Sagar-katte, Sindhuvalli, Yedayala.

There are also Inspection Lodges at Antarsante, Hunsur, Koppa, Krishnarajpet, Maddur (Mandya taluq), Mandya, Narsipur, Seringapatam, Yedatore and Yelwal.

Native travellers are accommodated in *chatrams* maintained at Balmuri, Bendravádi, Bhérya, Chamrajnagar, Dévámbudhi, Gundlupet, Himadgopal betta, Lingámbudhi, Maddur, Mandya, Mysore, Nanjangúd, Ságarkatte, Seringapatam, Tirumakúdlu and Yedatore.

## GAZETTEER

**Ashtagram.**—Before the Rendition, this was the name of a Division, which included the Mysore and Hassan Districts. Till 1882 it was also the name of a taluq, then changed to Seringapatam.

There were formerly two taluqs—Pattana Ashtagrám and Maisúr Ashtagrám, each of which originally contained eight villages or townships bestowed upon the Brahmans as charitable ináms, whence the name *ashṭa-gráma*, eight villages. The tract north of the Kávéri was called Paṭṭaṇa Ashṭagráma, as attached to Srirangapaṭṭaṇa (Seringapatam), and that south of the Kávéri, Maisúr Ashṭagráma, from its connection with the city of Maisúr (Mysore).

**Attikuppa.**—The name of a taluq and town, changed in 1891 to Krishnarájpet.

**Bettadpur.**—A village in the Hunsur taluq, 20 miles north-west of the kasba, on the Piriyapatna-Hassan road. Population 2,209.

The isolated conical hill of Bettadpur, 4,389 feet above the level of the sea, is a conspicuous object to all the country round. The place is the principal seat of the Sankéti Brahmans. It is said to have been in former times a Jain principality, founded in the tenth century by Vikrama Ráya, a fugitive from the inundation of Dváraka. He, by treachery, overcame some Bedar chiefs who opposed his settlement, and established himself in Vikramapatna,[1] having subdued a territory yielding a revenue of 7,000 pagodas. He was succeeded by his son Chengal Ráya, regarding whom some curious tales are related. His right ear, it is said, was like that of an ass—a secret known to none but himself and the barber who shaved him. The possession of the secret so troubled the latter that to relieve himself he whispered it to the

[1] This would seem to be the same as Mallarajapatna, now an insignificant village on the right bank of the Kaveri opposite to Ramnathpur (Arakalgud taluq, Hassan District).

sandal-tree in the courtyard of the palace, under which the king was accustomed to be shaved.[1] Some time after, the king being pleased with the performance of some tumblers, at their request presented them with the sandal-tree in the courtyard for the purpose of making a drum. They cut down the tree and made the drum. But when it was beaten it gave forth no other sound than the words the barber had whispered to the tree, and thus the secret became everywhere known.[2] Other stories about Chengal Ráya are that his arms reached down to his knees, and that the soles of his feet were covered with hair from his never putting them to the ground for fear of killing some living creature, which, according to the Jain faith, would be a heinous sin.

Chengal Ráya was evidently a powerful king. He built Bettadpur in consequence of a dream of his brother's, extended his territory till its revenue amounted to 12,000 pagodas, and formed with Nanjunda Arasu, the Lingáyit ruler of Piriyapatna, an alliance which was cemented by the marriage of Vira Raja, son of the latter, to Mallajamma, the daughter of Chengal Ráya. On this occasion he is said to have renounced the Jain faith for the tenets of the Lingáyits. Nanja Raja of Piriyapatna, 180 years afterwards, took the possession and granted the chief a few villages as a jágir. In 1645 Piriyapatna and Bettadpur were taken by the Mysore army under the dalavayi Dodda Raja. The jágir of the Bettadpur chief was, however, continued until resumed by Tipu.

On the hill of Bettadpur is a celebrated temple of Mallikarjuna. It has at some period been struck by lightning, whence the common story that the lightning once a year pays a visit to Isvara on the hill.

**Biligiri-rangan hills.**—A range of hills in the south-east of the Yelandur jágir, running north and south for nearly 10 miles. On the highest point, 5,091 feet above the level of the sea, is the temple of Biligiri Rangaswami, from which the hills take their name—in Sanskrit Svetádri. They are ascended on the Yelandur side by two ghats, one of which is three miles long, very steep and only practicable for pedestrians; the other, now overgrown, was nine miles long and just passable for horses. The slopes are tolerably thickly wooded, the following being the principal trees found: teak, sandalwood, honné, matti, bíté, kulé, kallubági, dadastu, jaldu, níra banni, bejilu, kuggi. Long grass everywhere covers the hills, often reaching from 10 to 18 feet in height, which, at the commencement of the hot season, is fired. The only inhabitants are the wild aboriginal tribe of Soligas, who

[1] The similar story of Midas will at once occur to the mind of the European reader.

[2] There is another tradition, in the south of the District, of a king named Lamba Karna Raya, the long-eared king. (*See* Terkanambi.)

occupy isolated hamlets, composed of five or six huts, made of mud and wattles and thatched with grass. Of wild animals, elephants are generally numerous ; bison and sámbar are common ; tigers, panthers, and bears are occasionally met with.

At the top of the ghát is a bungalow, near which is a cinchona plantation. A deep trench surrounds the garden to protect it from wild elephants, which are continually threatening it. With the exception of a small but thriving coffee estate, owned by the shánbhóg of the temple, there is no other plantation on this side of the Biligiri-rangans, although the soil and climate offer great advantages. Fever, which is prevalent at certain seasons, is one obstacle to settlers, and bad water, which at present has to be brought from tanks at some distance from the bungalow, is another. The temperature of the Biligiri-rangans is moderate, the thermometer seldom falling below 60° or exceeding 75°.

The temple, which is a short distance from the bungalow, is a shrine of great antiquity, but except from its situation, close to the brink of a precipice, presents no point of interest. It is said to have been repaired by Vishnuvarddhana Ráya. A car procession takes place in April, to which about 3,000 devotees resort. Some copper-plates at the temple record a grant in 1667 by Muddu Rája of Hadinad (*see* Yelandur) for the god, here called Bilikal Tiruvengalanátha. The revenue of the temple is derived from two villages granted by Púrnaiya, and amounts to Rs. 945 per annum. On the summit of a hill, 12 miles north from the bungalow, are the ruins of an old fort named Kanchi Kóte, said to have been built by Ganga Rája of Sivasamudram for his son-in-law.

**Chamarajnagar.**—A taluq in the south-east. Area 479 square miles. Head-quarters at Chámarájnagar. Contains the following hóblis, villages and population :—

| No. | Hoblis. | Villages. | Hamlets. | Villages classified. | | | Population. |
|---|---|---|---|---|---|---|---|
| | | | | Govern-ment. | Sarva-mánya. | Jodi. | |
| 1 | A'lúr ... ... ... | 13 | 11 | 12 | 1 | — | 11,239 |
| 2 | Bádarpura ... | 6 | 5 | — | 6 | — | 3,258 |
| 3 | Chámarájnagar ... | 19 | 16 | 19 | — | — | 16,152 |
| 4 | Haradanhalli ... ... | 36 | 10 | 34 | 2 | — | 7,938 |
| 5 | Honganúr ... ... | 16 | 2 | 16 | — | — | 6,672 |
| 6 | Kágalvádi ... ... | 8 | 8 | 8 | — | — | 9,033 |
| 7 | Kottalvádi ... | 26 | 1 | 26 | — | — | 6,328 |
| 8 | Santemáranhalli ... | 15 | 9 | 12 | 1 | 2 | 10,847 |
| 9 | Ummattúr ... ... | 8 | 2 | — | 8 | — | 5,453 |
| 10 | Uyyamballi ... ... | 32 | 7 | 28 | 4 | — | 14,330 |
| | Total ... | 179 | 71 | 155 | 22 | 2 | 91,250 |

*Principal places, with population.*—Chámarájnagar, 5,507; Rámasamudra, 4,693; Mangala, 3,379; Honganúr, 2,213; Kúdlúr, 1,994; Nágavalli, 1,897; Kágalvádi, 1,871; Ummattúr, 1,827; Kottalvádi, 1,767; Haradanhalli, 1,762; Saragúr, 1,689; Kudúr, 1,678; Chandakavádi, 1,619; Jotigondanapura, 1,614; Bágali, 1,392; Amachavádi, 1,369; Harve, 1,309; A'lúr, 1,253; Badanaguppe, 1,184; Ságade, 1,165; Tamadahalli, 1,112; Bendravádi, 1,074.

The taluq is watered by the Honnu-hole or Suvarnavati, which, rising beyond the southern frontier, flows with a north-easterly course past Rámasamudram and A'lúr into the Yelandur jágir. Near Attikalpur it is crossed by the Gajanur dam, whence springs the Bandigeri channel; and by the Hongalvadi dam, from which a channel of the same name runs to the large tank of Rámasamudram near Chámarájnagar. Temporary dams are constructed by the ryots of stakes, mats and sand after the monsoon is over and when the water of the river is consequently low. By these means are fed the Homma, Alurhalla, Alur Hosahalla, Saragur and Maralhalla channels. There are besides many large and small tanks.

Taken as a whole the taluq is remarkably rich and fertile, consisting of a fine, well-watered, and level plain stretching away north-westwards from the slopes of the Biligiri-rangan hills, which form its eastern and southern boundary. The low forest land at the foot of this range was probably well-populated in former times. The soils are of great variety, ranging from black and rich red to poor and gravelly. The poorer soils are on the slopes and watersheds towards the west, rapidly improving in depth and quality towards the east and in the valley of the Honnu-hole.

Jola is the staple dry crop; among the others, absence of cotton cultivation is remarked. The black soils produce almost all crops peculiar to such soil, including mulberry without irrigation; double crops in dry soil are not uncommon. In the wet lands comparatively little sugar-cane is raised. The gardens of areca, cocoa-nut and betel on the banks of the Honnu-hole are very fine. Date groves abound in all the hollows, when otherwise unoccupied, the tree being here very prolific. A very short neglect of gardens is sufficient to convert them into dense date-topes. There is some coffee cultivation, under European management. The original elephant keddahs are in the forests to the south-east.

The revenue settlement was introduced in 1877 into 30 villages, occupying a tract of 61½ square miles in the south-east, bounded by the Yelandur jágir on the north, the Biligiri-rangan hills on the east, and the Honnu-hole on the west, which it was intended to form into a jágir for the grandsons of the former Maharaja. But the general revenue settlement of the taluq was introduced in 1894. The area at this time was thus distributed :—

| | |
|---|---|
| Culturable (dry, 82,796; wet, 3,897; garden, 3,372)... ... | 90,065 |
| Inám villages ... ... ... ... ... ... | 42,575 |
| State forests (68,059); kávals (9) ... ... ... ... | 68,068 |
| Total acres | 200,708 |

The unoccupied area was 3,501 acres. The whole of the Bedarpur and Ummattur hoblis are inám, forming the endowments of the Chámarájesvara temple. The total revenue demand of the taluq for 1891-2 (15 months) was Rs. 1,65,000, and for 1892-3 it was Rs. 2,08,689.

The average annual rainfall at Chámarájnagar for 26 years (1870-95) has been as follows :—

| Jan. | Feb. | Mar. | April | May | June | July | Aug. | Sept. | Oct. | Nov. | Dec. | Year. |
|---|---|---|---|---|---|---|---|---|---|---|---|---|
| — | 0·12 | 0·43 | 1·39 | 4·60 | 1·05 | 0·75 | 2·12 | 2·47 | 4·82 | 2·43 | 0·50 ... | 20·68 |

The trunk road from Nanjangúd connects Chámarájnagar with the railway there and continues on to Coimbatore by the Hasanur ghat. A road from Gundlupet crosses this at the kasba and is carried on to Tirumakudal-Narsipur. A branch from the Nanjangúd road runs through Ummattur to Yelandur.

**Chamarajnagar.**—A town situated in 11° 55′ N. lat., 77° E. long., 36 miles south-east of Mysore, on the Hasanur ghat road, and 22 miles from the railway at Nanjangúd. Head-quarters of the taluq of the same name and a municipality.

| Population in 1891. | Males. | Females. | Total. |
|---|---|---|---|
| Hindus . ... ... ... ... | 1,935 | 2,106 | 4,041 |
| Muhammadans ... ... ... | 247 | 269 | 516 |
| Jains ... ... ... ... ... | 53 | 61 | 114 |
| Christians ... ... ... ... | — | 4 | 4 |
| Total ... | 2,235 | 2,440 | 4,675 |

It is situated in a plain composed of black cotton soil and is a thriving place. The principal Jain basti was erected in 1117, under the Hoysala king Vishnuvarddhana, by his general Punisa-Rája, who claims to have terrified the Todas, captured Nilagiri, and made himself master of Kerala or Malabar. Its present name was bestowed in 1818 by the Mahárája Krishna Rája Wodeyar of Mysore, who, on learning that his father, the unfortunate Chámaráj Wodeyar, was born there, resolved to dedicate the town to his memory. He accordingly changed the name from Arakoṭhára[1] to Chámarájnagar, and in 1825 founded there a large temple to Chámarájésvara. This he endowed in 1828 with sarvamányam villages yielding a yearly revenue of about Rs. 17,000 and an establishment consisting of an Amildar and 157 subordinates. As a work of art this temple contrasts unfavourably in point of durability and beauty with the old temple which it was intended to supersede, and from which most of the materials employed in its construction were procured. As in the temple at Nanjangúd, its outside walls are surmounted with representations of the different deities ranged in rows, so that each votary may find his patron saint without trouble. At about the same time the Rája had a palace erected at Chámarájnagar, an unshapely and ill-constructed building in the eastern style. A number of additional shrines in the temple were provided in 1850 and 1851 by some of the royal ladies.

Two miles east of the town is the populous suburb of Rámasamudram, containing 4,693 people, near to which are the ruins of an extensive city of antiquity, whose name, according to tradition, was Manipur.

| Municipal Funds. | 1892-3. | 1893-4. | 1894-5. | 1895-6. |
|---|---|---|---|---|
| Income ... ... ... ... ... | 699 | 1,103 | 1,075 | 1,989 |
| Expenditure ... ... ... .. | 1,593 | 1,755 | 1,236 | 2,644 |

**Chamundi.**—A rocky hill two miles south-east of the fort of Mysore, rising to a height of 3,489 feet above the level of the sea. Owing to its isolated position and precipitous sides it renders the position of Mysore conspicuous from afar. The oldest temple on the hill is that of Marbbala or Mahábales'vara, which was endowed by the Hoysala king Vishnuvarddhana in 1128, and in 1620 by the descendant of the Vijayanagar kings, ruling at Chandragiri.

The hill takes its name from the goddess Kálí or Chámundi, the consort of Siva, held to delight in blood, who is worshipped in a temple on the summit. Human sacrifices were common here in old times, but were rigorously put a stop to under the administration of Haidar. Krishna Rája Wodeyar III. repaired this shrine in 1827 and furnished it with a tower. In 1848 he presented it with the *simha-váhana* and other animal cars used in processions. A flight of stone steps leads to the top of the hill, and two-thirds of the way up, cut out of the solid rock, is a colossal figure of Nandi, the holy bull on which

[1] Properly *ari kuthára*, an axe to the enemy.

Siva is mounted in [the mythological sculptures. The height of the figure is not less than 16 feet; the animal is represented in a recumbent posture and hung with trappings and chains of bells. Although the carving is in no way extraordinary, yet the gigantic size, the correct proportions of the statue, and the labour that must have been expended on it, render it inferior to no work of art of the kind in South India. Dodda Deva Rája, who ascended the throne in 1659, and of whose character religion was the chief feature, was the author of this remarkable monument of devout zeal.

There is a bungalow at the top belonging to the royal family, which may be reached by a road carried along the northern slope, the distance by this way being 7 miles from Mysore.

**Chunchan-katte.**—A dam across the Kávéri, in Yedatore taluq, built in an advantageous position a short distance from the head of a narrow gorge called Danushkóṭi,[1] and a few hundred yards above the spot where the river falls from 60 to 80 feet in a succession of cascades. The Rámasamudram channel led off from this dam, together with the anicut itself, were constructed by Chikka Deva Rája Wodeyar, who came to the throne in 1672. The rapids in the river invest the spot with great sanctity: hence a large festival is held here annually in January, attended by upwards of 2,000 people.

**French Rocks.**—The hills so called at Hirodi (*see* below). The highest point is 2,882 feet above the level of the sea.

**Hirodi** or **French Rocks.**—A town, formerly a military station, 4 miles north of Seringapatam, on the Mysore-Nagamangala road.

It is now the head-quarters of the French Rocks Sub-Division, and a municipality. The Sub-Division was formed in 1882 and includes the Krishnarajpet, Malavalli, Mandya, Nagamangala and Seringapatam taluqs.

| Population in 1891. | Males. | Females. | Total. |
|---|---|---|---|
| Hindus... ... ... ... .. ... | 823 | 824 | 1,647 |
| Muhammadans ... ... ... ... | 268 | 364 | 632 |
| Christians ... ... ... ... ... | 73 | 118 | 191 |
| Total ... | 1,164 | 1,306 | 2,470 |

The French in Haidar's and Tipu's service were encamped here, whence its European name. A regiment of Madras Native Infantry was quartered in the cantonment until 1881, when it was given up as a military station.

[1] An old inscription describes it as Sita's bathing-place, and calls upon all who catch fish there to make an offering to her shrine.

| Municipal Funds. | 1892-3. | 1893-4. | 1894-5. | 1895-6. |
|---|---|---|---|---|
| Income ... ... ... ... ... | 507 | 1,006 | 1,354 | 1,304 |
| Expenditure ... ... ... ... | 252 | 568 | 696 | 758 |

**Ganjam,** or **Shahar Ganjam,** a village at the east end of the island of Seringapatam, being a suburb of the city (which see). It was established by Tipu Sultan, who, in order to provide it with an industrial population, transported thither twelve thousand families from Sira (Tunkur District), which had been the seat of the Mughal Government. The place was dismantled by him in 1799, under the impression that the British Army of invasion would make use of it as they did in 1792. After the capture of Seringapatam, the village was laid out afresh and rapidly regained prosperity, in spite of its reputation for unhealthiness. It contains a number of well-to-do merchants, and country cloths are made. The former paper manufacture has entirely ceased.

**Gopalswami betta.**—A lofty hill of extremely picturesque appearance, 10 miles south-west of Gundlupet, rising to a height of 4,770 feet above the level of the sea. An ascent of three miles leads to the top, and the base of the hill may be estimated at 16 miles in circuit. Its name is that of the shepherd god of the Hindus, an incarnation of Vishnu. In the puranas it is called Kamaládri and Dakshina Govardhangiri. The hill abounds in springs, and to its extraordinary moisture and the strata of argilla that compose it may be attributed its remarkable verdure. From a distance its summit appears surrounded by an entrenchment, the remains of the old walls carried round its sides. It is generally enveloped in clouds and mist, whence its name of Himavad Gópálswámi betta; but when the weather is clear it commands a most extensive view of Mysore and the Wainad. Inside the old fort is a temple dedicated to Gópálswámi, who is said to be heard blowing on his flute on certain occasions. Allusion has already been made to the history of the place (p. 221 : also Vol. I, p. 336). It was fortified by Somana Danáyak, and under the rule of the nine brothers named the Nava Danáyak, bore the name of Beṭṭada-koṭe or hill fort. The scene of the perilous leap by one of the Danáyaks on the north side, on the occasion of its capture, is still pointed out. At present the hill is uninhabited, except by two Brahmans belonging to the temple. An annual car festival is held there.

**Gundlupet.**—A taluq in the south. Area 544 square miles. Headquarters at Gundlupet. Contains the following hóblis, villages and population :—

| No. | Hóblis. | Villages. | Hamlets. | Villages classified. | | | Population. |
|---|---|---|---|---|---|---|---|
| | | | | Govern-ment. | Jodi. | Kayam-gutta. | |
| 1 | Gundlu ... ... ... | 30 | 5 | 30 | — | — | 15,726 |
| 2 | Hangala ... ... | 50 | 9 | 50 | — | — | 13,135 |
| 3 | Kelasúr... .. ... | 16 | 9 | 16 | — | — | 6,955 |
| 4 | Kútanúr ... ... | 30 | 14 | 30 | — | — | 8,497 |
| 5 | Rághavapura ... ... | 26 | 13 | 25 | — | 1 | 10,854 |
| 6 | Terakaṇámbi ... ... | 33 | 5 | 32 | 1 | — | 7,869 |
| | Total ... | 185 | 55 | 183 | 1 | 1 | 63,036 |

*Principal places, with population.*—Gundlupet, 4,022; Terakaṇámbi, 2,178; Kabbilli, 1,819; Hangala, 1,578; Kelasúru, 1,552; Báchahalli, 1,335; Hosapura, 1,328; Kadasoge, 1,258; Padagúr, 1,191; Bommalapura, 1,171; Huriyalla, 1,021.

The west and south of the taluq are occupied by extensive forests, covering 180 square miles, and including the Berambadi and Bandipur, reserved by the State. But these parts were probably more populous formerly. Pierced by good roads, affording egress both westward and southward, these forests present no inconvenience to the well-populated tracts lying east and north, except perhaps in being considered somewhat prejudicial to health. The inhabited portions of the taluq are separated from the vast forests beyond by a range of hills running parallel to the west and south boundary lines, and culminating in the Gópálswámi hill, which is situated at the angle where they diverge. There is also a range of hills to the north of Hangala hóbli, intervening between it and Terakaṇámbi and Gundlu hóblis.

The soils of the taluq vary considerably, running from good black or brown cotton soil to poor, shallow and rocky, the gradations being more marked in dry than in wet lands, which are more uniform in quality. The good soils generally are to the east and south-east, becoming more shallow as the forests and hills westward are approached.

Jola is the staple dry crop. Rági is also largely grown, but its cultivation is limited by the quantity of manure available, of which it requires a liberal allowance. Cowdung is the principal manure, and it is not so much used for fuel as elsewhere. A second crop of pulses or grain is commonly obtained off dry lands. Togari and avare are sown independently, with castor-oil, and not with jola or rági. The area under wet crops is small. A very superior kind of rice is raised under the Vijayapur tank, but the rest is quite ordinary, and the little sugar-cane grown is of poor quality. No leaf-manure is used even in rice cultivation. The gardens contain little or no areca-nut or cocoa-nut, but betel-leaf is extensively grown, and is of special quality and value. Along the banks of the Gundal river and its feeders are large groves of the toddy-palm.

This river flows through the taluq from south to north, and falls into the Kabbani at Nanjangúd. A masonry dam built across it near Komarvalli irrigates the lands in the neighbourhood. Along the southern boundary of the taluq runs the Moyár, which unites with the Bhaváni in the east beyond.

The revenue settlement was introduced in 1891. The area of the taluq was thus distributed :—

| | |
|---|---|
| Culturable (dry, 118,444 ; wet, 1,463 ; garden, 826) ... ... | 120,733 |
| Unculturable (including roads, village sites, &c.) ... ... ... | 114,361 |
| Forests (115,000) ; Inám villages (2,131) ... ... ... ... | 117,131 |
| Total acres ... | 352,225 |

The extent of unoccupied land was 7,645 acres. The total revenue demand for 1891–2 (15 months) was Rs. 1,10,615, and for 1892–3 it was Rs. 1,27,613.

The average rainfall for 26 years (1870–95) at Gundlupet, and for three years (1893–5) at the other station, was as follows :—

| | Jan. | Feb. | Mar. | April | May | June | July | Aug. | Sept. | Oct. | Nov. | Dec. | Year. |
|---|---|---|---|---|---|---|---|---|---|---|---|---|---|
| Gundlupet | 0·06 | 0·11 | 0·61 | 3·00 | 4·39 | 1·66 | 1·42 | 1·77 | 2·76 | 4·89 | 2·56 | 0·43 | ... 24·82 |
| Begur | — | 0·15 | 1·05 | 3·85 | 3·57 | 1·87 | 1·39 | 1·39 | 1·93 | 6·94 | 1·22 | — | ... 23·36 |

The Mysore-Ootacamund and Mysore-Gudalur road runs through Gundlupet, whence also there are roads eastwards to Chamarajnagar and westwards through Sultan's Battery to Cannanore. From Begur, 9 miles north of the kasba, there is a cross road to Sargur and Heggadadevankote.

**Gundlupet.**—A town situated in 11° 49′ N. lat. 76° 45′ E. long., near the left bank of the Gundal river, 36 miles south of Mysore, on the Mysore-Ootacamund road, and 24 miles from the railway at Nanjangúd. Head-quarters of the Gundlupet taluq, and a municipality.

| Population in 1891. | Males. | Females. | Total. |
|---|---|---|---|
| Hindus (with 1 Jain) ... ... ... ... | 1,843 | 1,566 | 3,409 |
| Muhammadans ... ... ... ... | 314 | 250 | 564 |
| Christians ... ... ... ... ... | 21 | 28 | 49 |
| Total ... | 2,178 | 1,844 | 4,022 |

The ancient name of Gundlupet was Vijayapura, and under this name it appears to have been held by the rulers of Terakaṇámbi for a long period. Chikka Deva Rája gave it its present appellation and first made it a place of note in 1674. This prince appears to have acquired an interest in the Gundal territory from the fact that his early life had been passed in confinement at Hangala, an obscure fort to the south of Gundlupet. There his father died, and no sacred stream being at hand, the body was conveyed to the Gundal river at Vijayapur and there burnt. Chikka Deva Rája, after performing the last rites under the eye of his guards, returned to his prison at Hangala. He afterwards built an agrahára near the site of his father's burning-place, enlarged the fortifications of the town, and constituted it the great commercial emporium of this part of his dominions. Over his father's tomb he founded a pagoda of Aparamita Paravása Déva,[1] which he richly endowed, and which remained in a flourishing state till the accession of Tipu Sultan, who withdrew its allowances. Nothing now remains of the agrahára, and the fine old temple has been allowed to fall into decay.

The rising town of Gundlupet gradually eclipsed the old fort of Terakaṇámbi in importance, and has ever since remained the chief town of the taluq, although often depopulated by fever. The fort of Gundlupet, a rude mud-and-stone structure, still remains, though somewhat ruinous. It was last repaired under the government of Krishna Rája Wodeyar III. The town has benefited by the opening of the railway to Nanjangúd, and considerable transit passes through it to the Nilagiris by the Segur and Gudalur ghats, and to the Wainad and Malabar.

| Municipal Funds. | 1892-3. | 1893-4. | 1894-5. | 1895-6. |
|---|---|---|---|---|
| Income ... ... .. ... ... | 1,045 | 1,278 | 1,119 | 2,428 |
| Expenditure ... ... ... ... | 992 | 1,842 | 2,056 | 3,245 |

**Gundal.**—The Gundal or Kaundinya river is formed by streams issuing from the southern hills stretching east from Gópálswámi betta. With a course due north, past the chief town, through the Gundlupet taluq, it enters the Nanjangúd taluq, where, continuing in the same general direction, it forms the Narsámbudhi tank and discharges itsel into the Kabbani at Nanjangúd. Though scarcely more than a monsoon stream, its waters are much utilized for irrigation. It is crossed

[1] The God of Perpetual Exile.

by an anicut at Halhalli. The reventue below the tank and its sluice channels amount to Rs. 4,906 from 470 kandis of land.

**Hadinaru,** more properly Hadi-náḍu,[1] a village in the Nanjangúd taluq, 5 miles north-east of the kasba, head-quarters of the Hadináru hóbli. Population, 1,857.

It is historically interesting as having witnessed the first step to power of the ancestors of the Mysore Rájas. Two young men, belonging it is said to the Yádava tribe, being induced to push their fortunes in the south, halted at Hadináru, probably in the 15th century. At that time the Wodeyar of the place, being of unsound mind, had "wandered forth into the wilds," and the pálégár of the neighbouring village of Kárugahalli, who was of the Toreyar caste, had taken advantage of the defenceless state of Hadináru to demand a daughter of the house in marriage. To this request the Wodeyar's family had been compelled to yield a reluctant assent, when Vijaya and Krishna, the two young adventurers from the north, appeared on the scene and espoused the cause of chivalry. By a stratagem they succeeded in slaying the low-caste pálégár of Kárugahalli, and the daughter of the Wodeyar, delivered from her persecutor, became the bride of Vijaya, who thereupon assumed the government of Hadináru and Kárugahalli, and is the ancestor of the Mysore Rájas. These two villages may therefore be considered as the nucleus of the Mysore State.

**Heggadadevankote.**—A taluq in the south-west. Area 621 square miles. Head-quarters at Heggadadevankote.

Contains the following hóblis, villages and population :—

| No. | Hóblis. | Vil-lages. | Ham-lets. | Villages classified. | | | | Popula-tion. |
|---|---|---|---|---|---|---|---|---|
| | | | | Govern-ment. | Sarva-mánya. | Jodi. | Kayam-gutta. | |
| 1 | Antarsante ... ... | 52 | 30 | 50 | 1 | 1 | — | 13,068 |
| 2 | Heggadadevankote ... | 57 | 27 | 56 | — | — | 1 | 14,187 |
| 3 | Jinahalli ... ... | 56 | 14 | 54 | 1 | — | 1 | 11,139 |
| 4 | Nemmanhalli ... ... | 48 | 14 | 44 | 2 | — | 2 | 8,519 |
| 5 | Saragúr... ... ... | 49 | 18 | 45 | 4 | — | — | 14,313 |
| | Total ... | 262 | 168 | 249 | 8 | 1 | 4 | 61,226 |

*Principal places, with population.*—Saragúr, 1,902 ; Belatur, 1,587 ;

[1] Wilks gives the name as Hadana. In Ganga inscriptions of the 10th century it appears as Adiráru : in a Hoysala inscription of 1196 it is called Hadinádu, and also in a Vijayanagar inscription of 1585. Hadinádu would represent the old Padinádu (*see* under Yelandur) or Ten naḍs, possibly the Punnáḍ Ten-Thousand (*see* above, p. 220).

Malali, 1,505; Kittúr, 1,443; Hebbelakuppe, 1,332; Bidagal, 1,309; Heggadadevankote, 1,295; Nérle, 1,124; Iṭna, 1,122; Ságati, 1,045; Mullúr, 1,002.

A large proportion of the taluq is covered with forest, especially in the west and south. The State teak forests of Kákankote, Begur and Ainur Márigudi, with other forests, occupy an extent of 130 square miles. In the first are situated the principal elephant keddahs.

The river Kabbani, rising in North Wainad, has a tortuous course through the taluq from south-west to north-east, passing near the town of Sargur. The west of the taluq is watered by the Nugu, which also has its source in Wainad, and with a northerly course falls into the Kabbani in the north, near the village of Hampapur. The Nugu is crossed by a dam at Lakshmanpura, whence springs an irrigation channel, 4 miles in length. But the principal irrigation channel is one drawn from an anicut on the Lakshmantirtha in Hunsur taluq.

Wherever land is cultivated it is found fertile and produces fine crops of rági. Except when the soil is poor, it is customary to raise two dry crops in the year. Red and dark brown soil is general. Wet cultivation is limited, partly owing to the unhealthiness of the irrigated tracts. There is little or no garden cultivation.

There is evidence that the taluq was probably far more populous in ancient times than it is now. Kittúr, called in an inscription of 1027 "the royal residence, the immense great city Kirttipura," was the capital of the Punnáḍ Ten-Thousand, which occupied the south of the Mysore District from the earliest times (*see* above, p. 220), and this must have exerted a great influence over all the neighbouring country. At a later period some part of this country was called the Bayal-nád, which was under the government of Kadamba chiefs, until subdued by the Hoysala king Vishnuvardhana, early in the 12th century.

The revenue settlement was introduced in 1884. The area of the taluq was thus distributed :—

| | |
|---|---|
| Culturable (dry, 76,367; wet, 3,725; garden, 321) ... ... | 80,413 |
| Unculturable (including roads, village sites, &c.) ... ... .. | 178,771 |
| Inám villages ... ... ... ... ... ... ... ... | 19,794 |
| Forests (83,254); kávals (12,228) ... ... ... ... ... | 95,482 |
| Total acres .. | 374,460 |

The unoccupied area was 9,323 acres. The total revenue demand for 1891–2 (15 months) was Rs. 90,170, and for 1892–3 it was Rs. 1,11,226.

The average rainfall at Heggadadevankote for 26 years (1870–95) was as follows :—

| Jan. | Feb. | Mar. | April | May | June | July | Aug. | Sept. | Oct. | Nov. | Dec. | Year. |
|---|---|---|---|---|---|---|---|---|---|---|---|---|
| — | 0·08 | 0·37 | 2·10 | 3·95 | 2·51 | 3·51 | 2·23 | 2·92 | 4·27 | 2·45 | 0·43 ... | 24·82 |

The Mysore-Manantody road runs through from north-east to south-west, and is crossed by a road from Hunasur through Heggadadevankote and Sargur to Begur on the Mysore-Ootacamund road.

**Heggadadevankote.**—The chief town of the taluq which bears its name, and a municipality. It is situated in a wild forest tract, 36 miles south-west of Mysore, on the Sargur-Hunasur road. The taluq head-quarters were at one time at Sargur during the monsoon, and for some years permanently. But in 1886 the head-quarters were re-established at Heggadadevankote.

| Population in 1891. | Males. | Females. | Total. |
|---|---|---|---|
| Hindus... ... .. ... ... ... | 587 | 579 | 1,166 |
| Muhammadans ... ... ... ... | 51 | 50 | 101 |
| Christians ... ... ... ... ... | 13 | 15 | 28 |
| Total ... | 651 | 644 | 1,295 |

The place can boast of considerable antiquity. Its puranic name was Brihad-bhánu-pura, and thither first the Pándus and then Janaméjaya are said to have gone, the latter being represented as the founder of the city. The Heggada Déva after whom it is now named, appears to have rebuilt the fort and restored in his own person the ancient line of rulers about the tenth century. The district was subsequently subdued by Vijayanagar, and only this town was granted to the chief as an estate, which was held as feudatory to Sri Ranga Ráyal at Seringapatam. It was conquered in 1624 by Chama Rája Wodeyar of Mysore, whose demands for submission Singappa Wodeyar the chief had contested by representing that he was related to Sri Ranga Ráyal and inherited his authority. An incident connected with its capture, related by Wilks, seems strongly to illustrate the character of the times:—"The Mysorean army attacked the place during the absence of its chief, Chenna Raj Wodeyar, on a distant expedition, and obtained a great booty. The simplicity of a vakíl, or negotiator, is preserved by tradition, who on the approach of the army came out to treat. 'My master,' (said he) is absent with the troops; the Ráni (queen) is in labour, and exceedingly alarmed at your approach; we have only fifty soldiers in the place, and the late rains have made two large breaches in the rampart, one on the southern and the other on the eastern face. To come at such a time is very improper and ungenerous.'" During the time of the Sultan, Heggadadevankote was constantly annoyed by invasions of the Wainad pálégárs.

| Municipal Funds. | 1892-3. | 1893-4. | 1894-5. | 1895-6. |
|---|---|---|---|---|
| Income ... ... ... ... | 230 | 205 | 215 | 383 |
| Expenditure ... ... ... | 331 | 152 | 195 | 853 |

**Hemavati.**—This river rises in the south-west of the Kadur District, and flows principally through the Hassan District (under which it is more fully described). In the Mysore District it runs from north to south in the west of the Krishnarajpet taluq, and flows into the Kávéri near Hoskote. There are five dams on it in this District, and as many channels, irrigating 4,264 acres. The Mandigere channel is taken off on the right bank from an anicut near the village of that name in Akkihebbal hóbli, and is now 27 miles long, discharging into the river near the village of Alambadi. It was at first only 15 miles in length; was extended 2 miles further in 1873; 6 miles in 1879; and 4 miles in 1881. The last 12 miles are thus known as the Hosanála. The Akkihebbal channel, 7 miles long, is on the same side of the river, and is drawn from an anicut in two sections, abutting on the island of Hosapattana, where there is an old deserted fort. The Hemagiri channel, 17 miles long, is taken off from an anicut at the foot of the Hemagiri hill. The land under it is mostly inám, and many complaints having arisen from ryots cultivating the other lands, regarding the management of the channel, which was in the hands of the inamdars, Mr. Bowring, the Chief Commissioner, persuaded the latter to assign one of their villages, Yachenhalli, for the purpose of the upkeep and improvement of the channel. The revenue derived from the village, about Rs. 1,000, is therefore paid into the treasury, and the channel is looked after by the Irrigation Department, with much benefit to all concerned. The Kallhalli channel, 8 miles long, is taken from an anicut near the village of the same name. The land under it is all assigned for the support of the Parakálaswámi. The Kannambádi channel is taken off from the Danáyakan-katte, near the junction of the Hemavati with the Kávéri. It is 14 miles long, and flows through the Kannambádi tank.

**Honnu Hole** or **Suvarnavati,** both meaning golden stream, the name of a river which rises in the mountains to the south-east of the District, near the Gajalhaṭṭi pass, and flowing north through the Chámarájnagar taluq and Yelandur jágir, enters the Coimbatore country, whence, passing to the west of Kollegála, it falls into the Kávéri opposite Kakkur near Talkád. The fertility which it spreads on either bank of the rich tract through which it flows is indicated by its name. It is crossed in Chámarájnagar taluq by two permanent dams: the Gajnur, near Attikalpur, giving rise to the Bandigere channel, 9 miles long; and the Hongalvadi, with channel of the same name, 15 miles long, which feeds the large Rámasamudra tanks close to the town of Chámarájnagar. By means of temporary dams, constructed when the water is low, of stakes, mats and sand, several smaller channels are fed, namely, the Homma, the A'lúrhalla and Hosahalla, the Sargur and Maralhalla. The revenue derived from all the above is upwards of Rs. 38,000. Besides these, the stream is dammed in the Yelandur jágir by the Ganganur anicut and feeds six channels, as well as seventeen large and eleven small tanks.

**Hunsur.**—A taluq in the west, till 1882 called Periyapatna, properly Piriyapatna. Area 672 square miles. Head-quarters at Hunsur. Contains the following hóblis, villages and population :—

| No. | Hóblis. | Villages. | Hamlets. | Villages classified. | | | | Population. |
|---|---|---|---|---|---|---|---|---|
| | | | | Government. | Sarvamánya. | Jodi. | Kayamgutta. | |
| 1 | Bettadapura ... ... | 30 | 38 | 29 | — | 1 | — | 15,036 |
| 2 | Bilikere ... ... | 66 | 18 | 63 | — | — | 3 | 11,465 |
| 3 | Chilkunda ... ... | 24 | 13 | 22 | 2 | — | — | 9,588 |
| 4 | Gaudagere ... ... | 26 | 11 | 25 | 1 | — | — | 7,101 |
| 5 | Háranhalli ... ... | 48 | 25 | 48 | — | — | — | 11,379 |
| 6 | Heggandúr ... ... | 72 | 21 | 70 | 1 | — | 1 | 9,612 |
| 7 | Kaggundi ... ... | 56 | 41 | 42 | 7 | 5 | 2 | 12,976 |
| 8 | Kirajáji... ... ... | 36 | 28 | 35 | 1 | — | — | 16,721 |
| 9 | Piriyapatna ... ... | 42 | 30 | 35 | 3 | 2 | 2 | 12,931 |
| 10 | Rávandúr ... ... | 12 | 31 | 12 | — | — | — | 6,462 |
| | Total ... ... | 412 | 256 | 381 | 15 | 8 | 8 | 113,271 |

*Principal places, with population.*—Hunsur, 5,141; Piriyapatna, 3,712; Bettadapura, 2,209; Kattemalalvádi, 1,934; Mákód, 1,608; Bannikuppe, 1,521; Kittúr, 1,494; Kampalapur, 1,433; Kuttavalli, 1,337; Gaudagere, 1,307; Kalkunike, 1,246; Chámráyankóte, 1,188; Bilikere, 1,165.

The Kávéri forms part of the western and northern boundary. The Lakshmantirtha runs through the south and east, a few miles within the limits of the taluq in those directions. It is crossed by several dams, which, with the channels issuing from them, are described in connection with the river. The principal hill is that of Bettadapura, rising to about 1,600 feet above the plain, and to 4,389 feet above sea-level. Thence westwards are some low ranges from which commences the great belt of forest which extends through the south-west of the District.

The surface of the country is very undulating, and from this cause not well adapted for irrigation from channels. But the soil being generally of a rich red description, rágí and other dry crops thrive remarkably well on it. The northern part is the most open, except on the extreme west, where it approaches the confines of Coorg. The centre and east are also open, but in places, especially in the kavals or grazing lands of the Amriṭ Mahal, scrub jungle is met with, and the nálas generally are covered with trees and bushes of wild date. The west and south are thickly wooded.

The soils vary from a loose greyish or reddish sandy soil to a firmer red, and to a rich black loam, of great fertility and depth. This prevails mostly in the north. Even the poorest soils, such as those in the Bilikere hobli, though shallow, yield excellent crops owing to a good sub-soil. It is customary to grow two dry crops in the year, especially in the south-west. Tobacco of a superior quality is grown near Beṭṭadapura. Rice cultivation is subject to the malarious fever which prevails in the irrigated lands. Sugar-cane is not now cultivated, though formerly it used to be. The grazing is exceptionally good.

The revenue settlement was introduced in 1884. The area of the taluq, exclusive of inams, was thus distributed :—

| | |
|---|---|
| Culturable (dry, 178,197 ; wet, 9,386 ; garden, 3,200) ... ... ... | 190,783 |
| Unculturable (including roads, village sites, &c.) ... ... ... | 140,960 |
| State forests and 37 kávals ... ... ... ... ... ... | 58,021 |
| Total acres ... | 389,764 |

The unoccupied area was 28,059 acres. The total revenue demand for 1891–2 (15 months) was Rs. 1,95,903, and for 1892–3 it was Rs. 2,26,307.

The average rainfall at Hunsur for 26 years (1870–95) was as follows :—

| Jan. | Feb. | Mar. | Apl. | May | June | July | Aug. | Sept. | Oct. | Nov. | Dec. | Year. |
|---|---|---|---|---|---|---|---|---|---|---|---|---|
| — | 0·03 | 0·51 | 2·28 | 5·88 | 3·02 | 3·25 | 2·89 | 3·81 | 6·07 | 2·18 | 0·65 ... | 30·57 |

The trunk road from Seringapatam branches 2 miles west of Hunsur to Mercara, *viâ* Piriyapatna and Fraserpet, and to Cannanore *viâ* the Periambadi Ghat. From Hunsur there is a road south to Heggadadevankote and Sargur, and one to Hanagod ; also one north-east to Yedatore. From Piriyapatna there are roads north to Bettadpur and Ramnathpur, west to Siddapur and Virarájendrapet in Coorg, and south to Anechaukur on the Cannanore road. There is also an unfinished road from Bettadpur to Fraserpet.

**Hunsur** or **Hunasur.**—A town situated in 12° 19′ N. lat. 76° 20′ E. long., on the right bank of the Lakshmantirtha, 28 miles west of

Mysore. Since 1865, head-quarters of the Piriyapatna taluq, from 1882 called the Hunsur taluq. It is also a municipality.

| Population in 1891. | Males. | Females. | Total. |
|---|---|---|---|
| Hindus... ... ... ... ... ... ... | 1,829 | 1,818 | 3,647 |
| Muhammadans ... ... ... ... ... | 717 | 708 | 1,425 |
| Christians ... ... ... ... ... ... | 39 | 30 | 69 |
| Total ... | 2,585 | 2,556 | 5,141 |

The trunk road from Seringapatam here branches off to Mercara and to Cannanore. The importance of the place is due to its being the head-quarters of the Amrit Mahal cattle-breeding establishment, an account of which will be found elsewhere. Besides this a tannery, a cumbly manufactory and timber yard were, until 1864, maintained by the Madras Commissariat. Boots, knapsacks, and pouches are still manufactured to a large extent by an enterprising native, who, in consideration of his having bought up the Government stock in hand, was permitted to use the tannery and adjoining premises free of rent. Cumblies of a better quality than are to be found elsewhere in the District are also produced, although these latter have been to some extent thrust out of the market by the importation of cheap English blankets. The wool of which they are made is obtained from a strain of the merino sheep, which the Government formerly maintained at Hunsúr. On account of the large manufacture of country carts to which the brisk traffic through Hunsúr between Mysore, Mercara and Cannanore has given rise, the town has received from the natives the cant name of Gaḍipaḷya. Extensive coffee pulping works have been erected, where the berry received from estates in Coorg is prepared for shipment to England.

| Municipal Funds. | 1892–3. | 1893–4. | 1894–5. | 1895–6. |
|---|---|---|---|---|
| Income ... ... ... ... | 2,422 | 4,050 | 3,485 | 3,744 |
| Expenditure ... ... ... | 2,807 | 2,915 | 3,379 | 3,363 |

**Ilavala** (*Yelwal*).—A village 9 miles north-west of Mysore, at the junction of the roads from Mysore and from Seringapatam to Coorg. Head-quarters of the Ilavála hóbli. Population 1,093.

On rising ground to the west is the Yelwal Residency, erected in the time of the Hon. Arthur Cole, on designs taken from the Enniskillen seat in Ireland. The extensive stables and out-buildings have lately been partly dismantled and the materials taken to Mysore to be used for some of the new offices there. The large park had become overgrown with *lantana*, and advantage has been taken of this to sow a great quantity of sandal seed, to the plants from which it acts as a nurse until they are grown up. A mile or two to the south was the old Hinkal race-course, with several bungalows (now in ruins) erected for the occupation of the chief officers and guests at the races. About 3 miles north is Sravana-gutta, with an abandoned Jain statue of Gomata, which resembles the colossal one at Yenur (South Kanara) in being represented with a grave dimpled smile.

**Kabbal-durga.**—A fortified conical hill in Malavalli taluq, rising to 3,507 feet above the sea. Owing to its precipitous sides, it would, if properly victualled and supplied with water, be almost impregnable. It is accessible only on one side, and even there the ascent is very laborious, the steps cut in the solid rock for part of the way not exceeding six inches in width. A pálégár named Gathék Rája is said to have built the fort. It was used as a penal settlement under the Hindu and Musalmán dynasties, and also under Mummadi Krishna Rája's government, and as the bad nature of the water, which appears almost poisonous, renders the hill pestilential, troublesome State prisoners were generally sent there. Colonel Wilks speaks of Kabbál-durga as a place of imprisonment, "where the dreadful insalubrity of the climate was mercifully aided by unwholesome food to shorten the sufferings of the victims." It was here that the hereditary rája, Cháma Rája, was sent to end his days by the daḷavâyi Deva Ráj. In 1864 the guns and ammunition were destroyed, and a small establishment of peons which had theretofore been maintained in the fort were removed, so that the stronghold is now uninhabited. Haidar Ali, who repaired the fort, re-named it Jáfarábád, but, as in nearly all cases where Musalmán names were substituted for Hindu by Haidar and his son, the former is forgotten and the latter has re-asserted itself.

**Kabbani, Kapini,** or **Kapila.**—A tributary of the Kávéri. It rises in the Western Ghats in North Wainad and enters Mysore at its south-western angle in Heggadadevankote taluq. Emerging from the dense jungles of Kákankote, it flows north-east past Nisana and Maggi, and winds its way to Sargur and Muttikere. Thence, turning eastwards, it receives the waters of the Nugu near Hampapura, and at Nanjangúd those of the Gundal. Passing Táyúr it falls into the Kávéri at Tirumakúdlu near Narsipur in Tirumakúdlu-Narsipur taluq, the confluence of the streams being esteemed a spot of pre-eminent sanctity.

It is a fine perennial river, averaging from 150 to 200 yards in breadth. During the dry season its body of water is not less than that of the Kávéri. There was formerly only one stretch of wet cultivation irrigated by the Kabbani,—jódi land, about 9 miles above Nanjangúd, on the left bank. But the recent extension of the Rampur channel for 32 miles has brought 1,367 acres under irrigation. At Nanjangúd the river is spanned by a broad but rudely constructed bridge, built by the daḷaváyi Deva Ráj about the middle of the 18th century.

**Kadamba.**—*See* Shimsha.

**Kalale.**—A village in Nanjangúd taluq, 3 miles south-west of Nanjangúd, close to the Mysore-Ootacamund road. Head-quarters of the Kaḷale hóbli. Population 2,067.

It is historically interesting from having been in former times the ancestral domain of the Daḷaváyis of Mysore. It is said to have been founded in the year 1504, by a connection of the Vijayanagar family, who with his descendants ruled the neighbouring country till the acquisition of Seringapatam by the Rájas of Mysore. Shortly after that event the Wodeyars of Mysore and of Kaḷale appear to have arrived at an agreement to unite their power. Thenceforth the Kaḷale family supplied the Daḷaváyi,[1] an hereditary minister and general of the Mysore State, while the Mysore Wodeyars continued to occupy the throne at Seringapatam, being distinguished by the appellation of Kartar (Curtur in old English documents), which means the ruler. Latterly the Daḷaváyis rendered the Rájas subservient to their interests, but were in their turn displaced by Haidar.

**Karighatta.**—A hill rising to 2,697 feet, in the Seringapatam taluq, east of the point where the Lókapávani joins the Kávéri. The annual festival (*játre*) held for one day in February or March attracts an assemblage of 20,000 people.

**Kaveri** (*Cauvery*).—The *Kabœris* of Ptolemy and the Greek geographers, the principal river in the Mysore State. It rises in Coorg, in the Sahyádri or Western Ghats, the reputed source being at Tala Kávéri. Flowing eastwards through Coorg as far as Siddapur, it there turns to the north, and touches the Mysore near Fraserpet, from which, as far as Kannagal, it forms for 20 miles the boundary between Mysore and Coorg. Continuing northwards for a few miles through the Arkalgud taluq of the Hassan District, near Konanur it turns to the south-east, which direction it maintains throughout the Mysore District.

Re-entering the latter near the anicut of Sáligram, it runs through a deep narrow gorge, suffering a fall of 60 to 80 feet in the rapids at Chunchankaṭṭe. With a short bend to the north from Yedatore to

[1] Formed from two Kannaḍa words,—*daḷa*, army, and *váyi* (for *báyi*), mouth,—the mouthpiece of the army, or the medium of commands to the army.

meet the Hemávati near Tippur, it resumes its south-east course and receives the Lakshmantirtha near Bhairapura. Lower down, where the stream branches to form the island of Seringapatam, the northern arm is fed by the Lókapávani. The growing river thence flows on to Narsipur, where its waters are replenished by those of the Kabbani. From this point, with a bend eastwards and southwards, it arrives at the ancient city of Talakad, all but buried in hills of sand. Again turning east, it is joined by the Suvarnávati or Honnu-hole, and thence forms the boundary between Mysore and Coimbatore for 40 miles. From near Talakad to the island of Sivasamudram it runs northwards.

The branches of the stream which enclose that island form the picturesque falls of Gagana Chukki on the Mysore side and of Bar Chukki on the Coimbatore side. The re-united stream, with a bed 300 feet lower, passes thence eastwards through a wild gorge, receives the Shimsha and the Arkavati from the north, and narrowing at one place to what is called the *mêke dhâṭu*, or Goat's Leap, quits the State at the point where the Coimbatore and Salem boundaries meet. In its further course it runs southwards, forming the boundary between those two Districts and receiving the Bhaváni and other streams. Thence, entering the Trichinopoly District in an easterly direction, it forms the island of Srirangam, and then spreads in a rich delta of fertility over the Tanjore District. The principal arm, under the name of the Coleroon, flows north-east, separating Trichinopoly and South Arcot from Tanjore, and falls into the Bay of Bengal near Devikotta.

The average breadth of the Kávéri in Mysore is from 300 to 400 yards, but from its point of confluence with the Kabbani to the Sivasamudram Falls it swells into a much broader stream. The maximum flood discharge, as gauged roughly at Bannur, is 239,000 cubic feet per second. The ordinary monsoon discharge, calculated at 4 feet in depth, is 18,000 cubic feet per second, but 6, 8 and 10 feet are not uncommon. The bottom of the river is for the most part composed of rocks, generally of granite character, which renders it unfit for navigation. In some places, however, where there is sufficient soil to admit of it, the bed of the river is laid out in vegetable gardens during the dry season when the water is very low. These gardens of melons and cucumbers have an exceedingly pretty effect. The first fresh in the river generally occurs about the middle of June. In August the flow of water begins to decrease, but the river is not generally fordable till the end of October. Its water is in some parts considered unwholesome by the natives, and at Seringapatam they attribute the fever which is there prevalent to its influence, being prejudiced against even bathing in it during certain months.

During the greater part of its course it is bordered on each bank by a rich belt of wet cultivation. There are, however, several breaks occasioned by the inadaptability of the country and deficiency of irrigation. The first of these is from the Sáligram anicut to Chunchankaṭṭe, about 5 miles on the right bank, the second from Yedatore to the Tippur anicut, a distance of 4 miles on the right bank, and the third from Narsipur in the Tirumakúdlu-Narsipur taluq to the boundary of the Coimbatore District, about 12 miles, also on the right bank.

The waters of the Kávéri are dammed by no less than twelve anicuts, from each of which one or more channels have been led off for purposes of irrigation. Two of the anicuts are situated in Hassan and will be described with their channels under that District.

The first dam thrown across the Kávéri in the Mysore District is the Aḷale Kaṭṭe, Yedatore taluq, a long straggling structure of rough stone and of irregular section; length 570 and breadth 4 yards: it supplies the Sáligram channels on the left bank, which run for a distance of 24 miles, passing the large village of Sáligram. The revenue realized is Rs. 18,361.

The next dam in order down the river is the Hanumanta Kaṭṭe, giving rise to the Mirle channel. It is irregular in section and built of rough stone, with a weir in its northern end. The channel is led off on the left bank and, after running for about a mile, divides into three branches, *viz.*, the Hosa nála, 6 miles in length, which receives the drainage of the Sáligram; the Hiri nála, 12 miles; and the Attikaṭṭe, 6 miles. The drainage of these unites in the valley, and is led off by a channel called the Hampapura, which, after a course of 16 miles, ends in the Gullige tank. The revenue derived from these channels is Rs. 20,811. The dam and channels were constructed by Chikka Déva Rája Wodeyar, and improved by Diván Púrnaiya.

Chunchankaṭṭe dam lies about two hundred yards below the last mentioned. It stretches tortuously across the river, and has a back facing. The dam is built in an advantageous position, a short distance from the head of a narrow gorge, and a few hundred yards above the Chunchan rapids, which are from 60 to 80 feet in height. The Rámasamudram channel led off from this dam has a course of 41 miles, and runs near to the important town of Yedatore. The cultivated area is about 4,300 acres, yielding a revenue of Rs. 25,809. Both dam and channel were constructed by Chikka Déva Rája Wodeyar.

The fourth anicut on the river is the Adagúr Kaṭṭe, giving rise to the Tippúr channel. It is composed of two separate dams of rough stone which abut on an island in the middle of the river. The channel has a course of 22 miles, and at its end joins the Anandur by means of an aqueduct thrown across the Lakshmantirtha river near the village of Ságarkatte, Mysore taluq. The greater part of the land below the channel is *inámti*, the revenue derived by Government being Rs. 4,089. Both dam and channel were constructed by Góvinda Náyaka, a pálégár chieftain.

Close to the village of Sítápur, in the Seringapatam taluq, is the Madad katte dam, a low straggling structure of rough stone, 776 yards in length and averaging 15 yards in breadth. From this dam the Chikkadévaráyaságar is led off, the finest channel in the Mysore country: it runs for 72 miles on the left bank of the river, irrigating an area of 13,737 acres, from which a revenue of Rs. 89,571 is derived. In its course it crosses the Anché Halla and Mosale Halla streams, and a small monsoon river called the Lókapávani near the station of French Rocks. Towards its end it feeds four important tanks, the Hosahalli, Kodagalli, Madagalli and Bannur, the last situated near the town of the same name. The channel passes the villages of Haravu, Kétanhalli, Nelmane, Patsómanahalli, Sethalli and Arekere, in its course. Both dam and channel were constructed by Chikka Déva Rája Wodeyar.

A few yards below the Madad katte is the Devaráya dam, giving rise to a channel of the same name on the right bank of the river. Its length is 18 miles, and the revenue derived amounts to Rs. 12,787.

Near the temple of Balmuri, a mile from the village of Belgula, is the Balmuri dam, giving rise to the Virjánadi channel on the right bank of the river. This channel is the second in importance in Mysore, running for 41 miles through the Seringapatam taluq: it passes the large villages of Pálhalli, Kalaswádi, Náganhalli, Nuganhalli and Hebbádi, and ends near the Ankanhalli tank. The revenue derived is Rs. 45,888, and the area irrigated is about 7,330 acres. By means of this channel, the former sugar and iron factories at Pálhalli used to be worked.

The eighth channel drawn from the Kávéri in the Mysore District is the Bangár Doddi. The dam is thrown across the Paschima-váhini branch of the river. The channel, after crossing the Paschima-váhini island, is led over a second branch of the Kávéri into the Seringapatam island by means of an aqueduct; it then divides into three branches, one enters the fort by means of an underground duct, a second terminates at the Darya Daulat garden, and the third, after traversing the island, ends at the Lál Bágh near the mausoleum of Haidar and Tipu. The revenue derived from irrigated land amounts to Rs. 5,632.

Next in order down the river is the Rámaswámi dam, giving rise to two channels, the Rámaswámi on the left bank in the Seringapatam taluq, and the Rájparamésvari on the right in the Tirumakúdlu Narsipur taluq. The Rámaswami has a course of 31 miles; for 12 miles it runs through the Bannúr hobli, then passing the large town of Sósile, ends about 8 miles from the town of Talakád. The revenue derived is Rs. 16,793, and the irrigated area is 3,104 acres. The Rájparamésvari runs for a distance of 21 miles and passes the villages of Rangasamudra, Gargésvari and Tirumakúdlu, irrigating an area of 1,848 acres, from which a revenue of Rs. 9,771 is derived. The land under the last three miles of the channel is sarvamánya. Dam and channels were constructed by Diván Púrnaiya.

The last dam on the river in the District is the Mádhava-mantri, situated near the village of Hemmige, about two miles above the town of Talakád. The main channel formerly ran through the town, but in consequence of the influx of sand during high winds from the celebrated sand hills, the course was altered to a few hundred yards north of the town. After running for about two miles, the channel divides into three branches, whose total length is 18 miles. The revenue derived is Rs. 13,677, the acreage 2,939. The main branch of the channel ends in the Jágír of Sivasamudram, a few miles above the celebrated Falls of the Kávéri.[1]

The river is spanned by bridges at Fraserpet, Yedatore, Seringapatam and Sivasamudram. Those for the roads at the two latter places are interesting specimens of native construction. Yedatore, Seringapatam and Talakád are the principal towns on the Kávéri. The phenomenon of the sand dunes which have enveloped the latter has been noticed elsewhere.

Alligators are numerous, but they have been seldom known to attack the fishermen, and the natives in general stand in no dread of them. Some of the varieties of fish found in the river are described under that head. Shoals of large fish are daily fed at Ramnathpur and Yedatore by the Brahmans.

In point of sanctity the Kávéri, also called the Dakshina Ganga, is perhaps inferior only to the Ganges: but this sanctity does not extend to the tributaries in the same degree. The reverence with which Hindus regard the Kávéri is exemplified in the nullah which was the work of, and bore the name of, the celebrated Divan Púrnaiya. This canal, which was drawn from the Kávéri about 30 miles above Seringapatam, was upwards of 70 miles in length and terminated at Mysore. It was carried over the Lakshmantirtha river by means of

[1] *See* Sivasamudram.

an aqueduct, so that although the nullah was partially available for irrigation, it is clear that not the least of Púrnaiya's object was to bring sacred water into the city of Mysore. Immense labour was expended on excavation, and in many places cuttings upwards of 100 feet deep were made through solid granite. But this ambitious work was, after all, ineffectual for the accomplishment of the end proposed, for the difference of levels made it impossible that in the absence of mechanical aids the Kávéri waters themselves could ever reach Mysore. The nullah, which in the crowded parts of the city had become little better than a deep and noisome sewer, has now been filled up within municipal limits, and sites have thus been provided for handsome streets and buildings. At the same time the coveted conveyance to the city of the sacred waters of the holy river has, with the help of modern science, been successfully effected by the erection near Anandur of turbines, by means of which the river water is forced up to a special reservoir at Mysore. The scheme was completed and the water made use of for the first time on the occasion of the installation of the present young Maharaja.

The supposed divine origin of the river is related in the Kávéri Mahátmya of the Agneya and Skánda puránas. She was first Vishnumáyá, a daughter of Brahma. By his direction she became incarnate in Lopámudrá, a girl formed by Agastya (with the view of her becoming his wife) of the most graceful parts of the animals of the forest, whose distinctive beauties (*mudrá*), as the eyes of the deer, &c., were subjected to loss (*lopa*) in her superior charms. Brahma gave Lopámudrá as a daughter to Kavéra muni, whence she acquired the name Kávéri. In order to secure beatitude for her new father, she resolved to become a river, the merit of whose waters in absolving from all sin and blessing the earth should accrue to him. But when she became of age, Agastya proposed to marry her. To reconcile the conflicting claims, Lopámudrá or the mortal part of her nature became the wife of Agastya, while Kávéri or the celestial part flowed forth as the river.

**Kittur.**—A large village on the right bank of the Kabbani, in Heggadadevankote taluq, south of the kasba. Population 1,443.

It is historically interesting as being identified with the Kitthipura or Kirthipura which was the capital of the Punnád Rájas (*see* above, p. 220, and Vol. I, p. 312). An inscription of the 11th century describes it as "the royal residence, the immense great city Kirthipura."

**Krishnarajpet.**—A taluq in the north-west, till 1891 called Attikuppa, and till 1882 forming part of the Hassan District. Area 424 square miles. Head-quarters at Krishnarájpet. Contains the following hoblis, villages and population :—

| No. | Hoblis. | Villages. | Hamlets. | Villages classified. | | | | Population. |
|---|---|---|---|---|---|---|---|---|
| | | | | Government. | Servamánya. | Jodi. | Kayamgutta. | |
| 1 | Akkihebbál ... ... | 60 | 14 | 43 | 16 | 1 | — | 15,434 |
| 2 | Chinkuruli ... ... | 62 | 37 | 52 | 8 | 1 | 1 | 16,065 |
| 3 | Kannambáḍi ... | 50 | 19 | 41 | 9 | — | — | 15,999 |
| 4 | Kikkéri ... ... | 60 | 20 | 59 | — | — | 1 | 13,064 |
| 5 | Krishnarájpéṭ ... | 67 | 21 | 66 | — | 1 | — | 16,350 |
| 6 | Santebáchihalli ... | 63 | 12 | 59 | 1 | 2 | 1 | 14,541 |
| | Total ... ... | 362 | 123 | 320 | 34 | 5 | 3 | 91,453 |

*Principal places, with population.*—Sindaghaṭṭa 1,874; Krishnarájpéṭ 1,662; Gummanhalli 1,629; Kannambáḍi 1,621; Hosaholalu 1,597; Kikkéri 1,574; Búkinkere 1,320; Maḍavankóḍi 1,130; Akkihebbál 1,020.

A number of villages from Chanraypatna and Hole Narsipur taluqs were added to the Kikkeri hobli in 1882, while the Melukote hobli was transferred to Seringapatam taluq, and some villages of Santebáchihalli to Nagamangala.

The drainage of the taluq is from north to south in a westerly direction, most of the streams discharging into the Hemavati, which runs along near the western border and joins the Kávéri in the south, on which side this latter river forms the boundary. On the eastern border are several rocky hills. There are some 284 tanks, at least 10 of which are of the first class. But the chief means of irrigation are the channels drawn from the Hemavati, of which there are five—the Mandigere, 27 miles long, irrigating 2,720 acres; the Akkihebbál, 7 miles long, irrigating 2,724 acres; the Hemagiri, 17 miles long, irrigating 1,460 acres, nearly all inám land; the Kannambaḍi, 14 miles long, irrigating 1,245 acres; the Kalhalli, 8 miles long, irrigating 328 acres.

The dry crop soils vary considerably, from good red in the low grounds to grey and sandy in the uplands, especially in Santebáchihalli and Chinkuruli hoblis. Black soil is rare and in small patches. The crops taken from the red and sandy soils are better than might be expected. The rice lands under tanks are fairly good, and in the east a coarse kind of rice, *doddi* or *karibhatta*, is raised without artificial irrigation. The gardens, especially those for cocoa-nuts, betel-leaf and plantains, are productive. But land under the river channels, though somewhat inferior in quality, is more sought after, on account of the perennial water supply. The irrigated tracts are also free from the fever which prevails in such lands in the taluqs to the west. The cultivation of sugar-cane is general, especially *marakabbu*.

Silk cloths of various kinds are manufactured at Sindaghatta. The raw silk brought from neighbouring taluqs is here spun into thread, dyed and woven.

The revenue settlement was introduced in 1886. The area of the taluq was thus distributed, excluding minor ináms :—

| | | |
|---|---|---|
| Culturable (dry, 108,453; wet, 9,114; garden, 3,326) ... | ... | 120,893 |
| Unculturable (including roads, tanks, village sites, &c.) ... | ... | 89,543 |
| Inám villages (33,306); 11 Amrit Mahal kávals (10,890) | ... | 44,196 |
| Total acres .. | ... | 254,632 |

The unoccupied area was 11,971 acres. The total revenue demand for 1891–2 (15 months) was Rs. 1,97,914, and for 1892–3 it was Rs. 2,13,489.

The average rainfall at Krishnarájpéṭ for 26 years (1870–95), and at the other station for three years (1893–5), was as follows :—

| | Jan. | Feb. | Mar. | Apr. | May | June | July | Aug. | Sept. | Oct. | Nov. | Dec. | Year. |
|---|---|---|---|---|---|---|---|---|---|---|---|---|---|
| Krishnarájpéṭ | 0·09 | 0·01 | 0·40 | 2·15 | 5·65 | 1·86 | 2·05 | 2·55 | 3·44 | 6·10 | 3·11 | 0·38 ... | 27·79 |
| Chinkuruli ... | — | 0·13 | 0·96 | 2·62 | 3·52 | 2·60 | 2·09 | 3·59 | 2·67 | 8·05 | 1·47 | — ... | 27·70 |

The main road from Seringapatam to Chanraypatna runs through the taluq from south-east to north-west, passing by Krishnarájpéṭ; from which there are roads north-east to Nagamangala and east to Melukote. There is also an unfinished road west to Akkihebbál and Bherya. A road from French Rocks runs to Kannambáḍi and continues westward as a cart track.

**Krishnarajpet.**—A small town situated in 12° 41′ N. lat., 76° 33′ E. long., 23 miles from the railway at French Rocks station, and 35 miles north-east of Mysore, on the Seringapatam-Chanraypatna road. Till 1891 it was called Attikuppa. Head-quarters of the Krishnarájpéṭ taluq, and a municipality.

| Population in 1891. | Males. | Females. | Total. |
|---|---|---|---|
| Hindus ... ... ... ... ... ... ... | 756 | 785 | 1,541 |
| Muhammadans ... ... ... ... ... ... | 68 | 50 | 118 |
| Christians ... ... ... ... ... ... ... | 2 | 1 | 3 |
| Total ... ... ... | 826 | 836 | 1,662 |

The place derives all its importance from being the head-quarters of the taluq.

| Municipal Funds. | 1892-3. | 1893-4. | 1894-5. | 1895-6. |
|---|---|---|---|---|
| Income ... ... ... ... ... | 419 | 459 | 676 | 747 |
| Expenditure ... ... ... ... ... | 938 | 694 | 709 | 1,080 |

**Lakshmantirtha.**—A tributary of the Kávéri. It rises in the Western Ghats, in the Brahmagiri which forms the southern frontier of Coorg. Its whole course is north-east. Entering Mysore two miles south of the village of Chikka Hejjur in Hunsur taluq, it flows past Hanagod, Hunsur and Kaṭṭe Maḷalvádi into the Yedatore taluq, where it falls into the Kávéri near the village of Ságarkaṭṭe. It is a perennial stream, and though a smaller river than the Kabbani, is considerably more utilized for irrigation. The following lands are irrigated from it. The right bank from Hanagod to Kaṭṭe Maḷalvádi ; the left bank from Kaṭṭe Maḷalvádi to the Seriyúr anicut ; both banks from the Seriyúr anicut to Marchahalli : the left bank from Marchahalli to Ságarkaṭṭe ; the right bank from Ságarkaṭṭe to the confluence with the Kávéri. It is crossed by seven dams.

The first dam thrown across the river is the Hanagód, below the village of the same name. It is built in the ordinary manner, of rough rubble stone, its strength being greatly augmented by the rocky formation of the river bed. The channel, which bears the same name, is led off on the right bank of the river, and after running for nine miles, divides into three branches, *viz.*, the Nellur 7, Hanumantapur 24, and Wudur 20 miles in length. The Nellur follows the course of the river, and ends in the Elephant tank near Hunasur. The Wudur and Hanumantapur, however, passing through a deep cutting, enter the watershed of the Kabbani river, the Wudur running in an easterly, the Hanumantapur in a southerly direction. Six tanks are fed by the Hanumantapur in its course, *viz.*, the Pudukóte, Nanjanhalli, Sówé, Harrupur, Belliganhalli, and Gudamanahalli. The total revenue derived from the Hanagód and branches, altogether 66 miles in length, irrigating 4,101 acres, is Rs. 18,245. The dense jungles which surround the channels interfere with extensive cultivation. The drainage from the Wudur and Hanumantapur channels is taken up by the Dásanpúr and Máikálwe ; the latter feeds the Karigal, Holléhundi and Parvatam tanks on the banks of the Kabbani.

The Rámenhalli, an old breached dam, is the next, about three miles up the river from Hunsur ; the channel was led off on the right bank, and ran for 20 miles, passing through the town of Hunsur.

The Kaṭṭe Maḷalwádi, situated near the village of the same name, about 4 miles below Hunasur, is the third dam on the river. The channel has a course of 11 miles along the left bank. The irrigated area is 509 acres, while the revenue derived is Rs. 2,520.

Near the village of Hundwádi is the Hangarhaḷḷi dam, giving rise to two channels, the Siriyúr and Husenpura. The former, on the left bank, runs for 11 miles, and yields a revenue of Rs. 1,753; the latter, on the right bank, has also a course of 11 miles, with a revenue of Rs. 3,246.

The fifth dam is the Marchahalli, giving rise to a small channel of the same name. The dam breached in 1864 and a new dam was constructed at a short distance above the site of the old one. The channel which runs along the left bank is 10 miles long and yields a revenue of Rs. 2,392.

The Ságarkaṭṭe dam, built by Divan Purnaiya near the village of the same name, gives rise to the Anandúr channel on the right bank. This channel was originally carried as far as Mysore, it having been the constructor's intention to supply the town with the river water; the design however failed, and the channel is in order for only 20 miles. The revenue derived is Rs. 7,278, on an irrigated area of 1,317 acres.

The Cholanhaḷḷi is the last dam on the river, about half a mile above its confluence with the Kávéri; the dam breached in 1864, but the irrigation under the channel is kept up by the drainage of the Anandúr, under which channel it runs for its whole length.

**Lokapavani** (world-purifier).—A small stream running to the Kávéri. It rises to the west of Nágamangala, and flowing with an easterly course past the French Rocks, receives the stream from the Moti Táláb, and enters the Kávéri opposite the Karighatta peak, off the north eastern point of the island of Seringapatam.

**Maddur.**—A town on the right bank of the Shimsha, 36 miles north-east of Mysore, on the Bangalore-Mysore railway and the Bangalore-Seringapatam road. It is a municipality, and till 1875 was the head-quarters of the separate Maddur taluq. This was for a time formed into a sub-taluq under Mandya taluq, but in 1886 was absorbed in that taluq.

| Population in 1891. | Males. | Females. | Total. |
|---|---|---|---|
| Hindus... ... ... ... ... ... | 769 | 846 | 1,615 |
| Muhammadans ... ... ... ... | 314 | 288 | 602 |
| Total ... | 1,083 | 1,134 | 2,217 |

Maddur, properly Marudúr, appears to have been formerly a place of importance, but has never recovered from the destruction to which it became subject during the war of Tipu with the English, and is unhealthy. There are two large Vishnuvite temples, dedicated to Narasimha and Varada Rája, which draw a nominal allowance from Government. A fine brick bridge of seven arches, constructed in 1850, spans the Shimsha, and has now been used for the railway as well as the road. Tradition claims for Maddur a great antiquity. It is stated to have been originally named Arjunapura, by Arjuna the Pandu prince, who arrived there on pilgrimage. The Shimsha also bears the name of the Kadamba, from a rishi who resided on its banks. Under the Gangas it formed part of the province of Chikka Gangavadi, and in later times Vishnuvardhana of the Hoysala line is stated to have given Maddur in inám to the Srivaishnava Brahmans. He is also stated to have built the Maddur tank and the temple of Varada Rája. The agrahara was called Narasimha-chaturvedimangalam, after his son. The fort was taken in 1617 by the Dalaváyi of Mysore, during the reign of Rája Wodeyar, and was rebuilt by Haidar Ali. It was dismantled by Lord Cornwallis in 1791 on his march to Seringapatam.

About three miles west of Maddur are the remains of an old fort named Nagarakere, which was inhabited 600 years ago by a páḷégár named Magurta Ráya. According to the popular legend, he was the son-in-law of Ganga Rája of Sivasamudram, and his wife was perpetually boasting of her father's splendour, declaring among other vaunts that she could hear her father's fort-gate, which was made of bell-metal, shut every evening at sunset. Incensed at this, her husband determined to prove his power superior to that of Ganga Rája, and marched an army against Sivasamudram, which he took and destroyed.

Four miles from the town is an unfinished tank, known as the Súlékere. It was commenced about 700 years ago by a woman of the dancing-girl caste, who died before it could be finished. It is estimated that its completion would cost a lakh and a half of rupees, and would bring more than a thousand kandis of wet land under cultivation.

There are cross roads from Maddur to Malavalli and the Kávéri Falls southwards, and to Huliyurdurga northwards.

| Municipal Funds. | 1892-3. | 1893-4. | 1894-5. | 1895-6. |
|---|---|---|---|---|
| Income ... ... ... ... ... | 358 | 260 | 804 | 800 |
| Expenditure ... ... ... ... | 1,064 | 461 | 622 | 1,108 |

**Malavalli.**—A taluq in the east. Area 391 square miles. Head-quarters at Malavalli. Contains the following hoblis, villages and population :—

| No. | Hoblis. | Villages. | Hamlets. | Villages classified. | | | Population. |
|---|---|---|---|---|---|---|---|
| | | | | Govern-ment. | Sarva-mánya. | Jodi. | |
| 1 | Arasinkere ... ... | 25 | 16 | 22 | 2 | 1 | 10,638 |
| 2 | Gauḍagere ... ... | 31 | 12 | 29 | 2 | — | 7,050 |
| 3 | Halagúr ... ... | 42 | 37 | 42 | — | — | 10,706 |
| 4 | Kiragával ... ... | 22 | 31 | 18 | 4 | — | 13,236 |
| 5 | Kúlagere ... ... | 35 | 25 | 29 | 5 | 1 | 12,111 |
| 6 | Malavalli ... ... | 29 | 20 | 26 | 1 | 2 | 15,152 |
| 7 | Purigál ... ... ... | 39 | 24 | 30 | 8 | 1 | 17,017 |
| | Total ... | 209 | 165 | 196 | 22 | 5 | 85,910 |

*Principal places, with population.*—Malavalli 6,308; Belakaváḍi 2,795; Kalkaṇṇu 2,221; Halagúr 1,847; Dod-Arasinkere 1,646; Kiragával 1,546; Purigál 1,209; Boṭṭanhalli 1,103; Boppagaudanapura 1,060; Kottanhalli 1,039.

The Kávéri forms the southern boundary, and receives towards the east the Shimsha, or Maddur Holé, into which all the waters of the taluq flow. At about the middle of the southern boundary the Kávéri divides into two branches, forming the island of Sivasamudra, and precipitating itself into deep ravines in the picturesque Kávéri Falls. The course of the Shimsha is at first east, but from the village of Sargur, where it is joined by the Kanva from the north, it runs south into the parent stream. Neither of these rivers is at present a source of irrigation, some channels which were formerly drawn from the Kanva having fallen out of repair. The latter part of the Ramaswami channel, drawn from the Kávéri near Bannur, irrigates lands in Purigal hobli, but they chiefly belong to the Jágírdár of Sivasamudra. All the remaining irrigated land is below the few tanks. The two largest, the Malavalli and Maranhalli tanks, are in the immediate neighbourhood of Malavalli, and their water, uniting into one channel, irrigates land to a distance of 9 miles. A large tank has also been recently formed by a dam across the Heb-halla, a tributary of the Shimsha, at Arasinkere.

The taluq generally is an undulating plain, except on the south-east, which is occupied by the Basavana betta State forest, and by hills of inconsiderable height: of these the principal are Kabbáldurga (3,507 feet), Basavana betta, Bemmanakandi betta, Tayalur betta, Singrajpur betta and Achala betta.

The soil in the south-eastern quarter of the taluq is mostly rocky and shallow: also in parts of the north-west. In the remaining parts it is generally red, with more or less admixture of sand. Towards the south-west the soil increases in depth, colour and fertility, until the rich soils, including patches of black soil, on the border of the Tirumakúdlu-Narsipur taluq are met with. The crops vary with the soils, jola, cotton and Bengal gram being grown to some extent in the better soils, while only rági, save, avare, togari and other pulses are grown in the poorer soils. The wet lands may be described as generally inferior, and there is an almost entire absence of sugar-cane cultivation. Mulberry is the chief crop in gardens, and it is grown even in dry lands, but in the latter case is poor. Areca, cocoa-nut and plaintains are sparsely represented. Silk and hides are the principal articles exported from the taluq. Halagúr was once the seat of a considerable iron industry, but owing partly to lack of fuel and charcoal, and partly to the competition of foreign iron, smelting has been almost abandoned. A project formed by Dr. Dhanakoti Ráju for reviving this industry, though not carried out, has been described in Vol. I, p. 534.

The revenue settlement was introduced in 1893. The area of the taluq was thus distributed:—

| | |
|---|---|
| Culturable (dry, 114,920; wet, 3,525; garden, 2,697) ... ... | 120,942 |
| Unculturable (including village sites, roads, &c.) ... ... ... | 64,947 |
| State forests and kávals (24,661); inám villages (38,780) ... | 63,441 |
| Total acres ... | 249,330 |

The unoccupied area was 4,479 acres. The total revenue demand for 1891-2 (15 months) was Rs. 85,640, and for 1892-3 it was Rs. 94,981.

The average rainfall at Malavalli for 26 years (1870-95) was:—

| Jan. | Feb. | Mar. | April | May | June | July | Aug. | Sept. | Oct. | Nov. | Dec. | Year. |
|---|---|---|---|---|---|---|---|---|---|---|---|---|
| 0·16 | 0·13 | 0·66 | 1·45 | 4·19 | 1·08 | 1·44 | 3·95 | 4·69 | 5·67 | 2·64 | 0·27 ... | 26·33 |

The Bangalore-Mysore road *viâ* Kankanhalli runs through Halagúr and Malavalli, and is crossed at Malavalli by the road from Maddur to Sivasamudram. There is also a road from Sosile through Belakavadi to Sivasamudram, with a branch from near Purigál to Talakád.

**Malavalli.**—A town situated in 12° 23′ N. lat., 77° 7′ E. long., 28 miles east of Mysore, at the intersection of the Mysore-Kankanhalli and Maddur-Sivasamudram roads, 18 miles south of the railway at Maddur. Head-quarters of the taluq of the same name, and a municipality.

| Population in 1891. | Males. | Females. | Total. |
|---|---|---|---|
| Hindus ... ... ... ... ... ... | 2,504 | 2,577 | 5,081 |
| Muhammadans ... ... ... .. | 248 | 283 | 531 |
| Christians ... ... ... ... ... | 19 | 8 | 27 |
| Total ... | 2,771 | 2,868 | 5,639 |

An inscription of 1685, in the time of Chikka Deva Rája, describes it as abounding in fruit-trees and filled with learned men. It formerly possessed a large fort, built of mud and stone, which is now ruinous. Haidar gave Malavalli in jágir to his son Tipu, so that it then enjoyed considerable prosperity, although it does not appear that the population was greater than it is now. Below the Malavalli tank is the site of a fruit garden which Tipu planted, now occupied by paddy-fields. About two miles from the town, and close to the new Mysore road, is the scene of the only engagement which took place between the British army under General Harris and Tipu Sultan, during the march of the former on Seringapatam in 1799. Bullets, &c., are frequently found in the neighbourhood after rain. After the action Tipu sent and destroyed Malavalli to prevent its being of any use to the British army.

| Municipal Funds. | 1892-3. | 1893-4. | 1894-5. | 1895-6. |
|---|---|---|---|---|
| Income ... ... ... ... ... | 735 | 614 | 1,827 | 1,646 |
| Expenditure ... ... ... ... | 1,521 | 665 | 1,037 | 1,564 |

**Mandya.**—A taluq in the north-east. Area 452 square miles. Head-quarters at Mandya. Contains the following hoblis, villages and population:—

| No. | Hoblis. | Villages. | Hamlets. | Villages classified. | | | | Population. |
|---|---|---|---|---|---|---|---|---|
| | | | | Government. | Sarvamánya. | Jodi. | Kayamgutta. | |
| 1 | Ane ... ... ... | 18 | 22 | 16 | 1 | 1 | — | 6,338 |
| 2 | A'takúr... ... ... | 27 | 24 | 26 | 1 | — | — | 9,496 |
| 3 | Basarálu ... ... | 45 | 29 | 43 | 2 | — | — | 10,494 |
| 4 | Dudda ... ... ... | 36 | 22 | 35 | 1 | — | — | 9,420 |
| 5 | Koppa ... ... ... | 30 | 30 | 29 | — | — | 1 | 10,052 |
| 6 | Kottatti ... ... | 29 | 14 | 26 | 3 | — | — | 11,246 |
| 7 | Kudargundi ... ... | 18 | 14 | 15 | 2 | — | 1 | 7,002 |
| 8 | Maddúr ... ... | 12 | 10 | 12 | — | — | — | 5,514 |
| 9 | Mandya ... ... | 23 | 14 | 19 | 1 | 1 | 2 | 12,800 |
| 10 | Muttegere ... ... | 24 | 11 | 23 | — | — | 1 | 3,949 |
| 11 | Tippúr ... ... ... | 22 | 11 | 17 | — | — | 5 | 6,720 |
| 12 | Yeleyúr... ... ... | 17 | 8 | 17 | — | — | — | 6,752 |
| | Total ... | 301 | 209 | 278 | 11 | 2 | 10 | 99,783 |

*Principal places, with population.*—Mandya 4,100; Maddur 2,392; Keregódu 1,513; Kestúr 1,422; Guttal 1,276; Honnalagere 1,237; Búdanúr 1,219; Sante Kanalagere 1,162; Besagarahalli 1,151; Yelechákanahalli 1,145; Holalu 1,137; Sátanúru 1,090; Kaudle 1,060; Kottatti 1,002.

The taluq was increased in 1875 by the addition of the Maddur taluq, with the exception of the Arasinkere hobli, joined to Malavalli; and in 1882 by the addition of the Koppa hobli from the Kunigal taluq.

The eastern portion is watered by the Shimsha or Maddur Holé, which is crossed 9 miles above the town of Maddur by the Maddur anicut, recently rebuilt of cut stone. It gives rise to the Maddur Ane channel, running altogether for a distance of 12 miles to the Maddur tank, and irrigating 1,090 acres. This also branches into the following channels:—Chamanhalli, 2¾ miles; Bairan, 2 miles; Vaidyanathapur, 3¼ miles; and Kemman, 5½ miles: altogether irrigating 1,910 acres. The remains are visible of another from the Chikka Holé to the Kestur tank, but this has been out of repair and not used for about 80 years. The western portion of the taluq is occupied by chains of rain-fed tanks, the drainage being south-easterly, towards the Shimsha. There are altogether over 200 tanks used for irrigation, of which Maddur tank is the largest, and 29 others are large. The wells are of no importance.

The country is gently undulating, and is only moderately wooded with banyan, ippe and other trees, there being no jungle, and only some small scrub on the eastern and north-western boundaries.

The soils for dry crops are as a whole poor, being sandy and gravelly, shallow and in some places very stony, especially in the uplands in the north. Black soil is rare. Good red soil occurs in the centre, and east of the Shimsha in the south. The soils in the wet lands are pretty uniform and of fair quality, except in those reclaimed under the new Maddur channel, and even here they are gradually improving from being brought under cultivation.

The usual dry crops are grown. The principal wet crop is rice. There is not much sugar-cane, but there is a good deal of mulberry in the east. The areca gardens were ruined in the famine. The gardens that now remain are not very good and contain chiefly cocoa-nut, plantains and mulberry, with minor crops of chillies, vegetables, &c. The honge trees are not here utilized for supplying manure to rice-fields as in Districts to the east. But hucheh-ellu or other inferior crop is grown in rice-lands after the harvest and is then ploughed in. Silt from tanks is largely used for manure both in wet and dry soils.

Sheep are numerous. A superior kind of *kambli* is made at Mandya, Sátanur, Mudagere and other places. Silkworms are largely kept by both Musalmans and Hindus, who send the cocoons principally to Channapatna, where the silk is reeled.

The revenue settlement was introduced in 1888, except in Koppa hobli, which was settled with Kunigal taluq in 1881. The area of the taluq was thus distributed:—

| | |
|---|---|
| Culturable (dry, 125,517; wet, 9,206; garden, 2,982) ... ... | 137,765 |
| Unculturable (including roads, village sites, &c.) .. ... ... | 94,262 |
| Inám villages ... ... ... ... ... ... ... ... | 23,753 |
| Total acres ... | 255,780 |

The unoccupied area was 11,785 acres. The total revenue demand for 1891–2 (15 months) was Rs. 1,96,560, and for 1892–3 it was Rs. 2,20,606.

The average rainfall at Mandya for 26 years (1870–95) and at the other stations for three years (1893–5) was as follows:—

| | Jan. | Feb. | Mar. | Apr. | May | June | July | Aug. | Sept. | Oct. | Nov. | Dec. | Year. |
|---|---|---|---|---|---|---|---|---|---|---|---|---|---|
| Mandya ... | 0·21 | 0·06 | 0·46 | 1·42 | 4·81 | 1·55 | 1·66 | 3·91 | 5·12 | 7·05 | 2·92 | 0·77 | ...29·94 |
| Koppa ... | — | — | 1·85 | 1·56 | 5·47 | 2·38 | 4·87 | 0·80 | 4·44 | 9·74 | 2·23 | — | ...33·34 |
| Lingarájchatra | — | 0·16 | 0·46 | 1·55 | 2·46 | 2·47 | 1·78 | 1·73 | 2·69 | 9·06 | 1·90 | 0·01 | ...24·27 |
| Maddur ... | — | 0·31 | 1·28 | 2·75 | 4·21 | 2·61 | 3·78 | 4·27 | 5·78 | 10·31 | 2·70 | — | ...38·00 |

These results are somewhat questionable, as other observations for the same periods make the annual rainfall at Mandya 25·71 and at Maddur 31·22.

The Bangalore-Mysore railway runs through the south of the taluq from east to west, with stations at Maddur, Mandya and Yeliyur. The Bangalore-Seringapatam trunk road is close alongside the railway. From Mandya there are roads north to Basarál and south to Bannur. From Maddur there are roads north to Huliyurdurga and south to Malavalli, Sivasamudram and the Kávéri Falls. There is also a road from Lingarájchatra to French Rocks.

**Mandya.**—A town situated in 12° 32′ N. lat., 76° 57′ E. long., 25 miles north-east of Mysore, on the Bangalore-Mysore railway and the Bangalore-Seringapatam road. Head-quarters of the Mandya taluq, and a municipality.

| Population in 1891. | Males. | Females. | Total. |
|---|---|---|---|
| Hindus ... ... ... ... ... ... | 994 | 945 | 1,939 |
| Muhammadans ... ... ... ... ... | 160 | 137 | 297 |
| Jains ... ... ... ... ... ... ... | 44 | 41 | 85 |
| Christians ... ... ... ... ... ... | 17 | 10 | 27 |
| Total ... | 1,215 | 1,133 | 2,348 |

The following is the mythological account of Mandya as contained in the local purána. In the Krita yuga, when the country was covered with thick jungle, a rishi who made *tapas* here, was in the habit of teaching the wild beasts to pronounce the sacred word Véda. On this account he named the place Védáranya, and established therein the god Janárdana or Varadarájáswámi, whose temple is still standing. During the same age another rishi set up the god Sakalésvaraswámi there. Vishnu appeared to him, and hence the place was re-named Vishnupura. Towards the end of the Dwápara yuga, a king, by name Indravarma, who was without issue, removed here in the hope of obtaining a son. His prayers were answered, and his son, whose name was Sómavarma, built a fort and agrahára, and nominated the site Mandévému, which has since been corrupted into Mandya.

But Mandya appears to be named after the native place, near Tirupati, of the first Brahman families who settled there; the village having been granted by Krishna Rája of Vijayanagar, in 1516, to Govinda Rája, twelfth in descent from Anantácháya, a disciple of the reformer Rámánujácharya, and a distinguished devotee of the idol Venkatesa at Tirupati. Mandya continued to remain a sarvamányam village for Sri Vaishnava Brahmans until the time of Tipu Sultan, who withdrew the allowance. He also removed the taluq cutcherry from Mandya to Keragod, but Purnaiya retransferred it to Mandya.

| Municipal Funds. | 1892-3. | 1893-4. | 1894-5. | 1895-6. |
|---|---|---|---|---|
| Income .. ... ... ... ... | 604 | 512 | 1,110 | 1,166 |
| Expenditure ... ... ... ... | 482 | 62 | 610 | 813 |

**Manipura.**—An ancient city of which the ruins are pointed out three miles south-east of Chamarajnagar. The legend regarding it has been given in the section on the history of the District.

**Melukote.**—A celebrated sacred town in the Seringapatam taluq, situated in 12° 40′ N. lat., 76° 43′ E. long., 20 miles north of the kasba, built on the rocky hills named Yadugiri, overlooking the Moti Táláb and the Kávéri valley. It is a municipality.

| Population in 1891. | Males. | Females. | Total. |
|---|---|---|---|
| Hindus ... ... ... ... ... | 1,304 | 1,367 | 2,671 |
| Muhammadans .. ... ... ... | 18 | 11 | 29 |
| Jains ... ... ... ... .. ... | 13 | 21 | 34 |
| Total ... | 1,335 | 1,339 | 2,734 |

*Mélu-kóṭe*, high or superior fort, is one of the principal sacred places in Mysore. When the Vaishnava reformer Rámánujácharya fled from the persecution of the Chola king, early in the 12th century, he took up his residence at Mélukóṭe and lived there for 14 years. It thus became the chief seat of the Sri Vaishnava sect of Brahmans, who reaped the benefit of the conversion by their apostle of the Hoysala king Bitti Deva, thenceforward called Vishnuvardhana, in obtaining assignments of all the most fertile tracts of land in the neighbourhood, especially of the *ashṭa gráma* (*see* above, p. 235) on either bank of the Kávéri.

The place suffered at the hands of the Muhammadans who wrecked Dorasamudra in the 14th century, as it was to Tondanur, now Tonnur, at the southern foot of the hill, that the Hoysala king at first retired. It was subsequently restored, in about 1460, by Timmanna Dannáyaka, lord of Nágamangala, who was the minister of the Vijayanagar king Mallikarjuna or Immadi Praudha Deva Ráya. The buildings must have been on a grand scale, as the remains of the Gopal Ráya gate on the south are of immense proportions. The former approaches are flagged with stones for a considerable distance. There is now a good road.

In 1771, the Mahrattas having encamped to the south of the hill after their victory over Haidar Ali at Chinkuruli, the Brahmans deserted Mélukóṭe, which was as usual plundered. For the sake of iron, the immense wooden cars belonging to the temples were set on fire, and the flames spreading to the religious buildings, some of them were entirely consumed. The principal temple is a square building, of great dimensions, but very plain, dedicated to Krishna under the name of Cheluva-pulle Ráya.[1] The original name of the idol appears to

[1] Although the image represents *Krishna*, it is commonly called *Chilla pulla Ráya*, or the darling prince; for *Chillapulla* is a term of endearment which mothers give to their infants, somewhat like our word darling. The reason of such an uncommon appellation being given to a mighty warrior is said to be as follows:—On *Ramanuja's* going to *Melukote*, to perform his devotions at that celebrated shrine, he was informed that the place had been attacked by the *Turc* king of *Delhi*, who had carried away the idol. The *Brahman* immediately set out for that capital; and on his arrival he found that the king had made a present of the image to his daughter; for it is said to be very handsome, and she asked for it as a plaything. All day the princess played with the image; at night the god assumed his own beautiful form, and enjoyed her bed; for *Krishna* is addicted to such kinds of adventures. This had continued for some time when *Ramanuja* arrived, and called on the image, repeating at the same time some powerful *mantrams*; on which the idol immediately placed itself on the *Brahman's* knee. Having clasped it in his arms he called it his *Chillapulla*, and they were both instantaneously conveyed to *Melukote*. The princess, quite disconsolate for the loss of her image, mounted a horse and followed as fast as she was able. She was no sooner near the idol than she disappeared, and is supposed to have been taken into its immediate substance; which in this country is a common

have been Ráma-priya. A more striking edifice is the temple of Narasimha, placed on the very summit of the rock. The large temple is richly endowed, having been under the special patronage of the Mysore Rájas, and has a most valuable collection of jewels. As early as 1614 we find Rája Woḍeyar, who first acquired Seringapatam and adopted the Vaishnava faith, making over to the temple and Brahmans at Mélukóṭe the estate granted him by the Vijayanagar king Venkatapati Ráya. There is also an inscription of 1785, showing that even Tipu Sultan granted some elephants for the temple. The Vairamuḍi[1] festival, which is the chief annual celebration, is attended by 10,000 people. The guru of the S'ri Vaishnava Brahmans, styled the Parakálaswámi, lives at Mélukóṭe and Mysore. The site of a ruined palace of the Mysore Rájas, adjoining the great temple, has now been laid out as a public garden.

The inhabitants are nearly all Brahmans, 400 of whom are attached to the great temple and receive thence a daily allowance, some of them being men of learning. There is also a class of temple servants of Sudra extraction, consisting of musicians, dancing-girls, and Vaishnava or Sátánanas. The only persons in the place who live by industry are a few families of weavers and some shopkeepers. Two classes of Holeyas or outcastes, called the Tirukula and Jámbavakula, are credited with having assisted Rámánuja in recovering the image of Krishna when it was carried off to Delhi, as related in the note at foot. Hence they have the privilege of entering the temple once a year to pay their devotions. The houses are roofed with tiles, and have an odd look from being covered with thorns. This is to keep off the monkeys, which are very numerous, and which, bearing a sacred character, it would be a grievous sin to destroy.

Cloths of good quality are made here, and ornamental punkahs or fans of the fragrant roots of the kuskus grass. There are many different kinds of rock on the hill. A strata of schistose mica which has decayed into a fine white clay is considered sacred. It is said to have been discovered by Emberumánár or Rámánuja and is used by the S'ri Vaishnava Brahmans for making the *náma* or sectarian marks on their foreheads. It is in such demand for this purpose, on account of its purity, that it is transported to distant places, even as far as

way of the gods disposing of their favourites. A monument was built for the princess, but as she was a *Turc*, it would have been improper to place this building within the walls of the holy place; it has therefore been erected at the foot of the hill, under the most abrupt part of the rock.—Buchanan, *Journ.*, I, 342.

[1] Said to be a corruption of the words *Vajra mukuti*, diamond crown. Stolen from Vishnu by a serpent who carried it to Pátála, it was recovered by Garuda, and presented to Krishna.

Benares. It is fabled to have been brought to Mélukóṭe by Garutman, the bird of Vishnu, from Sveta-dvipa (the white island) in the Kshira-samudra (the milk ocean).

| Municipal Funds. | 1892–3. | 1893–4. | 1894–5. | 1895–6. |
|---|---|---|---|---|
| Income ... ... ... ... ... | 1,007 | 1,058 | 1,737 | 1,749 |
| Expenditure ... ... ... ... | 902 | 613 | 1,440 | 2,336 |

**Moti Talab**, or lake of pearls, a large tank at Tonnur in Seringapatam taluq. It is formed by an embankment carried across a gap between two rocky hills, which stems the water of the Yádava nadi and other mountain torrents that there unite their streams. The mound, whose dimensions are given as 78 cubits high, 150 long, and 250 thick at the base, is said to have been constructed by Rámánujáchárya, the S'ri Vaishnava Brahman reformer, who had taken up his abode at the neighbouring town of Mélukóṭe. He named the tank Tirumalaságara. The superfluous water is let off through a channel which has been cut with great labour through one of the hills, at such a height as to enable it to water a great portion of the subjacent plain, which is three or four miles in extent. When the tank is full it contains a sufficient quantity of water to supply the cultivators for two years; but owing to failure of rain the water frequently continues lower than the opening of the outlet. Although the torrents bring down much sand, it so happens that the tank is never affected by that circumstance; for the two streams enter in such directions as to force all the sand towards the extreme corners, without diminishing the main depth. Nasir Jung, son of the Subadar of the Deccan, who visited it in 1746, gave it the name of Moti Talab or lake of pearls, an appellation to which its clear and beautiful water perhaps entitles it. The bank was breached and the water drained off by Tipu Sultan in 1798, to prevent its being used by an enemy besieging Seringapatam.

**Moyar.**—A river which forms the southern boundary of the Mysore State. It rises in the Múkarti hill in the Nilagiris and flows north-east, having there the name of Paikaré. On reaching the edge of the plateau, it turns west and falls in a succession of cascades, known as the Paikara Falls (the upper 180 feet, and the lower 200 feet), to the tableland below. It then, for the rest of its course, flows east, running at the bottom of the singular gorge called the Mysore ditch, from its presenting the aspect of a long deep moat as seen from the crest of the ghats. Finally, after separating the Nilagiris from the Eastern Ghats at the Gajalhatti pass, it joins the Bhaváni in the Coimbatore District, at Devanáyakankota, below the Rangaswami peak.

**Muduk-dore.**—A sacred hill near Talakad on the banks of the Kávéri, where the river takes a sudden turn to the south. On the hill is a temple dedicated to Mallikarjuna, whose játre, held for fifteen days in January or February, is attended by 10,000 people.

**Mugur.**—A large village in Tirumakúdlu-Narsipur taluq, situated 6 miles south by east of Narsipur. Head-quarters of the Múgúr hobli. Population 3,735.

It has a temple of Tibba Devi, which is the scene of an annual festival in December or January, resorted to by 2,000 people. There is also a palace belonging to one of the members of the Mysore royal family.

**Mysore.**—A taluq towards the centre. Area 322 square miles. Head-quarters at Mysore. Contains the following hoblis, villages and population :—

| No. | Hoblis. | Villages. | Hamlets. | Villages classified. | | | | Population. |
|---|---|---|---|---|---|---|---|---|
| | | | | Govern-ment. | Sarva-mánya. | Jodi. | Kayam-gutta. | |
| 1 | Anandúru ... ... | 19 | 5 | 14 | 4 | — | 1 | 5,644 |
| 2 | Ilavála ... ... | 19 | 19 | 16 | 2 | — | 1 | 7,290 |
| 3 | Kúdluhalli ... ... | 19 | 9 | 17 | 2 | — | — | 7,085 |
| 4 | Lingámbudhi ... | 23 | 19 | 20 | 2 | 1 | — | 8,830 |
| 5 | Mysore ... ... | 8 | 5 | 8 | — | — | — | 76,227 |
| 6 | Naváshahar ... ... | 5 | 2 | 5 | — | — | — | 2,237 |
| 7 | Sindhuvalli ... ... | 33 | 11 | 24 | 7 | — | 2 | 14,143 |
| 8 | Varakódu ... ... | 24 | 19 | 19 | 4 | — | 1 | 13,228 |
| | Total ... | 150 | 89 | 123 | 21 | 1 | 5 | 134,684 |

*Principal places, with population.*—Mysore, 74,048; Kadakola, 1,935; Udabúr, 1,736; Varakódu, 1,552; Yedakola, 1,520; Dhanagahalli, 1,482; Sindhavalli, 1,328; Vájamangala, 1,282; Ayirahalli, 1,164; Dúra, 1,119; Ilavála, 1,093; Tuptegála, 1,059.

The taluq was extended by the addition of the Naváshahar and Varakód hoblis from Mysore Ashtagram taluq in 1871. It lies between the Kávéri on the north and east, and the Kabbani on the south, though these rivers are beyond the boundaries and actually touch the taluq for a very short distance. The drainage is principally from north to south, to the Kabbani. The nature of the country is undulating. There are few hills, the only one of importance being the Chámundi hill, overlooking the city of Mysore from the south-east, and rising to about 1,000 feet above it. In the south-west there is a little scrub jungle, and wild date trees abound in all nálas and low-lying places.

A comparatively small extent of land is benefited by the river channels drawn from the Kávéri and the Lakshmantirtha. The Virajánadi and Devaráya channels irrigate a few villages to the east, and the Anandur channel a few in the north-west. There are 361 tanks, of which five are of the first class. The soil in wet lands is generally of superior quality, except under some of the channels. The soil in dry lands is mostly shallow and stony, with a large admixture of sand. But they vary much both in quality and depth. The prevailing colour is red. The dry crops are those usually grown in Mysore, there being two distinct seasons for sowing—the *káru* and the *hainu*. Rice and sugar-cane are grown under the channels, and the former under some tanks. Cocoa-nut, areca-nut, betel vines and plantains are largely grown, with vegetables and minor garden produce, around Mysore.

The revenue settlement was introduced in 1887. The area of the taluq was thus distributed :—

| | |
|---|---|
| Culturable (dry, 100,062 ; wet, 3,642 ; gardens, 4,191) ... ... | 107,895 |
| Unculturable (including village sites, roads, &c.) ... ... ... | 58,309 |
| Inám villages (28,958) ; 1 Amrit Mahál kával (759) ... ... | 29,617 |
| Total acres ... ... ... | 195,921 |

The unoccupied area was 11,514 acres. The total revenue demand for 1891–2 (15 months) was Rs. 1,62,786, and for 1892–3 it was Rs. 2,55,101.

The average rainfall at Mysore for 26 years (1870–95) was as follows :—

| | Jan. | Feb. | Mar. | Apr. | May | June | July | Aug. | Sept. | Oct. | Nov. | Dec. | Year. |
|---|---|---|---|---|---|---|---|---|---|---|---|---|---|
| Taluq Cutcherry | 0·10 | 0·11 | 0·58 | 1·97 | 4·90 | 2·17 | 2·21 | 3·00 | 3·22 | 6·74 | 1·54 | 0·36... | 26·90 |
| Jail Hospital ... | 0·10 | 0·07 | 0·63 | 2·14 | 5·65 | 2·25 | 2·27 | 3·11 | 3·81 | 7·58 | 2·28 | 0·60... | 30·49 |

The Mysore State railway passes through the taluq from north to south, with stations at Mysore and Kadakola. The Bangalore-Ootacamand road passes through Mysore, whence there are also roads to Bannur north-east, to Malavalli east, to Tirumakúdlu-Narsipur south-east, to the Wainad south-west, and *viâ* Yelwal on the north-west to Coorg and to Hassan.

**Mysore.**—The capital of the Province and residence of the Mahárája: situated in 12° 18′ north latitude and 76° 42′ east longitude, at the north-western base of the Chámundi hill.

It contains four suburbs and covers an area of 7½ square miles. The population numbers 74,048, of whom 36,691 are males and 37,357 females. The number of inhabited houses is 12,546; of which 197 are terraced, 10,462 tiled, and 1,887 thatched. The population is composed of the following classes :—

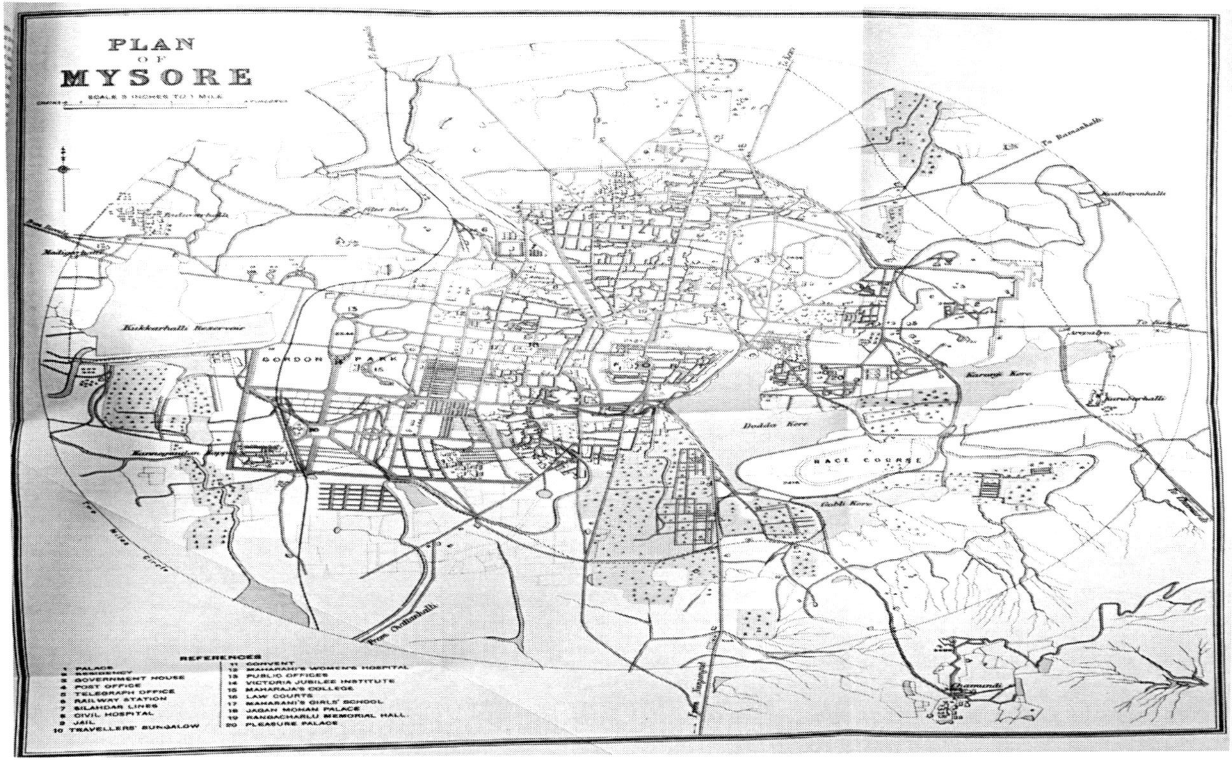
PLAN
OF
MYSORE
SCALE 3 INCHES TO 1 MILE
Kukkarhalli Reservoir
GORDON PARK
Karanji Kere
Dodda Kere
RACE COURSE
Gobli Kere
Chamundi
REFERENCES
1 PALACE
2 RESIDENCY
3 GOVERNMENT HOUSE
4 POST OFFICE
5 TELEGRAPH OFFICE
6 RAILWAY STATION
7 SILAHDAR LINES
8 CIVIL HOSPITAL
9 JAIL
10 TRAVELLERS' BUNGALOW
11 CONVENT
12 MAHARANI'S WOMEN'S HOSPITAL
13 PUBLIC OFFICES
14 VICTORIA JUBILEE INSTITUTE
15 MAHARAJA'S COLLEGE
16 LAW COURTS
17 MAHARANI'S GIRLS' SCHOOL
18 JAGAN MOHAN PALACE
19 RANGACHARLU MEMORIAL HALL
20 PLEASURE PALACE

| Population in 1891. | Males. | Females. | Total. |
|---|---|---|---|
| Hindus (with 237 Jains) ... .. ... ... | 28,315 | 28,738 | 57,053 |
| Muhammadans ... ... ... ... ... ... | 7,540 | 7,767 | 15,307 |
| Christians ... ... ... ... ... ... | 813 | 827 | 1,640 |
| Others (17 Parsis, 27 Sikhs, 4 Jews) ... ... | 23 | 25 | 48 |
| Total ... ... ... | 36,691 | 37,357 | 74,048 |

The population of the city was 57,815 in 1871, and 60,292 in 1881. It therefore increased by over 28 per cent. in the 20 years.

The city is built in a valley formed by two ridges, running north and south. There is also a slight ascent on the northern side. The streets out of the fort were comparatively broad and regular, and contained many substantial houses, some of them two or three storeys high. Within the fort, which is in the southern quarter, the streets were narrow and irregular, and most of the former houses had a mean and squalid appearance. But the great extension of the city, especially to the south-west, during recent years, and the immense improvements introduced on all sides have so completely transformed the place that persons who knew Mysore as it was twenty years ago would hardly recognise the present handsome and growing city, with its magnificent wide roads and imposing buildings.

The new portion of the town, called (after the late Mahárája) Chámarájapura, has more than doubled its area. Conspicuous on the high ground to the west, in Gordon Park, are the Public Offices, surmounted by a dome, with the statue of Sir James Gordon in front of the building. Close by are the Victoria Jubilee Institute and the pile of the Mahárája's College buildings, somewhat resembling a French château. Farther west are the groups of the Law Courts. The Maharani's Girls' School, Mari Mallapa's School, the Wesleyan Hardwicke College, and a Roman Catholic Church are among other large erections that catch the eye in this new quarter. A suitable railway station still remains to be built.

In the older parts of the city the changes have been equally striking. The most important perhaps has been the filling in of the portentous great drain known as Purnaiya's Nullah. Its place has been taken by a fine wide road, called Sayáji Rao road after the Gaikawar of Baroda. Other distinguished visitors have been similarly commemorated. One fine road is thus named the Albert Victor road; the new Devaráj Market has in front of it the Dufferin Fountain; and the Sayáji Rao road is flanked by the Lansdowne Bazaars, a picturesque two-storeyed range extending along the west of the Fort.

The *Fort* is of a quadrangular ground plan, three of the sides being about 450 yards in length, and the remaining or south side somewhat longer. The gates are situated on the north, south and west; those on the north and south are protected by out-works. Flanking towers command the curtain at frequent intervals; there is a casemate at the south-eastern, and a parapeted cavalier at the north-eastern angle, but the defences are mean and ill-planned. A ditch was carried round the fort and a sloping glacis, covered with houses abutting on it on all sides but the east, where the fort ditch is separated from the Dévaráj tank only by the high road to Nanjangud. The interior of the fort was crowded with houses, principally occupied by retainers of the palace. All this has now been changed. The ditch has been filled up and ornamental shrubberies and gardens laid out round the fort. The most crowded parts of the interior have been cleared out and general improvements introduced. In the open space outside the east gate are the Rangacharla Memorial Hall and other large buildings, and it is proposed to erect here an equestrian statue of the late Mahárája.

The palace of the Mahárája, which is situated inside the fort, facing nearly due east, is built in the ultra Hindu style, and, with the exception of a few paintings executed by European painters at various times in the palace employ, contains little trace of the influence of European art. The front, which is gaudily painted and supported by four elaborately carved wooden pillars, comprises the Sejjé or Dasara hall, an open gallery where the Mahárája is in the habit of showing himself to the people on great occasions, seated on his throne. This throne is one of the articles of interest in the palace. The original structure, which was of fig-wood overlaid with ivory, is generally stated to have been sent by Aurangzeb to Chikka Déva Rája in 1699; but some doubt has been thrown on this assertion by Colonel Wilks. The palace legend runs that it was discovered buried at Penugonda, by the founders of the Vijayanagar empire, Hakka or Harihara and Bukka, to whom its locality was revealed by an ascetic named Vidyáraṇya, and that it was handed down from dynasty to dynasty until it came into the possession of Rája Wodeyar. According to the same legend, it had once been the throne of the Pándus, who reigned at Hastinápura, and Kampula Rája is said to have brought it thence and buried it at Penugonda. It is certain, however, that the ivory throne was used by Chikka Déva Rája and his successors up to the accession of Tipu Sultan; that it was discovered in a lumber room of the Muhammadan palace after the downfall of Seringapatam, and employed at the coronation of the restored Rája. Since then it has entirely lost its original character, the ivory which covered the fig-wood of which the throne is made having been in its turn overlaid with gold and silver plating, which is carved into figures relating to Hindu mythology; the *simha*, or popular Hindu representation of a lion, whence the Sanskrit term for throne derives its name, being predominant, while the *hamsa*, a mythical bird, regarding which the legend runs that the head on which its shadow falls will once be encircled by a crown, surmounts the structure. As the crown in Travancore, so the throne is the peculiar emblem of royalty in Mysore, and on this account the Mysore Rája is distinguished by the appellation of Simhásanádhipati or ruler enthroned. Another seat, known as Bhadrásana or the auspicious seat, is used for minor ceremonies.

To revert to the palace, its principal gate opens on a passage under the Sejje, leading to an open yard. At the further or west side of this courtyard is the door leading to the women's apartments, which occupy most of the western portion of the palace.[1] The northern side comprises various offices, such as the armoury, library, &c.; and on the south are the rooms occupied by the Mahárája. Of these the most interesting is the Ambá viḻása, an upstair room sixty-five feet square and ten feet high, with a raised ceiling in the centre. It was here that the former Rája received his European guests and transacted the ordinary business of the day. A wooden railing separated that portion of the room in which the Rája's seat was placed from the rest, and the adjacent wall was hung with pictures, principally of officers connected at different periods with Mysore, which His Highness was accustomed to uncover and point out to his European visitors. The floor was of chunam, and, with the exception of the doors, which were overlaid with richly carved ivory or silver, there was no attempt at magnificence or display. This hall has been recently entirely renewed in more modern style, and the ceiling raised on handsome iron pillars. The sleeping and eating apartments of the Rája, which are for the most part small and confined, all opened upon the Ambá viḻása, and just outside it was the stall in which was kept the cow worshipped by His Highness. The chapel is adjacent. Although the palace had been almost entirely built since the year 1800, it was in very bad repair, and many of the tenements attached to it were crumbling to ruin. The only remaining portion of the palace of the old Hindu dynasty, which Tipu Sultan demolished, is a room in the interior, with mud walls of great thickness and stability. This is known as the Painted Hall, owing to the decoration of its ceiling, and is said to have been the state room of the old palace, which was a much less pretentious building. As

[1] In February 1897, this and other parts were damaged by fire, and are being rebuilt with more durable and less combustible materials.

with most oriental courts, there was no attempt at isolation, and except in front, where there is an open space, the palace was pressed close on all sides by the dwellings of the poorer inhabitants.

Opposite the northern gate of the Fort is a lofty building known as the Jagan Móhan Mahal, intended by the former Rája as an ornament to the town and a place of amusement for the European officers. The walls of the upper storey are painted with pictures, in many cases verging on the grotesque, representing the Rája in procession on shikár expeditions, and so forth. Another of the royal buildings is the Summer Palace, situated some distance east of the Fort. Here the late Mahárája received his instruction and the present Mahárája is doing the same. Adjoining it are the royal stables and a zoological garden. In the grounds is an old maze. In the same direction, to the south-east, is the new race-course, near the base of the Chamundi hill. The old race-course at Hinikal, some miles to the west, was given up in 1893.

The houses of the European residents are situated east of the town. The former Residency is now known as Government House, and is reserved for European guests. The front portion of the building, which possesses a large and handsome portico, was erected in 1805, under Major Wilks, and is of the Doric order of architecture. The back was added a few years later by Sir John Malcolm, and comprises one of the largest rooms without pillars in Southern India. It was designed by de Havilland. The present Residency is well situated on rising ground to the east, with an extensive view over Mysore. It was originally the residence of Dr. Campbell, the Durbar Surgeon in Sir Mark Cubbon's time. But Sir James Gordon, who had occupied it when guardian to the Mahárája, converted it into the Residency in 1881. Of the other European houses, one opposite the west gate of Government House awakens interest from the fact that it was built and for some time occupied by the great Duke of Wellington, then Colonel Wellesley.

The present town of Mysore cannot perhaps boast of much antiquity. But the place seems to have been known by its present name from the remotest times. For it corresponds with the Mahishmati of the Pándava prince Sahadeva's expedition mentioned in the Mahá Bhárata, and is the Mahisha to which the Maurya king Asoka sent a missionary in the 3rd century B.C. to proclaim the religion of Buddha. We find Maisunád or Maisur-nád mentioned in inscriptions of the 11th and 12th centuries, and the Yádava princes from Dváraka in Gujarat who, according to inscriptions, coming to worship their family god at Yadugiri or Melukote, became the founders of the Mysore house, are said to have been attracted by the beauty of the country to settle in the town of Mahishúr. But at the beginning of the 16th century its site was occupied by a village named Puragere. At this time the dominions of the Rája of Vijayanagar, the ancient city on the banks of the Tunga-bhadra, extended really or nominally over nearly the whole of South India. The tradition regarding the origin of the present Mysore dynasty, which savours of the age of knight-errantry, is given under Hadináru. The first of the line took the title of Wodeyar, and his successors gradually extended their little dominions until one of them named Bettada Cháma Rája divided his country between his three sons.[1] To Cháma Rája, surnamed Ból or the bald, he gave Puragere. Here a fort was either constructed or repaired in the year 1524, to which, from Mahishásura or the buffalo-headed monster whose overthrow was the most noted exploit of Káli or Chámundi, the name of Mahishúr (buffalo town), or in its Anglicised form Mysore, was again given. Fort after fort was subdued, and the limits of the country followed the progress of invading armies to the south. But till the beginning of the 17th century each successive Wodeyar or Arasu paid tribute to the viceroy of Seringapatam, who derived his power from the Rája of Vijayanagar; and an old manuscript affords a curious picture of the simplicity of the age and the poverty of the Mysore Arasu, who is stated to have been obliged to live on rági until a grant of wet land on the Kávéri from the viceroy at Seringapatam enabled him to procure rice for his table. But in proportion as the power of the viceroys became more and more effete, that of the Mysore Arasus grew stronger and stronger: the latter gradually evaded payment of tribute to the former, and in 1610, whether by fair means or foul is uncertain, obtained possession of Seringapatam itself, and with it what remained of the power and influence of the viceroys. Thenceforth Seringapatam became the seat of government of the Arasus.

It does not fall within the scope or purpose of this part of the work to follow the gradual expansion of the Mysore State under the Arasus, who in 1731 became subservient to the ends of the Dalaváyi or hereditary State minister and general; nor to describe the transformation of Mysore to a Musalmán state under the usurper Haidar Ali, who kept the representatives of the Hindu dynasty in the position of State prisoners in their own palace at Seringapatam. Haidar's son Tipu attempted to obliterate all traces of the Hindu ráj, and in pursuance of this policy caused the town and fort of Mysore, the ancient residence of the Rájas, to be razed to the ground, and deported all the inhabitants

[1] Wilks says:—"A grant is extant, dated in 1548, from Tim Ráj, probably the same to whom Hemanhally was assigned."—*Hist.*, Ch. II, p. 22.

to the neighbourhood of Seringapatam. The stones of the old fort he employed in building another fortress, on a slight eminence about a mile to the east, to which he gave the appellation, still retained by the site, of Nazarábád, or the place visited by the eye of the Almighty, and the remains of this fort are still to be seen.

The work, which, according to Major Wilks, could not have been of the slightest use in defending the country, was still unfinished at the fall of Seringapatam in 1799; and when it had been determined that the inauguration of the Rája, then a child of four years old, should take place at Mysore, it was discovered that, owing to the almost universal demolition of the place by Tipu, the workmen's huts at Nazarábád formed the only accommodation available for the performance of the ceremony. Into the best of these the young Rája was conducted and placed on the throne, while the work of rebuilding the palace of his ancestors was going on. The restoration of the fort was commenced at the same time, and for this purpose the stones which Tipu had removed to Nazarábád were brought back again. Owing to the presence of the court the town grew rapidly, and in time drew to itself much of the population of Seringapatam, which decreased as Mysore increased in importance. The Rája, at first through the Dewán Púrnaiya, continued to govern the country till 1831, when in consequence of disturbances in the north of Mysore a clause of the treaty of 1799 was put in force, and the government was vested in a Commission composed chiefly of British officers and subordinate to the Government of India.

The Rája still continued to reside in his palace at Mysore, and the settlement on him of one-fifth of the revenue of the country enabled him in a great measure to give reins to the princely liberality which formed the chief element in his character. He died at Mysore on the 27th of March 1868, aged 75, the oldest sovereign in India. It seemed almost hard to believe that the Rája who so short a time ago was on his throne in full possession of his faculties, was a man whose early childhood had been subject to the caprice of Tipu Sultan, and who remembered the great Duke of Wellington while yet in his prime: so completely had he outlived associations. Immediately after his death his adopted son, by name Cháma Rájéndra Wodeyar, a child of four years old, was proclaimed Mahárája, and in 1881 the country was restored to him and again placed under Hindu government. During his reign of 13 years took place the gradual transformation of Mysore into the handsome city it now promises to become. And after his lamented death at the close of 1894, his eldest son, then 10 years of age, was proclaimed Mahárája, under the regency of his mother, the Mahárání.

*Municipality.*—The municipality is conducted under Mysore Regulation III of 1888, and is presided over by the Deputy Commissioner, with the Town Magistrate as Vice-President. There are eight wards or municipal divisions, called Mohallas, of which a list is given in the margin. Besides the President and Vice-President there are 20 Municipal Commissioners, half of whom are either *ex-officio* or nominated by Government, and the other half elected. The privilege of election was granted in 1892, and out of 985 qualified voters 695 went to the polls. The Commissioners are elected for two years.

*Mohallas.*
I. Fort.
II. Lashkar.
III. Devarái.
IV. Krishnaráj.
V. Mandi.
VI. Chámaráj.
VII. Nazarábád.
VIII. I'rangéri.

Of the various improvements carried out in municipal limits many have been largely aided by Government funds and executed by the Public Works Department, as they were quite beyond the means of the municipality. In 1886 a complete system of drainage was provided for the Fort, and by the acquisition of houses on payment of compensation some broad streets were opened out, and the precincts of the palace greatly improved. The sanitation of some other parts of the old town are still very defective. The Municipal Report says that "in the Mandi, Lashkar and Devaráj Mohallas the houses are crowded together in all manner of ways, lanes in some places being too narrow even for one man to go through, and too crooked to admit of straight cuts of even 20 yards in their whole length. In these lanes also soak the sewage water of all the adjoining houses, so that only those long accustomed to the spots can walk there during nights without soiling their feet, and without knocking their heads against the walls of the houses." Proposals to improve these conditions are, notwithstanding, strongly opposed by the people generally. But a system of conservancy is being gradually introduced.

The most beneficial undertaking has been the provision of a pure water supply. For this purpose the Kukarhalli reservoir was formed towards the high ground on the west, and water has been for several years laid on to all parts of the city in iron mains, from which it is drawn off at hydrants and stand-pipes or fountains at all convenient points in the streets. A high level reservoir has also been constructed, the water in which is drawn from the Kávéri river near Anandur, and forced up with the aid of turbines erected there.

The operations connected with suitably laying out and populating the large western extension of Chámaráj pura, by sale of sites, &c., were entrusted to a special Building Committee. The results have been already generally described. An interesting movement has been the migration of a number of families of the weaver caste from Salem to settle in Mysore. For their accommodation a special site was granted in the new Mohalla, and a local sahukár has undertaken, with advances from Government, the erection of the necessary houses and buildings for them.

The following is a statement of the income and expenditure of the municipality for five years to 1895-6:—

| Receipts. | 1891-2. | 1892-3. | 1893-4. | 1894-5. | 1895-6. |
|---|---|---|---|---|---|
| Octroi ... ... ... | 59,687 | 60,226 | 58,048 | 58,650 | 60,000 |
| Tax on houses, buildings and lands ... ... ... | 14,611 | 11,692 | 11,993 | 15,000 | 15,000 |
| Licenses ... ... ... | 6,369 | 7,513 | 8,650 | 14,720 | 9,237 |
| Carriage tax .. ... ... | 797 | 247 | 567 | 470 | 470 |
| Tax on Animals ... ... | 1,487 | 499 | 848 | 930 | 930 |
| Mohatarfa ... ... ... | 9,624 | 8,230 | 7,964 | 9,000 | 9,000 |
| Rents ... ... ... | 4,625 | 4,311 | 6,915 | 5,320 | 6,130 |
| Fines ... ... .. ... | 25 | — | 6 | 50 | 10 |
| Miscellaneous ... ... | 5,769 | 7,058 | 13,402 | 5,380 | 6,250 |
| Adjustment of advances ... | — | 8,159 | 12,503 | — | — |
| Total Rs. ... ... | 1,02,994 | 1,07,945 | 1,20,896 | 1,09,520 | 1,07,027 |

| Expenditure. | 1891-2. | 1892-3. | 1893-4. | 1894-5. | 1895-6. |
|---|---|---|---|---|---|
| Head Office ... ... ... | 3,505 | 3,693 | 7,161 | 8,963 | 7,763 |
| Collection .. ... ... | 10,615 | 9,729 | 8,557 | 9,216 | 9,216 |
| Conservancy ... ... | 25,628 | 21,474 | 23,912 | 24,742 | 23,992 |
| Registration of Births and Deaths ... ... ... | 101 | 180 | 177 | 280 | 280 |
| Lighting ... ... ... | 5,632 | 6,202 | 5,328 | 7,760 | 6,260 |
| Public Works ... ... | 23,555 | 23,336 | 32,087 | 41,112 | 32,512 |
| Charitable Grants .. ... | 921 | 3,557 | 4,371 | 5,584 | 5,360 |
| Education ... ... ... | 11,915 | 10,222 | 9,346 | 9,696 | 9,696 |
| Miscellaneous ... ... | 9,119 | 22,094 | 10,195 | 14,593 | 14,793 |
| Advances ... ... ... | — | 7,724 | 7,792 | — | — |
| Total Rs. ... ... | 90,991 | 1,08,211 | 1,08,928 | 1,21,946 | 1,09,872 |

**Nágamangala.**—A taluq in the north, transferred from the Hassan District in 1882. Area 401 square miles. Head-quarters at Nágamangala. Contains the following hoblis, villages and population:—

| No. | Hoblis. | Villages. | Hamlets. | Villages classified. | | | | Population. |
|---|---|---|---|---|---|---|---|---|
| | | | | Government. | Sarvamánya. | Jodi. | Kayamgutta. | |
| 1 | Bindiganavile ... | 49 | 19 | 48 | — | 1 | — | 9,023 |
| 2 | Devalápura ... ... | 52 | 35 | 49 | — | 3 | — | 10,046 |
| 3 | Honakere ... ... | 86 | 50 | 71 | 1 | 12 | 2 | 17,450 |
| 4 | Nágamangala ... | 73 | 36 | 68 | 1 | 3 | 1 | 16,512 |
| 5 | Nelligere ... ... | 94 | 33 | 93 | — | 1 | — | 16,234 |
| | Total ... | 354 | 173 | 329 | 2 | 20 | 3 | 69,265 |

*Principal places, with population.*—Nágamangala, 2,938; Bellúr, 1,484.

The Shimsha forms part of the eastern boundary, and receives nearly all the smaller streams of the taluq. The Lokopávani has its source in the south-west. The country is generally pretty level, except for some low rocky hills in the north and west, more or less covered with scrub jungle. The principal point is called Chunchangiri. To the west of Nágamangala is a hill of talcose argillite, closely resembling potstone, and used by the natives in the same way for pencils. The number of tanks is about 130, of which some 30 are of considerable size; but many of them shallow from being silted up. There are no other means of irrigation.

The dry crop soils are mostly indifferent, sandy, gravelly and shallow soil being common. But good red soil is also met with; black soil is very uncommon. The soil of the wet lands is fairly good, but rather too sandy. Rági is the staple crop. In the vicinity of the rocky hills a coarse kind of rice is grown in situations where, from percolation of moisture, ordinary dry crops cannot be raised. Rice is almost the only wet crop, sugar-cane being rarely grown. The gardens are poor, and the famine destroyed all the areca-nut trees, leaving only a certain amount of cocoa-nut trees.

Sheep are everywhere abundant, and a sheep farm was at one time maintained by Government at Heriganhalli. But it was given up in 1863. The cattle, as a rule, are small, but fine draught-bullocks, which are bred locally, are met with in most villages and fetch a high price. Karadihalli is the centre of a tract specially given to the breeding and rearing of Hallikar cattle. Brass work of various kinds is an industry of Nágamangala.

In the middle of the 15th century there was a family of chiefs who called themselves Lords of Nágamangala. They were of the Lohita family, and inscriptions mention the following:—Singanna Wodeyar, whose wife was Sitámbika. His son, Timmanna Dannáyaka, whose wife was Rangámbika or Ranga Náyaki; he was minister to the Vijayanagar king Mallikárjuna or Immaḍi Prauḍha Deva Rája (1446–1467), and rebuilt Melukote. He was apparently the first who erected a fort on the island of Seringapatam. Deva Rája, son of Singaṇṇa Woḍeyar; he built a new dam on the Kávéri and led a channel from it to Harahu, now called Haravu. This family apparently did not survive the disaster which broke up the Vijayanagar empire. For at the end of the 16th century we find Nágamangala included in the territory bestowed upon Jagadeva Ráya of Channapatna (Bangalore District) for his gallant defence of Penugonda against the Muhammadans. From him it was taken by the Rája of Mysore in 1630. Being in the line of march of the Mahrattas to Seringapatam, it more than once suffered during the last century from their depredations, which have left their mark upon the taluq.

The revenue settlement was introduced in 1888. The area of the taluq was thus distributed :—

| | |
|---|---|
| Culturable (dry, 100,695; wet, 4,783; garden, 1,600) ... ... | 107,087 |
| Unculturable (including roads, village sites, &c.) ... ... ... | 125,905 |
| Inám villages ... ... ... ... ... ... ... ... | 8,926 |
| Forests (838); kávals (2,949) ... ... ... ... ... | 3,787 |
| Total acres ... ... | 245,705 |

The unoccupied area was 10,968 acres. The total revenue demand for 1891–2 (15 months) was Rs. 1,36,926, and for 1892–3 it was Rs. 1,48,616.

The average rainfall at Nágamangala for 26 years (1870–95), and at the other station for 3 years (1893–5) was as follows :—

| | Jan. | Feb. | Mar. | Apr. | May | June | July | Aug. | Sept. | Oct. | Nov. | Dec. | Year. |
|---|---|---|---|---|---|---|---|---|---|---|---|---|---|
| Nágamangala | 0·05 | 0·15 | 0·26 | 1·46 | 4·65 | 1·60 | 1·10 | 2·98 | 4·11 | 7·67 | 2·91 | 0·47 | ... 27·41 |
| Nelligere | — | 0·10 | 0·50 | 2·34 | 4·56 | 3·13 | 2·71 | 2·74 | 7·22 | 12·58 | 3·34 | 0·15 | ... 39·37 |

Another register for Nelligere for 4 years gives the annual average as 35·93.

The Bangalore-Hassan trunk road passes through the north of the taluq from east to west, and is crossed at Nelligere by the Seringapatam-Sira road, which runs north through French Rocks and Nágamangala. From the latter there is a road south-west to Krishnarájpet, and two unfinished roads west to Sravan Belgola and south-east to Basarál and Mandya.

**Nágamangala.**—A town situated in 12° 49′ N. lat., 76° 49′ E. long., on the Seringapatam-Sira road, 24 miles north of the railway at French Rocks, and 39 miles north of Mysore. Head-quarters of the Nágamangala taluq, and a municipality.

| Population in 1891. | Males. | Females. | Total. |
|---|---|---|---|
| Hindus ... ... ... ... ... ... ... | 1,041 | 1,041 | 2,085 |
| Muhammadans .. ... ... ... ... ... | 297 | 285 | 582 |
| Total ... ... ... | 1,338 | 1,326 | 2,667 |

It contains the remains of some fine temples and royal buildings. The inner fort was erected in 1270 by Chaimi Dannáyak, and a line of chiefs of the Lohita family continued to be lords of Nágamangala till the end of the 15th century or longer. The outer fort was erected in 1578 by Jagadeva Ráyal of Channapatna (Bangalore District), of whose dominions Nágamangala was one of the chief towns. It was captured in 1630 by Cháma Rája Wodeyar of Mysore. The town was reduced to ruins in 1792 by the Mahratta army under Parasu Ram Bhao, and 150,000 palm-trees were destroyed. Brass artistic work is made at Nágamangala.

| Municipal Funds. | 1892–3. | 1893–4. | 1894–5. | 1895–6. |
|---|---|---|---|---|
| Income ... ... ... ... ... | 534 | 581 | 908 | 984 |
| Expenditure ... ... ... .. ... | 368 | 399 | 956 | 1,125 |

**Nanjangud.**—A taluq in the centre southwards. Area 384 square miles. Head-quarters at Nanjangud. Contains the following hoblis, villages and population:—

| No. | Hoblis. | Villages. | Hamlets. | Villages classified. | | | | Population. |
|---|---|---|---|---|---|---|---|---|
| | | | | Govern-ment. | Sarva-mánya. | Jodi. | Kayam-gutta. | |
| 1 | Dásanúr ... ... | 17 | 8 | 17 | — | — | — | 7,043 |
| 2 | Dévanúr ... ... | 6 | 4 | 6 | — | — | — | 6,024 |
| 3 | Hadinâru ... ... | 8 | 9 | 6 | 2 | — | — | 7,100 |
| 4 | Heḍatale ... ... | 15 | 6 | 11 | 4 | — | — | 10,904 |
| 5 | Hura ... ... | 41 | 11 | 38 | 3 | — | — | 10,015 |
| 6 | Kalale ... ... | 49 | 15 | 34 | 11 | 3 | 1 | 18,689 |
| 7 | Nanjangúḍu ... | 28 | 16 | 21 | 6 | — | 1 | 17,839 |
| 8 | Rámpura .. ... | 15 | 12 | 15 | — | — | — | 6,654 |
| 9 | Táyúr ... ... | 20 | 18 | 16 | 2 | 2 | — | 13,106 |
| | Total ... | 199 | 99 | 164 | 28 | 5 | 2 | 97,374 |

*Principal places, with population.*—Nanjangúḍu, 6,912; Tagaḍúr, 2,805; Kalale, 2,067; Hadináru, 1,857; Devanúr, 1,742; Heḍatale, 1,622; Nerale, 1,574; Hullahalli, 1,517; Hemmaragála, 1,474;

Alaganji, 1,461; Ganaganúr, 1,415; Kudlapura, 1,378; Táyúr, 1,339; Hosakóṭe, 1,301; Belagali, 1,218; Debbúr, 1,156; Badanaválu, 1,149; Rampura, 1,107; Tummanerale, 1,094; Viradevanpura, 1,075; Kiragunda, 1,075; Kárya, 1,062; Dasanúr, 1,006.

The taluq was extended in 1882 by the addition of Táyúr hobli from Talakád taluq, and Devanúr and Dásanúr hoblis from Chámarájnagar taluq.

The Kabbani runs from west to east along the north of the taluq, and at Nanjangúd receives from the south the Gundal, which waters the central and eastern portions. There was not much wet cultivation, what there was depending upon rain-fed tanks. But the recent extension of the Rampur channel has brought more land under irrigation. The largest tank is the Narsámbudhi, two miles south of the kasba. A considerable quantity of jóla is grown.

Gold-mining has commenced at Wolgere, to the south-west of Nanjangúd. In the north-west of the taluq are some quarries of potstone intermixed in layers with schistose mica.

Nanjangúd is the present terminus of the Mysore State Railway from Bangalore. The Mysore-Trichinopoly road *viâ* the Hásanúr ghat runs through Nanjangúd, near to which the high road to Ootacamund branches off. There is also a road from Kaulandi to Yelandur. A road runs from Nanjangúd east to Tirumakúdlu-Narsipur, and west to Hullahalli, turning south to Hura. The road from Begur to Heggadadevankote crosses the south-west of the taluq.

The total revenue demand for 1891–2 (15 months) was Rs. 2,13,692, and for 1892–3 it was Rs. 2,50,172.

The average rainfall at Nanjangúd for 26 years (1870–95) was as follows:—

| Jan. | Feb. | March | April | May | June | July | Aug. | Sept. | Oct. | Nov. | Dec. | | Year. |
|---|---|---|---|---|---|---|---|---|---|---|---|---|---|
| 0·07 | 0·03 | 0·44 | 2·39 | 5·36 | 1·61 | 1·78 | 2·51 | 6·08 | 5·86 | 2·48 | 0·45 | ... | 26·66 |

**Nanjangúd.**—A town situated 12° 7′ N. lat., 76 45′ E. long., on the right bank of the Kabbani, 12 miles south of Mysore, at the point where the trunk road from Mysore branches to Ootacamund and to the Hásanúr ghat. Head-quarters of the Nanjangúd taluq, and a municipality. It is the present terminus of the Mysore State Railway.

| Population in 1891. | Males. | Females. | Total. |
|---|---|---|---|
| Hindus ... ... ... ... ... ... ... | 2,718 | 3,002 | 5,720 |
| Muhammadans ... ... .. ... .. | 319 | 343 | 662 |
| Jains ... ... ... .. ... ... ... | 13 | 14 | 27 |
| Total ... ... ... | 3,050 | 3,359 | 6,409 |

The early history of the place has been already related (p. 222). It is now noted for its temple dedicated to Nanjundésvara, an appellation given to Siva on account of one of his exploits in swallowing poison, and it is from this attribute of the god that the town derives its name. A temple of small dimensions is said to have existed from time immemorial. In one part of the temple are 66 images of Saiva saints, the *tiruttondar*, which may be of Chola origin, of the 11th century. But Karachúr Nandi Rája, and afterwards Púrnaiya, enlarged the temple to its present size. The former prince made Nanjangúd his favourite place of abode and fortified it. A celebrated car-festival, which lasts for three days, and is resorted to by thousands of devotees from all parts of South India, is held here at the end of March. The temple is 385 feet long by 160 broad, and supported by 147 columns. Some of the images are carved with great perfection of finish. Surrounding the outside of the temple are the figures of various deities with their names below, so that each votary can find his patron saint. The *gopura* was erected in 1845 by Mummadi Krishna Raja Wodeyar, and various shrines were added by the royal ladies down to 1853. This temple is inferior in point of sanctity to none in the Mysore District, and receives an annual allowance from Government of Rs. 20,197. At the point where a stream called the Chúrnavati from the tank runs into the Gundal or Kaundinya river is the Parasu Rama kshetra, with a temple of Parasu Rama. The moist earth around, called *mritika*, is considered an effective application for various skin diseases, and is being continually carried away to be used for such purposes. But the excavations speedily fill up again.

About a mile from Nanjangúd is a fine bungalow attached to the Mysore Residency, near to which is a rude stone bridge across the Kabbani, constructed about 120 years ago by Deva Ráj, the Dalavâyi of Mysore.

| Municipal Funds. | 1892-3. | 1893-4. | 1894-5. | 1895-6. |
|---|---|---|---|---|
| Income ... ... ... .. ... | 4,956 | 4,432 | 4,334 | 5,462 |
| Expenditure ... ... ... ... | 5,691 | 6,953 | 7,301 | 8,904 |

**Nidugatta.**—A village in the Mandya taluq, 18 miles north-east of the kasba, on the Bangalore-Mysore road. Population 805.

A large fair is held on Wednesday, attended by 2,000 people.

**Nugu,** also called the Bhrigu, an affluent of the Kabbani. It rises in Wainad and, entering the Mysore District in the south-west of the Heggadadevankote taluq, runs in a northerly direction, joining the Kabbani near the village of Hampapura on the Mysore-Manantody road. It is dammed by the Lakshmanpura anicut, from which issues a channel of the same name, 5 miles in length. The cultivation under the channel is of small extent, 297 acres, in consequence of the jungle surrounding. The revenue obtained amounts to Rs. 1,401. Gold dust in small quantities has been occasionally found in the bed of the stream, but never sufficient to repay the trouble of searching for it. It is supposed to be washed down from the source of the river in the Nellambur hills in Malabar.

**Palhalli.**—A village in Seringapatam taluq, on the right bank of the Kávéri, 3 miles west of Seringapatam, on the Seringapatam-Mercara road. Head-quarters of the Palhalli hobli. Till 1871 it was the kasba of the then Mysore Ashtagram taluq. Population 1,858.

It used to be well known for the now abandoned factories of the Ashtagram Sugar Works, a description of which will be found in Vol. I. of this work.

**Paschima-vahini.**—A sacred spot on the Kávéri, adjoining Seringapatam on the south-west, and a railway station. The river here makes a bend to the west, whence the name *paschima váhini*, the western stream, sometimes shortened into *pachiván*. The royal bathing ghat of the Mysore Rájas is here, together with many other bathing ghats. The Bangáradoḍḍi dam is on this stream, and gives rise to the channel of the same name, which waters the island of Seringapatam (*see* Seringapatam taluq).

**Piriyapatna.**—A town situated in 12° 21′ N. lat., 76° 9′ E. long., on the Mysore-Mercara road, 13 miles west by north of Hunsur. Formerly the head-quarters of the taluq which bore its name, now called Hunsur taluq. Population, 3,712.

According to tradition the place was visited in the mythological ages by Agastya, the first Brahman teacher who crossed the Vindhya mountains. Its ancient name was Singapattana, and here Karikala Chola Rája is stated to have formed a tank and erected a temple of Mallikárjunesvara. From inscriptions it appears that the place was one of the principal towns in the territory of the Changálva kings of Nanjaráyapattana (near Fraserpet in Coorg). They submitted to the Chola kings, and were thence designated Kulottunga-Chola-Changálvas. They claim to be descended from an original Changálva who was victorious over king Bijjala and assumed his titles. As Bijjala the Kalachurya king reigned from 1156 to 1167, this must be the period of Changálva. In his line was descended Nága, whose son was Ranga, whose son was Piriya, whose sons were Nanja and Mahadera, the former on the throne in 1521. Nanja's son was Nanjunda, his son Srikanṭha, his sons Vira (1559 and 1567), and Piriya (1586 and 1589).

Nanjunda Arasu, tradition says, passing that way to a marriage at Hanagod, was led by the circumstance of a hare starting up and biting the heels of his horse, which indicated *gandu bhúmi* or male soil, to erect a mud fort there. But it was Piriya Rája who replaced the mud fort by one of stone, established the péte, and called the town after himself—Piriyapattana. Another Nanja Raja followed, whose son, Rudra Gana or Piriya, was in power between 1597 and 1612. His son, Vira Raja, was on the throne in 1615, and during his reign the place was besieged for one year by Kanthirava Narasa Raja of Mysore. At last, when the fort was assaulted, Vira Raja, putting all his family and children to death, died fighting his enemies. During the reign of Tipu, Piriyapatna witnessed several conflicts between the Coorgs and Mysoreans, and the Víra Ráya, or Rája of Coorg, was confined within the fort for four years. On the approach of General Abercromby's army the houses of Piriyapatna were destroyed, and the fort was rendered useless to the enemy.

Owing to its position, the town is chiefly inhabited by traders, who export commodities, such as cotton and tobacco, to Coorg, Cannanore, &c. The large stone fort is in a ruinous condition. It was formerly infested by tigers, and even now it is said that cheetahs are occasionally found there. A pack of hounds is maintained in the neighbourhood by Mr. Murray Aynsley, and regularly hunted by planters from Coorg and other gentlemen.

**Saligram.**—A town in the Yedatore taluq, on the north bank of the Kávéri, 12 miles north-west of Yedatore, and a municipality.

| Population in 1891. | Males. | Females. | Total. |
|---|---|---|---|
| Hindus... ... ... ... ... ... | 1,532 | 1,579 | 3,111 |
| Muhammadans ... ... ... ... | 156 | 177 | 333 |
| Jains ... ... ... ... ... ... | 163 | 181 | 344 |
| Total ... | 1,851 | 1,937 | 3,788 |

It is esteemed sacred by the followers of Vishnu on account of its having been the residence of Rámánujáchári. There is also a considerable Jain population. Country paper used to be manufactured here.

| Municipal Funds. | 1892-3. | 1893-4. | 1894-5. | 1895-6. |
|---|---|---|---|---|
| Income ... ... ... ... ... | 587 | 660 | 688 | 1,290 |
| Expenditure ... ... ... ... | 1,118 | 251 | 453 | 2,073 |

**Sargur.**—A town situated in 12° N. lat., 76° 28′ E. long., on the right bank of the Kabbani, 36 miles south-west of Mysore, and a municipality. From 1864 to 1886 it was the head-quarters of the Heggadadevankote taluq.

| Population in 1891. | Males. | Females. | Total. |
|---|---|---|---|
| Hindus... ... ... ... ... ... | 744 | 818 | 1,562 |
| Muhammadans .... ... ... ... | 41 | 43 | 84 |
| Jains ... ... ... ... ... ... | 57 | 43 | 100 |
| Total ... | 842 | 904 | 1,746 |

There is nothing of special interest connected with Sargur. Its selection for the chief town was due to its open situation, free of the dense forests which cover most of the taluq and its being therefore more healthy.

| Municipal Funds. | 1892–3. | 1893–4. | 1894–5. | 1895–6. |
|---|---|---|---|---|
| Income ... ... ... ... ... | 330 | 330 | 305 | 671 |
| Expenditure ... ... ... ... | 809 | 394 | 456 | 1,304 |

**Seringapatam.**—A taluq in the centre northwards; till 1882 called Ashtagram. Area, 274 square miles. Head-quarters at Seringapatam. Contains the following hoblis, villages and population :—

| No. | Hoblis. | Villages. | Hamlets. | Villages classified. | | | | Population. |
|---|---|---|---|---|---|---|---|---|
| | | | | Government. | Sarvamánya. | Jodi. | Kayamgutta. | |
| 1 | Arakere ... ... | 20 | 13 | 16 | 4 | — | — | 9,890 |
| 2 | Belagola .. ... | 17 | 6 | 15 | — | 2 | — | 4,309 |
| 3 | Chandigál ... ... | 17 | 6 | 16 | 1 | — | — | 6,379 |
| 4 | Haravu... ... ... | 18 | 1 | 18 | — | — | — | 6,196 |
| 5 | Kirangúr ... ... | 19 | 12 | 18 | 1 | — | — | 10,918 |
| 6 | Kura ... ... ... | 1 | — | 1 | — | — | — | 12,553 |
| 7 | Kyátanhalli ... ... | 12 | 8 | 11 | 1 | — | — | 6,510 |
| 8 | Mélukóte ... ... | 27 | 9 | 24 | 2 | 1 | — | 7,054 |
| 9 | Pálhalli... ... ... | 5 | 1 | 5 | — | — | — | 2,609 |
| 10 | S'eṭṭihalli ... ... | 37 | 10 | 33 | 3 | — | 1 | 11,257 |
| 11 | Tirumalságarchatra ... | 37 | 9 | 35 | 1. | 1 | — | 7,567 |
| | Total ... | 210 | 75 | 192 | 13 | 4 | 1 | 85,242 |

*Principal places, with population.*—Seringapatam, 12,553; Arakere,

3,456; Mélukóṭe, 2,789; Hiróḍ, 2,470; Belagola, 2,148; Kirangúr 1,965; Pálhalli, 1,858; Sámanhalli, 1,417; Ukkaḍa, 1,414; Kurubar-Séttihalli, 1,240; Hiri Marali, 1,166; Mahadevapura, 1,148; Nagunhalli, 1,099.

The Kávéri runs through the south of the taluq, from west to east, forming several small islands near Belagola, and lower down the large one of Seringapatam. The Lókapávani from the north, uniting with a stream from the Móti Táláb on the west, runs south into the Kávéri off the north-east of the Seringapatam island, under the Karighatta peak. The country rising gradually on both sides of the Kávéri is naturally fertile, and for some distance from either bank is irrigated by fine channels drawn from the river, which follow the windings of the hills, and as they advance horizontally to the eastward send off branches to water the intermediate space. Of the anicuts or dams which force the water into the sources of these channels, there are five in this taluq. (1.) The Madad Kaṭṭe just beyond the border, in Krishnarajpet taluq, gives rise to the Chikkadevaráyaságara, the finest channel in the Mysore country, 10 or 12 yards wide, and 3 or 3½ deep, running for 72 miles on the left bank. It is carried across the Lókapávani by means of an aqueduct near the French Rocks, winds round the Karighatta hill, passes on to Arakere and terminates in the Bannur tank. (2.) The Devaráj Kaṭṭe is close to the former, and supplies the Devaráj channel on the right bank, which is 18 miles long and runs by Pálhalli into the Mysore taluq. (3.) From the Balmuri dam, a mile from Belagola, is drawn the Virjánadi channel, having a course of 41 miles on the right bank, of which 35 are in this taluq. (4.) The Bangáradoḍḍi dam is thrown across the *paschima váhini* or western stream of the river at Seringapatam.. The channel thence drawn is altogether 9 miles long. It is led by an aqueduct over a second stream into the island, where it divides into three branches, one entering the fort by an underground duct, a second running to the Darya Daulat Bágh, and the third to the Lál Bágh near the mausoleum of Haidar and Tipu. (5.) The Ramaswami dam, situated between Arakere on the left bank, and Mahadevapura on the right, gives rise to two channels, which are mostly out of this taluq—the Ramaswami, running for 30 miles on the left bank, and the Rájaparamesvari, running for 21 miles on the right bank. There is also an anicut on the Lakshmantirtha near Yedatore, from which an old channel called the Púrnaságara Nála passes through the Belagola hobli, but this is not now in use. A line of hills runs through the taluq north from the Kávéri, prominent peaks of which are Karighatta (2,697 ft.), French Rocks (2,882 ft.), and Yadugiri (3,579 ft.) at Melukote.

The soils under the channels are good, but of comparatively light order; towards the north-east there are some poorly populated and wild, but not very extensive, stretches of country. In the valleys and lowlands away from the channels there is a good deal of very fairly good soil. In addition to the cultivation of rice, which is general, sugar-cane of the kind known as *pattapatti* is extensively grown, especially under the first and third of the channels above mentioned. This found encouragement from the Ashtagram sugar works when they were in operation. The dry crops are those usual to the country, ragi being the principal, with which are sown avare and haralu. The gardens vary from those of the first class under channels to such as are merely hand-watered and planted with minor produce.

The revenue settlement was introduced in 1890. The area of the taluq was thus distributed :—

| | |
|---|---|
| Culturable (dry, 70,956; wet, 21,898; garden, 2,650) ... ... | 95,504 |
| Unculturable (roads, tanks, village sites, &c.), ... ... ... | 61,485 |
| Inám villages, 18,206; kávals, 191 ... ... ... ... ... | 18,397 |
| Total acres ... | 175,386 |

The unoccupied area was 7,937 acres. The total revenue demand for 1891–2 (15 months) was Rs. 2.74.463, and for 1892–3 it was Rs. 3.01.293.

The average rainfall at Seringapatam for 26 years (1870–95), and for 3 years (1893–5) at the other station was as follows :—

| | Jan. | Feb. | Mar. | Apr. | May | June | July | Aug. | Sept. | Oct. | Nov. | Dec. | Year. |
|---|---|---|---|---|---|---|---|---|---|---|---|---|---|
| Seringapatam ... | 0·23 | 0·04 | 0·58 | 1·63 | 5·27 | 2·13 | 1·91 | 2·97 | 3·58 | 6·72 | 2·24 | 0·67 | 27·97 |
| French Rocks ... | — | — | 0·48 | 3·19 | 4·24 | 2·32 | 1·10 | 3·25 | 4·48 | 7·19 | 1·34 | — | 27·59 |

The Bangalore-Mysore Railway runs through the middle of the taluq from east to south, with stations at French Rocks, Seringapatam, and Paschima Váhini. The trunk road is alongside the railway, with the one to Coorg going off to the west from Paschima Váhini. There are also roads from Seringapatam, north to French Rocks and Nagamangala, with a branch to Krishnarájpet and another to Melukote with continuation to the same place; and one south-east to Bannur. There is also a road from Lingarájchatra west through French Rocks to Kannambádi.

**Seringapatam.**—Properly S'rí-Ranga-paṭṭaṇa, is situated in 12° 25′ N. lat., 76° 45′ E. long., at the western or upper end of an island in the Kávéri, about three miles in length from west to east and one in breadth. The eastern end of the island is occupied by the prosperous suburb of Ganjam. Seringapatam, the head-quarters of the taluq of the same name and a municipality, stands on the Mysore State Rail-

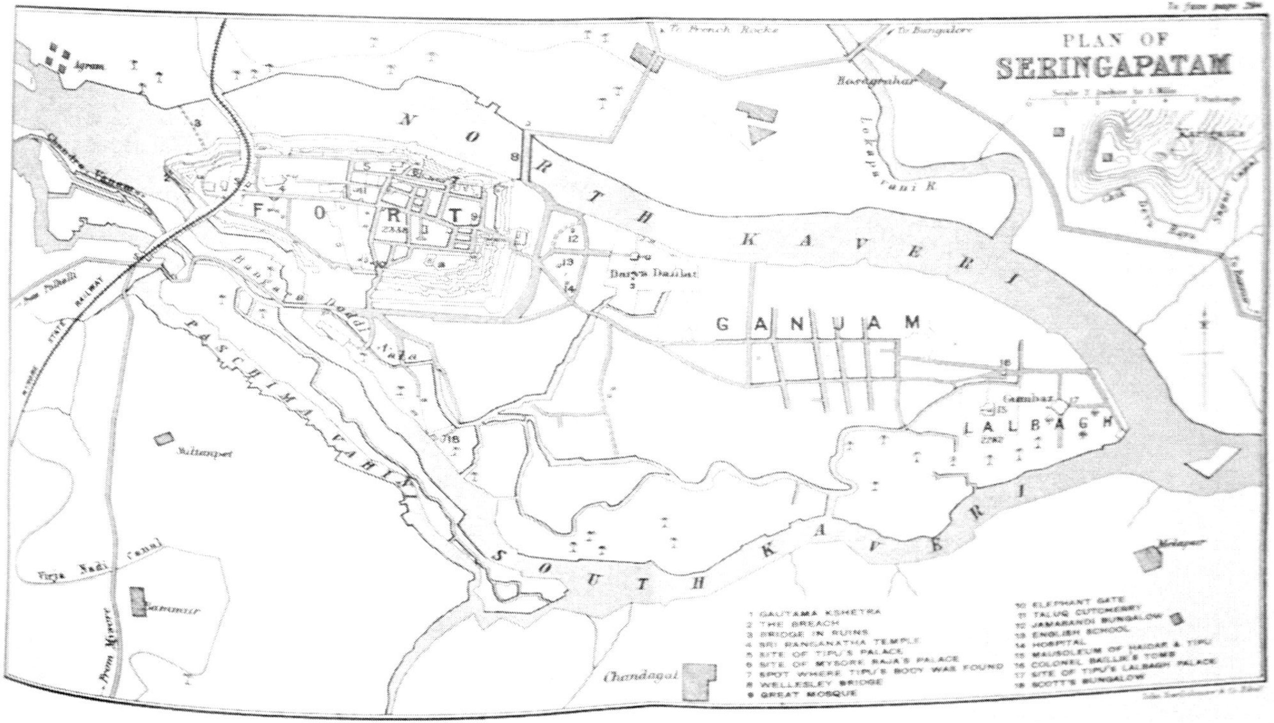

PLAN OF
SERINGAPATAM
NORTH KAVERI
SOUTH KAVERI
FORT
GANJAM
LALBAGH
PASCHIMA VAHINI
Darya Daulat
Gumbaz
Chandagal
Sultanpet
Agram
To French Rocks
To Bangalore
Lokapavani R.
Virja Nadi (anal)
From Mysore
1 GAUTAMA KSHETRA
2 THE BREACH
3 BRIDGE IN RUINS
4 SRI RANGANATHA TEMPLE
5 SITE OF TIPU'S PALACE
6 SITE OF MYSORE RAJA'S PALACE
7 SPOT WHERE TIPU'S BODY WAS FOUND
8 WELLESLEY BRIDGE
9 GREAT MOSQUE
10 ELEPHANT GATE
11 TALUQ CUTCHERRY
12 JAMABANDI BUNGALOW
13 ENGLISH SCHOOL
14 HOSPITAL
15 MAUSOLEUM OF HAIDAR & TIPU
16 COLONEL BAILLIE'S TOMB
17 SITE OF TIPU'S LALBAGH PALACE
18 SCOTT'S BUNGALOW

way and on the Bangalore-Mysore high road, 75 miles south-west from the former and 10 north-east from the latter.

| Population in 1891. | Males. | Females. | Total. |
|---|---|---|---|
| Hindus (with 2 Jains) ... ... ... | 4,997 | 5,592 | 10,589 |
| Muhammadans ... ... ... ... | 853 | 931 | 1,784 |
| Christians ... ... ... ... ... | 81 | 97 | 178 |
| Total ... | 5,931 | 6,620 | 12,551 |

In the earliest ages, Gautama rishi is related to have worshipped the Ranganáthaswámi whose temple is the principal Hindu building in the fort, and to have done penance in this the western or Paschima Ranganátha kshetra as distinguished from the eastern or Púrva Ranganátha kshetra at Srirangam near Trichinopoly.[1] The Gautama kshetra is a small island to the west of Seringapatam where the river divides. Under two large boulders on the north side of it is what is called the rishi's cave, now closed up. Opposite, on the north bank of the river, were found old Ganga inscriptions of the 9th century, referring to the Kalbappu hill at Sravana Belgola, and describing its summit as marked by the footprints of the munis Bhadrabáhu and Chandra Gupta.

In 894, during the reign of the Ganga sovereigns, a person named Tirumalaiya appears to have founded on the island, then entirely overrun with jungle, two temples, one of Ranganátha, and a smaller one of Tirumala Deva, enclosing them with a wall, and to have called the place Sri-Ranga-pura or pattana.[2] Subsequently, about 1117, Ramánujácharya, the celebrated apostle of the Vishnuvite sect, on fleeing from Dravida to avoid a confession of faith prescribed by the Chola Raja to be made by all his subjects, the object of which was to establish the superiority of Siva over Vishnu, took refuge in the Mysore country, where he succeeded in converting from the Jain faith the powerful Hoysala king, Bitti Deva, thenceforth known as Vishnuvardhana. This royal convert conferred on his apostle and his followers the tract of country on each side of the river Káveri at Seringapatam, known by the name of Ashṭagráma or eight townships, over which he appointed his own officers under the ancient designations of Prabhus and Hebbárs.

[1] The temples of Ranganáthaswámi on the three islands of Seringapatam, Sivasamudram and Srirangam are also called respectively those of Adi Ranga, Madhya Ranga, and Antya Ranga, or the Ranga of the beginning, the middle and the end.

[2] J. R. A. S. VIII, 6; *Mad. J. Lit. & Sc. XIV*, 13.

In 1454, Timmanna, a Hebbár descended from one of these, lord of Nágamangala, obtained, by a visit to Vijayanagar, the government of the district with the title of Danáyak, and permission to erect a fort at Srirangapattana. This he did with the aid of a hidden treasure he had discovered, and enlarged the temple of Ranganátha, making use of materials obtained from the demolition of 101 Jain temples at Kaḷasváḍi, a town 5 miles to the south. His descendants held the government until in 1495 Seringapatam passed into the direct possession of the Vijayanagar kings. For we learn from inscriptions that Narasa, the founder at that time of the second Vijayanagar dynasty, "quickly damming up the Kávéri when in full flood, crossed over and captured the enemy (unnamed) alive in battle. Taking possession of their kingdom he made the ancient Srirangapattana his own." The place was probably recognized as too important to remain in the hands of a nominal feudatory. It was eventually administered in the name of the Vijayanagar sovereigns by a viceroy known as the Sri-Ranga-Ráyal. Tirumala Rája, the last of these Ráyalu, was a relative of the royal family.

We have elsewhere seen how in 1610 Tirumala Raja, worn out with age and disease, surrendered his power to Rája Woḍeyar, the rising ruler of Mysore. There is a halo of mystery surrounding this transaction, and some authorities maintain that the viceroy intended his sway to descend to his kinsman the Rája of Ummattur, but the probability is that, foreseeing his inevitable subjugation by Rája Wodeyar, he made a virtue of necessity in retiring voluntarily. Thenceforth Seringapatam became the capital of the Rajas of Mysore, and continued to be the seat of government under the Musalman dynasty until its capture by the British in 1799.

But in the interval Seringapatam had been several times besieged, particulars of which will be found in Vol. I in the chapter on History. In 1638 by Ran-dulha Khan and the Bijapur forces, which were repulsed with great slaughter by Kanthirava Narasa Raja. Later in the same reign by Sivappa Nayak of Bednur, when the invaders were again driven off. But the king thought it prudent in 1654 to strengthen the fort, and to stock it with provisions and stores to enable it to stand a prolonged siege. In 1697 by the Mahrattas, when the bulk of the army was absent, engaged in the siege of Trichinopoly. But this attempt was also foiled and the enemy suffered a crushing defeat. In 1732 the Navab of Arcot sent a powerful army against Seringapatam, but it was met at Kailancha, near Channapatna, and driven in confusion below the Ghats. In 1755, when most of the forces were again absent at Trichinopoly, the Subadar of the Dekkan besieged the fortress, with the aid of a French force under Bussy. The latter was about to deliver the assault against the north-east angle, when the enemy were bought off for 56 lakhs. The treasury being empty, one-third was raised on the plate and jewels of the Hindu temples and the property and ornaments of the Raja, and for the remainder bills were given, which, however, were never redeemed. In 1757 by the Mahrattas under Báláji Rao, assisted by a European force. The place was reduced to extremity, and a compromise was made with the enemy for 32 lakhs; and as only 5 could be raised in cash, 14 taluqs were pledged for the payment of the rest. In 1759 the Mahrattas appeared in greater force under Gopal Hari, and the defence was entrusted to Haidar Ali, now risen to high command. After various successes he compelled the enemy to give up the pledged taluqs on payment of 32 lakhs in satisfaction of all demands. By a levy on all the public servants and wealthy people 16 lakhs were raised, and for the rest the bankers found the money on the personal security of Haidar, in consideration of the restored taluqs being placed under his direct management. Though not actually besieged, Seringapatam was taken possession of in June 1761 by Haidar, in consequence of the plots formed by the palace and the Hindu ministers to get rid of him, and his usurpation was from this time complete. The next attack on the fortress was in March 1771, by the Mahrattas under Tryambak Rao, after the disastrous defeat they had inflicted on Haidar at Chinkuruli. They blockaded Seringapatam for no less than 15 months, when a treaty was concluded on payment of 15 lakhs and the surrender of seven taluqs in the east and north as security for 15 lakhs more.

This brings us to the time of the two memorable sieges by the British in 1792 and 1799, in their wars against Tipu Sultan. On the former occasion the British army was commanded by Lord Cornwallis, the Governor-General. The first attempt against Seringapatam was made in 1791, but owing to the failure of supplies and the great sickness that broke out among men and cattle on the bursting of the monsoon, it was found necessary to bury the battering guns and retire to Bangalore, which was done by the route of Melukote, Nagamangala and Magadi. The operations against Seringapatam were resumed early in 1792, every provision having in the interval been carefully made for the success of the enterprise. The army arrived in sight of the fortress on the 6th of February, and that very night were carried out the masterly operations, led by Lord Cornwallis in person, by which the whole of Tipu's force was not only driven from the north of the river, but the British gained a firm position on the island itself, occupying Shahar Ganjam and all the east, including the Darya Daulat Bagh.

The following is a description of the place at that time by Major Dirom, who was a Staff officer with the army:—

The fort and outworks occupy about a mile of the west end of the island, and the Lál Bágh or garden about the same portion of the east end. The whole space between the fort and the Lál Bágh, except a small inclosure, called the Daulat Bágh, on the north bank near the fort, was filled, before the war, with houses, and formed an extensive suburb, of which the pettah of Shahar Ganjam is the only remaining part, the rest having been destroyed by Tipu to make room for batteries to defend the island, and to form an esplanade to the fort. This pettah or town of modern structure, built on the middle and highest part of the island, is about half a mile square, divided into regular cross streets, all wide, shaded on each side by trees and full of good houses. It is surrounded by a strong mud wall, and seemed to have been preserved for the accommodation of the bazar people and merchants, and for the convenience of troops stationed in that part of the island for its defence. A little way to the eastward of the pettah is the entrance into the great garden or Lál Bágh. It was laid out in regular shady walks of large cypress-trees, and full of fruit trees, flowers and vegetables of every description. The fort, thus situated on the west end of the island, is distinguished by its white walls, regular outworks, magnificent buildings and ancient Hindu pagodas, contrasted with the more lofty and splendid monuments lately raised in honour of the Mahomedan faith. The Lál Bágh, which occupies the east end of the island, possessing all the beauty and convenience of a country retirement, is dignified by the mausoleum of Haidar, and a superb new palace built by Tipu. To these add the idea of an extensive suburb or town, which filled the middle space between the fort and the garden, full of wealthy industrious inhabitants, and it will be readily allowed that this insulated metropolis must have been the richest, most convenient and beautiful spot possessed in the present age by any native prince in India.

After an examination of the defences, it was determined to attack the fortress on its northern face, and in case of necessity it seemed possible by repairing an old dam or embankment on the west to throw the water of the north branch of the river entirely into the other branch. The siege was pressed with vigour, and Tipu on his side was strenuously engaged night and day in strengthening the defences on the north side, and impeding the British operations by all the means in his power. But fortune was against him, and on the 23rd of February he was forced to agree to the terms proposed by Lord Cornwallis—namely, the surrender of half his dominions, the payment of three crores and thirty lakhs of rupees, the release of all prisoners detained from the time of Haidar Ali, and the delivery of two of his sons as hostages.

The siege of 1799 was under the command of General Harris, directed by the Governor-General, Lord Mornington (afterwards

Marquis Wellesley), who had come to Madras for the purpose. Since the former siege Tipu had greatly strengthened the fortifications. Double ramparts and double ditches were added to the northern and western faces, in addition to those on the eastern and southern faces, thus creating what was like a fortress within a fortress. Besides this, a new line of intrenchments was formed from the Daulat Bágh to the Periapatam bridge, within 600 or 700 yards of the fortress. How General Harris arrived before Seringapatam on the 5th of April, after defeating Tipu at Malavalli, and outwitting him in regard to his route, are described in the historical part of this work. The south-western angle was on this occasion chosen as the point of attack. In spite of Tipu's efforts to dislodge the enemy, especially by a vigorous sally on the 22nd led by his corps of Frenchmen, the works were steadily pushed on. And on the 26th a night attack, commanded by Colonel Wellesley, the future Duke of Wellington,[1] and followed up the next day, drove the Mysoreans from the last intrenchment they occupied outside the fortress. The final assault of the 4th of May, the circumstances attending the death of the Sultan, and all the events that followed upon it have been related in the chapter on History.

By this victory Seringapatam became the property of the British Government, who leased the island to Mysore for a fixed sum of Rs. 50,000 a year. Buchanan says the streets in the fort were narrower and more confused than in any place he had seen since leaving Bengal. The generality of the houses were very mean, although many of the chiefs were well lodged after their fashion. Tipu allowed no person to possess property in houses there. He disposed of the dwellings as he thought fit, and on the slightest caprice changed the tenants. The fort was for several years occupied by British troops, and to provide greater space within the walls the inner ramparts were thrown down and the inner ditch was filled up in 1800. The course of this ditch may now be traced by the line of tamarind trees planted along it when it was closed up. Seringapatam began rapidly to decline after the close of the war, and its decay was proportionate with the rise of Mysore. The population of the island, estimated by Buchanan to have reached at least 150,000 during the reign of the Sultan, before the expiration of a year had sunk to 32,000. Fever also gradually made its appearance and necessitated the removal of the troops to Bangalore, where the new Cantonment was formed in 1809. Seringapatam is now notoriously

[1] An incident of this affair was that Colonel Wellesley got separated from his troops and mixed up with the enemy, whom he mistook for them, and entered the fort along with them before he discovered his mistake, when fortunately he made his escape.

unhealthy for Europeans, and also for most natives; a severe attack of fever is generally the penalty of two or three nights spent in it or its vicinity. It is, however, strange that immediately after its occupation by the British, when the city is described by Buchanan as "a sink of nastiness," it does not appear to have been insalubrious. The increase in paddy cultivation may partially account for this change of climate, but the natives generally attribute it to the destruction of the sweet flag, a plant which formerly grew in profusion on the banks of the river, and was supposed to possess febrifugal properties.

The population continued still further to decline and was only 12,744 in 1852, falling still lower to 10,594 in 1871. But in 1891 it was again 12,551, and the advent of the railway, with stations at the Fort and at Paschima-váhini, together with improvements introduced by Municipal administration, have in recent years given it a somewhat more prosperous aspect. The railway cuts through the western part of the fort. With this exception the fortifications themselves are comparatively uninjured. On these the results of the breaching batteries are far more apparent than the work of time, and the fort is still so formidable that a great military authority who visited it a quarter of a century ago pronounced it the second strongest in India.

Although the fort is washed on its northern and western sides by the two branches of the river, and before the invention of rifled cannon had the advantage of not being commanded from any immediately adjacent height, it is to the ceaseless labour which must have been expended on it that it owes its great strength. The want of science which was apparent in long straight walls, square bastions, and glacis steep enough to shelter an assailant, was compensated for by deep ditches carried through solid granite, huge and massive walls, and lofty cavaliers.

The principal entrance was by what is known as the Elephant gate on the south side. This is not now used, the road being carried through a more convenient gateway made to the west of it. The Elephant gateway bears an inscription in Persian, stating that the foundation of the fort was laid in the year 1219 from the birth of Muhammad, that is of Tipu's Mauludi era, (1791 A.D.), when Jupiter was in the ascendant, Sagittarius and Libra were rising, Venus in twilight obscured by Jupiter, Mercury in conjunction with Virgo, Mars in Scorpio, the tail of the dragon in Pisces, and Saturn in Aries. The influence of these conjunctions was to show that the fort was fully equipped, and by the grace and mercy of God the Creator would remain permanent, free from all misfortune.

At the south-west angle of the fort may be viewed the breach made in 1799, the spot from which the storming party issued on the opposite side of the river being marked by two cannon fixed perpendicularly in the ground at the edge of the stream. Within the walls, surrounded by a high enclosure, are the remains of the Musalman palace, now converted into a sandal-wood store, but the greater part was demolished. A description of this palace has been given in Vol. I, as seen by Swartz in 1779, at p. 396, and as seen by Buchanan in 1800, at p. 520. Near the large temples of Srí Rangaswami, which is close by, are a few mud walls and a sunken granary, the relics of the ancient palace of the Ráyals or viceroys of Seringapatam and of the Rajas of Mysore.[1] The enclosure was for some years used as a gun-carriage factory. A large mosque erected by Tipu, with two tall minarets which are conspicuous from a great distance, is in front of the Mysore gate. The spot where Tipu fell is on the north face. Having been compelled to abandon the outer rampart, he attempted to escape into the inner fort through a narrow archway, but the crowd of fugitives from the British troops, who had already gained the interior, prevented this, and he was slain in an open space between the two walls. The archway in which he was wounded no longer exists. But a wooden door leading into a garden, about a hundred yards to the east of the sally-port, is pointed out as the spot where he was killed.

*Daryá Daulat Bágh.*—Just outside the fort, on the island, is the Daryá Daulat Bágh or "garden of the wealth of the sea," a summer palace which was Tipu's favourite retreat from business. Its graceful proportions, and the arabesque work in rich colours with which it is covered, render it very attractive. Mr. Rees, who has travelled much in India and Persia, says "The lavish decorations which cover every inch of wall from first to last, from top to bottom, recall the palaces of Ispahan, and resemble nothing that I know in India." Part of the walls are adorned with pictures in a style of broad caricature, representing Colonel Baillie's defeat at Conjeveram in 1780, Haidar and Tipu

[1] Of this building, Wilks says, that the Sultan, in removing the Raja's family from it, had intended to destroy it altogether, and gave orders for that purpose, which were afterwards changed. It was reported to him that several large apartments were full of books, chiefly of palm-leaf and cuduttums, and he was asked how they were to be disposed of. "Transfer them," says he, "to the royal stables as fuel to boil the cooltee (grain on which horses are fed)," and this was accordingly done. A small miscellaneous collection was preserved from this destruction by the pious artifice of a Brahmin, and in the confusion of the final siege fell into the hands of a British officer. Among the historical tracts which this collection contained was the record of a curious inquiry into the state of the family about the year 1716, for the purpose of ascertaining which of the branches had preserved the true blood of the house unpolluted by unworthy connections, when, out of thirty-one branches, thirteen were pronounced to be legitimate, and eighteen were excluded from he privilege of giving wives or successors to the reigning Rája.

as they appeared in public processions, and numerous figures of Rájas and pálégárs. These representations had been defaced by Tipu prior to the siege, but after the capture of Seringapatam were restored by Colonel Wellesley, who occupied the palace for some time. They were again allowed to become partially obliterated until Lord Dalhousie, during his tour in Mysore, caused them to be repainted by a native artist who remembered them as they were. Although the pictures have therefore twice undergone restoration it is probable that they are faithful prototypes of the original. The perspective is very bad, and the general effect is grotesque, but the artist has succeeded well in caricaturing the expression and attitude of the British soldier, and the Frenchmen under Lally must have been taken from the life.

*Lál Bágh.*—At the eastern end of the island towards the south is the Gumbaz or mausoleum which was built by Tipu for his father and in which he also is buried, as well as his mother. It is a square building surmounted by a dome, with minarets at the angles, and surrounded by a corridor which is supported by pillars of black hornblende. The interior is painted in lacquer with the tiger stripe, adopted by Tipu for military uniforms. The double doors inlaid with ivory were renewed by Lord Dalhousie. Each of the tombs is covered with a handsome pall. The mausoleum is supported at Government expense. A tablet on the tomb of Tipu contains some verses, in which the following expressions,—The light of Islam and the faith left this world; Tipu became a martyr for the faith of Muhammad; The sword was lost; The offspring of Haidar was a great martyr:—by the process called Abjad give 1213, the date of his death according to the Muhammadan era of the Hejira. A short distance from the entrance to the Gumbaz is the tomb of Colonel Baillie, erected in 1816 by his nephew, Resident at the Court of Lucknow. Of Tipu's palace which stood in the Lál Bágh nothing now remains. Buchanan in 1800 says of it, "Though built of mud, it possesses a considerable degree of elegance, and is the handsomest native building that I have ever seen."

The eastern portion of the island northwards is chiefly occupied by the suburb of Ganjam (see above, pp. 242 and 297). On rising ground called Sabbiráni Tittu, to the south of the Daulat Bágh, is a small monument to officers who fell in the final siege. Farther west, on the bank of the river, is Scott's bungalow. He was the officer in charge of the gun-carriage factory, and the Rája built this bungalow for him. In 1817 he lost his wife and children by a sudden death, which so affected him that he deserted the house and left the country. But the Rája directed that the house should remain as it was, untouched. Such of the old furniture and fittings as have not fallen to pieces by decay, therefore, still stand in the rooms, and the place is an object of melancholy interest to visitors.

On an elevated site opposite the north-west of the fort is Webbe's monument, erected by Purnaiya, and known as the ***rana-khamba*** or war pillar, from the fight that took place there in 1809 in connection with the short-lived mutiny of British officers in the Madras army (*see* Vol. I, p. 759).[1]

The island is watered from a canal, which is carried across the south branch of the river by an aqueduct constructed by Tipu. It rises a short distance above Seringapatam and irrigates the Darya Daulat Bágh and the garden attached to Haidar's mausoleum, as well as some rich sugar-cane fields on the island. Over the aqueduct is a bridge. The bridge across the northern branch was constructed by Purnaiya in 1804, and named the Wellesley Bridge in honour of the then Governor-General of India. It is an interesting specimen of native architecture. To the north-west of the fort may be seen the remains of a dam or bridge erected in the time of the viceroys of Vijayanagar.

| Municipal Funds. | 1892–93. | 1893–94. | 1894–95. | 1895–96. |
|---|---|---|---|---|
| Income ... ... ... ... | 10,366 | 10,317 | 11,488 | 15,298 |
| Expenditure ... ... ... | 11,147 | 9,455 | 9,431 | 10,792 |

**Shimsha** or **Shimshupa**, also called the Kadaba or Kadamba, and the Maddúr Holé—a tributary of the Kávéri. It rises to the south of Dévaráyadurga in Tumkur District, and flowing southwards through that District enters the Mysore District in the north-east of Mandya taluq. Pursuing a south-east course, it runs through Malavalli taluq and enters the Kávéri a few miles below the Falls at Sivasamudram. About nine miles north of Maddur is an anicut, rebuilt some years ago by the Public Works Department, of cut stone. From this dam is drawn the Maddur Aṇe channel on the right bank, which is 12 miles in length, and feeding the large Maddur tank, branches into four small channels, the Chamenhaḷḷi (2¾ miles), Bairan (2 miles), Vaidyanáthpúr (3¼ miles) and Kemman (5½ miles). Much mulberry is cultivated under these channels for the support of silkworms. The area irrigated from the channels is 3,000 acres, yielding a revenue of Rs. 18,889. The river is spanned near Maddur by a fine brick bridge of seven arches, constructed in 1850 for the Bangalore-Mysore road, and now used also for the Mysore State Railway.

[1] The details will be found in Colonel Malleson's monograph *Seringapatam, Past and Present.*

The valley of the Shimsha, under the Ganga kings, formed the province of Chikka Gangavádi, with its chief town at Honganur (Channapatna taluq).

**Sivasamudram.**—Though over the present boundary line of Mysore, this romantic spot is intimately associated with that country. It is on the south border of the Malavalli taluq, connected with the Railway and Bangalore-Seringapatam trunk road by a cross road from Maddur through Malavalli, 30 miles in length. The Kávéri here branches into two streams, each of which makes a descent of about 200 feet, in a succession of picturesque rapids and waterfalls. The principal island embraced within these torrents, called Heggura, but more generally known by the name of Sivasamudram or Sivanasamudram (sea of Siva), —the ancient city, of which a few vestiges are strewed around,—is about 3 miles long by ¾ of a mile broad.

Of its former history little is known; but the modern city appears to have been founded at the beginning of the 16th century by Ganga Rája, a representative probably of the Ganga kings, whose sovereignty in Orissa then came to an end. An inscription of 1604 records a grant to the temple by the chief of Hadinád. Through precisely the same mistake that occurred in the foundation of Chik Ballapur (Kolar District), the work was commenced before the appointed signal announced the lucky moment, and was therefore doomed to continue for only three generations. Ganga Rája, after a prosperous reign, was succeeded by his son Nandi Rája, who, to atone for a ceremonial offence, leaped into the cataract at Gagana Chukki on horseback with his wife. His son Ganga Rája the second enlarged the city greatly, and lived with much splendour. He had two daughters, whom he gave in marriage to the two chief Pálégars in the neighbourhood. The one was married to the Rája of Kilimale, a place now in ruins, about 12 miles from Satyagala. The other daughter was married to the Rája of Nagarakere, 3 miles east from Maddur. These marriages were very unhappy; for the pride of the ladies gave their husbands constant disgust. They were continually upbraided for not living in equal splendour with their father-in-law; and at length, having consulted together, they determined to humble their wives, by showing that their power was superior to that of Ganga Rája. Having assembled all their forces, they besieged Sivasamudra; but for a time had very little success.

The siege had continued twelve years without their having been able to penetrate into the island, when the two Rájas found means to corrupt the Dalaváyi or minister of Ganga Rája. This traitor removed the guards from the only ford, and thus permitted the enemy to surprise the place, while he endeavoured to engage his master's attention at the game of chess. The shouts of the soldiery at length reaching their ears, the prince started up from the game. The Dalaváyi, who wished him to fall alive into the hands of his sons-in-law, endeavoured to persuade him that the noise arose merely from children at play, but the Raja, having drawn his sword, first killed all his women and children, and then, rushing into the midst of his enemies, fought until he procured an honourable death. The sons-in-law on seeing this were struck with horror, and immediately threw themselves into the cataract at Gagana Chukki; and their example was followed by their wives, whose arrogance had been the cause of such disasters.

Jagadeva Ráyal of Channapatna, and Sri Ranga Raja of Talakad, the two most powerful of the neighbouring chiefs, then came, and removed all the people and wealth of the place. During the British march upon Seringapatam in 1791, Tipu Sultan, having destroyed every means of forage between Bangalore and the capital, drove all the inhabitants and cattle into the island of Sivasamudram, presenting a silent and desolate country to the advance of the army of Lord Cornwallis.

The island was overgrown with dense jungle, and the old bridges which connected it with the mainland on both sides had become impassable when in 1818 their repair was undertaken by Ramaswami Mudaliyar, a confidential servant of the Resident of Mysore. He expended several thousand pounds on the work and was rewarded by the British Government with the title of Janópakára Kámakarta or public benefactor. At the same time he was invested with a jágir composed of five villages from the British Government, yielding a revenue of Rs. 8,000 a year, and seven villages from the Mysore State, yielding Rs. 9,000 a year. The bridges are built of hewn stone pillars, connected by stone girders founded on the rocky bed of the stream, and though rude are good specimens of native construction. A bungalow was erected by the Jágirdar, near the road connecting the two bridges, for the accommodation of European visitors.[1]

*Gagana Chukki.*—On the western branch of the river, which forms the boundary between Mysore and Coimbatore, are the Gagana Chukki or Gangana Chukki falls, about two miles from the bungalow. The approach is by a steep path leading down from the tomb of Pir Ghaib, a Musalman saint. The stream here dividing so as to form a small island called Ettikur,[2] the parted waters dash with deafening roar over vast boulders of rock in a cloud of foam to unite again in the deep pool below, and with such violence that the column of vapour is at times

[1] He published an account of the place, with maps, in the *Madras Journal*, I, 83.
[2] Nellagana-tittu in Buchanan.

visible from Satyagala. "I have never," says Buchanan, "seen any cataract that for grandeur could be compared with this."[1]

*Bar Chukki.*—Grand and impressive as is the headlong turmoil of the waters in Gagana Chukki, the other falls, about a mile distant on the eastern branch of the river, being more easily viewed are generally more enjoyed. These are called the Bhar or Bar Chukki, and display a great volume of water, which in the rainy season pours over the hillside in an unbroken sheet a quarter of a mile broad. During the dry months it separates into several distinct falls of great beauty. In the centre is a deep recess in the form of a horse shoe, down which the principal stream falls, and having been collected into a narrow channel, rushes forward with prodigious violence and again falls, about 30 feet, into a capacious basin at the foot of the precipice. Hurrying on northwards, through wild and narrow gorges, the two streams unite again on the north-east of the island and continue their course to the east.

The most favourable time for visiting these Falls is during the rainy season, as in the winter months the island is excessively feverish.

**Somnathpur.**—An insignificant village on the left bank of the Kávéri in the Tirumakudlu Narsipur taluq, 5 miles north of Sósile, noted for the temple of Prasanna Chenna Késava. This elaborately carved structure is attributed to Jakanáchári, the famous sculptor and architect of the Hoysala kings, under whom Hindu art in Mysore reached its culmination. Though not on the scale of the unfinished temple at Halebid (Hassan District), the general effect is more pleasing, from the completion of the superstructure, consisting of three pyramidal towers or *vimána* surmounting the triple shrine; Prasanna Chenna Kesava occupying the central chapel, Gopála the one to the south, and Janárdana the one to the north. Round the exterior base are pourtrayed consecutively, with considerable spirit, the leading incidents in the Rámáyana, Mahá Bhárata and Bhágavata, carved in potstone, the termination of each chapter and section being indicated respectively by a closed or half-closed door. The number of separate sculptured images erected upon and around the basement, whose mutilated remains are shown around, was no less than 74.

The building, according to a fine inscription at the entrance, was completed in 1269, by Sóma, a member of the royal family and a high officer under the Hoysala king Narasimha III., who also founded the city which formerly surrounded it. Later grants were made by Ballála III. The vestibule is in ruins, and the images generally much

[1] *Journ.* I, 407. He had not, however, seen the falls of Gersoppa (Shimoga District).

damaged. Some clumsy attempts to repair this work of art appear to have been made recently.

There are also the ruins of a large Siva temple in the village, erected at about the same time.

**Sosile.**—A large village, in Tirumakudlu Narsipur taluq, on the left bank of the Kávéri at its confluence with the Kabbani. Head-quarters of the hobli of the same name, and a municipality.

| Population in 1891. | Males. | Females. | Total. |
|---|---|---|---|
| Hindus ... ... ... ... ... ... | 1,341 | 1,451 | 2,792 |
| Muhammadans ... ... ... ... ... | 109 | 132 | 241 |
| Total ... | 1,450 | 1,583 | 3,033 |

It contains the *matha* of the Vyása Ráya Swámi, the guru of the southern section of the Mádhva Brahmans, or those of Kannada and Telugu origin.

| Municipal Funds. | 1892–3. | 1893–4. | 1894–5. | 1895–6. |
|---|---|---|---|---|
| Income ... ... ... ... ... ... | 433 | — | 459 | 879 |
| Expenditure ... ... ... ... ... | 207 | — | 1,246 | 1,803 |

**Suvarnavati.**—*See* Honnu Hole.

**Talakad.**—A town of great antiquity, situated in 12° 11′ N. lat., 77° 5′ E. long., on the left bank of the Kávéri, 28 miles south-east of Mysore. It was the head-quarters of the Talakád taluq until 1868, when the kasba was established at Tirumakudlu Narsipur, 10 miles to the north-west, as being more central and accessible, and in 1882 the name of the taluq was changed to the latter. Population, 3,273.

The origin of the town is lost in antiquity; but one tradition is that its name was derived from two Kiráta brothers, Tala and Kádu, who, cutting down a tree which they saw wild elephants worshipping, discovered that it contained an image of Vishnu, and that the elephants were rishis transformed. The tree being miraculously restored, all obtained *moksha* and the place was named Tala-kádu, which was translated into Sanskrit as Dala-vana. Two stone images declared to represent the brothers are pointed out in front of the temple of Vedesvara. In a later age Rama is said to have halted here on his expedition to Lanka.

The earliest authentic notice of the city of Talekád or Talakád, in Sanskrit Dalavana-pura, is in connection with the Ganga line of kings.

Harivarma, ruling 247–266, was, according to an old chronicle, installed at Skandapura (said to be Gajalhaṭṭi, in the Coimbatore country, near where the Moyár flows into the Bhaváni), but resided in the great city of Dalavanapura in the Karnáta desa. Thenceforward Talakád became the capital of these powerful sovereigns, and there the subsequent kings of that line were crowned.

At the beginning of the 11th century the Gangas succumbed to the Cholas, who captured Talakád and gave it the name of Rájarajapura. But about a hundred years later it was taken by the Hoysala king Vishnuvardhana, who drove the Cholas out of Mysore. After this time we find that Talakád was composed of seven towns and five maṭhas or monastic establishments. The town of Máyilangi or Málingi, on the opposite side of the river, was also a large place, and had the name of Janantháthapura. Down to the middle of the 14th century it remained a possession of the Hoysalas, and then passed into the hands of a feudatory of the Vijayanagar sovereigns, whose line appears to be known as that of Soma Raja.

In 1634 it was conquered by the Mysore Raja under the following circumstances. Tirumala Raja, sometimes called Sri Ranga Ráyal, the representative of the Vijayanagar family at Seringapatam, being afflicted with an incurable disease, came to Talakád for the purpose of offering sacrifices in the temple of Védésvara. His wife Rangamma was left in charge of the government of Seringapatam; but she, hearing that her husband was on the point of death, soon after left for Talakád with the object of seeing him before he died, handing over Seringapatam and its dependencies to Rája Wodeyar of Mysore, whose dynasty ever afterwards retained them. It appears that Rája Wodeyar had been desirous of possessing a costly nose-jewel which was the property of the Ráni, and being unable to obtain possession of it by stratagem, and eager to seize any pretext for acquiring fresh territory, he levied an army and proceeded against Talakád, which he took by escalade; the Rája of the latter place falling in the action. The Ráni Rangamma thereupon went to the banks of the Kávéri, and throwing in the jewel, drowned herself opposite Málingi, at the same time uttering the three-fold curse,—"Let Talakád become sand; let Málingi become a whirlpool; let the Mysore Rájas fail to beget heirs."[1] The latter part is now happily of no effect.

The old city of Talakád is completely buried beneath hills of sand

[1] The following is what is known as the curse of Talakád, in the original:—

*Talakádu maral ágali.*
*Málingi maduv ágali.*
*Maisúru dhoregalu makkal illade hógali.*

stretching for nearly a mile in length, only the tops of two pagodas being visible. The sand hills used to advance upon the town at the rate of 9 or 10 feet a year, principally during the south-west monsoon, and as they press it close on three sides, the inhabitants were constantly forced to abandon their houses and retreat further inland. The town, however, is increasing in population, owing to the rich wet cultivation in the neighbourhood, derived from the Mádhava-mantri anicut and channel. More than thirty temples, it is stated, are beneath the sand. That of Kirti Nárávana is occasionally opened with great labour sufficiently to allow of access for certain ceremonies. The most imposing temple left uncovered by the sand is that of Vedesvara.

Steps have in recent years been taken (as suggested in the former edition of this work) to check the formation and advance of the sand-dunes, by planting suitable binding plants to prevent the sand lifting, and groves of trees, especially casuarinas, which grow so well in sand, in order to stop its drifting with the wind. These measures have been attended with a good deal of success. But without the directions of Government the people would do nothing, professing to look upon the phenomenon as the result of the curse before mentioned, and deeming it useless to fight against fate.

**Terakanambi.**—A town in Gundlupet taluq, on the Gundlupet-Chamrajnagar road, 7 miles east of the kasba. Head-quarters of the hóbli of the same name. Population 2,178.

A fair is held every Thursday, attended by 3,500 people.

The town is evidently of great antiquity, though its early history is somewhat obscure. There is a general agreement that its name was formerly Trikadamba-pura, and that it sprung out of a village called Kúdugallúr, standing where the *kúdu-gallu* or boundary stones united of three great countries—namely, Dravida, Kerala, and Hadinád or south-Karnáṭa. On the point of junction a temple to Trikadamba, the consort of the three-eyed Siva, was erected in the 6th century, by a king named Lamba Karna Ráya (the long-eared king) ruling the southern part of Karnáṭa; and hence the name of the town. This king, again, is stated to have belonged to the Kadamba line, and to be the same as Trinetra Kadamba, who would correspond with Mayúra-varma. Should this be true, it may be conjectured that the temple of Trikadamba marked the common boundary of the Ganga, Kerala, and Kadamba territories. Inscriptions show that Bayalnád (the Heggada-devankote taluq) was being ruled by chiefs of Kadamba descent until subdued by the Hoysalas.

The traditional list of rulers at Terakanámbi, among whom occurs a Mandava Ráya, king of Sivasamudra, throws little light upon its history until the time of the Hoysalas, who in turn were succeeded by the Vijayanagar dynasty. Harihara of that line appears to have added to the city. In the 16th century the chief of Ummattur held it for a short time, and then a number of freebooters of Telugu origin ravaged the country for some years, until Rája Wodeyar of Mysore took possession of it in 1624, after which period it became secondary in importance to Gundlupet. Under the Musalman dynasty Terakanámbi was the head-quarters of a taluq, which was further sub-divided into Avval Terakanámbi and Duyam Terakanámbi, but Purnaiya merged these in the Gundlupet taluq.

The fort of Terakanámbi was finally destroyed by the Mahrattas in 1747. Remains of five lines of fortification are still to be seen, and the site of the old palace is also pointed out, which, according to local tradition, was six storeys high. There are twelve temples in Terakanámbi of large dimensions, but ruinous. Several of them contain inscriptions.[1] The principal shrine is dedicated to Lakshmi Varadarájaswami, whose effigy was removed to Mysore by Krishna Rája III. These temples, as in most other parts of the District, are chiefly built of huge blocks of stone fitted to each other with great nicety, but their carving is not generally noteworthy. It appears as if the science of an inferior age to that in which they were founded had been brought to bear upon repairing them, so greatly inferior are some portions of them to others; an allowance of a few rupees is still devoted to keeping up most of them. In the neighbourhood of Terakanámbi are numerous old tanks, now disused, but indicating the former importance of the place.

**Tirumakudlu Narsipur.**—A taluq in the east, till 1882 called Talakád. Area 217 square miles. Head-quarters at Tirumakudlu Narsipur. Contains the following hóblis, villages and population:—

| No. | Hóblis. | Villages. | Hamlets. | Villages classified. | | | | Population. |
|---|---|---|---|---|---|---|---|---|
| | | | | Government. | Sarvamánya. | Jodi. | Kayamgutta. | |
| 1 | Bannúr ... ... ... | 5 | 3 | 5 | — | — | — | 7,045 |
| 2 | Bevinhalli ... ... | 22 | 13 | 15 | 6 | 1 | — | 10,533 |
| 3 | Múgúr ... ... ... | 8 | 6 | 5 | 1 | 1 | 1 | 9,174 |
| 4 | Rangasamudra ... ... | 25 | 7 | 15 | 3 | 7 | — | 8,296 |
| 5 | Sosale ... ... ... | 36 | 29 | 25 | 6 | 5 | — | 17,818 |
| 6 | Talakád ... ... | 14 | 15 | 9 | 1 | 3 | 1 | 13,274 |
| 7 | T. Narsipur ... ... | 28 | 21 | 28 | — | — | — | 17,314 |
| | Total ... ... | 138 | 94 | 102 | 17 | 17 | 2 | 83,454 |

[1] These are grants by the Ummattur chiefs, dated 1489 to 1504, and of the time of Krishna Raya (1520) and Venkatapati Raya (1640) of Vijayanagar, the latter grant being by Narasa Raja of Mysore.

*Principal places, with population.*—Bannúr, 4,925; Múgur, 3,735; Talakád, 3,273; Sosale, 3,033; Kempanapura, 2,005; Hosa Alagóḍ, 1,667; Tirumakudlu Narsipura, 1,650; Gargesvari, 1,631; Beṭṭahaḷḷi, 1,574; Holasál, 1,483; Doḍ Abbágalu, 1,339; Hemmige, 1,304; Binakanhalli, 1,210; Váṭálu; 1,201; Kaliyúr, 1,198; Nilasóge, 1,172; Somanáthpura, 1,160; Chidaravalli, 1,134; Hale Álagód, 1,051; Málingi, 1,041.

In 1882 the Bannúr and Bevinhalli hóblis were added to this taluq from the old Ashtagram taluq, while Táyúr hóbli was transferred from this to Nanjangud taluq, and in 1886 Purigáli hóbli to Malavalli taluq, together with the inám lands held by the Jágirdár of Sivanasamudram.

The taluq is watered by the Kávéri, which runs through it from north to south, with a wide serpentine bend towards the south, where it forms the boundary. The Kabbani also enters the taluq from the west and forms a junction with the Kávéri, but is not here utilized for agricultural purposes. The course of the Kávéri, on the other hand, may be traced by an almost unintermitting border of wet cultivation on each bank. The anicuts and canals are elsewhere described. In its course through this taluq the Kávéri takes the nature of a wide and shallow river with a sandy bed, and is fordable at several places except during a fresh. Along its banks and in the lowlands black soil predominates, and here good crops are obtained; but in the uplands, especially in the west of the taluq, the soil is very poor and does not repay cultivation without constant manuring. *Hain* is the almost universal season for crop on both wet and dry lands: the only standard *kár* crop being jóla, which is grown largely, principally on the black soil, the rich nature of which allows of the cultivation of cotton, wheat, or coriander seed as a *hain* crop during the same year.

With the exception of a little under 35 rain-fed tanks, all the wet land is dependent on the channels from the Kávéri. Hardly any bhara bhatta rice is grown. There are, however, several old tanks, most of which were breeched or fell out of repair during the Musalman rule. There is no jungle, and but little land is waste. There are extensive inam lands in this taluq; lands aggregating Rs. 10,205 annually are in the possession of relations and connections of the former Mahárája; and others yielding Rs. 13,000 were granted by that prince to Brahmans of his court. A few isolated rocky hills are found, the highest of which is Kundúr Beṭṭa on the frontier of Malavalli. The remainder of the taluq is level cultivated land.

The total revenue demand for 1891–2 (15 months) was Rs. 1,49,862, and for 1892–3 it was Rs. 1,69,266.

The average rainfall at Tirumakudlu Narsipur for 26 years (1870–95) was as follows :—

| Jan. | Feb. | Mar. | April | May | June | July | Aug. | Sept. | Oct. | Nov. | Dec. | | Year. |
|---|---|---|---|---|---|---|---|---|---|---|---|---|---|
| — | 0·02 | 0·61 | 2·44 | 5·64 | 1·92 | 1·23 | 2·99 | 4·35 | 6·78 | 2·00 | 1·04 | ... | 29·02 |

According to another record for the same period, the annual average is 25·87.

There are roads from Tirumakudlu Narsipur north-west to Mysore, north to Bannur and Seringapatam, and south-east to Talakád and Holesál. In each case the river has to be forded, as there are no bridges. There are also roads from Tirumakudlu Narsipur west to the railway at Nanjangud, and south to Múgúr and Santemarahalli. Another road runs east from Sósile to Sivasamudram and the Kávéri Falls, with a branch to Talakáḍ.

**Tirumakudlu Narsipur.**—A town situated in 12° 13′ N. lat., 76° 58′ E. long., at the junction of the Kabbani with the Kávéri, 20 miles south-east of Mysore, and 18 from the railway at Nanjangud. Head-quarters, since 1868, of the taluq of the same name, which, till 1882, was called the Talakád taluq. It is also a municipality.

| Population in 1891. | Males. | Females. | Total. |
|---|---|---|---|
| Hindus ... ... ... ... ... ... ... | 751 | 796 | 1,547 |
| Muhammadans ... ... ... ... ... ... ... | 57 | 41 | 98 |
| Christians ... ... ... ... ... ... ... | 2 | 3 | 5 |
| Total ... ... ... | 810 | 840 | 1,650 |

Narsipur is separated from Tirumakúdlu by the Kabbani, and is on the right bank of the two rivers, while Tirumakúdlu is on the tongue of land between the two where they unite. The above is the population of Narsipur; that of Tirumakúdlu is 679. This spot has always been considered specially sacred, and possesses two temples—one to Gunja Narasimha, which was repaired and embellished by the Dalaváyi of Mysore about 320 years ago, and is supported by an annual allowance of Rs. 958; and a second, situated at Tiruma-kúdalu (the most holy union), and dedicated to Agastyesvara, which receives annually Rs. 1,822, and has existed from time immemorial. The town of Narsipur is in no way noteworthy. Close to it on the south is Hosa Álagód, with a population of 1,667.

| Municipal Funds. | 1892–3. | 1893–4. | 1894–5. | 1895–6. |
|---|---|---|---|---|
| Income ... ... ... ... ... ... | 466 | 573 | 447 | 843 |
| Expenditure ... ... ... ... ... .. | 624 | 1,033 | 681 | 1,359 |

**Tonnur.**—Properly Tondanur, a village in the Seringapatam taluq, 10 miles north-west of Seringapatam. Population 546.

It is historically interesting as having been the refuge of the last of the Hoysala kings after the destruction of Dorasamudra by the Muhammadans in 1326. Here also is the splendid tank called the Moti Talab, lake of pearls (*q. v.*). There is a Musalman tomb close by, to Shah Salar Masaud Ghazi, bearing the date 760 Hijiri, or 1358.

**Ummattur.**—A village in Chámrájnagar taluq, on the Nanjangud-Yelandur road, 10 miles north of the kasba. Head-quarters of the hóbli of the same name. Population 1,827.

Ummattur was formerly an important principality under the Vijayanagar kings.[1] The Rája was related to the Sri Ranga Ráyal, or viceroy at Seringapatam, and to him Tirumala Rája, the last of the viceroys, seems to have formed the purpose of resigning his power, though compelled by circumstances to abdicate in favour of Rája Wodeyar of Mysore. Between the Mysore Rájas and the Ummattur Rájas there was naturally a strong feeling of enmity. This was shared by the house of Kalale, which the Ummattur chief had on one occasion nearly exterminated by a treacherous massacre of all its members, when one infant escaped. The latter grew up to restore the fortunes of his line, and a common interest, no less than relationship, formed the bond of union by which the Kalale chiefs became the Dalaváyis of the Mysore State. In 1613 Ummattur was subdued by Rája Wodeyar and annexed to Mysore. It is now an inám village, one of the endowments of the Chámrájesvara temple at Chámrájnagar.

**Varuna.**—A village in Varakod hóbli, Mysore taluq, a few miles south-west of Mysore. Population 520.

It is evidently, from the remains there, a place of great antiquity. There is a Ganga inscription of the 8th century. In the 10th century the place was in the possession of a chief named Goggi, who was of the Chalukya family. It was perhaps his daughter who became the wife of Bhillama,[2] one of the Yádava kings of Devagiri, earlier than the one mentioned in Vol. I, p. 342. In 1828 the queen Devájammanni of the Lakshmi-vilása had a temple erected here, made a tank and a tope, and granted endowments.

[1] The Wodeyars of Ummattúr undoubtedly for a long period exercised rule over the Nilagiris, and in their adversity found a refuge here, and for a time perhaps preserved their partial independence in the Malekota fort near Kalhatti. Near Malekota there are still living Bedar whose ancestors were in the service of the Ummattur Raja as tax-gatherers, and hence are still cordially hated by the Badagas, who, on the other hand, still call the Mysore Rajas their Kartas or lords.—Grigg's *Manual of the Nilagiri District*, pp. 268, 269.

[2] *See* Fleet's *Kan Dyn.*, new edition, p. 514.

**Yedatore.**—A taluq in the north-west. Area 234 square miles. Head-quarters at Yedatore. Contains the following hóblis, villages and population:—

| No. | Hoblis. | Villages. | Hamlets. | Villages classified. | | | Population. |
|---|---|---|---|---|---|---|---|
| | | | | Government. | Sarvamánya. | Jódi. | |
| 1 | Byádarahalli ... | 25 | 20 | 23 | 2 | — | 12,648 |
| 2 | Hanasóge ... ... | 29 | 18 | 16 | 13 | — | 10,313 |
| 3 | Haradanhalli ... | 22 | 14 | 22 | — | — | 9,193 |
| 4 | Mirle ... ... | 26 | 8 | 26 | — | — | 9,620 |
| 5 | Sálígráma ... ... | 20 | 9 | 20 | — | — | 11,279 |
| 6 | Tippur ... ... | 34 | 9 | 23 | 9 | 2 | 12,735 |
| 7 | Yedatore ... ... | 24 | 13 | 22 | 2 | — | 8,474 |
| | Total ... | 180 | 91 | 152 | 26 | 2 | 74,262 |

*Principal places, with population.*—Sáligráma, 3,788; Mirle, 2,511; Yedatore, 2,413; Tippúr, 1,811; Byádarahalli, 1,643; Haliyúr, 1,608; Kestúr, 1,599; Ballúr, 1,445; Sígaválu, 1,438; Bherya, 1,393; Gandhanhalli, 1,342; Hanasóge, 1,282; Hebbálu, 1,266; Hampápura, 1,160; Mélúru, 1,148; Kuppe, 1,065; Siddapura, 1,023; Chandigálu, 1,018.

The Hanasóge hóbli was transferred to this taluq from Arkalgud in 1882, and the Halli Maisur hóbli removed to the Hole Narsipur taluq. The Kávéri flows through the taluq from west to east, forming, in the latter direction, part of the northern boundary, where it receives the Hemavati from the north. The Lakshmantirtha runs along the eastern boundary to its confluence with the Kávéri. The great feature of the taluq is, therefore, the river channels drawn from the Kávéri, running for over 100 miles. The principal anicut on the Kávéri is at Chunchankatte, from which two channels are taken, one to the north of the river, and the other to the south. Of the former, the Saligram series are 24 miles long and irrigate 2,884 acres, yielding a revenue of Rs. 18,361. The Mirle series are 38 miles long, irrigate 3,110 acres, and realize Rs. 20,811. The Ramasamudram channel is 41 miles long, irrigates 4,300 acres, and brings in Rs. 25,809. The Tippur channel is taken from an anicut near Adagur. It is 22 miles long, irrigates 590 acres, and the revenue is Rs. 4,089. There is also an anicut on the Lakshmantirtha, near Malhalli, from which there is a channel on the north bank, irrigating 245 acres. There are about 140 tanks, of which 10 may be termed large, and that at Galagekere is fed by the river channel.

The country is gently undulating in character, there being neither hills nor jungle. Low scrub is met with in many places on the high grounds, and occasionally date topes in the valleys. The soils are not of a very high order, and may be described as fair average red and sandy, and of rather varying quality, under the channels especially. That under the Saligram, Mirle and Tippur channels is the best. Rági is the principal dry crop, sown in the early rains; oil-seeds, pulses and jola are also grown. Tobacco is cultivated in Byadarhalli. Only one crop of rice is raised in the year, the kinds chiefly grown being *kembhatta*, *kaddibhatta* and *bolamallige*. Sugar-cane has been given up, though grown to some extent formerly. The areca gardens suffered much from the famine, and the higher price of rice led to its substitution for areca in many parts. The other garden crops are plantain, betel-leaf, sweet potatoes, and various vegetables.

The revenue settlement was introduced into Hanasoge in 1884, and into the remainder of the taluq in 1885. The area of the taluq in the latter survey was thus distributed:—

| | |
|---|---|
| Culturable (dry, 73,107; wet, 10,631; garden, 1,816) ... | 85,554 |
| Unculturable (including village sites, &c.) ... ... ... | 27,565 |
| Inám villages (12,891); kávals (4,671) ... ... ... ... | 17,562 |
| Total area ... | 130,681 |

The unoccupied area was 5,574 acres, of which only 31 were wet or garden land. The total revenue demand for 1891–2 (15 months) was Rs. 2,21,676, and for 1892–3 it was Rs. 2,12,443.

The average rainfall for 26 years (1870–95) at Yedatore was as follows:—

| Jan. | Feb. | Mar. | Apr. | May | June | July | Aug. | Sept. | Oct. | Nov. | Dec. | Year. |
|---|---|---|---|---|---|---|---|---|---|---|---|---|
| — | — | 0·39 | 2·08 | 5·75 | 1·98 | 1·87 | 2·47 | 2·96 | 6·40 | 2·48 | 0·65 | ... 27·03 |

The Mysore-Hassan road runs through the east of the taluq from south to north westwards, crossing the river at Tippur, where there is as yet no bridge. From this road one branch runs west from Ságarkatte to Yedatore and onwards on the south side of the river, and another west from Hampapura to Saligram and farther on the north side. There is a cross road connecting Bherya and Saligram, and an unfinished road from Yedatore south to Hunsur.

**Yedatore.**—A town situated in 12° 28′ N. lat., 75° 27′ E. long., on the right bank of the Kávéri, 22 miles north-west of Mysore. Head-quarters of the Yedatore taluq, and a municipality. It is reached by a cross road from the Mysore-Hassan road, 8 miles north-west of Yelwal.

| Population in 1891. | Males. | Females. | Total. |
|---|---|---|---|
| Hindus ... ... ... ... ... ... ... | 917 | 1,044 | 1,961 |
| Muhammadans ... ... ... ... ... | 219 | 229 | 448 |
| Christians ... ... ... ... ... ... | 3 | 1 | 4 |
| Total ... ... ... | 1,139 | 1,274 | 2,413 |

A fair is held on Friday, attended by 250 people.

The town derives its name from the bend to the left (*yeḍa*) made by the river (*tore*) at this point, which invests it with peculiar sanctity. It was one of the places conquered by Rájendra Chola after his overthrow of the Gangas in the 11th century. A temple of Arkesvara, endowed by Mummadí Krishna Rája, occupies a prominent position, with bathing ghats leading down from it and an agrahára around.

| Municipal Funds. | 1892-3. | 1893-4. | 1894-5. | 1895-6. |
|---|---|---|---|---|
| Income ... ... ... ... ... | 450 | 577 | 644 | 1,124 |
| Expenditure... ... ... ... ... | 1,257 | 1,210 | 1,482 | 2,220 |

**Yelandur.**—A taluq in the south-east, forming the estate of a Jágirdar. Area 102 square miles. Head-quarters at Yelandur. Contains the following hóblis, villages and population :—

| No. | Hoblis. | Villages. | Hamlets. | Villages classified.[1] | | Population. |
|---|---|---|---|---|---|---|
| | | | | Sarva-mánya. | Jodi. | |
| 1 | Agara ... ... ... | 8 | 8 | — | 1 | 10,281 |
| 2 | Yaragamballi ... ... | 7 | 7 | 1 | 2 | 6,613 |
| 3 | Yelandúr ... ... | 10 | 9 | — | 1 | 14,502 |
| 4 | Biligiri Rangaswami betta | 1 | 9 | 1 | — | 358 |
| | Total ... ... | 26 | 33 | 2 | 4 | 31,754 |

*Principal places, with population.*—Agara, 5,218; Yelandúr, 3,566; Maddúr, 2,887; Honnúru, 2,803; Yaragamballi, 2,524; Kestúr, 2,450; Ambale, 2,383; Yeriyúr, 1,483; Gumballi, 1,102.

This small but rich tract is one of the most fertile and the most densely populated in the whole of Mysore. Along the eastern side

[1] The whole Jágir is sarvamányam with reference to the Mysore Government. The classification is that which is local to the Jágir.

are situated the Biligirirangan hills, running (within the Jágir) for about 10 miles north and south. The peak after which they are named rises to 4,195 feet above the sea. Teak, sandal, honne, matti and other valuable trees are found on their slopes. The only inhabitants of the range are the Soligas, who are permitted to cultivate free, within prescribed limits, in their own desultory and shifting mode, in return for which they guard the forest on the hills and render service in the temple on the summit on festive occasions.

The remainder of the Jágir, north-west of these hills and quite distinct from them, is one compact level stretch of land, traversed from south to north by the Honnu-holé or Suvarnavati, which is the sole source of irrigation. It possesses one anicut (at Ganaganur) and six channels and feeds the Agara tank, the water in which is practically unfailing. The level surface of the country, and the very slight rise of the river banks render dams unnecessary, for as soon as the river becomes at all full its water flows naturally into the channels. When the river water runs very low temporary dams are constructed, as in Chamrajnagar taluq, of stakes, mats, sand, &c. But it is proposed to construct a a permanent dam higher up the stream that will insure a permanent supply to the other large tanks, such as the Ambale, Yelandur, Yeriyur and Maddur. There are no rain-fed tanks worthy of mention, but some small ones near the Biligirirangans draw their water-supply from the hill streams.

The wealth of the Jágir is mainly due to the extraordinary fertility of the soil, which, except near the foot of the hills, is mostly a good black, free from the defects ordinarily found in it elsewhere. In the east, near the hills, the soil is red and sandy, but not poor. The garden crops are chiefly betel-leaf, areca, cocoa-nut and mulberry. The latter, indeed, is grown in all descriptions of land, garden, wet and dry. Sugar-cane is raised under the larger tanks and rice alone under the smaller ones. The staple dry crop is jola; togari and Bengal gram are also grown, but no cotton, though the soils are favourable for that crop. Rági is not much cultivated.

Silk is produced in large quantities, and piece goods are also manufactured. Brass is made into lamps and vessels at Yeragamballi. The principal markets resorted to are at Santemarahalli (Chamrajnagar taluq) and Kollegal (Coimbatore district).

There are inscriptions in the Jágir of the Ganga and Chola kings, and many of the time of the Hoysala kings. From the latter we learn that Yelandur was included in the Padináḍ province. This was also the case during the Vijayanagar period, towards the close of which the name gradually changes to the modern form of Hadináḍ, now represented by Hadináru (Nanjangud taluq). The kings of Padináḍ or the Ten Náds (*Padináḍugalam*) specially mentioned in connection with Yelandur are Singe-Depa; his son Rama, ruling in 1568; his younger brother Chenna; Tirumala Rája and Nanja Rája, the sons of the latter; Mudda Rája, son of Tirumala, ruling in 1654. It was subsequently absorbed into the Mysore territory.

In 1807 Yelandur was given in jágir by the British Government to Purnaiya in recognition of his services as Divan and Regent during the minority of the Rája. The *sanad*, countersigned by Sir John Malcolm, is drawn up in terms of high eulogy and appreciation of the great and faithful services rendered by the recipient. That sagacious minister, on being offered his choice of lands, is said to have chosen Yelandur; firstly, because it contained a never-failing supply of water; and, secondly, because it was (at that time) out of the beaten track of Government officials and travellers without being at too great a distance from the capital. But as he belonged to a Coimbatore family it seems more likely that, apart from the obvious natural advantages of the place, he chose it as being on the borders of Coimbatore and Mysore. The present Jágirdár is the great-grandson of Purnaiya.

The revenue settlement was introduced in 1896. The area of the Jágir was thus distributed:—

| | |
|---|---|
| Culturable (dry, 16,135; wet, 5,374; garden, 704) ... ... | 22,213 |
| Unculturable (roads, village sites, &c.) ... ... ... ... | 12,504 |
| Inam (principally Biligiri Rangaswami betta) ... ... ... | 30,341 |
| Total acres ... | 65,058 |

The unoccupied area was only 432 acres, of which 394 was dry crop land.

The average annual rainfall is about 25 inches.

There is a road from Kaulandi on the Nanjangud road, through Santemarahalli, which enters the Jágir on the west and passes through Yelandur and all the most populous parts, on north to Kollegal. This part of the road is through sticky black soil and is in bad order. There is also a road from Yelandur to the foot of the Ghats westward.

**Yelandur.**—A town situated in 12° 13′ N. lat., 77° 5′ E. long., on the Honnu-holé. The kasba of the Yelandur Jágir, and connected by road with the railway at Nanjangud, which is 26 miles distant, and thus with Mysore, 42 miles. Population 3,566.

Yelandur was from early times included in Padináḍ or Hadináḍ (corresponding perhaps with the ancient Punnád Ten Thousand) and was the seat of a wealthy principality at the time of the Vijayanagar sovereignty. The principal temple, that of Gaurisvara, was built by Singe-Depa, king of Padináḍ, in about 1450, and later kings of Padináḍ, or the Ten Náḍ country, granted endowments for it. The last Rája entered into alliance with the Mysore and Kalale chiefs, giving his daughter in marriage to one of the latter. A Jain named Vishálákaha Pandita, known as the Yelandur pandit, was the faithful adherent of Chikka Deva Rája during his captivity at Hangala, and on his accession to the throne in 1672 became his first minister. The celebrated Lingáyit poet Shaḍakshara Deva, who wrote the popular Rájasekhara Vilása in 1657, was a member of the Danagur maṭha near Yelandur.

The town is a thriving place, and many of the inhabitants are well to do. It contains a substantially built house of the Jágirdar. The portico of the Gaurisvara temple is a good specimen of the carving of the period. The inscription at the temple explains the name of the place as Eleyindúr, the town of the young moon; and compares the town to the eye or centre of a lotus, surrounded by eight petals, which are eight hills in the surrounding country—Svetasila (that is Biligiri) on the east, the Mallinátha hill near Kárápur on the south-east, the Suragi hill on the south, the Sankaresvara hill on the south-west, the Mallikárjuna hill near Jannúr on the west, the Sambhulinga hill on the north-west, Srisaila on the north, and the Nirmala hill on the north-east.

# HASSAN DISTRICT

## GENERAL DESCRIPTION

*Situation.*—A District in the west; situated between 12° 30′ and 13° 36′ north latitude, and between 75° 32′ and 76° 42′ east longitude. The greatest length is from north to south, about 75 miles; and the greatest breadth is from west to east, about 68.

*Area.*—The area is 2,641 square miles; of which 1,037½ square miles are under cultivation.

*Boundaries.*—It is bounded on the north by Kadur District; east by Tumkur and Mysore Districts; south by Coorg; and west by South Kanara, belonging to the Madras Presidency.

*Divisions.* — It is subdivided into the following seven taluqs. Alúr is a sub-taluq under Hassan taluq. Arsikere is the old Harnhalli taluq.

| No. | Taluq. | Area of Sq. Miles. | No. of Hoblis. | No. of Villages or Towns. | Population in 1891. | Per Sq. Mile. |
|---|---|---|---|---|---|---|
| 1 | Arkalgúd... ... ... | 262 | 6 | 289 | 75,812 | 290·12 |
| 2 | Arsikere ... ... ... | 490 | 6 | 358 | 65,306 | 133·27 |
| 3 | Bélúr ... ... ... | 338 | 7 | 395 | 75,470 | 222·69 |
| 4 | Chanaráyapatna ... ... | 413 | 7 | 377 | 78,211 | 189·37 |
| 5 | Hassan ... ... ... | 475 | 9 | 567 | 113,397 | 238·73 |
| 6 | Hole Narsipur ... ... | 233 | 4 | 226 | 50,894 | 218·42 |
| 7 | Manjarábád ... ... | 430 | 8 | 278 | 55,862 | 129·91 |
| | Total ... | 2,641 | 47 | 2,490 | 514,952 | 194·98 |

**Physical Features.**—The main body of the District consists of the Hémávati river basin. The only exceptions are certain outlying tracts along the west border—namely, the western portion of the Manjarábád taluq, which drains to the Nétrávati in South Kanara; and the Arsikere taluq, whose waters run north to the Vedávati in Chitaldroog. The Kávéri flows through a small portion of the south.

The course of the Hémávati in the District is at first south and then east. Running from north to south of Manjarábád taluq, it turns east along the Mysore and Coorg frontier, and continuing in the same direction, separates Hassan and Arkalgúd taluqs, and passing through

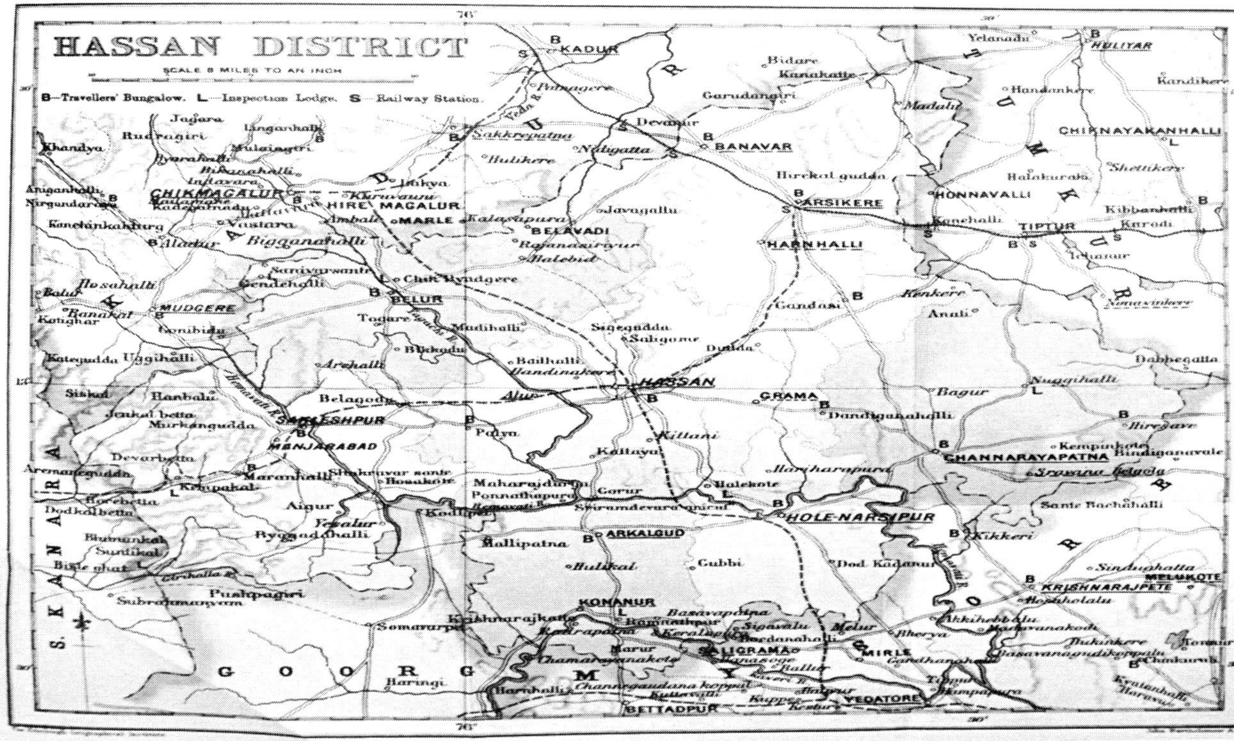
HASSAN DISTRICT
SCALE 8 MILES TO AN INCH
B—Travellers' Bungalow. L—Inspection Lodge. S—Railway Station.
KADUR
BANAVAR
ARSIKERE
TIPTUR
HULIYAR
CHIKNAYAKANHALLI
HONNAVALLI
CHIKMAGALUR
HIRE MAGALUR
MARLE
BELAVADI
HARNHALLI
BELUR
MUDGERE
HASSAN
GRAMA
CHANNARAYAPATNA
SAKLESHPUR
MANJARABAD
HOLE-NARSIPUR
ARKALGUD
KONANUR
SALIGRAMA
MIRLE
KRISHNARAJPETE
MELUKOTE
YEDATORE
BETTADPUR
S. KANARA
COORG
MYSORE
TUMKUR
KADUR

out Hole Narsipur taluq, leaves the District with a southerly course and falls into the Kávéri in the Mysore District. Its chief tributary is the Yagachi from the Belúr taluq, which joins it near Gorur, in Hassan taluq.

The Manjarábád side of the District, resting on the brow of the Western Ghats, forms a part of the Male-síme or Malnád, hill country, the remainder being Maidán or Bail-síme, plain country, also called Múḍu-síme or east country.

The mountains forming the western limit extend from the pass at the Bisale ghát to Jénkal-beṭṭa, including within a grand panorama the towering height of Subrahmanya or Pushpagiri, close to the south-west border, rising to 5,626 feet above the level of the sea; Devar-beṭṭa, (4,206 feet), Múrkan guḍḍa (4,265 feet),[1] and the superb Jénkal-beṭṭa (4,558 feet).[2] Besides the mountains in Manjarábád, there are low ranges of granitic hills running along the northern limits of the District through the Belúr, Hassan and Arsikere taluqs, marking the watershed which separates the Krishna and Kávéri river systems. The Indra-beṭṭa at Sravana-Belgola (3,309 feet) is noted for the colossal Jain statue on its summit. Some low hills pass through Hole Narsipur taluq towards Hassan and Channaráyapatna.

The general level of the country slopes with the course of the Hémávati, from the Ghat ranges towards the bed of the Kávéri in the south-east. At Belúr the height above sea level is 3,150 feet, at Hassan 3,084, at Sakleshpur 2,998; while at Channaráyapatna it is 2,771, and at Arsikere 2,666.

The Malnád or highland region, occupying the whole of the Manjarábád taluq and the western half of Belúr, has been thus graphically described by Major Montgomery, a former Superintendent. "The character of the country is generally undulating till on approaching the Ghats, when it becomes precipitous. Perhaps there is no scenery in India more beautiful than the southern part of this tract, adjoining the north-west of Coorg. It for the most part resembles the richest park scenery in England. Hills covered with the finest grass or equally verdant crops of dry grain, adorned and crowned with clumps of noble forest trees, in some instances apparently planted most carefully, and certainly with perfect taste. The highest and the most beautiful knolls have been generally selected as the spots on which to build the small mutts and other places of worship with which the country abounds, and the groves that surround or are in the vicinity of these are tended with the greatest care, and the trees composing them replaced as they die

[1] *Múru-kannu-gudda*, the hill of the three-eyed, *i.e.*, Siva.

[2] *Jénu-kallu-betta*, honey-rock hill.

off or are blown down. The southern differs from the more northerly and westerly parts of the Manjarábád taluq, in the absence of that succession of dense jungles which obscure the view, and in the soft character of the hills, which are in most instances quite free from the stunted date, and smooth as the lawn of a villa on the Thames. But the whole taluq is beautiful, and less wooded than Coorg or Nagar, though greatly partaking of the features of both."

The Maidán or lowland tract, forming the largest and most populous portion of the District, consists of an undulating plain country, generally cultivated, but here and there having extensive kávals or grazing lands. Patches covered with the wild date are common, and in some parts are limited tracts of stunted jungle growing upon a gravelly, gritty soil. The high-lying lands, particularly in the Hassan, Channaráyapatna and Hole Narsipur taluqs, have a singularly bare and bleak appearance and are frequently so stony that they are unfit for cultivation. They form, however, good gathering grounds for tanks, and the valleys below are rich and well wooded.

*Channels.*—The District partakes in the system of irrigation-channels which is so marked a characteristic of the Mysore District. The following table exhibits a summary of particulars regarding the most important. There are also a number of temporary channels for rice-fields in the Manjarábád country, and altogether a revenue is derived of Rs. 55,130 a year.

| Name of River. | Name of Anicut. | Name of Channel. | Length in Miles. | Acres Irrigated. | Revenue in Rupees. |
|---|---|---|---|---|---|
| Hemavati .. | Srirámadevar ... | North Channel .. | 47½ | 4,413 | 25,092 |
| | Srirámadevar ... | South Channel ... | 12 | 606 | 3,544 |
| Yugachi ... | Halvagal... ... | Halvagal.. ... | 6 | 184 | 914 |
| | Changarvalli ... | Changarvalli ... | 9 | 281 | 1,599 |
| | Chakratirtha ané | Chakratirtha ... | 2 | 130 | 749 |
| | Arehalli ané ... | Arehalli ... ... | 2 | 40 | 196 |
| | Kittur ané ... | Kittur ... ... | 9 | 559 | 2,557 |
| | Kudlur ... ... | Kudlur ... ... | 6 | 416 | 2,220 |
| | Madagatta ... | Madagatta ... | 8 | 550 | 2,501 |

**Rocks.**—Throughout the District, kaolin, felspar, quartz, and other materials suitable for the manufacture of earthenware are abundant. Kunker, a tufaceous nodular limestone, is found in many parts of the District, and is the only form of limestone rock known. It is found in alluvial valleys and on the banks of some streams, under or mixed with coloured clay. Potstone, from which the images at Halebid are carved, is found at four places in the Hassan and Belur taluqs. Hematite iron ore is obtained from the Bagadi hills in the Arsikere taluq, associated with granitic rocks, broken by trap protrusions.

Extensive traces of old gold mines have been found in some parts, and gold-mining on modern principles has been commenced at Harnhalli and Kempinkote, though as yet with little result.

**Soils.**—The soil of the Malnád is a rich red sedimentary, with forest loam in the jungles, and a red laterite soil on the grass-covered hills. The hills are of primitive formation, chiefly granitic, with a little iron ore. The products of this part are rice in the valleys, coffee and cardamoms in forest slopes.

The soils in the plains, surrounding the hills, are generally of a rich sedimentary character, easily worked, and affording fine crops of cereal or garden produce. On the tops of the rising grounds the soil is of course generally thinner and more sandy or gravelly than in the valleys, where on the contrary it is more clayey and darker in colour. There are also other extensive tracts with a gravelly sandy soil, resulting from the disintegration *in situ* of the primitive schists superimposed upon the granite. The black soil occurs, but only to small extent and in patches, chiefly in the Arkalgud, Channaráyapatna and Arsikere taluqs.

**Climate.**—The temperature of Hassan is slightly lower than that of Bangalore, the mean reading of the thermometer being 72·9°, and the daily range about 20°. The maximum has reached 97·6 in April, while the minimum has touched 42·7 in January. The heat during the hot months of March and April is much modified by the sea-breeze from the western coast, and by light fogs in the mornings and evenings. Owing to its proximity to the Western Ghats, and the moisture of the atmosphere from the numerous forest lands and marshy fields, the temperature of the Malnád is some degrees lower; but this scarcely compensates for the malaria generated by the extensive decomposition of vegetable matter. The European settlers generally suffer from miasmatic fever after the early rains, but they soon grow acclimatized and are ultimately better able to withstand it than the natives themselves, numbers of whom succumb each year to its attacks.

The following is a table of mean meteorological results from observations recorded at Hassan in 1894 and 1895:—

| 1894. | Barometer. | | | Thermometers. | | | | | | Aqueous Vapour. | | Wind. | | Rain. | | Cloud. | | |
|---|---|---|---|---|---|---|---|---|---|---|---|---|---|---|---|---|---|---|
| | Red. to 32° F. | Red. to Sea Level. | Daily Range. | Dry Bulb. Mean. | Dry Bulb. Max. | Dry Bulb. Min. | Dry Bulb. Range. | Wet Bulb. Mean. | Wet Bulb. Min. | Press. Inches. | Humidity. Per cent. | Daily Velocity Miles. | Mean Direction. | Fall, Inches. | Number of Days. | Mean. Per Cent. | No. of Days. Cloudless 10h. and 16h | No. of Days. Overcast. |
| | 26+ | 29+ | | | | | | | | | | | | | | | | |
| Jan. ... | ·902 | ·867 | ·121 | 69·5 | 81·1 | 54·7 | 26·4 | 55·5 | 50·3 | ·390 | 51 | 81 | E. | — | — | 37 | 5 | — |
| Feb. ... | ·911 | ·853 | ·126 | 72·9 | 85·3 | 56·9 | 28·4 | 57·4 | 52·1 | ·407 | 47 | 89 | E.S.E. | 0·01 | 1 | 23 | 8 | — |
| Mar. ... | ·857 | ·775 | ·127 | 77·9 | 89·5 | 64·1 | 25·4 | 62·0 | 58·0 | ·469 | 49 | 71 | S.S.E. | 2·36 | 6 | 46 | — | 2 |
| April... | ·810 | ·732 | ·120 | 77·7 | 88·3 | 65·8 | 22·5 | 65·3 | 61·2 | ·594 | 62 | 74 | S. by W. | 6·69 | 13 | 55 | — | — |
| May ... | ·800 | ·725 | ·111 | 76·8 | 86·5 | 65·6 | 20·9 | 65·3 | 61·0 | ·621 | 65 | 93 | W. by N. | 7·79 | 15 | 52 | — | — |
| June ... | ·758 | ·717 | ·073 | 72·3 | 78·7 | 64·9 | 13·8 | 64·7 | 61·0 | ·634 | 77 | 122 | W. by S. | 2·74 | 22 | 86 | — | 4 |
| July ... | ·780 | ·749 | ·065 | 71·1 | 77·1 | 64·0 | 13·1 | 63·6 | 60·0 | ·608 | 78 | 124 | W. | 2·81 | 22 | 89 | — | 6 |
| Aug. ... | ·761 | ·721 | ·085 | 71·7 | 78·3 | 64·2 | 14·1 | 64·2 | 60·6 | ·624 | 78 | 90 | W. by N. | 2·23 | 20 | 88 | — | 5 |
| Sept.... | ·793 | ·750 | ·099 | 72·4 | 80·4 | 62·9 | 17·5 | 63·9 | 60·5 | ·589 | 71 | 77 | W. by N. | 0·78 | 12 | 77 | — | 3 |
| Oct. ... | ·822 | ·780 | ·106 | 72·8 | 80·8 | 63·7 | 17·1 | 65·0 | 62·3 | ·602 | 72 | 61 | S.W. by S. | 10·99 | 18 | 73 | — | 3 |
| Nov. ... | ·902 | ·881 | ·100 | 70·0 | 77·5 | 60·7 | 16·8 | 62·9 | 59·2 | ·593 | 76 | 93 | E.S.E. | 2·18 | 7 | 64 | — | 3 |
| Dec. ... | ·915 | ·884 | ·117 | 69·8 | 80·0 | 56·5 | 23·5 | 60·2 | 55·2 | ·526 | 65 | 90 | E. | — | — | 32 | 2 | — |
| | 26+ | 29+ | | | | | | | | | | | | | | | | |
| Year ... | ·834 | ·786 | ·104 | 72·9 | 82·0 | 62·0 | 20·0 | 62·5 | 58·5 | ·555 | 66 | 89 | — | 38·58 | 136 | 60 | 15 | 26 |
| | | | | | | | | | | | | | | Total. | | | Total. | |

| 1895. | Barometer. | | | Thermometers. | | | | | | Aqueous Vapour. | | Wind. | | Rain. | | Cloud. | | |
|---|---|---|---|---|---|---|---|---|---|---|---|---|---|---|---|---|---|---|
| | Red. to 32° F. | Red. to Sea Level. | Daily Range. | Dry Bulb. | | | | Wet Bulb. | | Press. Inches. | Humidity. Per cent. | Daily Velocity Miles. | Mean Direction. | Fall, Inches. | Number of Days. | Mean Per Cent. | No. of Days. | |
| | | | | Mean. | Max. | Min. | Range. | Mean. | Min. | | | | | | | | Cloudless 10h. and 16h. | Overcast. |
| | 26+ | 29+ | | | | | | | | | | | | | | | | |
| Jan. ... | ·901 | ·862 | ·121 | 70·4 | 81·8 | 56·3 | 25·5 | 57·2 | 53·1 | ·395 | 51 | 69 | E. by S. | — | — | 28 | 8 | — |
| Feb. ... | ·906 | ·847 | ·124 | 73·5 | 85·5 | 58·5 | 27·0 | 57·5 | 54·0 | ·348 | 41 | 76 | E. by S. | 0·03 | 1 | 15 | 4 | — |
| Mar. ... | ·844 | ·749 | ·136 | 78·3 | 90·7 | 63·1 | 27·6 | 62·6 | 59·0 | ·460 | 45 | 77 | E.S.E. | — | — | 21 | 4 | — |
| Apr. ... | ·819 | ·732 | ·130 | 78·8 | 89·6 | 66·3 | 23·3 | 66·6 | 63·7 | ·588 | 59 | 79 | S. by W. | 2·25 | 7 | 47 | — | — |
| May ... | ·811 | ·731 | ·104 | 77·8 | 87·4 | 66·7 | 20·7 | 66·6 | 63·4 | ·612 | 62 | 107 | W. by S. | 5·19 | 11 | 48 | — | — |
| June ... | ·761 | ·708 | ·076 | 74·1 | 80·2 | 66·8 | 13·4 | 65·9 | 63·2 | ·620 | 73 | 121 | W. by S. | 4·41 | 20 | 80 | — | 10 |
| July ... | ·796 | ·773 | ·063 | 70·4 | 75·3 | 64·9 | 10·4 | 64·1 | 61·4 | ·605 | 80 | 126 | W. | 3·23 | 23 | 96 | — | 17 |
| Aug. ... | ·779 | ·746 | ·079 | 71·3 | 77·2 | 64·5 | 12·7 | 64·5 | 61·7 | ·612 | 78 | 96 | W. by N. | 3·44 | 20 | 88 | — | 8 |
| Sept. ... | ·813 | ·770 | ·099 | 72·7 | 80·3 | 64·1 | 16·2 | 64·8 | 62·4 | ·585 | 70 | 90 | W. | 3·95 | 15 | 76 | — | 1 |
| Oct. ... | ·831 | ·788 | ·105 | 73·0 | 79·6 | 65·3 | 14·4 | 66·0 | 63·8 | ·614 | 73 | 69 | S.S.E. | 5·64 | 16 | 83 | — | 4 |
| Nov. ... | ·920 | ·885 | ·103 | 71·4 | 79·5 | 60·5 | 19·0 | 62·0 | 58·5 | ·518 | 62 | 76 | E. by N. | 3·43 | 5 | 51 | 1 | — |
| Dec. ... | ·896 | ·875 | ·111 | 67·7 | 77·7 | 54·6 | 23·0 | 56·5 | 52·2 | ·409 | 55 | 94 | E.N.E. | 0·09 | 3 | 49 | 2 | 3 |
| | 26+ | 29+ | | | | | | | | | | | | | | | | |
| Year ... | ·840 | ·789 | ·104 | 73·3 | 82·1 | 62·6 | 19·4 | 62·9 | 59·7 | ·531 | 62 | 90 | — | 31·66 | 121 | 57 | 19 | 43 |
| | | | | | | | | | | | | | | Total. | | | Total. | |

*Rain-fall.*—The average annual rain-fall at Hassan is 32·94 inches, as deduced from the register for 26 years (1870–95). But the western districts bordering on the Ghats have a much heavier fall; the annual average at Sakleshpur being 83·55 inches, and at Aigur, near the Bisale ghat, as high as 100. At some of the western coffee estates even this is exceeded; the average at Byakarvalli Estate for 10 years being 110·26 and at Hulhalli Estate for 16 years 120·25. During the south-west monsoon, which prevails from the month of May till the middle of August, the weather is cold and raw; the rain-fall is continuous, with a few slight breaks. The *sóne* or drizzling rain extends as far as Gráma, 8 miles west of Hassan, and the condition of the surrounding vegetation distinctly shows the lines of demarcation which separate the Malnád from the Maidán country. The north-east monsoon also reaches the District, and the heavy showers which fall in October are of great value in filling the tanks in the Maidán taluqs.

The annual average by taluqs has been thus registered for the 26 years and for 10 years.

| | 26 Years. | 10 Years. | | 26 Years. | 10 Years. |
|---|---|---|---|---|---|
| Arkalgud ... ... | 26·33 ... | 28·27 | Gráma ... ... | 28·77 ... | — |
| Arsikere ... ... | 26·16 ... | 25·80 | Hassan ... ... | 32·94 ... | 31·57 |
| Balur ... ... | 29·88 ... | 31·00 | Hole Narsipur ... | 26·81 ... | 26·93 |
| Channaráyapatna... | 22·12 ... | 22·99 | Sakleshpur ... | 83·55 ... | 77·36 |

The actual annual rain-fall at Hassan has been registered as follows:—

| | | | | | | | |
|---|---|---|---|---|---|---|---|
| 1868 ... | 30·62 | 1875 ... | 22·63 | 1882 ... | 42·49 | 1889 ... | 31·80 |
| 1869 ... | 32·40 | 1876 ... | 18·06 | 1883 ... | — | 1890 ... | 30·55 |
| 1870 ... | 38·19 | 1877 ... | 38·55 | 1884 ... | — | 1891 ... | 29·92 |
| 1871 ... | 27·59 | 1878 ... | 29·01 | 1885 ... | — | 1892 ... | 29·57 |
| 1872 ... | 33·38 | 1879 ... | 34·11 | 1886 ... | 35·83 | 1893 ... | 30·35 |
| 1873 ... | 43·70 | 1880 ... | 33·23 | 1887 ... | 34·95 | 1894 ... | 33·88 |
| 1874 ... | 47·57 | 1881 ... | 16·12 | 1888 ... | 29·20 | 1895 ... | 29·71 |

**Vegetation.**—The upper slopes of the Ghats which form the western boundary of the District are clothed with magnificent virgin forests, containing, amongst other trees, the poon (*calophyllum angustifolium*), the some (*soymida febrifuge*), and blackwood (*dalbergia latifolia*). Some of these forests have been taken up for coffee and cardamom cultivation, but certain of them are reserved by Government as State forests—namely, the Kempuhole Ghat, Kaganeri Ghat, Kabbinale Ghat, and Bisale Ghat, all in the Manjarabad taluq. Owing, however, to their inaccessible position, these forests have as yet been worked only on a limited scale. The timber found in the coffee jungles bordering on the Ghats is of little value, with the exception of the honne (*pterocarpus marsupium*), the nandi (*lagerstrœmia microcarpa*), matti (*terminalia tomentosa*), heswa (*artocarpus hirsuta*), ebony (*diospyros ebenum*), and wild champaka (*michelia champaca*).

Lying more inland, in that tract of country in which the pure Malnad (hill country) merges into the Maidan (plain country), are the Gopigudda, Doddabetta, Hulkunda and Nagavara jungles. They contain chiefly inferior kinds of woods, with a quantity of nandi, matti and honne, much injured by indiscriminate felling. In the Arkalgud taluq, the only jungle worthy of mention is a strip of land lying on the borders of Coorg known as the Menasabetta, the value of which is at present very small from its having been overworked. In the Belur taluq is the Arehalli jungle, containing wood of the above description, but of little value from want of a road. There are also low matti jungles of some size near the Maharajandurga fort, and scrub jungle near the Síge-gudda in the Hassan and Hirikalgudda in the Arsikere taluqs. The babul (*acacia arabica*) is to be found growing in fields in parts of the Channaráyapatna and Hole Narsipur taluqs.

The pepper vine grows wild in the jungles of Manjarabad. The dindaga (*conocarpus latifolia*) and bévu (*melia azadirachta*), yielding gum, are met with in various places. The *rottleria tinctoria* is found in Manjarabad, the *morinda citrifolia* and *morinda ternifolia* in Belur, Manjarabad and Arkalgud. These yield the dyes known as *kapile* and *maddi*. The dyes called *papli chakki* and *patanga* are obtained, the former from the root of a scandent plant in Arsikere and Arkalgud, the latter from the bark of a small tree in Harnhalli. The jála or lac tree (*vatica*) is found scattered over several other taluqs, but not in Manjarabad, Arkalgud and Channaráyapatna. The síge kayi or soap nut (*mimosa abstergens*) is planted for village hedges in the east, but grows wild in Manjarabad and Belur. Except in the Ghat forests, sandal grows freely in the western taluqs in garden hedges and light jungle.

*Forests.*—The *State Forests* cover an area of 185 square miles. The following is a list of them, including 5 sandal reserves which occupy 3 square miles :—

| State Forests. | sq. m. | | sq. m. | Sandal Reserves. | acres. |
|---|---|---|---|---|---|
| Kempuhole Ghat | 16 | Burdalbore | 3 | Kemmanbore | 232 |
| Kaganeri ,, | 2 | Hagare | 3 | Gubbi | 428 |
| Kabbinale ,, | 23 | Byaba | 2 | Gandagere | 554 |
| Bisale ,, | 23 | Sige-gudda | 8 | Gubbi | 1,000 |
| Vijayapur | 5 | Baisur | 1 | Nakalgud | 185 |
| Hirikalgudda | 92 | Mallappan-betta | 1 | | |
| Doddabetta | 3 | Vantigudda | 1 | | |

*Plantations.*—There are 12 Forest plantations, covering 3,053 acres ;

and 8 Revenue plantations, covering 582 acres. *Avenues.*—There are 566 miles of road planted wlth avenues. *Groves.*—The number of topes or groves is 1,502, stocked with 57,141 trees.

**Cultivation.**—The following is a list of the ordinary crops cultivated :—

| Kannada. | Botanical. | English. |
|---|---|---|
| CEREALS. | | |
| Bhatta ... ... | Oryza sativa ... ... ... ... | Rice. |
| Godhi ... ... | Triticum aristatum ... ... ... | Wheat. |
| Jóla ... ... ... | Holcus sorghum ... ... ... | Maize. |
| Rági .. ... ... | Eleusine corocana ... ... ... | Rági. |
| Sáme ... ... ... | Panicum frumentaceum ... ... | Little millet. |
| PULSES. | | |
| Avare ... ... | Dolichos lablab ... ... ... | Cow gram. |
| Hesaru ... ... | Phaseolus mungo ... ... ... | Green ,, |
| Hurali ... ... | Dolichos uniflorus ... ... ... | Horse ,, |
| Kadale ... ... | Cicer arietinum ... ... ... | Bengal gram. |
| Togari ... ... | Cajanus indicus ... ... ... | Dholl. |
| Uddu ... ... ... | Phaseolus minimus ... ... ... | Black gram. |
| OIL SEEDS. | | |
| Haralu .. ... | Ricinus communis ... ... ... | Castor-oil. |
| Huchchellu ... ... | Guizotea oleifera ... ... ... | Wild gingelli. |
| Pundi ... ... | Hibiscus ... ... ... ... | Hemp. |
| Wollellu ... ... | Sesamum orientale ... ... ... | Gingelli. |
| MISCELLANEOUS. | | |
| Arale ... ... ... | Gossypium indicum ... ... ... | Cotton. |
| Hoge soppu ... ... | Nicotina tabaccum ... ... ... | Tobacco. |
| Menasina kayi ... | Capsicum annuum ... ... ... | Chilly. |

The number of acres under cultivation of the principal crops is thus returned for 1893: Rice 103,081, rági 287,458, wheat 80, other food grains 47,004, oil-seeds 32,670, sugar-cane 6,327, cotton 231, fibres 105, tobacco 1,939, cinchona 36, coffee 53,277, vegetables 3,455, cocoa-nut and areca-nut 25,677, other products 64,861.

Though the soil in many parts of the District is favourable, the ryots have directed little of their attention to the cultivation of wheat and cotton; the former is grown in the Arsikere taluq, and the latter in the Arsikere and Arkalgud taluqs.

*Tobacco* is cultivated to some extent on dry lands in parts of the Arsikere, Belur, and Arkalgud taluqs. The tobacco grown in the Arkalgud taluq is much prized for snuff, but that of Harnhalli and Belur is of inferior quality and is chiefly sold on the western coast for chewing.

The grain principally cultivated in the Malnad is *rice*, which, though of an inferior quality, grows most luxuriantly in the long winding valleys and in fields cut in terraces on their sides. At the head of each valley is generally a small tank with a common mud bund, which serves to collect a little water from the spring rising above it, to be used when the rains hang off; but artificial irrigation is generally rendered superfluous by the exceeding abundance and regularity of the rains, which continue in good seasons with but little intermission from May to November. The rice cultivated in the north-west of the Hassan taluq, and that grown in the Maidan taluqs on land irrigated by the channels leading from the anicuts thrown across the Kávéri, Hemávati and Yagachi rivers, is of a superior kind and bears comparison with the best table rice of Southern India. In other places in the Maidan country the crop is dependent on irrigation from tanks. In a few places where the means of irrigating is deficient, a coarse rice called bhar-doddi is raised, chiefly in the Arkalgud, Hole Narsipur and Channaráyapatna taluqs.

The *sugar-cane* grown is generally of the inferior kinds known as mara-kabbu and chaini-kabbu.

The rise in the price of rice, which has steadily taken place during the past few years, combined with years of drought, has lessened greatly the high estimation in which the possession of *cocoa-nut* and *areca-nut* palm gardens was once held. Many of the gardens are now much neglected, and the ryots no longer show the same avidity as they did formerly for this cultivation; which has the further disadvantage of not yielding a return till ten or twelve years after the trees are planted. The most valuable gardens are those situated in the Arkalgud taluq, where many of the Sankéti and Sri Vaishnava Brahman proprietors work in gardens themselves. The areca-nut produced is known as the volágra, and is not held in such high repute as that of Nagar. The cocoa-nuts of the Arsikere taluq, which are allowed to remain on the tree till they drop, are, however, much prized, and are largely exported in a dry state to Tiptur for the Bangalore and Bellary markets.

*Plantains* of good quality are grown to a considerable extent, and formerly every ryot in the Malnad had a few trees at the back of his house, but the cultivation has gradually yielded to that of coffee.

The cultivation of *coffee* takes rank as one of the most important products of the country. The rich red loam of the primeval forests which cover the slopes of the Malnad hills, is found to be well adapted for its growth. The cultivation of the berry, introduced first from Mecca by Baba Budan on the hills which bear his name in the Kadur District, was gradually extended into Manjarabad, and at the period of the assumption of the administration of the country by the British Government in 1831 was beginning to attract some attention. The cultivation of the plant did not, however, become general till Mr. Frederick Green opened the first European plantation in Manjarabad in 1843: since which period others, being assured of its success, have taken up jungle lands and invested capital largely in the enterprise. Every native in the Malnad has a few coffee-trees planted at the back of his house, and the Patels and principal Gauḍas have extended this cultivation till it embraces, in small plots, the whole of the jungles in which their villages are situated.

The following is the acreage under coffee in 1896 in the taluqs in which it is cultivated:—Manjarabad, 48,773; Balur, 10,301; Hassan, 1,117; Arkalgud, 110.

The *cardamom* plant is indigenous, being found growing wild in the densely wooded ravines on the verge of the Western Ghats. Its systematic cultivation has, for some years, been undertaken on a large scale.

**Wild Animals.**—The forests of the Malnad and the rocky hills in the Hassan, Arkalgud and Arsikere taluqs, give shelter to numerous wild beasts, amongst which the tiger, cheeta, bear, elk, spotted deer, jungle sheep and wild pig are the most common; black cheetas are occasionally shot in Manjarabad, and herds of elephants and bison visit the hilly tracts on the verge of the Ghats. Wolves and hyænas infest the Arsikere taluq, and antelope are plentiful in the kávals in the Maidan taluqs. Of the smaller mammalia, jackals, black and common monkeys, hares, squirrels, wild cats, sloths and porcupines are numerous. Otters are also found at the Krishnaraj anicut in the Arkalgud taluq and the Yettinhalla river in the Manjarabad taluq.

*Birds.*—Numbers of duck, teal, widgeon, a few wild geese and numerous waders visit the District in the cold season, and some remain to breed in the little tanks about Hassan and in the country to the west. Of the feathery tribes, jungle fowl, imperial pigeon, and peafowl are to be found in the jungles and gardens; and florican, bustard, and partridge on the plains. The *falco peregrinator* hawk is to be met with on the ghats in the Manjarabad taluq.

*Reptiles.*—Of the articulata, snakes and leeches are very numerous, especially in the forests of Manjarabad.

*Fish.*—The tanks and rivers are full of fish, of which the most esteemed for its taste is the mirl or maral.

**Domestic Animals.**—Owing to the number of kávals or pasture lands in the District belonging to the Amrit Mahal—some of considerable extent, such as the Síge-gudda kával near Hassan, affording rich pasturage and of sufficient size to maintain 2,500 head of cattle—may be attributed the possession by the more respectable class of ryots of a few cattle of superior breed. In the western taluqs the ploughing cattle are of diminutive size and of little value. Owing to the coarseness of the pasturage and the humidity of the climate, the mortality among the cattle in the Malnad is very great, so much so that the Gaudas have to replace their losses every few years by fresh purchases from the Maidan taluqs.

Draught cattle are numerous in Hassan, which is the great carrying taluq of the country, and supplies nearly all the carts required for the carriage of the rice and coffee of this District and of Kadur.

The live stock of the District in 1893 consisted of 516,894 cows and bullocks, 300 horses, 2,886 ponies, 2,382 mules and donkeys, 243,683 sheep and goats, 5,821 pigs, and 64,016 buffaloes.

## HISTORY

The earliest event supported by any evidence was a migration of Jains from Ujjain, under the leadership of Bhadrabáhu, one of the *sruta-kevalis* or hearers of the first masters, in order to escape a dreadful famine of twelve years' duration. He was accompanied by his principal disciple, Chandra Gupta, who is said to be identical with the great Maurya emperor, contemporary with the Macedonian conqueror Alexander the Great. While the emigrants were on their way to the Punnáta country (South Mysore) and the Chóla-mandala, their leader, Bhadrabáhu, died at Sravana Belgola, attended in his last moments by Chandra Gupta, who also died there twelve years later. These occurrences are recorded in an ancient inscription engraved on the surface of the rock at the summit of Chandra-betta at Sravana Belgola, and may be assigned to the 3rd century B.C. They invested the place with a sanctity which led to the subsequent formation of the well-known Jain settlement there. The colossal statue of Gomaṭesvara at the same place, on the summit of Indra-betta, bears at its foot inscriptions stating that it was erected by Chámuṇḍa Ráya. He was the minister and general of the Ganga king Ráchamalla II, and its date is probably 983.[1]

**Kadambas.**—During the first five centuries of the Christian era the west of the District was included with Tuluva (South Canara) as part of the Kadamba kingdom, whose capital was at Banavasi. After this the Kadambas became tributary to the Chalukyas, but we find Kadamba chiefs ruling as far south as Bayalnád (the Heggadadevankote taluq) down to the end of the 11th century.

[1] *See* my book, *Inscriptions at Sravana-Belgola.*

**Gangas.**—The Gangas, whose capital was at Talakád on the Kávéri, in the south-east of the Mysore District, were in possession of the whole of Mysore between the Western and Eastern Ghats from the 5th to the 11th century. The Jain establishment at Sravana Belgola (Channaráyapatna taluq) was in a special manner under their protection.

**Hoysalas.**—But the District is more particularly identified with the rise of the Hoysala power, and formed their ancestral kingdom. The origin of the line has been related in the general chapter on History (in Vol. I), and Sosevúr or Sasakapura, the home of Sala, the founder, has been identified by me with Angadi, which, though by recent changes in taluq boundaries it is now just within the Mudgere taluq of the Kadur District, is properly a village of the long-standing Balam or Manjarabad country. The dynasty arose in the 10th century, and continued in power to the middle of the 14th century. Their capital was Dorasamudra, the modern Halebid (Belur taluq), and the boundaries of the kingdom in the time of Vinayáditya (1047–1100), the son of Sala, were—on the west, Konkana (North Kanara) and Alvakheda (South Kanara); on the south, Báyalnád (Heggadadevankote taluq); on the east, Talakád (that is, not the city itself, but the province belonging to it; on the north, Sávimale (a hill not yet identified).

The kings had hitherto been adherents of the Jain faith, but Biṭṭi Deva, through the influence of a Vaishnava wife and the efforts of Rámánuja, the great Vaishnava teacher, who had taken refuge in Mysore from persecution by the Saiva king of the Chola country, embraced the religion of Vishnu and thence assumed his better known name of Vishnuvarddhana. He re-captured Talakád, which a century before had been taken by the Cholas, drove the latter out of Mysore, and possessed himself of all the old Ganga dominions. The Hoysalas had professed allegiance to the Chalukyas, but after this assumed independence. Ballála II (1172–1209) carried the Hoysala dominions up to the river Krishna, making Lakkundi in Dharwar his residence for a time; and Somesvara (1233–54) extended them southwards over the Chola country, where he took up his abode at Kannanur, near Trichinopoly. On his death there was a partition of his territories, the old Kannaḍa provinces, with the capital, going to Narasimha III, and the Tamil provinces, with Kolar District and the north of Bangalore District, going to Rámanátha. The territories were re-united under Ballála III (1291–1342), but the Muhammadans now appeared on the scene and brought the Hoysala power to an end. In 1311, an army under Kafur, the general of Ala-ud-Din, sacked Dorasamudra and returned to Delhi laden with spoils. In 1326 an expedition sent by

Muhammad III totally destroyed the city. The Hoysala prince retired at first to Tondanur (Tonnur, Mysore District), but lived at various places, such as Hosavidu (Hosur in Kolar District) and Unnámale (Trinomalee in South Arcot) maintaining an enfeebled power for about twenty years longer.

**Vijayanagar.**—In 1336 was founded the city of Vidyánagara, afterwards called Vijayanagara, the sovereigns of which eventually became paramount over all the countries south of the Krishna. They are stated to have taken peculiar interest in the province of Balam, now Manjarabad, and to have made great efforts to colonize it. Every encouragement was given to settlers of all castes by granting them land at little or no rent. The wealthier immigrants were made Patels and received large inams. This is the period at which, it is assumed, the inhabitants generally obtained a proprietary right in the land and the patels hereditary feudal powers. Later, all the west of this District was bestowed, with adjoining tracts above and below the Ghats, upon Vina Ramappa, a court musician.[1] After a reign of some years he abdicated, and the province of Balam, composed as above, and yielding a revenue of three lakhs of pagodas, was in 1397 made over by the rulers of Vijayanagar to Singappa Nayak, one of their generals and son of an old palegar named Manch Ayappa Nayak. The Balam palegars had their capital at Aigur and held the country for some generations.

The following is a tentative list of the Náyaks of Balam, with dates taken mostly from inscriptions:—

| Name | Date | Name | Date |
|---|---|---|---|
| Hiriya Singappa Náyak ... | 1397 | Venkatádri Náyak ... | ... 1646-56 |
| Manchayya Náyak ... ... | 1405 | Narasimha Náyak ... | ... 1658-65 |
| Chikka Singappa Náyak | | Venkatádri Náyak ... | ... 1671 |
| Hadapa Bayappa Náyak | | Krishnappa Náyak ... | 1686-1730 |
| Krishnappa Náyak ... | ... 1534-48 | Venkatádri Náyak ... | ... 1751 |
| Yarama Náyak | | Krishnappa Náyak ... | ... 1772-93 |
| Paddi Náyak | | Venkatádri Náyak ... | ... 1799 |
| Krishnappa Náyak ... | ... 1625-40 | | |

The fortunes of the family are further referred to below. Representatives are still in existence at Aigur.

At the end of the 16th century Jagadeva Ráyal, already mentioned in connection with his capital of Channapatna (Bangalore District), was invested with a territory extending over the east of the District.

**Mysore Rajas.**—Kikkeri, Sindhugatta, Nagamangala, and other places belonging to this government had gradually fallen to the Mysore Rájas, along with Channapatna, when in 1633 the Mysore army gained Channaráyapatna from the palegar of Hole Narsipur after a very long siege.

[1] A performer, as his name indicates, on the *vina* or Indian lute.

Shortly after this period we find Sivappa Náyak, of the Ikkeri principality in Nagar, attaining considerable power. So much so that Balam was overrun and held for 37 years, and shelter even extended to a descendant of the Vijayanagar house who had resorted for protection and help to this late dependent on its sovereign power. Sivappa Náyak established him in authority at Sakkarepatna and Belur, and even invaded Seringapatam in 1654 in his behalf. Peace was concluded between Mysore and Ikkeri in 1694, by which the six náds of Manjarabad were ceded to the old chiefs, and the remainder of the province of Balam was divided between the two contending parties. Except Manjarabad, the whole of the Hassan District has from this time formed a part of Mysore territory. On the capture of Bednur by Haidar Ali in 1762, Balam, which belonged to it, was allowed to remain in the hands of the chiefs on payment of an annual tribute of 5,000 pagodas.

The Arsikere taluq appears to have suffered greatly from the raids of the Mahrattas, and at one time was handed over to these freebooters as security for the payment of tribute: the villagers are then said to have raised for their defence those earthen towers which are yet to be seen in different parts of the taluq.

Krishnappa Náyak, who was ruling Balam in the time of Tipu Sultan, joined the army of Parasu Ram Bhao when advancing to co-operate with Lord Cornwallis against Seringapatam in 1792. On the conclusion of peace he fled to Coorg, fearing the Sultan's displeasure; but the latter induced him to return, and gave him the government of the Aigur-síme, forming the south of Balam. The rest of the province was attached to Mysore. Venkatádri Náyak, son of Krishnappa Náyak, was in possession of Aigur-síme at the fall of Seringapatam in 1799, and not only attempted to retain his independence but to extend his authority farther to the north. He was after two years seized at Uggihalli and as an example hanged, contrary to the wishes of Colonel Wellesley.

The Hassan District during the present century first formed part of the Patnada Ráyada, and was then called the Manjarabad Faujdári. From 1832 it was included in the Ashtagram Division. This was abolished at the Rendition in 1881, and in 1882 the Hassan District itself was reduced to a Sub-Division under Kadur District, with only four taluqs: Arsikere, Belur, Hassan (with Gráma sub-taluq), and Manjarabad. In 1886 the Hassan District, as at present constituted, was re-established, and in 1894 Alur was made the sub-taluq under Hassan instead of Grama.

## POPULATION

*Number.*—The population of the District is 514,952; of whom 255,044 are males and 259,908 females.

*Density.*—This gives 195 persons per square mile. The most thickly populated taluq is Arkalgud, where there are 290·12 persons to a square mile; next to which come Hassan, where the rate is 238·73, Belur 222·69, and Hole Narsipur 218·42. The most sparsely populated are Manjarabad, with 129·91 to the square mile, and Arsikere, with 133·27.

*By religion.*—According to religion the population is classified as follows:—

| Religions. | Above 15. | | Under 15. | | Total. | Per centage. |
|---|---|---|---|---|---|---|
| | Males. | Females. | Males. | Females. | | |
| Hindus ... ... ... | 150,040 | 154,650 | 95,424 | 96,551 | 496,665 | 96·44 |
| Muhammadans ... | 4,575 | 3,893 | 2,629 | 2,558 | 13,655 | 2·65 |
| Jains ... ... ... | 441 | 427 | 219 | 234 | 1,321 | 0·25 |
| Christians .. ... | 1,124 | 953 | 586 | 633 | 3,296 | 0·64 |
| Jews ... ... ... | 2 | 5 | 4 | 4 | 15 | — |
| Total ... | 156,182 | 159,928 | 98,862 | 99,980 | 514,952 | — |

*Increase.*—The following compares the statistics by taluqs according to the *khâneshumâri* accounts of 1853-4 with those obtained in the census enumerations of 1871, 1881 and 1891:—

| Taluq. | 1853-4. | 1871. | 1881. | 1891. |
|---|---|---|---|---|
| Arkalgud... ... ... ... | 57,017 | 76,184 | 66,157 | 75,812 |
| Arsikere ... ... ... ... | 29,753 | 74,720 | 50,656 | 65,306 |
| Belur ... ... ... ... | 53,830 | 75,821 | 67,538 | 75,470 |
| Channaráyapatna ... ... | 34,356 | 79,178 | 63,380 | 78,211 |
| Hassan ... ... ... ... | 43,460 } | 111,921 | 95,077 | 113,397 |
| Maharajandurga ... ... ... | 45,793 } | | | |
| Hole Narsipur ... ... ... | 30,294 | 50,941 | 37,783 | 50,894 |
| Manjarabad ... ... ... | 40,398 | 52,918 | 50,342 | 55,862 |
| Total ... ... | 334,901 | 521,683 | 430,933 | 514,952 |

Bearing in mind that some of the variations are due to redistribution of taluqs and to changes in the limits of the District, there was an apparent increase on the whole up to 1871 of 55·77 per cent. in 18 years. But the early enumeration was 25 per cent. in defect. The famine of 1877–8 sent down the total 17·39 per cent. by 1881, but it had risen again 19·5 per cent. by 1891. The net result may be stated at an increase of 20·61 per cent. in 38 years.

*Classes.*—Classified according to sources of livelihood and nationality the population is composed as follows :—

| | Number. | Per cent. |
|---|---|---|
| A. Agricultural ... ... ... ... | 200,013 ... | 38·84 |
| B. Professional ... ... ... ... | 31,416 ... | 6·10 |
| C. Commercial ... .. ... ... | 44,921 ... | 8·72 |
| D. Artisan and Village menial ... .. | 209,055 ... | 40·59 |
| E. Vagrant minor Artisans and Performers | 12,130 ... | 2·35 |
| Races and Nationalities ... ... ... | 16,966 ... | 3·27 |
| Others, not stated ... ... ... | 451 ... | 0·08 |

The castes or classes which number over 10,000 are the following, in order of strength. These account for 442,417, or 85·91 per cent. of the population :—

| | | | |
|---|---|---|---|
| Wokkaliga ... ... | 171,323 | Musalmán ... ... ... | 13,491 |
| Holeya ... ... ... | 87,055 | Neyigára ... ... ... | 12,808 |
| Lingáyita[1] ... ... | 67,231 | Mádiga ... ... ... | 11,190 |
| Kuruba ... ... ... | 40,730 | Panchála ... ... ... | 11,073 |
| Bráhmana ... ... | 17,060 | Agasa ... ... ... | 10,456 |

By far the most numerous class of Wokkaliga are the Gangaḍikára (126,433), and next the Nonaba (7,444). Of Brahmans the largest sects are Srivaishnava (4,063), Smárta (3,110) and Babbúr Kamme (2,368). Of Musalmáns, the Shekhs number 9,324, Pathans 1,828 and Saiyids 1,705. Of the Neyigára 9,726 are Devánga, and of the Panchála 8,179 are Akkasále.

**Agricultural Stock.**—The dead stock of the District includes 6,688 carts, 94,003 ploughs, and 22 boats.

*Tanks and Wells.*—There are 6,121 tanks, 97 canals, and 1,496 wells in the District.

**Towns.**—There are in the District 13 municipal towns, with a population of 38,906, composed (not including the recently formed ones, 6, 8 and 12) of 26,879 Hindus, 4,697 Musalmans, 376 Jains, 559 Christians and 15 Jews. The following is the list :—

| | | | |
|---|---|---|---|
| Hassan ... ... ... | 6,654 | Gráma ... ... ... | 2,184 |
| Hole Narsipur ... ... | 5,758 | Banavar ... ... ... | 2,017 |
| Arkalgud ... ... ... | 4,374 | Arsikere ... ... ... | 1,921 |
| Belur ... ... ... | 3,084 | A'lúr... ... ... ... | 1,822 |
| Channaráyapatna ... ... | 3,081 | Sravana Belgola ... ... | 1,763 |
| Konanúr ... ... ... | 2,433 | Sakleshpur ... ... ... | 1,591 |
| Harnhalli ... ... ... | 2,224 | | |

*Villages.*—The total number of *asali* or primary villages was 2,490, to which were attached 1,162 *dákhali* or secondary villages or hamlets. The following are the details :—

[1] There are also 11,638 included among Wokkaliga.

| Taluq. | Populated. | | Depopulated. | Classified. | | | | Total. |
|---|---|---|---|---|---|---|---|---|
| | Villages. | Hamlets. | | Government. | Sarvamánya. | Jodi. | Kayamgutta. | |
| Arkalgud ... ... | 260 | 211 | 29 | 254 | 19 | 16 | — | 289 |
| Arsikere ... ... | 314 | 223 | 44 | 353 | 1 | 1 | 3 | 358 |
| Belur ... ... | 359 | 186 | 36 | 339 | 8 | 48 | — | 395 |
| Channaráyapatna... | 371 | 78 | 6 | 373 | 4 | — | — | 377 |
| Hassan ... ... | 526 | 202 | 41 | 531 | 1 | 30 | 5 | 374 |
| Hole Narsipur ... | 188 | 124 | 38 | 206 | 5 | 13 | 2 | 226 |
| Manjarabad ... | 266 | 138 | 12 | 263 | 3 | 9 | 3 | 278 |
| Total ... | 2,284 | 1,162 | 206 | 2,319 | 41 | 117 | 13 | 2,297 |

**Great Festivals.**—The principal concourse of people occurs at the following religious festivals :—

At *Hassan*, the festival of *Hásnnamba*, held for 12 days in *Asvija bahula*, is attended by 4,000 people.

At *Belur*, during the *rathótsava* of *Kesava swami*, held for 5 days from 12th April, 5,000 people attend.

At *Hoskote*, Manjarabad taluq, *Kenchammana játre*, held twice a year, in the grove surrounding the vill·ge, first on the full moon day of *Vaishakha* and second on the same day of *K'ártika*, on each of which occasions 4.000 people assemble.

At *Tirupati* in Arsikere taluq, 3.500 people attend the *Venkatramana-swami rathótsava*, held for 5 days from 10th July.

At *Ramanathpur*, Arkalgud taluq, the *Subrahmanya* car festival lasts 8 days from *Márgasira suddha* 6, and attracts 3,000 people.

At *Hole Narsipur*, the car festival of Narasimhaswami is held for 10 days at the end of February, and 3,000 people assemble

**Fairs.**—The largest weekly fair in the District is held at Alur in the Hassan taluq, where about 3,000 people assemble every Wednesday.

**Vital Statistics.**—The birth-rate of the District in 1893–4 was 18·18 per mille of the population, and the death-rate was 14·35 per mille. There were 9,361 births registered, 4,872 of males and 4,489 of females. The number of deaths registered was 7,388, of which 3,899 were deaths of males and 3,489 deaths of females. The greatest number of deaths occurred in the month of August. By classes there were 6,426 deaths among Hindus, 195 among Muhammadans, and 767 among other classes. The causes of death were: from diseases—cholera 142, small-pox 296, fevers 4,106, bowel complaints 581 ; from injuries—suicide 21, wounds or accidents 86, snake-bite or wild beasts 13, all other causes 2,233.

## REVENUE

The following table exhibits the revenue of the District for five years, to 1895–6:—

| Items. | | 1891–2. | 1892–3. | 1893–4. | 1894–5. | 1895–6. |
|---|---|---|---|---|---|---|
| Land Revenue | ... | 11,00,442 | 11,22,096 | 11,80,832 | 12,55,316 | 12,28,375 |
| Forest ... | ... | 1,72,072 | 1,41,069 | 1,09,614 | 1,08,908 | 1,54,403 |
| Abkari ... | ... | 1,24,730 | 1,99,180 | 2,04,088 | 2,20,532 | 2,43,043 |
| Mohatarfa ... | ... | 30,514 | 31,972 | 31,884 | 25,782 | 26,195 |
| Sáyar ... ... | ... | 4,828 | 3,875 | 2,369 | 2,126 | 3,170 |
| Salt ... ... | ... | 460 | 215 | 360 | 303 | 298 |
| Stamps ... | ... | 71,125 | 62,661 | 61,219 | 65,476 | 70,040 |
| Law and Justice | ... | 15,898 | 14,228 | 16,039 | 15,005 | 18,630 |
| Police ... | ... | 102 | 36 | 149 | 99 | 169 |
| Public Works | ... | 8,352 | 9,199 | 6,837 | — | — |
| Miscellaneous | ... | 19,683 | 18,883 | 19,723 | 19,937 | 29,799 |
| Total | Rs. | 15,48,206 | 16,03,414 | 16,33,114 | 17,13,484 | 17,74,122 |

## TRADE

In a District so purely agricultural, the manufactures are almost exclusively such as are suited to a rural people. The most general are pottery, carpentry, weaving, rope-making, oil-pressing, &c., and the estimated annual outturn is approximately stated at about 17 lakhs.

*Cotton.*—The only good cloth manufactured is at Hole Narsipur. The produce of the looms in other parts of the country is of the coarsest description, the cloth being made either to order for the villagers or sold at the weekly markets.

*Silk.*—Musalmans at Channaráyapatna and Hole Narsipur earn a livelihood by making purses, silk cords and tassels.

*Wool.*—Cumblies or the coarse woollen blankets generally worn by the peasantry are manufactured in all the taluqs, save Manjarábád, by the Kurubar or shepherd class.

*Metals.*—A little iron ore is smelted at Bágadi in the Arsikere taluq. It is used chiefly for agricultural implements, but is of inferior quality, and no steel is manufactured.

The manufacture of brass and copper vessels is virtually a monopoly of the Jains residing at Sravana Belgola. Their pots are of excellent quality and meet with a ready sale at Mysore, and at the great annual festival at Subrahmanya in the South Kanara District.

Gold-mining, under European management, has been started in Arsikere and Channaráyapatna taluqs, but as yet with no satisfactory results. There are, however, extensive traces of old and abandoned workings.

*Oils.*—Under this heading may be added oil-mills, of which a large number are at work in the District, driven by bullock-power. The oil (castor, gingelli and wild gingelli) produced is mostly exported to Kanara, Coorg and to Birúr in the Kadur District.

*Bags.*—The manufacture of gunny bags gives employment to a few people, chiefly in the Arkalgud, Hole Narsipur and Channaráyapatna taluqs. Bags for the export of grain are also made from the bark of a tree called *gaja mara*, or elephant-tree. The trunk is steeped in water, after which the bark is removed entire by threshing it, in which state it is not unlike the leg of an elephant.

*Coffee.*—But the most important industry of the District is the cultivation of coffee, the produce of which, estimated at 15 to 20 lakhs of rupees a year, is mostly exported to Mangalore and the western coast preparatory to shipment to Europe.

*Exports and Imports.*—Though the exports of the District are large, the trade of the country is in the hands chiefly of outsiders, who frequent the different markets; there are therefore few merchants resident in the District of any wealth or importance. In addition to coffee, the articles exported are chiefly food grains. The imports consist of iron and of European cottons and woollens: ghee, areca-nut and cocoa-nut are also imported, together with salt.

**Marts.**—The great rice market is at Alúr in the Hassan taluq, about 7 miles from the kasba: it is attended by the ryots of the Malnad, who bring their rice in large quantities for sale, and by purchasers, many of whom come from great distances with carts and droves of bullocks for the conveyance of the rice purchased. Other important trading places are Yesalurpet, Kenchammana Hoskote and Channaráyapatna.

## COMMUNICATIONS

**Railways.**—The Southern Mahratta Railway from Bangalore to Poona crosses the north-west of the District for about 18 miles, with stations at Arsikere and Banavar. But a project has been prepared for a line from Arsikere, by way of Hassan and Manjarábád, to Mangalore, which would be of great importance for the District.

**Roads.**—In 1837 not a bridge had been constructed in the District, nor a road formed worthy of the name: the only means of carriage was by palanquins and pack bullocks. But now the District is intersected by several main lines of road, which connect all the towns of any importance, and afford easy means of communication with the large towns of Bangalore, Mysore, Bellary and Mangalore, to which places the trade of the country chiefly converges.

Of the passes to Mangalore and the country below the Western Ghats, there are two in Manjarábád—namely, the Manjarábád and Bisale. The Manjarábád Ghat road, on the grand trunk line from Bangalore to Mangalore, is towards the south of the Manjarábád taluq, and has been traced with great care. The gradients are from 1 in 20 to 1 in 14. The Bisale Ghat road is adapted principally for pack bullocks and foot passengers.

There are 127 miles of *Provincial roads* in the District, maintained at a cost of Rs. 23,120 a year. The length of *District roads* is 395 miles, costing Rs. 24,180. Particulars of each class of roads are given below:—

PROVINCIAL ROADS.

| | Miles. | Cost. |
|---|---|---|
| Bangalore-Mangalore road ... ... ... ... ... | 85 | 17,000 |
| Bangalore-Honnavar road ... ... ... ... ... | 20 | 4,000 |
| Banavar-Belur road ... ... ... ... ... ... | 13 | 1,040 |
| Hassan-Chikmagalur road ... ... ... ... ... | 9 | 1,080 |
| Total ... ... | 127 | Rs. 23,120 |

DISTRICT ROADS.

| | Miles. | Cost. |
|---|---|---|
| Manjarábád-Subrahmanya road ... ... ... ... | 39 | 3,900 |
| Arsikere-Channaráyapatna road ... ... ... ... | 28 | 2,520 |
| Hassan-Tiptur road ... ... ... ... ... ... | 24 | 1,920 |
| Hassan-Cannanore road ... ... ... ... ... | 37 | 1,850 |
| Yelwal-Hassan road ... ... ... ... ... ... | 33 | 1,650 |
| Arsikere-Huliyar road ... ... ... ... ... | 22 | 1,100 |
| Tiptur-Channaráyapatna road ... ... ... ... | 21 | 1,050 |
| Kattaya-Hallibail road ... ... ... ... ... | 19 | 950 |
| Dudda-Arsikere road ... ... ... ... ... | 16 | 800 |
| Seringapatam-Channaráyapatna road ... ... ... | 5 | 750 |
| Banavar-Sira road ... ... ... ... ... ... | 15 | 750 |

| | Miles. | Cost. |
|---|---|---|
| Channaráyapatna-Narsipur road ... ... ... ... | 13 | 650 |
| Narsipur-Arkalgud road ... ... ... ... ... | 13 | 650 |
| Anemahal-Mudgere road ... ... ... ... ... | 12 | 600 |
| Ayyahalli-Yesalurpet road ... ... ... ... ... | 12 | 600 |
| Banavar-Hiradi road... ... ... ... ... ... | 10 | 500 |
| Ramnathpur-Fraserpet road... ... ... ... ... | 8 | 480 |
| Hirisáve-Nuggihalli road ... ... ... ... ... | 9 | 450 |
| Arkalgud-Koolipet road ... ... ... ... ... | 9 | 450 |
| Hampapur-Ramnathpur road ... ... ... ... | 8 | 400 |
| Wongur-Mallipatna road ... ... ... ... ... | 8 | 400 |
| Channaráyapatna-Sravana Belgola road ... ... ... | 7 | 350 |
| Hassan-Saligram road ... ... ... ... ... | 6 | 300 |
| Sagarkatte-Ramnathpur road ... ... ... ... | 5 | 250 |
| Raji-Belur road ... ... ... ... ... ... | 5 | 250 |
| Banavar-Sakkarepatna road... ... ... ... ... | 2 | 160 |
| Bartavalli loop road ... ... ... ... ... ... | 3 | 150 |
| Palya-Belagod road ... ... ... ... ... ... | 3 | 150 |
| Kikkeri-Ippaya road... ... ... ... ... ... | 2 | 100 |
| Hullahalli loop road ... ... ... ... ... ... | 1 | 50 |
| Total miles | 395 | Rs. 24,180 |

**Accommodation for travellers.**—For the accommodation of European travellers stage bungalows have been built at the stations named below. Brahman kitchens are also provided in several.

*First Class.*—Arsikere, Channaráyapatna, Hassan, Sakleshpur.
*Second Class.*—Banavar, Belur.
*Third Class.*—Arkalgud, Dandiganhalli, Gandasi, Hirisáve, Hole Narsipur, Máranhalli, Pálya.

Natives are accommodated in *chatrams* in all the taluqs, and *musáfir khánas* have been built in Channaráyapatna, Dudda and Hirisáve.

## GAZETTEER

**Alur.**—A sub-taluq under Hassan taluq, formed in 1894, consisting of Alúr, Pálya and Ponnáthpur hoblis.

**Alur.**—A village in the Hassan taluq, 7 miles west of Hassan, close to the Hassan-Sakleshpur road. Till 1875 it was the head-quarters of the old Maharajandurga taluq, and in 1894 was made the head-quarters of a sub-taluq.

| Population in 1891. | Males. | Females. | Total. |
|---|---|---|---|
| Hindus .. ... ... ... ... ... | 745 | 733 | 1,478 |
| Muhammadans ... ... ... ... ... | 154 | 190 | 344 |
| Total ... ... | 899 | 923 | 1,822 |

The large weekly fair held here on Wednesdays is the chief rice market of the District. It is attended by the ryots of the Malnád, who bring their rice in large quantities for sale; and also by traders, many of whom come from great distances with carts and droves of bullocks for the conveyance of the rice purchased.

| Municipal Funds. | 1892-3. | 1893-4. | 1894-5. | 1895-6. |
|---|---|---|---|---|
| Income ... ... ... | 1,036 | 1,108 | 1,279 | 1,679 |
| Expenditure ... ... ... | 2,630 | 1,716 | 2,664 | 3,537 |

**Arkalgúd** or **Arakalgúdu.**—A taluq in the south. Area 262 square miles. Head-quarters at Arkalgúd. Contains the following hoblis, villages and population:—

| No. | Hoblis. | Villages. | Hamlets. | Villages classified. | | | Population. |
|---|---|---|---|---|---|---|---|
| | | | | Govern-ment. | Sarva-mánya. | Jodi. | |
| 1 | Arkalgúd ... ... | 35 | 67 | 32 | — | 3 | 12,792 |
| 2 | Basavapatna ... ... | 46 | 28 | 45 | 1 | — | 14,108 |
| 3 | Konanúr ... ... | 61 | 37 | 49 | 8 | 4 | 17,358 |
| 4 | Krishnarájkaṭṭe .. | 31 | 10 | 29 | 1 | 1 | 8,377 |
| 5 | Mallipatna ... ... | 60 | 36 | 55 | 2 | 3 | 10,007 |
| 6 | Marúr ... ... ... | 56 | 33 | 44 | 7 | 5 | 13,170 |
| | Total ... ... | 289 | 211 | 254 | 19 | 16 | 75,812 |

*Principal places, with population.*—Arkalgúd 4,374; Konanúr 2,433; Kerlápura 1,531; Basavapatna 1,333; Rudrapatna 1,068.

The taluq, which contained 10 hoblis (Gorur and Ponnathpur having been added in 1875 from the old Maharajandurga taluq), was abolished in 1882, and the hoblis were distributed among the adjoining taluqs. In 1886 the taluq was again formed with the 6 hoblis detailed above.

The Hemavati forms the entire northern boundary: the Kávéri runs through a portion of the south. From the Krishnarájkaṭṭe on the Kávéri the Kaṭṭepura channel runs along the south bank, past Rudrapatna; and the Rámnáthpur channel along the north bank, past Konanúr and Rámnáthpur to Basavapatna. Under these channels, although sugar-cane is but little grown, the rice crop is one of great yield and certainty. The kinds principally sown are *kembhatta*, *putbhatta* and *donibil.* The lands under tanks are of a very mixed character, and generally inferior in quality. Under the larger tanks, rice is followed by a crop of onions, which are very paying, and are extensively cultivated, especially in Arkalgúd hobli.

The west of the taluq, up to the borders of Coorg, is jungly and hilly, being on the skirts of the Malnád. The southern portion, along the Kávéri, besides paddy cultivation, supports numerous cocoanut and areca-nut gardens. But the areca-nut is the coarse variety or gódu, and it takes 50 trees to produce a manud of nuts. The gardens wind along sometimes in the southern valleys for two or three miles at a stretch. On the high watershed towards the centre there is much cultivation of tobacco, which is converted into snuff.

The taluq formed part of the Province of Balam until 1647, when it was conquered by the Rája of Mysore. In 1694 it was retaken from Sivappa Náyak of Ikkeri, into whose hands it had fallen, and has ever since been united to Mysore.

The revenue settlement was introduced in 1883. The culturable area of the taluq was thus distributed :—

Dry, 63,849 ; wet, 8,180 ; garden, 2,638 ... Total acres 74,667.

The total revenue demand for 1891–2 (15 months) was Rs. 1,47,148 and for 1892–3 it was Rs. 1,51,953.

The average rainfall at Arkalgúd for 26 years (1870–95) was as follows :—

| Jan. | Feb. | Mar. | Apl. | May | June | July | Aug. | Sept. | Oct. | Nov. | Dec. | | Year. |
|---|---|---|---|---|---|---|---|---|---|---|---|---|---|
| 0·01 | 0·01 | 0·17 | 1·88 | 3·45 | 3·17 | 5·48 | 2·46 | 1·99 | 4·73 | 2·43 | 0·55 | ... | 26·33 |

Another register for 10 years gives an average of 28·27.

A road from Hassan through Arkalgúd and Rámnáthpur to Piriyapatna runs through the taluq from north to south. This is crossed at Arkalgúd by the Narsipur-Manjarábád road through Kodlipet, running from west to east, and branching at Mallipatna to the Bisale Ghat. It is also crossed at Rámnáthpur by a road following the north bank of the river from Hampapur in Yedatore taluq to Fraserpet in Coorg, and there is a road running from it east on the south bank of the river to Yedatore.

**Arkalgud.**—A town situated in 12° 46′ N. lat., 76° 7′ E. long., 17 miles south of Hassan, on the Hassan-Piriyapatna and Kodlipet-Narsipur roads. Head-quarters of the Arkalgúd taluq, and a municipality.

| Population in 1891. | Males. | Females. | Total. |
|---|---|---|---|
| Hindus ... ... ... ... ... | 1,955 | 1,999 | 3,954 |
| Muhammadans... ... ... ... | 213 | 207 | 420 |
| Total ... | 2,168 | 2,206 | 4,374 |

The place is said to have been originally called *Arkapuri*, city of the sun, owing to Gautama rishi having there performed penance to that luminary. He also set up the image of Arkesvara, the erection of whose temple is attributed to a Chola king. The present town was founded about 1568 by Krishnappa Náyak, one of the Aigur chiefs, who changed the name to *Arkalgúdu*—abode of the sun. But old inscriptions give the name as Arakalgúdu. It was captured by Kanthirava Narasa Raj of Mysore in 1647, and subsequently by Sivappa Náyak of Ikkeri. In 1694 it was again besieged by Chikka Deva Raja and finally annexed to Mysore.

| Municipal Funds. | 1892–3. | 1893–4. | 1894–5. | 1895–6. |
|---|---|---|---|---|
| Income ... ... ... ... ... | 1,240 | 1,333 | 1,100 | 2,302 |
| Expenditure ... ... ... ... | 1,311 | 2,212 | 1,519 | 2,546 |

**Arsikere.**—A taluq in the north-east, till 1882 called Háranhalli. Area 490 square miles. Head-quarters at Arsikere. Contains the following hoblis, villages and population :—

| No. | Hoblis. | Villages | Hamlets. | Villages Classified. | | | | Population. |
|---|---|---|---|---|---|---|---|---|
| | | | | Government. | Sarvamánya. | Jodi. | Kayamgutta. | |
| 1 | Arsikere ... ... | 64 | 56 | 61 | — | 1 | 2 | 11,534 |
| 2 | Bánávara ... | 78 | 43 | 77 | — | — | 1 | 12,094 |
| 3 | Gandasi ... ... | 71 | 30 | 71 | — | — | — | 13,188 |
| 4 | Háranhalli ... | 50 | 43 | 49 | 1 | — | — | 9,332 |
| 5 | Jávagal ... ... | 44 | 16 | 44 | — | — | — | 7,242 |
| 6 | Kanagatte ... | 51 | 35 | 51 | — | — | — | 11,916 |
| | Total ... | 358 | 223 | 353 | 1 | 1 | 3 | 65,306 |

*Principal places, with population.*—Arsikere 2,472; Háranhalli 2,338; Bánávara 2,172; Kenkere 1,342; Mádálu 1,035.

The Bánávara and Jávagal hoblis were added from the Bánávara taluq, when it was abolished in 1882.

The surface of the taluq is very undulating, rising here and there into rocky hills covered with scrub jungle; these are most noticeable on the western border, where they form a pretty continuous chain. In the north are the Hirekal-gudda hills, on which is a temple of Tirupati, called Malekal Tirupati. The drainage of the taluq is northwards to the Vedavati. But there are few streams or tanks of any size. There are several Amrit-mahal kávals in the south, which has led to the breeding of a good stamp of cattle, in some demand in the Malnád.

The prevailing soil is of a sandy grey colour and often very stony, improving in quality in the hollows, but so poor on the high-lying lands as to be in many places unculturable. The wet lands vary from fair to good quality. Rági is grown everywhere, but in the west and south there is an extensive cultivation of chillies, for supply to the Malnád. The cocoa-nuts of this taluq, allowed to remain on the tree till they drop, are much prized and largely exported in a dry state, *kobri*, to Tiptur, for the Bangalore and Bellary markets. They are grown in the northern parts without irrigation in low-lying situations. The chief exports of the taluq are chillies, oil-seeds and rági from the south, and cocoa-nuts from the north.

There are numerous memorials throughout the taluq of the Hoysala kings, consisting of deserted temples and large stones covered with inscriptions. This country formed part of the territory bestowed by the Vijayanagar kings on Jagadeva Ráyal (of Channapatna, Bangalore District); on the overthrow of whose power it was seized by Timmappa Náyak of Tarikere, in whose family it remained till overrun together with the neighbouring districts by Sirappa Náyak of Ikkeri or Badnur in the 17th century. In 1690 it was incorporated in the Mysore by treaty with that state.

The revenue settlement was introduced in 1879. The area of the taluq at that time was distributed as follows:—

| | |
|---|---|
| Culturable (dry, 90,072; wet, 3,339; garden, 7,481) ... ... | 100,893 |
| Unculturable (including roads, village sites, &c.)... ... ... | 67,658 |
| Inám villages (1,973); 6 Amrit Mahal kávals (12,899) ... ... | 14,872 |
| Total acres ... | 183,423 |

The unoccupied area was 35,667 acres, of which 22,395 were dry land. The total revenue demand for 1891–2 (15 months) was Rs. 1,60,995 and for 1892–3 it was Rs. 1,86,722.

The average rainfall at Arsikere for 26 years (1870–95), and at the other station for 3 years (1893–5) was as follows:—

| | Jan. | Feb. | Mar. | Apl. | May | June | July | Aug. | Sept. | Oct. | Nov. | Dec. | Year. |
|---|---|---|---|---|---|---|---|---|---|---|---|---|---|
| Arsikere | 0·04 | 0·01 | 0·18 | 1·92 | 3·11 | 1·92 | 2·04 | 2·76 | 4·57 | 5·41 | 3·30 | 0·90 | ... 26·16 |
| Bánávara | — | — | 0·03 | 2·17 | 2·54 | 1·50 | 0·60 | 0·33 | 4·08 | 3·50 | 0·99 | — | ... 15·74 |

The railway from Bangalore to Poona runs through the taluq from east to west, with stations at Arsikere and Bánávar. Alongside of it is the Bangalore-Shimoga trunk road. From Arsikere there are roads south to Hassan, south-east to Channaráyapatna, and north to the Huliyár road. From Bánávar there is a road south-west to Halebid and Belur, and north-east to Huliyár. There is also a short cross road from Harnhalli eastwards to the trunk road.

**Arsikere** or **Arasiyakere.**—A town situated in 13° 19′ N. lat., and 76° 19′ E. long., 25 miles north by east of Hassan, on the Southern Mahratta railway. Head-quarters of the Arsikere taluq, and a municipality.

| Population in 1891. | Males. | Females. | Total. |
|---|---|---|---|
| Hindus... ... ... ... ... | 850 | 575 | 1,425 |
| Muhammadans ... ... ... | 163 | 100 | 263 |
| Jains ... ... ... ... ... | 12 | 3 | 15 |
| Christians .. ... ... ... | 121 | 97 | 218 |
| Total ... | 1,146 | 775 | 1,921 |

The town derives its name from a large tank, *Arasiya kere* or princess's tank, which was constructed under the Hoysalas in the 11th century. The fine ruined temples to the north, one of which is a special model of the Chalukyan style, and the inscriptions, show that it was a large place and of considerable importance. Under the Vijayanagar kings it passed into the possession of Jagadeva Ráya of Channapatna (Bangalore District); afterwards into that of Timmappa Náyak of Tarikere (Kadur District); and then into that of Sivappa Náyak of Ikkeri (Shimoga District); from whom it was acquired by Mysore by treaty in 1690. At a later period it was part of the Háranhalli taluq, which was one of those made over to the Mahrattas as security for the payment of tribute, and suffered the general destruction at their hands which reduced it to an insignificant village. In this condition it remained, with an evil reputation as the haunt of robbers who infested the high road. Since the advent of the railway in 1889, and the location here of the taluq head-quarters, it has developed into a rising and busy centre. It will be the junction for the line to Mangalore, and already the staff occupying the railway quarters accounts for the considerable number of Christians in the population.

| Municipal Funds. | 1892-3. | 1893-4. | 1894-5. | 1895-6. |
|---|---|---|---|---|
| Income ... ... ... ... | 1,777 | 1,836 | 1,608 | 2,212 |
| Expenditure ... ... ... ... | 1,736 | 1,912 | 1,608 | 2,971 |

**Banavar.**—A town in Arsikere taluq, 2 miles north-west of the railway station of the same name, on the Bangalore-Shimoga road. Head-quarters of the Banavar hobli, and a municipality.

| Population in 1891. | Males. | Females. | Total. |
|---|---|---|---|
| Hindus ... ... ... .. ... | 834 | 899 | 1,733 |
| Muhammadans ... ... ... ... ... | 180 | 92 | 272 |
| Jains ... ... ... ... ... ... | 11 | 1 | 12 |
| Total ... ... | 1,025 | 992 | 2,017 |

Till 1882 it was the head-quarters of a taluq named after itself, and included in the Kadur District. In 1886, on the formation of the Arsikere taluq, Banavar was absorbed in it and transferred to the Hassan District.

It is said to derive its name from *bána* (arrow), and *hora* (carry), Rama having there "carried the arrows" which Lakshmana had dropped from fatigue. An inscription of the 12th century spells the name Báṇavúru, arrow town. It seems in about the middle of the 11th century to have been the chief town of a territory ruled by Harihara Somes'vara Ráya, who was also the founder of Harnhalli. It was then included in the Hoysala kingdom. After the fall of Vijayanagar it was one of the places seized by the Ikkeri chiefs, but was eventually captured by Chikka Deva Rája in 1690 and annexed to Mysore. During his wars with the Mahrattas, Haidar Ali removed the people to form a new city at Nagapuri on the Hirekal hills, but the place proving unhealthy, they shortly returned to their original abodes.

| Municipal Funds. | 1892-3. | 1893-4. | 1894-5. | 1895-6. |
|---|---|---|---|---|
| Income ... ... ... ... | 667 | 597 | 618 | 1,164 |
| Expenditure ... ... ... ... | 747 | 670 | 580 | 1,364 |

**Belur.**—A taluq in the north-west. Area 338 square miles. Head-quarters at Belur. Contains the following hoblis, villages and population :—

| No. | Hoblis. | Villages. | Hamlets. | Villages classified. | | | Population. |
|---|---|---|---|---|---|---|---|
| | | | | Government. | Sarvamánya. | Jodi. | |
| 1 | Arehalli ... ... ... | 63 | 38 | 55 | 1 | 7 | 10,083 |
| 2 | Belúr ... ... ... | 37 | 18 | 28 | 3 | 6 | 13,715 |
| 3 | Bikkód ... ... ... | 64 | 23 | 54 | 1 | 9 | 7,671 |
| 4 | Halebídu ... ... | 60 | 56 | 53 | 2 | 5 | 17,168 |
| 5 | Mádihalli ... ... | 62 | 17 | 59 | — | 3 | 9,723 |
| 6 | Sanivársante ... ... | 56 | 7 | 48 | — | 8 | 7,102 |
| 7 | Tagare ... ... ... | 53 | 27 | 42 | 1 | 10 | 10,008 |
| | Total ... | 395 | 186 | 339 | 8 | 48 | 75,470 |

*Principal places, with population.*—Belúr 3,084; Belavádi 2,013; Halébídu 1,461; Arehalli 1,037; Rájansiriyúr 1,012.

The western portion of the taluq belongs to the Malnád, and for a short distance is bounded by the Hémávati, which separates it from Manjarábád. The Yagache flows through the central portion in a south-easterly direction, and its tributary the Berinji-halla joins it in the north. The country in the west is hilly and covered with jungle, the valleys, which are often deep, being cultivated with rice, and the hills, where the trees are of sufficient size, with coffee. In the east, the stony and rocky hills are either bare or partially covered with scrub jungle, the valleys are of greater breadth, and cultivated with rice, sugar-cane and dry crops. The intermediate portion of the taluq, in the vicinity of Belur and along the valley of the Yagache river, partakes of the nature of both east and west, but is generally more level and distinguished by extensive gravelly plains, covered with either short grass or dwarf date. The rice lands here lie in much larger stretches.

The Yagache and the smaller streams falling into it supply several small channels. The Bomḍihalli channel from the main stream runs for 4½ miles on the right bank, ending near Belur. The Kittur channel, drawn from a minor stream in the north-west, has a length altogether of 15 miles to the west. The Maddigatta channel, 8 miles long, is taken off from another small stream in the south. There is an old ruined dam at Ranagatta, apparently designed to carry water from the river to the Halebid tank, by a large channel, called Sangidevar kálve, the embankment of which is 15 to 20 feet high in some places.

The soils both wet and dry are poor in the west, gradually improving towards the east, until in the neighbourhood of Halebid dark soils of the best description are found, producing good crops of sugar-cane in the wet and often two crops in the year in the dry soils. Exceptions, however, occur, as in the stretch of black soil near Belur, and the poor high-lying dry soils near Halebid itself. A peculiar feature in the landscape in the south-west is the steep demarcation between high-lying and low-lying ground. Instead of the former merging gradually into the latter, it terminates abruptly, presenting an almost perpendicular scarp, varying in height from 50 to 100 feet. As the soil is very friable landslips are not uncommon, especially in the rains. In addition to the usual wet and dry crops, in the eastern hoblis tobacco is largely grown, of fair quality. In the Malnád, to the west, are several coffee plantations which occupy the isolated patches of forest called *uduve*. Of 13,000 acres under coffee, 1,550 are held by Europeans. Brass pots are made by the Jains at Tagare and other places. In the neighbourhood of Halebid is found the potstone which has been used in the elaborate carvings of the temples. The principal mart for this taluq and the surrounding country is Bikkód, the transactions at which are valued at Rs. 4,000 a week or 2 lakhs a year.

The taluq was in the heart of the Hoysala kingdom, the capital, Dorasamudra, being situated at Halebid. Subsequent to the destruction of that city, in the beginning of the 14th century, Belur was included in the province of Balam, which the Vijayanagar kings conferred, first upon Vina Rámappa, and then upon the Aigur chiefs. From these it was taken by Sivappa Náyak of Ikkeri, who bestowed it on the fugitive king of Vijayanagar, but in 1690 it was taken by Mysore.

The revenue settlement was introduced in 1877. The old rates of assessment seem to have been based partly on the Vijayanagar *varaha shist* and partly on Sivappa Náyak's *rekha shist.* It appears that no assessment was formerly demanded on account of dry land, except in a few villages to the south, where the *hakkal* or dry land was included in the assessment of wet lands. The area of the taluq in 1877 was thus distributed :—

| | |
|---|---|
| Culturable (dry, 79,311 ; wet, 28,853 ; garden, 1,439) ... ... | 109,603 |
| Unculturable (including grazing lands, roads, &c.) ... ... | 54,079 |
| Inám (27,158) ; 9 Amrit Mahal kávals (16,530) ... ... ... | 43,688 |
| Total acres ... | 207,370 |

The unoccupied area was 37,148 acres, of which 32,495 were dry land. The total revenue demand for 1891–2 (15 months) was Rs. 1,84,679 and for 1892–3 it was Rs. 2,13,496.

The average rainfall at Belur for 26 years (1870–95) was as follows :—

| Jan. | Feb. | Mar. | April | May | June | July | Aug. | Sept. | Oct. | Nov. | Dec. | Year. |
|---|---|---|---|---|---|---|---|---|---|---|---|---|
| — | 0.19 | 0·37 | 1·66 | 3·18 | 3·83 | 6·35 | 3·07 | 2·65 | 5·70 | 2·33 | 0·55 ... | 29·88 |

According to another register for 10 years the average is 31. But in the west of the taluq it is about 80 inches.

The Hassan-Chikmagalur road passes Belur, whence there are roads north-east through Halebid to the railway at Banavar, west through Mudgere to the Búnd ghat, and south to Sakleshpur.

**Belur.**—A town situated in 13° 10′ N. lat., 75° 55′ E. long., on the right bank of the Yagache, 28 miles south-west of the railway at Banavar, and 24 miles north-west of Hassan, on the Hassan-Chikmagalur road. Head-quarters of the Belur taluq and a municipality.

| Population in 1891. | Males. | Females | Total. |
|---|---|---|---|
| Hindus ... ... ... ... ... | 1,252 | 1,395 | 2,647 |
| Muhammadans ... ... ... | 211 | 194 | 405 |
| Jains ... ... ... ... ... | 18 | — | 18 |
| Christians ... ... ... .. | 5 | 9 | 14 |
| Total ... | 1,486 | 1,598 | 3,084 |

Belur, in the puranas and ancient inscriptions, bears the name of Velápura and Velur, and is styled the Dakshina Váranási or southern Benares. Its sanctity is due to the celebrated temple of Chenna Kesava, erected and endowed by the Hoysala king Vishnuvarddhana, on the occasion of his exchanging the Jain faith for that of Vishnu, in the beginning of the 12th century. The carving with which the temple is decorated rivals in fertility of design and perfection of finish that of the Halebid temple, and is attributed to the same master hand, that of the famous Jakanáchari. The incident related under Kaidala (Tumkúr District) would indicate that it was nearly his last undertaking. The annual festival, held for five days in April, is attended by 5,000 people. The image of Chenna Kesava is said to have been brought from the Baba Budan hills, but by some mistake that of the goddess being left behind, and her wounded pride forbidding the removal afterwards, the god is under the necessity of making a trip occasionally to the Baba Budan hills to see her. On these occasions he is said to make use of a large pair of slippers kept for the purpose in the temple. When they are worn out, it devolves upon the chucklers of Channagiri and Basvapatna (Shimoga District), to whom the fact is revealed in a dream, to provide new ones; in order to present which they are allowed to enter the courtyard of the temple.

The later history of Belur has already been given under the taluq.

| Municipal Funds. | 1892-3. | 1893-4. | 1894-5. | 1895-6. |
|---|---|---|---|---|
| Income ... ... ... ... | 1,905 | 2,255 | 2,248 | 3,330 |
| Expenditure ... ... ... | 1,806 | 3,342 | 3,664 | 4,650 |

**Channaráyapatna.**—A taluq in the east. Area 413 square miles. Head-quarters at Channaráyapatna. Contains the following hoblis, villages and population:—

| No. | Hoblis. | Villages. | Hamlets. | Villages classified. | | Population. |
|---|---|---|---|---|---|---|
| | | | | Government. | Sarvamányа. | |
| 1 | Anati ... ... ... | 49 | 18 | 49 | — | 8,853 |
| 2 | Bágúr ... ... ... | 57 | 4 | 57 | — | 9,568 |
| 3 | Channaráyapatna... ... | 53 | 13 | 53 | — | 13,498 |
| 4 | Dandiganhalli ... ... | 57 | 14 | 57 | — | 10,448 |
| 5 | Hirisáve ... ... ... | 53 | 6 | 53 | — | 10,374 |
| 6 | Nuggihalli ... ... | 56 | 6 | 56 | — | 11,123 |
| 7 | Sravana Belgola ... ... | 52 | 17 | 48 | 4 | 14,347 |
| | Total ... | 377 | 78 | 373 | 4 | 78,211 |

*Principal places, with population.*—Channarāyapatna 3,081; Sravana-Belgola 1,763; Nuggihalli 1,241; Hirísáve 1,232; Bágúr 1,055.

The taluq drains southwards to the Hemavati, the streams forming many large tanks. An elevated ridge runs along the north from east to west, a few small streams from which flow north and east to the Shimsha. It is a generally open and undulating country. Except a low ridge on the western boundary, the principal hills are the isolated peaks at the Jain settlement of Sravana-Belgola. The soil is mostly fertile and produces the usual wet and dry crops, but along the western border is generally shallow and very stony. The soil is of the ordinary light red and sandy description, going through few gradations, except near Nuggihalli where there is some soil of a colour approaching black. The pasture lands are very extensive and support large herds of cattle and sheep. There is a little irrigation from the Hole-Narsipur north channel. A considerable amount of the labour in the coffee districts is drawn from this taluq. It may prove to be rich in minerals, and gold-mining has recently been revived. Sravana-Belgola is noted for the manufacture of brass vessels. Small articles of silk are made by Muhammadans at Channaráyapatna.

This part of the District, after the overthrow of the Hoysala power, became one of the possessions of the chief of Hole-Narsipur. It was conquered by Chama Rája Wodeyar in 1633, and annexed to Mysore.

The revenue settlement was introduced in 1885. The area of the taluq was thus distributed:—

| | |
|---|---|
| Culturable (dry, 140,124; wet, 7,399; garden, 4,841) ... ... | 152,364 |
| Unculturable (roads, tanks, village sites, &c.) ... ... ... | 77,384 |
| Inam (2,939); kávals (14,640) ... ... ... ... ... | 17,579 |
| Total acres ... | 247,327 |

The unoccupied area was 51,742 acres, 50,586 being dry land. The total revenue demand for 1891–2 (15 months) was Rs. 1,89,870, and for 1892–3 it was Rs. 2,07,335.

The average rainfall at Channaráyapatna for 26 years (1870–95), and at the other stations for 3 years (1893–5) was as follows:—

| | Jan. | Feb. | Mar. | April | May | June | July | Aug. | Sept. | Oct. | Nov. | Dec. | | Year. |
|---|---|---|---|---|---|---|---|---|---|---|---|---|---|---|
| Channaráyapatna | — | 0·03 | 0·46 | 1·44 | 3·58 | 1·88 | 2·01 | 2·24 | 2·39 | 5·05 | 2·38 | 0·66 | ... | 22·12 |
| Bágúr ... ... | — | — | 0·12 | 0·51 | 1·75 | 0·70 | 0·60 | 1·57 | 2·71 | 4·58 | 1·53 | — | ... | 14·07 |
| Dandiganhalli ... | — | 0·21 | 0·31 | 3·05 | 0·67 | 2·73 | 1·05 | 5·96 | 2·32 | 4·46 | 1·27 | — | ... | 22·03 |

According to other records for 6 years the average at Bágúr is 15·32 and at Dandiganhalli 19·23.

The Bangalore-Hassan and Seringapatam-Shimoga roads cross at Channaráyapatna, whence there are roads to the north to Nuggihalli, and the railway at Tiptur, south-west to Hole Narsipur, and east to

Sravana-Belgola. From Nuggihalli there is a road to Hirésáve on the trunk road. There is also a branch road from Channaráyapatna to Bágúr and the main road.

**Channaráyapatna.**—A town situated in 12° 54′ N. lat., 76° 26′ E. long., 32 miles south by east of the railway at Arsikere, and 23 miles east of Hassan, on the Bangalore-Hassan road. Head-quarters of the taluq bearing the same name, and a municipality.

| Population in 1891. | Males. | Females. | Total. |
|---|---|---|---|
| Hindus ... ... ... ... ... ... | 1,186 | 1,300 | 2,486 |
| Muhammadans ... ... ... ... ... | 256 | 293 | 549 |
| Jains... ... ... ... ... ... ... | 8 | 14 | 22 |
| Christians ... ... ... ... ... ... | 18 | 6 | 24 |
| Total ... ... | 1,468 | 1,613 | 3,081 |

The town was originally called Koḷatur, and consisted only of an agrahára. Máchala Dévi and Sántala Dévi, two dancing girls, built the large tank on the north-east. About the year 1600 Lakshmappa Náyak, the chief of Hole-Narsipur, took the place from Puttagirija the Hebbár, and bestowed it as a jágir on his own son Channa Ráya, whom he had obtained by favour of the god Channaráyaswami, a name of Vishnu. To this deity a temple was erected, and the town was called *Channa-ráyapattana.*

The fort was built by a chief named Dodda Basavaiya, and when captured by Chama Rája Wodeyar of Mysore in 1633, was in possession of the chief of Hole-Narsipur. It was subsequently re-built by Haidar Ali, with a wet moat and traverse gateways, having suffered much in repeated attacks from the Mahrattas.

| Municipal Funds. | 1892-3. | 1893-4. | 1894-5. | 1895-6. |
|---|---|---|---|---|
| Income ... ... ... ... | 1,007 | 1,402 | 1,222 | 1,967 |
| Expenditure ... ... ... | 1,109 | 2,250 | 1,367 | 2,433 |

**Garudangiri.**—A conspicuous old hill-fort, 3,680 feet above the level of the sea, on the boundary of the District, about 7 miles north-east of Banavar. It was originally called Noṇabanakal, but received the present name on being fortified in 1660 by the Rája of Mysore, in order to be a protection to the frontier on that side, then overrun with jungle. In 1770 it was occupied by the Mahrattas under Tryambak Máma, after their defeat of Haidar at Chinkuruli, but was restored to Mysore on the conclusion of peace. On the death of Tipu Sultan it was delivered up to the British, and was garrisoned for some time by the Mysore troops.

**Grama.**—A large village, 7 miles east of Hassan, on the Bangalore road. From 1882 to 1894 it was the head-quarters of a sub-taluq of the same name, under Hassan taluq, comprising the Grama, Dudda and Kaṭṭáya hoblis. It is now the head-quarters of the Grama hobli, and since 1892 a municipality. Population 2,184.

From inscriptions it appears that it was founded in the 12th century by S'ántala Devi, queen of the Hoysala king Vishnuvarddhana, and was at first named S'ántigráma.

| Municipal Funds. | 1893-4. | 1894-5. | 1895-6. |
|---|---|---|---|
| Income ... ... ... ... | 414 | 428 | 774 |
| Expenditure ... ... ... ... | 241 | 375 | 782 |

**Halebid.**—A village in the Belur taluq, 18 miles south of the railway at Banavar, and 11 miles east of Belur, on the Belur-Banavar road. Head-quarters of the Halebid hobli. Population 1,461.

The village of *haḷe-biḍu*, old capital, marks the site of the ancient city of Dorasamudra, Dvárasamudra or Dvárávatipura, the wealthy capital of the Hoysala kings, founded early in the 11th century. The city was taken by the Muhammadan general Kafur in 1310, and plundered of immense wealth. In 1326 another Muhammadan army carried off what remained, and totally destroyed the city. The fallen king, after this event, took up his residence first at Tondanur (Tonnur, Mysore District), and then at other places far to the east of his dominions in the Tamil country.

The splendour of the city is attested not only by the account of the fabulous riches obtained from its conquest, as related by Muhammadan historians, but by its architectural monuments, which still rank among the masterpieces of Hindu art. The most remarkable of these are the Hoysaḷesvara and Kedáresvara temples.[1] The latter was the smaller, and a gem of art. But a banyan-tree, which had rooted itself in the *vimána* or tower over the sanctum, dislodged the stones, and many of the figures thrust out of the walls have been removed to the Museum in Bangalore. The large Hoysalesvara temple, though never completed, is in better preservation. The marvellous elaboration of ornamental sculpture round the walls, and the general architectural effect, have elicited from the highest authority on these subjects[2] the opinion that "taken altogether it is perhaps the building on which the advocate of

[1] *See* Vol. I, p. 514.

[2] Fergusson, *Hist. of Arch.*

Hindu architecture would desire to take his stand." The critique will be found more at length in another part of this work.

The plain Jain bastis, though cast completely into the shade by the ornate Saiva temples, are also striking buildings. The city is said to have originally contained no less than 720. Three only now remain, those of Adináthesvara, Sántisvara and Pársvanáthesvara, the latter of which is the largest.

Around a small hill called Benne-gudda are pointed out portions of the old wall, and the site of the palace to the east. South of the palace was the *áne gundi* or elephant pit. The position of the royal stables is indicated by the fields still entered in the revenue accounts as the *láya* (stables). Part of an aqueduct, by which the city was supplied with water from the Yagache, may be seen on the south. The balapam or potstone used in the sculptures is found on the Push-pagiri, or hill of flowers, near the town.

The only part that survived the general ruin was the potters' street, which it is said was spared on account of the shelter afforded by a potter to a distracted princess, whose two sons being beheaded at the instance of a royal mistress they had slighted, and herself forbidden the city, she cursed it as well as the royal family, predicting the speedy destruction of both, save only the potters' street.

**Haranhalli.**—A town in Arsikere taluq, 5 miles south of the kasba, on the Hassan-Arsikere road. Till 1882 head-quarters of a taluq of the same name. It is now the head-quarters of the Háranhalli hobli, and a municipality.

| Population in 1891. | Males. | Females. | Total. |
|---|---|---|---|
| Hindus ... ... ... ... ... | 960 | 980 | 1,940 |
| Muhammadans... ... ... ... | 133 | 151 | 284 |
| Total ... ... ... | 1,093 | 1,131 | 2,224 |

The fort is said to have been erected in 1070 by a chief named Somesvara Raya. The large Nagati tank was named after his daughter. There are several fine temples, partly in ruins, and other monuments, without the fort walls, which indicate the existence of a large city in former times. The inscriptions that are legible belong to the Hoysala rule. The later history of the place is the same as that of Arsikere (*see* above).

| Municipal Funds. | 1892–3. | 1893–4. | 1894–5. | 1895–6. |
|---|---|---|---|---|
| Income ... ... ... ... ... | 453 | 527 | 601 | 1,233 |
| Expenditure ... ... ... ... | 496 | 823 | 668 | 1,618 |

**Hassan**.—A taluq in the centre. Area 475 square miles. Head-quarters at Hassan. Contains, including the A'lúr sub-taluq, the following hoblis, villages, and population :—

| No. | Hoblis. | Villages. | Hamlets. | Villages classified. | | | | Population. |
|---|---|---|---|---|---|---|---|---|
| | | | | Govern-ment. | Sarva-mánya. | Jodi. | Kayam-gutta. | |
| 1 | A'lúr ... ... | 58 | 23 | 57 | — | — | 1 | 10,931 |
| 2 | Bailhalli ... ... | 58 | 12 | 52 | — | 5 | 1 | 10,779 |
| 3 | Dudda ... ... | 59 | 16 | 58 | — | 1 | — | 12,784 |
| 4 | Gráma ... ... | 62 | 22 | 59 | — | 3 | — | 13,531 |
| 5 | Hassan ... ... | 83 | 39 | 78 | — | 4 | 1 | 22,685 |
| 6 | Kattáya ... ... | 72 | 27 | 68 | 1 | 3 | — | 16,523 |
| 7 | Pálya ... ... | 48 | 24 | 39 | — | 8 | 1 | 6,077 |
| 8 | Ponnáthpura ... | 59 | 28 | 55 | — | 3 | 1 | 7,878 |
| 9 | Sáligáme ... ... | 68 | 11 | 65 | — | 3 | — | 12,209 |
| | Total ... | 567 | 202 | 531 | 1 | 30 | 5 | 113,397 |

*Principal places, with population.*—Hassan 6,654; Gráma 2,184; A'lúr 1,822; Kittani 1,177; Handinakere 1,070.

The A'lúr, Pálya and Chik-Kanagál hoblis were added in 1875 from Maharajandurga. The taluq was formed as at present in 1882, with Gráma as a sub-taluq, the latter comprising the Gráma, Dudda and Kattáya hoblis. In 1894 A'lúr was made the sub-taluq in place of Gráma, and includes the A'lúr, Pálya and Ponnáthpura hoblis.

The Hemavati forms the southern boundary. The Yagache flows through the west from north to south, receives most of the small streams, and joins the Hemavati near Gorúr. But a considerable water-course, running down through the east to the Hemavati, forms a chain of numerous tanks. The Yagache is dammed near Hassan, and supplies the Halvagal channel, 6 miles long. In the north is a group of hills called Síge gudda. There are some low hills on the south, separating the taluq from Arkalgud and Hole Narsipur.

The south-western hoblis are partly Malnád, Pálya being the most so, with fine breezy uplands, presenting in some parts the appearance of grassy open downs, and in others being covered with small scrub jungle. The climate and soils here are well suited to the production of rice of a superior description, but sugar-cane is raised only under special large tanks. Dry cultivation is little esteemed, and a crop once in three years is often deemed sufficient. Some 1,285 acres have been taken up for coffee. In the east of the taluq the villages are far apart, with extensive stretches of waste land which support large flocks of sheep. The soils, which run through many gradations, from light sandy grey to rich dark brown, are superior in the vicinity of the Yagache river, but deteriorate on the uplands as the river is receded from. Rági is the staple crop in dry lands and rice in wet, with a fair proportion of sugar-cane. Dod-rági is grown in the east, but gid-rági in the west, which admits in good years of an after crop of horse-gram. Fields in the east not adapted for rági are largely sown with chillies, between rows of castor-oil.

Hassan is the carrying taluq for the coffee districts which border it on the west, and supplies nearly all the carts required in this and the Kadur District. There is much good pasturage, and the large Síge guḍḍa kával, belonging to the Amrit Mahal, will maintain 2,500 head of cattle.

The taluq was included successively in the Chalukya and Hoysala dominions. It afterwards formed part of Balam and shared the fortunes of that province. It was incorporated with Mysore in 1690 by treaty with Ikkeri.

The revenue settlement was introduced into the Alúr, Pálya and Chik-Kanagál hoblis in 1881, and into the remainder of the taluq in 1882. The area was thus distributed :—

| | |
|---|---|
| Culturable (dry, 136,570 ; wet, 25,943 ; garden, 3,037) ... ... | 165,550 |
| Unculturable (including roads, tanks, village sites, &c.) ... ... | 61,160 |
| Inám (19,423) ; 26 kávals (40,208) ... ... ... ... ... | 59,631 |
| Total acres ... | 286,341 |

The unoccupied arable area was 63,537 acres, of which 59,107 were dry land. The total revenue demand for 1891-2 (15 months) was Rs. 2,78,876, and for 1892-3 it was Rs. 3,23,693.

The average rainfall at Hassan and Gráma for 26 years (1870-95) and at the other station for 3 years (1893-5) was as follows :—

| | Jan. | Feb. | Mar. | April | May | June | July | Aug. | Sept. | Oct. | Nov. | Dec. | | Year. |
|---|---|---|---|---|---|---|---|---|---|---|---|---|---|---|
| Hassan ... | 0·12 | 0·02 | 0·39 | 2·53 | 3·74 | 3·25 | 5·30 | 2·49 | 3·15 | 7·53 | 2·16 | 0·57 | ... | 31·25 |
| Gráma ... | 0·01 | 0·12 | 0·22 | 1·64 | 4·55 | 2·55 | 4·07 | 1·62 | 5·03 | 5·50 | 2·40 | 1·06 | ... | 28·77 |
| Kaṭṭaya ... | — | 0·07 | 0·45 | 2·99 | 4·77 | 4·79 | 2·93 | 2·18 | 1·66 | 9·03 | 3·80 | — | ... | 32·67 |

The fall in the west is probably about 65 inches.

The Bangalore-Mangalore trunk road by the Manjarabad Ghat runs through Hassan, and from this town there are roads north to the railway at Arsikere—with a branch from Dudda north-east to the railway at Tiptur,—north-west to Belur, south to Arkalgud—with a branch from Kaṭṭáya west to Hoskote,—and south-east to Hole Narsipur.

**Hassan.**—The chief town of the District, situated in 13° N. lat., 76° 9′ E. long., 25 miles south by west of the railway at Arsikere, and a municipality.

| Population in 1891. | Males. | Females. | Total. |
|---|---|---|---|
| Hindus ... ... ... ... ... | 2,448 | 2,469 | 4,917 |
| Muhammadans ... ... ... ... | 573 | 607 | 1,180 |
| Jains ... ... ... ... ... | 125 | 143 | 268 |
| Christians ... ... ... ... | 113 | 161 | 274 |
| Jews ... ... ... ... ... | 6 | 9 | 15 |
| Total ... ... ... | 3,265 | 3,389 | 6,654 |

The original town was at the adjacent village of Chennapatna. This was founded in the 11th century by Bukkana or Bukka Nayak, said to be an officer despatched by the Chola king to put down the depredations committed by neighbouring petty chieftains. In this enterprise he succeeded so well that he received permission to erect a fort and petta on the site of his encampment. He named the place Chennapatna, the handsome city, and made the large tank between it and Hassan. After a prosperous rule of 43 years Bukka Nayak died, and was succeeded by his son Búchi Nayak, who after 6 years was followed by his son Chennappa Nayak, and he after 45 years by his son Búcha Nayak. The latter died after 50 years without leaving male issue.

Chennapatna was then conferred by the Hoysala kings on Sanjíva Krishnappa Nayak. On one occasion a hare which he had started tcok to the town and entered the gates. While in great distress at this bad omen, Hásin-amma, the smiling goddess, appeared to him, and directed him to build a fort on the spot whence the hare had started, and where he would find her image. This he did and named the place *Hásana* after her. The present town therefore dates from the end of the 12th century. The sthala purána derives its name from a contraction of Simhásana-pura, and hither Janaméjaya is said to have come.

Hassan was included in the province of Balam and partook of its fortunes until annexed to Mysore in 1690, during the reign of Chikka Deva Raja Wodeyar.

| Municipal Funds. | 1892-3. | 1893-4. | 1894-5. | 1895-6. |
|---|---|---|---|---|
| Income ... ... ... ... ... .. | 7,994 | 8,123 | 9,568 | 9,876 |
| Expenditure ... ... ... ... ... | 8,060 | 13,287 | 8,930 | 10,358 |

**Hemavati.**—Golden, also called in Kannada *Yenne hole*, oily or shining river. One of the chief tributaries of the Kávéri. It rises just beyond the limits of the District, at Jávali, near Melbangádi, in Mudgere taluq, and flowing south is joined near the head of the Bund Ghat by the Sómávati. Continuing south through Manjarabad, past Sakleshpur, it receives from the south the Aigur river, near the place of that name, and the Kete halla at the Coorg frontier. Thence turning east, it crosses a small portion of Coorg, and re-entering Mysore receives from the north the Yagache near Gorur. With an easterly course it flows past Hole Narsipur to Ganni, some distance beyond which it bends round to the south, and runs down into the Kávéri, near Hoskote, in Krishnarájpet taluq. Its length within this District is 113 miles.

Its waters are dammed in several places, from each of which channels are led off. Only two are now in this District. The first dam is the Srirámdevar anicut in Hole Narsipur taluq. This work was originally constructed of rough stone by Danáyaka Hebbáraiya in 1533. It afterwards breached, and was three times repaired during the administration of the Dewan Purnaiya. The dam was 1,000 feet long and 24 feet high. In 1863 it again breached, since which a new anicut has been erected by the Public Works Department, at a cost of Rs. 2,78,504, a little below the former spot, on the principle now adopted of making the dam water-tight, which none of the others are. Two channels are led off from it, the Uttara or North channel, 47½ miles in length, on the left bank; and the Dakshina or South channel, 12 miles long, on the right. The former irrigates 4,413 acres, and the latter, which runs through the town of Hole Narsipur, 606 acres. The Madapur anicut, 10 miles below Hole Narsipur, breached in 1863. The channels irrigated 417 acres.

The Hémávati is crossed at Sakleshpur by a fine iron girder bridge of four spans, formed by lattice girders, each 120 feet long and resting on cylinders. It was finished in 1870 at a cost of Rs. 1,94,620.

The river is fabled to be the daughter of Daksha and wife of Isvara. The insult put upon the latter in not being invited to Daksha's sacrifice led to her casting herself into the fire, from which, when rescued, she was of the colour of gold (*hema*). Becoming incarnate as the daughter of Himavat, she performed penance with the view of being reunited to Isvara, who appeared to her and directed her to take the form of a river for the good of the world.

**Hole Narsipur.**—A taluq in the south-east. Area 233 square miles. Head-quarters at Hole Narsipur. Contains the following hoblis, villages and population :—

| No. | Hoblis. | Villages. | Hamlets. | Villages classified. | | | | Population. |
|---|---|---|---|---|---|---|---|---|
| | | | | Govern-ment. | Sarva-mánya | Jodi. | Kayam-gutta. | |
| 1 | Dod Káḍanúr ... | 49 | 45 | 47 | 1 | 1 | — | 11,852 |
| 2 | Gubbi ... ... | 29 | 22 | 24 | 1 | 4 | — | 7,675 |
| 3 | Halekóṭe ... ... | 79 | 16 | 75 | — | 2 | 2 | 13,812 |
| 4 | Hole Narsipur .. | 69 | 41 | 60 | 3 | 6 | — | 17,555 |
| | Total ... | 226 | 124 | 206 | 5 | 13 | 2 | 50,894 |

*Principal places, with population.*—Hole Narsipur 5,758; Harihara-pura 1,255.

The Hémávati runs through the taluq from west to east, and then turning south, forms a good part of the eastern boundary. The channels drawn from it are, the North channel of 47½ miles, and the South channel of 12 miles, both led off from the Srirámadevar dam. Another dam, the Mádápur, is breached. Near Hole Narsipur are a few isolated hills. Except for the channel irrigation, the taluq may be described as sterile. As the river is receded from, especially to the south, the uplands become bleak and unpromising. Even under the channels the soils are not very good, and in the taluq generally they are decidedly poor.

The taluq seems to have been the possession in the 12th century of a chief named Narasimha Nayak, who also owned Channaráyapatna. It was conquered from his descendants in 1667 by Dodda Deva Raja of Mysore.

The revenue settlement was introduced in 1884. The area of the taluq was thus distributed:—

| | | |
|---|---|---|
| Culturable (dry, 68,219; wet, 6,492; garden, 1,494) | ... ... | 76,205 |
| Unculturable (including roads, tanks, village sites, &c.) | ... ... | 30,413 |
| Inám (16,573); 8 kávals (8,202) ... ... ... | ... ... | 24,775 |
| Total acres | ... ... | 131,393 |

The unoccupied area was 25,613 acres, 25,136 being dry land. The total revenue demand for 1891-2 (15 months) was Rs. 1,05,716, and for 1892-3 it was Rs. 1,19,172.

The average rainfall for 26 years (1870-95) at Hole Narsipur, and for 3 years (1893-5) at the other station, was as follows:—

| | Jan. | Feb. | Mar. | Apr. | May | June | July | Aug. | Sept. | Oct. | Nov. | Dec. | Year. |
|---|---|---|---|---|---|---|---|---|---|---|---|---|---|
| Hole Narsipur ... | — | 0·03 | 0·60 | 2·03 | 3·78 | 2·05 | 2·76 | 2·44 | 3·06 | 6·17 | 3·11 | 0·78 | ... 26·81 |
| Srirámadevar dam | — | 0·11 | 0·31 | 3·79 | 4·33 | 2·90 | 1·18 | 1·17 | 2·07 | 7·24 | 2·12 | — | ... 25·22 |

The Mysore-Hassan road runs through the taluq from south-east to north-west, and is crossed at Hole Narsipur by the Channaráyapatna-Arkalgud road, running from north-east to west. There is also a cross road from the latter to near Kikkeri.

**Hole Narsipur.**—A town on the right bank of the Hémávati, situated in 12° 47′ N. lat., 76° 18′ E. long., 21 miles south-east of Hassan, on the Mysore-Hassan road. Head-quarters of the Hole Narsipur taluq, and a municipality.

| Population in 1891. | Males. | Females. | Total. |
|---|---|---|---|
| Hindus ... ... ... .. ... | 2,456 | 2,675 | 5,131 |
| Muhammadans ... ... ... ... | 301 | 297 | 598 |
| Jains ... ... ... ... ... | 14 | 15 | 29 |
| Total ... ... | 2,771 | 2,987 | 5,758 |

The fort was built in 1168 by Narsimha Náyak, a chief whose territories included Hole Narsipur and Channaráyapatna. The place was captured from his descendants in 1667 by the Raja of Mysore. The town is the residence of the guru of the Mádhva Brahmans of the Uttarádi branch. Cloth of good quality is made here. The manufacture of *goni* bags gives occupation to a good many people.

| Municipal Funds. | 1892-3. | 1893-4. | 1894-5. | 1895-6. |
|---|---|---|---|---|
| Income ... ... ... ... | 1,576 | 1,863 | 1,671 | 3,155 |
| Expenditure ... ... ... | 1,601 | 3,995 | 2,775 | 4,858 |

**Konanur.**—A large village on the left bank of the Kávéri in Arkalgud taluq, about 15 miles south-west of the kasba. Head-quarters of the Konanúr hobli, and since 1893 a municipality. Population 2,433.

It was the place to which Nanja Ráj was required to retire in 1759, and from which he was induced by Haidar under false pretences to return to power.

| Municipal Funds. | 1893-4. | 1894-5. | 1895-6. |
|---|---|---|---|
| Income ... ... ... ... ... ... ... ... | 498 | 594 | 1,000 |
| Expenditure ... ... ... ... ... ... ... | 204 | 562 | 956 |

**Malekal Tirupati.**—A temple on the Hirekal hills, near Arsikere. A flight of 1,700 steps leads to the top, the ascent of which is an efficacious substitute for a pilgrimage to the famous Tirupati in North Arcot.

**Manjarabad.**—A taluq in the west. Area 430 square miles. Head-quarters at Sakleshpur. Contains the following hoblis, villages and population :—

| No. | Hoblis. | Villages. | Hamlets. | Villages classified. | | | | Population. |
|---|---|---|---|---|---|---|---|---|
| | | | | Govern-ment. | Sarva-mánya. | Jodi. | Kayam-gutta. | |
| 1 | Belagód ... ... | 39 | 9 | 33 | — | 5 | 1 | 8,569 |
| 2 | Byágadahalli ... | 29 | 19 | 29 | — | — | — | 3,739 |
| 3 | Hánbálu ... ... | 30 | 20 | 30 | — | — | — | 5,105 |
| 4 | Hosakóte ... | 53 | 12 | 46 | 2 | 4 | 1 | 8,360 |
| 5 | Máranhalli ... | 24 | 11 | 24 | — | — | — | 5,105 |
| 6 | Sakleshpur ... | 40 | 17 | 39 | — | — | 1 | 9,086 |
| 7 | Sukravársante .. | 25 | 19 | 24 | 1 | — | — | 6,517 |
| 8 | Yesalúr ... ... | 38 | 31 | 38 | — | — | — | 9,381 |
| | Total ... | 278 | 138 | 263 | 3 | 9 | 3 | 55,862 |

*Principal places, with population.*—Sakleshpur 1,591 ; Yesalúr 1,338.

The northern hoblis were transferred in 1881 to the Múdgere taluq (Kadur District).

The whole taluq is Malnad, and comprises some of the most beautiful scenery in Mysore, flanked by the stupendous range of the Western Ghats.[1] The country to the east of the Hémávati is more open than that to the west. The Hémávati flows from the north-eastern angle down a part of the eastern border, and then crosses the taluq to the southern border, where it turns east, separating the taluq from Coorg. Near Aigur it receives the Aigur river; and on the Coorg frontier the Kete halla from the south. The western waters of the taluq flow down the Ghats to the Nétrávati in South Canara.

[1] The principal beauty lies in the wonderful contrasts which may be seen at a single glance. Scenery stern, rugged and precipitous is always to be enjoyed; but when you can contrast it, in almost a single glance, with the softest features of an English park landscape, the effect is heightened to an extraordinary degree. Even amongst the hills themselves the contrasts are very striking, and nature seems to have furnished in a single group every variety of mountain conceivable. In Europe the Pyrenees are the Pyrenees, and the Cheviots the Cheviots, with one common feature pervading each range of hills. But from a piece of elevated land not far from the spot where Arthur Wellesley pitched his camp of occupation, may be seen a complete amphitheatre of frontier mountains, presenting the greatest variety of character ; one an overhanging precipice of rock, from which you may drop a stone thousands of feet into the gorge below ; the next all grass, and softly rounded at the summit with cattle grazing on the slopes ; a third rising abruptly into a pointed peak, with feathery strips of jungle clothing the lower ravines, and extending far up the mountain-side ; while to the north of the group stretches a barren, serrated, rocky range, which in turn is broken by hills of a milder type.—Elliot, *Experiences of a Planter*, I, 42.

The soil on the hills is generally of a rich deep red, while in the valleys it is sometimes red and sometimes approaches to black. The grain principally cultivated is rice, which grows most luxuriantly in the valleys and fields cut in terraces on their sides, and in the western parts double crops are regularly raised. At the head of each valley is usually a small tank, with a common mud embankment, which serves to collect a little water from the spring rising above it, to be used when the rains hang off; but artificial irrigation is generally rendered superfluous by the exceeding abundance of the rains. Dry cultivation is found to the east of the river. To the west scattered patches of rági may be met with, but the practice is to grow it only once in 2 or 3 years or at even longer intervals.

The cultivation of coffee has assumed great importance. Though only half a century old, it has already, by attracting the investment of European capital and the settlement of European planters, changed the face of the country and revolutionised the old feudal customs and immunities of this region. Cardamoms are also cultivated in the western parts.

The old name of this part of the country was Balam, said to be derived from *bala*, strength. The history of the province has already been given, and the succession of Náyaks.

When the Aigur chief fled to Coorg in 1792, on the withdrawal of the British forces, he was invited back by Tipu Sultan and granted an estate yielding a revenue of 5,000 pagodas, composed of the mandes of Karodi, Yesalúr, Aigur, Bisale, and Uchangi. The remainder of the territory of Balam was annexed to Mysore, and a fort erected on one of the central heights for a garrison. The country being enveloped in fog when the Sultan inspected the works, he is said to have called it from that circumstance Manjarábád, "the abode of fog" (*manju*).

Manjarábád proper consisted of 6 náds, sub-divided into 36 mandes. Each mande had a patel, and one of these in each nád was the Nád Patel, a position of much local weight and influence. The senior Nád Patel was called the Shime Gauda, and had the precedence. Three of the nád patels were Lingáyits, and the other three Haḷe Wokkalu, ancient farmers. The mande and gráma patels were Devar Makkalu, God's children. The slaves, now free, were called Haḷe Makkalu, ancient children, and Holeyaru.

The houses of the patels are generally fortified, and in some instances surrounded with a deep fosse. Within these precincts they still maintain much of the authority they formerly exercised as feudal chiefs, each farm being complete in itself, and in respect to the requirements of daily life independent of its neighbours. Cloths, blankets, household utensils and such other articles as cannot be made up or manufactured in the house, are readily procured at the fairs held in different parts.

The patels and head men are a fine manly race, very superior to those of the plains. Their usual dress is a black cumbly, passed round the body and fastened over the left shoulder, leaving the right arm free. The waist is girded with a similar article, or with a cloth, generally dark blue with a white stripe. The turbans are mostly white, or dark blue with a small gold edging. The labourers have a similar dress of coarser material and usually wear a leather skull-cap. All classes carry a knife, and few are without a matchlock or musket.

The revenue settlement was introduced in 1882. The area of the taluq was thus distributed :—

| | |
|---|---|
| Culturable (dry, 34,395 ; wet, 40,220 ; garden, 315) ... ... | 74,930 |
| Unculturable (including roads, village sites, &c.) ... ... ... | 173,603 |
| 20 coffee estates and 1 state forest ... ... ... ... ... | 24,373 |
| Total acres ... ... | 272,906 |

The unoccupied area was 20,086 acres, of which 15,917 were dry land. The total revenue demand for 1891–2 (15 months) was Rs. 2,08,087, and for 1892–3 it was Rs. 2,33,457.

The average rainfall at Sakleshpur for 26 years (1870–95) was as follows :—

| Jan. | Feb. | Mar. | Apl. | May | June | July | Aug. | Sept. | Oct. | Nov. | Dec. | | Year. |
|---|---|---|---|---|---|---|---|---|---|---|---|---|---|
| 0·10 | — | 0·71 | 2·41 | 5·17 | 15·51 | 28·12 | 14·90 | 5·89 | 6·89 | 3·06 | 0·79 | ... | 83·55 |

But in the vicinity of the Ghats the average is considerably over 200 inches, diminishing every few miles to the east, until on the eastern border it is from 60 to 70 inches. At Hulhalli estate it is 120·25 ; at Byakarvalli estate 110·26 ; at Agalhatti estate 85·14 ; at Lakkunda estate 60·51.

The Manjarabad Ghat road from Hassan crosses the taluq through Sakleshpur ; and the Bisale Ghat road runs through the south. The taluq is intersected longitudinally by a road from Múdgere through Sakleshpur to Kodlipet and Arkalgud, giving off cross roads to Vangúr, to Yesalurpet, and by Kenchammana Hoskote to Pálya and Belur, and to Hassan.

**Sakleshpur.**[1]—A town on the right bank of the Hémávati, situated in 12° 57′ N. lat., 75° 51′ E. long., 24 miles west of Hassan, on the Bangalore-Mangalore road. Head-quarters of the Manjarabad taluq, and a municipality.

[1] By European coffee planters often called *Sucklassport.*

| Population in 1891. | Males. | Females. | Total. |
|---|---|---|---|
| Hindus... ... ... .. ... | 597 | 571 | 1,168 |
| Muhammadans ... ... ... | 236 | 146 | 382 |
| Jains ... ... ... ... ... | 12 | — | 12 |
| Christians ... ... ... ... | 17 | 12 | 29 |
| Total ... ... | 862 | 729 | 1,591 |

It owes its importance to the spread of coffee cultivation, for the traffic connected with which the Hémávati has been spanned at this point by an iron girder bridge, leading to the Manjarabad Ghat road, over which trade finds an outlet to the port of Mangalore. The town derives its name from a temple on the bank of the river, dedicated to Sakalesvara (*s'akala Is'vara*, the fragmentary Isvara, the linga having a small chip or dent).

| Municipal Funds. | 1892-3. | 1893-4. | 1894-5. | 1895-6. |
|---|---|---|---|---|
| Income ... ... ... ... | 1,961 | 2,875 | 2,953 | 5,297 |
| Expenditure ... ... ... | 1,622 | 5,473 | 4,392 | 7,445 |

**Sathalli.**—A village in the Hassan taluq, 10 miles south-west of the chief town. Population 795.

The village is interesting as being the centre of a Christian agricultural community, which had its origin in the labours of the well-known Abbé Dubois. Mr. Bowring says[1]: "There are twelve villages in the neighbourhood almost entirely inhabited by Christians, numbering about 1,000 souls. They are what are called caste Christians, that is to say, while following the Christian belief in all matters touching their faith and morals, they preserve their ancient social customs in everything which does not trench upon religion; and in respect to degrees of relationship in marriages and to succession to property have the same rules as their neighbours of the same caste who are not Christians." Attached to the church is a convent, where girls are taught by native nuns. There is a separate school for boys. The priests have also established a dispensary from which they supply medicine gratis to all comers.

**Sravana-Belgola.**—An important village, between two rocky hills in the Channaráyapatna taluq, 8 miles south east of the kasba. Head-quarters of the hobli of the same name, and since 1893 a municipality.

Population 1,763.

[1] *Eastern Experiences*, 82.

It is the chief seat of the Jain sect, being the residence of the principal guru. At the summit of Vindhya betta or Indra betta, 3,250 feet above the level of the sea, and about 400 feet above the village below, is the colossal statue of Gomaṭesvara, 57 feet high and surrounded with numerous sacred buildings. On Chandra betta there are also many temples, and between the hills a splendid tank (*beḷ-goḷa*). A considerable trade is carried on in brass utensils.

According to the tradition of the Jains, Bhadrabáhu, one of the *sruta-kevali*, as the immediate successors of the personal disciples of their founder Vardhamána or Mahávira are called, died here in a cave (still pointed out) on Chandra betta, while leading an emigration to the south from Ujjani, to escape a dreadful famine of 12 years' duration, which he had prognosticated. He is said to have been accompanied as his chief attendant by the celebrated emperor Chandra Gupta, who had abdicated the throne and, in accordance with Jain rules, adopted the life of a hermit. These events, which are borne out by rock inscriptions of great antiquity, though without a date, must be assigned to the third century B.C. The grandson of Chandra Gupta, it is said, paid a visit to the spot with an army, out of whose encampment arose the town of Sravana-Belgola, or Belgola of the Sravanas—*i.e.*, the Jains. The oldest basti on the hill is one dedicated to Chandra Gupta.

The gigantic statue was erected, as inscribed at its foot, by Chámuṇḍa Ráya, probably in 983. He was the minister and general of the Ganga king Ráchamalla. The name of the sculptor may have been Aritto Nemi. The surrounding enclosures were erected, as also inscribed at the foot of the statue, by Ganga Ráya, general of the Hoysala king Vishnuvarddhana. The image is nude and stands erect, facing the north, being visible for many miles round the country. The face has a serene expression; the hair is curled in short spiral ringlets all over the head, while the ears are long and large. The figure is treated conventionally, the shoulders being very broad, the arms hanging straight down the sides with the thumbs turned outwards, the waist small. From the knee downwards the legs are somewhat dwarfed. The feet are placed on the figure of a lotus. Representations of ant-hills rise on either side, with figures of a creeping plant springing from them, which twines over the thighs and the arms, terminating in a tendril with bunches of fruit. These symbolise the complete spiritual abstraction of a *yati*, absorbed and motionless during his long period of penance. Though by no means elegant, the image is not wanting in majestic and impressive grandeur. It was probably cut out of a rock which projected high above the hill, or the top of the hill itself may have been cut away. The figure has no support above the thighs. Though so old, the stone looks almost as fresh as if newly quarried. Within the enclosure around are 72 small statues of a similar description in compartments.

That Sravana-Belgola was an acknowledged seat of learning in early times is proved from the fact that a priest from there, named Akaḷanka Bhaṭṭa, was in 788 summoned to the court of Hemasitala at Kánchi, where having confuted the Buddhists in public disputation, he was instrumental in gaining their expulsion from the south of India to Ceylon. The temple was subsequently endowed by Narasimha and other Hoysala kings, but at the time of the conversion of Vishnu-varddhana to the Vaishnava faith by the reformer Rámánujáchári, the Jains suffered much persecution. Their influence at court, however, enabled them to bring about a compromise, which resulted, in the time of Bukka Ráya of Vijayanagar, in a declaration of tolerance, which was inscribed on stones and set up in public places. One is still at Sravana-Belgola and another at Kalya (Magadi taluq). The Jain establishment, which received the support of the Mysore Rajas as well as of the dynasties preceding them, was shorn, in common with others, of many of its privileges and emoluments by Tipu Sultan, and is now in a reduced condition. The place abounds in inscriptions,[1] some of the most interesting of which are those cut in the face of the rock on Chandra beṭṭa, in ancient characters a foot long.

| Municipal Funds. | 1894–5. | 1895–6. |
|---|---|---|
| Income ... ... ... ... ... ... ... | 347 | 359 |
| Expenditure ... ... ... ... ... ... | 260 | 385 |

**Yagache** or Badari, the chief tributary of the Hémávati. It rises in the Bábá Budan hills, and flowing south, receives the Berinji halla from the west, passes the town of Belur, and joins the Hémávati near Gorur in the Hassan taluq. *Yagache* in Kannada and *Badari* in Sanskrit is the name of the jujube tree (*zizyphus*).[2] There are three dams on the Yagache in this District, from which irrigation channels are led off. The Bomdihalli dam in Belur taluq, which is the first, provides irrigation for 290 acres from a channel of 4½ miles. The Halvagal dam, three miles west of Hassan, gives rise to a channel 6 miles long and irrigates 184 acres; and the Chengravalli dam, 3 miles from the point of confluence with the Hémávati, also feeds a channel 9 miles long and irrigates 281 acres.

[1] The whole, to the number of 144, have been published by me, with translations, in *Inscriptions at Sravana-Belgola*.

[2] For a legend connected with the name, *see* Vol. I, p. 470.

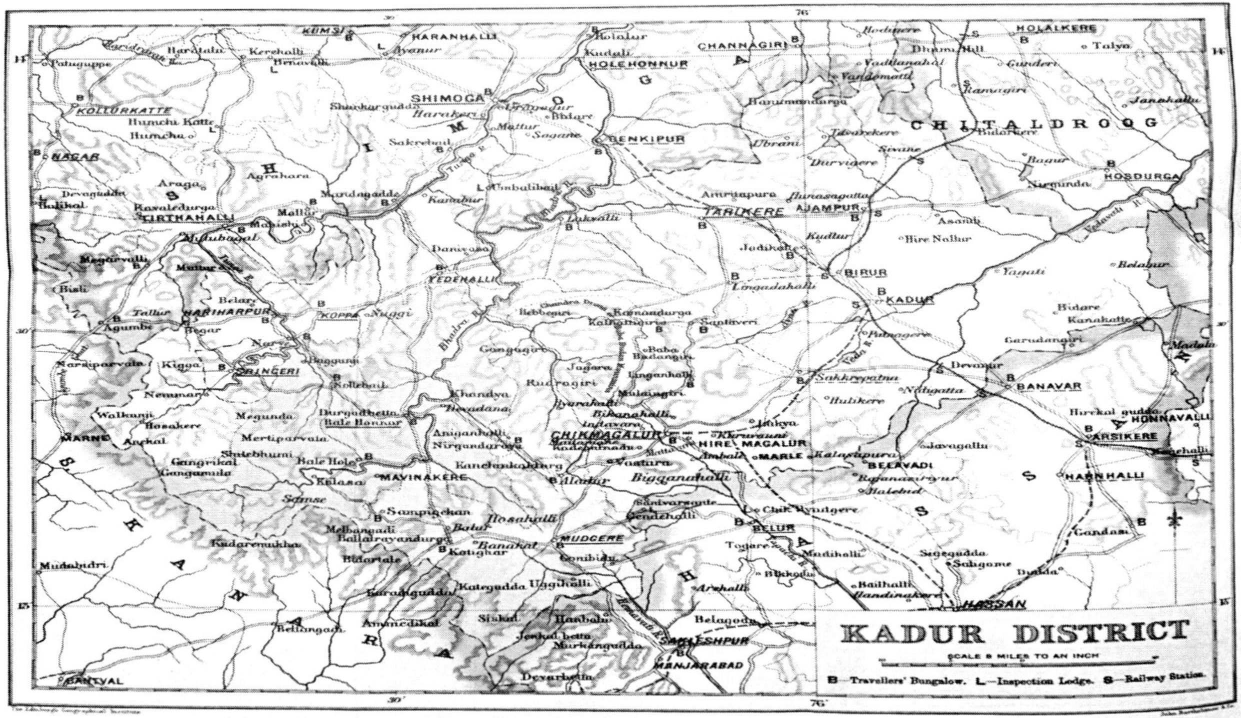
KADUR DISTRICT
SCALE 8 MILES TO AN INCH
B—Travellers' Bungalow. L—Inspection Lodge. S—Railway Station.
CHITALDROOG
SHIMOGA
HASSAN
CHIKMAGALUR
KADUR
BIRUR
TARIKERE
AJAMPUR
HOSDURGA
HOLALKERE
CHANNAGIRI
HOLEHONNUR
BENKIPUR
SHRINGERI
KOPPA
NARSIMHARAJAPUR
MUDGERE
BELUR
BANAVAR
ARSIKERE
HONNAVALLI
MANJARABAD
YEDEHALLI
TIRTHAHALLI
KOLLURKATTE
NAGAR
KUMSI
HARANHALLI
MAVINAKERE
HIRE MAGALUR
BELAVADI
HARNHALLI
SAKLESHPUR

# KADUR DISTRICT

## GENERAL DESCRIPTION

*Situation.*—The Kadúr District lies in the west of the State of Mysore, and was formed in 1863, with head-quarters at Kadúr, afterwards removed to Chikmagalúr. The District is situated between 12° 56′ and 13° 58′ north latitude and between 75° 8′ and 76° 25′ east longitude. Its greatest length is, from east to west, about 86 miles. Its greatest breadth, from north to south, is about 55 miles.

*Area.*—The area is 2,793 square miles. Of the whole extent 763 square miles are under cultivation, and 1,740 square miles unculturable.

*Boundaries.*—It is bounded on the north by the Shimoga District, on the north-east by the Chitaldroog District, on the east by the Tumkúr District, and on the south by the Hassan District. On the west the boundary is the chain of the Western Ghats, which separate it from South Kanara of the Madras Presidency.

*Sub-Divisions.*—It is sub-divided into the following taluqs. Bánávar taluq was abolished in 1882 and divided between Kadúr taluq and Arsikere taluq (Hassan District). At the same time Lakvalli taluq was abolished and Yedehalli sub-taluq formed, under Koppa taluq, which also includes the S'ringéri Jágír, with 5 hoblis. In 1897 Yedehalli sub-taluq was abolished and a new taluq called Bále Honnúr formed.

| No. | Taluq. | Area. sq. miles. | No. of Hoblis. | No. of Villages or Towns. | Population in 1891. | Per square mile. |
|---|---|---|---|---|---|---|
| 1 | Bále Honnúr ... ... | 410 | 5 | 87 | 33,186 | 80·94 |
| 2 | Chikmagalúr ... ... | 595 | 6 | 189 | 71,187 | 119·64 |
| 3 | Kadúr ... ... ... | 561 | 6 | 319 | 72,217 | 128·72 |
| 4 | Koppa ... ... ... | 466 | 5 | 114 | 34,728 | 96·29 |
| | S'ringéri Jágír ... | | — | 233 | 9,144 | |
| 5 | Múdgere... ... ... | 302 | 5 | 139 | 37,249 | 123·34 |
| 6 | Tarikere ... ... ... | 459 | 6 | 246 | 72,352 | 157·63 |
| | Total ... | 2,793 | 33 | 1,327 | 330,063 | 118·17 |

**Physical Features.**—The main part of the Kadúr District is composed of the most mountainous region included within the limits of Mysore. Bordered on the west by the mighty Ghat range, rising at this part into some of the loftiest peaks between the Himálayas and the Nilagiris; supporting on its centre the stupendous barrier of the Bábá Budan chain, of even superior elevation; between these towering masses, covered with a complete network of lofty hills whose altitude at certain points, as in the magnificent Merti peak of Kalasa, renders them conspicuous landmarks even in this neighbourhood of giant heights; while ranges of more modest pretensions extend throughout the north and east:—this District, with a slight exception eastwards, may truly be described as pre-eminently the Malnád or highland region.

Nor are these mountain tracts wanting in all those charms of wood and water which tend to soften the harsher features of so rugged a landscape. For though the summits rear themselves bareheaded into space, the slopes are thickly clad with primeval forest, through which the shining streams thread their often headlong way, fertilising the narrow valleys and open glades, till their waters descend to the level of the larger rivers, flowing in steep and sunken channels, whence daily issue dense mists that cover the face of the country, lifting as the heat of the morning sun increases in power.

In these vast solitudes the habitations of man are few and far between. A single homestead, hidden amid the luxuriance of tropical vegetation, is often the only sign of his presence for many miles around. Roads there are (or rather, thanks to the recent exertions of Engineer officers, were) none. No wheeled conveyance disturbed the peace of the well-nigh trackless woods, save where a space, annually cleared for the occasion, allowed the car of some popular god to be drawn a couple of hundred yards and back from his shrine in the depths of the forest. All the valuable produce of the country was, and to a great extent still is, transported on the backs of cattle, the rallying sounds from the belled leaders of the drove resounding far and wide.

The eastern or Maidán taluqs partake of the general features of that description of country in the other Districts, the transition from Malnád to Maidán being very abrupt and striking on approaching Lakvalli from the west.

The congeries of mountains within the area of the District, so far as they can be reduced to a system, seem to range themselves into a central north-and-south ridge, with a great loop or circle on either hand; while at the south-western angle of the District the Western Ghats make a bend inwards to the east, marking the initial point of the line which divides the northern from the southern waters of the Mysore. The main ridge above spoken of commences at Ballálráyandurga, and passing east of Merti gudda and Koppa-durga, separates the basin of the Bhadra from that of the Tunga, and runs up towards Mandagadde, connecting with the central range of the Shimoga District. On the west of this ridge is the valley in which Sringéri stands, enclosed with a girdle of mountains; while on the east of it and beyond the right bank of the Bhadra, is the Jágar valley, completely environed with the Bábá Budan mountains, which form as it were some gigantic out-work of the mighty Alpine wall.

The highest point in the District, and in Mysore, is Mulaina-giri in the Bábá Budans, which rises to 6,317 feet above the level of the sea. Of the companion heights in the same group, Bábá-Budan-giri is 6,214 feet, and Kalhatti-giri 6,155. The loftiest peak in the Western Ghats is the Kudure Mukh or Horse-face mountain, so called on account of its appearance from the sea, to which it presents a landmark well known to navigators of that coast. Its height is 6,215 feet. Another conspicuous mountain in the same range is the grand Ballálráyan-durga, 4,940 feet. The Gangámúla in Varáha parvata is 4,781, Woddin guḍḍa, 5,006, and Lakke parvata, 4,662. Of greater height is the superb hill of Kalasa called the Merti guḍḍa, situated in the heart of the mountain region to the west, and presenting, especially towards the north, a grand and symmetrical outline, towering above all the neighbouring heights. Its summit is 5,451 feet above the sea. Of other prominent peaks in the District, Kanchinkal-durga is 4,081 feet, and Sakunagiri 4,653. Koppa durga is 2,960.

The general level of the country lying along the south of the Bábá Budan and neighbouring ranges, which forms the water-parting between the northern and southern river-systems, is, at the Nirváni maṭha, 4,015 feet above the sea, at Chikmagalur 3,481, at Wastara 3,531, and at Aldur 3,454. The plains to the east of the District and the valleys in the west are a good deal lower, with a slope to the north. Thus at Kadúr the height is 2,553 feet above the level of the sea, and at Tarikere 2,235. At Sangamesvara it is 2,525, at B. Honnúr 2,516, at Baggunji katte, 2,481, at Sringéri 2,439, and at H riharpur 2,379.

The principal rivers of the District are the twin streams—the Tunga and the Bhadra, the latter running most of its course here. They both rise at Gangámúla in the Varáha parvata, situated in the Western Ghats at the point where the boundaries of the Koppa and Bále Honnúr taluqs meet. The Tunga flows north-east past Nemmár and Sringéri to near Baggunji, where it turns north by west, and passing Hariharpur, enters the Shimoga District, making a sharp turn to the north-east at the Bhiman-katte, and so to Shimoga. The Bhadra runs east for some distance past Kalasa, and then, turning north-east, flows with a winding course past Bále Honnúr and Khándya to Hebbe, where, receiving the Somaváhini from the Jágar valley, it continues to Lakvalli and thence flows on to Benkipur in the Shimoga District.

Of the southern streams the Hémávati has its source at Javali in Melbangádi, but almost immediately leaves this District and enters that of Hassan. The Berinji halla in like manner rises near Anur and shortly flows into Hassan District, where it joins the Yagache. The latter has its source near Sitalmalapan Kanive in the Bábá Budan range and runs through Hiremagalur towards Belur in Hassan.

On the east of the Bábá Budan range the Gauri-halla and the Avati are twin streams, rising near the peak of Mulainagiri. The first expands into the Ayyankere lake above Sakkarepatna, and issuing thence with the name of the Veda, skirts this town and flows north-east to Kadúr. The other, the northern stream, forms the large Madaga tank, and the two, uniting near Kadúr, continue into the Chitaldroog District under the name of the Vedavati.

The largest sheets of water are the two tanks or lakes in the gorges at the eastern base of the Bábá Budan mountains. The first of these, called the Ayyankere or Dodda Madaga-kere, is formed 4 miles north-west of Sakkarepatna by an embankment thrown across the river Veda, where it issues through the only outlet in the surrounding hills, a gap of about 1,700 feet in width, at the south-eastern foot of Sakunagiri. It is a beautiful expanse of water, about 7 miles in circumference, and dotted with several islands. Four channels are drawn from it, irrigating about 300 acres. The other tank, called the Madaga-kere or Kadúr Madaga-kere, has been similarly formed by embanking the sister stream, the Avati, at a point where the two hills called Sivanagiri and Hagrikangiri so nearly meet as to form a natural basin. The bund is 1,200 feet long.

The numerous perennial streams springing from the mountains of the District have been dammed at nearly every available point, giving rise to short channels which collectively supply a large amount of irrigation. The following table will shew the number and value of these useful works:—

| Name of River. | Number of dams. | Acreage irrigated. | Revenue in rupees. |
|---|---|---|---|
| Tunga and tributaries ... ... | 20 | 303 | 1,298 |
| Bhadra " ... ... ... | 18 | 325 | 1,396 |
| Hémávati " ... ... ... | 3 | 26 | 59 |
| Yagache ... ... ... .. | 16 | 1,941 | 22,593 |
| Veda and Avati ... ... ... | 49 | 1,568 | 31,210 |
| Other streams... ... ... ... | 9 | 765 | 4,729 |
| Total ... | 115 | 4,928 | 61,285 |

**Soils.**—Along the south of the Bábá Budan mountains is a rich tract of black cotton soil, whose fertility, enhanced by the command of an unfailing supply of water from the hill streams, is said formerly to have given to the plain of Chikmagalur the name of Honjavanige Sime, or land flowing with gold. The higher tracts of this region are generally gravelly. Black cotton soil also prevails in the neighbourhood of Ajjampur, together with red and gravelly soils. The western parts of Tarikere contain sandy and gravelly soils. About Yegate the earth seems poor and has a white chalky appearance. More to the south the soil is adapted to the cultivation of the cocoa-nut without irrigation, as in the adjoining parts of Tumkúr and Chitaldroog Districts.

The soil of the Malnád bears a general resemblance to that of the same region extending through the neighbouring Districts north and south.

*Minerals.*—Iron ore is largely obtained and smelted along the hills east of the Bábá Budan range, and those around Ubrani. Corundum is found in abundance near Kadúr and throughout the east. Traces of extensive old gold mines have been found in the neighbourhood of Ajjampur, and gold-mining is being revived under European management.

**Climate.**—At Chikmagalur, the head-quarters of the District, the mean annual temperature appears from the recorded observations to be between 72° and 73°. The following are given as readings of the thermometer:—

| 1891. | Mean. Max. | Mean. Min. | Highest reading. | Lowest reading. | 1892. | Mean. Max. | Mean. Min. | Highest reading. | Lowest reading. |
|---|---|---|---|---|---|---|---|---|---|
| May ... | 85 | 67 | 88 | 61 | May ... | 84 | 68 | 87 | 62 |
| July ... | 75 | 64 | 78 | 62 | July ... | 76 | 63 | 78 | 61 |
| December | 82 | 61 | 83 | 57 | December | 80 | 61 | 82 | 60 |

Situated in what was originally a treeless plain composed of black cotton soil, the heat would often be intense but for the neighbourhood of the mountains, the streams and breezes from which tend to moderate the temperature. A broad belt of trees has been planted completely round the town to form a protection against the high winds, which at certain seasons blow unchecked with great violence across the plain. The temperature of the Malnád districts often falls much lower, the cold in the early morning about Christmas being very sharp. Malarious jungle fevers are always prevalent at certain seasons, and neither Europeans nor natives are exempt from attacks.

*Rainfall.*—The average annual rainfall at Chikmagalur is 35·89 inches, calculated from the figures for 26 years (1870–95), though according to another register for 16 years it is 41·72. The monthly average is given under each taluq. The average annual rate for 26 years, and for 16 years, at other taluq stations, was as in the margin.

| | | |
|---|---|---|
| Kadur ... | 21·38 | 21·41 |
| Koppa ... | 116·90 | 119·89 |
| Mudgere ... | 97·47 | 102·50 |
| Tarikere ... | 27·85 | 31·88 |

On turning to the country lying within the Western Ghats a rainfall is recorded which far exceeds that of any other portion of Mysore, and is little less heavy than that of the wettest regions of the globe. At Hariharpur, the late head-quarters of the Koppa taluq, 166·14 inches fell in 1874. At Mudgere the fall was 193·81 in 1882, and of the coffee estates in that taluq 145·10 inches fell at Chethalli estate in 1895, and 155·9 at Kessel estate in 1892. The fall is heaviest in June, July, and August, during the south-west monsoon, the monthly average for those months being: at Koppa, 23·29, 42·9, 25·08; at Chethalli estate, 43·64, 42·98, 28·89; at Kessel estate, 30·31, 40·2, 21·11, with 10·54 in September.

**Vegetation.**—The west of the District is covered with some of the best forests in the country. This is especially the case with Lakvalli, which abounds in fine teak, and has for many years supplied the whole of western Mysore and the Bellary country with that timber, grown in the forests to the north of the Bábá Budans. Throughout the Jágar valley and most of the Koppa and Mudgere taluqs is a continuous stretch of valuable forest, densely clothing the hill-sides and giving shelter to much coffee cultivation. Sholas and hanging woods occupy almost every ravine and hollow of the Bábá Budans. The loftier heights are nearly always bare of trees, but clothed with much coarse grass and the dwarf date. The tree vegetation east and south of Santaveri is as a rule poor, and, even when the soil is better and the growth fair, there is but little good and useful indigenous timber. The eastern taluqs are generally devoid of trees. The date palm (*phœnix sylvestris*) grows profusely in parts, especially in Kadur, and the grazing is good. In the north of Tarikere are the jungles round Ubrani, which, though not yielding large timber, are valuable as affording a supply of fuel in so poorly wooded a neighbourhood. The sandal grows on the slopes of the hills leading up to the Bábá Budans from the south and east.

*Forests.*—The State Forests reserved in this District are that of Lakvalli, 47 square miles in extent; Gegargudda, 9 square miles; Basavankote, 15 square miles; and Muttodi, 17 square miles. *Teak plantations* have been formed at Lakvalli and at Hebbe, the extent of each being 375 acres at the former and 9 acres at the latter. There are also 3 other Forest plantations, occupying 46 acres, as well as 2 Revenue plantations. *Avenue trees* have been planted along 526 miles of public road; and 545 acres are occupied by 440 *topes* or *groves*, containing 15,912 trees.

*Cultivation.*—The following is a general list of the crops and other products of cultivation in the District:—

| Kannada. | Botanical. | English. |
|---|---|---|
| CEREALS— | | |
| Baragu ... ... ... | Panicum miliaceum .. | — |
| Bhatta ... ... ... | Oryza sativa ... ... | Rice |
| Godhi ... ... ... | Triticum aristatum ... ... | Wheat |
| Háraka ... ... ... | Panicum semiverticillatum | — |
| Jola ... ... ... | Holcus sorghum ... ... | Great millet |
| Navane ... ... ... | Panicum italicum ... ... | Italian millet |
| Rági .. ... ... | Eleusine corocana ... ... | Rági |
| Sajje ... ... ... | Holcus spicatus ... ... | Spiked millet |
| Same ... ... ... | Panicum frumentaceum ... | Little millet |
| PULSES— | | |
| Alasandi ... ... ... | Dolichos catiang ... ... | — |
| Avare ... ... ... | Dolichos lablab ... ... | Cow gram |
| Hesaru ... ... ... | Phaseolus mungo ... ... | Green gram |
| Hurali ... ... ... | Dolichos uniflorus ... ... | Horse gram |
| Kadale ... ... ... | Cicer arietinum ... ... | Bengal gram |
| Togari ... ... ... | Cajanus indicus ... ... | Pigeon pea, doll |
| Uddu ... ... ... | Phaseolus minimus ... ... | Black gram |
| OIL SEEDS— | | |
| Haralu ... ... ... | Ricinus communis .. ... | Castor-oil |
| Huchchellu or Ramtil ... | Guizotea oleifera ... ... | Wild gingelli |
| Kusumé ... ... ... | Carthamus tinctorius ... | Safflower |
| Wollellu ... ... ... | Sesamum orientale ... | Gingelli |
| VEGETABLES (Native)— | | |
| Agachi káyi ... ... | Corolina grandiflora ... | Linseed |
| Arisina ... ... ... | Curcuma longa ... ... | Turmer c |
| Badané káyi ... ... | Solanum melongena ... | Brinjal |
| Bendé káyi ... ... | Hibiscus esculentus ... | — |
| Bellulli ... ... ... | Allium sativum ... ... | Garlic |
| Genasu ... ... ... | Dioscorea atuleata ... ... | Sweet potato |
| Hágala káyi ... ... | Momordica charantia ... | — |
| Hiré káyi ... ... ... | Cucumis acutangulus ... | — |
| Jirige ... ... ... | Cuminum cyminum ... | Cummin seed |
| Kottambari bíja ... .. | — | Coriander seed |
| Kumbala káyi ... ... | Cucurbita pepo ... ... | Pumpkin |
| Mensina káyi ... ... | Capsicum annuum ... ... | Chilli |
| Mentya ... ... ... | Trigonella fœnum grœcum | Fenugreek |
| Mulangi ... ... ... | Raphanus sativus ... ... | Radish |
| Nirulli ... ... ... | Allium cepa ... ... ... | Onion |
| Padavala káyi ... ... | Trichosanthes anguina ... | Snake gourd |
| Sásive ... ... ... | Sinapis dichotoma ... ... | Mustard |
| Sunti ... ... ... | Ammomum zinziber ... | Dry ginger |
| Tondé káyi ... ... | Bryonia grandis ... ... | — |

| Kannada. | Botanical. | English. |
|---|---|---|
| MISCELLANEOUS— | | |
| Adike ... ... ... | Areca catechu ... ... | Areca-nut |
| Arale ... ... ... | Gossypium indicum ... | Cotton |
| Bále ... ... ... | Musa sapientum ... ... | Plantain |
| Bhangi ... ... ... | Cannabis sativa ... ... | Indian hemp |
| Kápi ... ... ... | Coffea arabica ... ... | Coffee |
| Gérubíja ... ... ... | Semicarpus anacardium ... | Marking nut |
| Hoge soppu ... ... | Nicotiana tabaccum ... | Tobacco |
| Kabbu ... ... ... | Saccharum officinale ... | Sugar-cane |
| Tengina káyi ... ... | Cocos nucifera ... ... | Cocoa-nut |
| Vílédele ... ... ... | Piper betle ... ... ... | Betel vine |
| Wóma ... ... ... | Sison amomum ... ... | — |
| Yélakki ... ... ... | Amomum repens ... ... | Cardamom |

Besides these, many kinds of European vegetables are grown with success in parts; among which, potatoes, French beans, cabbages, beetroot and knol kohl are the most common.

*Area under principal crops.*—The number of acres under rice cultivation is 107,165, wheat 490, rági 129,064, other food grains 77,087; oil seeds 12,850, sugar-cane 957, cotton 452, other fibres 106, tobacco 784, coffee 83,326, cinchona 279, fruit and vegetables 18,540, cocoanut and areca-nut 14,930.

The varieties of *paddy* raised in the district are fourteen, named as follows: késari, honusunga, kowde doḍḍi, kirvana, putta kirvana, kempu sanna bhatta, bilé sanna bhatta, kussadé, kesser bírá, sul bhatta, hola muradaga, putta bhatta, kumbár késari and kódi bhatta. Of these, kempu sanna bhatta, bilé sanna bhatta and putta bhatta are esteemed the best and fetch the highest prices.

The *areca* gardens, which occupy the moist and sheltered valleys throughout the west, produce the best description of nut in the country, that of Kalasa and its neighbourhood being in especially high repute.

The *coffee* cultivation of Southern India may be said to have had its origin in this District. For the plant was first introduced, in about the 17th century, by a Muhammadan pilgrim named Bábá Budan, who, on his return from Mecca, brought a few berries in his wallet and taking up his abode on the hills that now bear his name planted them near his hut. It was not, however, till about 1820 that the cultivation extended beyond his garden, and not till 20 years later that European enterprise was first attracted to it. One of the earliest European planters was Mr. Cannon, who formed an estate on the high range immediately to the south of the Bábá-Budan-giri, where the original coffee plants are still in existence, flourishing under the shade of the primeval forest.

The success of Mr. Cannon's experiment led to the occupation of ground near Aigur in South Manjarabad by Mr. Green in 1843, as stated under the Hassan District. Since 1860 estates have sprung up between these points with such rapidity that European planters are settled in almost a continuous chain of estates from the south-west of Shimoga to the southernmost limits of Manjarabad, not to mention Coorg and Wainad beyond.

The coffee zone in this District is estimated to cover about 1,000 square miles, extending over the whole western portion, and of this region one-tenth or more presents, as regards soil, aspect and shade, every condition necessary for successful cultivation. Within this area there were, in 1896, 160 square miles under coffee, as per particulars in the margin. There are altogether 543 European plantations, covering an area of 33,943 acres, assessed at Rs. 44,525, and 11,753 native plantations, occupying 66,406 acres, assessed at Rs. 61,608. The total area under mature plants is 55,510 acres, and under immature plants 25,685 acres. The remainder is not planted up. The gross average yield was estimated at 241 lbs. and 177 lbs. an acre on European plantations in 1895 and 1896 respectively, and 107 lbs. on native plantations. The total produce was nearly 12 million pounds of coffee.

| Taluq. | Acres. |
|---|---|
| Chikmagalur ... | 38,944 |
| Kadur ... ... | 767 |
| Koppa ... ... | 21,493 |
| Mudgere ... ... | 34,066 |
| Tarikere ... ... | 7,336 |

The *cardamom* grows wild in the malnád taluqs of the District, but owing to the extension of coffee estates it is no longer plentiful, except in the Kalasa and Melbangádi maganis. Its systematic cultivation has, however, been taken up by coffee planters, and in some parts with great success. The area under cardamom is 2,126 acres.

Of the *cinchona* plantation at Kalhatti on the Bábá Budans, and the results obtained by its cultivation, an account will be found in the section treating of that subject generally. The area under cultivation in 1895 was 279 acres, and the number of plants 127,243. The bark produced was only 150 lbs.

Some casual attempts seem to have been made to introduce the *tea* plant, but apparently without any valuable results. So also with the *mulberry*. To extend the growth of foreign *cotton*, a farm was established at Kadur under Mr. Meppin in 1849. But after a trial for five years it was given up as having produced no adequate results. The extent of land under cotton, which is confined to Kadur and Tarikere taluqs, is 452 acres.

**Wild Animals.**—The elephant is occasionally met with in Kig, Kerra and other remote parts of the Western Ghats, and bison throughout the Malnád. Tigers, panthers, and leopards are general, and the *shivanga* or hunting leopard is sometimes to be found. Among the smaller *felidæ* may be mentioned the tiger cat and the civet cat.

The wild boar is found all over the District and is very destructive to sugar-cane plantations, especially at the time when the young cane begins to throw out its tender shoots. The porcupine frequents all parts of the District.

Of the deer tribe, elk, spotted deer and antelope are less numerous than they used to be. The iguana, the mungoose and its enemy the coffee rat (*golunda eleita*) are common. Of squirrels, there are the flying squirrel, the large red squirrel and the common grey squirrel. Besides the lemur and the ape, the black monkey and the grey monkey abound in the forests.

*Birds.*—The bustard is common on the plains. The wild goose, duck, teal and snipe, the jungle-fowl and spur-fowl, partridges red and black, quail, peacock, pigeons blue and green, with doves of many varieties, are general. The buzzard and vulture, with various kites and hawks, are numerous.

The wooded tracts of the Malnád abound with birds of beautiful plumage, among which are hornbills, woodpeckers, and a great variety of smaller birds, as well as parrots and the talking mina.

*Reptiles.*—The cobra and the carpet-snake are the most venomous and most dreaded. Lizards are in great abundance and variety, and the bite of one kind is supposed to be poisonous. There are three kinds of scorpion general in the District; the large black rock-scorpion, the large red field-scorpion, and the little red house-scorpion. Leeches are very numerous and active during the rainy months. Spiders of immense size are found in the bamboo jungles on the banks of the Bhadra. The alligator is common in rivers and large tanks.

*Fishes.*—Fishes are abundant in both rivers and tanks. Besides the ordinary tackle of rod-and-line and nets, long conical baskets, called *hiruguli*, made of split bamboo interlaced with rushes, are used in catching them. The finest fish are found in the Tunga and Bhadra rivers and in the Madag, Ayyankere and Keresante tanks. The *mahseer*, probably the best freshwater fish in India, is sometimes caught in the rivers, and reaches to the weight of 20 lbs. At the S'ringéri maṭh and other sacred places on the banks of the rivers, fishes are daily fed and are so tame that a call will bring them in thousands to the surface. The Brahmans invariably throw the remains of their rice to the fish. Some of these are even adorned with jewellery, such as nose-rings, or ear-rings, and ornaments fastened to their tails.

The following are some of the principal fishes found in the District:—Kuchina murl (*ophiocephalus striatus*), bili korava (*ophio-*

*cephalus punctatus*), báli (*silurus*), havu (*macro gnathus*), gid pakke, aval minu, muru godu, kem minu, malla minu, gúginasibi, kare sanna, haladi, kuradi, halavu.

**Domestic Animals.**—The cattle of the District generally are poor in size and of inferior breed. The climate of the Malnád is very destructive to them, so much so that farmers of that region are forced to replenish their stock annually. The hardy buffalo, on the other hand, thrives in the moisture of the climate. Hence, in the plains, the she-buffalo is tended with even more care than the cow, as, apart from a large yield of milk, the sale of her male calves to purchasers from the Malnád is found to be very profitable. Though grazing is abundant in the hilly regions, it is of a coarse description, whence rágí and paddy straw are commonly given to the cattle on returning home in the evening. During the dry season in the plains, where grazing is not to be had, straw as above, with the stalks of jowari, navane, hurali, &c., are used as fodder, and even tender leaves of the date tree. These, however, afford no nourishment.

The live stock of the District consisted in 1893 of 256,722 cows, buffaloes and bullocks, 3,953 horses, ponies and donkeys, 66,943 sheep, goats and pigs.

## HISTORY

Few spots in the wild and romantic regions of this District, which contains the sources of the Pampa or Tungabhadra, the scene of memorable transactions recorded in the Rámáyana, are without a story connecting them with one or other of the heroes of the great Indian epics.

S'ringéri, as might be expected of the chief seat of Saiva Brahmanism, takes precedence of all other places in its claims to antiquity and historic fame. Its name is properly Rishya-S'ringa-giri. Here was the hermitage of Vibhándaka, and here the birthplace of his son Rishyas'ringa, a sage adorned with horns, who plays an important part in the opening scenes of the Rámáyana. He was begotten without a natural mother, and grew up in the wilderness never having seen or heard of a woman. At that time the kingdom of Anga was suffering from a great dearth, and the king Lomapáda was informed by his spiritual advisers that the only remedy lay in bringing thither the immaculate Rishyas'ringa. This, therefore, was resolved upon, and the princess Sánta to become his bride. But how to bring him was the question, for all feared lest they should alarm the unsophisticated youth and incur the wrath of the stern Vibhándaka, whose single glance could reduce them to ashes in a moment. At last the plan was agreed upon that a band of fair damsels should be sent in the disguise of hermits, who, by the attraction of their all-powerful wiles, should entice the young recluse away from his forest home. They arrive at Nárve near S'ringéri, and concealing themselves in the woods, watch for an opportunity when the father should be absent. Then issuing forth, by their sports and gambols they draw the attention of the young hermit, who, lost in wonder, directs them to his cell, duly performs the rites of hospitality and is soon bewitched with his charming guests. Next day he hastens to pay a visit to their pretended hermitage and being led on board a raft made to resemble an island is floated away in the society of his fair companions. How his approach to Anga brought rain, how he was married to the princess, how he then became the priest of king Dasaratha of Ayodhyá and performed the *asvamedha* or horse sacrifice, the celebration of which procured offspring to the childless monarch and resulted in the birth of Ráma, all this is fully related in the Bála Kánda of the Rámáyana.

Sakunagiri, a lofty hill on the bank of the Ayyankere near Sakkarepatna, is said to be so called from the omens (*sakuna*) that Hanuman, the monkey leader in Ráma's army, thence obtained, which guided him to the spot where the medicinal plant Sanjivini grew, that was used to revive Lakshmana from the swoon into which he fell on being wounded by Rávana.

Hiremagalúr is said to be situated in Siddha kshetra and to have been called Bhárgavapuri. It is made the scene of the celebrated *sarpa yága*, or serpent sacrifice, celebrated by Janamejaya Ráya in revenge for the death of his father Parikshit by the bite of a serpent. Under Shimoga District we may see that copper-plate inscriptions are there in existence professing to record grants made by Janamejaya to the Brahmans who took part in this *sarpa yága*. At Hiremagalúr a singular stone pillar, with a spear or flame-shaped head, is shown as the *yúpa stambha* or sacrificial post that was used on the occasion. Inscriptions at the place prove that Hiremagalúr was an agrahára in the time of the Gangas, in the 9th century.

Leaving the mythological period and the mention of places visited by Parasu Ráma, by Ráma and by Arjuna, three places in the District have traditions undoubtedly historical, though the exact period to which they relate is not clear. They, however, certainly belong to a period anterior to the rise of the Hoysala power. One of these, the ruined village of Halasur, near Lakvalli, is said to mark the site of Ratnapuri, a city founded by Vajra Makuta Ráya, the story of whose two sons, Chitrasékhara and Somasékhara and of the romantic adventure by which the younger obtained the hand of Rúpávati or Ratnávati, the fair princess of Nilávati-patna (Nirgunda) and with it the succession to that kingdom, is related under the Chitaldroog District.

Another ancient capital is Sakkarepatna. Its most celebrated king appears to have been Rukmángada, mentioned in the Mahá Bhárata, and *Hire-magaḷ-úru* (elder daughter's town), and *Chikka-magaḷ-úru* (younger daughter's town), the estates bestowed in dowry on the princesses of his house.

More definite than these is the historical acount of S'ringéri, whose celebrated maṭha on the Tunga is well known to have been established by S'ankaráchárya, the great Saiva reformer of the 8th century.

**Kadambas.**—The west of the District appears to have been subject from very early times to the Kadambas; while part of the frontier may have been included in Áḷuva-kheḍa, the territory of the Áḷuva, Áḷupa, or Áḷu kings, who seem to have ruled in South Kanara.

*Hombucha.*—The subsequent history of that part is connected with the S'ántara kings of Pomburchcha (Hombucha or Humcha, Shimoga District). In the account given of that line we see that they extended their dominions over the hill country southwards as far as Kalasa, and thence established their capital first at Sisila or Sisukali, at the foot of the Gháts in Mudgere, and finally at Kárkala in S. Kanara. They became at one time feudatories of the Chalukya sovereigns. But the numerous inscriptions of the Kárkala rulers with the general cognomen of Bairasu Wodeyar, surrounding the temple at Kalasa, date from the beginning of the 12th to the middle of the 16th century, those from the 14th downwards being made with permission of the Vijayanagar sovereigns.

**Gangas.**—All other parts of the District were in possession of the Gangas, as testified by inscriptions which occur in various parts. As far back as the 9th century we find mention in them of Piriyamuguḷi and Kiriyamuguḷi, which are the correct names of what are now called Hirimagaḷúr and Chikmagaḷúr. There seems, therefore, no foundation for the legend which derives the names from the elder and the younger daughter (*magaḷu*) of Rukmángada Ráya. The *muguḷi* is a useful tree, known botanically as *acacia suma*.

**Hoysalas.**—This District can claim the distinction of having given birth to the powerful Hoysala kings, who succeeded the Gangas, and who ruled Mysore from the 11th to the 14th centuries. For though their capital was in the Hassan District, their place of origin, Sosevúr or S'as'akapura, has been identified by me with Angadi in the south of the Mudgere taluq, where the existing temple of Vasantamma no doubt represents that of the goddess Vásantiká, the scene of the incident with the tiger which transformed Sala into Hoysala. Throughout the District the memorials of the Hoysala kings are abundant, especially east and south of the Bábá Budan mountains, in the neighbourhood of their capital Dorasamudra (Halebid, Hassan District). To the west their inscriptions are found at Khándya, and the fortified height of Ballála-Ráyan-durga bears witness to their rule. Aluva-khada was the early boundary of their kingdom under Vinayaditya.

**Vijayanagar.**—The foundation of the next paramount power, that of Vidyánagara, afterwards called Vijayanagara, is in some accounts ascribed to, and was certainly greatly promoted by, the sage and scholar Mádhava, entitled Vidyáranya or forest of learning. Wilson says: "Besides experience and talent Mádhava may have brought pecuniary aid to the undertaking. His title Vidyáranya and the scope of his writings show that he was a disciple of Sankaráchárya, and in all probability he was connected with the S'ringagiri (S'ringeri) establishment, the members of which, alarmed by the increasing numbers of the Jangamas and Jains and the approach of the Muhammadans, may have contributed their wealth and influence to the aggrandisement of the sons of Sangama." These were Bukka and Hakka or Harihara, the progenitors of the Vijayanagar line. Vidyáranya was their father's minister.

Under the Vijayanagar empire the west of the District, save the independent estate of S'ringéri, was mostly under the rule of the Karkala chiefs; the south formed part of the territory of Balam (Manjarabad, Hassan District) belonging to the Aigur chiefs; the north-east was included in the possessions of the Basvapatna or Tarikere palegars. The greater part of the District was subsequently, in the middle of the 17th century, overrun by Sivappa Náyak, the most distinguished of the Ikkéri or Bednúr chiefs. Sri Ranga Ráya, the representative of the Vijayanagar kings, resorted to his protection, and was by him established in the government of Sakkarepatna, Belur, and the neighbourhood. Meanwhile the Basvapatna territories had fallen a prey, first to the forces of Bijapur and then to those of the Mughals, and were in 1687 absorbed in the province of Sira.

**Mysore Rajas.**—The Rájas of Mysore, having in 1610 gained possession of Seringapatam and in 1687 of Bangalore, now carried their conquests to the west, and between 1690 and 1694 subdued all the south of the District. In the latter year a treaty was concluded between Mysore and Ikkéri, by which, with the exception of Aigur and

Vastára, the remaining conquests were retained as a part of the Mysore kingdom.

Haidar Ali in 1761 took possession of Sira, and after receiving or forcing the submission of its various dependencies, planned his expedition against Bednúr. This capital was taken in 1763, and the terrified Ráni escaped to Ballál-ráyan-durga. Thither a detachment was sent in pursuit, by which she was taken prisoner and conveyed to Maddagiri (Tumkúr District), appointed as the place of her confinement. By this conquest the Mysore dominion was extended over the whole of the Kadur country.

After the downfall of Tipu Sultan and the restoration of the Hindu ráj, the District formed part of the Nagara Ráyada or Subáyana. It was in the wild country north of the Bábá Budans that some of the abuses were practised with impunity which led to the insurrection of 1830. In December of that year, Rangappa Náyak, the head of the Tarikere family, secretly left Mysore, joined the insurgents and seized upon Kaldurga and Kámandurga. These forts were, however, recovered by the Mysore troops in February and March 1831, and the pálegar was put to flight. On the assumption of the government by the British in 1831, and the restoration of order, this part of the country was included in the Nagar Division. In 1863, it was formed into a separate District named after Kadur, where for a time the head-quarters were established. Before long, however, Chikmagalur was selected for the chief station as being more central, and a considerable town has there now sprung up.

In 1882 the Kadur District was extended by having Hassan attached to it as a Sub-Division, with 4 taluqs (Arsikere, Belur, Hassan and Manjarabad). But in 1886 the Hassan District was restored, and the Kadur District formed with its present limits. In 1897 the Yedehalli sub-taluq was abolished and the new taluq of Bále Honnúr was then established.

## POPULATION

*Number.*—The population of the District, according to the census of 1891, is 330,063, of whom 173,922 are males and 156,141 females.

*Density.*—Thus there are 118·17 persons to the square mile. The most thickly peopled taluq at the time of the census was Tarikere, with 160·42, followed by Chikmagalur and Kadur, with 127·6 and 127·36. The malnád taluqs of Koppa and Múdgere had only 88·55 and 95·97 per square mile.

*By religion.*—Arranged according to religion the following results are obtained :—

| Class. | Above 15. | | Under 15. | | Total. | Per-centage. |
|---|---|---|---|---|---|---|
| | Male. | Female. | Male. | Female. | | |
| Hindus ... ... | 105,394 | 90,043 | 57,453 | 58,091 | 310,981 | 94·21 |
| Muhammadans ... | 6,068 | 4,199 | 2,713 | 2,585 | 15,565 | 4·71 |
| Jains ... ... ... | 521 | 351 | 217 | 219 | 1,308 | ·39 |
| Christians ... ... | 1,273 | 407 | 283 | 246 | 2,209 | ·66 |
| Total ... | 113,256 | 95,000 | 60,666 | 61,141 | 330,063 | — |

*Increase.*—The following table compares the statistics for 1838, taken from Mr. Stokes' report, and those for 1853–4, according to the *khâne-shumâri* accounts, with the results obtained by census in 1871, 1881 and 1891.

| Taluq. | 1838. | 1853–4. | 1871. | 1881. | 1891. |
|---|---|---|---|---|---|
| Chikmagalur ... | 43,418 | 51,581 | 81,864 | 76,475 | 82,052 |
| Kadur ... ... | 23,878 | 47,828 | 70,639 | 56,820 | 72,217 |
| Koppa ... ... | 34,385 | 42,489 | 51,830 | 56,847 | 62,077 |
| Múdgere ... ... | — | 37,633 | 34,537 | 35,604 | 41,365 |
| Tarikere ... ... | 43,713 | 56,647 | 69,608 | 66,380 | 72,352 |
| Total ... | 145,394 | 236,178 | 308,478 | 292,126 | 330,063 |

The first column is wanting in the figures for Bánávar taluq, which should be included in Kadur; those for Vastára, now Múdgere, are included in Chikmagalur. The apparent increase between 1853 and 1871 was equivalent to 30·61 per cent., but 25 per cent. has to be allowed for defective enumeration. The famine sent down the total 5·3 per cent. by 1881, but it rose again 12·64 per cent. by 1891. The net result may be stated at an increase of 11·8 per cent. in 38 years.

*Classes.*—Classified according to sources of livelihood and nationality, the population is composed as follows :—

| | No. | Per cent. |
|---|---|---|
| A. Agricultural ... ... ... ... | 99,879 | 30·26 |
| B. Professional ... ... ... ... | 26,718 | 8·09 |
| C. Commercial ... ... ... ... | 33,335 | 10·09 |
| D. Artisan and Village Menial ... ... | 140,066 | 42·43 |
| E. Vagrant Minor Artisans and Performers | 11,832 | 3·59 |
| Races and Nationalities ... ... | 17,774 | 5 39 |
| Others, not stated ... ... ... | 459 | 0·13 |

The castes or classes which number 10,000 and over are the following, in order of strength. They represent a total of 217,389, or 65·86 per cent. of the population.

| | | | | | | | |
|---|---|---|---|---|---|---|---|
| Holeya... | ... 51,291 | Kuruba | ... 26,255 | Mádiga | ... | 10,448 |
| Wokkaliga | ... 39,169 | Bráhmana | ... 17,026 | Neyigára | ... | 10,217 |
| Lingáyita | ... 37,657[1] | Musalmán | ... 15,326 | Uppára | ... | 10,000 |

The most numerous classes of Wokkaliga are the Sáda (14,664), Gangadikára (13,386), and Nonaba (11,119). Among Kurubas, the Hálu Kuruba (17,017) predominate. Of the Brahmans the largest sects are the Srivaishnava (5,357), Smárta (2,384), Badaganád (2,073), and Tuluva (1,108). Of Musalmáns 10,912 are Shekhs, and 2,117 Pathans. Among the Neyigára there are 7,265 Devánga.

*Stock.*—The *agricultural stock* of the District consists of 5,448 carts and 51,212 ploughs; and the *manufacturing stock* of 670 cloth looms, 480 cumbly, and 9 girdle looms, with 2 for gunny cloth.

*Towns.*—The District contains 6 municipal towns, with a total population of 26,871, composed of 21,571 Hindus, 4,887 Muhammadans, 85 Jains, and 328 Christians. The following is the list:—

| | | | |
|---|---|---|---|
| Chikmagalur ... ... | 7,816 | Ajjampur ... ... ... | 2,890 |
| Tarikere ... ... ... | 7,056 | Kadur ... ... ... | 2,444 |
| Birur ... ... ... | 4,828 | Yedehalli ... .. ... | 1,837 |

*Villages.*—The total number of *asali* or primary villages in 1891 was 1,297, to which were attached 1,126 *dákhali* or secondary villages or hamlets. The following are the details:—

| Taluq. | Populated. | | Depopulated. | Villages classified. | | | | Total. |
|---|---|---|---|---|---|---|---|---|
| | Villages. | Hamlets. | | Government. | Sarvamánya. | Jodi. | Kayamgutta. | |
| Chikmagalur ... | 207 | 150 | 6 | 204 | 2 | 7 | — | 213 |
| Kadúr ... ... | 265 | 80 | 46 | 307 | — | 4 | — | 311 |
| Koppa ... ... | 160 | 611 | 3 | 163 | — | — | — | 163 |
| Sringéri Jágir | 225 | 26 | 8 | — | 233 | — | — | 233 |
| Múdgere ... | 132 | 197 | 5 | 135 | — | 2 | — | 137 |
| Tarikere ... | 212 | 61 | 28 | 234 | — | 6 | — | 240 |
| Total ... | 1,201 | 1,125 | 96 | 1,043 | 235 | 19 | — | 1,297 |

**Great Festivals.**—The most numerously attended religious festivals are the following:—

At *Sringéri*, Koppa taluq, during the *Navarátri mahotsava*, celebrated for 15 days from Asvija suddha 1st, when 10,000 people attend.

At *Pura*, Kadur taluq, where the *Mallésvara Devara játre*, held for 8 days from Phálguna suddha 10th, attracts 6,000 people.

At *Antargatte*, Tarikere taluq, 6,000 people collect for the *Ammana játre*, kept up for 15 days in the month of Mágha.

[1] Of this sect 25,783 besides are included in Wokkaliga.

At *Kárahalli*, Kadur taluq, 4,000 people come to the *Ammana játre*, held on the full moon day of Phálguna.

The same number keep the *Bettada Mallikárjuna Devara rathotsava* at *Sringéri* for a week from Mágha bahula 10th. The *Kártika dipotsava*, held at the same place on the full moon day of Kartika, is attended by 3,000 people.

At *Hosahalli*, Chikmagalur taluq, on the occasion of the *Nirvána Devara mathada játre*, lasting 3 days from Phálguna suddha 10th, 3,000 people assemble.

**Fairs.**—The largest weekly markets are mentioned below:—

| Place. | Taluq. | Day. | No. of Visitors. |
|---|---|---|---|
| Hanke ... ... | Chikmagalur .. | Sunday ... ... | 1,100 |
| Devarayapete ... | Do. ... | Wednesday ... | 3,000 |
| Pura ... ... | Kadur ... ... | Do. ... | 2,000 |
| Bírúr ... ... | Do. ... ... | Saturday ... ... | 1,000 |
| Keresante ... ... | Do. ... ... | Do. ... ... | 1,000 |

**Vital Statistics.**—The birth-rate of the District in 1893–4 was 18 per mille of the population, while the death-rate was 15·85 per mille. The number of births registered was 5,942, of which 3,103 were males and 2,839 females. The total of deaths registered was 5,231; of these 2,782 were males and 2,449 females.

The following were the causes of death registered: From diseases—cholera 44, small-pox 207, fevers 3,445, bowel complaints 753; from injuries—suicide 22, wounds or accidents 67, snake-bite or wild beasts 15, all other causes 678.

## REVENUE

The revenue of the District for five years is as contained in the subjoined statement:—

| Items. | 1891–2. | 1892–3. | 1893–4. | 1894–5. | 1895–6. |
|---|---|---|---|---|---|
| Land Revenue ... | 7,80,652 | 8,08,979 | 8,67,984 | 8,64,679 | 9,23,750 |
| Forests ... ... | 1,56,391 | 1,31,789 | 1,52,447 | 1,64,083 | 87,011 |
| Abkari ... ... | 87,593 | 2,32,889 | 2,67,858 | 2,94,524 | 3,16,573 |
| Mohatarfa ... ... | 20,565 | 20,893 | 16,739 | 15,786 | 15,389 |
| Sáyar ... ... ... | 1,14,023 | 1,05,061 | 79,970 | 1,02,625 | 1,05,645 |
| Salt ... ... ... | 1,845 | 895 | 1,377 | 659 | 747 |
| Stamps ... ... | 56,970 | 51,713 | 55,248 | 52,524 | 64,536 |
| Law and Justice ... | 17,303 | 16,056 | 19,079 | 17,810 | 19,861 |
| Police... ... ... | 328 | 119 | 319 | 227 | 140 |
| Public Works ... | 5,267 | 5,021 | 7,577 | — | — |
| Miscellaneous ... | 18,418 | 16,446 | 14,720 | 19,273 | 21,084 |
| Total Rs. ... | 12,59,355 | 13,89,861 | 14,83,318 | 15,32,190 | 15,54,736 |

## TRADE

The principal articles manufactured in the District are oils and oil cakes, piece goods, woollen kamblis, and glass bangles. Jaggory is also made, and there is some production of iron. A certain amount of catechu or terra japonica is also prepared.

The most important exports are coffee, pepper, cardamoms, rice and other food grains, and oil seeds, the various products of the District. It is only during the last 20 years that the Malnád parts have been opened up by a network of roads, and only since 1889 that the railway has run through a small part of the District. These agencies are effecting considerable changes in trade and the transport of commodities, the full effect of which can hardly yet be seen.

The principal old traffic between the Malnád and Maidán taluqs was through the following five kanaves or passes :—Talagudde, Talamakki, Birnahalli, Gantevináyakan and Sitalmallappan.

## COMMUNICATIONS

**Railways.**—The Southern Mahratta Railway from Bangalore to Poona runs through the east of the District for about 40 miles, with stations at Devanur, Kadur, Birur, Ajjampur and Shivani. A branch is also under construction from Birur, through Tarikere, to Shimoga.

**Roads.**—The length of the *Provincial roads* in the District is 219 miles, and of the *District roads* 404. The annual cost for the upkeep of the former is Rs. 37,975, and of the latter Rs. 24,305. The details of each class of roads are given below :—

PROVINCIAL ROADS.

| | Miles. | | Cost. |
|---|---|---|---|
| Bangalore-Honnavar road ... ... ... ... | 37 | ... | 5,500 |
| Kadur-Mangalore road ... ... ... ... ... | 62 | ... | 12,400 |
| Vastara-Koppa road ... ... ... ... ... | 49 | ... | 9,800 |
| Mudgare-Belur road ... ... ... ... ... | 11 | ... | 1,575 |
| Tarikere-Mangalore (Agumbi ghat) road ... ... | 53 | ... | 7,950 |
| Hassan-Chikmagalur road ... ... ... ... | 7 | ... | 700 |
| Total Miles | 219 | Rs. | 37,925 |

DISTRICT ROADS.

| | | | |
|---|---|---|---|
| Banavar-Sira road ... ... ... ... ... | 3 | ... | 150 |
| Banavar-Sakkarepatna road ... ... ... ... | 16 | ... | 800 |
| Birur-Ajjampur road ... ... ... ... ... | 9 | ... | 450 |
| Birur-Lingadahalli road ... ... ... ... | 10 | ... | 600 |
| Tarikere-Hosdurga road... ... ... ... ... | 21 | ... | 1,680 |

| | Miles. | Cost. |
|---|---|---|
| Shimoga-Yedehalli road | 11½ | 1,725 |
| Chikmagalur-Tarikere road | 35 | 2,800 |
| Baba Budan Hill road | 20 | 1,200 |
| Santaveri-Kalhatti road | 4½ | 225 |
| Chikmagalur-Yedehalli road | 40 | 3,200 |
| Uppahalli-Hirekolali road | 4 | 120 |
| Handi-Aldur road | 4 | 120 |
| Belur-Mudgere road | 8 | 320 |
| Anemahal-Mudgere road | 4½ | 225 |
| Kotigahar-Kalasa road | 27 | 2,700 |
| Balur-Magundi road | 11 | 440 |
| Tornamávu-Joladahál road | 6 | 240 |
| Bale Honnur-Kalasa road | 22 | 1,320 |
| Sollebail-Sringeri road | 13 | 300 |
| Sollebail-Balehole road | 18 | 1,080 |
| Narve-Naglapura road | 3 | 240 |
| Narve-Sringeri-Nemmar road | 15 | 300 |
| Sringeri-Kigga road | | 120 |
| Yedehalli-Mandagadde road | 10 | 500 |
| Yedehalli-Bale-Honnur road | 21 | 1,260 |
| Koppa-Badagi road | 6 | 180 |
| Koppa-Tirthahalli road | 5 | 250 |
| Koppa-Kalasapura road | 6 | 180 |
| Hariharpur-Kummakki road | 4 | 120 |
| Begur-Sringeri road | 8 | 100 |
| Mudgere-Baidavalli road | 8 | 240 |
| Magadi-Javagal road | 14 | 700 |
| Railway feeder roads in Kadur | 4½ | 180 |
| Nemmar-Heggan road | 6 | 180 |
| Doubla Estate road | 2 | 60 |
| Total Miles | 404 | Rs. 24,305 |

**Accommodation for travellers.**—The following places contain bungalows originally meant for the accommodation of European travellers. Many have Hindu kitchens attached.

*First Class.*—Chikmagalur, Kadur, Kalhatti.

*Second Class.*—Aldur, Bale Honnur, Koppa, Kotigahar, Lakvalli, Mathole, Mudgere. Sakkarepatna, Sollebail, Tarikere, Yedehalli.

*Third Class.*—Ajjampur. Aniganhalli, Bale-hole, Hariharpur, Jódikatte, Kalasa, Lingadahalli, Linganhalli, Narve, Sampigekán, Santaveri, Sringeri.

There are also inspection lodges at Attigundi, Bund ghat, Chik Agrahára, Kalasa, Kalasapura, Lakvalli, Madaga, Mollandur, Muttod, Pura, Sakkarepatna.

For native travellers Government *chatrams* are kept at Kadur and Tarikere ; with *musáfirkhánas* at Ajjampur, Aldur, Bale-Honnur, Chikmagalur, Jodikatte, Kadur, Koppa, Kotigahar, Mudgere, Sakkarepatna, Santaveri, Sollebail, Yedehalli.

## GAZETTEER

**Ajjampur.**—A town in the Tarikere taluq, on the Bangalore-Poona railway and the Tarikere-Hosdurga road, 14 miles east of the kasba. Head-quarters of the Ajjampur hobli, and a municipality.

| Population in 1891. | Males. | Females. | Total. |
|---|---|---|---|
| Hindus (with 4 Jains).. ... ... | 1,370 | 1,338 | 2,708 |
| Muhammadans ... ... ... ... | 109 | 73 | 182 |
| Total .. ... ... | 1,479 | 1,411 | 2,890 |

The site was originally occupied by the village of Keral. In the 17th century, Azim Khan, an officer of the Sira government, while hunting in the neighbourhood, was surprised at observing the hares turn upon his hounds and pursue them. The circumstance indicating a spot favourable for the purpose, he was directed to build the present fort, which was named after him *Ajim-pur*, now generally called Ajjampur.

A weekly fair is held on Tuesday, attended by 500 people. Black soil prevails in the neighbourhood, on which a considerable quantity of cotton is raised. Extensive old gold workings have been discovered in the vicinity, and a European company has commenced gold-mining.

| Municipal Funds. | 1891-2. | 1892-3. | 1893-4. | 1894-5. | 1895-6. |
|---|---|---|---|---|---|
| Income ... ... ... | 700 | 767 | 920 | 910 | 1,650 |
| Expenditure ... ... | 2,280 | 1,707 | 1,261 | 1,065 | 1,830 |

**Amritapura.**—A village a short distance north-east of Tarikere. Head-quarters of the Amritapura hobli. Population, 362. Contains the remains of a very fine and large temple of Amrites'vara, erected in 1197, in the time of the Hoysala king Vira-Ballála. It is in the Chalukyan style and was originally profusely sculptured with decorative details, even on the round Hindu battlements of the outer wall.

**Angadi.**—A village, 7 miles south of Múdgere, near Uggihalli. Population, 553. It is of special interest from my having identified it with the Sosevúr, Sasipura or Sasikapura, which was the birthplace of the powerful Hoysala line of kings, and the scene of the incident with the tiger which gained their progenitor Sala the throne and the name of Poysala or Hoysala (*see* Vol. I., p. 335). It contains a number of old inscriptions and remarkable ruined temples. There is some beautiful sculpture in what remains of the two Jain bastis. On the opposite side of the deeply sunk village path are the ruins of three fine temples, dedicated to Kes'ava, Pátála Rudra and Malles'vara. But the principal deity now worshipped is Vasantamma, who has a great reputation, and is probably the original Vásantiká Devi of the Hoysalas.

**Asandi.**—A village in Kadur taluq, about 5 miles east of Ajjampur. Population, 996.

Numerous old inscriptions and ruins in the place show that it was in ancient times of considerable importance. Under both the Gangas and the Hoysalas it was the chief city of a principality, which in the 8th century was governed by Vijayáditya, son of the king Sripurusha, and in the 12th and 13th centuries by a line of chiefs of Ganga descent.

**Ayyankere** or *Dodda Madaga-kere.*—A beautiful loch, surrounded with high hills and studded with islands, 4 miles west of Sakkarepatna. It is situated at the eastern base of the Bábá Budan range, being formed by embanking the perennial stream of the Gauri halla at the foot of Sakunagiri. Its outflowing waters are called the Veda, which unites, after a short course, with the Avati near Kadur and forms the joint stream of the Vedavati.

The construction of this magnificent reservoir is attributed to Rukmángada Ráya, the ancient king of Sakkarepatna. The embankment, formed of earth and stone, is about 1,700 feet long, and 300 feet high at the rear slope. The tank is very deep and contains in many parts 35 feet of water. The contents of the bund have been estimated at 605,760 cubic yards, and the quantity of water at 207,900 cubic feet, or 12,854,260 gallons.

There is a tradition that the bank was once on the point of breaching, when the danger which threatened the town of Sakkarepatna from inundation was announced by the guardian goddess of the lake to Honbilla, the *nirganti* or waterman. He obtained a promise from her that the catastrophe should be delayed until he returned with orders what to do from his master the king of Sakkarepatna; and hasting to the town delivered warning of the impending danger. The king sagely but inhumanly thought that, under the conditions of the promise, to prevent the return of the messenger would be for ever to avert the catastrophe. He accordingly had him killed on the spot and the embankment has stood ever since. A shrine has been erected at Sakkarepatna to the memory of the unfortunate man who was sacrificed for its stability, at which worship is still performed. Under the Hoysala kings considerable repairs were made to the bund. An inscription at the Ballálesvara temple, erected on a hillock towards the centre of the embankment, is of the time of Vira Narasimha, the middle of the 13th century.

Of the 4 channels drawn from the tank, the Mallappan kálve irrigates 18 acres; Basavan kálve, 170 acres; Uru kálve, 119 acres; and Kade kálve, 82 acres.

**Bábá Budan Mountains.**—The loftiest range on the Mysore table-land, situated in the centre of the District, to the north of Chikmagalur, between 13° 23′ and 13° 35′ north latitude, 75° 37′ and 75° 52′ east longitude. The form of the chain is that of a horse-shoe, with the opening to the north-west. The northern arm, commencing with the Hebbe hill (4,385 feet), stretches eastwards without interruption for about 15 miles; whence, bending southwards, it presents to the east an unbroken wall of more than 20 miles. The southern arm is formed by the Basvan gudda and Woddin gudda ranges. The character of the chain is that of a stupendous ridge, 6,000 feet above the level of the sea, and in some parts only a few yards wide at the summit, rising at intervals into loftier peaks. The summit of the hills consists of steep grassy slopes, well wooded in the ravines, through which flow perennial springs. The sides are densely clothed with forests, among which are numerous coffee plantations, as well as in the Jágar valley, which is one stretch of forest as far as the eye can reach.

The highest point is the symmetrical Mulaina-giri, 6,317 feet above the level of the sea. It is towards the south of the range and is the loftiest mountain between the Himálayas and the Nilagiris. Next to this, north-eastwards, is Bábá Budan giri, Váyu Parvata or Marut Saila, 6,214 feet. Near it are the sources of the Veda and Avati. The hollow which succeeds marks the shrine of Bábá Budan. The conspicuous conical peak on the outer verge of the eastern face is Deviramman gudda. A beacon is lighted here at the Dipavali festival, which is visible to all the surrounding country. Near the north-east angle is situated Kalhatti giri, 6,155 feet in height; north of which is Kalhatti bungalow, a hot weather retreat for European officials. These vast wilds and solitudes, with scarcely a human habitation, were, until a few years ago, well stocked with every variety of game, from the elephant and bison downwards. The advance of the coffee-planter has now forced back the savage denizens to remoter and more secluded spots. The Bábá Budan mountain was the cradle of the coffee cultivation of Southern India, and the slopes of the entire range, as well as the south of the forest-bound Jágar valley, are now occupied by coffee gardens, both European and native. The first European coffee plantation, opened out by Mr. Cannon in about 1840, is to the south of Bábá Budan giri, with other early estates.

Two roads pass along the eastern face from Chikmagalur to Tarikere, one over the summit and the other at a lower level. About midway in the latter, under Káman durga, is the settlement of Santavéri, from which a road, four miles in length, leads to Kalhatti. Santavéri is occupied chiefly by a colony of Lambánis. On the north-east of the mountains are the Abbe falls, a descent of 600 feet by a stream running to the Bhadra.

The range is called in the Hindu puránas Chandra Drona, but derives its present name from a Muhammadan saint who took up his residence on one of the southern slopes. He is stated to have reared coffee from seeds he obtained at Mocha, and thus to have introduced that important staple into India. A cave, containing what the Muhammadans assert to be the tomb of Bábá Budan, but the Hindus to be the throne of Dattátreya, is a venerated place of pilgrimage for adherents of both creeds. A Mussalman kalandar is the custodian of the cave, which is designated the southern Mecca, and well endowed. By the Hindus the reappearance of Dattátreya at the mouth of the cave, into which in ancient times he vanished, is looked for as a sign prophetic of the final avatár of Vishnu and the introduction of the millennium.[1]

Attigundi, about a mile from the cave, is the residence of the Kalandar and the principal village on the hills.

**Ballal-rayan-durga.**—A fine spreading hill in the Western Ghat range, crowned with extensive fortifications. It is situated in 13° 8′ N. lat., and 75° 29′ E. long., in the north-west angle of the Múdgere taluq, over against Kellaggur. The fortifications were erected, as its name indicates, by the Hoysala kings. The old entrance is to the north, through what is now the Horikán coffee plantation. There are two gates, the *diḍḍi bágalu* and the *simha bágalu*. The citadel is a small square fort on the highest point, overlooking the South Kanara District. To the east of it is the old tank, now a bog, overgrown with impenetrable bushes. The pass to Kanara, north of the droog, is tremendously steep, but was formerly in regular use. To this fortress the Ráni of Bednur fled for refuge on the capture of her capital by Haidar Ali in 1763, and hence she was sent by him as a prisoner to Maddagiri (Tumkur District.)

**Bálé-Honnur.**—A new taluq in the west, formed in 1897. Area about 410 square miles. Head-quarters at Bálé Honnúr. Contains the following hoblis, villages and population :—

[1] There is said to have existed a history of the Bábá Budan mountains in Persian, compiled in the time of the Bijapur kings. But it was borrowed in recent times by some official and at his death was among his effects, which were sold by auction. It is believed to have found its way to Mangalore, but I have been unable to trace it.

| No. | Hoblis. | Villages. | Hamlets. | Villages classified. | | | | Population. |
|---|---|---|---|---|---|---|---|---|
| | | | | Govern-ment. | Sarva-mánya. | Jodi. | Kayam-gutta. | |
| 1 | Baggunji ... ... | 14 | 67 | 14 | — | — | — | 4,104 |
| 2 | Bále Honnúr ... | 20 | 123 | 20 | — | — | — | 6,141 |
| 3 | Kalasa ... ... | 13 | 37 | 13 | — | — | — | 9,772 |
| 4 | Khándya ... ... | 17 | 10 | 17 | — | — | — | 4,943 |
| 5 | Megunda ... ... | 23 | 52 | 23 | — | — | — | 8,226 |
| | Total ... | 87 | 289 | 87 | — | — | — | 33,186 |

*Principal places, with population.*—Mávinakere, 3,662; Devadána, 1,166; Karikésari, 1,142; Kaṇabur, 1,081; Samse, 1,041.

The taluq was formed out of Bálé Honnúr hobli of the abolished Yedehalli sub-taluq, Megunda and Baggunji of Koppa taluq, Kalasa of Múdgere taluq and Khándya of Chikmagalur taluq. The river Bhadra runs through it from south to north, with high mountains on either side, especially on the west, from the Merti peak of Kalasa in the south to eastwards of Koppa droog in the north. The whole taluq is purely Malnád and full of grand and picturesque scenery. It is a network of lofty hills and sunken valleys, the former densely covered with forests, which shelter a continuous belt of coffee plantations, the latter occupied by steeply terraced rice flats and areca gardens. The dry cultivation is very limited and of little value.

This part of the country was at one time under the S'ántara kings of Hombucha and then under the Hoysalas.

**Bálé-Honnúr.**—A town (or rather group of villages) situated in 13° 20′ N. lat., and 75° 32′ E. long., on the west bank of the Bhadra. Head-quarters of the taluq of the same name. Population, with associated villages, 1,081.

There has always been a ford at this place over the Bhadra, but a fine bridge has now been built, increasing the importance of the town for through traffic. A little to the north is the Bálehalli maṭha, the seat of one of the principal gurus of the Lingáyit sect.

**Bhadra.**—The twin stream of the Tunga, which both united form the river Tungabhadra. It rises close to the Tunga in the Gangámúla peak in the Western Ghats, 15 miles west of Kalasa. With a tortuous course it flows first eastwards and then, being joined at Sangamesvara by the Anebidda halla from the south, turns north-north-east and runs past Khandeya, across the mouth of the Jágar valley, the drainage of which it receives in the Somaváhini at Hebbe. Thence, fed near

Lakvalli by streams from Kalhatti giri and Kal-durga, it continues, by Benkipur and Hole Honnur, to the point of confluence with the Tunga at Kudali in the Shimoga District. The extreme steepness of the banks prevents the waters being extensively utilized for irrigation, but there are 18 dams from which 325 acres are supplied with water. The dense forests through which it flows has procured it the reputation of being a less healthy stream than the Tunga. It is bridged at Bálé Honnúr, and at Benkipur for the Bangalore-Shimoga high road. It crosses the Tarikere-Agumbi ghat road between Yedehalli and Lakvalli.

**Birur.**—An important trading town in the Kadur taluq, on the Bangalore-Poona railway and the Bangalore-Shimoga road, 4 miles north by west of the kasba, and a municipality.

| Population in 1891. | Males. | Females. | Total. |
|---|---|---|---|
| Hindus (with 6 Jains) ... ... ... | 2,202 | 2,016 | 4,220 |
| Muhammadans ... ... ... ... | 354 | 236 | 590 |
| Christians ... ... ... ... | 14 | 4 | 18 |
| Total ... ... ... | 2,570 | 2,256 | 4,828 |

The merchants of Birur receive areca-nut from the Malnád districts in the west and export it to Bellary and Dharwar. A very large traffic is also carried on in the cocoa-nuts, grain and other produce of the surrounding country. The annual value of the transactions at Birur is stated at nearly 50 lakhs of rupees. Birur is the junction for the branch railway to Shimoga, and has been extended in recent years.

| Municipal Funds. | 1891–2. | 1892–3. | 1893–4. | 1894–5. | 1895–6. |
|---|---|---|---|---|---|
| Income ... ... ... ... | 2,595 | 2,633 | 2,705 | 3,775 | 8,108 |
| Expenditure ... ... ... | 4,929 | 2,916 | 5,585 | 9,633 | 9,052 |

**Bund Ghat.**—The Búnd Ghát (coffee ghat) is the principal outlet to the western coast from the south of the District. The Ghat road runs from Múdgere and is led through the Wombat-maraḍi or nine hills. The views from Kotigehára of the approach to and down the ghat are very fine. Near the head of the ghat is a hill, called Hulikal, with two boulders on it supposed to represent the petrified forms of a tiger and a bull. The descent is by easy gradients of 1 in 20 to 1 in 15.

**Chikmagalur.**—A taluq in the centre and south. Area about 595 square miles. Head-quarters at Chikmagalur. Contains the following hoblis, villages and population :—

| No. | Hoblis. | Villages. | Hamlets. | Villages classified. | | | | Population. |
|---|---|---|---|---|---|---|---|---|
| | | | | Government. | Sarvamánya. | Jodi. | Kayamgutta. | |
| 1 | Chikmagalur ... | 37 | 37 | 35 | 2 | — | — | 21,407 |
| 2 | Jágara ... ... | 14 | 23 | 14 | — | — | — | 4,796 |
| 3 | Kadagaluád ... | 17 | 5 | 17 | — | — | — | 4,979 |
| 4 | Lakya ... ... | 44 | 7 | 42 | — | 2 | — | 11,278 |
| 5 | Morle ... ... | 32 | 38 | 29 | — | 3 | — | 18,742 |
| 6 | Vastára ... ... | 38 | 27 | 36 | — | 2 | — | 9,985 |
| | | 182 | 137 | 173 | 2 | 7 | — | 71,187 |

*Principal places, with population.* — Chikmagalur, 7,816; Morle, 2,506; Hirimagalur, 2,028; Ambale, 1,690; Kuruvanni, 1,423; Matavára, 1,413; Kalasapura, 1,215; Bigganhalli, 1,146; Mailmane, 1,127; Byárahalli, 1,064; Indávára, 1,061; Bikanhalli, 1,009.

The north of the taluq is occupied by the lofty forest-clad circle of the Bábá Budan mountains, enclosing the wild Jágar valley. The southern, northern, and eastern slopes contain many coffee plantations. The tract of country around Chikmagalur consists of an elevated plain, composed of rich black soil, extending along the southern base of the Bábá Budan mountains and bounded east and west by inferior ranges of hills, which separate it from Sakkarepatna on one hand and from Vastára on the other. Apart from the excellence of the soil, it is watered by perennial streams issuing from the Bábá Budans, the principal being the Yagache, which flows south by east into the Hassan District. Such is the fertility of this tract that it received the expressive name of *hon-javanige* or land flowing with gold. It is very bare of trees but produces unfailing crops of wheat, Bengal gram, sugar-cane, rice, coriander, mentya, garlic, onions and kusumba. Neither cotton nor tobacco are grown, owing, it is said, to too much damp.

The western portion, which till 1875 formed part of the separate taluq of Vastára, borders the Malnád beyond and partakes of its character.

The country formed part of the territory of the Jain kings of Humcha and of their descendants the rulers of Karkala, latterly included in the Hoysala kingdom. Under the Vijayanagar empire it passed into the hands, first of the chief of Balam, and then into those of the Nayaks of Ikkeri. It was subdued by Chikka Deva Rája in 1690 and added to Mysore by treaty with Ikkeri in 1694; except the Vastára country, which fell to Mysore by Haidar Ali's conquest of Bednur in 1763.

The revenue settlement was introduced in 1880. The area of the taluq as constituted at that time was thus distributed :—

| | |
|---|---|
| Culturable (dry, 71,382; wet, 39,653; garden, 1,534) ... ... | 112,569 |
| Unculturable (village sites, roads, etc.) ... ... ... ... | 223,906 |
| Coffee estates (1,551), kavals (28,696), Inam villages (20,370) ... | 50,617 |
| Total acres ... | 387,092 |

The unoccupied arable area was 27,381 acres. The total revenue demand for 1891-2 (15 months) was Rs. 2,38,214, and for 1892-3 it was Rs. 3,18,967.

The average annual rainfall at Chikmagalur for 26 years (1870-95) has been as follows :—

| Jan. | Feb. | Mar. | Apr. | May | June | July | Aug. | Sept. | Oct. | Nov. | Dec. | | Year. |
|---|---|---|---|---|---|---|---|---|---|---|---|---|---|
| 0·20 | 0·19 | 1·06 | 2·21 | 4·92 | 4·48 | 6·07 | 3·28 | 3·03 | 7·39 | 2·41 | 0·65 | ... | 35·89 |

Another register for 16 years gives the annual average as 41·72.

There are roads from Chikmagalur north-east to the railway at Kadur, south-east to Hassan, south-west to Múdgere and Bund-ghat, with branches to Aldur and Bálé Honnur, north-west, past the mouth of the Jagar valley, to Yedehalli, and north to the Bábá Budans and to Tarikere.

**Chikmagalur.**—The head-quarters of the Kadur District, and of the Chikmagalur taluq; situated in 13° 18′ N. lat., 75° 51′ E. long., 25 miles from the railway at Kadur. It is also a municipality.

| Population in 1891. | Males. | Females. | Total. |
|---|---|---|---|
| Hindus ... ... ... ... ... | 2,660 | 2,652 | 5,312 |
| Muhammadans ... ... ... ... | 1,152 | 1,072 | 2,224 |
| Jains ... ... ... ... ... ... | 36 | 4 | 40 |
| Christians ... ... ... ... ... | 123 | 117 | 240 |
| Total ... ... | 3,971 | 3,845 | 7,816 |

It is situated in the valley south of the Bábá Budan range, in a fertile tract of black soil. Since the removal hither of the District head-quarters from Kadur, in 1865, it has enormously increased. The main bazaar street is a fine wide thoroughfare, more than 2 miles long, extending from the old fort of Chikmagalur to the village of Basavanhalli, which it includes. In fact, the place is often called by the latter name. A large fair is held on Wednesday, at which 3,000 people assemble. The wants of the neighbouring coffee districts have led to the settlement here of a number of Muhammadan traders and shopkeepers. The town, *úru*, is popularly supposed to be named after the *chikka magalu*, or younger daughter, of Rukmángada, the king of Sakkarepatna, being her dowry, as the contiguous village of Hiremagalur was that of the *hire magalu*, or elder daughter. But as stated above (p. 379), there seems to be no foundation for this derivation. There are inscriptions in the fort of the Ganga kings in the 9th century, and of the Hoysalas in the 13th century. At certain seasons the high east winds, to which the place is much exposed, render it unhealthy. A wide belt of trees has been planted completely round the limits of the station, in the form of an oval, to mitigate this evil. Besides the usual District offices, there are a club, hospital, high school and other public buildings.

| Municipal Funds. | 1891–2. | 1892–3. | 1893–4. | 1894–5. | 1895–6. |
|---|---|---|---|---|---|
| Income ... ... ... | 50,400 | 15,647 | 17,240 | 24,921 | 22,621 |
| Expenditure ... ... ... | 53,761 | 18,133 | 18,228 | 25,502 | 37,133 |

**Gangamula.**—The source of the Tunga and Bhadra rivers, situated in 13° 15′ N. lat., 75° 14′ E. long. The hill from which they issue, called the Varáha Parvata, is in the Western Ghats, on the confines of the Koppa and Bálé Honnur taluqs. The legend is that after Vishnu, incarnate as the Varáha or Boar, had raised up the earth from the waters of the ocean, into which a Daitya named Hiranyáksha had carried off and plunged it, he took his stand on this mountain, and the drops which trickled from his two tusks formed respectively the twin streams the Tunga and Bhadra. The Netrávati, a stream which flows west through S. Kanara, is supposed to rise at the same place, and to have sprung from the drops which fell from the eyes (*netra*) of the Boar. The *tunga* (long) left tusk was the one he used as his weapon, the *bhadra* (firm and strong) right tusk was the one on which he bore up the earth: this is the *dakshinonnata damshṭrágra* frequently invoked in inscriptions.

Mr. Bowring, who visited Gangámúla, says, "It is in truth a wild country, and has a desolate grandeur about it, seeming to be the end of the world. On every side tower up magnificent mountains, spreading for leagues in every direction, and covered with immense forests, while nowhere can one detect the faintest trace of human life, either in the shape of houses or of cultivation." It was to these solitudes that the father of Pandita Ramábái retired for many years, and here it was that he taught her Sanskrit.

**Hariharpur,** properly **Hariharapura.**—A village situated in 13° 30′ N. lat., 75° 22′ E. long., on the left bank of the Tunga, on the Tarikere-Agumbi road, 7 miles east of the Agumbi ghat. Till 1897 the head-quarters of the Koppa taluq. Population 1,089.

From inscriptions at the place it appears to have been an agrahára established in 1418 by Sábanna Wodeyar of A'raga (Tirthahalli taluq, Shimoga District) in the reign of Harihara Ráya of Vijayanagar, and named after the latter. Its importance has been mainly due to its being the taluq head-quarters.

**Hemavati.**—This river, a principal tributary of the Kávéri, is more fully described under the Hassan and Mysore Districts, in which most of its course is run. But it rises in this District, in Jávali, in the Melbangáḍi mágaṇi of the Múḍgere taluq. The reputed source is a spring, behind the house of Lakshmayya, a coffee planter, which is led through a stone bull into a square stone well. The stream runs in a south-east direction to the Hassan District, which it enters at the common boundary of Manjarabad and Belur.

**Hiremagalur.**—A large village, 1 mile south-east of Chikmagalur, largely inhabited by Sri Vaishnava Brahmans. Population 2,028.

It is said to be named from the *hire-magaḷu* or elder daughter of Rukmángada, the king of Sakkarepaṭṇa, having been bestowed on her as a dowry, but see above (p. 379). Its former name is stated to have been Bhárgavapuri. Here the emperor Janamejaya is related to have performed the *sarpa yága*, or serpent sacrifice, undertaken to avenge the death of his father Parikshit from the bite of a snake. The scene of this sacrifice is marked by a spear-headed stone pillar in the town, called the *yúpa stambha* or sacrificial post. It is said to be efficacious in restoring any one bitten by a serpent: the patient must circumambulate the pillar and bathe in the Siddha Pushkarini, a pond close by. The village is surrounded by a rich tract of black soil. Inscriptions at the place show that it was an agrahára in the 9th century in the time of the Ganga king Nitimárga, and in the 11th century in the time of the Hoysala king Vinayáditya. It contains some old temples, one dedicated to Kodaṇḍa Ráma and another to Paras'u, the axe of Paras'u Ráma.

**Kadúr.**—A taluq in the east; area 561 square miles. Head-quarters at Kaḍúr. Contains the following hoblis, villages and population :—

| No. | Hoblis. | Villages. | Hamlets. | Villages classified. | | | | Population. |
|---|---|---|---|---|---|---|---|---|
| | | | | Government. | Sarvamánya. | Jódi. | Kayamgutta. | |
| 1 | Bidare ... ... | 48 | 9 | 48 | — | — | — | 10,104 |
| 2 | Bírúr ... ... | 37 | 4 | 36 | — | 1 | — | 9,963 |
| 3 | Hirenallúr ... | 46 | 4 | 46 | — | — | — | 9,709 |
| 4 | Kaḍúr ... ... | 71 | 24 | 71 | — | — | — | 15,612 |
| 5 | Sakkarepaṭṇa ... | 42 | 24 | 40 | — | 2 | — | 13,434 |
| 6 | Yagaṭi ... ... | 67 | 15 | 66 | — | 1 | — | 13,395 |
| | Total ... | 311 | 80 | 307 | — | 4 | — | 72,217 |

*Principal places, with population.*—Bírúr 4,828; Kaḍúr 2,716; Sakkarepaṭṇa 1,846; Hulikere 1,210; Niḍigaṭṭa 1,144; Jilagúr 1,139; Paṭṇagere 1,097; Yagaṭi 1,042.

There have been frequent local changes in regard to the taluq. Originally, it appears, there were 4 taluqs, Kaḍúr, Yagaṭi, Garudangiri and Banavar. The two former belonged to the old Ikkéri kingdom, but were taken by the Mysore kings and given to the chief of Tarikere, in return for services in the field rendered by him. Haidar resumed them and annexed them to Mysore. Garudangiri was absorbed into Banavar, and about 1835 Yagaṭi was absorbed into Kaḍúr. In 1876 Kaḍúr and Banavar were formed into one taluq, named after Banavar, which was the chief town. In 1882 the head-quarters were removed to Kaḍúr, and in 1886, on the formation of the neighbouring Arsikere taluq, Kaḍúr taluq was reconstituted, with the addition of Sakkarepaṭṇa hobli from Chikmagalur, while portions of the old Banavar taluq, together with Banavar itself, were transferred from this District to Arsikere taluq in the Hassan District.

It is now virtually bounded on the west by the congeries of hills east of the Bábá Budan mountains, and those separating Chikmagalur from the Sakkarepaṭṇa valley, and on the south by the hills running up from Jávagal to the conspicuous height of Garudangiri. It is traversed through the middle, in a north-east direction, by the Vedavati, which is formed by the junction, south-east of Kaḍúr, of two streams, the Veda and Avati, and receives near Yagaṭi a stream from the south, called the Javagal-halla. The Veda and Avati both have their sources in the Bábá Budans; but the former comes through the Ayyankere and the latter through the Madagkere, the two largest tanks in that part of the country. These streams as they emerge from the hills have been dammed with great skill and a perennial water supply thus obtained.

Numerous channels are taken off from each, converting a considerable stretch of country into irrigated lands of special fertility. The general character of the taluq is that of a slightly undulating plain. Most of the waste lands are covered with wild date or *babul* trees. A large extent of waste lands is kept for grazing purposes, the number of cattle and sheep being very considerable. Soils of almost every quality are found, varying from black cotton soil of good quality to the poorest sand. Irrigated lands are of average quality, varying principally as the proportion of clay or sand predominates. A high class of tobacco is grown in the south and west. Cocoanuts are largely grown without irrigation, in low-lying sandy soils. The tree thrives best in the drier parts, where also the produce is superior in quality. Iron ore is obtained from Hogari-betta in the north-west.

The revenue settlement was introduced in 1878, and the area of the taluq as it then existed was distributed as follows:—

| | |
|---|---|
| Culturable (dry, 205,934; wet, 11,113; garden, 11,099) ... | 228,146 |
| Unculturable (roads, village sites, &c.) ... ... ... ... | 99,171 |
| Five Inám villages (5,291); 15 Amrit Mahal kávals (47,851) ... | 53,142 |
| Total acres ... | 380,459 |

The unoccupied arable area was 100,830 acres, nearly all dry crop land. The total revenue demand for 1891–2 (15 months) was Rs. 1,86,614, and for 1892–3 it was Rs. 2,12,476.

The average rainfall at Kaḍúr for 26 years (1870–95), and at Yagaṭi for 3 years (1893–5) has been as follows:—

| | Jan. | Feb. | Mar. | Apr. | May | June | July | Aug. | Sept. | Oct. | Nov. | Dec. | Year. |
|---|---|---|---|---|---|---|---|---|---|---|---|---|---|
| Kaḍúr | 0·12 | 0·03 | 0·34 | 1·24 | 3·27 | 2·39 | 1·98 | 1·19 | 2·32 | 5·53 | 2·03 | 0·94 ... | 21·38 |
| Yagaṭi | — | — | — | 2·89 | 2·39 | 1·61 | 1·85 | 1·06 | 2·66 | 7·49 | 1·88 | — ... | 21·83 |

The Bangalore-Poona railway runs through the taluq in a north-west direction, with stations at Devanur, Kaḍúr and Bírúr, where it turns north-east and enters the Tarikere taluq. From Bírúr a branch north-west to Shimoga is under construction. The Bangalore-Shimoga road is close alongside the railway, and there are roads from Kaḍúr south-west to Chikmagalur, and from Bírúr north to Ajjampur and west to Lingadahalli and the Bábá Budans. There is also a road from Sakkare-paṭṇa to Devanur and Banavar.

**Kadúr.**—A town situated in 13° 32′ N. lat., 76° 4′ E. long., on the Bangalore-Poona railway and the Bangalore-Shimoga road, 25 miles north-west of Chikmagalur. Head-quarters of the Kadur taluq and a municipality.

| Population in 1891. | Males. | Females. | Total. |
|---|---|---|---|
| Hindus (with 6 Jains) ... ... ... | 1,141 | 1,151 | 2,292 |
| Muhammadans ... ... ... ... | 89 | 52 | 141 |
| Christians ... ... ... ... ... | 5 | 6 | 11 |
| Total ... | 1,235 | 1,209 | 2,444 |

It was from 1863 to 1865 the chief town of the then newly-formed District, whence the latter obtained its name, and still later, till 1875, the head-quarters of the Kaḍúr taluq, which was then absorbed into Banavar taluq. In 1882 it was again made the taluq head-quarters, and in 1886 the taluq was again called after it.

From inscriptions and other monuments it is evident that a Jain settlement existed here in early times, connected with the Ganga kings. It was subsequently under the Hoysalas. During the sovereignty of the Vijayanagar kings, in the 14th century, the lands around Yemme Doḍḍi guḍḍa were conferred upon a dependent named Mada Nayak. At that time the agrahára of Narnapura occupied the present site of Kaḍúr, and the Nayak, when hunting one day in that direction, had his dogs turned back and pursued by an elk. This led to the foundation of the fort, called *Kaḍ-úru*, elk town, from *kaḍave*, an elk. The recent advent of the railway has increased its importance, as being the station for Chikmagalur and the coffee districts beyond.

| Municipal Funds. | 1891–2. | 1892–3. | 1893–4. | 1894–5 | 1895–6. |
|---|---|---|---|---|---|
| Income ... ... ... | 1,600 | 1,607 | 1,670 | 2,562 | 2,766 |
| Expenditure ... ... ... | 4,160 | 1,621 | 2,285 | 3,785 | 3,861 |

**Kalasa.**—A village in the Bálé-Honnur taluq, situated in 13° 14′ N. lat., 75° 26′ E. long., near the right bank of the Bhadra, by road 24 miles south-west of the kasba.

It is situated in a valley surrounded by the lofty hills of the Western Ghat range, and at the southern base of Merti, the grand hill of Kalasa. It contains a large temple dedicated to Kalasesvara, surrounded with inscriptions of the Bairasa Wodeyar family of Kárkala. The temple is said to have been founded by Shrutabindu, a king from the north, in order to atone for the sin of slaying animals in the chase. It was therefore probably a Jain temple originally. Mounds covering ruins on all sides point to the existence of a large town in former times. It was included in the dominions of Humcha and of the Kárkala chiefs descended therefrom. Subsequently it became the residence of the Aigur chiefs. The town then extended so as to include the present villages of Melangadi, Kilangadi, and Rudrapáda. Going through

Melangadi and keeping on to the river, a sacred bathing-place called Ambu-tírtha is reached, where the stream rushes very deep between some water-worn rocks. At one point is a large boulder, a big square-shaped stone placed horizontally on another. On the former is an inscription in Sanskrit, stating that Srí Madhvácharya brought and placed it there with one hand! The Kalasa territory was administered by three chiefs of a thousand villages, called Hebbáru. The areca-nut produced in the neighbourhood is reckoned the best in Mysore, being known as Desavara, in distinction from that grown in other Malnád parts, which is called Honnavara, and from Volágra, which is the produce of other inland gardens. Kalasa is connected with the Búnd ghat by a road through Bálur, and with the Agumbi ghat by a road running north through Baggunji.

**Khandeya.**—A village in Bálé-Honnur taluq, on the right bank of the Bhadra, where it makes a bend to receive the Anebidda-halla, 5 miles north-east of the kasba.

It appears to have been formerly a large place. There are some considerable old temples, the principal being one dedicated to Márkandesvara; also several inscriptions of the Hoysala and Vijayanagar kings. It is said to have been originally the hermitage of Márkanda rishi. He sought from Siva the boon of a son, and was required to choose between one who should be distinguished for his wisdom but die at the age of 16, and one who should be a fool and live a long life. The saint chose the former, and obtained Márkandeya. The distress of his mother as the time of his decease approached led to his discovery of his fate. But when Mrityu, the goddess of death, appeared to claim his life, Janárdana (Vishnu) offered to be the substitute, and Siva, moved by the youth's devotion, gave him victory over death. The place derives its name from Márkandeya, and the temples of Janárdana and Mrityunjaya (conqueror of death) commemorate his deliverance.

**Koppa.**—A taluq in the north-west. Area 466 square miles. Head-quarters, till 1897 at Hariharpur, now at Koppa. Contains the following hoblis, villages and population:—

| No. | Hoblis. | Villages. | Hamlets. | Villages classified. | | | | Population |
|---|---|---|---|---|---|---|---|---|
| | | | | Government | Sarvamánya. | Jódi. | Kayamgutta. | |
| 1 | Bellare ... ... | 14 | 45 | 14 | — | — | — | 5,048 |
| 2 | Dánivása .. | 43 | 208 | 43 | — | — | — | 10,709 |
| 3 | Hoskere ... ... | 13 | 27 | 13 | — | — | — | 4,623 |
| 4 | Kigga ... ... | 20 | 34 | 20 | — | — | — | 4,615 |
| 5 | Koppa .. ... | 22 | 76 | 22 | — | — | — | 9,733 |
| | Sringéri Jágir... | 233 | 26 | — | 223 | — | — | 9,144 |
| | Total ... | 345 | 416 | 112 | 223 | — | — | 43,872 |

*Principal places, with population.*—Sringéri, 1,987 ; Nuggi, 1,206 ; Hariharapura, 1,089.

The taluq is entirely Malnád and one of the wildest and most picturesque in the country. The most open portion is the Sringéri valley, which is traversed by the upper course of the Tunga. This river runs in a north-east direction as far as Narve, where it turns to the north-west. The watershed is in no part very distant, and the hill streams, though numerous, have not time to become of any size. The Sita and Begar hallas are the largest. The remaining three sides of the taluq are bounded by lofty mountains. From the Varáha parvata at Gangamúla, in the south-western angle, whence the Tunga and Bhadra take their rise, the Western Ghats run north, with such prominent points as Wolkonji, Sujibetta, Nemar and Kig. East from the same point stretch conspicuous ranges, culminating in the Merti peak of Kalasa, and thence northwards towards Koppa droog. The western and southern hills are mostly bare of trees at their summits, but are thickly wooded in the hollows. On proceeding eastwards the elevation of the tree zone rises, until only the highest hill-tops are devoid of forest. Most of the taluq is a succession of lofty hills and deep valleys, the latter, where not cultivated, being covered with jungle and heavy scrub.

The soil is a good red loam, whose fertility is yearly renewed by the decomposed vegetable matter which is washed down by the rain from the surrounding forests. Of dry crops, a little rági is grown for home consumption on high-lying *makki* lands ; but this is not reaped, only the heads are picked, and cattle turned in to eat the straw. Castor and other oil seeds are grown to a small extent as a second crop in some of the rice lands. The staple wet crop is rice, and a second crop is grown in some villages to the west. The sugar-cane is generally inferior and raised only in small patches for home use. The jaggory produced is too watery to crystallize and is commonly used, mixed with water, as a drink. But in the neighbourhood of Dánivása, in the north-east, where sugar-cane is largely grown, the juice is made into *sukkare bîja* or crystals, and afterwards manufactured into sugar. The principal garden crop is areca-nut, for which the taluq is renowned. The best gardens are in the south-east. Cardamoms are also a very valuable production, but require abundant and continuous moisture. Coffee cultivation has made great strides in the last 25 years. In 1870 Koppa and Nemar were the only coffee estates under European superintendence, whereas now this taluq is one of the principal centres for European coffee planters, and coffee is extensively cultivated in the hill ranges to the north and on the slopes of the Western Ghats.

The Sringéri jágir forms an endowment of the *maṭha* of the Smarta

Brahmans, founded in the 8th century by the Saiva apostle Sankaráchárya, as elsewhere related. The country, from its inaccessible character, was virtually independent, each mágani being the domain of some Heggaḍe or local chieftain. It was first included in the territories of the Humcha and Karkala rulers, and then in the Hoysala dominions. The religious establishment at Sringéri was intimately connected with the foundation of the Vijayanagar empire, and Harihara, one of the brothers from whom the royal line was descended, gave his name to the agrahara at Hariharapura. The Náyaks of Ikkéri gained possession of the territory on the overthrow of Vijayanagar, and in 1763, by the capture of Bednur by Haidar Ali, it was absorbed into the kingdom of Mysore.

The revenue settlement was introduced in 1880. The area of the taluq at that time was thus distributed:—

| | |
|---|---|
| Culturable (dry, 492; wet, 22,014; garden, 6,041) ... ... | 28,547 |
| Unculturable (roads, village sites, etc.) ... ... ... ... | 185,825 |
| 2 Inam villages ... ... ... ... ... ... ... | 28,932 |
| Total acres ... | 243,304 |

The unoccupied arable land was 1,752 acres. The total revenue demand for 1891–2 (15 months) was Rs. 3,31,885, and for 1892–3 it was Rs. 3,57,158.

The average rainfall has been estimated at 172 inches a year in the western portions and 108 in the eastern. But the following is the result of observations at taluq stations for 26 years (1870–95):—

| | Jan. | Feb. | Mar. | April | May | June | July | Aug. | Sept | Oct. | Nov. | Dec. | | Year. |
|---|---|---|---|---|---|---|---|---|---|---|---|---|---|---|
| Koppa | 0·19 | 0·13 | 0·41 | 1·66 | 3·72 | 23·29 | 42·90 | 25·08 | 9·56 | 7·40 | 2·11 | 0·45 | ... | 116·90 |
| Yedehalli | — | 0·16 | 0·29 | 2·07 | 3·76 | 9·92 | 16·59 | 10·02 | 5·14 | 5·23 | 2·57 | 0·47 | ... | 56·22 |

Other registers give an average of 119·89 at Koppa for 16 years and 53·64 at Yedehalli for 7 years.

The road from Tarikere to the Agumbi Ghat (the only one in the taluq 20 years ago) runs through Koppa, Hariharpur and the north. A cross road from Begar connects it with Sringéri and Nemar, and there is also a road from Sringéri to Kigga. From Hariharpur a road has been carried through Baggunji to Báḷe Honnur and Aldur. From Koppa there are roads to Sringéri, to Badagi, and to Tirthahalli. From Yedehalli there are roads to Báḷe Honnur, to Chikmagalur by the mouth of the Jagar valley, to Mandagadde, and to Shimoga by Umbalibail.

**Koppa.**—A village situated in 13° 16′ N. lat., 75° 24′ E. long., on the Tarikere-Agumbi Ghat road, 39 miles west of the railway at

Tarikere. Population, 782. Being appointed in 1897 as the head-quarters of the taluq, it is likely to rapidly increase in importance.

**Kudure Mukha.**—A peak in the Western Ghats and one of the loftiest points in Mysore, the summit being 6,215 feet above the level of the sea. It is situated on the frontier in the south-west of the District, at the point where the line of the Ghats bends more inland. The approach from the Mysore side is by way of Samse, the hill being sometimes called on the spot the Samse parvata. Its name of Kudure mukha, or Horse-face, is descriptive of its appearance seawards, where it is a well-known mark for navigators. The officials of Malabar have a bungalow at the top as a hot weather retreat, and a bridle path has been formed from the Malabar side, which is the easiest means of ascending the mountain.

**Lakvalli.**—A village in Tarikere taluq, on the right bank of the Bhadra, 13 miles west of Tarikere. Population, 1,358.

Till 1882 it gave its name to a taluq which included the Bábá Budan mountains and parts of what are now Koppa and Báḷe Honnur taluqs. West of it are vast forests on each side of the Bhadra, containing some of the most valuable teak timber in the country. Nowhere is the transition from Malnád to Maidán more abrupt or striking than here.

Lakvalli is close to the site of Ratnapuri, the ancient capital of Vajra Makuta Ráya. The neighbouring country subsequently formed part of the Humcha and Ganga territory; then of the Hoysala and Vijayanagar kingdoms. The palegars of Tarikere afterwards acquired some portion of it, but were forced to yield it to the Náyaks of Ikkéri. The overthrow of this latter power by Haidar Ali's conquest of Bednur in 1763 led to the absorption of the country into Mysore.

**Merti-gudda,** also called the Kalasa hill, is situated in the Báḷe Honnur taluq, in 13° 18′ N. lat., 75° 26′ E. long. It is the loftiest peak between the Bábá Budan and Western Ghat ranges, the summit being 5,451 feet above the level of the sea. To the north it presents a majestic conical aspect. Towards the south-west it is connected with two lower heights and is so surrounded on all sides with high hills that its true elevation does not appear except at a distance.

Mr. Bowring, who left few hills unscaled, says: "After a toilsome climb up its steep sides by the 'windy gorge,' one revels in a view which surpasses all expectation. On every side tower up hills of various shapes and sizes, stretching far away to the horizon, and presenting a wonderful spectacle of wild sublimity. The foot of the steep ridge which runs up to a sharp point forming the actual peak is called the Túral bágalu (entrance gate), and is in a gap between the Mérti Parvat and another hill to the south. A very tough pull of twenty-five minutes takes one hence to the summit, the higher of two peaks, between which there is a dip.

"The top of Merti is quite bare, but its sides are clothed with fine forests, in which are splendid specimens of the champaka tree, so much esteemed by natives for its fragrant white flowers; while one sees beneath, in secluded nooks and sheltered valleys, stretches of paddy land in successive layers, one below the other, and numerous gardens of areca-nut, which, in this remote corner, attains an excellence surpassing that of any other place where the fruit is grown. The sides of Merti, where the nature of the ground admits of it, are cultivated in a series of terraces, in which abundance of rice is grown, with a little coffee: this, however, does not succeed well, owing to the humidity of the climate."

**Mudgere.**—A taluq in the south. Area about 302 square miles. Head-quarters at Múḍgere. Contains the following hoblis, villages and population:—

| No. | Hoblis. | Villages. | Hamlets. | Villages classified. | | | | Population |
|---|---|---|---|---|---|---|---|---|
| | | | | Government. | Sarvamánya. | Jódi. | Kayamgutta. | |
| 1 | Banakal ... ... | 28 | 39 | 28 | — | — | — | 6,080 |
| 2 | Bidarnáḍ... ... | 14 | 3 | 14 | — | — | — | 6,107 |
| 3 | Góṇibíḍ ... ... | 29 | 44 | 28 | — | 1 | — | 9,001 |
| 4 | Mélbangáḍi ... | 21 | 11 | 21 | — | — | — | 6,880 |
| 5 | Múḍgere... ... | 46 | 66 | 45 | — | 1 | — | 9,181 |
| | Total ... | 138 | 163 | 136 | — | 2 | — | 37,249 |

*Principal places, with population.*—Bálúr, 1,433; A'ldúr, 1,355; Banakal, 1,200; Múḍgere, 1,149; Hosahaḷḷi, 1,051.

The taluq was formed in 1876 out of parts of Manjarabad, Belur and Vastára taluqs. In 1897 the Kalasa máganị was transferred to Báḷe Honnur taluq, and Bidarnád added from Chikmagalur. The taluq is Malnád and picturesque like all such country. The Hemavati has its source here and flows out at the south-east. The forests are not composed of such big trees as towards Lakvalli, but the hollows are well wooded and the many hanging woods on the hillsides impart great beauty to the landscape. The principal productions are coffee, areca-nut, cardamoms, rice and sugar-cane, the last in small quantity. The rice is dependent chiefly on springs in the hills from which watercourses are led. Dry crops are of no account and do not generally thrive. Coffee cultivation is extensive and important, and there are many estates under European superintendence. Tulu is much spoken by the labourers and others from South Kanara.

The nature of the Malnád country, its climate, the constitution of its society, and the character of its inhabitants, all conspire to produce a sort of semi-independence. There are some descriptive lines to the following effect which convey the same idea:—

| | |
|---|---|
| Hanneraḍu sávira guḍḍa | Káḍ-ella sampige |
| A'ru sávira daiva | U'r-ella heggaḍe |

Twelve thousand hills; six thousand demons: in every forest, champaka; in every village, a Heggaḍe (or local chief).

The hopeless inaccessibility of the country in past times, together with its natural fertility, seem to have whetted the rapacity of the governing powers, and the following is given as a history of the revenue exactions:—"The máganis were more or less subject, first, to the Virada or Varáha-shist of the Vijayanagar kingdom; then to the Rekha-shist of Sivappa Náyak; then to the additional imposts of other Ikkéri rulers, Pállegárs, and Haidar Ali, called Dasoha, Pagadi and Paṭṭi, or more generally Paṭṭi; then to the Paimáyish of Púrnaiya and the increased assessment imposed by him under the name of Shist-jásti and Kánike; and by the process of commuting the money-assessment of some of the best lands for a grain contribution for the use of the Rája's Módikhána; then to the impositions of over-zealous Amildars, mostly of this Minister's time, who, in villages rented in block to the Patels or other principal inhabitants, having found that these collected more than the Shist and Paṭṭi from the cultivators, carried this excess to account under the name of Beriz-jásti; then to the arbitrary exactions of the Amildar during the Rája's time, to which the Sharti system then in vogue necessarily gave rise; and then to the enhancement caused, after the assumption of the country by the British Government, by the Amildars to whom the duty of converting Púrnaiya's grain contribution into Suvarnádáya or money rent again was entrusted, and who settled the new money rates with reference to the Chadsál-jama or the highest share that had ever been realized, or with the aid of the more insidious Dhan-gutta system, which, professing nominally to levy only the grain rent, as a means of allaying the clamours of more suspicious ryots, levied a money rent in reality by compelling them to take the grain at an arbitrarily fixed price. Again, as in other Malnád parts, there was also the plan of compelling the ryots to keep in their holding every field they may at different times have taken either of their own accord or in consequence of pressure used to induce them to take up the holdings of their deceased relatives or neighbours, and to pay for these fields whether they were cultivated or waste. On the other hand, generally as a compromise necessarily due from the above extremely rigorous method of management to the actual exigencies of the revenue, it was customary to grant the concessions of the Shráya or Alave system, or reductions in whole or in part under the name of Tavaguf or Báki, of the Beriz-jásti or Paṭṭi, and even of the Shist, on the ground of the general excessiveness of the combined assessment, or of Ságuvali-nashṭa, Kula-nashṭa and Nisthalu, which suppose so much waste rice-land or supári garden, or of Alate-kammi and Hari-mara, which imply an actual deficiency either in the recorded extent of land or in the number of trees that should ordinarily be standing thereon in the supári gardens."

The revenue settlement, based on a regular survey, which put an end to all these irregularities, was introduced in 1881, except in Gonibid mágaṇi, which was settled in 1877 with Belúr taluq. The Kalasa mágaṇi, with an area of about 200 square miles, has now (1897) been transferred to Báḷe Honnur. Bearing these differences in mind, the following was the distribution of the area at the time of the settlement :—

| | |
|---|---:|
| Culturable (dry, 7,357 ; wet, 25,900 ; garden, 1,583) ... ... | 34,840 |
| Unculturable (roads, village sites, hittalus, etc.) ... ... ... | 230,864 |
| 13 Coffee estates ... ... ... ... ... ... ... | 6,086 |
| Total acres .. | 271,790 |

The unoccupied area was 5,511 acres. The total revenue demand for 1891–2 (15 months) was Rs. 1,47,590, and for 1892–3 it was Rs. 1,70,643.

The average rainfall at Múḍgere for 26 years (1870–95) has been as follows :—

| Jan. | Feb. | Mar. | April | May | June | July | Aug. | Sept. | Oct. | Nov. | Dec. | | Year. |
|---|---|---|---|---|---|---|---|---|---|---|---|---|---|
| 0·22 | 0·04 | 0·62 | 2·33 | 5·25 | 18·87 | 30·17 | 16·74 | 10·16 | 9·35 | 3·12 | 0·60 | ... | 97·47 |

Another register for 16 years makes the annual average 102·50.

The road from Chikmagalur to the Búnd Ghat runs through the taluq from north-east to south-west by Múḍgere, with branches from Kotigihár north to Báḷe Honnur and westwards to Kalasa. From Múḍgere there are roads east to Belúr, south to Manjarabad, and south-west to Uggihalli. But the best road to Belúr is from Anjur through Gonibid.

**Múḍgere.**—A village situated in 13° 8′ N. lat., 75° 41′ E. long., on the road from Chikmagalur to the Búnd Ghat, 19 miles south-west of

Chikmagalur. Head-quarters of the Múḍgere taluq. Population, 1,149. It owes its importance to being the taluq station. The road to Manjarabad also branches off here.

**Sakkarepatna.**—A village in the Kadur taluq, 11 miles south-west of the kasba, on the Kadur-Chikmagalur road. Population, 1,846.

A large weekly fair is held on Friday. At the car festival of Ranganátha, held in Vaishákha, as many as 3,000 rams are sacrificed in honour of the god.

Tradition relates that it was in olden times the capital of Rukmángada, a king mentioned in the Mahá Bhárata. Objects of interest in the town are the monument to Hon-billa, sacrificed for the stability of the Ayyankere (which see); a great gun, and an immense slab of stone, about 12 feet square and several inches thick, supported on 4 pillars. This is called Vira Ballála Chauki and is said to have been the royal seat of justice. During the time of the Vijayanagar kings the town became a possession of the Aigur or Balam chiefs. It was next taken by the Náyaks of Ikkéri. Sri Ranga Ráya, the fallen king of the Vijayanagar state, took refuge with the Ikkéri chief, who espoused his cause and established him in power at Sakkarepatna. But in 1690 it was taken by the Mysore army and retained by the treaty of 1694.

**Santaveri.**—A small village, principally composed of Lambánis, situated on the eastern face of the Bábá Budan mountains, just below Káman durga. It is on the Chikmagalur-Tarikere road, about midway between those two places. A road hence leads to Kalhatti and the summit of the mountains.

**Sringéri.**—A jágir in Koppa taluq, belonging to the chief *maṭha* of the Smárta Brahmans. It is administered in imitation of the Mysore revenue system, and contains the following hoblis, villages and population:—

| No. | Hoblis. | Villages. | Hamlets. | Population. |
|---|---|---|---|---|
| 1 | Chadravalli-pálu ... ... | 52 | 2 | 1,529 |
| 2 | Hejje Hounavalli-pálu... ... | 70 | 13 | 3,974 |
| 3 | Keḷa-pálu ... ... ... | 63 | 4 | 1,794 |
| 4 | Mélu-pálu ... ... .. | 43 | 7 | 1,764 |
| 5 | Silakaraḍi ... ... ... | 5 | — | 83 |
| | Total ... | 233 | 26 | 9,144 |

The jágir seems, from an inscription at the place, to have been granted as an endowment of the *maṭha* in 1346, by Hariyap-Oḍeyar (or Harihara, the first king of Vijayanagar), his four brothers—Kampaṇṇa,

Bukkaṇṇa, Márapa and Muddapa—son-in-law Ballappa Daṇṇáyaka, and the latter's son Sávaṇṇa. In an inscription of 1621 the Keladi king Venkaṭappa Náyak, who describes himself as grandson of Sadásiva Náyak, claims to have re-established Sringéri, from which it would appear that some interruption had occurred in the enjoyment of the jágir. It is about 8 miles long by 6 miles wide, and has the river Tunga running through it from south-west to north-east. The country is pure Malnád, and similar in character to the adjoining Koppa and Báḷe Honnúr taluqs. The revenue is estimated at Rs. 50,000 a year, which is supplemented by Rs. 12,000 from the Mysore State.

A road from Koppa to Nemár runs through Sringéri, where it is crossed by one from Begár to Báḷe Honnúr. There is also a road from Sringéri to Kigga.

**Sringéri.**—A sacred village on the left bank of the Tunga, situated in 13° 25′ N. lat., 75° 19′ E. long., in the Koppa taluq, 15 miles south-west of the kasba, and a municipality. Population, 1,987.

It is the head-quarters of the Jagad-guru, the high priest of the Smárta Brahmans, who is proprietor of the surrounding tract of country. *Sringéri*, *Sringa-giri* or *Rishya Sringa-giri* is related to have been the place where Vibhánḍaka rishi performed penance, and where Rishya Sringa, a celebrated character of the Rámáyana, was born. The latter, according to the narrative, grew up to man's estate without having ever seen a woman; when Lomapáda, king of Anga, was advised that if the youthful recluse could be brought to his city and married to the princess Sánta the drought which prevailed in his kingdom would be removed. In order to entice the young saint from his hermitage a bevy of fair damsels was despatched. They are said to have made their last halt at Nárve, a few miles from Sringéri, before essaying the power of their charms. Allurements, which even the most wary can rarely withstand, soon worked their effect on the unsophisticated youth. His curiosity being strongly excited to see more of these beautiful and gentle creatures so new to him, he was led away and conveyed to Anga. He afterwards became the priest of Dasaratha Ráya, and performed the *asvamedha* or horse sacrifice which resulted in the birth of Rama.

In subsequent times the great Saiva reformer Sankaráchárya settled here, as directed by the image of Sárad-amma or Sarasvati, which he had brought from Kashmir; and founded the spiritual throne which has been occupied down to the present day by as apostolical a succession as the papal chair. The 8th century is now proved to be the period of Sankaráchárya's religious conquests and revival of Siva worship. His opposition to the Buddhists and Jains, his destruction of their literature, and his polemical victories in all parts of India are matters of history. The Sringéri Swámi is a man of eminent learning and great sanctity. His claims to reverence are admitted by all votaries of Siva, whether of the Smárta or any other communion. The enormous sums obtained from the piety of his disciples during his tours in various parts are spent with a lavish hand in hospitality and works of charity so called. He is often away from his capital on such expeditions for several years.

Sringéri consists of a long street, with a loop on one side, encircling a small hill, Sringa-giri, on which stands a temple of Mallikárjuna. There are said to be 120 temples in the place, one being a Jain basti.[1] Many Brahman houses have a temple in the yard behind, of which the resident Brahman is the officiant. At the head of the street is the *maṭha* of the guru, within which is the temple of S'árad-amna, whose image is said to be of pure gold. At the side of the *maṭha* is the temple of Vidyás'ankara, an ornamental building of the Chalukyan style, on a raised terrace. Round the outer wall are sculptured images of various gods. At an angle on the right of the front entrance is a statue of Vyása, wearing a conical cap, the sacred thread and a *dhótra*; his right hand in the position called *abhaya hasta*. He is imparting instruction to S'ankaráchárya, whose statue, through the indentation of the plan, is at right angles to him. Sánkara has a palmyra leaf book in his left hand. These two figures, from being constantly anointed with oil, are quite black. Towards Vidyáranyapura, on the bank of the Tunga, is a small temple with an image of Sankaráchárya seated as a *yati*. This is where he is said to have disappeared from life.

Several large festivals occur during the year, the principal being the Navarátri. On these occasions all classes are not only fed at the expense of the *maṭha*, but cloths and bodices are distributed to the women, and pieces of money to the men. The fishes in the river are sacred and daily fed at certain pools. Besides Rs. 50,000 a year, the revenue of the mágaṇi, the cultivation of which is rice and areca-nut, the religious establishment is supported by a grant of Rs. 1,000 a month from the Mysore State.

**Tarikere.**—A taluq in the north-east. Area 459 square miles. Head-quarters at Tarikere. Contains the following hoblis, villages and population :—

[1] There is a good deal of toleration in religious matters in these parts, such as prevailed in the old times before sectarian prejudice became so bitter. Thus, the Lingáyits, I heard, are reconciled by being allowed to blow their conch-shells in the processions at S'ringéri. Jain inscriptions (as at Kalbasti) begin with the usual verse in praise of S'iva. A Jain temple at Horanád is served by a Havika Brahman.

| No. | Hoblis. | Villages. | Hamlets. | Villages classified. | | | | Population. |
|---|---|---|---|---|---|---|---|---|
| | | | | Government. | Sarvamánya. | Jodi. | Kayamguttta. | |
| 1 | Ajjampura ... | 55 | 16 | 54 | — | 1 | — | 19,010 |
| 2 | Amritapura ... | 41 | 5 | 41 | — | — | — | 10,742 |
| 3 | Lakvalli ... ... | 32 | 16 | 32 | — | — | — | 4,616 |
| 4 | Lingadahalli ... | 28 | 9 | 28 | — | — | — | 9,346 |
| 5 | Sivane ... ... | 48 | 10 | 45 | — | 3 | — | 15,496 |
| 6 | Tarikere ... ... | 36 | 5 | 34 | — | 2 | — | 13,142 |
| | Total ... | 240 | 61 | 234 | — | 6 | — | 72,352 |

*Principal places, with population.*—Tarikere, 7,056; Ajjampur 2,890; Sivane, 1,806; Lakvalli, 1,358; Kudlur, 1,250; Lingadahalli, 1,228; Durvigere, 1,015; Hunasagaṭṭa, 1,007.

This taluq is partly hilly and partly plain, the soil and climate being as varied as the configuration. Along the north are the Ubráni hills, which throw out short spurs into the plains. These were at one time covered with thick bamboo jungle. Around Ajjampur and up to the eastern border black cotton soil prevails, on which fine crops of wheat, cotton, Bengal gram, great millet, etc., are raised. All this portion of the taluq is perfectly bare of trees, and there is a good deal of saline efflorescence. In other portions red, sandy and gravelly soils are found, on which rági and different kinds of pulse are cultivated. The western portions of the taluq are semi-Malnád.

A portion of the Bábá Budan range enters the taluq in the south-west, the slopes of which are covered with heavy forest, partially cleared for coffee plantations. Fine iron ore is much worked in the Ubráni hills, and those at Lingadahalli at the foot of the Bábá Budans. In the hills near Ajjampur very extensive old gold workings have been discovered, and gold-mining is being revived under European superintendence by the Kadur-Mysore Company.

During the period of the Hoysala sovereignty the greater part of the taluq appears to have formed a principality, whose chief seat was at Kátur, a village near Tarikere. It was subsequently subdued by the Muhammadan forces which took Dorasamudra in the first part of the 14th century, but the line of chiefs seems to have been restored to power under the Vijayanagar sovereigns. After the fall of Vijayanagar, the pálegars of Basvapatna, being driven south by the invasions of the Bijapur army, gained possession of the country and founded Tarikere, from which they subsequently took their name. The territory eventually became subject to the Mughal government established at Sira, and so passed into the possession of Haidar Ali in 1761, and became a part of Mysore.

The revenue settlement was introduced in 1877. The area of the taluq at that time was distributed as follows :—

| | |
|---|---|
| Culturable (dry, 158,829; wet, 9,404; garden, 2,547) ... ... | 170,780 |
| Unculturable (roads, village sites, &c.) ... ... ... ... | 152,420 |
| Total acres ... ... ... | 323,200 |

The unoccupied area was 67,813 acres. The total revenue demand for 1891–2 (15 months) was Rs. 1,80,673, and for 1892–3 it was Rs. 2,02,937.

The following was the average rainfall at Tarikere for 26 years (1870–95), and at the other stations for three years (1893–5) :—

| | Jan. | Feb. | Mar. | April | May | June | July | Aug. | Sept. | Oct. | Nov. | Dec. | Year. |
|---|---|---|---|---|---|---|---|---|---|---|---|---|---|
| Tarikere ... | 0·16 | 0·12 | 0·28 | 0·87 | 2·63 | 3·39 | 6·44 | 3·60 | 3·02 | 5·00 | 1·88 | 0·46 ... | 27·85 |
| Ajjampur... | — | — | — | 2·73 | 2·98 | 3·17 | 3·47 | 2·40 | 2·94 | 2·95 | 0·85 | — ... | 21·49 |
| Sivane ... | — | — | — | ·2·70 | 2·21 | 7·57 | 2·87 | 1·70 | 2·34 | 3·33 | 1·01 | 0·08 .. | 23·81 |

Another register for 16 years makes the average annual rainfall at Tarikere 31·88.

The Bangalore-Poona railway runs near the south-east boundary, with stations at Ajjampur and Shivani. A branch from Birur is being made through Tarikere to Shimoga. The Bangalore-Shimoga road runs through Tarikere, whence there are roads west through Lakvalli to the Agumbi Ghat, east through Ajjampur to Hosdurga, and south along the eastern face of the Bábá Budans to Santaveri and Chikmagalur, as well as over the summit near Kalhatti. From Lingadahalli there is a road to Birur railway station, and from Santaveri a short road to Kalhatti bungalow and the summit of the mountains.

**Tarikere.**—A town, situated in 13° 42′ N. lat., 75° 52′ E. long., on the Birur-Shimoga railway and the Bangalore-Shimoga road, 35 miles north of Chikmagalur. Head-quarters of the Tarikere taluq, and a municipality.

| Population in 1891. | Males. | Females. | Total. |
|---|---|---|---|
| Hindus ... ... ... ... ... | 2,766 | 2,864 | 5,630 |
| Muhammadans ... ... ... ... | 696 | 647 | 1,343 |
| Jains ... ... ... ... ... | 25 | 1 | 26 |
| Christians ... ... ... ... | 27 | 30 | 57 |
| Total ... ... ... | 3,514 | 3,542 | 7,056 |

Tarikere appears to have had its origin in the town of Kátur, to the north-west,[1] founded at the end of the 12th century by one of the Hoysala kings, in obedience to the commands of the goddess Rénuka-paramésvari, who appeared to him in a vision. The town and neighbouring territory were bestowed, it is said, on a chief named Kanehada arasu. A descendant of his, named Káma Chakresvara Ráya, fortified Kámandurga on the Bábá Budans. The territory was afterwards subdued by Bukka Raya of Vijayanagar, and given to one of his Danáyaks, or generals. The latter was succeeded at his death by Sáluva Narsinga Raya, who transferred it to his brother Kártika Ráya, and retired to Benkipur. Krishna Ráya, the son of Kártika Ráya, constructed many useful irrigation works during his reign, among others the Tarikere-kaṭṭe-hole. His son-in-law, Hale Ráma Ráya, followed, in whose time the territory was subdued by the Bijapur army.

The territory of Kátur is said to have been subsequently bestowed upon Sarja Hanumappa Náyak, pálegar of Basvapatna, by the Mughals. A descendant of the same name, while hunting, saw a hare turn upon the hounds, and erected on the spot where this occurred the fort and town of Tarikere, so named from the number of *tari* trees (*mimosa catechu*) which grew there. The date assigned for this event is 1569. This line of chiefs, since known as the Tarikere pálegars, continued in power till subdued in 1761 by Haidar Ali, who annexed the territory to Mysore, granting the chief a maintenance allowance. The representative of the house took a leading part in the rebellion of 1830, which ended in the assumption of the government by the British. His son continued at large, creating disturbances, till 1834, when he was seized and hanged.

| Municipal Funds. | 1891–2. | 1892–3. | 1893–4. | 1894–5. | 1895–6. |
|---|---|---|---|---|---|
| Income ... ... ... | 4,485 | 4,311 | 5,134 | 6,093 | 6,925 |
| Expenditure... ... ... | 6,875 | 4,965 | 5,881 | 4,580 | 6,432 |

**Tunga.**—A river which rises in the same spot as the sister stream of the Bhadra—namely, at Gangámúla, in the Varáha peak of the Western Ghats, in the south-western angle of the Koppa taluq. Its

[1] In confirmation of this it may be stated that one of the standards for garden measurement in the western portion of the taluq, down to so late as 1849, was the *Hanuman áдya*, the measure of the left foot of the image of Hanuman at Hire Kátúr. Of such feet 18 were computed to be equal to one *káti*, and 100 kátis = 4,987 yards.

general course is north-east, but at Baggunji it turns to the north-west and keeps that direction to near Tirthahalli. Thence, with a sudden bend to the north-east, it takes its course past the town of Shimoga, and flows on to the point of confluence with the Bhadra at Kúdali; from which point commences the united stream of the Tungabhadra.

**Vastara.**—A village in Chikmagalur taluq, on the Chikmagalur-Mudgere road, 6 miles south-west of the kasba. Till 1875 it was the head-quarters of a taluq named after itself. Population, 882.

It is situated at the entrance to the Malnád country. The name is said to be a corruption of *vasu-dara*, land bestowed, that is, as an endowment. The foundation of the town is due to a Sántarasa, one of the Humcha kings, and it was subsequently held by their descendants the Pándya rulers of Sisugali and the Bairasa Wodeyars of Karkala. The chiefs of Balam and of Ikkéri in turn possessed it. Though taken by the Mysore army in 1690, it was one of the places restored to Ikkéri by the treaty of 1694. The conquest of Bednur by Haidar Ali in 1763 annexed it to Mysore.

**Vedavati** or **Haggari.**—A river which, after a lengthened course, principally through the Chitaldroog District, flows into the Tungabhadra in the Bellary District. It is formed by the union of two streams, the *Veda* and the *Avati*, which spring from the eastern side of the Bábá Budan mountains. The immediate source of the Veda is the Gauri halla, which, rising near Mulainagiri, flows eastwards, and is embanked at a gorge near Sakunagiri, expanding into the Ayyankere. The stream, on leaving this tank, takes the name of the Veda, and, skirting the town of Sakkarepatna, flows north-east to Kadur. The Avati also rises near Mulainagiri, and after forming the Madaga tank, continues east to Kadur. The two streams unite at Tangli, 3 miles south-east of Kadur, and form the Vedavati, which shortly enters the Chitaldroog District.

**Yedehalli.**—A town in Koppa taluq, 14 miles north-east of the kasba, on the Tarikere-Agumbi road. Till 1882 it was the head-quarters of the Lakvalli taluq, and then till 1897 the head-quarters of the Yedehalli sub-taluq attached to Koppa taluq. It is a municipality.

| Population in 1891. | Males. | Females. | Total. |
|---|---|---|---|
| Hindus (with 3 Jains) ... ... ... | 701 | 727 | 1,428 |
| Muhammadans ... ... ... ... | 199 | 208 | 407 |
| Christians ... ... ... ... | 1 | 1 | 2 |
| Total ... ... ... | 901 | 936 | 1,837 |

Yedehalli is said to be so called because there was formerly a S'iváchára maṭha here, at which food (*yeḍe*) was given every day to travellers. The town consists of two portions, the fort and the petta, which are a considerable distance apart. At the end of the 16th century it belonged to the pálegars of Tarikere, and afterwards fell into the hands of the Ikkéri chiefs. It is the residence of several wealthy merchants, being an entrepôt for the produce of the Malnád and a place of considerable traffic between the east and west of the country.

| Municipal Funds. | 1891-2. | 1892-3. | 1893-4. | 1894-5. | 1895-6. |
|---|---|---|---|---|---|
| Income ... ... ... | 858 | 845 | 1,030 | 737 | 1,224 |
| Expenditure ... ... | 1,496 | 1,142 | 1,118 | 563 | 1,422 |

SHIMOGA DISTRICT
SCALE 8 MILES TO AN INCH
B—Travellers' Bungalow. L—Inspection Lodge. S—Railway Station.
DHARWAR
CHITALDROOG
KADUR
KANARA
RANIBENNUR
HARIHAR
DAVANGERE
UCHANGIDURGA
BANAVASI
MUDI
SORAB
SIRALKOPPA
MASUR
SIDDAPUR
BILGI
SHIKARPUR
HONNALI
BELAGUTTI
NYAMTI
SAGAR
KUMSI
HARANHALLI
SHIMOGA
HOLEHONNUR
CHANNAGIRI
BENKIPUR
TARIKERE
AJAMPUR
BIRUR
KOLLURKATTE
NAGAR
TIRTHAHALLI
SHANKARANARAYANA
BASRUR
KUNDAPUR
KOTESWAR
SHIRUR
BAIDUR
UPPUNDA
KALTOD
KOPPA
HARIHARPUR
SRINGERI
YEDEHALLI

# SHIMOGA DISTRICT

## GENERAL DESCRIPTION

*Situation.*—A District in the north-west; situated between 13° 28′ and 14° 38′ north latitude, and between 74° 41′ and 76° 9′ east longitude. Its greatest length is 95 miles from east to west. From north to south the longest line is 80 miles.

*Area.*—Its area is computed at 4,009 square miles; of which 1,132 square miles are under cultivation, and 2,463 square miles unculturable and waste.

*Boundaries.*—It is bounded on the east and south by the Chitaldroog and Kadur Districts respectively, on the north by Dharwar, and on the north west by North Kanara, both belonging to the Bombay Presidency, and on the west by South Kanara of the Madras Presidency.

*Divisions.*—The Ságar Sub-Division, formed in 1891, comprises the Sorab, Ságar and Nagar taluqs. The whole District consists of the following taluqs. Kumsi is a sub-taluq under Shimoga taluq.

| No. | Taluq. | Area, sq. miles. | No. of Hoblis. | No. of Villages or Towns. | Population. | Per sq. mile. |
|---|---|---|---|---|---|---|
| 1 | Channagiri ... ... | 465 | 5 | 243 | 74,218 | 159·60 |
| 2 | Honnáli ... ... ... | 329 | 3 | 167 | 63,527 | 193·09 |
| 3 | Nagar ... ... ... | 529 | 6 | 204 | 42,841 | 80·98 |
| 4 | Ságar ... ... ... | 666 | 6 | 246 | 58,999 | 88·58 |
| 5 | Shikárpur ... ... | 428 | 6 | 197 | 64,404 | 150·47 |
| 6 | Shimoga ... ... ... | 659 | 7 | 393 | 94,716 | 143·72 |
| 7 | Sorab ... ... ... | 461 | 6 | 306 | 70,047 | 151·94 |
| 8 | Tírthahalli ... ... | 472 | 5 | 244 | 59,229 | 125·48 |
| | Total ... | 4,009 | 44 | 2,000 | 527,981 | 131·69 |

**Physical features.**—A line drawn from Talguppa to Anantapur and thence to the Ghats through Masarur and Kavaledurga, with one from this last point to Kodachádri Parvata, would nearly correspond with the watersheds which separate the main lines of drainage. All the streams to the south, east and north of the line flow to the Tungabhadra; those on the west to the Sharavati, and those on the south-west to the Gargita. The main part of the District therefore consists of the western slopes of the upper Tungabhadra valley.

This river is formed by the union, at Kudali, of the Tunga and the Bhadra, of which the former runs most of its course within this District, in a north-easterly direction. From the point of confluence of the united streams the river runs north to the frontier, which it follows north-eastwards to beyond Harihara, receiving on the left bank the Choradi and on the right the Haridra. Thence, leaving the Mysore, it runs north, separating Madras from Bombay until joined on the left by the Varada, when again turning north-east, it marks the boundary between Madras and the Nizam's dominions, and receiving on the right the Haggari or Vedavati, flows past Hampe, the site of the ancient cities of Kishkindha, Anegundi and Vijayanagar, into the Krishna beyond Karnul.

The Sharavati rises near Kavaledurga and, uniting with the Haridravati on the right, pursues a north-west course to the frontier. Thence turning west it hurls itself down the Ghats by the Jóg or far-famed Falls of Gersoppa, a sheer descent of over 900 feet, and runs into the sea at Honavar (Honore).

The streams rising between Kodachádri Parvata and Kavaledurga flow west or south-west into the sea at Kundapur, the principal one being the Gargita, which descends to S. Kanara from the head of the Haidar Ghar Ghat.

The western side of the District, resting upon the Ghats, is very mountainous and covered with magnificent forest, the highest point being the Kodachádri Parvata, a fine peak situated 10 miles north-west of Nagar. Its elevation is 4,411 feet above the level of the sea. Govardhangiri in Ságar, and Chandragutti in Sorab, are also conspicuous hills, the height of the latter being 2,794 feet.

The interior of the District is crossed at the central watershed by a chain of hills running from Mandagadde on the Tunga northwards, between Anantapur and Kumsi, towards Sorab, and by a range from Atavádi westwards through Ikkéri to Tálguppa. On the east are two lines of low, stony hills stretching from the south of Channagiri to the frontier, one following the course of the Tungabhadra northwards, the other crossing that river near Hole Honnur and passing near Shikarpur. The south-west around Nagar and Kavaledurga is full of hills.

The general elevation of the District along the watershed is about 2,100 feet above sea level, falling to 1,900 in the east and west. The height of Anantapur has been determined as 2,101 feet; east of which, Shimoga is 1,899 and Benkipur 1,872; while on the west, Tálguppa is

1,956, Ságar 1,973, Kollur Katte 1,928, Nagar 1,887, and Haidarghar 1,896. The head of the chasm at the Falls of Gersoppa is 1,670 feet.

The greater part of the District is reckoned as Malnáḍ or hill country, which, roughly speaking, may be described as occupying all to the west of a line drawn from Shikarpur to Gajanur; the eastern portion being Maidán or Bailu síme, open country. The whole of the first-named region presents a range of scenery abounding with every charm of tropical forests and mountain wilds. Trees of the largest size stand thickly together over miles of unbroken ranks, their giant trunks entwined with creepers of python dimensions, their massive arms decked with a thousand bright blossoming orchids. Birds of rare plumage flit from bough to bough. From the thick woods, which abruptly terminate on verdant swards, bison issue forth in the early morn and afternoon to browse on the rich herbage, while large herds of elk pass rapidly across the hillsides. Packs of wild dogs cross the path, hunting in company, and the warning boom of the great *langur* monkey is heard from the lofty trees. The bamboo forest has beauties of its own, whether waving in immense fronds of delicate green foliage, or whitening with its rice-like grain. Lively gardens of the elegant areca palm, for which Nagar is famous; the *káns* of Sorab, with the rich hues of wild cinnamon and the sombre green of the jack, intermingled with the truncated leaf of the *bagni* palm, and the waving bunches of the pepper vine; the magnificent avenues of the *dhúpa* tree in Ságar:—all unite to vary the attractions of a region replete with every natural beauty. The view from the head of the descent to the Falls of Gersoppa is probably one of the choicest bits of scenery in the world.

The features of the open country are tame in comparison with those of the woodland tracts, but there is much that is picturesque in the fertile taluq of Channagiri with its large Súḷekere lake, the finest reservoir with one exception in the south of India.

**Rocks.**—Laterite is abundantly found and quarried in the western taluqs. The square blocks form the most common building material, being used not only for dwelling-houses, but for bridges and other public erections. Broken up it forms metalling for roads.

*Minerals.*—Iron ore is extracted in some parts. On the summit of the Ghats stones are frequently found possessing magnetic properties, as at Kodachádri. Gold is widely diffused and a broad auriferous tract extends throughout the eastern half of the District. Gold-mining under European direction has been commenced in the Honnáli gold-field and south of Benkipur on the Bhadra.

**Soil.**—The general substratum of laterite in the western taluqs, wherever it approaches the surface, checks vegetation. The soil in the rice valleys, so characteristic of the Malnáḍ, is loose and sandy, while that of garden lands is stiff and clayey. The richest soil of the District is in the north-east, from the Súlekere northwards. The black soil here prevails, as also around Nyámti and Belgutti in Honnáli taluq.

**Climate.**—Approaching as it does at one point within 8 miles of the sea, and extending eastwards nearly 100 miles, the District presents much variety of climate in different parts. For about 25 miles from the Ghats the south-west monsoon is felt in full force, the annual fall of rain at Nagar being from 150 to 170 inches. East of this line, however, the quantity rapidly diminishes, being at Shimoga about 31, and at Channagiri only about 25, or less. At Shimoga, which is 40 miles from the nearest Ghats, the south-west monsoon often produces nothing more than driving clouds with a strong steady breeze and moist cool atmosphere, with occasional drizzle and a few days of moderately heavy rain. East of the junction of the Tunga and Bhadra, the wind blows during the height of the monsoon with much force, but the clouds which are carried along with it rarely break. The heaviest rains on this side are in May and October, and come in thunder-storms from the eastward. The order of the seasons has been observed as follows by Mr. Stokes:—

"In the middle of March, or a little before the commencement of the Hindu year, the weather becomes close and hot, the prevailing wind from the west being frequently interrupted by calms. In the course of the next fifteen days thunder-showers fall, which are sometimes very violent, and the first or second is usually a hail-storm, the hailstones varying from the size of a musket-ball to that of a pigeon's egg. These occasional showers continue through the month of April, but the heat is relieved on the western side of the District by the sea-breeze, which is felt distinctly at Shimoga. In May the weather gets still more uncertain, and before the close of the month one or more violent squalls occur, accompanied with heavy rain. About the end of the first week in June the south-west monsoon generally sets in and blows almost without intermission until the end of July or middle of August. A break then ensues, which lasts for 15 or 20 days, usually with a clear sky and little wind or rain. The monsoon, however, returns again, sometimes with much force, and continues till the end of September, when the weather again becomes unsettled, and thunder-storms from the east alternate with hot sunshine, till about the 10th of October, soon after which the north-east monsoon sets in. A dry north-east wind, mostly with a clear sky, blows daily from nine o'clock A.M. till sunset; sometimes with great violence. The rapidity with which evaporation goes on during this wind is astonishing. The roads which have been broken up into deep quagmires become in a few days dusty, and not a vestige is left of the numerous pools which had been visible all over the country. The water in the paddy fields is dried up, and the crops, till then green, become immediately dry. At this time the nights are calm and very clear, and a heavy dew falls. The mornings are very cool and sometimes foggy. The cold increases till about the 10th of January, and from the middle of December till the end of January the thermometer at daylight is not often more than 50°; the cold then moderates, and the sea-breeze is sometimes felt in the evening and at night, and commonly brings with it a heavy fog, which in the Malnád is so thick in the morning that objects cannot be seen at the distance of 10 yards. It seldom clears till past nine o'clock.

*Temperature.*—The following are given as the results of thermometric observations at Shimoga in 1892, the latest procurable:—

| — | Mean. Max. | Mean. Min. | Highest Reading. | Lowest Reading. |
|---|---|---|---|---|
| May ... ... | 92·45 | 56·23 | 98 | 53 |
| July ... ... | 84·71 | 55·94 | 92 | 55 |
| December ... | 83·85 | 54·40 | 85 | 49 |

The average temperature in the preceding years was:—

| | 9 A.M. | 3 P.M. | | 9 A.M. | 3 P.M. |
|---|---|---|---|---|---|
| 1890 ... | 74·98 ... | 78·73 | 1891 ... | 69·83 ... | 78·20 |

*Rainfall.*—The average annual rainfall at Shimoga, calculated on the observations recorded for 26 years (1870–95) is 34·50 inches, or, according to another register for 14 years, 36·99 inches. As previously stated, this rate is very greatly exceeded in the Malnád districts according to their greater or less proximity to the Ghats. The monthly average is given under each taluq, but the average annual rate at other taluq and sub-taluq stations was as follows:—

| | | | |
|---|---|---|---|
| Channagiri ... ... ... | 25·90 or 26·34 | Ságar ... ... ... | 71 06 or 69·71 |
| Honnáli ... ... ... | 22·69 „ 22·99 | Shikárpur ... ... | 30·13 „ 31·33 |
| Kumsi ... ... ... | 38·94 | Sorab ... ... .. | 56·20 „ 57·48 |
| Nagar ... ... .. | 184·43 „ 192·59 | Tirthahalli ... ... | 116·10 „ 110·35 |

The actual annual fall at Shimoga has been recorded as below:—

| | In.c. | | In.c. | | In.c. | | In.c. |
|---|---|---|---|---|---|---|---|
| 1837 ... | 27·4 | 1846 ... | 32·7 | 1855 ... | 15·6 | 1864 ... | 34·7 |
| 1838 ... | 15·8 | 1847 ... | 31·3 | 1856 ... | 24·7 | 1865 .. | 34·1 |
| 1839 ... | 31 | 1848 ... | 33·6 | 1857 ... | 22·1 | 1866 ... | 36·3 |
| 1840 ... | 23·9 | 1849 ... | 39·5 | 1858 ... | 33·4 | 1867 ... | — |
| 1841 ... | 23·8 | 1850 ... | 38·5 | 1859 ... | 31·8 | 1868 ... | 34·8 |
| 1842 ... | 29 | 1851 ... | 20·3 | 1860 ... | 20·5 | 1869 ... | 26·27 |
| 1843 ... | 15·3 | 1852 ... | 42·8 | 1861 ... | 25·8 | 1870 ... | 42·74 |
| 1844 ... | 30·7 | 1853 ... | 29·4 | 1862 ... | 24·7 | 1871 ... | 35·28 |
| 1845 ... | 24·1 | 1854 ... | 26·1 | 1863 ... | 31·3 | 1872 ... | 64·46 |

| | In.c. | | In.c | | In.c. | | In.c. |
|---|---|---|---|---|---|---|---|
| 1873 ... | 29·12 | 1884 ... | 31·82 | 1888 ... | 38·40 | 1892 ... | 26·51 |
| 1874 . | 39·89 | 1885 ... | 39·60 | 1889 ... | 40·70 | 1893 ... | 34·10 |
| | | 1886 ... | 38·30 | 1890 ... | 35·05 | 1894 . | 26·07 |
| 1882 ... | 56·57 | 1887 ... | 36·64 | 1891 ... | 29·80 | 1895 ... | 37·30 |
| 1883 .. | 47·57 | | | | | | |

**Vegetation.**[1]—The Western Ghats and the country immediately below them are covered with magnificent evergreen forest. Many of the hills are heavily wooded up to their summits. In some parts the undergrowth is dense, elsewhere the forest is open, and on all sides trees with clear stems to the first branch of from 80 to 100 feet meet the eye. The great bulk of these trees can scarcely be realized except by actual measurement. The more valuable kinds are poon, wild jack, ebony, somé, heigni, erool, dúpada mara, the large dévadáram, gamboge and a species of cedar. The wealth of timber in these forests is almost entirely unproductive, owing to the inaccessible nature of the country.

More to the east, as far as a line from Anavatti to midway between Shikárpur and Honnáli and thence to Sakrebail, is a rich and productive belt of vegetation, including the káns of Sorab, areca palm and cardamom gard. , and the rich rice-flats of Ságar, Nagar and Tirthahalli. Within this tract are the State and District forests. The more important trees are teak, black wood, honne, matti, sampaji, arsentéga, alale, biridi, bilvára, bági, ságade or chendála, jambe, dindiga, hulvati or námadári, húnal and mashi, jani, kadaga, kuli, kaltéka, nelli, navaládi, nandi, pachári, shi-anvige, tapasi, and kendatsal.

Teak, not of the largest size, is found in Shikárpur, Kumsi and Sakrebail. Bamboo is abundant everywhere. Sandal is most plentiful in Sorab, Ságar and Nagar taluqs. It also grows in parts of Shimoga and Shikárpur, and a little in Channagiri and Honnáli.

The taluq of Sorab abounds with káns, many of which are cultivated with pepper vines, and sometimes coffee. The sago palm (*caryota urens*) is also much grown for the sake of its toddy. These káns are apparently the remains of the old forests, which appear once to have stretched as far east as Anavatti. At the present day at Anavatti itself there is no wood, and the surrounding country is clothed with either scrub jungle or small deciduous forest, generally pentapterous. Káns are found also in Ságar, Nagar, and the other Malnád taluqs, but those in Sorab are, from their number, situation and accessibility, the most valuable.

The Ságar taluq is not so thickly wooded as that of Sorab, except along the Ghats. The adjoining taluq of Nagar possesses heavy forests

[1] Compiled from the Annual Report of the Forest Department.

in the west (though several of the hills are cleared), but the wood grows generally in large káns, which are scattered unequally over the taluq. Going south to Tirthahalli much fine timber is found to the north of the Tunga, while to the south of the river the country is comparatively open. From Mandagadde in this taluq is a long stretch of wooded country, which runs north *viâ* Hannigeri through portions of the Shimoga taluq to the confines of Sorab and Ságar. In this strip there is good teak, much fine second-class timber, and a vast quantity of *inga xylocarpa*, which is largely used for making charcoal for the iron mines that abound near Masrúr, Shrigeri and other places in Anantapur and Shimoga.

Between Shikárpur and Kumsi is a belt of jungle, parts of which have been placed on the State forest lists. In the eastern portions of Shikárpur and Honnáli taluqs there is comparatively little wood. Between Shikárpur and Sorab is a quantity of small pentapterous jungle near Udagani and Sirálkoppa, which only requires conservation to grow up into a valuable second-class forest.

The Honnáli taluq is poorly wooded. Near Malébennúr, in the low hills to the east of the Tungabhadra, are the remains of old jungles, which apparently yielded small timber and much fuel. In Channagiri there is very little wood; in the south-west of the taluq is a small jungle.

*Forests.*—The reserved or State Forests occupy an area of 355 square miles, according to the following detailed statement:—

| Name. | Sq. miles. | Name. | Sq. miles. |
|---|---|---|---|
| Shankargudda, Butanbail | 37 | Are Telgadde | 1 |
| | | Karadi-betta | 30 |
| Sakrabail | 23 | Belandur | 25 |
| Male Bennur | 11 | Chandrakal | 11 |
| Telagadde | 5 | Gangavansara | 25 |
| Kukvada Ubrani | 70 | Chandragatti | 6 |
| Chorna Yedehalli | 10 | Bettadakurli | 3 |
| Masarur | 10 | Kavadi | 2 |
| Kumsi | 20 | Malandur | 11 |
| Kunchinhalli | 6 | Umblibail, Hunsekatte | 16 |
| Togarsi | 1 | | |
| Kavali | 1 | Aldhara | 17 |
| Basava Nandihalli | 3 | Purdhai | 10 |

*Plantations.*—There are 9 Forest plantations, occupying an area of 873 acres; and 2 Revenue plantations, covering 411 acres. *Avenue trees* have been planted on 611 miles of public road, giving a total of 126,654. *Groves* or topes number 261, containing 9,045 trees.

**Cultivation.**—Rice is the principal cultivated product of the District, of which more than 60 kinds are enumerated. Areca-nut is extensively grown in Nagar, Ságar and Tirthahalli, that of the first-named place being considered superior to any in the Province. Sugar-cane is largely reared in Shikárpur. Honnáli chiefly produces different kinds of dry grains as well as cotton. Pepper grows wild in the forests of Nagar and Sorab, while cardamoms are produced in the jungles about Agumbi, though not so good as those raised in areca gardens.

The sowing of rice commences in April and continues on till well in July. Reaping commences in November, and by the end of February or so is concluded. By the close of March, or a little after, the grain is threshed, and by the close of April or May is ready for the market.

The following are the names of the different kinds grown in the District:—

| | | |
|---|---|---|
| Sakaláti sanna | Chekkali bhatta | Varnagilli bhatta |
| Dásar ,, | Jangali ,, | Chale ,, |
| Nerlagiri ,, | Hasar meluge bhatta | Nerogoli ,, |
| Putti ,, | Kare dádi ,, | Haluganna ,, |
| Bili ,, | Hunse huvina ,, | Kamariganna bhatta |
| Kempu ,, | Bidane bija ,, | Kempu dádi banna sále |
| Marutra ,, | Kalave ,, | Bili ,, |
| Nirlagiri ,, | Togarigina ,, | Nirada ,, |
| Gauri ,, | Siddasále ,, | Billikana hegge |
| Bhangár kaddi bhatta | Sómasáli ,, | Juddi ,, |
| Mentyasále ,, | Jírige sáli ,, | Mardara ,, |
| Kesari ,, | Motalingana ,, | Putti ,, |
| Hasar kesari ,, | Hasibilevina ,, | Sampige dála |
| Kempu ,, ,, | Bili hasadi ,, | Betta kendála |
| Hanesále ,, | Mara hasadi ,, | Bále suli |
| Keruvina ,, | Kugalli ,, | Hunkal mardiga |
| Ambe mori ,, | Kírvannana ,, | Kavade doddiga |
| Hasadi ,, | Hasangana ,, | Kambu tige |
| Haralu honisana ,, | Kodde ,, | Pusta manjari |
| Hudri ,, ,, | Kurni ,, | Bili mundakara |
| Jolasina ,, | Gúgigonda ,, | Kempu ,, |

Next to rice the most important wet crop is sugar-cane, of which the principal varieties cultivated are ***kiri kabbu***, ***mara kabbu***, ***rastali***, and ***pattapatti*** or ***rám rastali***. Planting operations commence in January and continue till June. The crop takes a twelvemonth or more to arrive at maturity, when it is cut and for the most part converted into jaggory, which is ready for the market about July of the year following that in which the cane was put down.

The coffee zone of the District is estimated to extend over 1,000 square miles, but a considerable portion of this area is not of the most favourable description. The number of plantations is 250, of which only half-a-dozen belong to Europeans. The area actually under coffee is 979 acres, distributed in the following taluqs:—Nagar, 165; Ságar, 5; Shimoga, 129; Tirthahalli, 680.

In 1861 an effort was made to stimulate the production of cotton, by the establishment in convenient localities of cotton gins manufactured in a workshop set up at Shimoga, and by the distribution of

American and Egyptian seed. But the attempt, owing to various causes, among others unfavourable seasons and the ravages of insects, to which the foreign plants seemed more particularly liable, was abandoned after a trial for two years.

*Channels.*—There are 165 anicuts on the rivers of the District and their feeders, from which are drawn channels for irrigation, having an aggregate length of 168 miles 1,007 yards. The following are the particulars:—

| Feeders of what Stream. | No. of Anicuts. | Length of Channels. |
|---|---|---|
| Sharavati ... ... ... ... ... ... | 70 | m. 26 y. 102 |
| Varada... ... ... ... ... ... ... | 51 | 40 328 |
| Choradi ... ... ... ... ... ... | 12 | 33 780 |
| Tunga ... ... ... ... ... ... ... | 29 | 68 1,557 |
| Tungabhadra ... ... ... ... ... ... | 3 | ... |

*Acreage under Crops.*—The number of acres cultivated with the principal crops in 1892 was:—Rice, 202,422; wheat, 525; other food grains, 315,243; oil seeds, 3,750; sugar-cane, 7,920; cotton, 1,633; fibres, 340; tobacco, 290; coffee, 707; vegetables, 2,400; cocoa-nut and areca nut, 18,859.

*Crops.*—The following list shows the quantity and value of each article of produce in the District, together with the quantity and value exported and imported in one year:—

| Kannada. | Botanical. | English. | Produced in the District. | | Exported. | | Imported. | |
|---|---|---|---|---|---|---|---|---|
| | | | Quantity. | Value. | Quantity. | Value. | Quantity. | Value. |
| | | | Tons. | Rs. | Tons. | Rs. | Tons. | Rs. |
| CEREALS. | | | | | | | | |
| Bhatta ... ... | Oryza sativa ... ... | Rice ... ... ... | 144,772 | 50,67,020 | 44,000 | 15,40,000 | — | — |
| Gódhi ... ... | Triticum aristatum ... | Wheat ... ... | 117½ | 10,855 | — | — | 100 | 28,000 |
| Háraka ... ... | Panicum semiverticillatum | — | 50 | 200 | — | — | — | — |
| Jola ... ... | Holcus sorghum ... ... | Great Millet ... | 20,000 | 7,00,000 | 10,000 | 3,50,000 | 1,000 | 28,000 |
| Navane ... ... | Panicum italicum ... | Italian millet ... | — | — | — | — | — | — |
| Rági ... ... | Eleusine corocana ... | Ragi ... ... ... | 35,340 | 9,89,520 | 4,000 | 1,12,000 | — | — |
| Sajje ... ... | Holcus spicatus ... ... | Spiked millet .. | 7 | 100 | — | — | — | — |
| Same ... ... | Panicum frumentaceum ... | Little millet ... | 400 | 5,000 | — | — | — | — |
| PULSES. | | | | | | | | |
| Alasandi ... | Dolichos catiang ... ... | — | 20 | 900 | — | — | 20 | 900 |
| Avare ... ... | Dolichos lablab ... ... | Cow gram ... ... | 188 | 11,698 | 85 | 5,288 | 103 | 6,400 |
| Hesaru ... ... | Phassolus mungo ... | Green gram ... ... | 82 | 7,654 | 53 | 4,946 | 145 | 13,530 |
| Hurali ... ... | Dolichos uniflorus ... | Horse gram ... ... | 734 | — | 157 | 8,792 | 710 | 39,760 |
| Kadale ... ... | Cicer arietinum ... ... | Bengal gram ... | 125 | 9,333 | 73 | 5,450 | 145 | 10,820 |
| Korasáni ... | — | Panic seed ... ... | 158 | 11,060 | 58 | 4,060 | 86 | 5,600 |
| Togari ... ... | Cajanus indicus .. ... | Pigeon pea, doll ... | 80 | 4,480 | 30 | 1,680 | 353 | 19,760 |
| Uddu ... ... | Phaseolus minimus ... | Black gram ... ... | 70 | 6,334 | 14 | 1,306 | 110 | 10,260 |
| OIL SEEDS. | | | | | | | | |
| Agase ... ... | Linium usitatissimum ... | Linseed ... ... | 7 | 250 | — | — | — | — |
| Dod haralu ... | Ricinus communis ... | Castor ... ... | 532 | 37,250 | 24 | 1,700 | 285 | 19,950 |
| Ollellu ... ... | Sesamum orientale ... | Gingelli ... ... | 125 | 14,080 | 33 | 3,470 | 66 | 7,390 |
| Pundi .. ... | Hibiscus cannabinus ... | Dekhan hemp ... | 7 | 50 | — | — | — | — |

| Kannada. | Botanical. | English. | Produced in the District. Quantity. | Produced in the District. Value. | Exported. Quantity. | Exported. Value. | Imported. Quantity. | Imported. Value. |
|---|---|---|---|---|---|---|---|---|
| | | | Tons. | Rs. | Tons. | Rs. | Tons. | Rs. |
| VEGETABLES. | | | | | | | | |
| Bellulli ... ... | Allium sativum ... ... | Garlic ... ... | 3 | 450 | — | — | 6 | 900 |
| Kotambari ... | Coriandrum sativum ... | Coriander ... ... | 2½ | 600 | — | — | 7 | 1,800 |
| Mensinakáyi ... | Capsicum annuum ... | Chilly ... ... | 150 | 18,160 | 62 | 7,440 | 230 | 27,600 |
| Mentya ... ... | Trigonella fœnum grœcum | Fenugreek ... ... | 4 | 740 | 1 | 186 | 4 | 740 |
| Nirulli ... ... | Allium cepa ... ... | Onion ... ... | 70 | 6,000 | 3 | 2,000 | 3 | 2,000 |
| Sásive ... ... | Sinapis dichotoma ... | Mustard ... ... | 210 | 8,000 | 150 | 2,500 | 3 | 200 |
| Sunti ... ... | Amomum zinziber ... | Dry ginger ... ... | 1 | 180 | — | — | 1 | 180 |
| MISCELLANEOUS. | | | | | | | | |
| Adike ... ... | Areca catechu ... .. | Areca-nut ... ... | 3,800 | 16,72,000 | 3,750 | 16,50,000 | — | — |
| Arsina ... ... | Curcuma longa ... ... | Turmeric ... .. | 7 | 2,100 | — | — | 14 | 4,200 |
| Bále hannu .. | Musa sapientum ... ... | Plantain ... No. | 3,200,600 | 6,500 | 150,000 | 2,130 | 100,000 | 700 |
| Ganja ... ... | Cannabis sativa ... ... | Hemp ... ... | — | — | — | — | — | — |
| Hatti ... ... | Gossypium indicum ... | Cotton ... ... | 171 | 15,372 | 33 | 2,970 | 15 | 1,300 |
| Hogesoppu ... | Nicotiana tabaccum ... | Tobacco ... ... | 9 | 3,600 | 5 | 2,000 | 100 | 40,000 |
| Hunase ... ... | Tamarindus indica ... | Tamarind ... ... | 255 | — | 1,700 | 1,36,000 | 2 | 160 |
| Kabbu ... ... | Saccharum officinale ... | Sugar-cane ... ... | 3,194 | 2,55,578 | — | — | — | — |
| Kobbari ... ... | — | Dry cocoa-nut ... | — | — | — | — | 105 | 27,300 |
| Menasu ... ... | Piper nigrum ... ... | Black pepper ... | 93 | 61,580 | 77 | 52,080 | — | — |
| Sige káyi ... | Mimosa abstergens ... | Soap-nut ... ... | 50 | 4,500 | 25 | 2,250 | — | — |
| Tengina káyi ... | Cocos nucifera ... ... | Cocoa-nut ... No. | 117,000 | 4,680 | 10,200 | 408 | 350,000 | 12,250 |
| Yelehambu .. | Piper betle ... ... | Betel leaf ... Bl. | 80,000,000 | 12,48,000 | 40,000,000 | 6,34,000 | 200,000 | 2,000 |
| Yélakki ... ... | Amomum repens ... | Cardamom ... ... | 23 | 77,640 | 21 | 72,376 | — | — |

Besides the articles contained in the above list, almost all the varieties of native vegetables are grown in gardens; where also are reared different kinds of fruits, such as mango, orange, lime, citron, guava, jack, jambalum, rose-apple, custard-apple, pine-apple, and rámphal (bull's heart).

The places to which the agricultural productions of the District are exported are:—Dharwar, Canara, Bellary, Birur, Chitaldroog, Harihar, Davangere, Koppa, Yedehalli, and Tarikere. The imports are chiefly from Dharwar, Canara, Coompta, Bellary, Kadur and Chitaldroog districts, Chiknayakanhalli, Mysore and Bangalore.

**Wild Animals.**—The larger game is most abundant in Ságar, where bison are common and elephants occasionally met with. Tigers, panthers and bears, which are the most feared by the people, are found principally to the west of Shimoga and in Shikárpur. In Channagiri their numbers have been very greatly reduced. The wild boar, so destructive to crops, abounds in Channagiri, Nagar and other parts. Sambar, chital and jungle sheep are general in the wooded tracts. Elephants latterly became so numerous and destructive to the crops that attempts were made to reduce their numbers by shooting. But this was found ineffectual, and Keddah operations were started, resulting in the capture of over 60 elephants at Sakrebail at the end of 1894.

*Birds.*—Wild geese, ducks, and teal frequent the tanks in Channagiri and Shimoga, while pea-fowl and jungle-fowl are to be had in the woods.

*Reptiles.*—The crocodile is to be found in some of the streams, especially in the Tunga and in the tanks communicating with it.

**Domestic Animals.**—The best cattle in the District are to be met with in Channagiri, where there are several large kávals belonging to the Amrit Mahal. About Shimoga the bullocks are a short, thickset breed, well adapted for agricultural purposes. The cows are very indifferent and give but little milk. Buffaloes are reared for the Malnad, the females being reserved for the dairy. These powerful animals are much used in Shikárpur for all purposes, some being of enormous size. Droves of pack bullocks are kept in Nagar for the transport of grain to the coast. They are small in size and poorly nourished. During the rainy season they are driven to the large pasture grounds of Ságar, the grass in which, though very coarse, is considered good for cattle, as they thrive here better than in any other part of the Malnad. Asses are numerous in the neighbourhood of Shimoga, where also a few sheep and goats of inferior breed are reared.

*Live Stock.*—The District in 1893 contained 420,876 cows and buffaloes, 2,094 horses and ponies, and 46,771 sheep and goats.

## HISTORY

There are four copper-plate inscriptions in the District claiming to be grants made by the Pándava emperor Janamejaya, son of Parikshit, of the Lunar line. This is the monarch to whom the Mahá Bhárata was originally recited. The grant at the Bhímankaṭṭe maṭha, near Tirthahalli, is dated in the year 89 of the Yudhishṭhira era, or B.C. 3012. The king is stated to be ruling at Kishkindha, and to have made the grant in the presence of the god Harihara, on the spot where his great-grandfather Yudhishṭhira had rested on the bank of the Tungabhadra.[1] The other three grants—Gauj, Kuppagadde and Begur, in Shikárpur taluq—profess to be grants made by Janamejaya to the officiating priests at the *sarpa yága*, or serpent sacrifice, which we have seen (under Kadur District) is supposed to have been performed at Hiremagalur. In these inscriptions the king is said to be ruling in Hastinapura, and to have made the grants in the presence of the god Harihara, at the confluence of the Tungabhadra and the Haridra. Their period, if genuine, would be about 3102 B.C., the commencement of the Kali-yuga, when Janamejaya is said to have reigned.[2] The date of the Ganj agrahára plates was calculated by the Astronomer Royal, Sir G. Airy, to be really 1521 A.D., but this seems to have arisen from a mistake in the details as given to him. A native astronomer worked out the date for me as 3066 B.C. But an inscription discovered by me, dated Saka 366 (A.D. 444), expressed in similar terms but attributed to a Chálukya king Vira Nonamba, has thrown some light on the question, and in publishing it[3] I examined the parallel passages and gave reasons for assigning all of them to about 1194 A.D. These and some other grants of a questionable character seem to be connected in some way with Henjeru (*see* Hemavati, Tumkur District) and Harihara (Chitaldroog District).

The legend of Jamadagni and Renuka (*see* Vol. I, p. 275) is also applied to this District, and at Chandragutti the latter is said to have performed the *sahágamana* and became a *sati*, leaving to her son Parasu Ráma the fulfilment of a curse upon Kártiviryárjuna, the murderer of her husband.

Another place of undoubted antiquity is the village of Kubattur, in

[1] Buchanan was shown a copy of an inscription at Banavási said to be dated in 168 of the Yudhishṭhira era.—*Jour.*, II, 362.

[2] In Prinsep's *Useful Tables* Janamejaya is assigned to 1300 B.C. on the authority of Prof. Wilson according to the *Bhágavata Purana.*—Thomas, *Ind. Antiquities*, II, 237.

[3] *Ind. Ant.*, VIII, 89; *Mys. Ins.*, lxx.

Sorab. Its former name was Kuntala-nagara, and tradition declares it to have been the capital of Chandrahása, the romantic story of whose life (*see* Vol. I, p. 283) occurs as an episode in the Mahá Bhárata,[1] and is related at length in the popular Kannada poem, the Jaimini Bhárata.

**Mauryas** and **Guptas.**—The earliest authentic history relating to the District is connected with the Mauryas. An inscription at Bandanikke (Shikárpur taluq) says that they ruled over Kuntala, and in this province some parts of the Shimoga District were certainly included. The discovery by me of Edicts of As'oka in Chitaldroog District has placed beyond doubt the fact of Maurya rule in the north of Mysore in the middle of the 3rd century B.C. We have also the statement in the *Mahawanso* that As'oka sent a *thero* to Banavási to proclaim the Buddhist faith. Another inscription, at Kupatur, says that "Nágakhanḍaka (Shikárpur taluq) was protected by the wise Chandra Gupta, an abode of the good usages of eminent Kshatriyas." In the Samudra Gupta inscription at Allahabad a list is given of kings in Southern India who submitted to him; among these, according to one reading of the passage,[2] was Oṭṭúraka, he of Oṭṭúr. Again, in the Mahákúṭa inscription near Bádámi, in Bijapur,[3] the Chálukya king Kírttivarma is said to have subdued (besides the Mauryas, Kadambas and Gangas) among others, a king of Vaṭṭúr. These are doubtless the same place, and may be identical with the Oṭṭúr to the north of Sorab.[4] In the Kadamba inscription at Tálgunda, too, described below, it is implied that the king Kákusthavarma gave his daughter in marriage to a Gupta king.

**Satavahanas.**—The next guides we have to the history of those early times are the inscription discovered by me at Malavalli (Shikárpur taluq), and one previously known at Banavási, which show that Háritiputra Sátakarni, an Ándrabhritya or S'átaváhana king, was ruling in those parts in about the 2nd century A.D.

**Kadambas.**—The Kadambas followed the S'átaváhanas, and are specially identified with Banavási, which was their original capital, and is mentioned in connection with As'oka in the 3rd century B.C., and by Ptolemy in the 2nd century A.D. The fine inscription discovered by me at Tálgunda (Shikárpur taluq) has given us for the first time what appears to be an authentic account of their origin and rise to power, free from the numerous legends that have become mixed up

[1] *See* translation in Talboys Wheeler's *Hist. Ind.*, I, 522.

[2] Fleet's *Early Gupta Kings*, p. 7 of Inscriptions.

[3] *Ind. Ant.*, XIX, 7.

[4] The oldest inscriptions now there are Ráshṭrakuṭa, of the 10th century.

with the subject. The information derived from this source, and all others available, has been summarized in the chapter on History in Vol. I.

**Gangas.**—While the Kadambas were exercising sovereignty in the west of the District, the Gangas were established in the east, and Mandali and Purali, on the river, close to Shimoga, one to the south and the other to the north, seem to have been places of importance under their rule. In the 4th century the Ganga king Mádhava II married the Kadamba king's sister; and in the 10th century the Banavase Twelve Thousand (the Shimoga District), with other provinces, was formally transferred to the Gangas by the Ráshtrakútas.

**Chalukyas.**—The Chálukyas, claiming to be of the Lunar line and former rulers of Ayódhyá, first crossed the Narmada or Nerbudda and appeared in the Dekkan in the person of Jayasimha, who, in the 4th century, defeated and destroyed the Ráshṭrakúta or Ratta prince. He was subsequently killed in a contest with the Pallava king, but his immediate successors subdued the whole of the Kuntala country, and by the 5th century had established their capital at Vátápi, now Bádámi, in the Bijapur district. In the 6th century they profess to have subdued the Kadambas and Gangas. The former became their feudatories, but the latter remained independent, though they must have retired from much of the Shimoga District. In the 7th century the Chálukyas separated into two families, the Eastern Chálukyas fixing their capital at Vengi, in the Godávari District, and the Western Chálukyas continuing to rule from Bádámi. The Shimoga District was under the latter, forming the Banavase Twelve Thousand province, with its seat of government at Belgámi (Shikárpur taluq). But in the 8th century the Western Chálukyas were overcome by the Ráshṭrakútas, and did not regain supremacy for two hundred years.

**Ráshtrakútas.**—This line of kings exercised a great influence over the Mysore country, especially in the north-west. Their capital was Mányakheta (Malkhed in the Nizam's dominions). They at first seized and imprisoned the Ganga king, and appointed their own viceroys to govern his territories. But eventually they reinstated him and entered into alliance with the Gangas. In the 10th century there were intermarriages between the families, and in return for Ganga help in defeating the Cholas, the Banavase Twelve Thousand, and other provinces were again added to the Ganga kingdom by the Ráshṭrakútas.

**Humcha.**—At the time of the commotions in the 7th century we find a Jain principality established at Pomburchcha or Hombucha (Humcha, in Nagar taluq), founded by Jinadatta, of the Solar race, and prince of the northern Mathura (on the Jumna, near Agra). This event is assigned to the year 500 of the fifth Kali yuga of the Jains, or 159 B.C. It seems more probable that the dynasty arose after the power of the Kadambas had been circumscribed by their superiors, the Chálukyas. Under the latter, Humcha kings, bearing successively the title of S'ántana or S'ántara Deva, can be traced by inscriptions in the 10th and 11th centuries. Jinadatta brought under his sway all the country as far as Kalasa (Kadur District); then, descending the Ghats to Sisila or Sisukali, finally established his capital at Karkala (S. Kanara), appointing lieutenants at Barkur, Bangádi, Múḍu Bidare and Mulki. The territories thus acquired yielded a revenue of 9 lakhs of pagodas above and 9 lakhs below the Ghats. His successors, under the general title of Bhairasu Wodeyar, continued in power down to the 16th century, being subordinate in turn to the Chálukyas, the Hoysalas, and the Vijayanagar kings, until their territories were subdued by the Keladi chiefs. The last of them, it is said, having no son, divided his territories among his seven daughters.

**Chalukyas.**—In 973 Taila retrieved the fortunes of his dynasty by destroying the Ráshṭrakúṭas, and restored the Chálukya empire, which became more powerful than under the early kings. The capital was now established at Kalyána (in the Nizam's Dominions). The Kalyána dynasty was at the zenith of its glory in the 11th century, under Vikramáditya, who established the Chálukya Vikrama era, used in subsequent inscriptions for nearly 200 years. During this period the Banavase Twelve Thousand was one of the most important provinces of their empire. In 1155 the Chálukya king was dethroned by his general, Bijjala Deva, of the Kalachurya line, a family which had been originally subdued at the same time as the Ráshṭrakúṭas or Rattas. The Chálukya power thus came to an end. The king retired to Banavási, and a feeble remnant of the state appears afterwards to have survived, first at Annigere, in Dharwar, and then in the Konkan, for about a century later. The name then disappears from history.

**Kalachuryas.**—The Kalachuryas possessed themselves of most of the Chálukya dominions, including the Banavase Twelve Thousand, and ruled at Kalyána for three generations, down to 1182. During the reign of Bijjala Deva, before mentioned, it was that the Lingáyit religion which prevails throughout the Kannada and Telugu countries arose, its founder, Basava, being his prime minister, whose sister, famed for her beauty, the king had married. No mention occurs after the 12th century of the Kalachuryas.

**Hoysalas.**—This brings us to the time when the Hoysalas of Dorasamudra (Halebid, Hassan District) had subdued the whole of

Mysore. Among the provinces ruled by Vishnuvarddhana of that line are included Banavási. Vira Ballála, advancing north of the Tungabhadra, came into collision with the Yádavas of Devagiri (Daulatabad). Between the forces of these two powers several engagements took place. At one time, in the 12th century, the Hoysalas advanced as far as the Krishna. A century later the Yádavas appear by inscriptions to have secured the allegiance of the Kadambas and gained possession of the northern parts of the District.

The Muhammadans now appear on the scene. Dévagiri was reduced in 1294 by Ala ud Din, and twenty years later the Yádava line was extinguished. Dorasamudra was sacked in 1310 by Káfúr, and totally destroyed in 1326, which terminated the Hoysala power.

**Vijayanagar.**—The Vijayanagar empire next arose, the foundation of that city on the Tungabhadra being assigned to the year 1336. Within its dominions were ultimately comprised all the countries south of the Krishna. Towards the close of its ascendancy were established the houses of the Keladi, Ikkeri or Bednur chiefs in the west, and the Basvapatna or Tarikere chiefs in the east.

*Keladi.*—The origin of the former, who were Lingáyits, is as follows. Bhadraiya, a Malava Gauda of Keladi, is said to have discovered a hidden treasure, which, after sacrificing two of his slaves, he took possession of, and therewith built a fort. He next visited the court of Vijayanagar and obtained from Sadás'iva Ráya, then ruling, a grant of the government of Barkur, Mangalur, and Chandragutti, with the title of Sadás'iva Náyak.[1] His successor transferred the capital to Ikkéri. Venkatappa Náyak threw off dependence on the fallen Vijayanagar sovereign, and in 1639, during the reign of Virabhadra Náyak, the capital was again removed and established at Bednur. Sivappa Náyak was a most able administrator, and conquered as far as Shimoga eastwards, with all Kanara westwards. He succeeded to the government in 1645, and is the most celebrated of the line, not only for the extent of his conquests, but for his politic regulations, elsewhere described. We have seen in the history of the Mysore, Hassan and Kadur Districts how he overran the province of Balam; also how he granted protection to Sri Ranga Ráya, the fugitive king of Vijayanagar, establishing him in a government at Belur and Sakkarepatna, and even adventuring to besiege Seringapatam in his behalf. Sivappa Náyak died in 1660, and the government continued in the same family till 1763, when Bednur was captured by Haidar Ali, and the District thus

[1] The Jain account is that the last of the Humcha kings became a Sivabhakta, taking the name of Gante Wodeyar; that he was the progenitor of the Keladi family, and that owing to his change of faith the provincial governors threw off their allegiance.

annexed to Mysore. The Ráni Virammáji, with her adopted son, fled to Ballálráyandurga (Kadur District), a strong fortress at the head of the Kudakal pass; but being surrounded by Haidar's troops, she was taken prisoner and sent to Maddagiri (Tumkúr District).

The Keladi, Ikkéri or Bednúr State was the most considerable of those that were absorbed into the present Mysore territories by the victories of Haidar Ali, and its conquest was always acknowledged by him to have established his fortune. Some details of its history are therefore here given, for a portion of which I am indebted to a manuscript favoured by Mr. F. M. Mascarenhas of Mangalore (a complete stranger to me), who has also written a History of Canara and other works relating to that interesting region. A notice of his document, which was late in reaching me, was printed in the former edition of this work as an Appendix to Vol. III, Coorg.[1]

The following is the list of the chiefs as given by him. It agrees generally with one taken by Mr. Stokes from a *kadata* or black book at Keladi, and appears to be more correct than one given by Buchanan:—

| | | |
|---|---|---|
| 1. | Chaudappa Náyak, son of Hulibailu Basappa ... ... ... | 1499–1513 |
| 2. | Sadás'iva Náyak, son of 1 ... ... ... ... ... ... | 1513–1545 |
| 3. | Sankanna Náyak I, son of 2 ... ... ... ... ... ... | 1545–1558 |
| 4. | Sankanna Náyak II, younger brother of 3 ... ... ... ... | 1558–1570 |
| 5. | Rámarája Náyak, son of 3 ... ... ... ... ... ... | 1570–1582 |
| 6. | Venkatappa Náyak I, younger brother of 5 ... ... ... ... | 1582–1629 |
| 7. | Vírabhadra Náyak, grandson of 6, and son of Bhadrappa Náyak ... | 1629–1645 |
| 8. | S'ivappa Náyak, grandson of 4, and son of Siddappa Náyak ... | 1645–1660 |
| 9. | Venkatappa Náyak II, younger brother of 8 ... ... ... .. | 1660–1661 |
| 10. | Bhadrappa Náyak, son of 8 ... ... ... ... ... ... | 1661–1663 |
| 11. | Somas'ekhara Náyak I, younger brother of 10 ... ... ... | 1663–1671 |
| 12. | Channamáji, widow of 11 ... ... ... ... ... ... | 1671–1697 |
| 13. | Basappa Náyak I, adopted son of 12 ... ... ... ... ... | 1697–1714 |
| 14. | Somas'ekhara Náyak II, son of 13 ... ... ... ... ... | 1714–1739 |
| 15. | Basappa Náyak II, nephew of 14, and son of Vírabhadrappa Náyak | 1739–1754 |
| 16. | Channa Basappa Náyak, adopted son of 15 ... ... ... ... | 1754–1757 |
| 17. | Virammáji, widow of 15 ... ... ... ... ... ... | 1757–1763 |
| 18. | Somas'ekhara Náyak II, adopted son of 17. | |

The 18 chiefs ruled 265 lunar years, 1 month and 25 days.

The circumstances under which the family first rose to power are described under Keladi, and the reason of the transfer of their capital to Ikkéri. Sadás'iva Náyak received that name from Sadás'iva Ráya of Vijayanagar, in reward for his services against the forces of Ahmednagar, and his success in putting down various rebellious chiefs in Tuluva or South Kanara, which he overran as far as Kasargod, in witness of which a stone pillar was erected by him there. The two

[1] "I have consulted," he says, "two Canarese manuscripts, one of which came to me from Bednore, and another from Kundapur in South Canara."

Sankanna Náyaks who followed were sons of different mothers. The elder after a time made over the government to his brother, and set out on a pilgrimage to all the holy places in India, from Rames'vara in the extreme south to Kedarnath, Nepal and Kashmir in the Himálayas. When at Delhi he is said to have defeated in the presence of the court a celebrated prize-fighter, named Ankush Khan, who had affixed a sword to the gate of the city as a challenge to all comers. During his travels the god Aghores'vara appeared to him at Paidana and Virabhadra at Avali, in consequence of which, on his return to his country, he set up the latter at Keladi and the former at Ikkéri. According to Buchanan, he did not resume his power, but lived in retirement for the rest of his days. But it would appear that he did take up the government again, and was successful in various contests against the Muhammadans and in Kanara. It was during the reign of Sankanna II that the Vijayanagar empire was overthrown by a confederacy of Muhammadan powers. The Keladi chief seems to have embraced the opportunity to overrun the territories of Baira Devi.

But it was Venkatappa Náyak who assumed independence, and had to encounter the invasion of the Bijapur forces under Randulha Khan, which he succeeded in driving back. During his reign the dominions of his house were extended north and east to Másur, Shimoga, Kadur, and Bhuvanagiri (Kavaledurga), while on the west and south they were carried to the sea at Honore by the conquest of the queen of Gersoppa —the pepper queen of the Portuguese—a feudatory of Bijapur, and down as far as to the borders of Malabar, his power being so firmly established that he was able to add 50 per cent. to the land assessment throughout a great part of Kanara. He came into collision with the Portuguese by espousing the cause of the queen of Olaya against the Bangar rája, who was an ally of theirs, and ousting him from his territory. The Portuguese, being at the time engaged in expeditions against Persia and Malacca, and desiring to gain the alliance of Venkatappa in order to secure the trade in pepper and keep it out of the hands of the English and Dutch, the viceroy at Goa sent him an embassy in 1623. An Italian nobleman, Pietro della Valle, who had been wandering for some years through Turkey, Egypt, Arabia and Persia, accompanied the ambassador to Ikkéri, and has left an account of his journey. He mentions the fine wide level road from Ságar to Ikkéri, and the splendid avenue of trees on either side. These are the magnificent *dhupa* trees, of which many may still be seen. He also came upon a woman performing *sati*, whom he endeavoured, without success, to save from the flames. *Mástikal* of the later Vijayanagar period are numerous in Sorab and neighbouring parts, and the rite must have been very prevalent. He afterwards travelled alone through the country, "marching at his pleasure; and as the roads throughout the dominions of Venkatappa were very secure he descended the ghats slowly."

Vírabhadra Náyak, by an embassy to the Bijapur sultan, stopped a formidable invasion by Randulha Khan, assisted by the rájas of Sunda and Bilgi, and the chiefs of Tarikere and Banavar. He then removed the capital to Bednur. Sivappa Náyak, his general, subsequently subdued Tulava, and Bairasa Wodeyar of Karkala, invading Malayála and entering Coorg.

Sivappa Náyak was one of the most distinguished of the line. He greatly enlarged Bednur, assisting merchants and artisans from all parts to settle there. His expeditions in Mysore extended over Balam to Vastara, Sakkarepatna and Hassan. He introduced the land assessment called *shist*. Father Leonardo Paes, who travelled in Kanara at the time, says that he had collected enormous treasure after his thorough conquest of Canara; that his possessions extended from the Tudry river to Kasargod or Niles'var; and that he had a standing army of from forty to fifty thousand men. There were more than 30,000 Christians among his subjects, originally natives of Goa and Salsette. Sri Ranga Ráya, the fugitive king of the Vijayanagar dynasty, fled to him for refuge in 1646, and Sivappa Náyak not only gave him the government of Belur and Sakkarepatna, but attacked Seringapatam on his behalf, gaining the *soubriquet* Piṇḍa of Ikkéri, Minḍa of Mysore. Father Vincent, a Barefoot Carmelite friar, mentions in his travels the wealthy Musalman merchant Shah Bandari Isak, who was a favourite of the chief, and traded on the western coast and at Bednur.

There were frequent contests in subsequent reigns between the Mysoreans and the forces of Bednur; also several invasions by the Bijapur armies. In the time of Bhadrappa Náyak the latter are said to have taken Bednur and besieged Bhuvanagiri, whither the chief, with his family, had retired; but a peace was eventually concluded. In 1664 Sivaji made a sudden descent on the coast of Canara, sacked Barcelore or Kundapur, and sailed back to Gokarna, plundering all the adjacent tracts, and levying heavy contributions from the rich mercantile towns, of which the English factory at Carwar paid £112 sterling.

Somasekhara was murdered by his nobles, as stated by Dr. John Fryer of the English Navy, who was then at Carwar, and there were many intrigues regarding the succession, as he had no son. But, according to information given to Buchanan, he went mad, and during the paroxysms of his disease committed great enormities, ripping up pregnant women with his own hands, and for the gratification of his lust seizing every beautiful girl that he met. At length he was assassinated by a Brahman named Somaya, who, though he had rid them of a monster, was nevertheless put to death by the Sivabhaktas, as they considered that he had brought to an end the principal dynasty that professed their creed. His widow, Channamáji, carried on the government, "by and with the authority," Dr. John Fryer says, "of one Timmanna Náyak, who from a toddy-man has, by his cunning polity more than true prowess and valour, raised himself to be General and Protector." The Rani adopted a son, and Timmanna Náyak, who kept them both under restraint, was killed in battle, on which things began to return to the regular current. The Rani's forces took Basavapatna and other places to the east. Harikere she fortified and named it Channagiri, after herself. She also gave shelter to Ráma Rája, the son of Siváji, when he was in hiding from the Mughals, until he could escape to his own country.

Basappa Náyak, her adopted son, next came to the throne. He seems to have been devoted to works of charity. All ascetics, of whatever faith, who came to his dominions in the winter, were provided, it is said, with an umbrella and a blanket. All wayfarers were fed at the *dasoharas*. At nightfall men were sent into the streets with cooked rice for wanderers, and milk for young children. As an atonement for the murder of Somasekhara, he imposed an extra assessment of $\frac{1}{10}$th of an anna, or $\frac{1}{160}$th of the standard rent, to provide funds for erecting *chhatras* and feeding pilgrims.

Somasekhara II is said to have attacked Sira, and taken Ajjampur, Sante Bennur, and other places from the Mughals. Basappa Náyak was called Buddhi, or the Wise. Jacobus Canter Visscher, writing of this period, says :—"The Bednore Prince is much more magnificent and powerful than those of Malabar. His kingdom produces many peculiar commodities, such as sandalwood, which is found there in great abundance, as well as rice." He calls Bednore the granary of all southern India. He also writes :—"The city (Bednur) where the Rája holds his court lies some leagues inland, and is connected with the seaport by a fine road, planted with trees, which the inhabitants are obliged to keep in excellent order. This road is so secure that any stranger might go and sleep there with bags full of money, and nobody would molest or rob him, for if such a thing occurred the people in the neighbourhood would not only be severely punished, but would be forced to make good the money." It was during this reign, in 1748, that the intrigues of Dupleix released Chanda Sahib from the Mahrattas at Sattara, as a candidate for the Navábship of the Carnatic, in opposition to Muhammad Ali, the English candidate. Bednur was then at war with Chitaldroog, and both sought the countenance of Chanda Sahib, who was marching leisurely to the south, awaiting information from his partisans. He was induced to side with Chitaldroog, but in the decisive battle of Mayakonda, on the 24th of March 1748, the Chitaldroog forces suffered complete defeat, and their chief, Madikeri Náyak, was slain. The son of Chanda Sahib had been killed by his side, and he himself fell into the hands of the enemy, who were taking him in triumph to Bednur. But informing his Musalman guards of his prospects, they marched off with him to the French instead, and he eventually took Arcot in 1750. On the other hand, in 1752 the French were forced to surrender at Trichinopoly to Major Lawrence. Chanda Sahib escaped to the Tanjore general under a promise of being conveyed to some French settlement, but was basely stabbed by him, and his head sent to his rival, Muhammad Ali. The latter gave it to Nanja Ráj, the Mysore commander, who despatched it to Seringapatam, where it was exposed for three days over one of the gates. To return to Bednur. In 1751 a treaty was concluded between the Raja and the chief of the English factory at Tellicherry.

An adopted son succeeded Basappa, but on remonstrating with his adoptive mother on her amours, which had become a public scandal, he was put out of the way by a Jeṭṭi dislocating his neck in the bath, and Virammáji occupied the throne in her own name, adopting a son as her successor. But her notorious character, and an imposition of 50 per cent. additional tax in order to buy off the Mahrattas, who threatened the country, had alienated the people, and Haidar's invasion now followed. The chief of Chitaldroog, whom he had just subdued, introduced to him a pretender, Channa Basappa, professing to be the prince who was thought to have been murdered. Haidar saw the use to be made of him, and invaded Bednur in January 1763, ostensibly to restore him to the throne, though even the troops nicknamed him the Ghaib, or resurrection rája. At Kumsi Haidar found the former prime minister of Bednur in prison, and obtained from him such information, that refusing all the offers of money made by the Rani to buy him off, which were raised in amount the nearer he approached, he pressed on to Bednur. Diverting the attention of the garrison by a feigned attack at the barriers, he entered with a column by a secret path revealed to him by the prime minister, and captured the city in March 1763. The Rani, with her paramour and adopted son, fled to Ballálráyandurga, leaving orders to set fire to the palace. The inhabitants *en masse* took shelter in the surrounding woods, and the triumphant Haidar, extinguishing the flames and sealing up the houses, acquired a booty estimated at twelve millions sterling. The Rani, her lover, and her adopted son were all seized by Haidar and transported to the fortress of Maddagiri (Tumkur District), together with even the pretender whose cause he had ostensibly espoused. They were liberated when the Mahrattas took Maddagiri. Virammáji died on the way to Poona, and Somasekhara ended his days there unmarried.

*Basvapatna.*—The founder of the Basvapatna family appears to have been Dhúma Rája, who coming from, it is said, Vijayanagar, formed an alliance with a Bedar family, and established himself at the Dhumi hill, near Holalkere. His son, Kongana Náyak, built the fort of Basvapatna, and subdued a territory extending from Harihar and Kumsi to Tarikere and Bágur. Hanumappa Náyak, who succeeded, appears to have been confirmed in these possessions by the Vijayanagar sovereign, and to have founded Sante Bennur. The family were driven from their northern possessions by the Bijapur army under Ran-dulha Khan in 1636, and then established themselves at Tarikere (Kadur District).

At the beginning of the 18th century the north-east of the District was the scene of much contest between the Chitaldroog and Bednur troops, culminating in 1748 in the decisive battle of Mayakonda, in which, as already described, Madakeri Náyak, the palegar of Chitaldroog, was slain, and Chanda Sahib, the claimant to the Nabobship of Arcot, who had espoused his cause, was captured by the Bednur army. The Nawab of Sávanur then held it for a short time, until the whole, with Bednur, was included in Mysore by the conquests of Haidar Ali. His successes in Sunda and Sávanur led to an invasion by the Mahrattas in 1765, repeated on several occasions afterwards. From the devastation of Shimoga and the open country in 1791 by the army under Parasuram Bhao a famine ensued.

In January 1783, when Tipu Sultan succeeded his father, Mysore being still at war with the English, a force from Bombay, under General Mathews, landed at Kundapur, and carrying by assault the formidable defences of the Hosangadi pass—which bristled with a continuous series of batteries and breastworks, headed at the top by the strong fort of Haidarghar, the whole held by about 17,000 men—occupied Bednur or Haidarnagar on the 27th, the governor having fled. But an expedition which began so well was doomed to end in disaster. The English general was deluded into a false security, and instead of making adequate preparations for defence, scattered his force in various detachments over the country. On hearing of this the Bombay Government superseded him by another officer, but on his way the latter was captured by pirates and killed. Tipu appeared in

April with a large army, recovered Kavaledurga and Haidarghar on one side, and Anantapur on the other, and invested Bednur. The garrison held out till the 30th, when they were forced by starvation to capitulate, which they did on condition of being sent to the coast. But, in violation of the terms, they were marched off in irons, some to Chitaldroog, but the majority to Seringapatam, where numbers were put to death with the most inhuman cruelties.

After the death of Tipu Sultan and the restoration of the Hindu government in 1799, parts of the District were ravaged by Dhundia Wahag, a prisoner at Seringapatam who had obtained release at the time of the capture; but he was speedily put down by Colonel Wellesley, being killed in a cavalry charge led by that illustrious warrior in person. The tranquillity thus restored continued until 1830. But during the greater part of this time the principal authority had been left too much in the hands of one family. Every office was gradually filled with Deshasta Brahmans, who made themselves obnoxious to the Lingáyits. A system of secret plunder was connived at, of which they and their patrons reaped the benefit. At the same time the mode of farming the revenue laid the people under burdens from which there was no redress. Matters grew to such a pitch that in 1830 the gauḍas and ryots assembled in kúṭas or indignation meetings at Basvapatna and Honnali. The discontent was fomented by a pretender to the Bednur throne, named Budi Basavappa, who formed insurgent bands; and these again were shortly joined by Rangappa Náyak, the head of the Tarikere family, and by numbers of Thugs, professional stranglers. The Raja's troops failed to put down the now open revolt, and he was obliged to seek the aid of a British force. The suppression of the insurrection in 1831 was followed by an inquiry into the causes which had led to it, and as the result of that investigation the government was placed under British Commissioners. The District has since that time not only enjoyed the blessing of peace, but has advanced in a course of prosperity which has effectually obliterated all traces of the disorders by which it was previously afflicted.

In 1862 the Shimoga District, with Kadur and Chitaldroog, were formed into the Nagar Division. In 1879 the Division was abolished. In 1882 Davangere taluq was transferred to this District, but in 1886 reverted to Chitaldroog.

# POPULATION

*Number.*—The entire population of the District, according to the census of 1891, was 527,981, of which number 275,884 were males and 259,296 females.

*Density.*—This gives 131·69 persons to the square mile. The Honnáli taluq was the most thickly peopled at the time of the census, containing 193·09 persons to the square mile. In Channagiri there were 159·60, in Sorab 151·94, and in Shikárpur 150·47. The most sparsely populated taluqs were Nagar, with 80·98, and Ságar, with 88·58.

*By Religion.*—The following table represents the numbers according to religion :—

| Religion. | Above 15. | | Under 15. | | Total. | Per centage. |
|---|---|---|---|---|---|---|
| | Males. | Females. | Males. | Females. | | |
| Hindus ... ... | 165,397 | 144,492 | 91,826 | 90,996 | 492,711 | 93·32 |
| Muhammadans ... | 9,743 | 8,593 | 6,027 | 5,834 | 30,197 | 5·71 |
| Jains... ... ... | 1,268 | 965 | 589 | 600 | 3,422 | 0·64 |
| Christians ... ... | 770 | 363 | 264 | 254 | 1,651 | 0·31 |
| Total ... | 177,178 | 154,413 | 98,706 | 97,684 | 527,981 | — |

*Increase.*—The following figures compare the estimates of population in 1838, as given in Mr. Stokes's Report, and in 1853–4 according to the *khâneshumâri* accounts, with the numbers ascertained in the census periods of 1871, 1881, and 1891 :—

| Taluq. | 1838. | 1853–4. | 1871. | 1881. | 1891. |
|---|---|---|---|---|---|
| Channagiri ... ... | 38,363 | 43,948 | 69,593 | 65,267 | 74,218 |
| Honnáli ... ... | 39,525 | 49,925 | 59,067 | 55,976 | 63,527 |
| Nagar ... ... ... | 33,621 | 55,587 | 42,605 | 43,665 | 42,841 |
| Ságar ... ... ... | 42,575 | 60,206 | 60,038 | 59,210 | 58,999 |
| Shikárpur ... ... | 40,476 | 58,484 | 63,310 | 63,510 | 64,404 |
| Shimoga ... ... | 51,389 | 64,878 | 93,457 | 95,828 | 94,716 |
| Sorab ... ... ... | 42,529 | 60,072 | 67,073 | 66,514 | 70,047 |
| Tirthahalli ... ... | 15,650 | 34,079 | 51,715 | 56,561 | 59,229 |
| Total ... | 304,128 | 427,179 | 506,858 | 506,531 | 527,981 |

In the first period of 15 years the total increased apparently at the rate of 40·4 per cent., and in the second period of 18 years at the rate of 16·8 per cent. The great advance in the former period bears ample testimony to the beneficial effect of the restoration of order under British rule, following upon the disturbances which had devastated the country for some years previously. But as the census of 1871 shows that previous estimates were 25 per cent. too low, it seems that the population remained almost stationary, or even slightly declined, in the 38 years to 1891. The famine of 1877–8 apparently had no effect in diminishing the population in this District. The increase in the 20 years from 1871 to 1891 has been only 4·16 per cent., but it is a hopeful sign that the whole of this has occurred in the last decade.

*Classes.*—Arranged according to occupation and nationality, the population may be classified as follows :—

| | | No. | Per cent. |
|---|---|---|---|
| A. | Agricultural ... ... ... ... | 181,317 ... | 34·34 |
| B. | Professional ... ... ... ... | 44,088 ... | 8·35 |
| C. | Commercial... ... ... ... ... | 68,423 ... | 12·96 |
| D. | Artisans and Village Menial ... ... | 158,541 .. | 30·02 |
| E. | Vagrant Minor Artisans and Performers | 43,431 ... | 8·22 |
| | Races and Nationalities ... ... ... | 31,948 ... | 6·05 |
| | Others, not stated ... ... ... ... | 333 ... | 0·06 |

The following are the largest castes or classes, those which number over 10,000, in order of strength. These account for 464,256, or 87·93 per cent. of the population :—

| | | | | | |
|---|---|---|---|---|---|
| Wokkaliga ... | 135,069 | Beda ... ... | 25,678 | Agasa ... ... | 13,103 |
| Lingáyit[1] ... | 72,800 | Kuruba... ... | 23,683 | Pancháła ... | 11,927 |
| Holeya... ... | 38,000 | Mádiga... ... | 23,017 | Uppára... ... | 10,956 |
| Musalmán ... | 30,015 | Wodda... ... | 14,918 | Idiga ... ... | 10,944 |
| Bráhmana ... | 29,374 | Lambáni ... | 14,127 | Mahrata ... | 10,645 |

The most numerous classes of Wokkaliga are the Sáda Lingáyit (39,669), Halepaika (12,576), Gangadikára (9,081), Nonaba (8,552), and Kunchatiga (8,082). Of Musalmáns 18,834 are Shekhs. The principal Brahman sects are Smárta (7,051), Desastha (3,804), Badaganád (3,522), Havika (3,235), Drávida (2,996), and Chitpávan (2,081). Of Kuruba 9,719 are Hálu Kuruba. Of Wodda there are 8,171 Mannu Wodda. Among Pancháła the Akkasále number 6,846.

**Stock.**—The *agricultural stock* of the District in 1892 consisted of 18,795 carts and 85,111 ploughs. The *manufacturing stock* consisted of 1,156 looms for cloth, 387 for *kamblis*, 4 for girdles, 26 for *goni*, and 1 for carpets; also of 98 oil-mills—namely, 3 of stone and 95 of wood.

**Tanks.**—The District contains 8,611 tanks.

[1] There are also 48,221 included among Wokkaliga.

**Dwellings.**—The total number of houses in 1892 was 103,159. Next to Shimoga, the taluqs of Honnáli and Sorab contain the largest number of first-class houses.

**Towns and Villages.**—The District contains 14 municipal towns, with a population of 44,782, composed of 35,232 Hindus, 147 Jains, 8,612 Muhammadans, and 791 Christians. The following are the towns, with population :—

| Town | Population | Town | Population |
|---|---|---|---|
| Shimoga ... ... ... | 11,340 | Tirthahalli... ... ... | 2,359 |
| Shikárpur ... ... ... | 5,011 | Benkipur ... ... ... | 2,270 |
| Channagiri... ... ... | 3,787 | Sirálkoppa... ... ... | 2,125 |
| Honnáli ... ... ... | 3,467 | Sorab ... ... ... | 1,661 |
| Nyámti ... ... ... | 3,102 | Kumsi ... ... ... | 1,656 |
| Hole Honnur ... ... | 2,947 | Nagar ... ... ... | 1,576 |
| Ságar ... ... ... | 2,857 | Kollúrkaṭṭe ... ... | 624 |

The total number of *asali* or primary villages in 1891 was 2,000, to which were attached 1,551 *dákhali* or secondary villages or hamlets. Of the former 1,807 were populated and 193 depopulated. Government villages numbered 1,931, sarvamánya 9, jóḍi 58, and káyamgutta 2.

**Great Festivals.**—The principal concourse of people occurs at the undermentioned festivals :—

At *Togarsi*, Shikárpur taluq, during the *Mallikárjuna játre*, held for 5 days in March, 10,000 people assemble.

On the bund of the *Súlekere*, Channagiri taluq, 10,000 assemble for the *Siddésvara rathótsava*, held for 3 days in February.

At *Shikárpur*, Shikárpur taluq, 5,000 people come together for the *Huchcha Ráya rathótsava*, which lasts for 3 days in April.

At *Chikka-Hulikere*, Channagiri taluq, on the occasion of *Mahesvari játre*, lasting for 3 days in December, 6,000 people assemble.

At *Chandragutti*, in Sorab taluq, 5,000 people collect together during the *Renukammana rathótsava*, held for 8 days in Chaitra.

An equal number assemble at *Tirthahalli*, Tirthahalli taluq, for *Rámesvara rathótsava*, celebrated for 3 days in Márgasira.

At *Humcha*, in Nagar taluq, the *Padmávati Ammana rathótsava*, lasting 7 days in March, attracts 4,000 people.

A similar concourse takes place at *Jénukal gudda*, Nagar taluq, during the *Jénukal Ammana játre*, held for 15 days in September : at *Rampur*, Honnáli taluq, during the *Hálswami játre*, lasting 4 days in Mágha : at *Ságar*, during the *Mári* feast, held for 3 days : on the banks of the *Tungabhadra*, Shimoga taluq, during the *Sangamésvara játre*, held for 3 days in April.

At *Belgávi*, Shikárpur taluq, 3,000 people come together for the car festival of *Kedáresvara* and *Basavanna Devaru*, lasting 3 days in March.

At *Pillangéri*, Shimoga taluq, during the *Srinivasa Devara rathótsava*, held for 2 days in May, 3,000 people assemble.

There are 2,000 people at each of the following:—At *Márikoppa*, Honnáli taluq, for *Haladamma rathótsava*, 5 days in Asvija: at *Nelli*, same taluq, for Hariamma festival in February: at *Keladi*, Ságar taluq, for *Rámesvara rathótsava*, 3 days in Phálguna: at the *Rámachandra maṭha*, Nagar taluq, for 10 days in March: at *Sampekaṭṭe*, same taluq, for *S'ambhulinga rathótsava*, 3 days in March.

**Fairs.**—The following are the largest weekly fairs held in the District:—

| Place. | Taluq. | Day. | No. of Visitors. |
|---|---|---|---|
| Shimoga ... ... | Shimoga ... ... | Tuesday ... ... | 1,500 |
| Benkipur ... ... | do. ... ... | Monday ... ... | 1,000 |
| Hole Honnur ... | do. ... ... | Saturday ... ... | 1,000 |
| Anaveri ... ... | do. ... ... | Thursday ... | 1,000 |
| Ayanur ... ... | do. ... ... | Sunday ... ... | 1,000 |
| Nyámti ... ... | Honnáli ... ... | Friday ... ... | 1,000 |
| Sirálkoppa ... ... | Shikárpur ... | Sunday ... ... | 3,000 |
| Shikárpur ... ... | do. ... ... | Saturday ... ... | 1,500 |
| Ságar ... ... | Ságar ... ... | Thursday... ... | 2,000 |

**Vital Statistics.**—*Births.*—The number of births registered in the District in 1893-4 was 9,963, of which 5,135 were of males and 4,828 of females. This gives a birth-rate of 18·87 per mille of the population.

*Deaths.*—The number of deaths registered in the same period was 11,279, being 5,942 of males and 5,337 of females. The death-rate was thus 21·36 per mille of the population.

As the death-rate exceeded the birth-rate it is possible that the statistics for the latter are defective. The Local Fund report gives for rural parts only, 9,626 births and 9,675 deaths in 1894-5, with 10,072 births and but 7,756 deaths in 1895-6.

Of the 11,279 deaths in 1893-4 there were 7,123 due to fevers, 1,139 caused by bowel complaints, 217 by small-pox, and 2 by cholera, while 141 were due to injuries—namely, 20 to suicide, 105 to wounds from accidents, 16 to snake-bite or wild animals.

*Medical Relief.*—Besides the hospital at Shimoga, there are dispensaries at all the taluq and sub-taluq head-quarters, and at Benkipur. Eight trained native midwives are employed in villages, who attended 393 cases in the year.

## REVENUE

The revenue of the District for 5 years to 1894–5 is shown in the statement below :—

| Items. | 1890–1. | 1891–2. | 1892–3. | 1893–4. | 1894–5. |
|---|---|---|---|---|---|
| Land Revenue ... | 12,75,754 | 12,88,794 | 13,11,218 | 13,22,880 | 13,27,737 |
| Forests ... ... | 3,69,130 | 3,90,296 | 3,95,137 | 4,41,462 | 4,62,524 |
| Mohatarfa ... ... | 30,996 | 29,894 | 29,728 | 29,001 | 21,923 |
| Abkári ... ... | 27,575 | 75,069 | 2,01,077 | 2,13,487 | 2,20,673 |
| Sáyar ... ... ... | 2,14,134 | 3,26,713 | 2,22,817 | 2,15,837 | 2,85,604 |
| Salt pans ... ... | 622 | 177 | 156 | 339 | 153 |
| Stamps ... ... | 63,536 | 91,163 | 72,251 | 77,763 | 77,990 |
| Law and Justice ... | 12,050 | 17,957 | 15,397 | 15,785 | 14,816 |
| Police ... ... ... | 120 | 155 | 197 | 113 | 18 |
| Public Works ... | 6,302 | 6,509 | 5,008 | 4,041 | — |
| Other Items ... ... | 18,144 | 20,963 | 22,454 | 20,007 | 20,188 |
| Total Rs. ... | 20,18,363 | 22,47,690 | 22,75,440 | 23,40,715 | 24,31,626 |

## TRADE

**Manufactures.**—The chief articles of manufacture in the District are coarse cotton cloths, *kamblis*, iron articles, brass and copper vessels, earthenware, and jaggory. A few striped carpets are made at Shikárpur; some pieces of chintz in Shimoga and Ayanur, coarse brown paper being also at one time manufactured in the former place; stone jugs in Tirthahalli; hand-mills in the Honnáli taluq, and ropes of sanab, pundi, leather and leaves of the date-tree.

*Oils.*—The different kinds of oil made in the District are generally gingelli, castor, ramtil, cocoa-nut, linseed, safflower, pundi and caron, but the oil of sandal, cinnamon and nága sampige (*michelia champaca*) are occasionally extracted.

**Art.**—The District is noted for its beautiful sandal-wood carving, of which industry Sorab is the principal seat.

**Commerce.**—*Exports.*—The statement below exhibits the principal articles exported, together with the annual quantity and value thereof:—

| Article. | | Quantity. | Value. | To what place. |
|---|---|---|---|---|
| | | | Rs. | |
| Kamblis ... | No. | 5,600 | 5,900 | Kadur District, &c. |
| Iron ... | Mds. | 3,500 | 700 | Bombay *viâ* Coompta in N. Kanara |
| Iron articles ... | No. | 1,100 | 2,500 | Dharwar, &c. |
| Silver do. .. | ,, | 20 | 500 | Dharwar. |
| Steel do. ... | ,, | 50 | 250 | do. |
| Wooden do. ... | ,, | 5,030 | 5,900 | do. |
| Gingelli oil ... | Mds. | 900 | 5,700 | Kadur District. |
| Jaggory ... ... | ,, | 80,000 | 90,000 | Dharwar, &c. |
| Leather ... ... | No. | 12,750 | 17,450 | Bellary, &c. |
| Leather articles | ,, | 15,000 | 10,000 | Dharwar. |
| Earthenware ... | ,, | 157,200 | 16,570 | do. |
| Rattan articles ... | ,, | 2,000 | 125 | do. |
| Bamboo & date mats | ,, | 2,520 | 1,230 | do. |
| Hemp do. | ,, | 130 | 505 | Kanara. |

*Imports.*—The imports are as given in the subjoined table :—

| Article. | | Quantity. | Value. | From what place. |
|---|---|---|---|---|
| | | | Rs. | |
| Cotton ... .. | Mds. | 75 | 425 | Kadur, &c. |
| Cotton thread ... | ,, | 352 | 5,316 | Bombay, Bangalore, &c. |
| Piece goods ... | No. | 88,430 | 12,22,150 | Bellary, Dharwar, Bombay, Bangalore, Madras. |
| Kamblis ... | ,, | 60,200 | 74,000 | Dharwar, Chitaldroog. |
| Iron ... ... | Mds. | 1,470 | 5,300 | Coompta. |
| Brass utensils ... | ,, | 1,280 | 16,980 | Dharwar, Hubli, Kanara. |
| Bell metal vessels | ,, | 6,110 | 11,976 | Dharwar. |
| Silver articles ... | No. | 1,422 | 7,448 | Dharwar, Bombay, &c. |
| Copper vessels ... | ,, | 33,220 | 29,880 | Dharwar, &c. |
| Golden ornaments | Seers. | 78 | 45,200 | Dharwar. |
| Wooden articles | ... | 250 | 500 | Madras, Bombay, &c. |
| Gingelli oil ... | Mds. | 9,000 | 45,000 | Kadur, Dharwar. |
| Castor oil ... | ,, | 9,500 | 46,000 | Bangalore, Kadur, &c. |
| Jaggory ... ... | ,, | 2,000 | 2,280 | Dharwar. |
| Gunpowder ... | ,, | 43 | 1,860 | Madras, &c. |
| Leather articles | No. | 2,000 | 2,000 | Bombay, Kanara, &c. |
| Earthenware ... | ,, | 1,000 | 400 | Dharwar, &c. |
| Rattan articles... | ,, | 400 | 80 | Bangalore. |

## COMMUNICATIONS

**Railways.**—A branch of the Southern Mahratta railway is under construction from Birur (Kadur District) to Shimoga, through Benkipur.

**Roads.**—The length of *Provincial Roads* in the District is 220 miles, supported at an annual cost of Rs. 26,390. *District Roads* covera distance of 412 miles, and cost Rs. 23,215 a year for up-keep. Details of each class of road are subjoined :—

PROVINCIAL ROADS.

| | Miles. | Cost. |
|---|---|---|
| Bangalore-Honavar road | 72 | 10,080 |
| Tarikere-Mangalore road | 7 | 700 |
| Shimoga-Harihar road | 31 | 1,860 |
| Shimoga-Mangalore road | 58 | 7,250 |
| Shimoga-Haidarghar road | 52 | 6,500 |
| Total | 220 | Rs. 26,390 |

DISTRICT ROADS.

| | Miles | Cost |
|---|---|---|
| Chitaldroog-Benkipur road | 30 | 1,800 |
| Channagiri-Honnali road | 20 | 1,000 |
| Benkipur-Umbalibail road | 12 | 600 |
| Shimoga-Yedehalli road | 18 | 1,800 |
| Shimoga-Hole Honnur road | 9 | 225 |
| Shimoga-Sorab-Sirsi road | 66 | 3,960 |
| Siralkoppa-Hirekerur road | 9 | 540 |
| Siralkoppa-Hanagal road | 21 | 1,050 |
| Sorab-Siddapur road | 10 | 500 |
| Ayanur-Honnali road | 21 | 1,050 |
| Kumsi-Honnali road | 4 | 200 |
| Anantapur-Tirthahalli road | 33 | 1,650 |
| Anantapur-Kollurkatte road | 16 | 800 |
| Anantapur-Shikárpur road | 9 | 450 |
| Sagar-Benavalli-Kollurghat road | 22 | 1,100 |
| Guddekoppa-Kollurkatte road | 10 | 500 |
| Sagar-Siralkoppa road | 22 | 2,200 |
| Ulavi-Sorab road | 8 | 240 |
| Gersoppa Falls road | 2 | 200 |
| Honnali-Shikárpur road | 23 | 1,150 |
| Honnali-Tumminakatte road | 6 | 300 |
| Tirthahalli-Hulikal road | 14 | 700 |
| Kollurkatte-Kollurghat road | 11 | 880 |
| Sirivanti-Kaule road | 2 | 50 |
| Irankanive-Basavankanive road | 3 | 90 |
| Kudarikonda road | 2 | 60 |
| Lakshmipur-Mavinakar road | 9 | 450 |
| Total | Miles 412 | Rs. 23,215 |

**Accommodation for Travellers.**—Dák bungalows for the accommodation of Europeans have been erected at the following stages, with native kitchens separately built for most of them :—

*First Class.*—Shimoga, Jóg.

*Second Class.*—Anantapur, Benkipur, Honnáli, Kumsi, Ságar, Talguppe.

*Third Class.*—Agumbi, Anavatti, Benavalli, Channagiri, Holalur, Kodachádri, Kollurkatte, Malur, Mandagadde, Mégarvalli, Nagar, Sakrebail, Saulanga, Shikárpur, Sorab, Súlekere, Tirthahalli.

Native travellers rest in the *chatrams* built at Agumbi, Anantapur, Benkipur, Chílur, Hádigal, Honnáli, Mahishi, Maḷur, Manḍagadde, Mégarvalli, Shikárpur and Shimoga.

A large *chatram* and *ghat*, on the bank of the Tunga at Shimoga, called after the founder, Courpalais Chatram, has been recently constructed, providing separate accommodation for Hindus, Muhammadans and Christians.

## GAZETTEER

**Anantapur.**—A village in the Ságar taluq, 15 miles south-south-east of the kasba, on the Shimoga-Gérsoppa road. In 1838 it was included in Nagar taluq, but afterwards, till 1875, was again the head-quarters of a taluq bearing its own name. It is now the head-quarters of the Anantapur hobli. Population, 426.

The name of the town, it is stated, should be *Anandapura*, bestowed upon it in the time of Somasekhara Náyak, of the Keladi family, on account of the *ánanda*, or pleasure, he enjoyed in the company of a mistress named Champaka Sárisi who lived here. But there are several inscriptions of the Chálukyas on the spot, dated in the 10th century, which show that it was a place of importance long before the rise of the Keladi house. From one of these it appears that the town was originally named after Andásura, who, in the account of Humcha, it will be seen opposed himself to Jinadatta in the 8th century, and was defeated. It was several times the subject of attack during the commotions of Haidar and Tipu's time, and during the insurrection of 1830.

Besides the high road from Shimoga to Ságar, there are cross-roads hence to Shikárpur northwards, and to Kollurkatte and Tirthahalli southwards.

**Araga.**—A village in Tirthahalli taluq, a few miles north of the kasba. Population, 454.

In old inscriptions it is called the capital of the Male-rájya, or hill kingdom, and was in the Sántalige Thousand. The S'ántara kings of Hombucha owned it under the Chálukyas. In the 14th century, and later on under Vijayanagar, it comprised 3 cities and 18 *kampanas*, and gave its name to the kingdom of A'raga, which was governed by a prince of the royal family. The Keladi chiefs next held it, until they were subverted by the conquests of Haidar Ali.

**Bandalikke** or **Bandanikke.**—A ruined and deserted village in the north of Shikárpur taluq. It was in the earliest times the capital of the Nágarakhanda Seventy, which an inscription informs us was ruled by the "wise Chandra Gupta." It contains many ruined temples of large dimensions and wonderful sculpture. There are more than thirty important inscriptions, ranging from Saka 834 to 1369, and containing records of the Ráshṭrakúṭas, Chálukyas, Kalachuryas, Hoysalas, Yádavas and Vijayanagar kings. The place was probably destroyed by the Muhammadans after the fall of Vijayanagar.

**Basvapatna.**—A ruinous town situated in 14° 12′ N. lat., 75° 52′ E. long., in the north-west of the Channagiri taluq, 16 miles north-north-west of the kasba. Population, 1,218.

Basvapatna, properly Basavapattana, is situated in a narrow valley enclosed with hills, and was the original possession of the Basvapatna chiefs, afterwards known as the Tarikere Pálegárs. The founder of the family was Dhúma Rája, said to have come from Vijayanagar. When hunting in the forest where Basvapatna now stands he came upon the abode of the Beda who grazed his cattle there, and who had a beautiful daughter. Becoming enamoured of her he proposed to marry her, but her father was unwilling to give her to a man of a different caste. Dhúma Rája then obtained his consent by a promise that he would settle there, and that her sons should succeed him in the government. He established himself at the Dhúmi hill, and had two sons, Kongana Náyak and Rámappa Náyak, of whom the former succeeded his father, and built the fort of Basvapatna. During his rule he also subdued a territory extending from Anantapur to Máyakondu and from Harihar to Tarikere. He was followed at Basvapatna by Víra Hanumappa Náyak, he by Immadi Hanumappa Náyak, and he by Huchchu (mad) Hanumappa Náyak. In the time of Kongana Náyak, the next ruler, the place was taken by the Bijapur army under Randulha Khan. This was in 1636, and the chief then retired to Tarikere, which from that time became the residence of the family. Basvapatna was subsequently taken by the Bednur chief, who built a second or outer wall to the fort. It was next captured by the Mughals, and during the time that Dilávar Khan was governor of Síra, seems to have enjoyed much prosperity for twenty years.[1] It afterwards changed hands several times, being held by the Mahrattas for seven years, and by Haidar Ali, who destroyed the fortifications. The Mahrattas under Parasu Ram Bhao ruined the town in 1791. The fort was repaired after 1799, but the place has never recovered its former prosperity.

[1] Buchanan mentions a mosque near the fort which was celebrated as being the first abode of Bábá Budan before he went south to the hill which bears his name in Kadur District.

**Bednur.**—(*See* Nagar.)

**Belagavi** or **Balagami.**—A village remarkable for its antiquities, situated in 14° 24′ N. lat., 75° 18′ E. long., in Shikárpur taluq, 14 miles north-west of the kasba. Population, 1,470.

*Baḷḷigáve, Baḷḷigámve, Baḷḷigráme, Baḷḷipura* or *Baḷipura*, as its name is variously written in old inscriptions (the latter seldom) was, under the Chálukya and Kalachurya sovereigns, the capital of the Banavase nád, or Banavase Twelve Thousand province. It was a place of such antiquity, even in the 12th century, as to be styled the mother of cities, the capital of ancient cities, the *anádi rájadháni*, or immemorial capital, and is said to derive its name from the rákshasa Bali. On account of its religious merit it was called the Dakshina Kedára, and it also had the name of Kamaṭha. It contained five *maṭhas* and three *puras*, the former belonging respectively to the votaries of Vishnu, Siva, Brahma, Jina and Buddha. Its prosperity continued under Hoysala Vira Ballála and the Yádavas. The place abounds with inscriptions, of which there are eighty-four, nearly all dated earlier than the close of the 13th century. There is little doubt that the city fell a prey to the Muhammadan armies which overturned the Yádava and Hoysala powers soon after. The ruined temples of Kedáresvara, Pancha Linga, Kaiṭabhesvara, Somesvara and Tripurahantesvara are rich with carving which is not surpassed in taste and finish by any in Mysore, the handiwork, according to tradition, of the famous Jakanáchári.[1]

**Belagutti.**—A village situated in 14° 12′ N. lat., 75° 35′ E. long., in the Honnali taluq, 5 miles north-west of Nyámti. Population, 2,644.

It was the residence of a line of chiefs subject to the Chálukya and Yádava kings. The inscriptions at the place are all of the 12th and 13th centuries. From these it is ascertained that *Belegavatti* was the original form of the name. The following chiefs are mentioned as ruling there:—Malli Devarasa in 1196, Isvara Devarasa in 1216, Simhala Devarasa in 1232, Bira Devarasa in 1249.

**Benkipur.**—A town on the right bank of the Bhadra, at the point where the high road to Shimoga crosses the river, and where there will be a railway station. It is 12 miles south by east of Shimoga, and a municipality.

[1] The two fine *dvárapálaka* at the entrance to the Mysore Museum, were brought from the Pancha Linga temple.

| Population in 1891. | Males. | Females. | Total. |
|---|---|---|---|
| Hindus ... ... ... ... ... ... ... | 773 | 836 | 1,609 |
| Muhammadans... ... ... ... ... ... | 320 | 326 | 646 |
| Christians ... ... ... ... ... ... | 11 | 4 | 15 |
| Total ... ... | 1,104 | 1,166 | 2,270 |

There are the remains of a fine triple temple of Narasimha, of the early Vijayanagar period, never finished. The name of the town is properly Bankipura, for Vankipura, from Sanskrit *vanki*, a bend in a river, such as occurs here, making it a sacred spot.

| Municipal Funds. | 1892-3. | 1893-4. | 1894-5. | 1895-6. |
|---|---|---|---|---|
| Income ... ... ... ... ... | 576 | 765 | 682 | 1,400 |
| Expenditure ... ... ... .. | 716 | 760 | 967 | 1,228 |

**Bhadra.**—One of the two main streams whose union forms the Tungabhadra. It rises in the Western Ghats at Gangámúla in the Varáha Parvata, on the western frontier of the Kadur District, and flowing north-east along the western base of the Bábá Budan mountains, enters this District in the south of the Shimoga taluq. Thence, running due north past Benkipur and Hole Honnur, it unites with its sister stream the Tunga at Kudali, about 8 miles north-east of Shimoga. It is bridged at Bále Honnur, and at Benkipur.

**Bilesvara betta,** or *Agastya Parvata*, a hill near Humcha in the Nagar taluq, from which several of the streams in the District spring: namely, the Haridravati, flowing north-west to the Sharavati; the Sharmanavati, which runs in the same direction into the former; the Kumadvati, running north and falling into the Tungabhadra; and the Kushavati, running south into the Tunga.

**Chandragutti.**—A high-peaked hill in the west of the Sorab taluq, formerly fortified, with a village of the same name at its base on the east. Population 713.

The hill is said to have been originally of such a height that it obscured the moon, whence the name *Chandra-gupti*, but it was reduced to its present size by a rákshasa during his contest with Krishna, who hid here. The summit is 2,836 feet above the level of the sea. It was the early stronghold of the Kadamba kings of Banavási, and the town below was the residence of Trinetra Kadamba. In modern times it was one of the first acquisitions of the Ikkeri chiefs, but was destroyed by the palegar of Bilgi in the time of Haidar

Ali. The place was afterwards taken successively by Parasu Ram Bhao, and by Dhundia, neither of whom held it more than a few months. On the hill is a temple dedicated to Rénuka, the mother of Parasu Ráma.

**Channagiri.**—A taluq in the east. Area 465 square miles. Head-quarters at Channagiri. Contains the following hoblis, villages and population:—

| No. | Hoblis. | Villages. | Hamlets. | Villages classified. | | Population. |
|---|---|---|---|---|---|---|
| | | | | Govern-ment. | Kayam-gutta. | |
| 1 | Basavapatna ... ... ... | 26 | 2 | 26 | — | 10,033 |
| 2 | Channagiri ... ... ... | 74 | 1 | 73 | 1 | 23,883 |
| 3 | Nallúru ... ... ... | 63 | — | 63 | — | 18,401 |
| 4 | Sante Bennúru ... ... | 48 | 1 | 48 | — | 15,483 |
| 5 | Ubráni ... ... ... | 32 | 2 | 32 | — | 6,418 |
| | Total... ... ... | 243 | 6 | 242 | 1 | 74,218 |

*Principal places, with population.*—Channagiri, 3,787; Sante Bennúru, 1,643; Nallúr, 1,624; Vaddanahálu, 1,558; Hodigere, 1,237; Tyávanige, 1,237; Pándomaṭṭi, 1,222; Kattalagere, 1,218; Devarahalli, 1,123; Somalapura, 1,097; Dáginakaṭṭe, 1,072; Chirudoni, 1,036; Távarekere, 1,036.

The south and west are crossed by lines of hills, the streams from which unite to form the great Súlekere tank, 40 miles in circumference, and thence flow north in what is called in old inscriptions the river Haridra to the Tungabhadra at Harihar. The remaining parts of the taluq consist of an open country with very extensive grazing lands. Hence the cattle are superior to those in other parts of the District. In the north is a fertile tract containing much garden and sugar-cane cultivation. The cultivation of the black soil below, and the red soil around, the Súlekere, so long neglected that the wild date had invaded all the neighbourhood and made it extremely unhealthy, has been in recent years promoted by clearing the jungle and other measures conducive to that end. The hills to the west of the taluq are included in the auriferous belt running north from the Bábá Budan mountains.

The revenue settlement was introduced into the south of the taluq in 1870, and into the north in 1871. The area was thus distributed:—

| | | |
|---|---|---|
| Culturable (dry, 170,517; wet, 6,665; garden, 1,413) | ... | 178,595 |
| Unculturable (including roads, tanks, village sites, &c.) | ... | 73,495 |
| Total acres | ... | 252,090 |

The unoccupied arable land was 79,813 acres. The total revenue demand for 1891-2 (15 months) was Rs. 1,99,516, and for 1892-3 it was Rs. 2,07,340.

The average annual rainfall at Channagiri for 26 years (1870-95), and at Joladahál for 3 years (1893-5), was as follows:—

| | Jan. | Feb. | Mar. | Apr. | May | June | July | Aug. | Sept. | Oct. | Nov. | Dec. | Year. |
|---|---|---|---|---|---|---|---|---|---|---|---|---|---|
| Channagiri ... | 0·10 | 0·02 | 0·23 | 1·46 | 2·93 | 3·49 | 4·98 | 3·63 | 3·60 | 3·82 | 1·40 | 0·24 ... | 25·90 |
| Joladahál ... | — | — | 0·01 | 1·76 | 2·96 | 6·09 | 7·50 | 7·00 | 3·81 | 5·66 | 1·06 | — ... | 35·85 |

According to another register for 23 years the annual average is 26·34 at Channagiri.

The Benkipur-Chitaldroog road passes through Channagiri, from which place there is a road north, running west of the Súlekere, up to Male Bennúr, with one from Súlekere east to Sante Bennúr and the railway at Sásalu. The Bangalore-Poona railway runs a few miles beyond the eastern border of the taluq.

**Channagiri.**—A town situated 14° 1′ N. lat., 75° 59′ E. long., 14 miles west of the Holalkere railway station, and 33 miles north-east of Shimoga, on the Benkipur-Chitaldroog road. Head-quarters of the Channagiri taluq, and a municipality.

| Population in 1891. | Males. | Females. | Total. |
|---|---|---|---|
| Hindus (with 8 Jains) ... ... ... | 1,469 | 1,624 | 3,093 |
| Muhammadans ... ... ... ... | 340 | 351 | 691 |
| Christians ... ... ... ... ... | 3 | — | 3 |
| Total ... ... | 1,812 | 1,975 | 3,787 |

It is the residence of several Lingáyit merchants, but derives most of its importance from being the taluq station.

| Municipal Funds. | 1892-3. | 1893-4. | 1894-5. | 1895-6. |
|---|---|---|---|---|
| Income ... ... ... ... ... | 1,226 | 1,345 | 1,365 | 2,423 |
| Expenditure ... ... ... ... | 1,266 | 1,570 | 3,619 | 5,153 |

From inscriptions it would appear that in early times this part of the country was in possession of the Gangas and governed from Asandi (Kadur District). In the twelfth century it formed part of the Chálukya dominions, and was included in the Nonambarádi Thirty-two Thousand province, over which the Pándya Rája at Uchchangi ruled. Under Vijayanagar, in the sixteenth century, it was still under the Uchchangi district, and attached to Sante Bennúr. At the end of the seventeenth century the town was captured by the Bednur army, and named Channagiri after the reigning queen Channamáji, who erected the fort and granted the place as an estate to her sister.

**Gersoppa,** Falls of.—*See* Sharavati.

**Govardhangiri.**—A hill on the western frontier of the Ságar taluq, overlooking the old town of Gérsoppa, said to have been fortified by Jinadatta, the founder of the Humcha state.

"It is in the remotest corner of Mysore, and has rarely been visited by Europeans. It stands on a promontory, the rock on all sides being precipitous, save an approach from the south-east, which is limited to a narrow neck of land on which are two causeways called *sárá*, strongly fortified by outposts called *ukhaḍs*, and with tremendous ravines on either side. A difficult path then leads down to a third causeway, above which towers up the fort on one side, while on the other a rugged and devious path, commanded for some distance by the fortress, leads down to the plain country beneath. The fort is in fair repair, but is now deserted and overgrown with jungle, though the old pass is still used by traders, who carry down to Gérsoppa on pack-bullocks the rice grown in the upper country, which finds a ready sale. The road is frightfully steep and rough, and it is a marvel how any laden animal can traverse it; yet 50,000 bullocks yearly descend and ascend it, carrying down grain and bringing up salt for consumption in the Malnád." [1]

**Hole Honnur.**—A small town in Shimoga taluq, on the right bank of the Bhadra, 9 miles north-east of Shimoga, and a municipality.

| Population in 1891. | Males. | Females. | Total. |
|---|---|---|---|
| Hindus ... ... ... .. ... | 1,170 | 1,290 | 2,460 |
| Muhammadans ... ... ... ... | 235 | 252 | 487 |
| Total ... ... | 1,405 | 1,542 | 2,947 |

In Haidar Ali's time Hole Honnúr was given in jágir to the officers of the Sowars, and a great many Mahrattas are settled there, most of whom have still one or more members of their family in the Sowar department.

| Municipal Funds. | 1892-3. | 1893-4. | 1894-5. | 1895-6. |
|---|---|---|---|---|
| Income ... ... ... ... ... ... | 756 | 1,082 | 1,005 | 1,900 |
| Expenditure ... ... ... ... ... | 978 | 1,140 | 1,596 | 2,158 |

[1] Bowring, *East. Ex.*, 120.

**Honnali.**—A taluq in the north-east. Area 329 square miles. Head-quarters, in 1869 fixed at Nyámti, were again transferred to Honnáli in 1882. Contains the following hoblis, villages and population :—

| No. | Hoblis. | Villages. | Hamlets. | Villages classified. | | | | Popula-tion. |
|---|---|---|---|---|---|---|---|---|
| | | | | Govern-ment. | Sarva-mánya. | Jodi. | Kayam-gutta. | |
| 1 | Belagutti ... ... | 54 | 2 | 53 | — | 1 | — | 20,814 |
| 2 | Honnáli ... ... | 50 | — | 47 | — | 2 | 1 | 18,444 |
| 3 | Sásivehalli ... | 63 | 1 | 58 | 1 | 4 | — | 24,269 |
| | Total ... | 167 | 3 | 158 | 1 | 7 | 1 | 63,527 |

*Principal places, with population.*—Honnáli, 3,467; Nyámti, 3,102; Belagutti, 2,644; Kundúr, 1,482; Soratúr, 1,196; Kulambi, 1,070; Kulagaṭṭe, 1,053.

The Kumsi hobli was made a separate sub-taluq under Shimoga in 1882, and Kundúr mágani was at the same time transferred to Honnáli from Channagiri. The taluq is crossed from south to north by the Tungabhadra, and bounded east and west by lines of low stony hills. The northern and eastern parts consist of dry crop country of unusual fertility, good black soil being common, and cotton and jowari the leading products. The extreme west, on the other hand, may be considered a purely rice country, with sugar-cane as usual intermixed, rágí being the staple dry crop grain. The central part partakes of a mixed character between the two. Very rich black soil prevails around Nyámti and Belagutti, and much money was made in this neighbourhood during the American War of 1864–5 by the growth of cotton. The Honnáli gold-field (*see* Vol. I) is at the foot of the hills in the south-west, of which the Kalva Rangan peak (3,388 feet) is the highest point within the District.

The revenue settlement was introduced in 1874. The area of the taluq at that time was thus distributed :—

| | | |
|---|---|---|
| Culturable (dry, 125,834; wet, 10,922; garden, 721) | ... | 137,477 |
| Unculturable (including roads, tanks, village sites, &c.) | ... | 94,034 |
| Total acres ... | ... | 231,511 |

The unoccupied arable area was 42,387 acres. The total revenue demand for 1891–2 (15 months) was Rs. 1,57,192, and for 1892–3 it was Rs. 1,75,232.

The average annual rainfall at Honnáli for 26 years (1870–95), and at the other station for 3 years (1893–5), was as follows:—

| | Jan. | Feb. | Mar. | Apl. | May | June | July | Aug. | Sept. | Oct. | Nov. | Dec. | | Year. |
|---|---|---|---|---|---|---|---|---|---|---|---|---|---|---|
| Honnáli ... | 0·10 | 0·08 | 0·33 | 1·47 | 3·34 | 3·05 | 3·57 | 2·38 | 2·52 | 4·17 | 1·44 | 0·24 | ... | 22·69 |
| Saulanga... | — | — | 0·40 | 0·62 | 1·63 | 3·74 | 5·25 | 1·74 | 3·54 | 5·14 | 1·86 | — | ... | 23·92 |

The road from Shimoga to Harihar passes through Honnáli, where the river has to be forded. From Honnáli there is a road southwards through Nyámti to Ayanur, and one west to Shikárpur. The Shimoga-Shikárpur road passes through Saulanga, and there is a road from Nyámti east to Sásivehalli.

**Honnali.**—A town situated in 14° 15′ N. lat., 75° 42′ E. long., on the left bank of the Tungabhadra, 24 miles north of Shimoga, on the Shimoga-Harihar road. It is a municipality, and was till 1869 the head-quarters of the Honnáli taluq, which were then fixed at Nyámti, but were again transferred here in 1882.

| Population in 1891. | Males. | Females. | Total. |
|---|---|---|---|
| Hindus (with 15 Jains) ... ... ... | 1,327 | 1,354 | 2,681 |
| Muhammadans ... ... .. ... | 369 | 395 | 764 |
| Christians ... ... ... ... ... | 17 | 5 | 22 |
| Total ... ... | 1,713 | 1,754 | 3,467 |

Honnáli is said to have borne the puranic name of Bháskara kshetra. By the Muhammadan government it seems to have been called Bidiri. Honnáli means "gold-bearing," but the Mackenzie MSS. state that the name is derived from Honnu and anala, "gold of fire," the tradition being that fire is the father of gold. An inscription, however, gives it as Suvarṇṇáli, which is the same as Honnáli. The fort is occupied principally by Vaidika Brahmans, and the town by Lingáyit traders in grain. The place belonged to Vijayanagar, and after the overthrow of that power in the 16th century was seized by a chief named Múgidora Mara Náyak. In spite of attacks from the Tarikere chiefs, he held it till ousted by the Bijapur conquests in the 17th century. On the fall of Bijapur, Honnáli was captured by the Bednur State, with which it was connected until taken by Haidar Ali, and annexed to Mysore. It was one of the centres of the insurrection of 1830. Honnáli is the residence of a Naváb of Afghan descent. "The founder of the family was a Jamaud Afghan named Abdul Nabi Khán, an officer of the court of Delhi, who received an estate from the emperor in Dharwar along with the Naváb of Sávanur. Since the death of Naváb Kutb-ul-Mulk, during the siege of Seringapatam, the Honnáli chiefs have possessed little but a barren title."[1]

| Municipal Funds. | 1892-3. | 1893-4. | 1894-5. | 1895-6. |
|---|---|---|---|---|
| Income ... ... ... ... ... | 1,047 | 1,110 | 1,300 | 1,830 |
| Expenditure ... ... ... ... | 2,197 | 1,091 | 1,670 | 2,031 |

**Humcha.**—A Jain village situated in 13° 51′ N. lat., 75° 16′ E. long., in the Nagar taluq, 12 miles east of Nagar. Population, 997.

The correct name is *Hombucha*, also written in old inscriptions *Pomburchchha* and *Paṭṭi Pomburchchha.* It was the capital of a principality founded by Jinadatta, who is said to have come from Mathura, in Upper India. His father, Sahakára, had a son Mardatta by a Kiráta woman, at whose instigation an attempt was made to get Jinadatta out of the way in order to secure the succession for her son. Jinadatta was accordingly sent on a certain errand bearing the offering of a lime, which was to be the signal of their victim to the executioners appointed to murder him. But Mardatta, meeting him on the way, offered to relieve him of the message, and was consequently slain. Jinadatta, advised by his mother, fled, taking with him a small golden image of Padmávati. He was pursued by a force of 1,200 men sent by his father, but on exhibiting the image of Padmávati they were transported back to a distance of 150 miles. He continued his wanderings until he arrived at the spot where Humcha now stands. Being weary, he tied his horse to a *kari lakki* tree and fell asleep, when the goddess revealed to him that he was to be the founder of a kingdom in that place, and directed him to touch her image with his horse's bit, which, on his doing so, was instantly changed into gold. The story of the golden bit gained him the support of a local chief against the army of his pursuers, who now again appeared. They at last surrendered and entered his service, whereupon, being provided with funds by the goddess, who converted into gold all the iron brought into contact with her image, he commenced the building of the city. He also erected a temple to Padmávati over the tree under which he had slept—the same, it is said, which is now growing out of the side of the temple. All these things being accomplished, the golden image vanished, the king being directed to one of stone, in which the goddess would reside, and which was duly set up in the temple. These events happened, according to the account of the late Humcha swami, Devendra Tirtha Bhattáraka, in the year 500 of the 5th Kali yuga (or 159 B.C.).

[1] Bowring, *East. Ex.*, 107.

An inscription of the 11th century traces the descent of Jinadatta to Ráha, of the Ugra-vams'a, lord of the Northern Madhura, who was a successful leader in the Bhárata war in Kuru-kshetra, on account of which he received a *s'ankha*, or conch shell, and the *vánara dhvaja*, or monkey flag, from Náráyana. After several kings had ruled in succession to him there came Sahakára, who turned a cannibal.[1] To him and to his wife Sriyá-devi was born Jinadatta. Disgusted at his father's character, the latter fled to the south. On his way he slew an *asura* named Simharada, and thus obtained the *simha lánchhana*, or lion signet. He also slew Andhakásura and founded Andhásura, a place which still bears the same name, immediately to the east of Anantapur. Then, coming to Kanakapura, the modern Humcha, he slew Kanakásura, and drove away Kara and Karadúshana, who were in Kundada-kóṭe, the hill near Agumbi. Pleased at his exploits, the goddess Padmávati entered into the *lakki* tree (still shown growing out of her temple) at Kanakapura, gave it the name of Pombuchcha, and made it the capital of his kingdom. According to another statement, he was aided in establishing his kingdom by his *guru*, named Siddhánta-kírtti. After several kings had ruled, there were S'ri'kesi and Jayakesi. The former had a son Ranakesi. He was followed by several kings, after whom came Hiranyagarbha, who drove out the kings of Yadhivása and subdued the Sántalige Thousand Nád (the present Tirthahalli taluq). He took the name of Vikrama S'ántara, and was succeeded by the following S'ántara kings:—Chági S'ántara, Vira S'ántara, Kannara S'ántara, Tyági S'ántara (who married a Kadamba princess), Nanni S'ántara, Ráya S'ántara, Chikka Vira S'ántara, Ammana Deva, Tailapa Deva (who married a Ganga princess), Bira Deva S'ántara (who married Ganga and Nolamba princesses), and his brother Barmma Deva S'ántara, ruling in 977. This genealogy is sufficient to warrant our placing Jinadatta in the 7th or 8th century. The grants continue to the 12th century, and give us the later names of Ammana, Taila, Káma, Jagadéva and Bammarasa.

Jinadatta subdued the country as far as Kalasa (Kadur District), and fortified the hill of Govardhangiri on the western frontier of the Sagar taluq. He or his descendants afterwards removed the capital first to Sisila or Sisukali and then to Karkala, both in S. Kanara; establishing lieutenants in Barkur, Bangádi, Mudu Bidare and Mulki, and obtaining from the possessions a revenue of 9 lakhs above the

[1] An inscription at Harihara contains a curious allusion to a king who, possessed by an evil spirit, became a cannibal, and in order to gratify his taste settled as a barber at Kálanjara, where he was slain by Krishna, one of the earliest of the Kalachurya princes.

ghats and 9 lakhs below. His successors at Karkala adopted the title of Bairasu Wodeyar, which was taken by all the line subsequently. The Jains say that Gante Wodeyar adopted the faith of the Sivabhaktar or Lingáyits, on which the lieutenants refused to obey him and declared their independence, and that he was the progenitor of the Keladi chiefs who afterwards subdued the territory. The grants existing at Kalasa of the Bairasu Wodeyars of Karkala date from the end of the 12th to the 16th century, and are made under the Hoysala and Vijayanagar sovereigns.

The existing ruins of Humcha, situated at the foot of the Bilesvara hill, said to be the source of seven streams, indicate the site of a large town. The name Hombucha, golden bit, is considered to confirm the story of its origin, while that of Govardhangiri, given to the chief's first stronghold, points to his connection with the celebrated hill so called near Mathura.

**Ikkeri.**—A village situated in 14° 8′ N. lat., 75° 5′ E. long., in the Ságar taluq, 3 miles south of the kasba. Population, 239.

*Ik-kéri* (the two streets) was, from about 1560 to 1640, the capital of the Keladi chiefs, afterwards removed to Bednur. Ikkéri continued, however, to be the nominal capital, the Rajas were called by its name, and the coins were called Ikkéri pagodas and fanams, although, in fact, the mint was removed. Its walls were of great extent, forming three concentric enclosures. In the citadel was the palace, of mud and timber, adorned with carving and false gilding. The only vestige of its former greatness is the temple of Aghoresvara, a large and well-proportioned stone building. On the floor in front of the shrine are the effigies of three of the Keladi chiefs, doing obeisance, with the name inscribed above each. One of them, Huchcha (mad) Somasekhara, is represented as manacled and fettered. The distance between the central pillars was adopted as the standard measure for garden land. A rod of this length, equal to 18 feet 6 inches, was the space called *dáya* allowed for one tree, and the shist was fixed on 1,000 such *dáya* at various rates.

**Kavale-durga.**—A hill in a wild and inaccessible region, in the west of the Tirthahalli taluq. It rises to 3,058 feet above the sea. The place is said to be the Kámyaká-vana in which the Pandus lived for some time during their exile. They are related to have erected the ancient fortifications, of great size and strength, on the hill. Bhima threw the Bhimankaṭṭe across the Tungabhadra, so as to turn the course of the river towards their abode. But the rishis performing penance lower down the stream, finding the water cut off, complained to Dharma Raya, who requested Bhima to release the stream, which he did by making the three existing openings in the dam. The hill was in later times called Bhuvana-giri, and was a stronghold of the Bednur chiefs. A large slab of stone in the palace, 8 feet by 7 feet, called the Ráni's Cot, and well carved, has an inscription on it bearing date in the year Bháva, corresponding to 1694.[1] The present name Kavaledurga, guarding hill-fort, was given to the hill on its capture by Haidar Ali.

The old town, formerly head-quarters of what was, till 1882, called the Kavaledurga taluq, is to the west of the droog.

**Keladi.**—A village situated in 14° 13′ N. lat., 75° 5′ E. long., in Ságar taluq, 4 miles north of the kasba. Population, 1,388.

It is interesting as the place whence the Ikkéri chiefs derived their origin, which is thus related. Two brothers named Chavuda Gauḍa and Bhadra Gauḍa, living in the village of Hale-bayal, in the Keladi taluq of the Chandragutti pargana, had two servants or slaves, named Yádava and Murári, who cultivated their masters' fields. A cow they had was discovered to shed her milk over a certain ant-hill, which, on digging into, Chavuda Gauḍa found contained a linga, over which, therefore, he built a small temple. A little time after, the servants, when ploughing, turned up an old sword, which they put into the thatch of the house, intending to make a scythe of it. But they discovered that if a crow perched on the shed the sword leaped out in the form of a serpent and killed it. On this Chavuda Gauḍa took it and, carefully cleaning it, kept it in his house, giving it the name of Nágaramuri. At another time the ploughshare struck against the ring of a cauldron, which contained treasure. Afraid to disturb it, Chavuda Gauḍa covered it up again, but that night had a dream, in which he was directed to offer a human sacrifice and take the treasure. On hearing this his two slaves volunteered to be the victims on condition that their memory was preserved. All the preparations being made, the place was dug up at night, and the slaves, after ablutions, prostrated themselves to the cauldron and were beheaded with the sword Nágaramuri.

With this accession of wealth the Gauḍas raised a small force and began to subdue the neighbouring villages. But they were seized and sent to Vijayanagar by orders from the king, and there put into custody. Hearing that a pálegar near Balihalu was rebellious, they made an offer through the court musicians to punish him if allowed to do so. Permission being given, they went with a force and killed the pálegar, on which they were released and confirmed in the possession of the places they had captured, receiving from the king a seal (*sikha*

[1] This cot is now in the Victoria Institute at Mysore.

*moharu*). The town of Keladi was then founded, together with the temple of Rámésvara.

One day while the Gauḍa was hunting, a hare turned upon his hounds, indicating heroic virtue in the soil of the place in which this occurred. He therefore removed his town to the spot, calling it Ikkéri. His son and successor, with the sanction of Sadásiva Ráya the Vijayanagar sovereign, took the name of Sadásiva Náyak.

Two mounds, called Kalte, at the entrance to Keladi are pointed out as the scene of the human sacrifices. The principal building in the place is the double temple of Rámésvara and Virabhadra, a large and plain structure.

**Kodachadri.**—A lofty mountain in the west of the Nagar taluq and a conspicuous landmark. Its height is 4,411 feet above the sea. It rises more than 2,000 feet above the level of the villages below, and is clothed with splendid forests. From Nagavadi, at the head of the Kollur ghat, it is 4 miles distant, and from this point the ascent is 3 miles. The first portion of the hill is very steep and difficult to ascend. Above this is a temple to the Huli Deva, tiger god, whose image is provided with thirty-two arms. The top of the hill, which from a distance has a bluff appearance, is in reality a narrow ridge, in many places only 12 feet across, with a precipice on either side. It commands an extensive and splendid view over the Western Ghats and Kanara.

On the west the hill descends almost perpendicularly for 4,000 feet, and the Kanara forests lie spread out below. The sea appears quite close, and on a clear day the vessels are discernible with the naked eye. The bay and town of Kundapur lie opposite. But for the very limited level space on the top, and the difficulty of access, this hill would make a most desirable sanitarium, having a beautiful climate, and so near the sea that it catches the earliest breath of the sea-breeze. There is a small bungalow at the top.

**Kudali.**—A sacred village in Shimoga taluq, at the confluence (*kúdali*) of the Tunga and Bhadra, where they unite to form the Tungabhadra, about 9 miles north-east of Shimoga. Population, 949.

It is the seat of a maṭha connected with the one at Sringéri, the original Guru having been appointed by the Sringéri Swámi about 500 years ago to minister to the Smártas of Mahratta descent. There is also a maṭha of the Mádhva sect. Notwithstanding their being subject to the Kúḍali gurus, the Mahrattas under Parasuram Bhao plundered and burnt the place in 1791, and were consequently threatened with excommunication, which was averted by timely gifts. There are three old temples at Kúdali, dedicated to Brahmes'vara, Narasimha and Rámes'vara.

Of inscriptions at the place the one with the oldest pretensions is on copper plates at the Brahmes'vara temple, professing to be a grant by the emperor Rukmángada ruling at Ayódhyá. The Sringéri maṭha has one, also on copper, dated S'aka 1075, a grant by a Kadamba king named Purandara Ráya. Of those on stone, the oldest are of the Hoysala period. One records a grant to the Rámanátha temple by Vira-Ballála (III) on the return of his son from Delhi, whither apparently he had been taken in the Muhammadan invasion. Later grants are by the Vijayanagar kings, and the Sringéri maṭha has copper grants by the Keladi chief Somasekhara Náyak in the 17th century.[1]

**Kumadvati** or **Choradi.**—An affluent of the Tungabhadra. It rises in Agastya Parvata or the Bilesvara hill near Humcha, and flowing north near Kumsi and Shikárpur, receives at the latter place a stream on the left from Anantapur. Continuing north, it forms the large Masur Madaga tank on the frontier, and turning north-east, runs into the Tungabhadra at Mudanur, some distance above Harihar.

It is stemmed by twelve anicuts, giving rise to channels 33 miles in total length.

**Kumsi.**—A town on the Shimoga-Gérsoppa road, 14 miles north-west of Shimoga. Head-quarters of the Kumsi sub-taluq (composed of Kumsi and Háranhalli hoblis), and a municipality.

| Population in 1891. | Males. | Females. | Total. |
|---|---|---|---|
| Hindus ... ... ... ... ... | 694 | 680 | 1,374 |
| Muhammadans ... ... ... ... | 159 | 122 | 281 |
| Christians ... ... ... ... ... | 1 | — | 1 |
| Total ... ... | 854 | 802 | 1,656 |

From inscriptions at the place it appears that its correct name is Kumbase, and that it was granted as an endowment by Jinadatta Ráya of Pomburcha (Humcha) for the Jain temple there. Kumsi was formed into a sub-taluq under Shimoga taluq in 1882.

| Municipal Funds. | 1892-3. | 1893-4. | 1894-5. | 1895-6. |
|---|---|---|---|---|
| Income ... ... ... .. ... | 674 | 656 | 771 | 1,208 |
| Expenditure... ... ... ... ... | 826 | 998 | 781 | 1,169 |

[1] The Chola king Rájéndra-Deva claims to have gained a great victory over the Chálukyas in the middle of the 11th century at Kúdali-sangam, which, as Dr. Hultzsch thinks, may be this place. On the other hand, it may be one near S'ris'aila.

**Madagada-kere** or **Masur-Madaga-kere.** — A large tank in Shikárpur taluq, 7 miles north of the kasba, on the frontier. It is formed by embanking the waters of the Choradi or Kumadvati, at a point where it runs through a gorge in a low chain of hills. The original bund was 660 feet wide at top and 90 feet high, and according to an Arabic inscription on the spot it was at one time repaired by the Navάb of Sávanur. The sheet of water—second only to the Súlekere—thus formed irrigated a large extent of land in Dharwar. When the tank breached many years ago, the bund was reconstructed on a smaller scale, in consequence of which a considerable tract of rich land, formerly included in the bed of the tank, was left bare. This was soon taken up for cultivation, and as many as thirty-five villages have sprung up around, contributing Rs. 45,000 more to the Mysore revenue than was formerly realized. Should the embankment be ever raised to its original standard, as at one time contemplated, most of these villages would be submerged.

**Malavalli.**—A village in the north of Shikárpur taluq, about 9 miles from Siralkoppa. Population, 588.

Of interest on account of a pillar discovered by me there bearing an inscription of Háritiputra Sátakarni, probably of the second century; the oldest in Mysore next to the Edicts of Asoka. From this it appears that the original name of the village was Maṭṭapaṭṭi.

**Nagar.**—A taluq in the south-west. Area 529 square miles. Head-quarters, till then at Nagar, were transferred to Kollúrkatte in 1893. Contains the following hoblis, villages, and population :—

| No. | Hòblis. | Villages. | Hamlets. | Villages classified. | | Population. |
|---|---|---|---|---|---|---|
| | | | | Govern-ment. | Jodi. | |
| 1 | Haritála ... ... ... | 5 | 25 | 5 | — | 1,028 |
| 2 | Humcha ... ... ... | 37 | 48 | 37 | — | 6,424 |
| 3 | Jála ... ... ... ... | 22 | 55 | 22 | — | 7,139 |
| 4 | Kerehalli ... ... ... | 55 | 107 | 54 | 1 | 8,768 |
| 5 | Nagara ... ... ... | 31 | 30 | 31 | — | 11,191 |
| 6 | Paṭṭaguppe ... .. ... | 54 | 111 | 54 | — | 8,291 |
| | Total ... ... ... | 204 | 376 | 203 | 1 | 42,841 |

*Principal places, with population.*—Nagar, 1,576 ; Humcha, 997.

The Nagar taluq was extended in 1832–3 by amalgamating with it the Anantapur taluq, but the latter was re-established in 1857–8. In 1875 a portion of it was again added to Nagar.

The taluq is enclosed on three sides by hills, the drainage of which flows north-west, uniting in the Sharavati. But the streams in the south-west of the taluq run directly down the Ghats westward and discharge into the sea at Kundapur, forming in S. Kanara the three rivers Gargita, Chakra nadi, and Mudur. The Honnár hobli in the north-west is an isolated bit of country belonging to S. Kanara, and forming part of the endowments of the temple at Kollur below the ghats. The principal mountain is the Kodachádri parvata in the north-west, to the north of which is the Kollur ghat. The other pass to the coast is by the Haidar Ghar or Hosangadi ghat in the south-west.

This is a purely Malnad taluq. The whole is densely wooded, the southern part being composed of a perfect cluster of hills, in a basin formed by which Nagar, the capital formerly called Bednur, is situated. The Sharavati flows from south to north, and its valley may be said to be the most open portion of this very inaccessible country. The Rámachandrapur Nála is a small stream which flows very close to and almost parallel with the Sharavati, and joins it near the boundary of the taluq. To the west of the valley in which these two streams flow the appearance of the country becomes wilder and wilder as the Ghats are approached, and these are here more precipitous than usual, and present few natural outlets. The rise towards the crest of the Ghats is very rapid, a height of 4,411 feet being attained at Kodachádri, a mountain on whose summit meet the three boundaries of South Kanara, Nagar, and Ságar taluqs. Tŏ the east of the Sharavati and to the north generally the country is more level, although the extent of jungle appears to suffer no diminution; but it changes considerably in character, the proportion of timber trees seeming to be greater than to the west, where the soil is more shallow, with much laterite.

The productions of the country are areca-nut, pepper, cardamoms, and rice. Dry crops are not raised anywhere. The areca-nut is reputed to be of very fine quality, but the gardens have been much neglected. They largely belong to Brahmans, who are dependent on labour imported from the coast for their cultivation. The forests are chiefly *káns*, there being but little deciduous forest; what there is being found chiefly to the north and east, towards Anantapur. Rice is exported to the coast, and areca-nut to Bellary and Walájapet by way of Bírur. All other articles of consumption, and cloths of every description are imported from the plain countries; about one-fourth by the merchants who come to buy areca-nut, and the rest by ryots from Tirthahalli, Avinhalli, and Kollur, either on bullocks or by porters.

The revenue settlement was introduced in 1877, except in the Haritala and Kerehalli hoblis, which were settled in 1874 when they formed part of the Anantapur taluq. The area of the taluq was thus distributed in the survey of 1877 :—

| | | |
|---|---|---|
| Culturable (dry, 8,169 ; wet, 31,268 ; garden, 2,255) | ... | 41,692 |
| Unculturable (including roads, tanks, village sites, &c.) | ... | 189,136 |
| Total acres | ... | 230,828 |

The unoccupied arable land was 10,775 acres. The total revenue demand for 1891–2 (15 months) was Rs. 1,82,026, and in 1892–3 it was Rs. 1,63,997.

The average rainfall at Nagar for 26 years (1870–95), and at the other station for 3 years (1893–5), was as follows :—

| | Jan. | Feb. | Mar. | Apl. | May | June | July | Aug. | Sept. | Oct. | Nov. | Dec. | Year. |
|---|---|---|---|---|---|---|---|---|---|---|---|---|---|
| Nagar ... | 0·14 | — | 0·12 | 0·86 | 3·92 | 42·07 | 72·03 | 40·02 | 15·02 | 7·89 | 2·02 | 0·34 | ...184·43 |
| Kollúrkaṭṭe | — | — | 1·24 | 2·79 | 1·79 | 25·79 | 26·11 | 24·12 | 3·69 | 5·43 | 1·22 | — | ... 92·18 |

Another register for 22 years makes the annual average at Nagar 192·59 inches.

Considerable attention has been paid in recent years to improving the communications of the taluq, by a system of roads radiating from Kollúrkaṭṭe. There are thus roads east to Ayanur, and north to Ságar and to Anantapur ; with the Ghat roads to the coast south, through Nagar and Haidarghar to the Hosangadi ghat, and west to the Kollúr ghat. There is also a road from Anantapur south through Humchada-kaṭṭe to Tirthahalli, and one is projected from Hulikal near Haidarghar to Tirthahalli. A branch from the Ságar road connects with the Kollúr ghat road.

**Nagar.**—A town situated 13° 50′ N. lat., 75° 6′ E. long., on the Kollúrkaṭṭe-Haidarghar road. Head-quarters till 1893 of the Nagar taluq, and has a municipality.

| Population in 1891. | Males. | Females. | Total. |
|---|---|---|---|
| Hindus ... ... ... ... ... | 702 | 716 | 1,418 |
| Muhammadans ... ... ... ... | 64 | 64 | 128 |
| Christians ... ... ... ... ... | 19 | 11 | 30 |
| Total ... ... | 785 | 791 | 1,576 |

It was originally a small village, called, from the nature of the forest around, Bidaru haḷḷi, bamboo village, and contained a temple of Nilakantha, the property of a Brahman named Honne Kambli Bhatta. About 1640, under the name of Bidarúr or Bidanúr (Bednur), it became the capital of the Keladi chiefs, who transferred the seat of their government hither from Ikkéri. Being in the direct course of trade by the Hosangadi ghat, it rapidly increased in size and importance, until there was a prospect of the houses reaching the number of a lakh, which would entitle it to be called a Nagara. The walls were 8 miles in circumference, and had 10 gates, named the Dilli, Kodial, Kavaledurga, &c. The palace was on a hill in the centre, surrounded with a citadel, and the whole city was encircled by woods, hills and fortified defiles, extending a great way in circumference.

Sivappa Náyak, whose conquests have been elsewhere described, did much to improve and enlarge the town, and his successors ruled here undisturbed till 1763, at which time their territories extended from Sante Bennur and Holalkere in the east, over the whole of South Kanara to the western coast. In that year Haidar Ali, having conquered all the northern parts of Mysore, advanced upon this capital. The Ráni Virammáji, having in vain tried to buy him off with offers of large sums of money, took to flight, ordering the palace to be fired if the treasures could not be saved. The terror-stricken inhabitants fled *en masse* to the woods. Haidar pressed on, and, storming the town, extinguished the flames of the palace and gained possession of a booty estimated at twelve millions sterling in value.

In pursuance of the intention to make it a *Nagara*, he gave the place the name of Haidar-Nagar, and greatly increased its trade. He built a palace outside the fort, established in the town his principal arsenal, which employed many hands in the manufacture of arms and ammunition, and continued the mint, where coins were first struck in his name, the Haidari pagodas, and much money was coined during his reign. He gave great encouragement to merchants, and endeavoured, but with little success, to introduce the cultivation of mulberries and the rearing of silkworms.

The place suffered much during the wars with Tipu Sultan. It was captured by the British in February 1783, under General Matthews, and surrendered at the end of April. During the sieges the palace and the town were burnt. Tipu rebuilt the palace, and endeavoured to restore the town, but his regulations for the protection of internal trade dealt a severe blow to its prosperity. He also appointed a Kázi, who pulled down the Christian church and Hindu temples, broke to pieces numerous inscriptions on stone, and erected a mosque from the ruins. In the insurrection of 1830, Nagar, as it was called after 1789, again became the object of attack. But from the time that the court was removed the place lost its prospects, as it never obtained a footing as a mercantile town between the table-land and the coast, being merely a place of transit. Mr. Stokes, writing in 1838, says :—"Nagar and its vicinity exhibit traces of great decline in wealth and population.

It has nearly lost its trade, for which, from the difficulty of access, it is not naturally well adapted." Under the Rája's government it gave its name to the Nagar Faujdari, which included the present Districts of Shimoga and Kadur. From 1831 that name was changed to Nagar Division, and from 1863 to 1881, when Divisions were abolished, the Nagar Division was composed of the Shimoga, Kadur and Chitaldroog Districts. Nagar has latterly benefited by the opening out and improvement of the ghat-roads, but the transfer of the taluq head-quarters to Kollúrkaṭṭe in 1893 further tends to diminish its importance.

| Municipal Funds. | 1892–3. | 1893–4. | 1894–5. | 1895–6. |
|---|---|---|---|---|
| Income ... ... ... ... ... | 486 | 512 | 497 | 642 |
| Expenditure ... ... ... ... | 621 | 578 | 554 | 669 |

**Nyamti.**—A town situated in 14° 9′ N. lat., 75° 38′ E. long., on the Honnáli-Ayanur road. Head-quarters from 1869 to 1882 of the Honnáli taluq, and is a municipality.

| Population in 1891. | Males. | Females. | Total. |
|---|---|---|---|
| Hindus (with 2 Jains) ... ... ... | 1,383 | 1,494 | 2,877 |
| Muhammadans ... ... ... ... | 118 | 107 | 225 |
| Total ... ... | 1,501 | 1,601 | 3,102 |

Nyámti is a town of very modern date, the petta having been established in the time of the Divan Purnaiya. Being situated between the Malnád and the Maidan regions, a considerable trade is carried on by the merchants, who are all Lingáyits, in exchanging the products of both tracts. The grain of the Malnád and the jaggory of the neighbouring taluqs, which can be stored in this dry climate for some time without risk of damage, with areca-nut from Nagar and Koppa, are forwarded to Bellary, Dharwar, &c., in return for cloths and other articles, which are sent to the Malnád and Kanara. During the American war of 1864–5 much money was made here by the cotton trade.

| Municipal Funds. | 1892–3. | 1893–4. | 1894–5. | 1895–6. |
|---|---|---|---|---|
| Income ... ... ... ... ... | 1,483 | 1,412 | 1,630 | 2,754 |
| Expenditure ... ... ... ... | 2,156 | 2,846 | 2,367 | 3,368 |

**Sagar.**—A taluq in the west. Area 666 square miles. Headquarters at Ságar. Contains the following hoblis, villages, and population:—

| No. | Hoblis. | Villages. | Hamlets. | Villages classified. | | Population. |
|---|---|---|---|---|---|---|
| | | | | Govern-ment. | Inam. | |
| 1 | Anantapura... ... ... | 61 | 40 | 61 | — | 8,070 |
| 2 | Bárangi ... ... ... | 35 | 73 | 35 | — | 6,801 |
| 3 | Ikkéri ... ... ... | 57 | 90 | 57 | — | 10,541 |
| 4 | Karúr ... ... ... | 33 | 51 | 33 | — | 9,887 |
| 5 | Ságara ... ... ... | 32 | 25 | 32 | — | 11,840 |
| 6 | Tálaguppe ... ... ... | 28 | 31 | 28 | — | 11,860 |
| | Total ... ... ... | 246 | 310 | 246 | — | 58,999 |

*Principal places, with population.*—Ságar, 2,869; Keladi, 1,388; Kánale, 1,317; Taḍagalale, 1,045; Nellúr, 1,026.

This taluq occupies the most westerly projection of Mysore, being at one point not more than 8 miles from the sea. The west and greater part of the north and south are bounded by the Ghats, a spur from which crosses the taluq from west to east, passing south of Ikkéri and parting the western from the northern streams. The Sharavati runs through the middle from south to north-west, receiving near Bárangi the Yenne Hole. On touching the frontier it turns west, and descending the Ghats in the far-famed Falls of Gersoppa, flows to the sea at Honavar. The principal stream running north is the Varada, which rises near Ikkéri. The chief heights are Deva-konda and Govardhangiri.

The taluq is considered purely Malnád, but there is a considerable difference between the south-western and north-eastern portions, separated mostly by the river Sharavati. The rice-fields in the former bear a double crop annually, but the gardens, stocked with areca palms, pepper and cardamoms, are somewhat inferior. This tract presents the appearance of a rolling stretch of bare hill-tops, the sides and valleys densely wooded, the latter occupied by the gardens. The scenery is surpassingly beautiful, and the climate, in the hottest time of the year, is cool and pleasant. The people live in separate homesteads, and village communities, so far as living in one place is concerned, are unknown. The remaining portion of the taluq is comparatively level and open, but the climate is not so good as in the other part. Only one crop of rice can be raised annually, but some of the gardens are remarkably fine. The people, as a rule, live together in villages, but still there are many homesteads scattered here and there, principally to the south-west.

The forests, although on the whole extensive, are not in compact masses, nor are they very productive. Excepting the great Hinni forest, which lies to the south of the Gersoppa Falls, the remainder are chiefly *káns*, or tracts of virgin evergreen forest, in most of which pepper grows abundantly self-sown and uncared for, but little of the produce being collected owing to the depredations of monkeys. There are also towards the south patches of evergreen forest, generally only a few acres in extent, with very sharply-defined limits. There is a thick undergrowth of a low plant called Goravi katige. Deciduous timber trees are rare. Inside one of these patches of forest the growth of trees and underwood is so dense that it is difficult to pass through; on emerging, suddenly hardly a bush will be visible for the hundreds of yards or more of grassy open which may intervene between the patches. The real cause of this alternation of bare ground and densely-wooded patches is to be found in the laterite formation. Wherever the hard bed of laterite is near the surface wood refuses to grow. Towards the east the forest is gradually disappearing before the inroads of garden cultivators, who mercilessly strip and clear the Bayan Betta, as they are called, in order to obtain the *soppu*, or leaf manure, which is indispensable for their gardens.

In the káns the soil is rich and deep, but in most of the taluq the soil is hard and shallow, with much laterite. Ságar is essentially a garden taluq, and rice cultivation is also extensive. Dry crops are of no account, and raised on the same ground only once in three or four years. The rice is largely exported by the ryots themselves, chiefly to Gersoppa, by way of the Govardhangiri and Hinni ghats; but that of the southern máganis is often sent to Bhatkala or Baidur. Areca-nut is exported principally towards Bellary, though some goes also to Walajapet and to Birur. Cardamoms and pepper are taken to the Kanara and Dharwar markets.

At first under the Kadambas, this country subsequently was subject to the rule of the Sántara kings of Pomburcha, as feudatory to the Chálukyas. Various governors of the Banavase Twelve Thousand, appointed by the Chálukyas, Hoysalas and Yádavas, held sway over it from the 12th century, until under Vijayanagar the Keladi chiefs arose to power, of whose territory it formed a part until taken by Haidar and annexed to Mysore.

The revenue settlement was introduced in 1874. The area of the taluq was thus distributed in 1892:—

| | |
|---|---|
| Culturable (dry, 27,790; wet, 41,282; garden, 4,224) | 73,296 |
| Unculturable (including roads, tanks, village sites, &c.) ... | 349,932 |
| Total acres ... | 423,228 |

The unoccupied arable area was 29,057 acres. The total revenue demand for 1891–2 (15 months) was Rs. 3,97,453, and for 1892–3 it was Rs. 4,14,295.

The average rainfall at Ságar for 26 years (1870–95) was as follows:—

| Jan. | Feb. | Mar. | Apl. | May | June | July | Aug. | Sept. | Oct. | Nov. | Dec. | | Year. |
|---|---|---|---|---|---|---|---|---|---|---|---|---|---|
| 0·12 | 0·02 | 0·28 | 1·89 | 2·85 | 14·19 | 26·86 | 12·94 | 5·23 | 5·22 | 1·28 | 0·18 | ... | 71·06 |

Another register for 23 years makes the annual average 69·71.

The high road from Shimoga to the Gersoppa Falls runs through Anantapur and Ságar. From Ságar there are roads north to Sirálkoppa, with a branch to Sorab, and south to Kúllurkaṭṭe, with a branch to the Kollur ghat. From Anantapur there are roads south-west to Kúllurkaṭṭe and Nagar, and south to Tirthahalli. The passes to the coast are the Gersoppa, Hinni, and Govardhangiri to Honavar; the Hogavadi to Bhatkal; and the Karni and Kollur to Baidur. Regular roads have been constructed through the first and last of these; the others are only fit for pack bullocks, which are largely used.

**Sagar.**—A town on the left bank of the Varada near its source, situated in 14° 10′ N. lat., 75° 5′ E. long., 40 miles west-north-west of Shimoga, on the Shimoga-Gersoppa road. Head-quarters of the Ságar Sub-division and of the Ságar taluq, and a municipality.

| Population in 1891. | Males. | Females. | Total. |
|---|---|---|---|
| Hindus ... ... ... ... ... | 1,376 | 1,013 | 2,389 |
| Muhammadans ... ... ... .. | 219 | 183 | 402 |
| Jains ... ... ... ... ... ... | 12 | 1 | 13 |
| Christians ... ... ... ... ... | 34 | 19 | 53 |
| Total ... ... | 1,641 | 1,216 | 2,857 |

This town is one of the chief depôts for the areca-nut trade, and contains some wealthy merchants. Pepper, sandalwood and other products of the Malnád are exported by them to the Madras districts east and north, and to parts of Bombay in the west, the returns being made chiefly in cloths.

The town has been recently extended to the west by a quarter named Chamarájendra Péte, in memory of the late Maharaja's visit.

| Municipal Funds. | 1892–3. | 1893–4. | 1894–5. | 1895–6. |
|---|---|---|---|---|
| Income ... ... ... ... ... | 2,128 | 2,030 | 1,857 | 2,923 |
| Expenditure ... ... ... ... | 3,271 | 2,241 | 2,753 | 3,282 |

**Sante Bennur.**—A village in Channagiri taluq, on the road from Súlekere to Sásalu railway-station. Head-quarters of the Sante Bennúr hobli. Population, 1,643.

It was called Sante Bennúr on account of the large weekly fair (*sante*) held there, and to distinguish it from Male Bennúr, Ráni Bennúr, and others of the name. It was founded, probably in the 16th century, by a chief of the Basavapatna family, on the spot where a hare had been observed to turn upon the hounds, which indicated heroic soil. The settlement of traders and merchants was encouraged, and a large petta sprung up. Hanumappa Náyak, one of the chiefs, erected a palace at Sante Bennúr, and had a skilfully-constructed *honḍa* or reservoir made in front of the ancient temple of Ranganátha, faced round with flights of steps, and with ornamental pavilions at the angles and in the centre. The one in the middle, called the Vasanta mantapa, had a fountain playing from the top. After the capture of Basavapatna the town was taken by the Musalman forces of Bijapur, under Randulha Khan, who destroyed the temple and erected in its place a mosque of very large dimensions. Hanumappa Náyak, who had been forced to retire to Tarikere and Kaldurga, was greatly incensed at this, and watching his opportunity planned a night attack, in which he put to death the Muhammadan governor, and desecrated the mosque with the blood of hogs, pulling out a stone from the walls of each compartment. The Tarikere chiefs eventually regained the place and held it until it was taken by Chitaldroog early in the 17th century. In 1717 it was captured by the Bednúr chiefs, who fortified it, and in spite of repeated attacks by Chitaldroog, retained it till 1761, when it fell into the hands of Haidar Ali. In common with other places in the neighbourhood it was plundered and destroyed by the Mahrattas under Parasu Ram Bhao in 1791. The mosque, never used since its desecration, and the *honḍa*, with its ruinous but graceful pavilions, are the only points of interest now left.

**Sharavati.**—A river which rises at Ambu-tirtha, near Nonabar, in the Tirthahalli taluq. It takes a north-westerly course by Fatte-petta, receives the Haridravati on the right below Paṭṭaguppe, and the Yenne Hole on the left above Bárangi. On arriving at the frontier it bends to the west, and precipitating itself down the celebrated Falls of

Gersoppa, and passing that village (properly *Géru-sappe*), which is really some 18 miles distant, discharges into the sea at Honávar in N. Kanara. The name Sharávati, arrow-born, is in allusion to its flowing from the Ambu-tirtha, which was formed by a stroke of Rama's arrow. The stream is crossed by 70 anicuts, from which small channels are drawn having an aggregate length of 26 miles.

The magnificent *Falls of Gersoppa*, or Jóg, that is, the waterfall, as they are called by the natives, are unquestionably the grandest natural beauty in Mysore, rich as it is in splendid scenery. They eclipse every other Fall in India and have few rivals in any part of the world. "While excelled in height by the Cerosoli and Evanson cascades in the Alps, and the Falls of the Arve in Savoy, the Gersoppa cataract surpasses them in volume of water precipitated; and while much inferior to Niagara in volume, it far excels those celebrated Falls of the New World in height."[1] They are situated in 14° 14′ N. lat., and 74° 50′ E. long., on the borders of Mysore and N. Kanara, 62 miles from Shimoga in the former and 30 from the port of Honávar (Honore) in the latter. Their existence appears to have been unknown at the time of Buchanan's journey in 1800. The Sharávati, flowing over a very rocky bed about 250 yards wide, here reaches a tremendous chasm, 960 feet in depth, and "performs (as Captain Newbold has expressed it) this stupendous lover's leap from the chains of the giant Ghats into the arms of his ocean-rescued[2] mistress—prolific Kanara."

The water comes down in four distinct falls, presenting a scene of transcendent grandeur and sublimity, whose effect is greatly heightened by the wild and beautiful country around, covered with a wealth of luxuriant vegetation. The Rája Fall[3] pours in one unbroken column sheer to the depth of 830 feet. Half way down it is encountered by the Roarer, another fall, which precipitates itself into a vast cup and then rushes violently downwards at an angle of forty-five degrees to meet its famous compeer. A third fall, the Rocket, shoots downwards in a series of jets; while the fourth, called the Dame Blanche, is an

[1] The height of the Cerosoli cascade is 2,400 feet; that of Evanson 1,200 feet and the Falls of the Arve 1,100 feet. At Niagara, a river two miles across, contracted to less than half its former breadth, is hurled over a precipice 164 feet high in two great sheets into the basin below.—*J. A. S. B.*, xiv, 421.

[2] Alluding to the legend of the formation of the western coast by Parasu Rama.

[3] By various visitors this has been called the Grand fall, the Main fall, and the Horse-shoe fall. The Rája after whom it is now generally named was the Sode Rája of Sirsi, who proposed to erect a little shrine or mandapa on the spot, the lines for the foundation of which may be seen on the stone just above the Rája's rock which projects over the chasm.

These falls are perhaps unique as a scene of natural beauty in India free from all signs of idolatry.

Undine-like cascade gliding quietly over the mountain side in a sheet of foam.

The most favourable time for visiting these glorious works of nature is in the cold season, when the river is low enough to admit of crossing to the Mysore side, whence the best views are obtained. During the monsoon the place is enveloped in a dense cloud of vapour, through which rises the thunder of the invisible mighty waters in their fearful descent. There are good bungalows on both the Mysore and the Bombay sides, immediately at the head of the falls. Close by the latter is a slab of rock projecting over the verge of the gulf, by lying down on which and peering over the best view is obtained of the appalling abyss from above, rendered more striking by the continual flight across it of myriads of rock pigeons, which find a congenial home in the face of the cliffs.

"I lay down flat on this shelf (says a visitor in the month of August, fifty years ago) and drew myself up to its edge, over which as I stretched my head a sight burst on the view which I shall never forget and can never hope to describe. I have since looked down the fuming and sulphurous craters of Etna and Vesuvius, but have never experienced the sensations whioh overwhelmed me in the first downward gaze into this (*hibernice*) volcano of waters: for so it looks; a chaotic scene that rivets with basilisk fascination the gaze of the spectator. It was with great reluctance and with an intense feeling of depression that I withdrew my head, drenched in spray, from the brink of the precipice. One might almost gaze for ever on this abyss in which a mighty mass of water appears eternally burying itself in a mist-shrouded grave. The clouds of spray which continually ascend heavenwards in slow and majestic wreaths appear to typify the shadowy ghosts of the entombed waters."

The Falls are seen to greatest advantage from the selected points of view which have been cleared on the Mysore bank, the most popular being Watkins's platform. From this side a descent may be made to the pool below, the water in which is 130 feet in depth. But this is a difficult undertaking and the re-ascent extremely laborious. The view looking upwards from below is generally considered far less impressive than from the other points, as regards the Falls themselves, but the grandly rugged features of the chasm and the winding gorge in which it is prolonged are more clearly seen in all their savage nakedness.

The varying effects of light and shade at different hours are extremely beautiful. A lovely rainbow spans the waters in the afternoon, rising with the declining sun, and even lunar rainbows are said to be formed in certain aspects of the moon. Rockets and blazing torches or bundles of straw cast over on a dark night, throw out a fitful glare upon the jaws of the abyss, producing weird and solemn effects as viewed from the Rája's Rock. No words can suffice to adequately describe the charms of a scene replete with every element of the sublime, combining in one superb panorama so many varying aspects both of terror and of beauty, all instinct with the life, the force and play of moving waters.

"The precipice over which the water falls affords a fine section of gneiss and its associated hypogene schists, which dip easterly and northerly away from the Falls at an angle of about 35°. The gneiss is composed of quartz and felspar, with both mica and hornblende, and alternates with micaceous, talcose, actinolitic, chloritic and hornblende schists, imbedding (especially the latter) iron pyrites. These rocks are penetrated by veins of quartz and felspar and also of a fine grained granite, composed of small grains of white felspar, quartz and mica. The mass of hypogene rocks has evidently been worn back several hundred feet by the erosion and abrasion of the cataract; the softer talcose and micaceous schists have suffered most. Rock basins are frequent in the bed of the river, which is worn in the rock and rugged with water-worn rocky masses." [1]

Two officers of the Indian Navy, deputed by Government to measure the Falls, arrived there on the 6th of March, 1856. Their account of the feat, written in the old bungalow book, is as follows :—

Threw a light flying bridge across the chasm from the tree overhanging the Roarer, to the rock westward of that called the Rája's rock. To this slung a cradle of light bamboo, capable of holding two people comfortably. The cradle traversed on one single and two double blocks, through which rove the four hawsers composing the bridge. We had previously placed the bridge from the Rája's rock to the tree, but found that the lead line would not, from any single part of the bridge, plumb clear of the Roarer, or the rocks on either side ; thus proving beyond a doubt that the pool had never before been plumbed from the sides of the chasm.

In the forenoon of the 12th of March, all arrangements being completed and provision made against remote contingencies, we made the passage in the cradle from side to side, halting in the centre to pour a libation to the guardian spirits of the chasm. The arrangements being found perfectly satisfactory, we proceeded to plumb the pool. The cradle with one person was eased away to a distance of 47 feet from the tree. The lead line was lowered from the shore through a block (*vulgo*, a pulley) on the cradle, passing down through its centre. The plummet consisted of 7 lbs. of hard lead placed in the centre of an annular life-buoy slung horizontally, the whole weight being about 18 lbs. When the lead reached the pool, the

[1] *J. A. S. B.*, xiv, 420.

life-buoy floated it, and thus the lead man in the cradle felt the loss of weight. Having during our service had a little experience in deep water, we knew that a loss of 20 lbs. from a plumb-line of upwards of 100 fathoms would be scarcely appreciable, and so we found it. But by hauling up half a fathom and letting go suddenly, the life-buoy made a discernible splash in the water. A mark was then placed on the line by the block, and the angle of its dip taken with a theodolite on the brink of the precipice near the tree, at the hypotenusal distance of 47 feet. This gave the perpendicular depression of the cradle below the instrument (on a level with the tree) as 14 feet, which, added to the line paid out, 815 feet, gave the exact depth 829 feet.

In the afternoon we descended the ravine, and with a raft of a few bamboos and three boats' breakers, paddled and sounded all round and across the pool, having previously, from above, turned off a great part of the Roarer into the Rocket. We found that 22 fathoms was the greatest depth anywhere. This sounding was taken very near the west side, about 30 yards from the head of the pool or base of the Grand Fall. We climbed the rock on which the Roarer falls, and when about 30 feet up it, the stream, which before had been mild rather, came down with great force on our devoted heads, and we had to "hold on by our eyelids" to prevent being washed off.

By measuring a base we ascertained the horizontal distance between the centres of the Kanara and Mysore bungalows[1] to be 710 yards; between the Rája's rock and the tree that plumbs the Roarer, 74 yards. The top of the Rája's rock is 5 feet below the level of the above-mentioned tree. A plumb-line lowered from this tree into the bed of the Roarer measured 315 feet.

On the 15th of March, broke up our bridge, from which we had taken several satisfactory views of the chasm, and descended by a rope into the cup of the Roarer, where we breakfasted, and afterwards, with some little difficulty at one point, passed down by the side of the Roarer, and reached a position at the back of the Grand Fall, whence the Rocket and Roarer were seen to the right of it. From this place only can you have a correct idea of the great depth of the cavern in front of which the Grand Fall drops. The sky clouded over and thunder pealed when we were below. The effect was grand in the extreme. At 5 P.M. reached the top of the cliff in safety.

The new Kanara bungalow is 1,670 feet above the level of the sea, the old one 1,850. The old Mysore bungalow was 30 feet lower than the last; the new one, built at what was known as Palmer's platform, is still lower.

**Shikárpur.**—A taluq in the north. Area 428 square miles. Head-quarters at Shikárpur. Contains the following hoblis, villages and population:—

[1] This was the old Mysore bungalow, no longer in existence.

| No. | Hoblis. | Villages. | Hamlets. | Villages classified. | | Population. |
|---|---|---|---|---|---|---|
| | | | | Government. | Jodi. | |
| 1 | Bellandúr ... ... ... | 23 | 13 | 20 | 3 | 5,419 |
| 2 | Hosúr ... ... ... | 21 | — | 21 | — | 5,927 |
| 3 | Mugalagere... ... ... | 39 | 5 | 39 | — | 9,515 |
| 4 | Shikárpura ... ... ... | 42 | 3 | 39 | 3 | 16,254 |
| 5 | Tálagunda ... ... ... | 36 | 1 | 34 | 2 | 12,667 |
| 6 | Udagaṇi ... ... ... | 36 | — | 36 | — | 14,622 |
| | Total ... ... ... | 197 | 22 | 189 | 8 | 64,404 |

*Principal places, with population.*—Shikárpur, 5,011; Sirálkoppa, 2,125; Isúr, 1,703; Sálur, 1,490; Belagávi, 1,470; Tagarti, 1,223; Bilakí, 1,024; Kaḍenandihalli, 1,033; Begúru, 1,014.

The taluq is crossed from south to north by the Choradi or Kumadvati, which forms the large Masur-Madak tank on the northern frontier. There are lines of low hills on all sides, covered with jungle, which gives shelter to numerous tigers, cheetas, and other wild beasts.

Being on the border where Malnád and Maidán meet, it partakes of the characteristics of both. Except for the Jambur hills running down into the middle from the north, the gently undulating surface is unbroken, and where uncultivated is covered with low scrubby jungle, which in the south and west rises into forest. The soils are chiefly reddish-brown and grey, very light and friable, and containing much sand, except in the low-lying grounds, where they are much darker in colour and more clayey. In the extreme north, however, and on the banks of the Choradi, dark brown and black soil of a superior description is found, on which wet crops are raised. In the east, where dry crop cultivation is the most successful, the soil is less sandy and more like loam, except in the high-lying wet crop land.

The main cultivation is sugar-cane and rice, especially the former, to which crop the energies of the ryots are chiefly directed, and on the successful maturing of which the prosperity of the taluq rests. Dry crops in the west are poor, chiefly rági, horse-gram, and castor-oil. In the east the dry crops are much better, and cotton and jola grow well in some villages. The principal export of the taluq is jaggory, which mostly goes to Dharwar, and rice, which is sent in various directions. Sirálkoppa is the chief market for grain, and Shikárpur for cloth.

The taluq is a perfect museum of antiquities, and no part of Mysore is richer in remains and records of the past. It is here that I have found evidence of the rule of the S'átaváhanas and Guptas, and the true history of the early Kadambas. Bandanikke was the chief city of the Nágarakhanda Seventy, and Belgávi of the great Banavase Twelve Thousand province, which was one of the chief possessions of succeeding dynasties, the Chálukyas, the Ráshtrakútas, the Gangas, the Hoysalas, the Yádavas, and others, down to the time of Vijayanagar and the Keladi or Bednur chiefs, overwhelmed in the conquests of Haidar Ali.

The revenue settlement was introduced in 1873, when the area of the taluq was distributed as follows:—

| | | |
|---|---|---|
| Culturable (dry, 60,173; wet, 42,545; garden, 1,613) | ... | 104,331 |
| Unculturable (including roads, tanks, village sites, &c.) | ... | 106,083 |
| Total acres ... | ... | 210,414 |

The unoccupied arable area was 26,927 acres. The total revenue demand in 1891–2 (15 months) was Rs. 2,60,105, and in 1892–3 it was Rs. 3,90,082.

The average rainfall for 26 years (1870–95) at Shikárpur, and for 3 years (1893–5) at the other station, was as follows:—

| | Jan. | Feb. | Mar. | Apl. | May | June | July | Aug. | Sept. | Oct. | Nov. | Dec. | Year. |
|---|---|---|---|---|---|---|---|---|---|---|---|---|---|
| Shikárpur ... | 0·09 | 0·11 | 0·29 | 1·06 | 2·97 | 4·39 | 8·16 | 4·16 | 2·81 | 4·60 | 1·27 | 0·22 | 30·13 |
| Sirálkoppa... | — | — | 0·34 | 0·89 | 1·35 | 6·31 | 9·38 | 6·00 | 1·31 | 9·69 | 0·78 | — | 36·05 |

According to another register for 23 years the average at Shikárpur is 31·33.

From Shikárpur there are roads to Shimoga, Anantapur, Honnáli, and Sirálkoppa. From the latter there are roads to Hire Kerur and the railway at Byádgi, to Anavatti, to Sorab, and to Ságar.

**Shikárpur.**—A town near the right bank of the Choradi or Kumadvati, situated in 14° 16′ N. lat., 75° 25′ E. long., 33 miles north-west of Shimoga, with which it is connected by road. Head-quarters of the Shikárpur taluq, and a municipality.

| Population in 1891. | Males. | Females. | Total. |
|---|---|---|---|
| Hindus ... ... ... ... ... | 874 | 892 | 1,766 |
| Muhammadans ... ... ... ... | 174 | 153 | 327 |
| Total ... ... ... | 1,048 | 1,045 | 2,093 |

The town appears to have been founded by one Maliya, and after him originally called Maliyanhalli. The Keladi chiefs on gaining possession changed the name to Mahádanpur. During the time of either Haidar or Tipu, it received its present name of Shikárpur or Shikáripur, hunting or hunter's town, from the abundance of game there met with during a royal hunt. The old fort at the western end is now in ruins.

| Municipal Funds. | 1892-3. | 1893-4. | 1894-5. | 1895-6. |
|---|---|---|---|---|
| Income ... ... ... ... ... | 1,541 | 1,536 | 1,731 | 3,148 |
| Expenditure ... ... ... ... ... | 1,752 | 1,388 | 1,657 | 3,110 |

**Shimoga.**—A taluq in the south-east. Area 659 square miles. Head-quarters at Shimoga. Contains the following hoblis, villages and population :—

| No. | Hoblis. | Villages. | Hamlets. | Villages classified. | | | Population. |
|---|---|---|---|---|---|---|---|
| | | | | Government. | Sarvamánya. | Jódi. | |
| 1 | Benkipur ... .. ... | 72 | 25 | 65 | 1 | 6 | 11,911 |
| 2 | Bidare ... ... ... | 44 | 17 | 34 | 2 | 8 | 9,350 |
| 3 | Háranhalli ... ... | 59 | 3 | 56 | — | 3 | 12,023 |
| 4 | Holalúr ... ... ... | 51 | 11 | 44 | 4 | 3 | 16,409 |
| 5 | Hole Honnúr ... ... | 55 | 1 | 54 | — | 1 | 15,066 |
| 6 | Kumsi ... ... ... | 34 | 5 | 34 | — | — | 5,560 |
| 7 | Shimoga ... ... ... | 78 | 37 | 62 | — | 16 | 24,397 |
| | Total ... ... | 393 | 99 | 349 | 7 | 37 | 94,716 |

*Principal places, with population.*—Shimoga, 11,504 ; Hole Honnúr, 2,947 ; Háranhalli, 2,288 ; Benkipur, 2,270 ; Harakéri, 1,728 ; Kumsi, 1,656 ; Mattúr, 1,377 ; Ayanúr, 1,157 ; Sógáne, 1,101 ; Uragaḍúr, 1,099.

Kumsi and Haranhalli máganis were added to this taluq from Honnáli in 1882.

The Tunga and the Bhadra, entering the taluq on the south, flow northwards and unite at Kudali, 9 miles north-north-east of Shimoga, whence the Tungabhadra continues north with a winding course. The greater part of the taluq on the west and south is covered with hills and forest, abounding in tigers, cheetas, bears, and other wild animals. The ancient divisions were Gájanur-pál to the west of the Tunga, Yeḍatore-pál between the rivers, and Benkipura east of the Bhadra.

The cultivation of the taluq lies almost all in the level valleys of the rivers, but owing to the width and the depth below the level of the country of their channels, their waters are not made use of for irrigation. On the other hand, the force of the currents, especially in the Tunga, serves to float timber towards the plain country. The hills in the south-west are covered with forest ; those in the east bear only stunted teak; the northern hills contain nothing better than scrub jungle. Laterite is almost entirely absent. The soils on either bank of the Tungabhadra, to the north, are very rich, and the climate remarkably favourable to dry cultivation. In the rest of the taluq the soils are, generally speaking, light and sandy, but the dry crop soils, though as a rule poor, are in some few spots of a rich dark colour. Rági is the staple crop in the red soils, but black soils, which are confined to the north and north-east, produce a variety of crops, including jola, cotton, and oil-seeds. The rice lands are mostly of poor quality and not specially productive. A small amount of sugar-cane is grown. The gardens produce a little areca-nut, with betel-leaf and plantains.

The revenue settlement was introduced in 1875. The area of the taluq was thus distributed :—

| | |
|---|---|
| Culturable (dry, 79,550; wet, 36,289; garden, 1,490) ... | 117,329 |
| Unculturable (including roads, village sites, &c.) ... ... | 245,482 |
| Total acres ... ... | 362,811 |

The unoccupied arable land was 30,288 acres. The total revenue demand for 1891–2 (15 months) was Rs. 2,94,993, and for 1892–3 it was Rs. 3,39,798.

The rainfall in the taluq varies very much between the south-west and the north-east. The following was the average for 26 years (1870–95) at Shimoga and Kumsi, and for 3 years (1893–5) at the other stations :—

| | Jan. | Feb. | Mar. | April | May | June | July | Aug. | Sept. | Oct. | Nov. | Dec. | Year. |
|---|---|---|---|---|---|---|---|---|---|---|---|---|---|
| Shimoga ... | 0·13 | 0·02 | 0·49 | 1·94 | 3·61 | 4·98 | 7·78 | 4·52 | 3·73 | 5·25 | 1·66 | 0·39 | ...34·50 |
| Kumsi ... | — | 0·03 | 0·19 | 2·43 | 3·30 | 6·85 | 10·22 | 5·28 | 4·31 | 4·08 | 2·10 | 0·15 | ...38·94 |
| Ayanur ... | — | — | 0·35 | 1·24 | 3·41 | 9·27 | 11·07 | 5·59 | 3·18 | 8·57 | 1·34 | — | ...44·02 |
| Benkipur . | — | — | 0·38 | 2·33 | 2·91 | 4·24 | 5·71 | 5·42 | 3·04 | 7·84 | 2·36 | — | ...34·23 |

Another register for 14 years makes the annual average at Shimoga 36·99 inches.

A railway is under construction from Birur through Benkipur to Shimoga. The high road from Bangalore to Gersoppa passes through Shimoga, whence there are roads northwards to Honnáli and Harihar, south-west to Tirthahalli and the Agumbe Ghat, and north-west to Shikárpur. From Benkipur there are roads north-east to Channagiri and Chitaldroog, and south-west to Umbalibail and Yedehalli. From Ayanur there are roads west to Kollúrkaṭṭe and north to Nyámti and Honnáli. A short road connects Kumsi and Háranhalli.

**Shimoga.**—The chief town of the District, situated in 13° 55′ N. lat., 75° 38′ E. long., on the left bank of the Tunga, 171 miles north-west of Bangalore, on the Bangalore-Gersoppa road, and at the terminus of the railway under construction from Birur.

| Population in 1891. | Males. | Females. | Total. |
|---|---|---|---|
| Hindus ... ... ... ... ... | 3,905 | 4,001 | 7,906 |
| Muhammadans ... ... ... ... | 1,416 | 1,503 | 2,919 |
| Jains ... ... ... ... ... ... | 32 | 10 | 42 |
| Christians ... ... ... ... ... | 233 | 240 | 473 |
| Total ... ... .. | 5,586 | 5,754 | 11,340 |

Shimoga derives its name either from *Shiva-mukha*, the face of Shiva, or from *Shimoge*, sweet pot, an appellation given to it by a rishi who here found the savoury herbs which he compounded for his daily meal. From inscriptions it appears that Mandali, a suburb of Shimoga to the south, was an important place in early times under the Gangas. This part of the country was, at a later period, ruled by the Chálukyas and the Hoysalas, after which it was included in the dominions of Vijayanagar. Little is known of its history but that from the 16th century it was one of the possessions of the Keladi or Ikkéri chiefs. The place was taken by Haidar in his invasion of Bednur, and he subsequently brought a number of carpenters here from Mangalore to make lighters or barges for navigating the river. But they proved to be of no use. A battle was fought in the neighbourhood of Shimoga in 1798, between the Mahrattas under Parasu Ram Bhao and Tipu Sultan's forces under Muhammad Reza, the Benki Naváb, when the latter, being forced back on Haidarnagar (Bednur), Shimoga was besieged. The garrison was forced to capitulate, and the Mahrattas plundered and burnt the town. The scattered survivors of the population returned on the withdrawal of their army, but after the fall of Seringapatam the place was again pillaged by Dhundia Wahag, who left Shimoga and the neighbouring villages a heap of ruins. Being made the head-quarters of the District and of the late Nagar Division, it has gradually risen in population and wealth, which is likely to increase when the railway is finished.

| Municipal Funds. | 1892-3. | 1893-4. | 1894-5. | 1895-6. |
|---|---|---|---|---|
| Income ... ... ... ... ... | 13,961 | 14,365 | 16,560 | 17,478 |
| Expenditure ... ... ... ... | 14,320 | 15,007 | 17,000 | 22,896 |

**Siralkoppa.**—A mercantile town in the Shikárpur taluq, 11 miles north-west of the kasba, and a municipality.

| Population in 1891. | Males. | Females. | Total. |
|---|---|---|---|
| Hindus (with 1 Jain) ... ... ... | 799 | 817 | 1,616 |
| Muhammadans .. ... ... ... | 270 | 239 | 509 |
| Total ... .. ... | 1,069 | 1,056 | 2,125 |

It is of importance as forming a point of communication between Ságar, Sorab, and other parts of Mysore, and the Dharwar, Kanara, and Bellary Districts. It is the principal depôt for jaggory, which is largely prepared in this taluq and exported by the merchants of Sirálkoppa in exchange for piece goods, *kamblis*, &c. A large fair is held on Sunday.

| Municipal Funds. | 1892–3. | 1893–4. | 1894–5. | 1895–6. |
|---|---|---|---|---|
| Income ... ... ... ... ... | 1,197 | 1,293 | 1,388 | 2,300 |
| Expenditure ... ... ... ... | 1,763 | 1,341 | 1,744 | 2,899 |

**Sorab.**—A taluq in the north-west. Area 461 square miles. Head-quarters at Sorab. Contains the following hoblis, villages and population :—

| No. | Hoblis. | Villages. | Hamlets. | Villages classified. | | | Population. |
|---|---|---|---|---|---|---|---|
| | | | | Government. | Sarvamánya. | Jodi. | |
| 1 | A'navatti ... ... ... | 52 | 7 | 50 | — | 2 | 18,667 |
| 2 | Chandragutti ... ... | 40 | 28 | 39 | 1 | — | 8,287 |
| 3 | Kyásanúr ... ... ... | 84 | — | 84 | — | — | 9,874 |
| 4 | Soraba ... ... ... | 56 | 17 | 55 | — | 1 | 14,614 |
| 5 | Tavanandi... ... ... | 39 | 8 | 38 | — | 1 | 11,232 |
| 6 | Telagadde... ... ... | 35 | 3 | 35 | — | — | 7,373 |
| | Total ... ... ... | 306 | 63 | 301 | 1 | 4 | 70,047 |

*Principal places, with population.*—Múdi, 2,578; Uddari, 1,743; Soraba, 1,661; Kubattúr, 1,314; A'navatti, 1,269; Kuppagadde, 1,228; Tattúr, 1,137; Jeḍe, 1,043.

The Varada runs along the western side, forming in some places the boundary, and at one point, near Banavási, leaving and re-entering the taluq. The minor streams unite in the Dandavati, which, rising near Sorab, flows north and west into the Varada near Jeḍe. The principal hill is Chandragutti in the west, rising to 2,794 feet above the level of the sea.

Except Chandragutti mágani, the taluq is gently undulating, the bottoms of the valleys being occupied by rice-fields and gardens. Above the wet lands are stretches of open dry crop fields, called *hakkal*, and on the highest ground are the *káns*. The woodland scenery of the taluq is unique, on account of these patches of forest. These are composed of some of the finest forest to be found in the south of India, detached in small portions, with clearly demarcated lines. This arrangement is due to the position of the laterite which forms the substratum of the whole taluq. Outside the forest, on the higher ground, the soil is only about 4 inches in depth; while within, 15 feet from the edge, it is deep and rich enough to support the largest forest trees. These káns are full of the wild pepper vine, the produce of which used to be largely gathered; but the most valuable product now is the juice of the *bagani* palm, which is extracted for toddy by the Halepaikas.

Rice, jaggory, and areca-nut are the chief products of the taluq. The areca palm gardens are larger and more numerous in the south and west than in the other parts, and often contain cardamoms. On the areca trees attaining a certain size, betel and pepper vines are trained up the stem. Rice and sugar-cane cultivation are universal, and the crops good and certain. When the rice has been cut and stacked, the ground while still damp is ploughed up and left fallow till the early rain in May, no Vaisákh crop being raised.

The revenue settlement was introduced into 19 northern villages in 1868, and into the remainder of the taluq in 1871. The area of the taluq was thus distributed :—

| | | |
|---|---|---|
| Culturable (dry, 72,021 ; wet, 52,707 ; garden, 1,464) | ... | 126,192 |
| Unculturable (including roads, village sites, &c.) ... | ... | 124,492 |
| Total acres ... ... | ... | 250,684 |

Of the unculturable area 32,477 acres are *kán*. The unoccupied arable area was 27,874 acres. The total revenue demand for 1891–2 (15 months) was Rs. 2,89,269, and for 1892–3 it was Rs. 2,96,197.

The average rainfall at Sorab for 26 years (1870–95) was as follows :—

| Jan. | Feb. | Mar. | Apl. | May | June | July | Aug. | Sept. | Oct. | Nov. | Dec. | Year. |
|---|---|---|---|---|---|---|---|---|---|---|---|---|
| 0·19 | 0·01 | 0·23 | 1·26 | 2·63 | 10·67 | 19·89 | 10·15 | 4·82 | 5·04 | 1·13 | 0·18 | 56·20 |

Another register for 23 years makes the annual average 57·48.

There is a road through Sorab from Sirálkoppa to Siddapur; one south from Sorab to Ságar, with a branch from Ulavi to Sirálkoppa; and one north to Banavási. A road from Sirálkoppa runs through A'navatti towards Hánagal.

**Sorab.**—A town situated on the right bank of the Dandavati, in 14° 23′ N. lat., 75° 10′ E. long, at the junction of roads from Ságar and Sirálkoppa, 54 miles north-west of Shimoga by road. Head-quarters of the Sorab taluq, and a municipality.

| Population in 1891. | Males. | Females. | Total. |
|---|---|---|---|
| Hindus (with 5 Jains) ... ... ... | 702 | 726 | 1,428 |
| Muhammadans ... ... ... ... | 137 | 96 | 233 |
| Total ... ... ... | 839 | 822 | 1,661 |

Sorab derives its name from Surabhi, the cow of plenty, which—together with Nanda, Bhadra, Susilya, and Sumana, four other celestial cows—used daily to shed milk over the image of Ranganátha on the bank of the Dandavati. It is the principal residence of the *gúḍigars* or sandalwood carvers, whose delicate and elaborate workmanship is generally well known. The articles of their manufacture chiefly in demand are boxes, caskets, and cabinets. These are completely covered with minute and complicated designs of vegetation and scroll work, interspersed with figures from the Hindu pantheon; the general effect of the profuse detail being extremely rich. The carving of Sorab is considered superior to that of Bombay or Canton, and being a very tedious process, requiring great care, is expensive. The *gúḍigars* will imitate admirably any designs that may be furnished them. Boards for album-covers, the plates from Jorrocks's Hunt, and cabinets surrounded with figures in high relief of knights in mediæval armour, have thus been produced for European gentlemen with great success.

| Municipal Funds. | 1892-3. | 1893-4. | 1894-5. | 1895-6. |
|---|---|---|---|---|
| Income ... ... .. ... ... | 751 | 840 | 1,100 | 1,764 |
| Expenditure ... ... .. ... | 917 | 890 | 1,430 | 1,938 |

**Sulekere**, the largest tank or artificial reservoir in Mysore, is situated in the middle of the Channagiri taluq. Its margin is said to be 40 miles round, and next to the Kambham tank in Kadapa, is probably the finest reservoir in Southern India.

Its name is derived from *súḷe*, courtesan, and *kere*, tank. "The local legend asserts that this woman was a king's daughter, who, having formed a connection with some divinity, built, as an expiatory act, the tank, which submerged the town of her father, who cursed her as a prostitute. The work is a very fine one, and the reservoir receives the drainage of twenty square miles, all of which pours into the gorge where it is built, (the main stream bearing the name of Haridra or Haridravati). The embankment is of no great length, the defile between the adjacent hills being narrow: but it is of stupendous width, height, and strength, though not quite straight. It has resisted successfully the floods of centuries, but owing to the great pressure of the volume of the water in the tank, the difficulty of properly working with rude plugs the enormous sluices was immense, and the latter in course of time became much injured, and could not be utilized. (The old wooden plugs have now been replaced by iron ones.) Of the two sluices, that to the north was called the Sidda, and that to the south the Basava, and both were in bad order. During the drought which prevailed some years ago, advantage was taken of the circumstance to repair the sluices, which a man could pass through with ease, although the first adventurer was encountered by a cobra on entering the northern one. The channels had also fallen into disrepair, and the great extent of land immediately below the tank (reputed to be more than 20,000 acres) was covered by a dense date jungle; so that the vast supply of water afforded by this magnificent reservoir flowed uselessly away to the river Tungabhadra, near Harihar. (The channels have now been fully repaired, and hundreds of acres of sugar-cane are grown under them. The feverish jungle, formerly so dreaded by cultivators, has given place to smiling gardens.) It is a remarkable fact that notwithstanding the damaged state of the sluices and the great force of the water when escaping through them, the embankment has always remained firm and uninjured, a satisfactory proof of the solidity of the structure." [1]

The construction of the tank is assigned to the 11th or 12th century, and remains are pointed out, said to have belonged to Svargavati, the city which was submerged. Its king was Vikrama Ráya, who, having no children, adopted the son of the Gauda of Billahalli. This youth received the name of Ragi Raya. But a daughter was subsequently born to the king in reward for his devotion to Siva. She was called S'ántava, and was the heroine of the story. At the east end of the embankment is a temple of Siddesvara, in front of which are some defaced inscriptions. One appears to be a Vijayanagar grant of the 16th century. There is said to be a stone dated S'aka 1311, in the tank. A large festival is held at the temple at the time of Sivarátri.

**Talagunda.**—A village in Shikárpur taluq, about 2 miles north-east of Belgámi. Population, 967.

The original village was an agrahára called Sthánagundúr, and was

[1] Bowring, *East. Ex.*, 105.

the place in which the Kadamba king Mukanna or Trinetra established the Brahmans he had brought from Ahichchatra. According to some accounts there were 12,000 Brahmans of thirty-two families, and according to other accounts 32,000. The place is rich in ancient inscriptions, the most important of which is on a pillar discovered by me in front of a ruined temple. It is of about the 5th century, beautifully engraved in what are called box-headed characters, and contains in high-flown Sanskrit verses the only apparently authentic account that has been found of the origin and rise of the Kadamba dynasty.

**Tirthahalli.**—A taluq in the south-west, till 1882 called Kavaledurga. Area, 472 square miles. Head-quarters at Tirthahalli. Contains the following hoblis, villages and population :—

| No. | Hoblis. | Villages. | Hamlets. | Villages classified. | | Population. |
|---|---|---|---|---|---|---|
| | | | | Government. | Jodi. | |
| 1 | Agrahára ... ... ... | 41 | 81 | 41 | — | 10,167 |
| 2 | Águmbi ... ... ... | 41 | 270 | 41 | — | 15,800 |
| 3 | Áraga ... ... ... ... | 57 | 97 | 57 | — | 11,872 |
| 4 | Mandagadde ... ... ... | 63 | 94 | 62 | 1 | 9,046 |
| 5 | Muttúr... ... ... ... | 42 | 130 | 42 | — | 12,344 |
| | Total ... | 244 | 672 | 243 | 1 | 59,229 |

*Principal places, with population.*—Tirthahalli, 2,359; Tallúr, 1,104; Mulbágal, 1,018.

The Tunga enters the taluq in the south and takes a northerly course to a point west of Tirthahalli, where it is joined by the Begarhalla from Sringéri. It then runs east, forming for some distance the boundary between the Shimoga and Kadur Districts. All the minor streams, said to number seventy-five, run into the Tunga, except a few in the north-west, which flow into the Sharavati. The taluq is essentially Malnád in its nature, hills, forests, areca-nut gardens and running streams being the prevailing characteristics. The whole taluq is hilly, especially the west, which touches the Ghats and is covered with splendid forest. The chief heights are Kavaledurga, Kabbinada-gudda, and Kundada-gudda, the latter, which is near Agumbi, being a very conspicuous point. Iron stone of a superior quality is obtained at Kabbinada-gudda (iron hill), the iron made from which the natives hold to be as good as steel.

The east and south of the taluq is heavily wooded. The undulating country in the centre and north is more open, the unculturable portions being usually covered with grass and bushes. Heavy forest prevails in the west, the tops of the hills only being bare. Open patches often occur in the forest, owing to laterite cropping up near the surface, allowing only of the growth of a little poor white grass. In the vicinity of large stretches of garden the forest has often almost disappeared, owing to reckless cutting of trees to provide leaf manure for the areca gardens.

The principal productions are areca-nut, pepper, cardamoms, and rice, with a little coffee. Sugar-cane is grown for local consumption only. The areca-nut is considered as of better quality than that of Nagar, and only a little inferior to that of Kalasa and Ságar. The whole of it is exported to Walája by way of Birur, and to Bellary and Channagiri taluqs. The pepper is exported to Kanara, and cardamoms to Haveri in Dharwar. A small quantity of cardamoms is produced spontaneously in the jungles about Agumbi, but this is not so good as what is produced under the shade of areca gardens. The rice grown is mostly of the coarser varieties. In the high-lying rice lands, called Makki, a little rági or other dry crop is raised. Coffee cultivation was introduced in 1847, but there are no European coffee gardens, and the native gardens are few and carelessly tended. The káns contain less pepper than those of Sorab and Ságar, but they are valued for the toddy extracted from the *bagini* palms. Much of the cultivation of the taluq is in the holding of Brahmans and Námdári Gaudas, who, in addition to their own field hands, formerly slaves, and even now in the wilder parts fed, clothed, housed, and married by their masters, are dependent on labour from below the Ghats. These below-ghat coolies can always be recognized by the peculiar cap, made out of the spathe of the areca palm, which both men and women are accustomed to wear.

Large vessels of *balapam* or potstone are made at Kavaledurga, and silver cups at Tirthahalli.

This part of the country formed the Sántalige Thousand which is mentioned in many old inscriptions. Under the Chálukyas the S'ántara kings of Hombucha held possession. At a later period, and during the time of the Vijayanagar sovereignty, it was called the Âragada-rájya or Âraga kingdom. Eventually the Keladi chiefs acquired it, and Kavaledurga was their principal stronghold. This was captured by Haidar Ali, and the country annexed to Mysore.

The revenue settlement was introduced in 1878. The area of the taluq was thus distributed :—

| | |
|---|---|
| Culturable (dry, 10,537 ; wet, 42,918 ; garden, 6,593) ... | 60,048 |
| Unculturable (including roads, village sites, &c.) ... ... | 242,724 |
| Inám village ... ... ... ... ... ... ... | 1,885 |
| Total acres | 304,657 |

The unoccupied arable land was 9,767 acres. The total revenue demand for 1891–2 (15 months) was Rs. 4,54,107, and for 1892–3 it was Rs. 4,39,495.

The average rainfall at Tirthahalli for 26 years (1870–95), and at the other station for 3 years (1893–5), was as follows :—

| | Jan. | Feb. | Mar. | April | May | June | July | Aug. | Sept. | Oct. | Nov. | Dec. | Year. |
|---|---|---|---|---|---|---|---|---|---|---|---|---|---|
| Tirthahalli | 0·01 | — | 0·49 | 1·61 | 2·67 | 22·58 | 42·99 | 25·02 | 8·50 | 9·39 | 2·17 | 0·67 | 116·10 |
| Agumbi ... | — | — | 0·41 | 1·23 | 6·53 | 79·46 | 93·82 | 84·06 | 30·92 | 18·38 | 1·35 | — | 316·16 |

Another register for the same period makes the average at Tirthahalli 110·35.

The main road from Shimoga to the Agumbi Ghat passes through Tirthahalli, and is met at Agumbi by the Tarikere and Koppa road. From Tirthahalli there is a road north to Anantapur, and roads are proposed south to Koppa and west to Hulikal on the Hosangadi Ghat. From Mandagadde, with the river between, there is a road to Yedehalli.

**Tirthahalli.**—A town situated in 13° 41′ N. lat., 75° 17′ E. long., on the left bank of the Tunga, 35 miles south-west of Shimoga, on the Shimoga-Agumbi road. Head-quarters of the Tirthahalli taluq, and a municipality.

| Population in 1891. | Males. | Females. | Total. |
|---|---|---|---|
| Hindus (with 3 Jains) ... ... ... | 1,026 | 840 | 1,866 |
| Muhammadans ... ... ... ... | 194 | 124 | 318 |
| Christians ... ... ... ... ... | 99 | 76 | 175 |
| Total ... ... ... | 1,319 | 1,040 | 2,359 |

The town derives its name from the number of *tirtha* or sacred bathing-places in the Tunga at or near this spot. A pool at one of the cylindrical hollows scooped out by the water in the rocky bed is a favourite spot for cleansing away sin by ablution. The formation of the hole is ascribed to Parasu Rama, who made it with his axe. At the Ramesvara festival, held for three days in Márgashira, thousands of people pass through the hole. At that season the river can be crossed by stepping over the great boulders in the bed, the difficult places where there is a rush of water being temporarily bridged over by the Brahmans.

It is the principal centre of trade for the Nagar and Koppa taluqs, valued at five to six lakhs a year, one-half of which results from transactions at the Ramesvara festival. Cocoa-nuts and cocoa-nut oil are imported from Kanara by the Agumbi and Hulikal ghats, and various kinds of pulse, piece-goods, cattle, &c., from the maidán taluqs.

There are two maṭhs, the Havika maṭh on the town side, and the Putiki maṭh on the opposite side. To this place all the people of the Malava caste resort from Kanara and Nagar to be branded with a religious stamp, *mudra dhárana*, by their priest the Koppada Dásaiya, who comes here from Koppa. Three miles up the river is the Mulbágal maṭh, and a mile higher the Bhimankaṭṭe maṭh, which claims a fabulous antiquity.

| Municipal Funds. | 1892–3. | 1893–4. | 1894–5. | 1895–6. |
|---|---|---|---|---|
| Income ... ... ... ... ... | 1,654 | 1,848 | 1,242 | 2,000 |
| Expenditure .. ... ... ... | 2,261 | 2,815 | 1,413 | 2,667 |

**Tunga.**—This river rises in the Western Ghats, at Gangámúla in the Varáha parvata (Kadur District), close to the twin stream of the Bhadra. Its course is at first north-east past Sringéri to Baggunji, where it turns north-west and continues in that direction to near Tirthahalli. Thence, bending round for some distance to the east, it eventually flows north-east past Shimoga to Kúḍali, where it unites with the Bhadra. Near Mandagadde it branches for a short distance into seven streams, hence called Yélukálu shílu, which prevents the passage of rafts of bamboos and timber during the dry season when the water is low. Its banks are not so steep as those of the Bhadra, and it is generally esteemed a more healthy stream, its current being more rapid and the banks less shut in by dense forest. A project was formed some years ago by the Madras Irrigation Company for damming the river either at Tirthahalli or at Mallúr, and constructing an immense reservoir, all the requisite surveys for which were made.

**Tungabhaḍra.**—This famous river, the chief tributary of the Krishna, is formed at Kúḍali, 9 miles north-north-east of Shimoga, by the confluence of the twin streams Tunga and Bhadra.

From this point its general direction is north, but it winds so as to form three loops before reaching Honnáli. Thence with a more direct course it runs north, and receiving the Choradi or Kumadvati on the left, bends to the north-east, following the Mysore frontier to Harihara, where it is joined by the Haridra from the Súlekere on the right. Running again north along the boundary, it quits this State and, continuing north-west and north, separates the Madras and Bombay Presidencies. From the point where the Varada enters it on the left the river turns north-east and, flowing past the village of Hampe, between the sites of the celebrated cities of Kishkindha, Anegundi or Hastinávati, and Vidyánagara or Vijayanagara, forms the common boundary of Bellary and the Nizam's Dominions, receiving on the right the Haggari or Vedávati. Soon after this its course is directly east, along much of the Karnul and Haidarabad frontier. Passing Karnul it enters the Krishna a few miles beyond, at Kúḍali Sangam or S'ris'aila.

The river is never dry, but the channel being full of rocks will not admit of floats in the hot season when the water is low. In the rainy season it swells prodigiously, and forms an extremely rapid aud muddy stream, 10 or more feet higher than the rocks. It is easily fordable in the dry season; at other times ferry-boats are used for crossing at favourable spots, where the banks approach one another and the water is deep. Alligators abound in it. The maximum flood discharge determined for the Harihara bridge was 207,843 cubic feet per second, the ordinary monsoon discharge being roughly calculated at 30,000.

The river is crossed at Harihara by a fine bridge of stone and brick, consisting of 14 elliptical arches of 60 feet span each. It was completed in 1868, at a cost of 3½ lakhs of rupees. There is another magnificent bridge of 52 piers at Rampur, in Bellary, where the North-West line of the Madras Railway crosses the river.

The ancient and puránic name of the river is the Pampá, by which it is mentioned in the Rámáyana, and which still survives in the name of the village Hampé, at the Pampa kshetra, the site of the celebrated ancient and modern capital cities previously mentioned. The name Tungabhadra occurs in the Bhágavata Purána. The mythological origin of the river, as given in the Tungabhadra Mahátmya of the Brahmánda Purána, is to the following effect:—Hiranyáksha, son of Kasyapa Rishi by Diti Dévi, seized the earth and bore it down to the lower world. The Brahmans having no ground to stand upon, discontinued their usual rites and sacrifices. The demi-gods, being thus deprived of their usual offerings, complained to Vishnu, who, assuming the form of a *varáha* or boar, plunged into the ocean, entered the lower world, destroyed the demon, and brought up the earth again. The perspiration arising from this exertion of the boar trickled down its tusks as it rested on the Varáha parvata and formed two streams, that from the left tusk being the Tunga and that from the right tusk the Bhadra. A third stream, the Netravati, is supposed to have its origin in the same place from the *nétra*, or eyes of the boar.

**Varada.**—A tributary of the Tungabhadra. It rises at Varadá múla, near Ikkéri, and running north past Chandragutti and Banavási, turns to the north-east, which direction it keeps till it leaves the

Mysore. Entering Dharwar it flows north, and, bending round gradually to the north-east some distance south of Bankapur and Sávanur, runs with an easterly course into the Tungabhadra at Gulnatha, below Havanur.

It is stemmed by 51 small anicuts in Ságar and Sorab, giving rise to channels having a total length of 36 miles.

The ***Vara-dá*** (boon giving) river originated, according to legend, in the Bhagirathi water poured from his conch by Náráyana (Vishnu) on the head of Siva at Varadá múla, the hermitage of Sringa muni, in order to subdue the flame of austerities which threatened to consume the gods; performed by Siva to atone for his sin in pulling off one of Brahma's five heads.

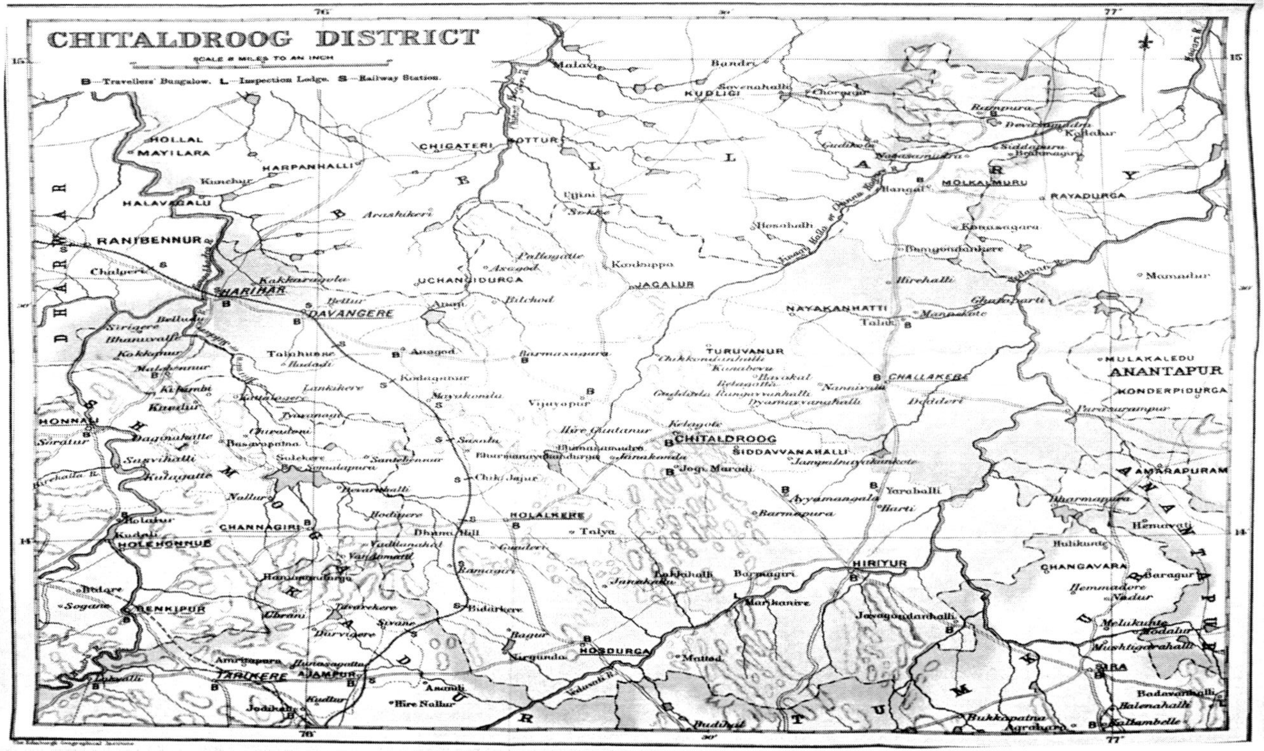
CHITALDROOG DISTRICT
SCALE 8 MILES TO AN INCH
B—Travellers' Bungalow. L—Inspection Lodge. S—Railway Station.

# CHITALDROOG DISTRICT

## GENERAL DESCRIPTION

*Situation.*—A District in the north. Its situation, taking the extreme limits, is between 13° 40′ and 15° 2′ north latitude, 75° 42′ and 77° 6′ east longitude; but owing to a long and narrow projection into Bellary northwards the main part of the District does not extend beyond 14° 40′ north latitude. Its greatest length from north to south is about 88 miles, the greatest breadth from east to west about 100 miles. The arm jutting north into Bellary is 32 miles long, by from 5 to 12 broad.

*Area.*—The area is 4,022 square miles, of which 1,650 square miles are cultivated, and 1,531 square miles are unculturable.

*Boundaries.*—It is bounded on the north by the Bellary District, and on the east by the Anantapur District, both of Madras; on the south-east by Tumkúr District, south-west by Kadur District, and west by the Shimoga District, all of Mysore; while on the north-west it is bounded by the Dharwar District of Bombay.

*Divisions.*—It is divided into the following taluqs, the sub-taluqs being Hosdurga, under Holalkere taluq; and Harihar, under Dávangere taluq:—

| No. | Taluq. | Area in sq. miles. | No. of Hoblis. | No. of Villages or Towns. | Population in 1891. | Per sq. mile. |
|---|---|---|---|---|---|---|
| 1 | Challakere ... ... | 790 | 4 | 191 | 60,711 | 76·84 |
| 2 | Chitaldroog ... | 531 | 4 | 189 | 66,546 | 125·31 |
| 3 | Dávangere ... ... | 552 | 8 | 262 | 94,565 | 171·31 |
| 4 | Hiriyúr ... ... | 807 | 5 | 215 | 54,302 | 67·28 |
| 5 | Holalkere ... ... | 681 | 6 | 329 | 67,051 | 98·45 |
| 6 | Jagalúr ... ... | 371 | 3 | 169 | 38,229 | 103·04 |
| 7 | Molakálmuru ... | 290 | 2 | 97 | 32,560 | 112·27 |
| | Total ... | 4,022 | 32 | 1,452 | 413,964 | 102·92 |

**Physical Features.**—The whole of this comparatively arid District is included in the valley of the Védavati or Haggari, with the

Tungabhadra running for a few miles along the north-western boundary. The Védavati enters the District in the south-west and flows in a north-east direction to a few miles beyond Hiriyúr. From this point, where the stream begins to take the name of Haggari, it runs north, within a few miles of the main eastern boundary, and leaves the District near the eastern base of the Molakálmuru projection. During the hot months it is for the most part dry, but supplies a number of wells sunk in the sandy bed.

The District is crossed from south-south-east to north-north-west by a belt, about 20 miles broad, of intermittent parallel chains of low hills, mostly bare and stony, through which are several *kanives*, or passes. The eastern line runs from the west of Hiriyúr up to Chitaldroog (3,229 feet), and thence, with a break for some distance, continues from Kankuppa hill (2,721 feet) to the frontier. The summit of Jogi Maraḍi to the south of Chitaldroog, one of the highest points in this range, is 3,803 feet above sea-level. The western parallel commences at Hosdurga (3,226 feet), and passes by Máyakonda to Anaji. Around Molakálmuru in the north are some detached clusters of rocky hills. Of these, Nunke Bhairava hill is 3,022 feet, Jatinga Rámesvara hill 3,469, and Santigudda 2,595. This part of Mysore, says Mr. Bruce Foote, is "occupied by a tract of country of singular beauty. The bold, rocky hills which rise out of it in every direction are divided from each other by equally picturesque valleys full of fine trees, amongst which tamarind trees, pre-eminent for their love of granitic soil, abound. The road from the travellers' bungalow at Hanagal (on the Bangalore-Bellary high road), which skirts the south side of the line of hills for the first five miles, and for the next four passes right through them, takes one through scenery not easily forgotten for its striking beauty in grand rocks and rich vegetation."[1]

Except in the region of the hilly belt, the whole extent of the District north and east is an open and level plain, entirely destitute of picturesque features, but presenting at certain seasons in favourable spots a vast expanse of verdant cultivation. Though there are no trees there is abundance of excellent pasture, while the black and dreary-looking soil seems only to require the contact of water to develop its productiveness. To the north and west of Chitaldroog the surface of the country is undulating and covered with thick and rich grass. Trees are few in number.

The general level of the District is about 2,000 feet above the sea.

[1] Geology of the Bellary District (*Memoirs of the Geological Survey of India*, Vol. xxv).

At Chitaldroog it is 2,383, but at Hiriyúr it is 1,965, while at Harihar, probably the lowest point in Mysore, it is only 1,830.

**Rocks.**—The hills in the south-east are of secondary formation. They run in straight lines in various directions, and are bare of trees, but have a green appearance in the wet season from the growth of long hill-grass upon them. They are almost constantly covered at the top with a kind of magnetic ironstone, which withstands the decomposing powers of the air and water much longer than the lower parts of the hills. These seem to be composed of ferruginous clayey slate. Through the surface of the soil appear perpendicular layers of slate, which are often intersected with quartz or marl. The slate is iron-shot and always decomposing and red.

The hills to which Chitaldroog belongs are composed of the prevailing gneiss of Mysore, the felspar being in some places of a fine red, in others of a silvery white colour. When this rock begins to decompose it assumes a slaty form, the layers of which are pretty thick, but as the disintegration advances it scales off in thin laminæ which are very brittle, and in them the mica is more apparent than in the fresh rock.

The lower ridges north and west of Chitaldroog consist of a compound in which chlorite, oxide of iron, and sometimes hornblende prevail. They often form basins of considerable size, which have a very fertile soil. Many of them are naked, but some are covered with fine grass and produce trees of a middling size.

West of these ranges of hills descends an extensive and variegated valley leading towards the Tungabhadra. The lower country is variously intersected with ridges, some of which are high, and all contain in their rocks much iron and magnesia. North of Máyakonda the country becomes long waving. Here and there are single hills of short ranges, the former mostly gneissic or granitic, the latter slaty. The nearer the river is approached the more black cotton soil and marl abound. Along its course the former predominates, and below it are beds of mica slate.

*Minerals.*—Clay ironstone constitutes some ranges of hills near Chitaldroog. Drawing slate is also found in the neighbourhood. Schorl in quartz is met with near Harihar. Potstone and actinolite occur frequently in nests near Mattod. It has a considerable admixture of iron, and when decomposed becomes quite red. Asbestoid is found in the potstone near Talya, and ligniform asbestos among the Máyakonda hills. Lamellar actinolite at Harihar. A mineral resembling brown spar occurs near Talya and Anaji. Near the former place and others among the Chitaldroog hills is found iron glance. Carbonate of soda is abundant. The hills running up from Hiriyúr by Chitaldroog, to the frontier at Jagalur and Anaji, form part of the auriferous tract called the Central or Chiknáyakanhalli band (*see* Vol. I, p. 50).

*Soils.*—The black cotton soil prevails throughout the taluqs north and west of Chitaldroog, interspersed with sandy and gravelly tracts. In the west a red and loamy soil occupies the valleys. In the south the soil contains much common salt, and on that account is favourable to the growth of cocoa-nut trees, of which there are large plantations. The eastern taluqs have a light sandy soil abounding in springs. These *talpargis* or spring heads may be tapped at short distances from each other. The water is either conducted by narrow channels to the fields, or a *kapile* well is constructed, from which the water is raised by two or four bullocks. These wells extend from Maddagiri up to Molakálmuru, but do not for the most part, except in the Chitaldroog taluq, cross to the westward of a nearly central line drawn from north to south. In the Tumkúr District the water is near the surface, but in the greater part of Pávugada the wells require to be cut through a soft porous rock composed of decomposed hornblende, which, however, forms a wall of tolerable durability. North and west of this the water is still lower, and hard strata of rock have sometimes to be perforated before the springs are reached.

**Climate.**—The climate, as compared with that of other parts of the Mysore, may be described as drier and hotter: a difference due to the lower elevation, the less abundant rainfall, and the absence over a large proportion of the District of considerable inequalities of surface, which might tend to retain moisture and moderate the radiation from extensive and bare plains of black or whitish grey soil. In the western taluqs during the hottest season a cool western breeze often sets in soon after nightfall, and blows during the greater part of the night.

*Temperature.*—From the recorded observations the mean average temperature throughout the year is ascertained to be about seventy-seven degrees Fahrenheit. Captain Chalmers deduced 78·25° as the average from a register kept from 1837 to 1841, but the readings were taken at different places in moving about the old Chitaldroog Division, which included the Tumkúr District.

The following tables contain the mean recorded results for 1894 and 1895. In the former year a maximum of 98·4 was registered in March, and a minimum of 53 in January. In the latter year the maximum was 100·4 in May, and the minimum 51·2 in December.

| 1894. | Barometer. | | | Thermometers. | | | | | | Aqueous Vapour. | | Wind. | | Rain. | | Cloud. | | |
|---|---|---|---|---|---|---|---|---|---|---|---|---|---|---|---|---|---|---|
| | | | | Dry Bulb. | | | | Wet Bulb. | | | | | | | | | No. of Days. | |
| | Red. to 32° F. | Red. to Sea Level. | Daily Range. | Mean. | Max. | Min. | Range. | Mean. | Min. | Press. Inches. | Humidity. Per cent. | Daily Velocity Miles. | Mean Direction. | Fall Inches. | Number of Days. | Mean. Per cent. | Cloudless 10 h. and 16 h. | Overcast. |
| | 27+ | 29+ | | | | | | | | | | | | | | | | |
| Jan. . | ·556 | ·873 | ·128 | 73·3 | 83·5 | 61·1 | 22·4 | 57·5 | 53·6 | ·376 | 45 | 183 | E. by S | 0·00 | — | 20 | 14 | — |
| Feb. . | ·558 | ·853 | ·136 | 77·7 | 88·5 | 64·6 | 23·9 | 58·4 | 54·3 | ·355 | 37 | 182 | S.E. by S. | 0 00 | — | 11 | 18 | — |
| Mar. . | ·488 | ·752 | ·140 | 83·3 | 94·1 | 70·8 | 23·3 | 62·4 | 58·6 | ·418 | 37 | 150 | S.W. by S. | 0·41 | 1 | 30 | 5 | — |
| April . | ·433 | ·693 | ·142 | 83·9 | 94·6 | 71·7 | 22·9 | 66·0 | 62 6 | ·528 | 46 | 181 | W. by S. | 0·85 | 7 | 34 | — | — |
| May . | ·419 | ·689 | ·136 | 81·7 | 92·1 | 70·0 | 22·1 | 67·2 | 64·1 | ·587 | 54 | 227 | W. | 4·63 | 10 | 34 | 3 | — |
| June . | ·362 | ·648 | ·092 | 78·6 | 86·7 | 69·8 | 16·8 | 67·7 | 65 2 | ·629 | 64 | 294 | W. by S. | 0·72 | 10 | 86 | — | 3 |
| July . | ·387 | ·698 | ·078 | 75·2 | 82·0 | 68·0 | 14·0 | 66·7 | 64·4 | ·628 | 72 | 297 | W. by S. | 2·97 | 20 | 89 | — | 6 |
| Aug. . | ·378 | ·681 | ·103 | 75·6 | 82·4 | 68·4 | 14·0 | 67·1 | 65·0 | ·634 | 71 | 271 | W. by S. | 2·05 | 14 | 89 | — | 3 |
| Sept. . | ·412 | ·715 | ·119 | 75·9 | 83·8 | 67·4 | 16·4 | 66·3 | 63·9 | ·603 | 67 | 258 | W. | 1·59 | 8 | 78 | — | 6 |
| Oct. . | ·454 | ·760 | ·126 | 75·7 | 83·1 | 67·2 | 15·9 | 66·2 | 63·6 | ·610 | 67 | 165 | S.W. by W. | 5·56 | 18 | 68 | — | 5 |
| Nov. . | ·563 | ·894 | ·108 | 71·3 | 79·2 | 61·7 | 17·5 | 61·8 | 58·3 | ·529 | 66 | 181 | S E. by E. | 3·46 | 4 | 53 | 1 | 3 |
| Dec. . | ·574 | ·895 | ·120 | 72·9 | 82·1 | 61·8 | 20·4 | 59·4 | 55·7 | ·433 | 52 | 204 | E. by S. | 0·00 | — | 21 | 12 | — |
| | 27+ | 29+ | | | | | | | | | | | | | | | | |
| Year . | ·465 | ·763 | ·119 | 77·1 | 86·0 | 66·9 | 19·1 | 63·9 | 60·8 | ·528 | 57 | 216 | — | 22·24 | 92 | 51 | 53 | 26 |
| | | | | | | | | | | | | | | Total. | | | Total. | |

| 1895. | Barometer. | | | Thermometers. | | | | | | Aqueous Vapour. | | Wind. | | Rain. | | Cloud. | | |
|---|---|---|---|---|---|---|---|---|---|---|---|---|---|---|---|---|---|---|
| | | | | Dry Bulb. | | | | Wet Bulb. | | | | | | | | | No. of Days. | |
| | Red. to 32° F. | Red. to Sea Level. | Daily Range. | Mean. | Max. | Min. | Range. | Mean. | Min. | Press. Inches. | Humidity. Per cent. | Daily Velocity Miles. | Mean Direction. | Fall Inches. | Number of Days. | Mean. Per cent. | Cloudless 10h. and 16h. | Overcast. |
| | 27+ | 29+ | | | | | | | | | | | | | | | | |
| Jan. . | ·554 | ·865 | ·127 | 74·1 | 84·5 | 61·7 | 22·8 | 58·4 | 54·5 | ·394 | 46 | 176 | E. by S. | — | — | 14 | 17 | — |
| Feb. . | ·550 | ·842 | ·131 | 78·3 | 88·9 | 66·0 | 22·9 | 59·1 | 55·2 | ·366 | 37 | 179 | S.E. by S. | — | — | 6 | 16 | — |
| Mar. . | ·482 | ·746 | ·137 | 83·3 | 94·5 | 70·2 | 24·3 | 62·3 | 58·0 | ·422 | 37 | 157 | S. | — | — | 17 | 8 | — |
| April . | ·446 | ·709 | ·149 | 83·2 | 94·2 | 70·5 | 23·7 | 66·2 | 62·6 | ·538 | 48 | 161 | S. by W. | 3·97 | 8 | 35 | 2 | — |
| May . | ·427 | ·690 | ·135 | 82·6 | 93·7 | 70·1 | 23·6 | 67·7 | 64·6 | ·585 | 52 | 228 | W. | 7·87 | 8 | 40 | 4 | — |
| June . | ·374 | ·668 | ·090 | 77·4 | 85·3 | 68·7 | 16·6 | 68·4 | 65·9 | ·670 | 70 | 237 | W.S.W. | 4·75 | 16 | 76 | — | 9 |
| July . | ·404 | ·720 | ·081 | 73·9 | 80·1 | 67·3 | 12·8 | 66·9 | 64·8 | ·645 | 77 | 281 | W. by S. | 3·16 | 21 | 95 | — | 17 |
| Aug. . | ·397 | ·706 | ·099 | 74·7 | 81·5 | 67·6 | 13·9 | 67·1 | 64·9 | ·641 | 74 | 255 | W. | 1·83 | 17 | 87 | — | 7 |
| Sept. . | ·439 | ·744 | ·121 | 75·8 | 83·7 | 67·3 | 16·3 | 66·9 | 64·4 | ·625 | 70 | 213 | W. by S. | 3·37 | 12 | 80 | — | 3 |
| Oct. . | ·473 | ·781 | ·119 | 75·6 | 82·5 | 67·5 | 15·0 | 67·1 | 64·4 | ·642 | 70 | 148 | S.S.E. | 4·82 | 16 | 79 | — | 3 |
| Nov. . | ·580 | ·902 | ·110 | 72·8 | 80·8 | 62·7 | 18·0 | 62·5 | 58·9 | ·527 | 61 | 142 | E. | 3·11 | 4 | 41 | 4 | — |
| Dec. . | ·564 | ·900 | ·118 | 70·0 | 78·7 | 59·3 | 19·3 | 57·3 | 53·6 | ·407 | 53 | 189 | E. | 0·11 | 3 | 42 | 8 | 4 |
| | 27+ | 29+ | | | | | | | | | | | | | | | | |
| Year . | ·474 | ·773 | ·118 | 76·8 | 85·7 | 66·6 | 19·1 | 64·2 | 61·0 | ·539 | 58 | 197 | — | 32·99 | 105 | 51 | 59 | 43 |
| | | | | | | | | | | | | | | Total. | | | Total. | |

*Rainfall.*—The average annual rainfall at Chitaldroog, calculated from the observations for 26 years (1870–95), is 24·85, or, according to another statement, 24·23. The average monthly fall is given under each taluq. The average annual rate for the remaining taluq or sub-taluq stations for the same period was as follows:—

| | For 26 years. | | Other Returns. | | For 26 years. | | Other Returns. |
|---|---|---|---|---|---|---|---|
| Challakere ... | 17·37 | or | 18·50 | Hosdurga ... | 22·47 | or | 22·24 |
| Dávangere ... | 19·65 | ,, | 21·05 | Jagalúr ... ... | 17·71 | ,, | 18·88 |
| Hiriyúr ... ... | 16·78 | ,, | 17·15 | Molkálmurn ... | 21·14 | ,, | 22·46 |
| Holalkere ... | 25·60 | ,, | 23·92 | | | | |

The distribution of rain diminishes as a rule from south-west to north-east. Hiriyúr and Challakere taluqs especially form a comparatively rainless tract, receiving in some parts less than ten inches in the year. From the tables it appears that the heaviest rainfall in the District is generally in October, at the break of the north-east monsoon. Hence the distress occasioned by a failure of the rains at that season, followed as it is by severally totally dry months, including in rapid succession the coldest, and then the hottest period of the year.

The actual annual rainfall at Chitaldroog has been thus recorded:—

| | | | | | | | |
|---|---|---|---|---|---|---|---|
| 1868 ... | 21·27 | 1875 ... | 12·14 | 1882 ... | 28·84 | 1889 ... | 30·13 |
| 1869 ... | 22·90 | 1876 ... | 8·39 | 1883 ... | 35·30 | 1890 ... | 19·63 |
| 1870 ... | 26·85 | 1877 ... | 12·05 | 1884 ... | 18·31 | 1891 ... | 18·92 |
| 1871 ... | 25·33 | 1878 ... | 27·15 | 1885 ... | 26·34 | 1892 ... | 22·58 |
| 1872 ... | 26·38 | 1879 ... | 24·55 | 1886 ... | 22·39 | 1893 ... | 28·55 |
| 1873 ... | 31·15 | 1880 ... | 32·66 | 1887 ... | 23·17 | 1894 ... | 22·24 |
| 1874 ... | 34·31 | 1881 ... | 12·94 | 1888 ... | 26·47 | 1895 ... | 32·98 |

**Vegetation.**—This District is almost throughout a "dry and thirsty land." It has no forest. Great undulating plains, covered frequently with nothing but stones and a dwarf species of mimosa (called locally the *hote jáli*, and armed with vicious looking and formidable spines from one to four inches in length), are dotted at wide intervals, with villages lying in the hollows, having sometimes a few trees round them. These are the characteristics of fully one-third of the District. The whole taluq of Challakere answers generally to this description, but where there is any water in the soil there are some fine cocoa-nut gardens. The pastures, too, during the cooler months of the year, are good, and the Amrit Mahal has extensive grazing grounds in Dodderi, Tallak, Hosdurga, and other parts of the District.

Standing on the low range of hills near the Mári Kanave, the view which meets the eye is not, during the rainy months, altogether so desolate. Looking up the valley of the Védávati towards Hosdurga a few more trees are seen, and the country is not so very bare. To the south and south-east, along the Hiriyúr hills, there are jungles of the kárâchi (*hardwickia binata*). Again, between Bommagondankere and Hángal, in the taluq of Molakálmuru, is another tract of country covered with the kárâchi. In the same taluq, to the east of the kasba town and on the borders of the Bellary District, is a small fuel jungle among hills; and in the western corner of the Jagalúr taluq is another of tolerable dimensions. Not far from the town of Chitaldroog are a few small patches of acacias, and on the Jógi maṭṭi, a hill near Chitaldroog, are a few bamboos and some poor trees of second-class timber.

Yet the soil would not be unproductive if it only had water. Near Jagalúr and Bommagondankere, and one or two other spots where irrigation is possible from either tanks or wells worked by *kapile*, heavy crops are taken. On the high lands where the soil is a disintegrated rock, the dry crops, provided sufficient rain falls, are good.

The quantity of timber for building purposes is, as may be supposed, very limited; and the large towns draw their supplies chiefly from more favoured districts. In the villages the huts are very poorly built. The stems of cocoa-nut trees and wood obtained from dead fruit-trees growing in gardens are much used, and not unfrequently the scapes of the common aloe are used both as joists and uprights.

Mr. Bowring remarks: "It is not improbable that this portion of Mysore may have been less sterile formerly, as on many of the hills traces are to be seen of forests cut down long ago. In fact, old records mention the existence of fine timber where such has wholly disappeared, owing, no doubt, to the reckless way in which the cultivators have cut down whatever they required for agricultural implements, regardless of the destruction caused to young trees and saplings. No one ever thought of planting new trees to replace those that had been felled, and so, as population increased and agriculture spread, the few remaining forests rapidly disappeared. The denudation of trees under which the District suffers has probably had much to do with the prevailing drought, there being scarcely any vegetation to arrest the passage of the monsoon clouds, which float onwards without depositing their valuable contents."

*Avenues* have been planted along the public roads as in other Districts, but with little effect, and the trees are kept alive with much difficulty. There were 425 miles thus planted up to 1895. At the same period there were 28,172 trees in 868 *groves*, covering 784 acres.

**Forests.**—The reserved State forests are Jogimatti, 7¼ square miles, and Nirtadi-gudda, 5½ square miles. *Plantations.*—There are three Forest plantations, covering 92 acres, and nine Revenue plantations, covering 251 acres. *Groves.*—There are 820 groves or topes in 798 villages, planted with 25,097 trees. *Avenues* have also been planted on both sides of 417 miles of road.

**Cultivation.**—Chitaldroog, Hiriyúr, Máyakonda, Dávangere, and Bilchod produce cotton, which is also grown, though in smaller quantities, in Anaji, Kankuppa, and Molakálmuru. Flax for the manufacture of linseed oil is raised in Dávangere, Kankuppa, and Bilchod. All the northern taluqs produce wheat, jola, navane, sugar-cane, and chenna. Rice is less abundant. Cummin seed is grown in the north-east. In the south, about Mattod, are extensive groves of cocoanut trees, growing, as in the neighbouring parts of Tumkur, in the dry lands without irrigation. The cultivation in the south-west consists of the ordinary dry crops raised on red soil. All along the east the *kapile* wells are largely used in raising crops by irrigation, including rági, which on the Bellary border is cultivated in no other way.

The following are the principal crops cultivated in the District :—

| Kannada name. | Botanical name. | English name. |
|---|---|---|
| CEREALS. | | |
| Baragu ... ... | Panicum milaceum ... ... ... | — |
| Bhatta ... ... | Oryza sativa ... ... ... ... | Rice. |
| Godhi ... ... | Triticum aristatum ... ... ... | Wheat. |
| Háraka ... ... | Panicum semiverticillatum ... ... | — |
| Jola .. ... ... | Holcus sorghum ... ... ... | Great millet. |
| Navane ... ... | Panicum italicum ... ... ... | Italian millet. |
| Rági ... ... ... | Eleusine corocana ... ... ... | Rági. |
| Sajje ... ... ... | Holcus spicatus ... ... ... | Spiked millet. |
| Sáme ... ... ... | Panicum frumentaceum ... ... | Little millet. |
| PULSES. | | |
| Avare ... ... | Dolichos lablab ... ... ... | Cow gram. |
| Hesaru ... ... | Phaseolus mungo ... ... ... | Green gram. |
| Hurali ... ... | Dolichos uniflorus ... .. ... | Horse gram. |
| Kadale ... ... | Cicer arietinum ... ... ... | Bengal gram. |
| Korasáni ... ... | — ... ... ... | Panic seed. |
| Tadagani ... ... | Dolichos catiang ... ... ... | — |
| Togari ... ... | Cajanus indicus ... ... ... | Pigeon pea, doll. |
| Uddu... ... ... | Phaseolus minimus ... ... ... | Black gram. |
| OIL SEEDS. | | |
| Haralu ... ... | Ricinus communis ... ... ... | Castor oil. |
| Huchchellu ... ... | Guizotea oleifera ... ... ... | Wild gingelli. |
| Wollellu ... ... | Sesamum orientale ... ... ... | Gingelli. |
| VEGETABLES (NATIVE). | | |
| Bellulli ... ... | Allium sativum ... ... ... | Garlic. |
| Jirige ... ... ... | Cuminum cyminum ... ... ... | Cummin seed. |
| Kottambari ... ... | — ... ... ... | Coriander. |
| Mensina káyi ... | Capsicum annuum ... ... ... | Chilly. |
| Mentya ... ... | Trigonella fœnum grœcum ... ... | Fenugreek. |
| Nirulli ... ... | Allium cepa ... ... ... ... | Onion. |
| Saute káyi ... ... | Cucumis sativus ... ... ... | Cucumber. |

| Kannada name. | Botanical name. | English name. |
|---|---|---|
| MISCELLANEOUS. | | |
| Adike ... ... | Areca catechu ... ... ... | Areca nut. |
| Arale ... ... | Gossypium indicum ... ... ... | Cotton. |
| Bále ... ... ... | Musa sapientum ... ... ... | Plantain. |
| Hoge soppu ... ... | Nicotiana tabaccum ... ... ... | Tobacco. |
| Hunase ... ... | Tamarindus indica ... ... ... | Tamarind. |
| Kabbu ... ... | Saccharum officinale ... ... ... | Sugar-cane. |
| Sanabu ... ... | Crotolarea juncea ... ... ... | Country hemp. |
| Tengina káyi ... | Cocos nucifera ... ... .. | Cocoanut. |
| Viledele ... ... | Piper betle ... ... ... ... | Betel vine. |

*Area under principal crops.*—The cultivation of rice covered in 1893 an area of 34,954 acres; wheat, 1,152; other food grains, 730,659; oil seeds, 64,538; sugar-cane, 296; cotton, 44,676; fibres, 947; tobacco, 1,494; other crops, 10,762.

**Wild animals.**—The tiger, panther, bear, hyæna and wild hog infest more or less all the hilly and wild tracts. Deer are to be found chiefly in Hiriyúr, Chitaldroog and Holalkere taluqs.

*Birds.*—All kinds of wild fowl are very numerous in the secluded tanks in the south of the District. Pelicans may be seen about Mattod.

**Domestic animals.**—The cattle vary greatly in size and strength, some of the largest and finest in the south of India being occasionally bred, while the ordinary run of those employed by the ryots, both for domestic and agricultural purposes, is of small size and stature. The best cows and oxen are bred in Chitaldroog and the taluqs to the north and east of it. Buffaloes are finest in the neighbourhood of Chitaldroog.

The best sheep, and those which yield the finest wool, are bred in the north-western parts of the District. In the south and west they are slightly inferior, while those of Hiriyúr are considered still less valuable.

*Live Stock.*—The number of cows and bullocks in 1893 was 235,118; buffaloes, 63,334; horses and ponies, 1,998; donkeys, 4,383; sheep and goats, 316,300.

## HISTORY

The plates existing in Shimoga District, which profess to record grants made at Harihara by the emperor Janamejaya in 3066 and 3022 B.C., have been referred to under that District, and in the general chapter on History in Vol. I.

**Mauryas.**—But the oldest authentic inscriptions found in Mysore, and indeed in Southern India, are the Edicts of Asoka discovered by me in 1892 in Molakálmuru taluq; and no older inscriptions have come to light anywhere in India. This discovery carried back the history of Mysore to the 3rd century B.C., and threw a new light on the condition of the Peninsula at that period. The accounts of Bhadrabáhu and Chandra Gupta at Sravana Belgola (Hassan District) had connected Mysore with the Mauryas, but the Edicts of Asoka made it clear that the north of the country, probably the province long afterwards known as Kuntala, was a component part of the Maurya empire.

**Satavahanas.**—The next link in the chain of evidence for the early history of the District was the find of Buddhist lead coins on the site of the ancient city of Chandrávali, immediately to the west of Chitaldroog. One at least of the coins bore the name of the S'átavá-hana king Pulomáyi, and in conjunction with the inscription of Háritiputra Sátakarni, discovered by me in Shikárpur taluq (Shimoga District), left little doubt that the S'átaváhanas held sway over the north of Mysore in the 2nd century A.D.

**Kadambas.**—The Kadambas succeeded the S'átaváhanas, and there is probably a trace of them in an old inscription at Anaji, which may be of the 4th century, and which mentions a great battle between a Pallava king named Naṇakkása and a king named Krishnavarma, doubtless a Kadamba. The latter suffered so complete a defeat that the prince S'ivanandavarma retired in consequence from the world. Banavasi was the chief Kadamba capital, but Uchchásringi is also mentioned as an important seat of their government, and this corresponds either with Uchchangi-durga near Dávangere, or with a hill of the same name, but also called Hire-A'ryara-durga, near Molakálmuru, some Kadamba inscriptions being found here. A rock inscription of Chandiyammarasa, to the south-west of Chitaldroog, is also probably Kadamba.

The *Chálukyas* in the 6th century reduced the Kadambas to the condition of feudatories, and soon extended their dominion over this District in their contests against the Pallavas. But in the 8th century the *Ráshṭrakútas* became supreme, and so remained for two hundred years. Under them part of the District seems to have been attached to the Kadambalige nád.

**Nolambas.**—But the distinctive ruling race in the District at this time was the Noḷambas or Noṇambas, a branch of the Pallavas, and their territory was the Nolambaváḍi or Noṇambaváḍi Thirty-two Thousand, called in an inscription a girdle for her loins (*kaṭi-núpura*) to the Lady Earth. They had a capital at Penjeru or Henjeru, now Hemavati, close to the eastern point of Hiriyúr taluq, but they also had a city, Nolambapattana, of which only the name remains, to the east of Chitaldroog, near Aymangala, properly Ayyapamangala, so named after a Nolamba king, as also was Nannivála.

The *Chálukya* power was revived at the end of the 10th century, and their government of Noḷambavádi was at one time under the prince Vishnuvarddhana Vijayáditya, who had his capital at Kampili (in the Puryabhadra in Bellary District) and then under the prince Jayasingha Noḷamba Pallava, who also ruled over Banavase. From about the middle of the 11th to the end of the 12th century, the government was hereditary in a family of Páṇḍyas, of whom Tribhuvana Malla Páṇḍya Deva, Vijaya Páṇḍya Deva, Vira Páṇḍya Deva, and another Vijaya Páṇḍya Deva are mentioned; whence the region, or some portion of it, was also called the Páṇḍya rájya and the Páṇḍya manḍala. Its capital at this time was at Uchchangi-durga (near Dávangere). In the latter part of the period, though subordinate to the *Kalachurya* kings who supplanted the Chálukyas, these Pándyas appear to have affected some degree of independence. They claim to be of the Yádava race and lords of Kánchipura.

**Hoysalas.**—At the close of the 12th century the District was absorbed in the kingdom of the Hoysalas, whose capital was at Dorasamudra (Halebid, Hassan District). Nolambavádi and Nirgunda were both provinces of the Hoysala dominions, and descendants of the Ganga kings appear to have continued to rule over the latter as subordinate governors. The north-east, as far as Niḍugal, was subdued by Vishnuvarddhana, and Molakálmuru by Vira Ballála.

For about 15 years from 1270, the *Yádava* kings of Devagiri (Daulatabad) gained some advantage over the north-western parts of the District, and the seat of the provincial government was apparently established by them at Betúr, near Dávangere, which, however, is also described as having long before been the capital of some local chieftain.

In 1287 the Hoysalas had recovered their possessions in this part of Mysore, but the seat of government seems to have been transferred to Bemmattana-kallu, the present Chitaldroog. Before long both Devagiri and Dorasamudra were taken and sacked by the Muhammadans, and the two royal lines were brought to an end.

**Vijayanagar.**—From the middle of the 14th century, under the Vijayanagar sovereigns, who next became paramount, Bemmattana-kallu continued the chief town of the District. But subordinate to this sovereignty, in the course of the 15th century, arose the various palegars who held tracts of country on feudal tenure. The most considerable of these were the chiefs of Chitaldroog and Niḍugaḷ.

*Chitaldroog.*—The Chitaldroog family were of the Beda or Boya caste, corresponding with the Kirátas of Sanskrit writers. Hunters and mountaineers, as the names indicate, they belonged to one of the hill tribes who subsisted by hunting and tending cattle. The accounts of their origin are somewhat confused, but it appears that three families emigrated from Jadikal-durga, in the neighbourhood of the shrine of Tirupati, and settled at Nirutadi near Bharmaságar about 1475. The son and grandson of one of the leaders, named respectively Hire Hanumappa Náyak and Timmana Náyak, afterwards took up their residence at Matti in Hadadi hobli, Dávangere taluq. The latter, called Kámagéti Timmana Náyak, was appointed in 1508, by the Vijayanagar king, as Náyak of Holalkere, and afterwards to the same office in Hiriyúr and eventually in Chitaldroog. The hill at this place he fortified, and so conducted himself that a force was sent against him.[1]

On this occasion Timmana Náyak distinguished himself as the hero of a most extraordinary adventure. Stealing into the camp at night, with the intention of carrying off the horse of Sáluva Narasinga Ráya, the prince who commanded, he accidentally roused the groom. Hastily hiding among the litter, he lay quiet to escape observation, when the groom, driving in afresh the peg for the heel ropes, as luck would have it sent it right through the hand of the concealed chief. The latter bore the pain without moving, and when all was again still, releasing himself by cutting off the hand which was pinned to the ground, he succeeded in carrying off the horse in triumph. This unexampled proof of fortitude, while it attached to him more closely his immediate followers, showed the besieging army that no intimidation would be effectual with such an opponent. A peace was therefore, it is said, concluded, and Timmana Náyak invited to Vijayanagar, the sovereign of which expressed the greatest admiration of his courageous exploit. After successfully aiding the royal troops in an expedition against Kulburga, he visited the capital and was rewarded with many honours. At a later period he incurred the royal displeasure and was imprisoned at Vijayanagar, where he died.

[1] According to another account, Timmana Náyak came with a small body of armed men from a place called Madakeri below the Ghats, 10 *gau* distant from Tirupati, and entered the service of the palegar of Basvapatna. Some quarrel arose about a mistress that Timmana Náyak kept at Matti, and he took refuge at Máyakonda, whence, on being pursued, he escaped to the jungle at Guntanur. Collecting a band, he commenced plundering on every side, and erected a small fort called Rangapatna near Haleyúr. The neighbouring palegars of Harpanhalli, Nidugal, and Basvapatna, being much annoyed by his depredations, united against him and with the aid of some troops from Vijayanagar marched upon Rangapatna. Timmana Náyak was then forced to retire to Chitaldroog, where he was closely besieged, when the incident related in the text occurred and led to his formal recognition as one of the chiefs dependent on Vijayanagar.

His son, Obana Náyak, was in the next reign appointed Náyak of Chitaldroog. He took the name of Madakeri Náyak, and on the fall of Vijayanagar in 1564 assumed independence. In 1602 he was succeeded by his son Kastúri Rangappa Náyak, during whose warlike reign the possession of Máyakonda, Sante Bennúr, Holalkere, Anaji, Jagalúr and other places was contested in several battles with the Basvapatna palegar, and they remained as parts of the Chitaldroog territory. At the chief's death in 1652 his possessions yielded a revenue of 65,000 Durgi pagodas. Madakeri Náyak, his son, was next installed, and ruled till 1674. He extended the dominions, principally eastwards, until they yielded 100,000 Durgi pagodas.

An adopted son named Obana Náyak next succeeded, but after a few months was put to death by the dalaváyis, who were dissatisfied with his management. His son Súrakánta Rangappa then took the government, but on refusing to the troops the customary gratuities on the accession of a new master, they mutinied and killed him. Chikkanna Náyak, a younger brother of Madakeri Náyak, was next invited to the throne and installed in 1676. After forcing the Harpanhalli chief to raise the siege of Anaji, he was under the necessity of defending Harihar against the Muhammadans. This he effected by the following stratagem. Causing, on the approach of night, lights to be fixed to the branches of the trees and horns of the cattle at his encampment near the Báti hill, and the musicians to play as usual on their instruments as if the army were still there, he marched with nearly the whole force by a circuitous route and threw himself into the fort from the west, and thus drove off the besiegers. He formed alliances by marriage with the Ráyadurga and Basvapatna chiefs, and died in 1686. His brother Madakeri Náyak succeeded, but was imprisoned by the dalaváyis, who set up Rangappa.

But in 1689 Kumára Barmappa Náyak assumed the government and reigned till 1721. He was principally remarkable for the extent of his benefactions and the number of his children. It was during this period that the Mughals overran the Carnatic possessions of Bijapur and established their government at Sira, of which province Basavapatna and Budihál were made parganas, and to which Chitaldroog and the other neighbouring estates of palegars became tributary.

His son Madakeri Náyak, who came next, was engaged in continual hostilities against Harpanhalli, Sávanúr, Bednúr, and the Mahrattas under Siddoji or Hindu Rao, the father of Morári Rao. He was generally successful in his engagements and annexed a large tract of country on the north-east, extending beyond Molkálmuru, conquered from Ráydurga. In 1748 he secured the alliance of Chanda Sáhib, who, released from prison at Sattara through the designs of Mons. Dupleix, was marching south. But in the battle of Máyakonda, the Chitaldroog army encountered with disastrous result that of Bednúr, which was assisted by the confederate forces of Ráydurga, Harpanhalli and Sávanur. Madakeri Náyak was slain, in single combat on elephants, by Somasekhara Náyak, the Harpanhalli chief; Chanda Sahib's son fell at his side, and he himself was taken prisoner by the Bednúr troops. But having made known his hopes and designs regarding the Naváb-ship of the Carnatic to the Musalman officers of the latter, they released him and joined his standard.

Kastúri Rangappa Náyak, son of Madakeri, succeeded, and with the aid of Morári Rao retook Máyakonda. He made various expeditions to the north and south, in the latter of which he gained some possessions in the Budihál country. He at the same time kept up a friendship with the Subadar of Sira, who, it is said, invested him with the titles of Tallári and Nád-gauda of Sira. He died in 1754 without issue, and Madakeri Náyak, the son of Barmappa Náyak, was acknowledged as his successor.

Placed between the Mahrattas on one side and Haidar Ali on the other, this chief occupied a perilous position. In 1762 he was summoned by the latter, to whom the palegars of Ráydurga and Harpanhalli had submitted. Madakeri Náyak procrastinated, on which Haidar overran the whole country with his cavalry, and the chief was forced to compromise by paying a fine of two lakhs of rupees and an annual tribute. At this time, a pretender to the throne of Bednúr, announcing himself as Channa Basavaiya, whom it was supposed had been murdered, had sought protection and assistance from Chitaldroog. Haidar Ali soon saw the use that could be made of him, and in 1763 the united armies of Mysore and Chitaldroog invaded the Bednur country, with the ostensible object of restoring the rightful king. The result of the expedition has been related in the history of the Shimoga District. Haidar, having accomplished his purpose, sent the pretender, called in joke the Ghaib (or resurrection) Rája, to Maddagiri (Tumkur District) as a prisoner, along with the Bednur Ráni.

In 1777, when Haidar Ali was threatened with a formidable invasion by the allied armies of the Mahrattas and of Nizam Ali, the Chitaldroog palegar having received information which led him to consider that Haidar's fortune would shortly be reversed, held back from sending the usual contingent of troops to his assistance. Haidar, posted in a strong position at Gutti, found means to avert the danger, and immediately marched upon Chitaldroog to punish it, rejecting the offers of the chief to pay a large fine. The siege was maintained for some months without success, when an arrangement was entered into and a fine of thirteen lakhs of pagodas levied on the chief. But the advance of the Mahrattas forced Haidar to destroy the siege works and hasten to the north-west before the whole was paid, and the palegar, still doubting to which side fortune might incline, evaded the order to accompany the army with his troops. The Mahratta campaign failed, from the mutual jealousy of the leaders and other causes, and Haidar, after a successful career of conquest over all the country between the Tungabhadra and the Krishna, once more sat down indignant before Chitaldroog. But only by the treachery of the Muhammadan officers in the palegar's service was the place at last taken in 1779. Madakeri Náyak, on finding himself betrayed, threw himself on Haidar's mercy. He and his family were sent as prisoners to Seringapatam; while to break up the Bedar population, whose blind devotion to their chief had so prolonged the contest, he removed 20,000 inhabitants to people the island of Seringapatam, and of all the boys of proper age formed regular battalions of captive converts or Chelas, who in following wars were of great service to him.

*Niḍugal.*—The founder of the Niḍugal family appears to have come from the neighbourhood of Bijapur, and claimed to be a Kshatriya. According to tradition, he was born of a girl of that caste, whose family had settled at Dodderi, Harti, and Sarvad in the Bijapur country. At the age of seven she conceived by the Sun, and her father Timma Raja, to avert disgrace, exposed the infant to which she gave birth on a *tippe* or dunghill. The child was found by a cowherd named Kamma, who brought him up as his own. After a time the cowherd removed to Kamlapur near Vijayanagar, where there was an enclosure for the exhibition of tiger fights. On one occasion, when the king Krishna Raya was present, a tiger got loose and ran among the cattle, on which the boy killed it with his axe. The king made inquiry regarding a youth of such bold spirit, and on hearing his story took him away from the cowherd, alleging that as a foundling he belonged to the State. At the same time, from the fact of his having been found on a *tippe*, he gave him the name of Tippana Náyak.

Some time after he defeated a noted champion athlete, who had prevailed against all other opponents at the Court, and put him to death; for which exploit he was granted a tract of country in the east of the Chitaldroog District, to be cleared of jungle and formed into an estate. Settling at Machisamudra, Gosikere, and Challakere, he built Dodderi and Harti, naming them after the towns of his ancestors; and took possession of the country extending from Chitaldroog to Pávugada, and from Molkálmuru to Sira. At his death, which must have happened in the latter half of the 16th century, he divided his territory among his seven sons.

On the invasion of the country by the Bijapur army the descendants of these were driven from their respective possessions, and Timmana Náyak, who had lost Dodderi, retired to the hill of Niḍugal, which he fortified; and there the family long remained, paying to Sira a tribute of 3,000 pagodas. On the capture of Sira by Haidar Ali in 1761, the Niḍugal chief, also called Timmana Náyak, submitted to the conqueror, who imposed on him a tribute of 7,000 pagodas and the supply of 300 men. Subsequently, while accompanying Tipu Sultan in the expedition against Mangalore, he fell ill; and when at the point of death was compelled to sign a letter relinquishing his territory and ordering his son Hottana Náyak to deliver it up to the governor of Chitaldroog. Possession was at once taken, and Hottana Náyak, with his brother, were sent as prisoners to Chitaldroog and thence to Seringapatam, where they were put to death when the British army ascended the Ghats.

**Mysore Raj.**—On the overthrow of the Muhammadan government and the formation of the present kingdom of Mysore, the Chitaldroog country was included in it, and formed the Chitrakal Ráyada, Subayana or Faujdári. The west and south suffered during the insurrection of 1830. Under the subsequent British management, the Chitaldroog Division included the Chitaldroog and Tumkur Districts, with head-quarters at Tumkur. In 1863 that Division was broken up, by joining the Chitaldroog District to the Nagar Division, and the Tumkur District to the Nundydroog Division. In 1879 the Divisions were abolished, and in 1882 Chitaldroog was reduced to a Sub-Division under Tumkur District. In 1886 the Chitaldroog District was re-established, but Pavugada taluq remained a part of Tumkur District.

## POPULATION

*Number.*—The population of the District by the census of 1891 consists of 209,590 males and 209,394 females, or altogether 413,984 persons.

*Density.*—It will thus be seen that there are 102·92 persons to a square mile—a comparatively low rate, due to the extent of the District and the barrenness of a considerable portion of it. The Dávangere taluq was the most thickly peopled when the census was taken, the ratio being 162·41 persons per square mile, followed by Chitaldroog taluq, with 125·72, and Jagalur taluq, with 103·04. The scantiest population was in Hiriyúr taluq, with only 67·28 per square mile. Challakere taluq had only 76·84, and Molkálmuru 83·48.

*By religion.*—According to religion the population is thus distributed, adults being shown separately from children :—

| Religion. | Above 15. | | Under 15. | | Total. | Per cent. |
|---|---|---|---|---|---|---|
| | Male. | Female. | Male. | Female. | | |
| Hindus ... ... | 123,134 | 118,081 | 76,433 | 77,224 | 394,872 | 95·38 |
| Muhammadans ... | 5,668 | 4,972 | 3,803 | 3,739 | 18,182 | 4·39 |
| Jains ... ... | 266 | 172 | 117 | 84 | 639 | 0·15 |
| Christians ... ... | 117 | 69 | 49 | 49 | 284 | 0·06 |
| Others (6 Parsis, 1 Jew) | 3 | 3 | — | 1 | 7 | — |
| Total ... | 129,188 | 123,297 | 80,402 | 81,097 | 413,984 | — |

*Increase.*—The following figures compare the estimates of population in the *khâneshumâri* accounts of 1853–4, with the numbers recorded in the census periods of 1871, 1881, and 1891 :—

| Taluq. | 1853–4. | 1871. | 1881. | 1891. |
|---|---|---|---|---|
| Challakere ... ... ... ... | 22,144 | 57,187 | 45,747 | 60,711 |
| Chitaldroog ... ... ... ... | 34,720 | 75,442 | 50,834 | 66,546 |
| Dávangere ... ... ... ... | 60,823 | 94,006 | 72,749 | 94,565 |
| Hiriyúr ... ... ... ... | 30,785 | 61,866 | 40,163 | 54,302 |
| Holalkere ... ... ... ... | 33,493 | 78,336 | 47,249 | 67,051 |
| Jagalúr ... ... ... ... | 26,710 | 40,311 | 28,437 | 38,229 |
| Molakálmuru ... ... ... | 22,133 | 28,405 | 25,332 | 32,560 |
| Total... ... ... | 230,808 | 435,553 | 310,511 | 413,964 |

Some of the differences are due to redistribution of taluqs and to changes in the limits of the District. There was an apparent increase in the first 18 years up to 1871 of 88·97 per cent., and even allowing 25 per cent. of defective enumeration in the early estimate, as was shown to be required at the actual census, there still remains the high rate of 63·97 per cent., an eloquent testimony to the security and prosperity of the District. But the great famine of 1877–8 fell with severity upon Chitaldroog, and the population went down 28·7 per cent. by 1881. It has since again risen 33·31 per cent. in the 10 years to 1891, indicating considerable elasticity in the population. The net result may be stated at an increase on the whole of 43·49 per cent. in 38 years.

*Classes.*—Classified according to occupation and nationality, the population is composed of the following divisions :—

| | Nó. | | Per cent. |
|---|---|---|---|
| A. Agricultural ... ... ... ... ... | 88,393 | ... | 20·86 |
| B. Professional ... ... ... ... ... | 15,427 | ... | 3·72 |
| C. Commercial ... ... ... ... ... | 52,708 | ... | 12·73 |
| D. Artisan and Village Menial ... ... .. | 148,712 | ... | 35·92 |
| E. Vagrant Minor Artisans and Performers ... | 90,148 | ... | 21·77 |
| Races and Nationalities ... ... ... ... | 18,473 | ... | 4·46 |
| Others, not stated ... ... ... ... ... | 123 | ... | 0·02 |

The following are the largest castes or classes, those which number over 10,000, in order of strength. These account for 330,628, or 79·86 per cent. of the population.

| | | | |
|---|---|---|---|
| Beḍa ... ... .. | 71,607 | Golla ... ... ... | 31,505 |
| Wokkaliga ... ... | 69,560 | Kuruba ... ... ... | 25,398 |
| Lingáyit[1] ... ... | 61,325 | Musalmán ... ... | 17,219 |
| Mádiga ... ... ... | 37,086 | Woḍḍa ... ... ... | 16,928 |

The most numerous classes of Wokkaliga are the Sáda (27,988), Kunchaṭiga (10,758), Reḍḍi (8,056), and Nonaba (3,865). Among the Kuruba, Hálu Kuruba number 9,882. Among Musalmáns, the Shekhs (10,912) predominate. There are only 5,993 Brahmaṇs altogether, the most numerous sects being Des'astha (1,412) and Baḍaganád (1,193).

**Stock.**—There were 11,731 carts and 61,120 ploughs in 1893, which form the *agricultural* stock of the District. The *manufacturing* stock included 2,757 cloth looms, 1,500 kambli, 69 girdle, 1 góni, and 1 carpet loom, besides oil-mills which number 115.

*Tanks.*—The District contains 872 tanks.

**Dwellings.**—First-class houses at the same period numbered 15,968, tenanted by 79,840 people, while those of an inferior description numbered 74,857, with 334,144 occupants. The best houses are most numerous in Dávangere taluq. Hiriyúr and Chitaldroog follow next in order.

**Towns and Villages.**—The District contains nine municipal towns, with a population of 33,800, composed of 27,785 Hindus, 5,531 Muhammadans, 310 Jains, 6 Parsis, 167 Christians, and 1 Jew.

The following are the towns, with the population of each :—

| | | | |
|---|---|---|---|
| Dávangere ... ... | 8,061 | Holalkere ... ... | 2,557 |
| Harihar ... ... ... | 6,385 | Molakálmuru ... ... | 2,421 |
| Chitaldroog ... ... | 4,946 | Hosdurga... ... ... | 2,061 |
| Hiriyúr ... ... ... | 2,863 | Challakere ... ... | 1,710 |
| Jagalúr ... ... ... | 2,796 | | |

[1] There are also 31,853 included among Wokkaliga.

The total number of *asali* or primary villages in 1891 was 1,452, to which were attached 189 *dákhali* or secondary villages or hamlets. Of the former 1,185 were populated, and 267 depopulated. Government villages numbered 1,415, and inám villages 37—namely, 10 sarvamánya, 20 jóḍi, and 7 káyamgutta.

**Great festivals.**—The largest religious festivals are held at the following places:—

At *Náyakanhaṭṭi*, Challakere taluq, on the occasion of the *Tippa Rudra* car festival, held on Pushya bahula first and two subsequent days, about 10,000 people assemble.

At *Kotegudda*, Jagalur taluq, 8,000 people come together for the *Virabhadra Deva* festival, lasting from 17th to 21st March.

At *Kalladevarpura*, Jagalur taluq, the car festival held from 19th to 22nd April, attracts 6,000 people. The same number attend the *Ammana* festival at *Bevinhalli*, in Hiriyúr taluq, celebrated for seven days from full moon day of Chaitra.

At *Hiriyúr*, Hiriyúr taluq, 5,000 people come together during the *Tyára Mallesvara* festival, kept up for a week from full moon day of Mágha.

At *Murgi maṭha*, in Chitaldroog taluq, 4,000 people collect on the 11th day of Asvija, on account of the *Murgi maṭha* festival.

At *Gurusiddapura*, Jagalur taluq, 3,500 people attend the *Chavudesvara* festival, which lasts from 1st to 3rd March.

At *Mári Kanave*, Hiriyúr taluq, 2,500 people assemble for the *Máramma játre*, held for five days from Vaisákha suddha 5th.

At *Yaraballi*, Hiriyúr taluq, 3,000 people come to a similar *játre*, for five days from Vaisákha full moon day.

At *Devapur*, Hosdurga sub-taluq, more than 2,000 people assemble on the occasion of the *Keriyagalamma jáṭre*, which lasts for eight days in Pushya.

At *Dávangere*, the *Durgamma játre*, held once in two years in Phálguna, is attended by 8,000 people.

At *Harihar*, the car festival of *Harihareswara*, held on the full moon day of Mágha, attracts 5,000 people.

At *Hale Báti*, Dávangere taluq, 5,000 people celebrate the car festival of *Pránadeva* in the month of Pushya; and at *Avergola*, in the same taluq, a similar festival on Mágha bahula 5th, is attended by 2,000 people.

At *Nunke Bhairava gudda*, near Molakálmuru, a festival in honour of *Nunke Bhairava* is held for eight days from Vaisákha suddha 5th, and attracts 2,500 people.

At *Gaurasamudra*, Challakere taluq, the *Máramma játre*, held for four days from Bhádrapada suddha, is attended by 3,000 people.

**Fairs.**—The largest weekly fairs are the following:—

| Place. | Taluq. | Day. | No. of Visitors. |
|---|---|---|---|
| Dávangere ... ... | Dávangere ... | Sunday ... ... | 2,000 |
| Chitaldroog ... | Chitaldroog... | Monday ... ... | 1,000 |
| Harihar ... ... | Dávangere ... | Tuesday .. ... | 2,000 |
| Jagalur ... ... | Jagalur ... | Saturday ... ... | 2,000 |

**Vital Statistics.**—The birth-rate of the District in 1893–4 was 23·27 per mille of the population, and the death-rate was 13·50 per mille. The number of births registered was 9,634—namely, 4,848 of males and 4,786 of females. The number of deaths registered was 5,590, of which 2,843 were deaths of males and 2,747 of females. The following were the causes of death:—Diseases—cholera, 22; smallpox, 508; fevers, 3,052; bowel complaints, 432; injuries—suicide, 2; wounds or accidents, 78; snake-bite or wild beasts, 13; all other causes, 1,355.

## REVENUE

The following statement exhibits the revenue of the District for five years to 1895–6:—

| Items. | 1891–2. | 1892–3. | 1893–4. | 1894–5. | 1895–6. |
|---|---|---|---|---|---|
| Land Revenue ... | 6,18,867 | 6,39,004 | 6,57,623 | 6,63,643 | 6,91,052 |
| Forests ... ... | 20,296 | 20,411 | 15,397 | 25,579 | 21,406 |
| Abkari ... ... | 1,40,230 | 2,10,826 | 2,16,177 | 2,19,975 | 2,23,156 |
| Mohatarfa ... ... | 41,944 | 42,210 | 37,418 | 34,106 | 33,684 |
| Sáyar... ... ... | 5,824 | 5,597 | 3,405 | 7,148 | 5,731 |
| Salt ... ... ... | 8,949 | 9,105 | 10,740 | 8,740 | 9,571 |
| Stamps ... ... | 24,140 | 28,002 | 29,143 | 29,055 | 29,660 |
| Law and Justice ... | 5,258 | 7,371 | 8,221 | 5,889 | 6,798 |
| Police ... ... | 20 | 105 | 26 | 27 | 11 |
| Public Works ... | 8,414 | 3,135 | 6,858 | — | — |
| Miscellaneous ... | 9,651 | 12,013 | 12,738 | 14,265 | 15,773 |
| Total Rs. ... | 8,83,593 | 9,77,779 | 9,97,746 | 10,08,427 | 10,36,842 |

## TRADE

**Manufactures.**—The most general manufactures of the District are those of *kamblis* or camblets and piece goods.

*Woollen Fabrics.*—The kamblis or woollen blankets, which are generally 4 cubits wide by 12 long, are manufactured of the finest description in Dávangere and Jagalur taluqs, both white and black, as well as checked. Some have been turned out to the value of Rs. 200 and Rs. 300, of so fine a texture that they could be rolled up into a hollow bamboo, and were considered impervious to water. But the price of the more expensive kinds usually made, the wool being taken from the first shearing of the sheep, varies from Rs. 25 to Rs. 40. Coarser descriptions, costing from R. 1 to Rs. 12 each, are made in Chitaldroog, Challakere, and more or less in all the other taluqs. Towards Molkálmuru they may be had as cheap as 10 annas.

*Cotton Fabrics.*—These are produced in greatest quantity in the neighbourhood of Harihar, in Chitaldroog taluq, and in the north of Molkálmuru. At the first are made women's and men's cloths, towels, napkins, sheets, girdles, and tape. The price of cloth varies from R. 1 to Rs. 25 a piece, $2\frac{1}{2}$ to 3 cubits wide, and from 6 to 12 long for men's wear, 12 to 18 for women's. At Chitaldroog are manufactured white sheets, men's cloths and inferior women's cloths, the latter costing from R. 1 to Rs. 6 each. At Devasamudra and other villages north of Molkálmuru are woven cloths of the kind generally worn by Wokkaliga and Banajiga women, valued at from Rs. 2 to Rs. 10 each. White cloths are also made, costing from 8 annas to Rs. 3 a piece. Coarse cloths are made to some extent in all the taluqs, and in Dávangere and Hosdurga cotton thread is largely spun by the women. In the latter, red and coloured handkerchiefs are made.

A large cotton ginning factory has been established at Dávangere by Messrs. Binny & Co., of Madras.

*Silk Fabrics.*—The silk manufactures are confined to the Molkálmuru and Harihar taluqs. In the former, silk cloths suited for men and women, with scarves and turbans of the same material, are made, varying in price from Rs. 10 to Rs. 150. Women's cloths, of cotton and silk interwoven, are also manufactured, costing from Rs. 3 to Rs. 40 each. At Harihar white-and-black check cloths are woven, of raw silk imported from Bangalore.

*Metal Manufacture.*—This consists principally of *iron*, with some *steel*, and is carried on in the Hiriyúr, Hosdurga, and Chitaldroog taluqs, in the neighbourhood of the central hill ranges. The ore is first melted and the metal procured in balls or lumps : these are afterwards hammered into bars or pigs for use, or converted into steel as required. The iron articles manufactured are tools and implements of various kinds for agricultural and industrial purposes. From steel are made swords, daggers, knives, &c. *Brass* vessels and utensils are made north of Molkálmuru by Panchálas, varying in price from 8 annas to Rs. 60. Similar articles, as well as lamps, are made in Hosdurga taluq.

*Glass.*—The manufacture of bangles or coloured glass bracelets, so largely worn by native women, is carried on at Mattod.

Of other manufactures, that of *paper* was formerly an important branch, especially in Challakere taluq, the size of the paper made in which was the standard of a measure called the Dodderi *gaz* or yard. The material used for the manufacture was old *ganni*, and the paper was of the kind called whitey-brown and unglazed. *Rez* or emery for blotting ink is made at Mattod.

Articles of *leather*, such as slippers, buckets, and cords for *kapile* wells, &c., are made in the Molkálmuru taluq, costing from 2 annas to Rs. 5 each; and also sieves, baskets, mats, &c., of *bamboo*. Blue and red *dyes* are made at Harihar, the former from indigo, the latter from the root and bark of two kinds of tree, called *malagina kone* and *patanga*.

**Marts.**—The chief mart in the District is Dávangere. But there is also considerable traffic between the Nagar Malnád and the eastern districts through Holalkere and Huliyár; and with Bellary and districts to the north through Tallak and other places in Challakere taluq. There are agents of Bombay houses at Dávangere for the purpose of buying up oil seeds, &c.

## COMMUNICATIONS

**Railways.**—The Southern Mahratta Railway from Bangalore to Poona runs through the west of the District from south to north-west for about 52 miles, not far from the boundary. There are stations at Hosdurga Road, Rámagiri, Holalkere, Chik Jájur, Sásalu, Máyakonda, Kodaganur, Tolahunse, Dávangere, and Harihar.

**Roads.**—The *Provincial Roads* in the District have a total length of 207 miles, and cost for up-keep Rs. 25,940 yearly. The *District Roads* cover 245 miles, and are maintained at an annual expense of Rs. 13,280. Particulars are given below of the length and cost of each:—

PROVINCIAL ROADS.

| | Miles. | Cost. |
|---|---|---|
| Salem-Bellary road | 89 | 12,460 |
| Bangalore-Dharwar road | 72 | 8,640 |
| Chitaldroog-Benkipur road | 29 | 3,480 |
| Shimoga-Harihar road... | 17 | 1,360 |
| Total | 207 | Rs. 25,940 |

DISTRICT ROADS.

| | Miles. | Cost. |
|---|---|---|
| Holalkere-Huliyar road ... ... ... ... | 27 | 2,160 |
| Hosdurga-Bidarkere railway feeder ... ... ... | 6 | 240 |
| Hiriyur-Huliyar road ... ... ... ... ... | 22 | 1,320 |
| Challakere-Pavugada road ... ... ... ... | 28 | 840 |
| Challakere-Nayakanhatti road ... ... ... ... | 12 | 600 |
| Nayakanhatti-Jagalur road ... ... ... ... | 16 | 480 |
| Hángal-Ráyadurga road ... ... ... ... | 6 | 300 |
| Hiriyur-Hosdurga road ... ... ... ... ... | 26 | 1,040 |
| Hiriyur-Mári Kanave road ... ... ... ... | 4 | 160 |
| Chitaldroog-Challakere road ... ... ... ... | 18 | 2,160 |
| Channagiri-Sante Bennur-Sásalu road ... ... ... | 5 | 200 |
| Vijapur-Ujani road ... ... ... ... ... | 31 | 1,550 |
| Anagod-Kodaganur road ... ... ... ... | 5 | 200 |
| Anaji-Uchchangidurga road ... ... ... ... | 2 | 80 |
| Dávangere-Hadadi road ... ... ... ... | 10 | 500 |
| Harihar-Harpanhalli road ... ... ... ... | 7 | 350 |
| Tarikere-Hosdurga road... ... ... ... ... | 10 | 500 |
| Chitaldroog station roads ... ... ... ... | 10 | 600 |
| Total ... | 245 | Rs. 13,280 |

**Accommodation for travellers.**—Europeans travelling in the District find accommodation in the *dák bungalows* built at the stations named below. Brahman kitchens are attached to several.

*First Class.*—Chitaldroog, Dávangere, Harihar, Hiriyur.

*Second Class.*—Bharmaságar, Bommagondankere, Challakere, Holalkere, Male Bennur.

*Third Class.*—Ayamangala, Anagód, Hángal, Hosdurga, Javangondanhalli, Jogimatti, Rampur, Talak, Vijapur.

Native travellers rest in the *chatrams* maintained by Government at Bharmaságar, Chitaldroog, Hangal, Harihar, Hiriyur, Sánekere and Talak.

## GAZETTEER

**Betur** or **Bettur.**—A village in Dávangere taluq, 2 miles north of the kasba. Population, 1,183.

It appears to have been the old capital of a principality. At the end of the 13th century it was taken by the Devagiri general and made the seat of government during the ascendancy of the Yádava kings of Devagiri over the northern parts of the Hoysala dominions.

**Challakere.**—A taluq in the north-east, till 1882 called Doddéri taluq. Area, 790 square miles. Head-quarters at Challakere. Contains the following hoblis, villages and population :—

| No. | Hoblis. | Villages. | Hamlets. | Villages classified | | | | Population. |
|---|---|---|---|---|---|---|---|---|
| | | | | Government. | Sarvamânya. | Jodi. | Kayamgutta. | |
| 1 | Challakere ... ... | 47 | 3 | 46 | — | — | 1 | 17,088 |
| 2 | Náyakanhaṭṭi ... | 47 | 8 | 47 | — | — | — | 10,402 |
| 3 | Parasurámpura ... | 51 | 4 | 50 | — | 1 | — | 15,331 |
| 4 | Talak... ... ... | 46 | 10 | 45 | 1 | — | — | 17,890 |
| | Total ... | 191 | 25 | 188 | 1 | 1 | 1 | 60,711 |

*Principal places, with population.*—Náyakanhaṭṭi 2,468; Challakere 1,710; Ghataparti 1,644; Nanniválu 1,279; Mannekote 1,276; Irehalli 1,430; Parasurámpura 1,101: Doddéri 1,001.

From 1875 to 1886 Mòlakálmuru taluq was included in this taluq.

The Vedavati flows through the east from south to north, and receives various nálas, the most important of which are the Garni from near Chitaldroog, and the Náyakanhaṭṭi from that village. The surface of the taluq is comparatively flat, with a few rocky ridges or bare hills. Date groves occur in some parts, and groups of bábul in the beds of tanks and along the river. Except for these, the taluq generally presents a bleak and barren appearance. No less than 104 square miles are occupied by Amrit Mahal kávals.

The soil is mostly red and sandy, but in the south-west corner there is some good black soil. The surface of the ground is often covered with loose stones, solid rock constantly crops up, and enormous boulders are found even in cultivated fields. In many villages the soil is impregnated with saline matter, which causes a white efflorescence on the surface. This soil is cultivated, but produces very poor crops. The tanks are numerous, but few are of the first class. Wells are more relied upon, many of which are formed from *talpargis* or spring heads. Great attention is paid to the cultivation of rice and other irrigated cereals, as well as to the cocoa-nut and areca-nut gardens, but dry crop cultivation is carried on in a slovenly and careless manner. Sajje and sáve are the principal dry crops, but castor-oil, horse gram, rági, and javari are also grown. The two latter, however, as well as wheat, navane and tobacco, are almost always raised in irrigated lands. Cotton is grown in small quantities, chiefly in the black soil.

The revenue settlement was introduced in 1872. The area of the taluq at that time was thus distributed :—

| | | |
|---|---|---|
| Culturable (dry, 251,169; wet, 4,934; garden, 9,434) ... | ... | 265,537 |
| Unculturable (including roads, tanks, village sites, &c.) ... | ... | 102,205 |
| 3 Inam villages (5,760); 22 Amrit Mahál kávals (66,560) | ... | 72,320 |
| Total acres | ... | 440,062 |

The unoccupied arable area was 151,299 acres, 148,061 of it being dry crop land. Of the present taluq 153,480 acres are cultivated, and 192,335 unculturable. The land revenue for 1891-2 (15 months), was Rs. 93,852, and for 1892-3 it was Rs. 98,347.

The average rainfall at Challakere for 26 years (1870-95), and at the other stations for 3 years (1893-5), was as follows:—

| | Jan. | Feb. | Mar. | April | May | June | July | Aug. | Sept. | Oct. | Nov. | Dec. | Year. |
|---|---|---|---|---|---|---|---|---|---|---|---|---|---|
| Challakere | — | 0·02 | 0·23 | 0·84 | 3·28 | 1·21 | 1·23 | 1·75 | 3·91 | 2·45 | 2·36 | 0·09 | ... 17·37 |
| Náyakanhaṭṭi | — | 0·13 | 0·08 | 1·34 | 1·65 | 1·48 | 0·56 | 1·08 | 1·52 | 3·92 | 1·62 | — | ... 13·38 |
| Talak ... | — | — | 0·13 | 1·75 | 1·28 | 1·91 | 1·04 | 0·73 | 4·88 | 5·38 | 0·85 | — | ... 17·95 |

Another register for 23 years makes the annual average at Challakere 18·50 inches.

The Bangalore-Bellary high road runs through the taluq from south to north, being met at Challakere by a road from Chitaldroog. There are also roads from Challakere north-west to Náyakanhaṭṭi and east to Pavugada.

**Challakere** or **Chellakere.**—Head-quarters of the Challakere taluq, situated in 14° 18′ N. lat., 76° 43′ E. long., on the Bangalore-Bellary road, 18 miles east-north-east of Chitaldroog, with which it is connected by a road. It is a municipality.

| Population in 1891. | Males. | Females. | Total. |
|---|---|---|---|
| Hindus (with 9 Jains) .. ... ... | 800 | 790 | 1,590 |
| Muhammadans .. ... .. ... | 67 | 49 | 116 |
| Christians ... ... ... ... ... | 3 | 1 | 4 |
| Total ... .. ... | 870 | 840 | 1,710 |

There is little of interest in the place, which derives most of its importance from being the taluq kasba. The residents are chiefly Lingáyit traders. To the same sect belongs the temple of Chellakere-amma, the principal building.

| Municipal Funds. | 1892-3. | 1893-4. | 1894-5. | 1895-6. |
|---|---|---|---|---|
| Income ... ... ... ... ... | 473 | 525 | 534 | 782 |
| Expenditure... ... ... ... .. | 514 | 509 | 446 | 714 |

**Chitaldroog.**—A taluq in the centre. Area 531 square miles. Head-quarters at Chitaldroog. Contains the following hoblis, villages and population :—

| No. | Hoblis. | Villages | Hamlets. | Villages classified. Government. | Sarvamánya. | Jodi. | Kayamgutta. | Population. |
|---|---|---|---|---|---|---|---|---|
| 1 | Bharmaságara ... | 55 | 6 | 52 | 1 | 1 | 1 | 13,933 |
| 2 | Chitaldroog... ... | 57 | 23 | 50 | 1 | 6 | — | 26,270 |
| 3 | Gunṭanúr ... ... | 59 | 10 | 59 | — | — | — | 13,608 |
| 4 | Turavanúr ... ... | 18 | 6 | 18 | — | — | — | 12,735 |
| | Total ... | 189 | 45 | 179 | 2 | 7 | 1 | 66,546 |

*Principal places, with population.*—Chitaldroog, 4,946; Turavanúr, 4,444; Siddavvanhalli, 2,968; Dyamavvanhalli, 1,662; Chikkondanahalli, 1,620; Jampalnáyakankote, 1,323; Guḍḍa Rangavvanhalli, 1,300; Kúnabévu, 1,225; Bharmaságara, 1,127; Kelagote, 1,083; Híre Guntanúr, 1,081; Háyakal, 1,074; Jánukonda, 1,071.

A range of hills running north and south divides the taluq into two almost equal portions. Towards the north the range is narrow and the hills bare and insignificant, but south of Chitaldroog it spreads out into greater width and the hills are loftier and peculiarly striking in appearance. The country to the east and west of the above range is comparatively flat and free from jungle. To the east black soil preponderates, while to the west the country for the most part is composed of red soil.

The western half has a better water supply than the eastern. In it is situated the large Bhimasamudra tank, about 3½ miles in length by 2 in breadth. Dry crops are cultivated principally on the eastern side of the taluq, and consist of jola, cotton, navane, gram, &c. The crops of the western side are jola, rági, togari, &c., the rági being frequently sown in garden and rice lands. The kind of rice cultivated is sal bhatta, which requires little water and thrives upon the rainfall alone, though generally planted near a tank or nullah in case of need.

Chitaldroog was once remarkable for the manufacture of silk and cloths of good description, but at present kamblis and cotton cloths are alone woven in that town, and in Turavanur and Siddavvanhalli, where also dyers in red carry on their trade. The caste called Reddis are very numerous in the eastern parts of the taluq, so much so that it is often spoken of as the Reddi country.

The east and north of the taluq are included in an auriferous tract, in which land has been taken up for gold-mining.

The revenue settlement was introduced in 1867. The area of the taluq at that time was thus distributed :—

| | |
|---|---|
| Culturable (dry, 190,011 ; wet, 6,200 ; garden, 3,070) ... ... | 199,281 |
| Unculturable (including roads, village sites, &c.) ... ... ... | 106,872 |
| Total acres ... | 306,153 |

The unoccupied arable land was 62,447 acres, mostly dry crop land. Of the present taluq 159,384 acres are cultivated, and 113,226 unculturable.

The land revenue for 1891–2 (15 months) was Rs. 1,02,167, and for 1892–3 it was Rs. 1,05,567.

The average rainfall for 26 years (1870–95) at Chitaldroog, and for 3 years (1893–5) at the other station was as follows :—

| | Jan. | Feb. | Mar. | Apl. | May | June | July | Aug. | Sept. | Oct. | Nov. | Dec. | Year |
|---|---|---|---|---|---|---|---|---|---|---|---|---|---|
| Chitaldroog | 0·19 | 0·03 | 0·33 | 1·41 | 3·43 | 2·57 | 2·68 | 2·89 | 3·61 | 4·98 | 2·34 | 0·39 | ... 24·85 |
| Vijapur ... | — | 0·17 | — | 1·80 | 0·65 | 3·36 | 3·09 | 2·25 | 1·99 | 1·40 | 1·42 | — | ... 16·13 |

The high road from Hiriyur to Harihar runs through the taluq from south east to north-west, and is crossed at Chitaldroog by a road from the Holalkere railway station in the south-west to Challakere in the north-east. There is also a road from Vijapur to Jagalur and the frontier northwards.

**Chitaldroog.**—The chief town of the District, situated in 14° 14′ N. lat., 76° 27′ E. long., 24 miles from the Holalkere railway station, and on the Bangalore-Harihar road, 126 miles north-west of Bangalore. It is a municipality.

| Population in 1891. | Males. | Females. | Total. |
|---|---|---|---|
| Hindus ... ... ... ... ... | 1,873 | 2,114 | 3,987 |
| Muhammadans ... ... ... ... | 439 | 473 | 912 |
| Jains ... ... ... ... ... .. | 16 | 6 | 22 |
| Christians ... ... ... ... ... | 14 | 11 | 25 |
| Total ... ... ... | 2,342 | 2,604 | 4,946 |

The town, which is surrounded with a line of fortifications and includes an inner fort, is built at the north-eastern base of a dense cluster of rocky hills, very extensively fortified. The history of the place has already been related in connection with that of the District. There are many inscriptions on the hill, of the Chálukyas, the Hoysalas, and the Vijayanagar kings, dating from the 11th to the 15th century. Its name at that time was Bemmattanakalla or Bemmattanúru. According to legend a giant named Hiḍimbásura was here slain by Vrikódara or Bhima, one of the Pándus. The present name of the place is derived either from *Sitala-* or *Chitrakal-durga*, meaning spotted or picturesque castle, or *Chatrakal*, umbrella rock, the umbrella being the ensign of royalty. To the south-west is a striking lofty hill of this form, considered sacred by both Hindus and Musalmans. At the top is a pillar and shrine of Dhavalappa or Siddesvara. The Muhammadans call it the tomb of Saad-ulla. There is also another hill south of Chitaldroog, with a shrine at the summit dedicated to Obala-devi, and held specially sacred by the Bedas.

The mahal or palace in the inner fort, erected by Tipu Sultan, with a fine fruit garden attached, is used as the cutcherry. Before it stands an immense trough for watering elephants, which was found on the hill, formed out of a single stone. In the town, water is laid on to all the streets from the Timmanhalli tank, a short distance to the south. The principal temple is one of two storeys, dedicated to Uchchangi-amma. The extensive fortifications, batteries and works of masonry forming the *méldurga* or upper hill-fort, which includes 14 temples, present many points of interest. The remains of the fort and palace of the palegars, which were of mud, are still to be seen, with the site of a pleasure garden. The formidable stone fortress, as it now is, was erected under Haidar and Tipu, by whom also were constructed the immense granaries and pits for storing oil and ghee. Chitaldroog was for some years garrisoned by British troops, but given up on account of its unhealthiness.

Besides the usual District offices, which are beyond the fort walls, 3 miles to the north-west is situated the Murgi maṭh, the residence of the chief guru of the Sivabhaktas or Lingáyits. It is a large and well-built edifice. In one part is an ingenious water wheel. The name of the maṭh is said to be derived from *múru-gi*, the three *gi-s*, namely *yógi*, *jógi* and *bhógi*. There is a fine maṭh belonging to the guru on the hill, but it is deserted owing to his inability, on account of the opposition of other sects in the town, to visit it with all the insignia of his authority, one of which is a lighted torch by day.

To the west, among a wildly rugged and picturesque group of hills, is the Ankli maṭh, of recent establishment. There is here a curious long series of subterranean chambers, now regularly built round with masonry and thickly covered with plaster. They are entered by a good stone staircase, which leads down to rooms of various sizes at different levels. In them are shrines, lingas, baths and pedestals, apparently for *yógásana*. The style of their present architecture may be from 300 to 500 years old, but the caverns no doubt existed long before. When and for what purpose they were originally formed or occupied is unknown. When the Ankli maṭha was first established, about 40 years ago, they were found deserted, and the entrance choked up with a thick growth of bushes. They are now merely used for storing things in. At the Panchalinga cave, near the entrance, is an inscription of 1286, in the reign of the Hoysala king Nárasimha III, recording a grant by his minister Perumále.

In this quarter, immediately to the west of Chitaldroog, are traces of an ancient city, consisting of very large-sized bricks, and remains of pottery. Coins are frequently found after heavy rains. In 1888 a large find was made of Buddhist leaden coins, one of which bore the name of the Andhra or S'átaváhana king Pulumáyi, of the 2nd century. According to tradition the city was called Chandrávali, and extended as far as the four points, Náralgundi, Báralgundi, Huligundi and Basavangundi. Huligundi is to the north of the Ankli maṭha, and Basavangundi is to the north-west of the Cholagatta hill, near Gárihatti village.

About three miles south of Chitaldroog is the Jogi maṭṭi or maraḍi, one of the highest points in the District, being 3,803 feet above the level of the sea. It is surrounded with hills and is overgrown with bamboo, stunted teak and other trees. A road has been made to it and a plantation commenced. It is a convenient resort during the intense heat of the hot months.

| Municipal Funds. | 1892-3. | 1893-4. | 1894-5. | 1895-6. |
|---|---|---|---|---|
| Income ... ... ... ... ... | 4,785 | 4,755 | 7,005 | 7,954 |
| Expenditure ... ... ... ... | 5,184 | 7,331 | 4,223 | 7,652 |

**Davangere.**—A taluq in the north-west, including Harihar subtaluq. Area, 552 square miles. Head-quarters at Dávangere. Contains the following hoblis, villages, and population :—

| No. | Hoblis. | Villages. | Hamlets. | Villages classified. | | | | Population. |
|---|---|---|---|---|---|---|---|---|
| | | | | Government. | Sarvamánya. | Jodi. | Kayamgutta. | |
| 1 | A'nagóḍ ... ... | 23 | — | 23 | — | — | — | 5,336 |
| 2 | Anaji ... .. | 28 | 1 | 27 | — | — | 1 | 9,021 |
| 3 | Dávangere ... | 43 | 2 | 41 | — | — | 2 | 20,000 |
| 4 | Hadaḍi ... ... | 39 | — | 39 | — | — | — | 11,455 |
| 5 | Harihar ... | 41 | — | 40 | — | 1 | — | 17,330 |
| 6 | Male Bennúr ... | 45 | — | 44 | 1 | — | — | 18,773 |
| 7 | Máyakonḍa .. | 43 | 3 | 41 | 2 | — | — | 12,650 |
| | Total ... | 262 | 6 | 255 | 3 | 1 | 3 | 94,565 |

*Principal places, with population.*—Dávangere, 8,061; Harihar, 6,385; Male Bennúr, 1,909; Máyakonda, 1,646; Sirigere, 1,348; Hadaḍi, 1,266; Laukikere, 1,200; Bettur, 1,183; Bellúḍu, 1,135; Kákkaragola, 1,082; Kokkanúr, 1,011.

This taluq (to which that of Harihar was united in 1875, and formed into a sub-taluq in 1892) has the Tungabhadra running along its western boundary, into which the Haridra from the Súlekere flows at Harihar. The south-west is bounded by the chain of hills trending the right bank of the Bhadra and Tungabhadra from Ajjampur north-west to the frontier. Except where a low range of hills crosses the taluq from the east of Máyakonda to the east of Anaji, it consists of a wide unbroken level plain, sloping down to Harihar and the river in the north-west, upon which the insignificant Báti hill makes a conspicuous figure, while Uchchangi-durga, beyond the border, looms formidably upon the north-east horizon.

Black soil prevails in the west, and stony or gravelly soil in the east; but these are often intermixed, together with patches of red. The chief crops cultivated are jola, cotton, and rági, of which the ryots use the former principally for food. Rice and sugar-cane are grown to a small extent only under tanks.

The taluq is noted for the manufacture of kamblis, of which some of the finest texture are valued as high as from Rs. 200 to Rs. 300. Coarse cotton cloths are largely woven in the villages. More than half the population consists of Sivabhaktas or Lingáyits.

This country was probably owned by the Kadambas at the beginning of the Christian era. It afterwards formed part of the province of Nonambaváḍi under the Chálukya and Hoysala kings, the seat of government being at Uchchangi-durga. The Yádavas of Devagiri held it for some years, making Bettur the chief town. It then fell a prey to the Muhammadan incursions by which the Hoysala dominion was overthrown, but on the rise of the Vijayanagar empire was enriched by its kings, from Harihara Ráya downwards. On the downfall of that State the principal places in the taluq were seized by the chiefs of Bednur and Tarikere, until taken, some by the Naváb of Sávanur, and some by the palegar of Chitaldroog, who in their turn were forced to yield them to Haidar Ali; since when, with occasional possession by the Mahrattas in the latter part of last century, they have remained attached to Mysore.

The revenue settlement was introduced into the old Harihar taluq in 1865, and into Dávangere taluq in 1866. The area at that time was distributed as follows:—

| | |
|---|---|
| Culturable (dry, 293,466 ; wet, 3,185 ; garden, 2,121) ... ... | 298,772 |
| Unculturable (including roads, village sites, &c.) ... ... ... | 53,716 |
| Inam ... ... ... ... ... ... ... ... ... | 27,911 |
| Total acres ... | 380,399 |

The unoccupied arable land was 127,452 acres. The present taluq has 238,775 acres cultivated, and 54,958 unculturable. The total land revenue for 1891–2 (15 months) was Rs. 1,64,166, and for 1892–3 it was Rs. 1,64,870.

The average rainfall at Dávangere for 26 years (1870–95), and at the other station for 3 years (1893–5) was as follows:—

| | Jan. | Feb. | Mar. | April | May | June | July | Aug. | Sept. | Oct. | Nov. | Dec. | Year |
|---|---|---|---|---|---|---|---|---|---|---|---|---|---|
| Dávangere | 0·02 | — | 0·24 | 0·79 | 2·40 | 2·17 | 2·69 | 2·07 | 3·84 | 4·31 | 0·97 | 0·15 | 19·65 |
| Harihar ... | — | 0·04 | 0·15 | 1·44 | 2·04 | 1·80 | 2·11 | 1·38 | 1·82 | 5·25 | 1·32 | — | 17·35 |

Other registers make the average for 19 years at Dávangere 21·05, and for 4 years at Harihar 18·19.

The Southern Mahratta railway from Bangalore to Poona runs through the taluq from south-east to north-west, with stations at Máyakonda, Kodaganur, Tolahunse, Dávangere, and Harihar. The Bangalore-Harihar high road passes by Anagod and Dávangere, while from Harihar there is a road south-westwards to Shimoga *viâ* Male Bennúr. From Dávangere there are roads south to Hadaḍi and east to Anaji. From A'nagóḍ there is a road south to the railway and to Holalkere, and one north to Anaji.

**Davangere.**—One of the most important seats of trade in the Province, situated in 14° 28′ N. lat., 75° 59′ E. long., on the Bangalore-Poona railway and the Bangalore-Harihar road, 38 miles north-west of Chitaldroog. Head-quarters of the Dávangere taluq, and a municipality.

| Population in 1891. | Males. | Females. | Total. |
|---|---|---|---|
| Hindus... ... ... ... ... ... | 3,351 | 3,428 | 6,779 |
| Muhammadans ... ... ... ... | 604 | 571 | 1,175 |
| Jains ... ... ... ... ... ... | 45 | 9 | 54 |
| Christians ... ... ... .. ... | 26 | 27 | 53 |
| Total ... ... ... | 4,026 | 4,035 | 8,061 |

Dávangere was originally an obscure village, forming one of the suburbs of Bettur. Haidar Ali gave it as a jágir to a Mahratta chief named Apoji Rám, who encouraged merchants to settle there. He died without heirs, but the place continued to increase under the encouragements given by Tipu Sultan, and it is now the most populous town in the Chitaldroog District. The merchants are principally Sivabhaktas or Lingáyits. The increase in population, especially since the advent of the railway, has made it necessary to extend the town to the east.

The most valuable trade here is that which is carried on with Wallajapet in North Arcot on the one side, and Nagar and Ságar on the other. Areca-nut and pepper, the produce of the latter, are sent to the former; and Madras goods imported from Europe, China, Bengal, and the eastern islands, together with salt, obtained in return; which, as well as kamblis made in the neighbourhood, are transmitted to Nagar and Ságar. There is also a large trade in cotton, and a cotton ginning factory has been established by Messrs. Binny & Co. of Madras. Agents of Bombay houses are stationed here for the purchase of oil-seeds, &c.

| Municipal Funds. | 1892–3. | 1893–4. | 1894–5. | 1895–6. |
|---|---|---|---|---|
| Income ... ... ... ... .. | 3,890 | 5,100 | 8,030 | 10,300 |
| Expenditure ... ... ... ... | 3,651 | 5,388 | 7,980 | 11,006 |

**Dodderi.**—A village in Challakere taluq, 4 miles east of the kasba. Population 1,001.

It was founded by the progenitor of the Nidugal family of chiefs (see p. 463 above), and it was here that Khasim Khan, the Mughal governor of Sira, being surprised while conveying a large treasure, by a Mahratta force under Danoji Ghorpada, assisted by the palegar of Chitaldroog, appears to have committed suicide to avoid disgrace. His body was afterwards taken to Sira and buried there. From this time Dodderi remained in the possession of the Chitaldroog chief until it was taken by Haidar Ali. Down to 1882 it gave its name to the taluq now called Challakere, and was long the head-quarters. It was once celebrated for its paper manufacture, and the size of the sheets regulated the Dodderi *gaz* or yard, which was a standard measure of length.

**Haggari.**—The principal stream of this name, sometimes called Hire Haggari by way of distinction, is also known as the Védávati, and is described under that designation. But there are in this District a Haggari and a Chinna Haggari besides. For a description of the latter see Janaga-halla.

The remaining stream is formed by the outflow of the Anaji tank, whence running northwards, almost along the boundary, it continues in the same direction through the Bellary country to the Tungabhadra.

**Harihar.**—A sub-taluq under Dávangere taluq, comprising the Harihar and Male Bennur hoblis.

**Harihar.**—An ancient town, situated in 14° 31′ N. lat., 75° 51′ E. long., on the right bank of the Tungabhadra, at the Mysore and Dharwar frontier. Till 1875 it was the head-quarters of a taluq bearing the same name, now united to Dávangere, from which it is 9 miles west. It is a railway station and a municipality.

| Population in 1891. | Males. | Females. | Total. |
|---|---|---|---|
| Hindus ... ... ... ... ... ... ... | 2,384 | 2,487 | 4,871 |
| Muhammadans ... ... ... ... ... | 712 | 715 | 1,427 |
| Jains ... ... ... ... ... ... ... ... | 19 | 5 | 24 |
| Christians (with 1 Jew) ... ... ... ... | 39 | 18 | 57 |
| Parsis ... ... ... ... ... ... ... ... | 2 | 4 | 6 |
| Total ... ... ... | 3,156 | 3,229 | 6,385 |

According to legend this spot was the capital or stronghold of a giant named Guha or Guhásura, whose extent was such that its eastern gate was at Uchchangi-durga, the southern at Govinahálu, the western at Mudanur, and the northern at Airani. The giant, having by his penance obtained from Brahma the boon of exemption from death at the hands either of Hari (Vishnu) or of Hara (Siva), became in consequence such a tormentor of gods and men that Vishnu and Siva, in order to counteract the spell, combined into one form of Harihara and destroyed him. The descent of this incarnation was at Kudalur, the confluence of the Tungabhadra and the Haridra, where its footprints are still pointed out. The expiring giant prayed that the place might be named after him, whence it was called Guháranya kshétra.

There are numerous inscriptions around the great temple, the earliest of which (passing over one on copper of the 7th century, which refers to another part) are dated in the 12th century. In the time of the Chálukya kings Harihara appears to have been an ancient agrahára, possessed by 104 Brahmans, and included in the province of Noṇambaváḍi, administered by governors bearing the name of Páṇḍya. The present highly ornate temple of Hariharesvara, was erected in 1223 by Polálva, a general and minister of the Hoysala king Narasimha II, and some additions were made in 1268 by Soma, the general under a subsequent king of the same name and dynasty, and the founder of Somanáthpur (Mysore District) with its splendid temple. In 1277 Sáluva Tikkama, commander of the forces of the Devagiri king Rámachandra, appears as erecting a temple to Mahadeva, in honour of the preceding king so named. Many benefactions were bestowed down to the 16th century by the Vijayanagar kings, one of the founders of which line, Hakka, assumed the name of Harihara Ráya.

After the fall of Vijayanagar the place was seized by the Tarikere chiefs, who erected the fort. From them it was taken by the Navàb of Sávanur, who granted it in jágir to Shir Khan. While in possession of the Muhammadans the temple was left intact, but the roof was used for a mosque, a small Saracenic doorway being made into the tower for the pulpit. Harihara was subsequently sold to the chiefs of Bednur, for, it is said, a lakh of rupees. The Mahrattas next held possession, until it was subdued by Haidar Ali in 1763. Since that time it has been thrice taken by the Mahrattas.

Until 1865 a native regiment was stationed in the cantonment two miles north-west of Harihar. In 1868 was completed the splendid bridge across the Tungabhadra, over which runs the trunk road from Bangalore to Dharwar. It is of stone and brick, built in 14 elliptical arches of 60 feet span, and cost nearly 3½ lakhs of rupees. There is also now a separate bridge over the river for the railway.

| Municipal Funds. | 1892-3. | 1893-4. | 1894-5. | 1895-6. |
|---|---|---|---|---|
| Income ... ... ... ... ... | 2,545 | 2,978 | 4,440 | 4,309 |
| Expenditure ... ... ... ... | 3,670 | 6,190 | 4,487 | 4,582 |

**Hiriyur.**—A taluq in the south-east. Area 807 square miles. Head-quarters at Hiriyúr. Contains the following hoblis, villages and population :—

| No. | Hoblis. | Villages. | Hamlets. | Villages classified. | | | | Population. |
|---|---|---|---|---|---|---|---|---|
| | | | | Government. | Sarvamánya. | Jódi. | Kayamgutta. | |
| 1 | Aymangala ... | 39 | 14 | 38 | — | 1 | — | 16,924 |
| 2 | Dharmapura ... | 22 | 2 | 22 | — | — | — | 7,930 |
| 3 | Hiriyúr .. ... | 60 | 3 | 57 | 1 | 1 | 1 | 15,141 |
| 4 | Javanagondanhalli | 32 | 2 | 32 | — | — | — | 5,979 |
| 5 | Lakkihalli ... | 62 | 1 | 61 | — | 1 | — | 8,328 |
| | Total ... | 215 | 22 | 210 | 1 | 3 | 1 | 54,302 |

*Principal places, with population.*—Hiriyúr, 2,863; Maradidevigere, 1,712; Aymangala, 1,223; Harti, 1,116; Maradihalli, 1,106; Dharmapura, 1,050.

Hiriyúr is reckoned one of the most barren taluqs in Mysore, and, compared with the rest of the country, an almost rainless region.

Throughout the west it is crossed by the parallel ranges of the low rocky and hilly belt which runs in a north-westerly direction through the centre of the District. Making its way through the gaps in these hills, with a course nearly at right angles to their general direction, the Védávati flows north-east across the centre of the taluq to some distance beyond Hiriyúr, where it turns north.

The south-western hoblis are peculiarly barren in appearance. They consist chiefly of large masses of hills, scantily clothed with jungle and generally capped with black rock. No gardens or tanks relieve the harshness of the landscape. Everywhere, to the very fields, stones cover the ground; pure soil is rarely met with, and then only at the very lowest parts of the valleys. But the rocks in this part are reported to be auriferous, connected with the Chiknáyakanhalli band. If the reefs should prove to be of sufficient value for mining, the aspect of the country might soon undergo a great change. In the north-west, Aymangala is a flat and stony country, but contains a large quantity of black soil. For the remainder of the taluq, an abrupt and decided line, almost identical with the course of the high road from Hiriyúr to Bangalore, separates black soil from red. All to the north is flat and composed chiefly of black soil; whilst to the south the country is at first stony and broken, and then hilly and composed of red soil.

In the black soils jola and cotton are the principal productions, but wheat and Bengal gram are grown in soil silted up behind embankments made for that purpose. In the red soil rági and avare are the chief crops, but togari, castor-oil and horse gram are also grown. The garden cultivation is very inferior, and some rice is grown under tanks.

The contact of water alone seems required to quicken the fertility of the dreary and barren tracts in much of this taluq, so much so that a single good season of rain enriches the ryots with comparatively little labour. The construction of a dam across the Védávati near Barmagiri at the Mári Kanive, the last of the narrow gorges through which it passes the hills, has been long proposed, as a means of providing irrigation for this rainless land which would convert it into an expanse of rice-fields. But there appears to be some uncertainty as to the data on which such a scheme must be based, and the project is from time to time postponed. Another similar project is the Kumbar-katte.

Though cultivation is wanting, manufacture is busy in the Mattod hobli and the neighbourhood of the hills. Iron is smelted at Arsingundi, Chikka Byáldakere and other villages. At the latter there is an extensive manufacture of shoes for bullocks and horses. At Mattod are glass works, formerly very extensive. The principal article made is bangles or glass bracelets for women.

The revenue settlement was introduced in 1868 and 1869. The area of the taluq at that time was thus distributed :—

| | |
|---|---|
| Culturable (dry, 314,036; wet, 3,724; garden, 8,076) ... ... | 325,836 |
| Unculturable (including roads, tanks, village sites, &c.) ... ... | 358,264 |
| Total acres ... | 684,100 |

The unoccupied arable land was 146,423 acres. The total land revenue for 1891–2 (15 months) was Rs. 61,521, and for 1892–3 it was Rs. 64,900.

The average rainfall at Hiriyúr for 26 years (1870–95), and at the other station for 3 years (1893–5), was as follows :—

| | Jan. | Feb. | Mar. | Apr. | May | June | July | Aug. | Sept. | Oct. | Nov. | Dec. | Year. |
|---|---|---|---|---|---|---|---|---|---|---|---|---|---|
| Hiriyúr ... | 0·10 | 0·06 | 0·14 | 0·92 | 2·78 | 1·80 | 1·25 | 1·21 | 2·95 | 3·81 | 1·39 | 0·37 ... | 16·78 |
| Yaraballi | — | 0·70 | 0·59 | 1·93 | 2·09 | 2·26 | 0·39 | 0·38 | 1·83 | 5·03 | 1·67 | — ... | 16·87 |

Another register for 21 years makes the annual average at Hiriyúr 17·15 inches.

The high road from Bangalore branches at Hiriyúr to Bellary northwards and to Chitaldroog north-west. There is also a road connecting Hiriyúr with Huliyar, and another connecting it with Hosdurga, with a branch from Barmagiri to the Mári Kanive.

**Hiriyur.**—A town situated in 13° 57′ N. lat., 76° 40′ E. long., on the right bank of the Védávati, at the bifurcation of the Bangalore high road to Bellary and to Chitaldroog. Head-quarters of the Hiriyúr taluq, and a municipality.

| Population in 1891. | Males. | Females. | Total. |
|---|---|---|---|
| Hindus (with 15 Jains) ... ... ... ... | 1,172 | 1,115 | 2,287 |
| Muhammadans ... ... ... ... ... ... | 313 | 251 | 564 |
| Christians ... ... ... ... ... ... | 7 | 5 | 12 |
| Total ... ... ... | 1,492 | 1,371 | 2,863 |

*Hiri-úru*, the great town, was founded, apparently, in the 16th century, by a chief from Máyasamudra, named Kesava Náyak, the virtue of the spot being discovered by the incident of a hare turning on the hounds. The family of the founder continued in possession for three generations, under Naula Allapu Náyak, Konchappa Náyak, who built the big temple, and Rangappa Náyak. During this time settlers were encouraged to take up their residence in the town, and it reached a prosperous condition. It was then taken, first by the Bijapur army and afterwards by the palegar of Chitaldroog, whose ancestor, before coming to power, had held the office of Náyak of Hiriyúr under the

Vijayanagar kings. In 1762 it was captured by Haidar Ali, and suffered very severely during the subsequent contests of that ruler and the Mahrattas, whose devastations brought on a famine which swept off all the inhabitants.

Its unhealthy condition led to an attempt in recent times to remove the town to a higher site on the other side of the river, where the taluq offices have been built; but the people, as usual, are loath to leave the neighbourhood of the ancient temples, one of which, dedicated to Tára Mallésvara, has a lofty tower erected by the Chitaldroog palegar. East of the old town the Védávati is bridged for the high road.

| Municipal Funds. | 1892–3. | 1893–4. | 1894–5. | 1895–6. |
|---|---|---|---|---|
| Income ... ... ... ... ... | 760 | 755 | 773 | 1,116 |
| Expenditure ... ... ... ... .. | 988 | 774 | 785 | 1,008 |

**Holalkere.**—A taluq in the south-west, till 1882 called Hosdurga, which was then made a sub-taluq under it. Area 681 square miles. Head-quarters at Holalkere. Contains the following hoblis, villages, and population:—

| No. | Hóblis. | Villages. | Hamlets. | Villages classified. | | | | Population. |
|---|---|---|---|---|---|---|---|---|
| | | | | Government. | Sarvamánya. | Jodi. | Kayamgutta. | |
| 1 | Bágúr ... ... ... | 60 | 18 | 58 | — | 1 | 1 | 11,504 |
| 2 | Barmanáyakandurga ... | 53 | 1 | 53 | — | — | — | 10,422 |
| 3 | Holalkere ... ... | 48 | 6 | 47 | 1 | — | — | 13,754 |
| 4 | Hosdurga ... ... | 70 | 18 | 68 | — | 2 | — | 11,216 |
| 5 | Rámagiri ... ... | 41 | 2 | 41 | — | — | — | 10,166 |
| 6 | Tálya ... ... ... | 57 | 4 | 57 | — | — | — | 9,989 |
| | Total ... ... | 329 | 49 | 324 | 1 | 3 | 1 | 67,051 |

*Principal places, with population*:—Holalkere, 2,938; Hosdurga, 2,061; Bágúr, 1,156; Jánakal, 1,097; Gunḍéri, 1,078; Rámagiri, 1,062.

The taluq consists of a long narrow strip of country, lying to the west of the central belt of hills, which from Hosdurga northwards form much of the eastern boundary. The north is also occupied by hills, and there is a group on the west covered with low jungle. The rest of the taluq is comparatively flat, with a preponderance of red soil, but good black soil occurs near Andnur and Rámagiri. The good and bad soils are very intimately interspersed throughout the taluq. Long stretches of good grazing exist in different parts, but especially in the centre. The country is intersected by many fair-sized *nálas*, and the Vedávati runs in a direction from south-west to north-east across the southern extremity.

The most common dry crops are jola and rági. Cotton is grown, but to no extent. Iron is worked in the Gunḍéri hobli, and in Hosdurga there are a good many workers in brass.

The oldest inscriptions in the taluq are Ráshṭrakúṭa, of the 10th century, and show this part of the country as being then attached to the government of the Kadambalige Thousand náḍ, which I have not been able to identify. The Chálukyas, the Hoysalas, and the Vijayanagar kings succeeded in turn. Under the two first the two great provinces of the Nonambaváḍi 32,000 and the Gangaváḍi 96,000 are constantly mentioned, and there is reason to believe that their boundaries met somewhere near Rámagiri.

The revenue settlement was introduced in 1868. The area of the taluq at that time was thus distributed.—

| | | |
|---|---|---|
| Culturable (dry, 181,858; wet, 2,656; garden, 1,352) | ... | 185,866 |
| Unculturable (including roads, tanks, village sites, &c.) | ... | 106,778 |
| Total acres | ... | 292,644 |

The unoccupied arable land was 77,242 acres, nearly all dry crop land. Of the present taluq 137,760 acres are cultivated, and 202,880 acres unculturable. The total land revenue for 1891–2 (15 months) was Rs. 97,228, and for 1892–3 it was Rs. 1,01,067.

The average rainfall at Holalkere and Hosdurga for 26 years (1870–95), and at the other stations for 3 years (1893–5), was as follows :—

| | Jan. | Feb. | Mar. | April | May | June | July | Aug. | Sept. | Oct. | Nov. | Dec. | | Year. |
|---|---|---|---|---|---|---|---|---|---|---|---|---|---|---|
| Holalkere | — | 0·01 | 0·18 | 1·28 | 2·65 | 2·18 | 3·54 | 3·27 | 4·64 | 4·09 | 3·61 | 0·15 | ... | 25·60 |
| Hosdurga | 0·06 | 0·06 | 0·21 | 1·51 | 3·41 | 2·45 | 2·50 | 1·58 | 2·93 | 4·58 | 2·87 | 0·31 | ... | 22·47 |
| Dhumi | — | — | 0·52 | 0·57 | 1·63 | 5·26 | 6·34 | 4·04 | 1·13 | 3·48 | 0·70 | — | ... | 23·67 |
| Rámagiri | — | — | 1·49 | 1·74 | 1·96 | 3·84 | 2·02 | 2·42 | 1·42 | 4·77 | 1·05 | — | ... | 20·71 |

Other registers make the average for 22 years at Holalkere 23·92, for 12 years at Hosdurga 22·24, and for 2 years at the two other places 25·99 and (?) 12·39.

The Southern Mahratta railway from Bangalore to Poona runs throughout the west of the taluq, from south to north, with stations at Bidarkere or Hosdurga Road, Rámagiri, Holalkere, Chik Jájúr, and Sásalu. There is a road from Channagiri through Holalkere to Chitaldroog, with one from Huliyar through Hosdurga to Dávangere, most of it close to the railway line. There are roads from Hosdurga to the railway at Bidarkere, to Ajjampur and to Hiriyúr. Also a road from Sásalu to Sante Bennúr and Súlekere.

**Holalkere.**—A town situated in 14° 2′ N. lat., 76° 15′ E. long., 4 miles east of the Holalkere railway station, and 20 miles south-west of Chitaldroog, on the Chitaldroog-Shimoga road. Head-quarters of the Holalkere taluq, and a municipality.

| Population in 1891. | Males. | Females | Total. |
|---|---|---|---|
| Hindus ... ... ... ... ... ... | 986 | 1,066 | 2,052 |
| Muhammadans ... ... ... ... ... | 204 | 209 | 413 |
| Jains ... ... ... ... ... ... | 42 | 40 | 82 |
| Christians ... ... ... ... ... ... | 7 | 3 | 10 |
| Total ... | 1,239 | 1,318 | 2,557 |

As Polalakere, it appears to have been an important Jain settlement in the 10th century. The present town seems to have been founded in the 14th century, by a Boya gauda, under the protection of the Dhumi chief Doḍḍaṇṇa Náyak. In course of time it fell into the hands of the palegars of Basvapatna; and in 1475, Timmanna Náyak, the progenitor of the Chitaldroog family, obtained from Vijayanagar his first appointment as Náyak of Holalkere. It remained in possession of the Chitaldroog family till taken by Haidar Ali, and suffered, in common with all the neighbouring parts, from repeated Mahratta invasions.

Its situation on the high road, near the foot of the pass which leads to Chitaldroog, and a large weekly fair combined to make it a thriving town, and its prosperity has been promoted by the advent of the railway and the location here of the taluq head-quarters.

| Municipal Funds. | 1892-3. | 1893-4. | 1894-5. | 1895-6. |
|---|---|---|---|---|
| Income ... ... ... ... ... ... | 887 | 955 | 964 | 1,593 |
| Expenditure ... ... ... ... ... | 1,151 | 1,020 | 1,189 | 1,539 |

**Hosdurga.**—A sub-taluq under Holalkere taluq, composed of the Hosdurga and Bágúr hoblis. Till 1882 it gave its name to what is now the Holalkere taluq.

**Hosdurga.**—A town situated in 13° 48′ N. lat., 76° 21′ E. long., at the northern base of the hill from which it is named, 11 miles east of the Bidarkere or Hosdurga Road railway station, and 19 miles south of Holalkere, on the Huliyar-Tarikere road. Head-quarters of the Hosdurga sub-taluq, and a municipality.

| Population in 1891. | Males. | Females. | Total. |
|---|---|---|---|
| Hindus ... ... ... ... ... | 881 | 900 | 1,781 |
| Muhammadans ... ... ... ... | 91 | 85 | 176 |
| Jains ... ... ... ... ... ... | 53 | 51 | 104 |
| Total ... ... ... | 1,025 | 1,036 | 2,061 |

*Hosa durga*, the new hill-fort, appears to have been erected in 1675 by Chikkanna Náyak, the palegar of Chitaldroog; for the purpose of covering his operations against Bágur, the chief town of that quarter, then in possession of the Muhammadans and attached to Sira. In 1708, a Jangam priest, driven out of Bágur, took refuge with the Chitaldroog palegar, and was by him commissioned to build the petta below the hill and procure settlers to reside there. Eventually the place was taken by Haidar Ali and, with the exception of temporary occupations by the Mahrattas, has ever since been attached to Mysore.

| Municipal Funds. | 1892–3. | 1893–4. | 1894–5. | 1895–6. |
|---|---|---|---|---|
| Income ... ... ... ... | 982 | 1,099 | 1,060 | 1,847 |
| Expenditure ... ... ... | 1,866 | 1,461 | 1,134 | 1,823 |

**Jagalur.**—A taluq in the north, till 1882 called Kankuppa. It was in that year made a sub-taluq under Chitaldroog, but restored as a taluq in 1886. Area 371 square miles. Head-quarters at Jagalúr. Contains the following hoblis, villages and population:—

| No. | Hoblis. | Villages. | Hamlets. | Villages classified. | | Population. |
|---|---|---|---|---|---|---|
| | | | | Govern-ment. | Jodi. | |
| 1 | Bilichód ... ... ... | 61 | 7 | 61 | — | 14,490 |
| 2 | Jagalúr ... ... ... | 76 | 15 | 75 | 1 | 18,189 |
| 3 | Sokké ... ... ... | 32 | 2 | 32 | — | 5,550 |
| | Total ... ... | 169 | 24 | 168 | 1 | 38,229 |

*Principal places, with population.*—Jagalúr, 3,249; Sokké, 1,790; Bilichód, 1,250; Pallagaṭṭe, 1,070.

The country is slightly undulating, except where a low and rugged range of hills, somewhat thickly covered with thorn jungle, runs from Kankuppa to the north-west. East of these lies an auriferous band continuous with one from Chitaldroog. There are no water-courses. The Janaga-halla flows along the eastern side; and the stream from the Anaji tank, also called the Chinna Haggari, along the western. Here, too, there is an auriferous band.

Dividing the taluq into two nearly equal portions by a line from Basavankote through Kankuppa to Chikmallanhalli, the country to the north of this may be described as composed almost entirely of light and sandy soil, except among the hills in the north-west, where in some few places a rich red soil has been formed in the valleys by deposit of the finer particles of the decomposed rocks. All the better descriptions of soil are south of the line. The black soil is rather intimately interspersed with the surrounding red and sandy soils, but predominates in Jagalúr and Bilichód. Probably one-fourth of the whole extent of cultivable soil in the taluq is either black or good brown soil.

Cotton and white jola are grown exclusively on the black soil. Rice and sugar-cane are largely cultivated, the latter of the small kind called *hulíu kabbu*. The only extent of garden land is under the Jagalúr tank. Much rice is grown on the banks of the Janaga-halla.

The revenue settlement was introduced in 1867. There was at that time under cultivation an area of 94,590 acres (dry, 91,075; wet, 1,150; garden, 2,365). The present taluq consists of:—

| | |
|---|---|
| Culturable (dry, wet and garden) ... ... ... ... ... | 147,200 |
| Unculturable (including roads, village sites, &c.) ... ... ... | 89,600 |
| Total acres ... | 236,800 |

The unoccupied arable area is 36,480 acres. The total land revenue for 1891–2 (15 months) was Rs. 52,326, and for 1892–3 it was Rs. 54,229.

The average rainfall at Jagalúr for 26 years (1870–95) was as follows:—

| Jan. | Feb. | Mar. | Apr. | May | June | July | Aug. | Sept. | Oct. | Nov. | Dec. ... | Year. |
|---|---|---|---|---|---|---|---|---|---|---|---|---|
| — | 0·01 | 0·08 | 1·24 | 2·16 | 1·34 | 1·69 | 2·14 | 3·77 | 2·51 | 2·65 | 0·12 ... | 17·71 |

Another register for 24 years makes the annual average 18·88.

The only road is from south to north through Jagalúr and Kankuppa. A road is proposed from Jagalúr east to Náyakanhatti.

**Jagalur.**—A town situated in 14° 31′ N. lat., 76° 24′ E. long., 28 miles north-by-west of Chitaldroog, with which it is connected by a road from Vijapur. Head-quarters of the Jagalúr taluq, and a municipality.

| Population in 1891. | Males. | Females. | Total. |
|---|---|---|---|
| Hindus... ... .. ... ... ... ... | 1,311 | 1,210 | 2,521 |
| Muhammadans ... ... ... ... ... | 142 | 126 | 268 |
| Christians ... ... ... ... ... ... | 4 | 3 | 7 |
| Total ... | 1,457 | 1,339 | 2,796 |

The population consists mostly of Lingáyits. There is little of interest about the place, which derives its importance from being the taluq head-quarters, removed here from Kankuppa in about 1868. The houses are all built of an iron-shot slaty stone, and flat-roofed. Jagalúr has a large tank.

| Municipal Funds. | 1892-3. | 1893-4. | 1894-5. | 1895-6. |
|---|---|---|---|---|
| Income ... ... ... ... ... | 855 | 763 | 780 | 1,200 |
| Expenditure ... ... ... ... | 1,173 | 1,086 | 893 | 1,100 |

**Mari Kanive.**—A pass in the eastern line of the Chitaldroog hills, through which the Védávati issues to the open country of Hiriyur. So far back as Buchanan's time it was pointed out as a spot peculiarly favourable for the construction of a dam across the gorge, whereby an immense reservoir would be formed capable of irrigating the adjoining thirsty plains and converting them into a vast expanse of rice cultivation. The project, however, though much money has been spent on surveys and measurements, has not yet been commenced.

**Mattod.**—A village in the Hosdurga sub-taluq, 10 miles east of the kasba, near the right bank of the Védávati. Population 880.

It is celebrated for its glass works, at one time more extensive than they are now. The articles made consist entirely of bangles, the rings worn round the wrists of native women. They are of five colours—black, green, red, blue and yellow. The furnaces are constructed in a high terrace, built against the inside of the fort wall, but many of them seem to have long been disused. Only two are now in good repair. The process of manufacture is described in the first part of this work. All the materials are found in the neighbourhood.

Mattod was the seat of a line of palegars, whose founder was named Giriyappa Náyak. He was a handsome man, of great stature and prodigious strength, which he exercised in catching the wild beasts of the neighbourhood. Venkatpati Ráya, hearing of him through the Búdihál chief, sent for him to Penugonda, where, an elephant one day breaking loose, he had an opportunity of displaying his powers; for the infuriated animal could not be secured until Giriyappa Náyak boldly seized him by the tusks and fastened a rope to his trunk. For these and other feats he was, about 1604, made palegar of Lakavanhalli, his native place, with a grant of villages yielding a revenue of 9,000 pagodas. In 1710, Dodala Náyak, a descendant, built the fort of Mattod. He at the same time adopted the Lingáyit faith. His son, Sangappa Náyak, distinguished himself at the court of Seringapatam by riding a most vicious and unmanageable horse which would allow no one to mount it; and when the courtiers, jealous of his success, pelted him with limes to embarrass him, he drew a sword and divided them as he rode swiftly about after them.

Hálappa Náyak next succeeded, and after him Siddappa Náyak. He was the second son, but inherited the beauty, stature and prowess of his line; on which account his father had allowed him to supersede the eldest son, Dodala Náyak. The latter thereupon repaired to Chitaldroog, the palegar of which took up his cause, and defeating the younger brother, installed the elder in his place, subject to a tribute of 2,000 pagodas. On Siddappa Náyak's being taken prisoner to Chitaldroog, the daughter of the palegar of that place fell in love with him. His being a Lingáyit would have made their union impossible had he not been a Boya by descent. Eventually it was arranged that he should marry her and be restored to his government. His son Hálappa Náyak was induced by the growing power of Haidar Ali to assist the latter in the first siege against Chitaldroog. On Haidar's withdrawal the palegar of Chitaldroog in revenge took Mattod by assault, plundered the town and carried Hálappa off to prison. Chitaldroog was next year taken by Haidar and Hálappa released, but he never regained his territory.

**Molakalmuru.**—A taluq in the north-east, from 1882 to 1886 made a sub-taluq named Hángal, under Challakere taluq, but then restored to a taluq. Area 290 square miles. Contains the following hóblis, villages and population:—

| No. | Hóblis. | Villages. | Hamlets. | Villages classified. | | | Population |
|---|---|---|---|---|---|---|---|
| | | | | Government. | Sarvamánya. | Jodi. | |
| 1 | Devasmudra ... ... | 52 | 11 | 48 | 2 | 2 | 16,094 |
| 2 | Molakálmuru ... ... | 45 | 7 | 43 | — | 2 | 16,466 |
| | Total ... | 97 | 18 | 91 | 2 | 4 | 32,560 |

*Principal places, with population.*—Molakálmuru, 2,421; Devasamudra, 1,977; Konaságara, 1,908; Roppa, 1,822; Nágasamudra, 1,677; Rámpura, 1,579.

This taluq is a long and narrow strip of country jutting into the Bellary district. A few isolated villages on the west are entirely separated from the body of the taluq. The surface is very undulating, and except where cultivated rice and garden lands exist, is covered with rocks and loose stones. A range of bare, rocky hills of considerable height stretches right across the taluq, running from a south-easterly in a north-westerly direction. When the range approaches the western boundary it becomes split up into numerous elevations of different heights, which singly or in groups are scattered about in all directions, and some of which from the size and fantastic shapes of the enormous boulders of which they are composed present a very remarkable appearance. More than one-third of the whole surface is occupied by these hills, which are so barren that not a blade of grass or a tree will grow upon their sides. A tract of nearly 9 square miles in the south is occupied by kammar (*Hardwickia binnata*) jungle, but the distribution is thin and the trees have been pollarded and much denuded. It seems a pity that steps are not taken to replant and conserve this valuable wood. The southern half of the taluq is comparatively level, but the soils are of the poorest kind, comprising the light red and sandy descriptions, and there is no black soil whatever.

The Janaga-halla, after running along the western boundary for a short distance, suddenly turns to the east, and flowing in a north-easterly direction, with the name of Chinna Haggari, receives the drainage from the bare, rocky hills around, and unites with the Vedávati in the Bellary district. All the tanks of any importance are close to the river, and receive their supply from it by means of channels varying in length from a mile to five miles. These channels are little used for direct irrigation.

The principal feature in the cultivation is the lands irrigated from wells, which exist in almost every village, and under which, as a rule, two crops are obtained annually, chiefly rice; but betel-leaf, tobacco, wheat and javari are also grown. Betel-leaf is extensively cultivated in Devasamudra and Rámpura for the Bellary market. Except under irrigation the soils are peculiarly unfertile, and dry crops are but little attended to, the ryots devoting all their capital and skill to the cultivation of the wet lands.

Kamblis, coarse cotton cloths, women's cloths with silk borders, and tape for belts are the principal manufactures. The women's cloths are chiefly made at Molakálmuru. Iron ore, brought from the Kúmáraswámi hill in Sundur, is smelted in one or two villages.

This part of Mysore has lately acquired a special interest from my discovery here in 1892 of Edicts of Asoka. None have ever been found before in the South of India, and this find has been pronounced by high authority as marking an epoch in Indian archæology. It effectually lifts the veil which has obscured the ancient history, and leaves no doubt that the Maurya empire of the 3rd century B.C. extended as far as to include the north of the Mysore country. The

Edicts found were in three places, close around the village of Siddapura (possibly the Isila to which the Edicts were addressed), engraved on rocks on either side of the Janagahalla—one at Brahmagiri, another at the Timmanna rocks, and the third at the top of the Jatinga Rámesvara hill. Here Jatáyu is said to have fallen in attempting to rescue Sita from Rávana.

The next oldest inscriptions in the taluq are also at the latter place and at the Nunke Bhairava hill. Those of the former are Chálukya of the 10th and 11th centuries, and show us Vishnuvarddhana Vijayáditza ruling the Nolambavadi 32,000, which thus included Molakálmuru, with his capital at Kampili, on the Tungabhadra in Bellary district. He was followed by Jayasingha, younger brother of Vikramáditya VI, and having, among others, the titles of Nolamba Pallava. The inscriptions at the Nunke Bhairava hill are Kadamba, and it is possible that the Uchchangi-durga to the north of Molakálmuru, also known as Hire-A'ryara-durga, hill fort of the old A'ryas, may be the Uchchásringi which was one of the Kadamba seats of government. In the time of the Hoysalas we find a line of rulers of the Solar race, that is of Chola descent, who held Nidugal (*see* above, p. 163), in possession of Háneyakote, which was then the name of the Brahmagiri fort, and of which there is perhaps a reminiscence in Hángal or Háneyagal. The fort was captured in the 12th century by Vira Ballála, who changed the name to Vijayagiri.

Under the Vijayanagar kings, in the 15th century, Molakálmuru seems to have belonged to the chiefs of Ráyadurga, 7 miles to the east. One of them, named Bomma Náyak the Foolish, gave it up to Mallappa Náyak of Hatti (now called Náyakanhatti) in exchange for some white cattle, of which he owned a rare and valuable breed. It was before long conquered by the palegars of Chitaldroog, in whose hands it remained till captured by Haidar Ali and annexed to Mysore.

The revenue settlement was introduced in 1872. The area of the taluq at that time was thus distributed :—

| | |
|---|---|
| Culturable (dry, 83,604 ; wet, 2,766 ; garden, 5,995) ... ... | 92,365 |
| Unculturable (including roads, tanks, village sites, &c.) ... ... | 87,254 |
| Total acres ... | 179,619 |

The unoccupied arable land was 34,466 acres, nearly all dry crop land. The total land revenue for 1891–2 (15 months) was Rs. 49,458, and for 1892–3 it was Rs. 50,023.

The average rainfall at Molakálmuru for 26 years (1870–95) and at the other station for 3 years (1893–5) was as follows :—

| | Jan. | Feb. | Mar. | April | May | June | July | Aug. | Sept. | Oct. | Nov. | Dec. | Year. |
|---|---|---|---|---|---|---|---|---|---|---|---|---|---|
| Molakálmuru | 0·01 | 0·01 | 0·14 | 0·56 | 2·00 | 2·08 | 1·60 | 2·35 | 5·18 | 5·27 | 1·84 | 0·10 | 21·14 |
| Rámpura | — | — | — | 0·77 | 1·70 | 0·97 | 1·63 | 1·56 | 3·72 | 5·88 | 1·25 | — | 17·48 |

Other registers for 10 and 5 years make the annual average 22·46 and 15·73 respectively.

The Bangalore-Bellary high road runs throughout the taluq from south to north, with a road from Hángal east to Molakálmuru and Ráyadurga.

**Molakalmuru.**—A town situated in 14° 44′ N. lat., 76° 48′ E. long., 38 miles south of the railway at Bellary, on a cross-road from Hángal, which is on the Bangalore-Bellary high-road, to Ráydurga. Head-quarters of the Molakálmuru taluq, and a municipality.

| Population in 1891. | Males. | Females. | Total. |
|---|---|---|---|
| Hindus ... ... ... ... ... ... ... | 991 | 950 | 1,941 |
| Muhammadans ... ... ... ... ... | 229 | 251 | 480 |
| Total ... ... | 1,220 | 1,201 | 2,421 |

The place is entirely surrounded by barren stony hills, among which, just above the town to the north, is a large reservoir, constructed by the Hatti chief in the name of his mother. Near to it a good echo is obtained from the *kúguva bande* or shouting stone, and in the east of it is a boulder on which is inscribed a *yamaka* verse in praise of Kálidása. To the north-west of this is the Nunke-Bhairava hill, on which, in a remarkable enclosed valley or ravine, with no visible outlet at either end, is an ancient temple of that name, served by a succession of Gosáyins from Northern India. Inscriptions show that the proper name of the god is Lunkes'vara, and it appears to have been set up in the 10th century by a Kadamba prince. The Kadambas also had a fort here called the Lunkeya-kote.

The ancient history has been given under the taluq. In modern times, under the Vijayanagar State, it belonged to the chief of Ráydurga, 7 miles to the east. After the fall of Vijayanagar, the Ráydurga palegar Bomma Náyak, surnamed the Foolish, gave up Molakálmuru to Mallappa Náyak of Hatti (now called Nayakanhatti) in exchange for some white cattle, of which he owned a rare and valuable breed. Mallappa Náyak, finding water on the hill, fortified it and lived there. But in the time of his son the place was taken by the palegar of Chitaldroog, in whose family it remained till captured by Haidar Ali and annexed to Mysore.

| Municipal Funds. | 1892–93. | 1893–94. | 1894–95. | 1895–96. |
|---|---|---|---|---|
| Income ... ... ... ... | 933 | 833 | 816 | 1,680 |
| Expenditure ... ... ... | 1,444 | 916 | 807 | 1,720 |

**Nayakanhatti.**—Formerly called Hatti, a large village in the Challakere taluq, 14 miles north-west of the kasba. Population 2,468.

The traditional history of this place relates that one Kotte Malla Náyak, the owner of numerous flocks and herds of superior cattle, living in the forests of Kara-male and Komma-male, to the east of the Srisaila mountains, was compelled by drought and famine to move elsewhere in quest of forage. He ultimately arrived, with 1,200 head of cattle, besides cows and sheep, in the neighbourhood of Hatti; where, finding abundant pasturage, he settled, obtaining permission from Vijayanagar to clear some of the forest, erect villages and bring the region under cultivation. A *bhát* or eulogist one day visited him, and was so liberally rewarded for his flattering verses that on repairing to court he extolled the Náyak in such extravagant terms as to excite the jealousy of the king, who sent a force to apprehend him. Mallappa Náyak, having no other resource, urged his cattle to charge the troops, which were completely routed by these novel defenders. The king, indignant at the repulse, offered a large reward to anyone who would bring the Náyak prisoner to him, but none would venture. Finally some courtesans undertook the task, but failed with all their seductive arts to get him into their power. Surprised at their failure, they questioned the genuineness of his virtue unless it could stand the test that all his cattle would run to him at the sound of his voice. He immediately mounted on a rock and called out in his usual manner, when all the herds and flocks ran and assembled round him. The report of the courtesans aroused the highest respect for Malla Náyak on the part of the king, who conferred on him all the country round Kondarpi-durga, with the title of palegar.

One of his descendants, in the third generation, separated with his cattle from the others and founded Hatti as a residence for himself. At a later time Budi Malla Náyak of this family rendered important military aid to Vijayanagar, and by victory over a jeṭṭi or wrestler at court obtained the name of Bhima, and thereupon built Bhimankere. Afterwards, when Bomma Náyak the Foolish was palegar of Ráydurga, Malla Náyak at his request gave him 2,000 red and 1,000 white cattle, and received in exchange the hill of Molakálmuru. This he fortified and thence extended his possessions; but in the time of his son it was seized by Barmappa Náyak of Chitaldroog, who confined the palegar to his original estate at Hatti. This, too, was shortly taken by Hiré Madakeri Náyak and annexed to Chitaldroog; of which it remained a part till captured by Haidar Ali.

Náyakanhatti contains a celebrated tomb and temple dedicated to a Mahá-purusha or saint of the Lingáyits, named Tippe Rudraiya, who lived about 200 years ago, wrought miracles and became the spiritual preceptor of the Hatti palegars. The large sums bestowed upon him by the faithful he devoted to the enlargement and repair of tanks, and to other works of public benefit which entitle his name to be held in honour.

**Nirgunda.**—A village in the Hosdurga taluq, 7 miles west of the kasba. Population 345.

This now insignificant village is interesting as marking the site of one of the most ancient cities in Mysore of which there is authentic record. Nirgunda was the capital of a Jain principality of the same name, included in the Ganga empire, 1,500 years ago. According to tradition, it was founded in B.C. 160 by a king from the north, named Nilasekhara, son of Rája Paramesvara Ráya, who gave it the name of Nilávati-patna. He was succeeded by Virasekhara, and their descendants continued to be independent sovereigns of their country.

From the Nágamangala plates we know that Dundu, with the title of Nirgunda Yuva Rája, and after him his son Parama Gula, with the title of Sri Prithivi Nirgunda Rája, ruled early in the 8th century. The legend of the place proceeds to the reign of Vikrama Ráya of this house, in whose time occurred a romantic incident. Two princes, Somasekhara and Chitrasekhara, sons of Vajra Makuṭa Ráya, came secretly to Nilávati from Ratnapuri (near Lakvalli, Kadur District) for the purpose of securing for the younger the hand of Ratnavati or Rupávati, the king's daughter, famous for her beauty. Having rendered themselves invisible, they penetrated at night to the king's bed-chamber and attached to his arm a paper containing their demand. The king on discovering it was much perplexed; but a lion having taken refuge in a pleasure garden near the town and become a terror to the people, he caused it to be proclaimed that the princess would be given in marriage to whomsoever should destroy the lion. The two brothers, who lodged in disguise at a dancing-girl's house, sallied forth next night, killed the beast and, cutting off its tail, returned to their concealment. In the morning, Mára, a washerman of the town, finding the lion dead, cut out its tongue, and carrying it to the king, presented himself as the champion to be rewarded with the hand of the princess. While preparations for this distasteful marriage were going on, the princes appeared before the palace in the guise of strolling musicians, with the lion's tail tied to their lute. This drew attention to them and the truth came out, which ended in Ratnavati being married to Chitrasekhara.[1] Vikrama Ráya, dying without issue, left the kingdom to his son-in-law. His descendants were Bala Vira and Narasimha. About this time the Hoysala kings captured Nilávati, and some epidemic seems to have led to its desertion soon after. Bágúr, a short distance to the north, was subsequently founded, and became the capital of the region in place of Nirgunda or Nilávati. Mounds of ruins and several old temples are still in existence around the village, with an old Hoysala inscription of 1065.

**Vedavati**, or Haggari, the principal river in the District, a tributary of the Tungabhadra. It is formed by two streams, having their sources on the eastern side of the Chandra Drona or Bábá Budan mountains (Kadur District). The Veda, which is the chief one, forms the beautiful Ayyankere lake, whence issuing, it passes to the south of Sakkarepatna and then turns north-east. Near Kadur it is joined by the other stream, the Avati, and further on by the streams from the hills near Halebid and Harnhalli on the south, and those from the hills around Ubráni on the north.

With a direct north-east course, the Vedávati now enters the Chitaldroog District, passing about midway between Hosdurga and Mattod; and penetrating the central belt of hills, it issues thence by the pass called the Mári Kanive, to the south of Barmagiri-durga, and continues in the same direction past Hiriyur, to about seven miles beyond. Here, on receiving the streams from Sira and Hagalvadi, it turns northwards, taking the name Haggari, said to be derived from *hagga-ari*, freeing from the bonds (of sin).

Winding through an open country, it leaves the Mysore about 5 miles north of Ghataparti in Challakere taluq and enters the Bellary District, with for some distance a north-east course. It then again turns north, and at a point nearly parallel with the furthest limit of Mysore on that side, receives the Janagahalla or Chinna Haggari from Molakálmuru. Continuing north, and leaving Bellary about 10 miles to the west, it flows into the Tungabhadra some distance to the south of Huchahalli.

It is a very shallow river and though impassable except by boats in the monsoon, in the dry season it presents a broad bed of sand, in which, however, *kapile* wells are readily formed. In the Bellary country the river is supposed to be gradually changing its bed. At Moka, 12 miles from Bellary, the sandy bed is two miles broad.

[1] For the continuation of the story, describing the marvellous adventures by which Somasekhara won the hand of a princess of Hemavati (p. 182 above), *see* my *Coorg Gazetteer*, pp. 94 *ff*.

The river is bridged for the trunk road at Hiriyur (the first bridge erected in Mysore under the British Government), and for the Bellary Branch railway at Permadevanhalli. The project of embanking the stream at the narrow gorge of the Mári-Kanive and thus creating, at a cost of about 15 lakhs, an immense reservoir that would irrigate 50,000 acres of the fertile but arid plains of Hiriyur, is a proposal of long standing, still under consideration. A great number of small channels are drawn from the Vedávati in the Kadur District.

# APPENDIX

## GLOSSARY OF JUDICIAL AND REVENUE TERMS

### And other Words occurring in Official Documents

A'bád ... ... ... Populous ; cultivated.

Abkári ... ... ... Revenue derived from duties levied on the manufacture and sale of inebriating liquors, and on intoxicating drugs ; excise.

Achkat ... ... ... The total area of land attached to a village. When applied to irrigation, it means the total extent of land capable of being watered by any particular work.

Adavu ... ... ... Mortgage with or without possession ; deposit.

A'dhára ... ... ... Security ; pledge ; recognizance ; bail ; an exhibit.

A'dhár rékh ... ... Base line.

Adhikára ... ... Cognizance ; jurisdiction ; authority.

Agrahára ... ... A village held by Brahmans on a favourable tenure.

Ain jama ... ... Actual receipts or credits.

Aivaj ... ... ... Amount of money.

A'kár ... ... ... Area (of a field).

A'kárband ... ... A register showing the area and rate of assessment in detail of each survey number.

Alavi ... ... ... Progressive rental for improvement of land, or rent commencing at a low rate and increasing gradually year by year till the maximum limit is attained.

Amal ... ... ... Business ; operation.

A'mad ... ... ... Imports.

Amildár, Amil ... ... A native collector in charge of a taluq.

Amal jári ... ... Execution, particularly of a decree.

Amánat, Anámat ... Deposit.

Amáni ... ... ... Lands or other sources of revenue held under the direct management of Government officials.

| | |
|---|---|
| Amín ... ... ... | A bailiff in the Judicial Department. |
| Amma ... ... ... | Small-pox. |
| Amrái ... ... ... | Tope of trees ; grove ; the receipts from produce of such are entered under the head *amrái.* |
| Amrit Mahál ... ... | A department for improving the breed of cattle for Government purposes. |
| Anche ... ... ... | Post. |
| Anche chíla, anche bastu | The leather wallet containing letters and papers carried by the postal runners. |
| Anche kachéri ... ... | Post Office. |
| Anche mane, anche-yavara gudisalu ... | Postal runners' hut. |
| Ancheyava ... ... | Postal runner. |
| Andáz, Andáj ... ... | An estimate. |
| Angadi ... ... ... | A shop. |
| Angadi terige ... ... | Tax on shops. |
| Anna chhatra, Anna satra | A building for the accommodation of travellers where food is also supplied. |
| Ane, Anekat (anicut) ... | A masonry or brick dam across a river or stream for the purpose of raising the water and distributing it by side channels to the land on each side that would otherwise not benefit by the overflow. |
| Anúrádha ... ... | A rain commencing between 17th and 29th November ; paddy is sown at this time. |
| Anwádidár ... ... | A re-mortgagee ; the mortgagee who holds the property from the proprietor being called Bhogyadár. |
| Archaka ... ... ... | The officiating priest of a pagoda. |
| Ardhamánya ... ... | Land granted on a light quit-rent ; generally half rent, as its name implies. |
| Ardhamányadár ... | A man who holds as a mányam, lands assessed at half the usual rates, |
| Are ... ... ... | Mahratta. |
| Aridra ... ... ... | A rain commencing between 19th June and 2nd July. Paddy, cotton, &c., are sown at this season. |
| Arzi, Arji, Urzee ... | A petition addressed by an inferior to a superior; *vice versâ*, it would be a tákíd ; among equals it would be a yadásht ; an address ; a memorial. |
| Asal ... ... ... | Principal ; original stock. |
| Asámi ... ... ... | An individual. |
| A'shúr khána ... ... | An open building reserved by Muhammadans for the exhibition of the *panja* during the Muharram ; at other times it affords shelter to poor Muhammadan travellers. |

| | |
|---|---|
| A'slésha ... ... ... | A rain commencing between 31st July and 13th August. Gram and mangoes are sown at this time. |
| A'sti ... ... ... | Property; riches; real or personal goods. |
| Aswini ... ... ... | A rain commencing between the 11th and 23rd April. Ground tilled at this season. |
| A'yakat ... ... ... | The total area of land attached to a village; when applied to irrigation it means the total extent of land capable of being watered by any particular work. |
| Ayya, Ayyanavaru ... | A Lingáyit priest and teacher. |
| Azmáish taríkh ... ... | On probation. |
| | |
| Báb ... ... ... | An item; head of accounts. |
| Baddi ... ... ... | Interest. |
| Bádige ... ... ... | Rent. |
| Badli ... ... ... | A substitute acting for an absentee on leave. |
| Badti ... ... ... | Increase, especially of pay. |
| Bágáyat ... ... ... | Garden lands, the assessment on which is levied according to the number of trees; the rate varying according to the fertility of the soil. |
| Bahal ... ... ... | Reinstatement. |
| Bakshi ... ... ... | Head of an office. |
| Balagai ... ... ... | Pariahs of the right hand caste in Mysore and other Kannada countries. |
| Bandára ... ... ... | A store room or treasury. |
| Saraswati Bandára ... | A library. |
| Bandi, bandy ... ... | A cart or conveyance. |
| Bándinavaru ... ... | Officials of the Revenue Survey and Settlement Department |
| Bandhi khána ... ... | A jail or lock-up. |
| Bánd, Bándu ... ... | An earthen embankment used as a survey mark. |
| Banjar ... ... ... | Waste land. |
| Báodi, Báoli ... ... | A well. |
| Bár ... ... ... | Mysore Infantry. |
| Bárábalóti ... ... | Village officials, consisting of 12 persons—viz., Gauda, Shanbhog, Panchángi, Talvár, Tóti, Nírganti, Agasa, Náyinda, Kumbára, Lohár, Badagi and Agasále. |
| Barávard ... ... | Pay abstract. |
| Bartaraf ... ... ... | Dismissal. |
| Bárigát ... ... ... | Body-guard. |
| Bárika ... ... ... | A menial among the village servants; a deputy talári, who is employed to watch the crops, from the growing crop to the granary. |
| Basti ... ... ... | A populous town; a Jain temple. |
| Bastu ... ... ... | A bundle of records or papers. |

| | |
|---|---|
| Batái, Batáyi ... ... | Division of the crop between the cultivator and the landlord, or the Government in that capacity. |
| Batavád ... ... ... | Disbursement ; payment ; distribution. |
| Bázár ... ... ... | A market. |
| Bédaru ... ... ... | Hunters ; poachers |
| Bé-chirákh ... ... | Without lamp ; deserted. Applied to an uninhabited village. |
| Beddalu ... ... ... | Dry land. |
| Bele ... ... ... | Crop. |
| Bella ... ... ... | Jaggory, a kind of molasses. |
| Bépár ... ... ... | Trade. |
| Bépári ... ... ... | A merchant or trader. |
| Bériz ... ... ... | The full revenue obtainable. |
| Bésáya .. ... ... | Cultivation. |
| Bésige kála ... ... | Hot weather ; dry season. |
| Besta ... ... ... | A fisherman ; palankeen bearer. |
| Betta ... ... ... | A hill. A Jain place of worship at the summit of a hill, consisting of an unroofed enclosure surrounding a colossal image. |
| Bé-várasu ... ... | A term generally applied to property left by persons without heirs ; unclaimed. |
| Bhága ... ... ... | Partition ; share. |
| Bhang, Bhangi ... ... | Hemp used in making an intoxicating and stupefying preparation which is smoked like tobacco. |
| Bhára márga ... ... | Transit duty. |
| Bharani ... ... ... | A rain commencing between 27th April and 2nd May. Various kinds of grain are sown at this season. |
| Bharti ... ... ... | Export. |
| Bhatamánya ... ... | A small portion of rent-free land granted to Brahmans. |
| Bhatamányadára ... | A Brahman holding rent-free lands. |
| Bhata vritti ... ... | A small portion of rent-free land granted to Brahmans. |
| Bhatta (Batta) ... ... | Extra pay or allowances to public servants ; an allowance to temporary peons, serving summonses and other processes of courts ; travelling allowance ; paddy. |
| Bhatti ... ... ... | A still. |
| Bhatti sunka ... ... | Still-head duty. |
| Bhávi ... ... ... | A well. |
| Bhéti ... ... ... | An interview ; visit. |
| Bhógya ... ... ... | Mortgage with possession. |
| Bhúmi ... ... ... | Land, generally applied to culturable land. |
| Bídi ... ... ... | A street. |

| | |
|---|---|
| Bidige ... ... ... | Second day of the bright or dark half of a lunar month. |
| Bíjavari ... ... ... | Area of land calculated according to the quantity of seed required for sowing in it. |
| Billeyava ... ... | A peon or man wearing a belt. |
| Bílu ... ... ... | Waste, uncultivated land. |
| Birádári ... ... ... | A troop of Silahdars in the Mysore Horse, consisting generally of 12 men. |
| Bitti, Bégári ... ... | Gratuitous labour exacted from ryots on account of Government. |
| Bógyadar, Bhógyadár ... | A mortgagee who holds the property from the proprietor. |
| Bombe ... ... ... | An image, idol, doll. |
| Boond ... ... ... | Coffee. |
| Bóyi ... ... ... | A palankeen-bearer. |
| Brahmádáya ... ... | Land belonging to Brahmans. |
| Brinjári ... ... ... | A tribe resembling gipsies, who wander about and earn a livelihood as carriers of grain, &c. |
| Buddhivanta ... ... | Wise man; the elder or *prud'homme* of a village or community. |
| Bund ... ... ... | The embankment forming a tank or reservoir. |
| | |
| Canteroy pagoda (Kanthiráya varaha) | A coin named after Kanthirava Raya, worth 10 gold fanams. |
| Chadsál ... ... ... | Year in which a maximum amount of revenue was derived. |
| Chákara ... ... | A menial among the village servants; a deputy talári, who is employed to watch the crops, from the growing crop to the granary. |
| Chákari ... ... ... | Appointment. |
| Chakbandi ... ... | Boundaries. |
| Chalan ... ... ... | List of letters despatched, made by the postmaster and sent with them. |
| Chalavádi ... ... | A low caste. The servant of a Linga merchant carrying a large ladle with chain and bell on his shoulders. Menial servant under the head merchant of a town. |
| Chambár ... ... | Currier and shoemaker. |
| Chapávane ... ... | Concealment, generally applied to unauthorized cultivation. |
| Chátála, Sátáṇi ... ... | A class of Sudras; followers of Vishnu, and wearing no top-knot. |
| Chatra, Chhatra ... | An inn; a resting-place for travellers. |
| Chaṭṭegára ... ... | A half-caste; an East Indian. |
| Chaubíne ... ... | Beams. |
| Chaukasi ... ... | To lessen the price; to haggle. |

Chauk, Chowk ... ... A place where four roads meet; a square.
Chauthái... ... ... A fourth part.
Chávadi ... ... ... A small public office; a police station.
Chela ... ... ... A Hindu boy seized in early life and forcibly made a Muhammadan by order of Tipu; these boys as they grew up were incorporated in a military corps, retaining the name of Chelas.
Chengúli.. ... ... Day labourer.
Chhápa kágada... ... Stamp paper.
Chilre ... ... ... Small coin; change. Petty; trifling; sundry.
Chitta ... ... ... A rain commencing between 8th and 20th September. Millet and gingelli oil-seeds are sown at this time.
Chitte, Chitta ... ... Accounts.
Choon kud ... ... Soil containing minute fragments or nodules of limestone.
Chóri ... ... ... Theft.
Chóri mál ... ... Stolen property.
Chór inám ... ... Land enjoyed free of rent by stealth or unauthorizedly.
Choul bhúmi ... ... Salt or saline efflorescence.
Chout, Chaut ... ... The tribute or contribution formerly levied by the Mahrattas.
Chuki ... ... ... A mistake or error.
Chungadi ... ... Interest.

Dacoit ... ... ... A robber, especially one of a gang of housebreakers who plunder with the aid of torches.
Dacoity ... ... ... A torch robbery.
Dafedár ... ... ... Head peon having charge of ten or more persons.
Daftar, Duftur ... ... Records; the place where records are kept.
Daftar ilákha ... ... A department in which accounts connected with revenue are kept.
Daga ... ... ... Deceit; fraud.
Dákhale ... ... ... Reference; authority.
Dákhal ... ... ... Admission.
Dákhale gráma... ... A subordinate village included in a large one.
Dalaváyi (Dulwoy) ... The hereditary commander of the forces.
Daláyita, Daláyat ... A peon.
Dalláli ... ... ... A broker.
Dámásháyi ... ... A proportionate share.
Dána, Dána shásana ... A gift, a deed of gift.
Dana ... ... ... Cattle.
Danda ... ... ... Fine.
Dandu ... ... ... An army: a cantonment.
Darbár (Durbar) ... A court; a royal court; an audience or *levée*.

| | |
|---|---|
| Darkhást ... ... | An application to rent land ; a tender ; a petition. |
| Daróde ... ... ... | Robbery. |
| Darógha, Daróga ... | A native officer ; superintendent ; or manager. |
| Daryáfti ... ... ... | An inquiry ; trial. |
| Dasavanda ... ... | Land granted to a person for repairing or building a tank, on condition of paying in money or kind one-tenth or some small share of the produce. |
| Dast-aivaz ... ... | A voucher ; a written document. |
| Dastúri ... ... ... | According to custom ; a customary allowance or perquisite. |
| Daul ... ... ... | Estimate ; valuation. |
| Dáyádi ... ... ... | Cousin ; a distant relation from the same male stock. |
| Deha-jháda, Dahazada | Census ; an account showing the number of houses, shops, cattle, population, looms, ploughs, &c., of which a town or village consists. |
| Dévádáya ... ... | Lands endowed rent free for pagodas. ... |
| Dévánga... ... ... | A sect of weavers. |
| Dévastháma ... ... | A temple. |
| Dhani ... ... ... | A master. |
| Dhanishta ... ... | A rain commencing between 3rd to 15th February. |
| Dhárane... ... ... | Market rate ; price ; value. |
| Dharmakarta ... ... | Temple-warden. |
| Dhársód... ... ... | System of giving and taking equally in order to ensure a straight boundary. |
| Dhore ... ... ... | Master ; King. |
| Dhruva pairu ... ... | Standing crops. |
| Diván (Dewan)... ... | Minister. |
| Doddi ... ... ... | A pound for cattle. |
| Dóli (dhooly) ... ... | A litter like a palankeen. |
| Domba ... ... ... | A tumbler or juggler. |
| Dóni ... ... ... | A boat, especially one hollowed out of a log. |
| Doopun ... ... ... | Liable to be washed away by running water. |
| Drishyádhára ... ... | Mortgage without possession. |
| Durga (Droog) ... ... | A hill-fort. |
| Duddu ... ... ... | A copper coin, three of which go to an anna. |
| Du-fasal ... ... ... | Raising two crops a year on the same land. |
| Durast ... ... ... | Repair. |
| | |
| E'kabhógya ... ... | Undivided possession held by only one. |
| Ekkalu gadde ... ... | Alluvial soil. |
| Ere bhúmi ... ... | Black soil. |
| E'ri ... ... ... | Bund of a tank. |
| E'ru ... ... ... | A plough, or plough-and-oxen. |
| E'ru kánike ... ... | Plough-tax. |
| | |
| Faisal ... ... ... | Decision ; judgment. |

Fakír ... ... ... Muhammadan mendicant.
Fanam (*hana*) ... ... A small coin of either gold or silver, worth 14 duddu = 4 annas 8 pie.
Fasal ... ... ... Crop.
Fasli ... ... ... The revenue year.
Férisht ... ... ... A list; a catalogue; an inventory.
Firka ... ... ... Subdivision of a hobli; the charge of one shanbhog.

Gadde ... ... ... A paddy-field; an irrigated field.
Gádi ... ... ... A cart or conveyance.
Gána ... ... ... An oil-mill.
Gána terige ... ... A tax on oil-mills.
Gandha ... ... ... Sandal.
Gániga ... ... ... The owner of an oil-mill.
Ganna ... ... ... Sugar-cane.
Gauda ... ... ... The head man of a village; the head of village police.
Gávada, Gau ... ... A distance of about 12 miles.
Ghalige ... ... ... A Hindu hour = 24 English minutes.
Gida gávalu ... ... A forest watchman.
Giráki ... ... ... Demand; saleable.
Girivi ... ... ... A mortgage.
Go bhúmi ... ... Land set apart for grazing; pasture land.
Gochu ... ... ... Soil containing large nodules of limestone.
Golla ... ... ... A milkman. A subordinate official employed in the treasury in carrying money-bags, &c.
Go mála ... ... ... Land set apart for grazing; pasture land.
Góni ... ... ... Gunny; a coarse cloth made of hemp.
Goravi kólu ... ... A fire-stick used instead of a torch.
Gósáyi ... ... ... A sect who never marry, and whose profession is traffic, the profits of which go to a chief guru called Mahant.
Goshwára ... ... An abstract; a *résumé*.
Gudára ... ... ... A tent.
Gudli ... ... ... An implement with a short handle fixed at right angles, used for digging instead of a spade.
Gumásta ... ... An accountant; an agent; a steward; a representative; a confidential factor.
Gunta, Goonta ... ... Land measure = 121 square yards.
Gutigedár ... ... A contractor.
Gutta, Gootta ... ... A rock, or rocky hill.

Habba ... ... ... A feast; festival.
Hádi ... ... ... A road.
Hadlu ... ... ... Grass land covered with water; a waste rice-field.

Hádya ... ... ... Land covered with low brushwood and small trees from which fire-wood, leaves, &c., for manuring the fields, are taken.

Hága ... ... ... One-fourth of a fanam.

Hagévu ... ... ... A subterraneous granary.

Hak, hakku ... ... A right.

Haláku ... ... ... Disorder.

Hálat ... ... ... The excise duty levied on areca-nut, cardamom, pepper and tobacco, on removal from the place of their production. Export duty levied on coffee.

Hale Paika ... ... Toddy drawers in the Nagar country.

Halige mara ... ... A plank used in levelling the fields after seed is sown.

Hana ... ... ... Money ; a fanam.

Hangámi ... ... Temporary.

Hankalu ... ... ... A reaped field.

Haradári ... ... A league = 3 miles ; a measure of extent containing 2,000 fathoms, or about two miles and a half ; a kos.

Harkár ... ... ... Guide ; personal attendant.

Harkat ... ... ... Obstacle ; obstruction.

Haráz ... ... ... Auction.

Hásal ... ... ... Postage ; tax.

Hasta ... ... ... A rain commencing between 24th September and 7th October ; millet and gingelli oil-seeds are sown at this time.

Hastántra ... ... Cash balance.

Havaldár, Havildar ... A sergeant.

Havéli, Sarkár havéli ... A large house for the accommodation of Government servants.

Heggade ... ... Head man of a village ; the head of village police ; in some parts of the Province rent-free lands are assigned for their support.

Hamsáya ... ... The rate of assessment paid on neighbouring lands taken as the standard in assessing lands newly cultivated.

Henda ... ... ... The juice of the date-palm ; toddy ; which ferments and becomes intoxicating.

Hingáru, Hingári ... The latter rains, from July to November ; the north-east monsoon.

Hisse ... ... ... Share ; partition.

Hóbli, Hóbali ... ... The subdivision of a taluq.

Hoblidár... ... ... A commandant of a *hobli* of peons.

Hola ... ... ... A field.

Holeya ... ... ... Pariah ; outcaste.

Hole ... ... ... A stream ; river.

| | |
|---|---|
| Honnu ... ... ... | Half an Ikkeri pagoda (gold) value Rs. 2—4—0. |
| Hukum ... ... ... | A written order from a superior. Ordinary order. |
| Hulasu ... ... ... | Looking well, generally applied to crops ; thrifty. |
| Hulbanni takhta .... | Statement showing the grazing purchased by each individual. |
| Hulgával, Hulbigával, Hullugával ... ... | Pasture land. |
| Hulgával sunka... ... | Grazing dues. |
| Hundi, Hoondee ... | A bill of exchange. |
| Huzúr, Hoozoor, Hujúr | The presence. The chief officer (European) of the district. |
| Huttuvali ... ... | The produce of a garden or field, or of any trade ; the amount of an assessment, rent, income, revenue. |
| Ijáfe ... ... ... | Increase, especially of pay. |
| Ijára, Ijáre ... ... | Contract or lease, generally applied to the farming of revenue. |
| Ijárdar, Izardar... ... | A contractor ; a farmer of liquor shops. |
| Ilákhe ... ... ... | A department. |
| Inám ... ... ... | A gift ; reward, a grant of land or money by Government as a reward for services rendered, or in consideration of services to be performed, or for religious or charitable purposes. |
| Inámti, Inámati ... | Free of tax or rent. |
| Inámdár... ... ... | The holder of a rent-free grant. |
| Irawára ... ... ... | The total produce before division under the *batayi* system. |
| Irsál patti ... ... | List of remittance of cash sent to the treasury ; an invoice. |
| Isam ... ... ... | An item ; a head of charge. |
| Istihár ... ... ... | A notification ; proclamation. |
| Isvi ... ... ... | The Christian era. |
| Jádamáli, Jhádmáli ... | A sweeper employed in cleaning office rooms. |
| Jafti ... ... ... | Attachment of property, confiscation. |
| Jágir ... ... ... | Rent-free lands granted for services rendered to Government. |
| Jágírdár ... ... ... | Holder of lands free of assessment, generally as a reward for meritorious service. |
| Jáhir náma ... .... | A notice or summons. |
| Jamábandi ... ... | The annual settlement made under the ryotwar system. |
| Jamádár... ... ... | A commandant of a *hobli* of peons ; a commissioned officer in the Mysore Horse. |
| Jamá kharch ... ... | Receipts and expenditure. |
| Jamín ... ... ... | Land. |

| | |
|---|---|
| Jámín ... ... | ... Bail; security. |
| Jamíndár ... | ... A landholder. |
| Jámíndár ... | ... A surety. |
| Jangama... ... | ... A Lingáyit priest. |
| Janti kallu ... | ... A boundary or demarcation mark, composed of three stones in a line. |
| Jantri ... ... | ... Tables used for calculation. |
| Jári ... ... | ... Current; in force. |
| Jaríb ... ... | ... Measurement. |
| Jári inámti ... | ... Rent-free land. |
| Jatka ... ... | ... A small, close, two-wheeled conveyance drawn by a pony. |
| Játre ... ... | ... Annual fair, usually occurring on the occasion of a festival. |
| Jauli ... ... | ... A term applied to cloths of all kinds; piece goods. |
| Iaván, Javána ... | ... A peon; an inferior officer who acts as a guard and a messenger. |
| Iaváb ... ... | ... An answer. |
| Javábdári ... | ... Responsibility. |
| Jéshta ... ... | ... Third lunar month corresponding to June and July. A rain commencing between 30th November and 12th December. Paddy is sown during this time. |
| Jhadti ... ... | ... Examination of an account. |
| Jhár patrak ... | ... Statement showing the number and description of trees in each survey number. |
| Jiddu ... ... | ... Jealousy; anger. |
| Jindagi ... ... | ... Property; estate. |
| Jiráyiti ... ... | ... Cultivation; farming. |
| Jítagára ... ... | ... A hereditary labourer or slave. |
| Jódi ... ... | ... Quit-rent; grant of land or village on lighter assessment than the proper revenue. |
| Jódídár ... ... | ... A ryot holding as *inám*, lands or village on reduced assessment, varying according to circumstances. |
| Jódidár takhta ... | ... A record of the settlement of the amount of Jódí to be paid upon each wattan or varttane. |
| Jógi ... ... | ... A class of religious mendicants. |
| Joti (banna) phana | ... An oil manufacturer of the Lingáyit caste. |
| Joyisa ... ... | ... An astrologer. |
| Junárdár... ... | ... An inferior official performing the duties of a vernacular clerk. |
| Jurmáne... ... | ... A fine. |
| Kabúláti... ... | ... An agreement or engagement in writing. |
| Kabúliyat banjar | ... Waste land left by the occupant. |

| | |
|---|---|
| Kachéri (cutcherry) ... | An office; a court. |
| Kachha kharadu ... | A rough account. |
| Kada ... ... ... | Debt. |
| Kadame ... ... ... | A deficiency. |
| Kadangu ... ... | A trench or ditch in garden. |
| Kadata (Cuduttum) ... | A cloth covered with a composition of charcoal and gum, and used instead of a slate for writing and keeping accounts on. |
| Kádagi ... ... ... | A basket or pannier put on a pack bullock. |
| Kaifiyat ... ... ... | A deposition. |
| Kai kágada ... ... | A recognizance. |
| Kalási ... ... ... | A lascar; a subordinate who pitches and takes care of tents. |
| Kálave ... ... ... | A channel or stream, generally for irrigation. |
| Kalla ... ... ... | A thief. |
| Kálu ... ... ... | A fourth part of anything. |
| Kámáti ... ... ... | Day labourer. |
| Kambli (cumbly) ... | A coarse woollen blanket or camblet, used by all classes for protection against wet and cold, and for sleeping in at night. |
| Kambli Kuruba... ... | A lower class of Sudras. |
| Kammi jásti patti ... | Statement showing increase and decrease. |
| Kamshara ... ... | Reduction to a lower grade. |
| Kandáya, kandáyam .... | Land-tax; money assessment. |
| Kandi, Khandaga (Candy) | Land measure = 20 kudus or 10,000 square yards for wet and garden land; and = 20 kudus or 64,000 square yards for dry land. Grain measure = 120 kudus or 4 bushels 12·8 pts. |
| Kanikapille (conicopilay) | An overseer. |
| Kantu ... ... ... | Stipulation of payment; instalment. |
| Kapile ... ... ... | An apparatus for raising water from a well or tank for irrigating fields, worked by men or by oxen on an inclined plane. |
| Karagupadi ... ... | Duty on goods where they are consumed or sold, in contradistinction to *sthal bharti*, which is levied at the place of production; sale. |
| Káranji ... ... ... | A reservoir or fountain. |
| Karáru ... ... ... | An agreement. |
| Kárkháne ... ... | A manufactory; a workshop. |
| Karnam (Curnum) ... | Village accountant. |
| Kártika fasal ... ... | November paddy crop. That for April and May is Vaisákha fasal. |
| Káru ... ... ... | The wet season. |
| Kasba, Kasaba ... ... | The chief town of a district or division. |
| Kásu ... ... ... | A pie-piece. |
| Kasúri ... ... ... | Neglect; fault. |
| Kattadaka ... ... | A written agreement. |

Katte ... ... ... Anicut or dam in a river or stream ; a pond ; a custom-house.

Kattu ... ... ... Court papers or proceedings.

Kattu kálve ... ... Feeding channel to a tank.

Kauldar ... ... ... A ryot holding lands on special agreement.

Kával ... ... ... Ground reserved for pasturing cattle.

Kere ... ... ... A tank.

Kéri ... ... ... A small street with houses on both sides ; a hamlet.

Khaidi ... ... ... A prisoner.

Khaidu ... ... ... Imprisonment.

Khajáne, Khazána ... Treasury.

Kháné shumári... ... Census. An account showing the number of houses, shops, cattle, population, looms, ploughs, &c., of which a town or village consists.

Kharchu ... ... ... Expense.

Kháte ... ... ... A holding or occupancy.

Kháyam ... ... ... Fixed ; permanent.

Kháyamguttadár ... Holder of land or a village on a fixed and unalterable assessment.

Kháyam guttige ... Fixed assessment or rent.

Khush básh ... ... A private person of independent means.

Khún ... ... ... Murder.

Khurd-bard ... ... Embezzlement of public money.

Killedar ... ... ... A police inspector ; a commandant of a fort.

Kistu ... ... ... An instalment of the annual assessment paid by holders at stated times.

Kistu bandi ... ... A document given to a landholder showing the instalments payable by him.

Kodagidár ... ... A holder of land under a tank, free of or on nominal assessment for having repaired or restored it, and on the further condition of his keeping in good order the said irrigation work on which the land below depends for its supply of water.

Kódi ... ... ... The weir of a tank or reservoir.

Kola ... ... ... A reservoir with stone steps down to the water's edge.

Kóla ... ... ... The stocks ; *kai kóla*, hand-stocks, *kálu kóla*, leg-stocks.

Kolaga ... ... ... One-twentieth of a khandaga.

Kólkár, Kólukára ... A stick-bearer ; a peon.

Kole róga ... ... A rot or disease which attacks areca palms.

Kól áta ... ... ... A stick-dance, or dance accompanied with striking of sticks ; practised at the Dasara by school-boys who, accompanied by their masters, go about the streets reciting Maharnavami padyas and receiving presents.

Kolli ... ... ... A stream or rivulet.
Kólu ... ... ... A pole; a rod.
Komati, Komatiga ... Traders.
Konga ... ... ... A class of servants of Tamil origin.
Koppalu ... ... ... The suburbs or outlying villages of a town.
Korama .... ... ... A wild race inhabiting the forests and mountains.
Kottige ... ... ... An outhouse or shed, generally for cattle.
Kotvál (cutwal)... ... An official whose principal duty is to furnish supplies to travellers.
Krayadár ... ... Purchaser.
Kudu ... ... ... Land measure = 16 *padis* or *pailis* or 500 square yards for wet and garden land, and = 16 *padis* or *pailis* or 3,200 square yards for dry lands. Grain measure = 8 seers or 13·44 pints.
Kula ... ... ... A single farmer; a tenant.
Kula nashta ... ... Loss of a tenant.
Kulavádi... ... ... A menial among the village servants; a deputy talári, who is employed to watch the crops, from the growing crop to the granary.
Kulavar, Kulavaru ... A term applied to accounts and returns made out with reference to the cultivators, as distinguished from accounts prepared according to the holdings.
Kulavar-chitte, Kulavar-patte A detailed account of the land cultivated by each holder.
Kulavar-jamabandi ... Individual settlement.
Kumri ... ... ... A term applied to cultivation carried on by felling a tract of forest, burning the wood, and raising a crop of grain on the clearing, which is abandoned in the following year, and a fresh clearing made somewhere else. This practice is now prohibited.
Kurige ... ... ... A sowing machine and plough combined.
Kurrul ... ... ... Clayey soil, which when dry turns very hard, which does not easily absorb water, and which if once wetted does not dry soon. It is sometimes so bad that even grass will not grow on it.
Kushki ságuvali ... Dry cultivation.
Kushki ... ... ... A term applied to unirrigated land.

Labbe ... ... ... Muhammadan converts of Tamil origin.
Ládar ... ... ... A class of Mahratta Sudras.
Lakkote ... ... ... An envelope; a sealed letter.
Lál Bágh ... ... A pleasure garden.
Lambáni... ... ... A tribe resembling gipsies, who wander about and earn a livelihood as carriers, sometimes called Brinjaries.

| | |
|---|---|
| Lashkar ... ... ... | A cantonment. |
| Lavájame ... ... | Establishment of a department drawing pay. |
| Lavani faisal patrak ... | Record of the final settlement of each Survey number in the village. |
| Lekkha ... ... ... | Accounts ; an account. |
| Léva dévi ... ... | Dealings, generally in money. |
| Lingáyit, Lingáyita ... | A follower of Siva wearing the *linga*. |
| Lúti ... ... ... | Plunder. |
| Mádiga ... ... ... | A chuckler ; currier and shoemaker. |
| Máf ... ... ... | Pardon, remission. |
| Máfi rahadári ... ... | Passport granted for the conveyance of goods from one place to another for which duty had already been paid. |
| Mágani ... ... ... | Subdivision of a taluq, corresponding to a hobli or nád. |
| Magga ... ... ... | A weaver's loom. |
| Magha ... ... ... | A rain commencing between 14th and 27th August. Tobacco and wheat are sown at this time. |
| Maharnavami ... ... | A feast observed on the 9th day of the 7th lunar month ; the last day but one of the Dasara, on which arms are worshipped. |
| Mahasulu ... ... | Octroi ; toll ; crop. |
| Mahazar... ... ... | Award of a panchayat, or jury. |
| Maidán ... ... ... | A plain ; the plain country, or *Bail shime*, as distinguished from the *Malnád* or hill region. |
| Male ... ... ... | Rain. |
| Male kála, Male gála ... | Rainy season. |
| Málika ... ... ... | Owner. |
| Malnád, Malenád ... | Hill country ; the western part of Mysore. |
| Mámaledár ... ... | A native collector in charge of a taluq ; an Amildar. |
| Mámúl, Mámúli ... | Established ; customary ; usual. |
| Mana ... ... ... | A maund. |
| Mande ... ... ... | Subdivisions of a hobli in Manjarabad, corresponding to a *firka* or *phut mágani*. |
| Manegár, Manegára ... | An agent ; a native accountant ; an overseer. |
| Mane terige ... ... | House-tax. |
| Mantapa ... ... | A place built for worship in front of a temple or on the bank of a river, or by the side of a well ; also a place in which an idol is deposited. |
| Mánya ... ... ... | Exempt from taxes or imposts. |
| Máru kukke ... ... | A small basket or muzzle put on bullocks to prevent them from feeding. |
| Masalat ... ... ... | Counsel ; plot. |
| Masbálchi ... ... | A torch-bearer or lamplighter. |
| Mashál chóri ... ... | Torch robbery. |
| Matha (mutt) ... ... | House of a priest ; a school-house. |

| | |
|---|---|
| Matha vritti ... | ... Land granted rent-free to a math. |
| Maund ... ... | ... A weight equal to 40 seers or 24 lbs. |
| Méda, Myáda ... | ... A caste, or a member of it, occupied in cutting and selling bamboos, or making and vending bamboo baskets, &c. |
| Méla ... ... | ... A band of actors. |
| Meládhikári ... | ... Superior officer. |
| Méstri (maistry) | ... A subordinate employed in supervising a work; a native overseer; a chief builder, carpenter, &c. |
| Minahu ... ... | ... Till; until. |
| Mirási ... ... | ... An allowance or perquisite, sometimes paid in money and sometimes in kind; generally applied to grain, &c., given to village officials or head-men by the ryots. |
| Mobalagu ... | ... Amount of money. |
| Móchi ... ... | ... A class of cobblers who make saddles, native slippers, &c. |
| Mohar, mohur ... | ... A seal; stamp. |
| Mohatarfa ... | ... Taxes levied on looms, houses, oil-mills, shops, &c. |
| Mokhtiyár-náma | ... Power of attorney. |
| Mokhtesar ... | ... Head of a department. |
| Mrigasira ... | ... A rain commencing between 5th and 18th June. Paddy, cotton, &c., are sown at this season. |
| Muchchalike ... | ... A deed of agreement. |
| Muchchi... ... | ... A man employed in public offices to make ink, mend pens, provide papers, seal letters, bind books, and the like. |
| Mufat, muft ... | ... Free from payment. |
| Múkuppe ... | ... A mode of cultivation by which a crop is divided into three parts, of which one is for the rent of the ground, another for labour, and the third for the seed and implements. |
| Múla ... ... | ... A rain commencing between the 12th and 25th December. Cummin, coriander, tobacco and other seeds are sown at this time. |
| Mulki ... ... | ... Pertaining to revenue |
| Mungári, Mungáru | ... The early rains, from April to June. The former or early season for cultivation. The south-west monsoon. |
| Múnshi (moonshee) | ... Reader and interpreter; vernacular clerk. |
| Munsif ... ... | ... A subordinate civil judge. |
| Musáfir khána ... | ... A rest-house for native travellers. |
| Mutálfka... ... | ... An agent. |
| Mutfarkhát ... | ... Stipend; pension. |
| Mutsaddi, Mutsaddy | ... An agent; a native accountant. |
| Muzarái ... ... | ... A department for the control of temple funds and other religious property. |

Nádári ... ... ... Poor; helpless.

Nádiga ... ... ... Village accountant. With hardly an exception they are of the Brahman caste. The office is hereditary in common with those of all the other village officials. In some places they hold land free of rent, and in others on light assessment. In some few places a fixed money allowance is given. In all instances there are certain fixed fees payable to them in money or in kind by the ryots.

Nádu, nád ... ... A district; a subdivision of a taluq corresponding to a hobli.

Nagad gutta ... ... Money assessment.

Nagadi ... ... ... Relating to cash transactions or accounts connected with treasury finance.

Nagadiyát ... ... Money assessment.

Nakásh ... ... ... Map or plan.

Nakshe ... ... ... A plan.

Nazar ... ... ... Offerings to a sovereign.

Nazarána (nuzzerana) ... Compulsory offerings.

Namúne ... ... ... A specimen or sample.

Nán parvarish ... ... Allowance to a child till able to provide for himself.

Nánya ... ... ... The change of money, as rupees, annas, &c.; any coin.

Názar ... ... ... Sheriff; an officer of a court who is charged with serving processes, &c.

Négalu ... ... ... A plough.

Nikále ... ... ... Final disposal.

Nímtán ... ... ... Testing of survey.

Nirakh-náma ... ... Price current of market rates, &c

Nirakh ... ... ... Rate; fixed price.

Nírganti ... ... ... Regulator and distributor of water to irrigated lands.

Níru gandáya ... ... Water cess.

Nirúpa ... ... ... A written order from a superior.

Nóta ... ... ... Sight; examination of money.

Nuksán, Luksán ... Loss; damage.

Nyáya ... ... ... Justice.

Ole, wóle ... ... A palmyra leaf, or manuscript written on palmyra leaf.

Oopulwat ... ... Excess of moisture from surface springs.

Ooturwut ... ... A sloping surface.

Paddhati... ... ... Usage; custom.

| | |
|---|---|
| Padi, Páili ... ... | Land measure = 31¼ square yards for wet and garden land, and 200 square yards for dry land. |
| Pádya ... ... ... | The first day of the bright or dark half of a lunar month. |
| Pahne súd ... ... | Statement showing old and new survey numbers, names of fields, description of tenure, names of occupants, &c. |
| Paigast ... ... ... | A detective. |
| Páikari ... ... ... | Temporary tenant, or one who resides in one village and cultivates land in another. |
| Paimáyish ... ... | Measurement of land. |
| Pairu ... ... ... | Crop. |
| Paksha páta ... ... | Partiality. |
| Palla ... ... ... | One hundred seers. |
| Pallikúta... ... ... | A village school. |
| Pálu ... ... ... | Waste land. |
| Pálu kandáya ... ... | A term applied to assessment paid on land left fallow or untilled. |
| Pancháyit, Panchayat, Pancháyati, Panchá-yattu. | A jury; a popular jury or committee of five persons. |
| Panchami ... ... | Fifth day of the bright or dark half of a lunar month. |
| Pancháñga ... ... | A calendar; an almanac. |
| Panch-báb ... ... | Five items of excise: toddy, liquor, tobacco, ganja, and betel. |
| Panchéru ... ... | Five seers, or ⅛th of a maund. |
| Pandit (pundit) ... ... | A learned man; a physician. |
| Panju ... ... ... | A torch. |
| Pantóji ... ... ... | A village schoolmaster. |
| Parabhári ... ... | Assignment; delivery. |
| Parampóku ... ... | Uncultivable land. |
| Párpatyagára, Párpate-gár | Manager or supervisor of a chatram or temple. |
| Paricháraka ... ... | A Brahman temple-servant. |
| Párikhattu ... ... | A deed of dissolution of partnership or of parcenership; a written receipt and acquittance. |
| Pasaráyé... ... ... | Market fees. |
| Páshandi ... ... | A heretic; a schismatic. |
| Patela, patel (potail) ... | Head man of a village; the head of village police; in some parts of the Province rent-free lands are assigned for their support. |
| Patna shetti ... ... | A title given to the principal men of towns next to the *Shettis*, a *Shetti* being in some respects similar to a Mayor and a *Patna shetti* to an Alderman. |

| | |
|---|---|
| Patra ... ... ... | A bond. |
| Pattana, patna (putten) | A town. |
| Patte (putta) ... ... | A title-deed granted by Government. |
| Patte ... ... ... | Apprehension; detection. |
| Pattedar... ... ... | A leaseholder. |
| Patti ... ... ... | A list. |
| Pávu, páu ... ... | One-fourth of a seer. |
| Péshkár ... ... ... | A revenue officer next in rank to the Amildar. |
| Peshkash (peshcush) ... | The fixed payment made by zamindars to Government. |
| Péte, petta ... ... | Market; a trading town. |
| Pharári ... ... ... | A runaway. |
| Phasalu ... ... ... | Crop. |
| Phidvi ... ... ... | Servant. |
| Phiryád ... ... ... | A complaint. |
| Phod ... ... ... | Subdividing fields. |
| Phútkúl patrak ... ... | A detailed statement of occupancies when two or more are included in one and the same Revenue Survey number, with area and assessment of each. |
| Phút mágani ... ... | Subdivision of a mágani. |
| Pót pahni ... ... | An inspection statement like *Pahni súd.* |
| Pramána ... ... | Oath. |
| Pránta, prántya... ... | Locality. |
| Prativádi ... ... | Defendant. |
| Pubba ... ... ... | A rain commencing between 28th August and 10th September. |
| Pudavat ... ... ... | Investments, generally of money, made by persons for the upkeep or maintenance of temples and other charitable institutions. |
| Pújári ... ... ... | The officiating Brahman or priest of a temple. |
| Punarvasu ... ... | A rain commencing between 3rd and 16th July. Paddy, cotton, &c., are sown at this season. |
| Punya ... ... ... | Good lot or fortune. |
| Purvabhádra ... ... | A rain commencing between 2nd and 14th March. |
| Purvásh. áda ... ... | A rain commencing between 26th December and 7th January. Cummin, coriander, tobacco, and other seeds are sown at this time. |
| Pushya ... ... ... | A rain commencing between 17th and 30th July. Gram and mangoes are sown at this time. |
| Puróhita... ... ... | A family priest. |
| Raddi, reddi ... ... | A Telugu designation for the head man of a village, the head of village police. In some parts of the Province rent-free lands are assigned for their support. |
| Raddu ... ... ... | Repeal; cancel. |

Raft ... ... ... Export.
Rahadári ... ... A passport.
Raita, raiyat, ryot ... A cultivator; a farmer.
Rájináma, rázináma ... A deed of consent; an acquittance; settlement of a dispute; a resignation of office.
Rakta kodagi ... ... Land given free of rent to the family of a person wounded or killed in battle.
Raktaván ... ... An official whose business it is to supply ink.
Rási ... ... ... A heap, generally of corn.
Rázi, Ráji ... ... Mutual consent.
Régada ... ... ... Black cotton soil.
Reswut ... ... ... Want of cohesion among the constituent particles of the soil, arising from the presence of fine sand.
Revati .. ... ... A rain in some places commencing between 28th March and 11th April. The land is ploughed at this time.
Risále ... ... ... A detachment in the Mysore Horse.
Risáldár ... ... ... Officer commanding a detachment.
Riváz ... ... ... Rate of assessment; usage.
Róhini ... ... ... A rain commencing between 22nd May and 4th June. Paddy, cotton, &c., are sown during this rain.
Rójináma, róju ... ... Daily cash account of receipts and disbursements.
Rokka ... ... ... Money; cash.
Rúbkári ... ... ... Extract from a resolution or a letter addressed by an equal to an equal.
Ruju ... ... ... Proof; signature.
Rusum ... ... ... An allowance; fee.
Rúba-rúb (roob roob) ... Personally; in person.

Sabab ... ... ... An excuse; reason; cause.
Sádilwár ... ... ... Contingent expenses, usually applied to money allowed for the purchase of stationery.
Ságuvali-chítu ... ... Written permission to cultivate land given to a ryot on his application to take up land being accepted.
Ságuvalidár ... ... Cultivator.
Saza ... ... ... Punishment.
Sákshi ... ... ... A witness.
Sála ... ... ... Debt.
Sál jháda ... ... Annual return or statement.
Sámán ... ... ... Baggage; articles.
Sambala ... ... ... Pay; salary.
Sammat ... ... ... A subdivision of a taluq, corresponding to a hobli.
Sammati ... ... ... Consent.
Sampádane ... ... A perquisite; allowance; gains not authorized.

**Samstháná** ... ... A district or territory belonging to a native chief, or a temple; a state.

**Sandáya** ... ... ... Repayment.

**Sángada** ... ... ... A ferry-boat formed of two *dónis* joined together, with a deck or platform upon them.

**Sanad, sunnud** ... ... A grant; a diploma; a charter; a patent; a document conveying to an individual emoluments, titles, privileges, offices, &c., under the seal of the ruling authority.

**Sanaddár** ... ... One who holds a written authority or *sanad* from the ruling power to hold land or office.

**Sante** ... ... ... A fair; a market-place.

**Sante pasaráyi** ... ... Market fees.

**Sarbaráyi** ... ... Furnishing supplies.

**Saráfa, Shroff** ... ... An examiner and sorter of coins; money changer. An official employed in treasuries to test and count coins.

**Sarhad** ... ... ... Boundary; limit.

**Sarkár, circar** ... ... Government.

**Sar amin, Sur ameen** ... A sub-magistrate.

**Sarásari** ... ... ... Average.

**Sáráyi** ... ... ... Arrack.

**Sardár** ... ... ... An officer; a European gentleman.

**Sarvádhikári** ... ... General agent.

**Sarvamánya** ... ... Land granted on entirely free tenure.

**Sávukára, sowcar** ... A rich man; a merchant.

**Sawár, sowar** ... ... A trooper.

**Sáyar** ... ... ... Transit duties; miscellaneous revenue.

**Sékada** ... ... ... Percentage.

**Ser, seer** ... ... ... Grain measure = Rs. 84 in weight, or 1·68 pints. A weight = 24 tolas.

**Servegára** ... ... A chief herdsman in the Amrit Mahal.

**Sétuve** ... ... ... A bridge.

**Shaka** ... ... ... Era; especially the era of Sáliváhana, commencing A.D. 78.

**Shánabhóga, Shánbhóg** Village accountant; with hardly an exception they are of the Brahman caste. The office is hereditary in common with all the other village officials. In some places they hold land free of rent, and in others on light assessment. In some few places a fixed money allowance is given. In all instances there are certain fixed fees payable to them in money or in kind by the ryots.

**Shanabu** ... ... ... Hemp used in making a coarse cloth called *góni*.

**Shásana** ... ... ... A stone slab or brass or copper plates on which memorial inscriptions, grants to temples, &c., are recorded.

| | |
|---|---|
| Shékdár ... ... ... | Revenue officer in charge of a hobli or sub-division of a taluq. |
| Shendi ... ... ... | Toddy. |
| Shetti ... ... ... | A title borne by Komati and Lingáyit merchants. |
| Shikmidár ... ... | Sub-cultivator. |
| Shilku ... ... ... | Balance; remainder. |
| Shirastedár, Sheristadar | Head of a revenue or judicial office. |
| Shiváyi jama ... ... | Miscellaneous receipts credited to Government. |
| Shraya ... ... ... | Progressive rental for improvement of land, or rent commencing at a low rate and increasing gradually year by year till the maximum limit is attained. |
| Shrotriyadár ... ... | The holder of a village, or a certain extent of land granted on easy rent in perpetuity, or for a limited number of lives (generally as a reward for public service) to Brahmans only. |
| Sibbandi... ... ... | An establishment. |
| Siledar,Silahdar,Silladar | A lancer; a trooper. |
| Silsila banjar ... ... | Government unoccupied waste land. |
| Subédár, Soobahdar ... | A provincial governor; a native collector in charge of a taluq. |
| Súd ... ... ... | A tabular statement. |
| Suggi ... ... ... | Harvest time. |
| Sukáliga, Sukáligaru ... | A tribe resembling gipsies who wander about and earn a livelihood as carriers; sometimes called *Brinjaries*. |
| Sunka ... ... ... | Toll; octroi; custom. |
| Supári ... ... ... | Areca-nut. |
| Suphardu ... ... | Possession; care. |
| | |
| Tagáde ... ... ... | Importunity in urging the settlement of a claim or payment of a debt; dunning. |
| Tagair ... ... ... | Dismissal from service. |
| Taggu ... ... ... | Dearness; high price. |
| Tahanáma ... ... | An agreement. |
| Takávi (tuccavee) ... | Recoverable advances of money to ryots to enable them to cultivate. |
| Tákid ... ... ... | An order. |
| Takrár ... ... ... | Dispute. |
| Táku ... ... ... | A certain portion of land, generally applied to fields. |
| Talári, talavára... ... | Village watchman and scout, whose duty is to give information to officers, &c., to guide travellers, &c., his only remuneration being the grant of a small extent of rent-free land. In some villages where there is no Talári the duties are performed by the Toti, his deputy. |

Tálúk, taluq, talook ... A division of a district under the management of an Amildar.
Támbra shásana ... Grant or inscription engraved on copper plates.
Tammadi ... ... The officiating priest of a pagoda.
Tamsúku ... ... A bond ; a written document.
Tankasále ... ... A mint.
Tapásini ... ... Examination of classers' tests.
Tappál ... ... ... Post.
Tappe ... ... ... Relay or set of bullocks or bearers posted for travellers.
Tapsíl ... ... ... Detail.
Taradúd... ... ... Adoption of prompt measures.
Tari ... ... ... Wet—*i.e.*, irrigated—land.
Tárík ... ... ... Date.
Tasdík ... ... ... Allowance to temples, chatrams, &c.
Távu ... ... ... A place.
Teppa ... ... ... A raft.
Téru ... ... ... An idol car.
Tevari, tevaru ... ... Division between the fields ; a border or small bank of grass bounding a field, commonly called *bund* or *badhu*.
Thána, Tháne ... ... A police station.
Tírpu ... ... ... A decision.
Tirve ... ... ... Land-tax.
Tola ... ... ... A rupee's weight = $\frac{1}{40}$ part of a pound avoirdupois.
Tópu ... ... ... A grove of trees, generally called *tope*.
Toreya ... ... ... A class of bearers.
Tóṭa ... ... ... A garden.
Tóṭi ... ... ... A menial among the village servants ; a deputy talári, who is employed to watch the crops from the growing crop to the granary.
Túbu ... ... .. The sluice of a tank or reservoir.
Tukadi ... ... ... District.

Udave ... ... ... Jungly tract fit for coffee plantation, a term used in Nagar and Hassan.
Ukkada (ookad) ... A station at the side of a road where tolls are collected.
Ulame ... ... ... Land given to a sub-cultivator.
Ulamedár ... ... A sub-cultivator.
Uligadavaru ... ... Peons.
Umbali ... ... ... A village or plot of ground free of rent.
Umbalidár ... ... The holder of a rent-free village or land.
Umedvár ... ... A volunteer official ; one who works without pay in hope of ultimately gaining a situation.
Uru ... ... ... A village ; a county.

| | |
|---|---|
| Uttára, Uddhára ... | Remission of land-rent on account of imperfectly ripened crops from inclemency of season and failure of rain. In Nagar it is used for Inámti. |
| Vadda, Woddar ... | A tank digger; a worker in stone. |
| Vádi ... ... ... | Plaintiff. |
| Vahivat ... ... ... | Usual procedure. |
| Vaidya ... ... ... | A physician. |
| Vaja ... ... ... | Reduction; deduction. |
| Vaisákha phasal ... | May crop. |
| Vakálat náma ... ... | Power of attorney. |
| Vakíl ... ... ... | An agent; attorney. |
| Vákmúla, vánmúla ... | A deposition. |
| Válaga uttára ... ... | Rent-free land granted to musicians. |
| Valase ... ... ... | Fugitives; people moving *en masse* from alarm or fear of an invasion. |
| Vára ... ... ... | Tenure of land, the half of the produce of which is given to the landlord instead of rent. |
| Váragára ... ... | A sub-lessee who gives half the produce of the land he cultivates to the owner. |
| Varaha ... ... ... | The coin called a pagoda. |
| Várasdár ... ... | Claimant. |
| Varga, warg ... ... | A ledger; a farm or holding having a separate number in the revenue accounts. There are sometimes two or three or even more holdings in one *Varga*. |
| Vargadár ... ... | A leaseholder (in Nagar); in other parts of the province the term means a transferee. |
| Vartamána ... ... | News; information. |
| Vartaka ... ... ... | A merchant. |
| Varushásana ... ... | Annual allowance. |
| Vasha ... ... ... | Possession; care; charge. |
| Vasúl ... ... ... | Collection; receipts. |
| Váyide ... ... .. | An instalment; a term. |
| Vichárane ... ... | An inquiry. |
| Vighalige ... ... | The sixtieth part of a *ghalige* or Indian hour. |
| Villéd-ele, Vílyad-ele ... | Betel-leaf. |
| Visa ... ... .... | A sixteenth part of anything. |
| Visha-háku ... ... | To poison. |
| Vivara ... ... ... | Particulars. |
| Vrittidár... ... ... | Proprietor of small grants of land free of rent, or on a light rent, to Brahmans only. |
| Vyápára... ... ... | Trade. |
| Vyájya ... ... ... | A quarrel; a lawsuit. |
| Walsur ... ... ... | Soil with a mixture of sand. |

Wasúl báki ... ... Statement showing full particulars of each occupant's entire holdings under the old and new systems.
Wolágra... ... ... Internal; home produce.
Wola-ságuvalidár ... Sub-cultivator.
Wottu ... ... ... Total.

Yádasht, Yádástu, Yádi A memorandum.
Yajamána ... ... Master; lord; owner; proprietor; husband.
Yála, Yela ... ... An auction.
Yedagai ... ... ... A member of the left-hand caste; currier and shoemaker.
Yele hambu ... ... Betel-vine.
Yedaru chítu ... ... A counterpart agreement; an engagement given by the tenant of an estate held under lease or mortgage to pay a consideration annually for its occupancy; also a writing given by the purchaser of land to the proprietor, engaging to give it back on receiving his money again within a stipulated period.
Yéta, Yáta ... ... A lever for raising water from a well; a well from which water is raised by such an instrument. In some places it is called a pikota.

Zirát ... ... ... Cultivation.

# ADDENDA ET CORRIGENDA

## VOL. I.

Page Line

12 Note[1] Add, "Mr. Bruce Foote, in his Geology of the Bellary District (*Mem. Geol. Surv. Ind.*, Vol. XXV.), says :—Captain Newbold did far more to elucidate the Geology of Southern India up to the establishment of the Geological Survey than all the other writers and investigators of the subject taken together, and his work deserves full notice, for most of it was well done according to the geological views prevalent in his day . . . . The principal point on which his views cannot now be accepted is his assumption that the schistose bands in the peninsula have been brought into their present positions by being broken through by great outbursts of granite. At first sight this appears to be the case, but on closer and more extended examination of the country this idea is found to be untenable, for the old granitoids are nowhere seen to be irrupted into the schists; on the contrary, the latter were deposited on the former by quiet, long-continued sedimentary action. This is, of course, a total change of the relative positions of the two rock series: the granitoids assume their true position as the true fundamental rocks of the country, and the schists are seen to be vastly younger in age than Newbold supposed them to be.

The granitic intrusions in the schist series which Newbold regarded as intrusions of the granitoid mass, are all found to be intrusions of much younger pegmatoid veins, and of very small extent and importance."

13 5 Before "Metamorphic Rocks" insert, "Archæan or."

13 7 To "Southern India" add as note[1], "The schists are not, in the modern sense of the term, *hypogene schists;* they are truly and unmistakably sedimentary formations associated with contemporary trap-flows, and whatever metamorphism they have undergone since their deposition is due to great movements of the earth's crust, which led to their being bent up into great folds forming huge synclinals and anticlinals. When this had happened a period of vast erosive action ensued, and thousands of feet in thickness of the schistose series were removed, and the underlying granitoid foundation was again exposed; while much of the eroded material was re-deposited as the rocks of the younger Kadapa and Karnul systems. The equivalents of Newbold's *hypogene schists* (in the Bellary district) belong to the system I have called the Dharwar system. . . .

The greater mass of the Dharwars consists of schists, hornblendic, chloritic, and argillaceous; but the associated traps, and more especially the hæmatitic quartzites, from their superior hardness and durability, occupy in many places much the most prominent positions; while, from the same reasons, the taluses they have given rise to in the hilly tracts are of extraordinary extent, and cover up much of the softer rocks, and mislead one as to their real extent.

The Dharwar rocks were originally deposited over very much larger areas than they now occupy, and very probably extended across the whole, or nearly the whole, peninsula. How far they may have extended to the north it is not possible at present to say, for the northern extremities of several of the Dharwar tracts are hidden under younger geological formations—*e.g.*, the Kaladgi and Bhima series, and the Deccan trap along the upper course of the Kistna river. To the southward the Dharwar rocks extend into and across

**Page Line**

the valley of the Kavéri almost to the northern slope of the Nilgiris. . . . The Dharwar system was exposed to great contortion and deformation at a very remote geological period, and this had been followed by a vast period of denudation, during which the enormous folds into which they had been forced previously were largely eroded, and cut up into the great bands in which they now occur. In general structure these bands are of two types—in the one, the band is a narrow synclinal fold, or a series of narrow synclinals echeloned after each other at exceedingly acute angles. In the second type, the band shows a natural erosion boundary on one side, and on the other is faulted down against and among the underlying granitoids. It is owing to these faultings down into the older rocks that the softer schistose members of the system have in many cases escaped from being entirely denuded away.—Bruce Foote, *loc. cit.*, pp. 22 and 74."

81 heading Omit "Fruit."
211 heading For "Tudas" read "Todas."
285 13 For "now" read "near."
340 34 For "Chalasaravi (probably in the south of" read "Bayal-nád (Wainád, in."
419 Note[1] Add, "Welsh says:—Though a short, swarthy-looking man, and rather inclining to fat, he was as hardy and active in body as in mind; and even when far advanced in life, he would ride thirty or forty miles a day, and chase a hare, an antelope, or a fox, with all the fire and vigour of youth. In short, when Colonel Sir Barry Close died in England, he left not a superior, and few, if any, equals, in the service."
441 16 For "now" read "in 1878."
478 38 For "affords" read "afford."
542 6 For "hippe" read "ippe."
543 21 For "hippe" read "ippe."
764 11 For "1886" read "1876."

## VOL. II.

11 28 For "*curacus*" read "*curcas.*"
47 Note For "1794" read "1784."
53 20 For "it seems probable" read "it is now settled."
,, 21 For "the matter," &c., read "the cost of maintenance being borne in the proportion of one-third by the Military department for the army, and two-thirds by the Municipality for the civil population."
137 4 Add, as note, "Mackenzie, writing in 1801, says:—The fort of Colar is far from being strong or tenable in any degree. It is throughout built of mud, with a kind of *fausse braye* and a very shallow ditch round it. The western gateway is very intricate, and as long as one good half of the whole fort, but the eastern one is hardly protected at all. There is a cavalier near to the west gate which commands the fort and surrounding tract. The works were in perfect repair at the time I surveyed them."
218 20 Add, as note, "Orders have been issued to close the keddahs for the present, from July 1897, and to employ the trained elephants in moving timber."
223 Note Substitute, "Takkola has now been identified by Dr. Hultzsch with a place near Arkonam in North Arcot district."
271 15 For "Anantácháya" read "Anantácharya."
311 32 For "breeched" read "breached."
380 9 For "A'ḷuvakhaḍa" read "A'ḷuvakheḍa."
427 18 For "Ganj" read "Gauj."
500 7 For "in the Purybhadra" read "on the Tungabhadra."
517 1 For "Bemmattanakalla" read "Bemmattanakallu."

# INDEX

MAP OF
MYSORE
NORTH KANARA
DHARWAR
BELLARY
ANANTAPUR
KADAPA
CHITALDROOG
SHIMOGA
TUMKUR
BANGALORE
HASSAN
S. KANARA
COORG
MYSORE
SALEM
ARCOT
MALABAR
NILGIRI
COIMBATORE

# OPINIONS

ON THE

# GAZETTEER OF MYSORE AND COORG.

## FIRST EDITION.

"Of Mysore, Dr. Hunter observes that the volumes compiled by Mr. Lewis Rice, Director of Public Instruction (who has also compiled that for Coorg), are better than anything he himself has been able to do even for Bengal. Mysore will shortly return to native rule, and these volumes form an invaluable record of what an episode of honest English administration has effected for an Indian State."—*Abstract of Reports of the Surveys in India for* 1876–7. (*Published by order of Her Majesty's Secretary of State for India in Council.*)

"Mr. Rice has done his work so well that we look forward with interest to the publication of his promised Gazetteer of Coorg. . . . He combines a comprehensive grasp of his entire subject with the faculty of lucid exposition, and also a careful attention to details."—*Academy.*

"A mine of information about the country. . . . Evidently written *con amore*, it shows great care and research, great knowledge of the language and literature of the country, and a thorough appreciation of the subject in hand."—*Calcutta Review.*

"The work (volume on Coorg) seems well done, and Mr. Rice's industry is worthy of all praise. No one in any way interested in Coorg will fail to find some notice of the subject specially interesting to him: and many persons not specially interested in the country will find matters of general interest. The songs alone render the book worthy of notice."—*Madras Mail.*

"In particular the volumes of . . . Mr. Rice on Mysore form models of administrative research."—*Sir W. W. Hunter, in Preface to Imperial Gazetteer of India.*

"Extremely glad the work was put into such good hands, for you have rendered a great service both to Government and to the people."

"A perfect *répertoire* of information."

"Has done more for Mysore than any one since the days of Buchanan."

"Those who enjoy reading history in the guise of romance may do so in the Gazetteer of Mysore by Mr. Lewis Rice."

"Reliable and readable work."—(*Various.*)

"Mr. Rice's Gazetteer of Mysore and Coorg, and other works—writings and collections—are solid productions, of inestimable value, already regarded as standards, and sure to be regarded as such for generations to come."—*Bangalore Spectator.*

*By the same Author.*

MYSORE INSCRIPTIONS, translated for H.M. Secretary of State for India, from Photographs in the India Office and original sources. With Introduction and Map. 1879. Price Rs.6.

FIND OF ROMAN COINS NEAR BANGALORE, with facsimiles. 1891.

EDICTS OF ASOKA IN MYSORE, with Illustrations. 1892.

"Cette découverte fera époque dans l'archéologie indienne."—*Presidential Address (by M. Senart), Académie des Inscriptions, Paris.* "The most important epigraphic discovery which was made in India during the year 1892. These inscriptions have created no small stir in the learned world."—*Presidential Address (by Sir Charles Elliott), Asiatic Society.*

# MYSORE ARCHÆOLOGICAL SERIES.

## EPIGRAPHIA CARNATICA.

I. COORG INSCRIPTIONS, translated for Government. With Illustrations. 1886. Price Rs. $2\frac{1}{2}$.

II. INSCRIPTIONS AT S'RAVANA BELGOLA, a chief seat of the Jains. With Illustrations, Introduction, Text and Translations. 1889. Price Rs.12.

"Important volume."—*Vienna Oriental Journal.* "The editor has spared no pains in making the results of his long and arduous work of decipherment available to the student."—*Trübner's Record.* "A very valuable book."—*Presidential Address (by Mr. Beveridge), Asiatic Society.* "To all who wish to study Indian architecture of a particular class we recommend the volume as the best available professionally useful book on the subject."—*Indian Engineering.*

III. INSCRIPTIONS IN THE MYSORE DISTRICT. PART I. 1894. Price Rs.12.

"The numerous and various points of interest which the new epigraphic discoveries in Mysore offer, entitle Mr. Rice to the hearty congratulations of all Sanskritists, and to their warm thanks for the ability and indefatigable zeal with which he continues the archæological explorations in the province confided to his care."—*Dr. G. Bühler, in Academy.* "Supplies a great desideratum, as it contains S'aka dates for several Chola kings whose inscriptions in the Madras Presidency are only dated in years of the reign."—*Dr. Hultzsch, in Report for 1894-5.* "The volume redounds to the credit of the author . . . His work is always thorough, and in all the volumes he has published he has shown a comprehensive grasp of his subject, and placed before his readers most useful, lucid and detailed reports."—*Madras Mail.*

IV. INSCRIPTIONS IN THE MYSORE DISTRICT. PART II. [*Now ready.*

(*In the Press.*)

INSCRIPTIONS IN THE

V. HASSAN DISTRICT.

VI. KADUR DISTRICT.

VII. SHIMOGA DISTRICT. PART I.

VIII. SHIMOGA DISTRICT. PART II.

IX. BANGALORE DISTRICT.

X. KOLAR DISTRICT.

XI. CHITALDROOG DISTRICT.

XII. TUMKUR DISTRICT.

ON SALE BY THE CURATOR, GOVERNMENT BOOK DEPÔT, BANGALORE.

REPORT ON THE MYSORE CENSUS OF 1881. Compiled for Government. With Statistical Tables and Map. 1884. Price Rs.4.

"Has done good service to Mysore by the information he has given to the world in this valuable Census Report."—*Surgeon-General Balfour, in St. James's Gazette.*

CATALOGUE OF SANSKRIT MANUSCRIPTS IN MYSORE AND COORG. Compiled for Government. 1884. Price Rs.3½.

"Reichhaltiger Katalog, dessen Studium jedem Sanskritisten angelegentlich empfohlen werden kann."—*Professor Jolly, in Oesterreichische Monatsschrift für den Orient.*

AMARAKOS'A, the *Nāmalingānus'āsana* of Amara Simha, with Kannada and English meanings. Third Edition. Price As.12.

---

## BIBLIOTHECA CARNATICA.

I. KARṆĀṬAKA-BHĀSHĀ-BHŪSHAṆA, by Nāgavarmmā, the oldest grammar extant of the language. In Sanskrit sūtras, with Commentary, and Introduction. 1884. Price Rs.2½.

II. KARṆĀṬAKA-S'ABDĀNUS'ĀSANA, by Bhaṭṭākalanka-Deva. In Sanskrit sūtras, with its two commentaries—*Bhāshā-Manjarī* and *Manjarī-Makaranda*: an exhaustive treatise on the grammar of the language, completed in 1604. With Introduction on the Literature of Karnātaka. 1890. Price Rs.10.

"The author was evidently a profound grammarian."—*Professor Kielhorn.*

III. PAMPA-RĀMĀYAṆA, the *Rāmachandra-Charita-Purāṇa* of Abhinava-Pampa or Nāgachandra; an ancient Jain poem of the 12th century. With Introduction and Analysis of the poem. Revised Edition. 1892. Price Rs.4½.

IV. PAMPA-BHĀRATA, the *Vikramārjuna-Vijaya* of Pampa; an ancient Jain poem of 941. With Introduction and Analysis of the poem. [*Now ready.*

V. KAVIRĀJAMĀRGGA, by *Nripatunga*, a treatise of the 9th century on *alankāra*; the oldest Kannada work of which manuscripts have actually been found. With Introduction by K. B. Pathak. [*Now ready.*

VI. KĀVYĀVALOKANA, by Nāgavarmmā. [*In preparation.*

ON SALE BY THE CURATOR, GOVERNMENT BOOK DEPÔT, BANGALORE.